FUNDAMENTALS OF FEDERAL INCOME TAX LAW

THIRD EDITION

William D. Popkin
Walter W. Foskett Professor of Law
Indiana University at Bloomington
School of Law

CASEBOOK SERIES

Library of Congress Cataloging-in-Publication Data

Popkin, William D.
Fundamentals of federal income tax law / by William D. Popkin.
3rd ed.
p. cm. — (Cases and materials series)
"Times Mirror books."
Includes index.
ISBN # 0-8205-3185-5
1. Income tax—Law and legislation—United States—Cases.
I. Title. II. Series: Cases and materials.
KF6368.P668 1998
343.7305'2—dc21
98-10822
CIP

MATTHEW BENDER & CO., INC
EDITORIAL OFFICES
2 PARK AVENUE, NEW YORK, NY 10016-5675 (212) 448-2000
201 MISSION STREET, SAN FRANCISCO, CA 94105-1831 (415) 908-3200

PREFACE TO THE THIRD EDITION

The third edition incorporates the changes made by the 1996 and 1997 amendments to the Internal Revenue Code. A major pedagogical point to be made about these changes is what they tell us about the tax legislative process — congressional posturing with questionable policy impact (*see, e.g.*, the child tax credit; the medical and educational savings incentives; the 18% long term capital gains rates in the next century; and new IRA rules).

The only major organizational change in the book is to put some introductory capital gains material in Chapter 3 (Defining Income). A lot of what comes later depends on knowing a little about the preferential rate on capital gains (*e.g.*, recapture; fair market value deduction for charitable contributions). So it is helpful to have some of that information introduced early. It fits well into Chapter 3 because there has always been a lingering thought that capital gain is not fully income, even though *Eisner v. Macomber* admitted this type of "realized" accretion into the income category.

PREFACE TO THE SECOND EDITION

The second version of this casebook is a sharp departure from the first in one major respect. As the complexity of the tax law has increased, the best course is to return to basics. To that end, the material is sharply pared down to less than 500 pages. Fundamental structural themes are presented and their implications explored but without as much elaboration as is customary in most basic income tax materials.

The issues are explored through consideration of statutory text, cases, and administrative rules, along with supplementary comments, problems and questions. The supplementary material permits more detailed exploration underlying issues and encourages exploration of the code's underlying structure and policy. The teacher can decide which issues to pursue in what depth, perhaps exploring the particular areas of special interest with additional material.

Despite the diminished length of the book, I find that there is more than enough material for a basic four-hour course. In fact, I often lack time to cover some of the more detailed material about tax shelters (chapter 16), carved out income interests (chapter 20), and the accrual method relating to economic performance (chapter 23).

Part I introduces all the major issues in the income tax law—the rate structure and taxable units, assignment of income, income definitions (including basis), gifts, taxable years, and tax expenditures.

Part II focuses on the consumption part of the income definition, dealing with income in-kind, business deductions, personal insurance and personal losses, and the charitable deduction.

Part III deals with savings—deprecation and loss deductions, and the distinction between current expenses and capital expenditures.

Part IV explains limits on deductions: (a) requirements that expenditures be ordinary, necessary, and reasonable; public policy limits; political expenditures; expenses to produce tax exempt income; (b) limits on the interest deduction; (c) loans, basis and tax ownership, including limits on net loss deductions and the rules dealing with tax shelters; and (d) the alternative minimum tax.

Part V considers the taxation of appreciated gain: (a) nonrecognition rules; (b) capital gains and losses; (c) carved out income interests; and (d) deferred payments.

Part VI deals with timing and accounting methods. Many earlier chapters also deal with timing (*e.g.*, original issue discount, and the distinction between current expenses and capital expenditures), but Part VI focuses on accounting—primarily cash and accrual methods, including economic performance rules.

The book makes a special effort to deal with those aspects of the code which have become fundamental in recent years: phantom tax rates; the tax on marriage; disallowing deductions as a proxy for taxing a payee; the schedularization of the code through net loss limitations with carryover provisions; and (of course) the many ways in which time value of money issues arise (original issue discount; prepayment for consumption; "interest free" loans; and carved out income interests).

One pedagogical objective from the earlier version persists. Tax law continues to be an ideal course for teaching statutory interpretation. The material permits exploration of the following basic interpretive issues: (a) plain meaning (in its various guises of ordinary usage and term of art); (b) whether a term means the same thing in tax code as in other legal setting (such as "marriage," "property," and "interest"); (c) legislative history; and (d) legislative purpose. Specific interpretive doctrines are also considered, such as: (a) legislative reenactment and inaction; and (b) *expressio unius est expressio alterius*. We also approach tax avoidance as a problem of statutory interpretation.

The book also presents materials about how tax law is made. Chapter 6, about tax expenditures, provides a window on the legislative process and on the point-counter-point of agency and legislative rules.

SUMMARY OF CONTENTS

DETAILED TABLE OF CONTENTS

Page

Chapter 4 Gifts

Chapter 5 Taxable Year

Chapter 6 Tax Expenditures and the Legislative Process

PART II
PERSONAL CONSUMPTION AND BUSINESS EXPENSES

Chapter 7 Income In-Kind

Page

PART I

BASIC CONCEPTS

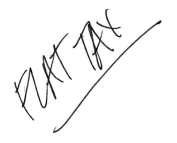

CHAPTER 1

TAX BASE, TAX RATES, AND TAXABLE UNITS

§ 1.01 TAX BASE

Taxable income. The "tax base" for any tax is the amount by which tax rates are multiplied to compute the tax. For the income tax, the tax base is "income." More precisely, it is something the statute defines as "taxable income." That figure is computed by first identifying "gross income," and then subtracting deductions to arrive at taxable income. The deductions come in two categories. First, you subtract certain deductions to reduce gross income to "adjusted gross income." (These are often called "above the line deductions.") Second, you subtract additional deductions to reduce adjusted gross income to "taxable income." (Most of these are called "below the line deductions," or "itemized deductions." *§ 63(d)*.)

The relevant statutory sections are *§ 61* (gross income); *§ 62* (adjusted gross income); and *§ 63* (taxable income).

Standard deduction. Why does it matter whether a deduction reduces gross to adjusted gross income or reduces adjusted gross to taxable income? One reason is that taxpayers can elect not to itemize deductions and instead take a standard deduction. *§ 63(b), (c)*. A taxpayer can*not* take *both* the itemized deductions and the standard deduction. If, however, the deduction is "above the line" (if it reduces gross to adjusted gross income), the deduction *and* the standard deduction are both available.

Itemized deductions. Itemized deductions come in two categories. Some itemized deductions must be added together and only the total over 2% of adjusted gross income is deductible. *§ 67*. Other itemized deductions are deductible without regard to the 2% floor.

Horizontal equity. These rules sound very mechanical, but they have a serious impact on different groups of taxpayers. The significant policy issue is one of "horizontal equity" — who is like someone else, so that they should pay the same tax. Exclusions or deductions available to one taxpayer but not another treat taxpayers differently. Do they deserve "different" treatment? If not, horizontal equity is violated.

Types of deductions. Here is a short (and very incomplete) list of typical above the line deductions; and itemized (below the line) deductions. Note carefully that neither *§ 62* nor *§ 63* allows deductions — these sections only tell you how to compute taxable income based on deductions allowed by some other section. The basic sections *allowing* deductions are *§ 162* (business expenses), and *§ 212* (investment expenses). Numerous personal expenses are deductible as well (*see* cites in *§ 67(b)(1–5)*).

Some basic themes should emerge from the list. Typical above the line deductions are business deductions, except those incurred by employees. Business deductions incurred by employees are usually below the line, except for reimbursed expenses, which are above the line. Do you see why the teacher of this course might rather have her employer reimburse expenses, than have her employer pay the reimbursement as a taxable wage, followed by the employee taking a deduction for the expense?

Typical below the line deductions are small deductions which the IRS has difficulty auditing (usually subject to the 2% floor), and nonbusiness expenses which the tax law wants to encourage (usually not subject to the 2% floor).

EXPENSES

Above the line	**Below the line** 2% floor	**Below the line** No 2% floor
(§ 62)	(§ 67(a))	(§ 67(b))
Business, except by employees	Employees, if not reimbursed	Charitable Medical
Employees, if reimbursed	Investment (other than interest)	Certain state taxes
		Certain investment and home loan interest

Deduction for personal exemptions. The discussion has not mentioned one important deduction — the deduction for personal exemptions. Generally speaking, each individual is entitled to one such deduction for himself or herself, and for certain dependents (we'll explain "dependents" later — typically, a child in the household will be a dependent). The personal exemption deduction is available to all individual taxpayers, whether or not they take the standard deduction. *§§ 151; 63(a); 63(b)(2).*

Inflation adjustments. The dollar figures in the code are sometimes adjusted for inflation — for example, *§ 63(c)(4)* (standard deduction) (tax year 1998 — $7,100 for married couple filing joint returns; $4,250 for single taxpayer); *§ 151(d)(4)* (personal exemption deduction) (tax year 1998 — $2,700 per deduction).

§ 1.02 TAX RATES

Progressivity. The income tax is taxable income times the tax rate. Income tax rates are progressive — meaning that the tax rate increases on *additional* amounts of income. I did not say that taxpayers with higher income pay tax at a higher rate on *all* their income, only that the tax rate increases on additional income. Another way of saying the same thing is that the "marginal" tax rate increases with additional income.

A progressive rate ladder, illustrated below, helps you understand the concept of progressivity. Each rung of the ladder represents additional income. Using the tax rates in *§ 1(a)* on married couples, there are five rungs, taxable at the following rates: 15%, 28%, 31%, 36%, and 39.6%. The top two rungs were adopted in 1993; previously, the top marginal tax rate was 31%. The dollar figures in *§ 1* are adjusted for inflation after 1993 so that an increase in taxable income that does not increase purchasing power will not push a taxpayer into a higher bracket. *§ 1(f)*.

Progressive Rate Ladder (§ 1(a)) — Tax Year 1998

Taxable Income	Tax Rate
>278,450	39.6%
>155,950 to 278,450	36%
>102,300 to 155,950	31%
>42,350 to 102,300	28%
0–42,350	15%

Marginal tax rates. The top tax rate to which a taxpayer is subject is called the marginal tax rate. In the above chart, a taxpayer with $350,000 taxable income is subject to a 39.6% marginal tax rate. That is different from the average tax rate on all taxable income. The average tax rate is the total tax divided by taxable income. It is lower than the marginal tax rate, when the tax on lower rungs of the ladder is less than the tax on the top rung.

The marginal tax rate is critical for tax planning. For example, a taxpayer who can shift income subject to the top rate to other lower-rate taxpayers in the family can reduce the total family tax. The marginal tax rate is also critical for deciding whether to earn *more* money.

Problem: Computing taxable income. Work out this problem. Be sure to use the tax rates for married couples. Notice that there is a different rate structure for unmarried individuals and heads of households. *§ 1(b), (c)*. The reasons for the different rate structures are explained later in this chapter.

Husband earns $60,000 income as an employee. Wife earns $65,000 as a free lance (non-employee) author. The husband has $4,000 employer-reimbursed business expenses while traveling; and $2,900 unreimbursed employee business expenses. The wife has $5,000 of her own business expenses for equipment and supplies. The couple pays $4,500 state and local property and income taxes, and $4,000 interest on a home loan, both of which are below the line deductions, not subject to the 2% floor. They have two children, ages 5 and 8, who live in their household and receive all of their support from their parents. *What is the couple's gross income, adjusted gross income, and taxable income? What is their average and marginal tax rates?*

Effect of deductions and credits in a progressive tax. One of the effects of progressive tax rates is that the value of a deduction increases as the marginal tax rate increases. You can see this by redoing the above problem on the assumption that the couple has only one child — that is, one less deduction for personal exemptions. What is the value of the deduction for the second child? What is the value of a $1,000 deduction for someone in the 39.6% bracket?

A tax "credit" reduces the tax, not taxable income. A credit expressed as a percentage of a dollar figure reduces tax by the same amount regardless of the marginal tax rate. For example, a credit for a dependent child equal to 20% of $2,000 per child reduces tax by $400 per child in all cases, even for a taxpayer in the 15% marginal tax bracket.

Is this last statement entirely accurate? Suppose a couple with two children has $3,000 total earnings. Would this taxpayer benefit by substituting a $400 credit for a deduction for personal exemptions? How could you change the law to give this couple the benefit of the credit?

"Phantom" marginal tax rates. The earlier problem of the couple with $125,000 earnings raises an important policy issue — should people with high income enjoy (1) the benefit of lower tax rates on lower amounts of income; (2) the benefit of the personal exemption deductions; and (3) the benefit of itemized deductions? Suppose you said "no" — those with higher income should *not* enjoy these benefits. The tax code sometimes says "no."

That sounds easy enough. Just tell those with higher incomes that they cannot be taxed at lower rates on their "lower-bracket" income; and that they cannot take personal exemptions or itemized deductions when their income rises above a certain threshold. Well, it is not so easy. A simple sounding policy may be mechanically difficult to implement.

First, define "higher income." At what income should tax benefits be lost?

Second, how should the benefit be reduced? Can you say, for example, that everyone with adjusted gross income over $300,000 loses the benefit of tax rates below 39.6%? No, you can't. Do you see why? Suppose the ay 39.6%

$310,000
−278,450
31,550

tax law said that. Assume you have $300,000 adjusted gross income from earnings and are offered an additional $10,000 compensation. Would the marginal tax rate on that added $10,000 be more than 100% (that is, would you lose more in higher taxes than you earned from the income increase)?

Under current law, the benefit of the lower tax rate on lower amounts of income is *not* lost by individuals with higher income. Corporations, however, do lose the benefit of the lower rates as their incomes rise over certain thresholds. *§ 11(b)(1) (flush paragraph).*

Problem: Disappearing personal exemption deductions. Work out this problem for tax year 1998. A married couple has $186,800 of earnings and four personal exemptions in 1998. One spouse is offered a salary increase of $20,000. By how much does their income tax increase? This problem illustrates how the current law phases out the deduction for personal exemptions for people with higher income. *§ 151(d)(3).* The rationale for the rule is that the personal exemption deductions are primarily aimed at getting low income people off the tax rolls, both to lower their taxes (although they still pay social security taxes), and to reduce administrative burdens. The effect of the rule is to raise the *marginal* tax rate when adjusted gross income exceeds the "threshold amount" (defined in the statute as $150,000 for a married couple, but adjusted for inflation — for tax year 1998, the threshold is $186,800), until the tax benefit is lost.

For those who are mathematically inclined, the increase in marginal tax rates from disappearing personal exemption deductions, imposed on each $2,500 of income over the threshold amount, is:

$$\frac{.02 \times p \times \# \times \text{marginal tax rate}}{2,500}$$

where p = the personal exemption deduction amount; and # = the number of personal exemptions.

In addition, the deduction of *certain* itemized deductions (after applying the 2% floor) is reduced as an individual's income rises above the "applicable amount" ($100,000, adjusted for inflation — for tax year 1998, $124,500). The effect, again, is to raise marginal tax rates. *Certain* itemized deductions are reduced by 3% of adjusted gross income over the "applicable amount," except that the reduction cannot exceed 80% of itemized deductions subject to the reduction. *§ 68.* There is no point in memorizing this complexity, but there is a point in reading about it. You should ask this question. Why doesn't the tax law just raise the tax rates on people with higher incomes? Why go through the complexity of gradually depriving them of certain itemized deductions? The answer is that rate increases are politically unpopular.

§ 1.03 DEDUCTION FOR DEPENDENTS

In the problem we just discussed, the children had no income and were supported by their parents. They were obviously "dependents" within *§ 152*. The category of dependents is not limited to children, but includes all of the individuals listed in *§ 152(a)*, if the taxpayer provides over one-half of their support. The deduction is permitted if the dependent's gross income is less than the "exemption amount," which is the amount allowed as a personal exemption deduction in the relevant tax year. There are a few exceptions to the income ceiling. The most important exception permits parent to take deductions for a dependent child even if the child's income if over the ceiling, if the child is under age 19, or is a full-time student and is not age 24 or older.

[A]—Dependent children and the taxable unit

The income of parents and children is generally not combined into one taxable unit, but there are code provisions which move in that direction. Before the Tax Reform Act of 1986 a parent could take a personal exemption deduction for a child *and* the child could also take a personal exemption deduction for herself. That is no longer true. If a child is eligible to be taken by a parent as a personal exemption deduction, the child cannot also take the deduction. How might this affect children at college with summer earnings?

Of course, the child can still take the standard deduction (for tax year 1998, $4,250), but there are limits. A dependent child's standard deduction cannot exceed the *greater* of (1) (a) earned income (typically, income from personal services) plus (b) $250 (adjusted for inflation beginning in 1999); or (2) $700 (for tax year 1998). (The "plus $250" provision was added in 1997. Is that aimed at children with small bank accounts?) The purpose of this rule is to prevent higher income parents shifting investment income (such as dividends and interest) to a child, thereby sheltering the investment income by a high standard deduction. The rule is not, however, limited to investment income from property received from a parent. *§ 63(c)(5)*.

Yet another provision prevents shifting investment income to a child under age 14. This so-called "kiddie tax" taxes the child *at the parent's tax rate* (if higher than the child's rate) on investment income which exceeds twice the standard deduction available to offset the dependent child's investment income (for tax year 1998 — two times $700, or $1,400). *§ 1(g)*. There is no kiddie tax if parents elect to be taxed on their children's income.

[B]—Defining support

The following case grapples with the meaning of "support." "Support" is not limited to items included in gross income. The rental value of a home is "support" but is not gross income. What emphasis do the following opinions place on administrative concerns and nontax policy?

BARTSCH v. COMMISSIONER

41 T.C. 883, 885-88 (1964)

TIETJENS, JUDGE: . . .

Section 152(a) defines a dependent as any of enumerated individuals (including the mother of the petitioner) over half of whose support, for the calendar year in which the taxable year of the taxpayer begins, was received from the taxpayer.

The problem here is whether petitioner is entitled to add the value of her "services" to her mother to her out-of-pocket expenses in that regard. If she can do so under the statute, then the claimed mother dependent can be held to have received over half of her support from petitioner and petitioner can have the dependency exemption, and the head of a household status, as well.

We think this cannot be done and accordingly hold that Anna did not receive over half her support in the taxable year from the taxpayer, her daughter.

. . . [T]he Treasury promulgated section 1.152-1 of the Income Tax Regulations which provided in part: The term "support" includes food, shelter, clothing, medical and dental care, education, and the like. Generally, these items of support are measured in terms of the amount of expense incurred by the one furnishing such items. However, if the item of support furnished an individual (either by himself or others) is in the form of goods, services, or other benefits, it will be necessary to measure the amount of such items of support in terms of its fair market value.

However, . . . the Treasury amended the above regulation by substituting for the last two sentences in the above quotation the following: Generally, the amount of an item of support will be the amount of expense incurred by the one furnishing such item. If the item of support furnished an individual is in the form of property or lodging, it will be necessary to measure the amount of such item of support in terms of its fair market value.

Thus, the reference to valuing services in determining the amount of support was deliberately deleted from the regulations. . . .

To use what has become a cliche: taxation is a practical matter. . . . Taxpayer and her mother lived together in a home owned by the mother. Each performed household tasks commensurate with her physical capacities. Neither charged or collected from the other for such tasks on a monetary basis. Yet our taxpayer would have us place a value on what she "did" for her mother in order to claim her as a dependent. We attach no opprobrium to her claim; but we are reluctant to say, in the absence of specific statutory direction, and in the face of the equivocal regulatory history, that the taxpayer is entitled to her claim.

We find nothing in the statute requiring that such services as taxpayer rendered to her mother are to be "valued" in computing the "support" which she furnished her mother for dependency exemption purposes. Without clear statutory direction, it is beyond our comprehension why or how such services must be measured in the market place, or anywhere. How can a quantum meruit be put upon a daughter's care for an aged mother?. . . . The term "support" in the Code must mean something more than furnishing the ordinary kindnesses and helpfulness and the cooking and the cleaning and the dishwashing that one able member of the household furnished another less able. These things are not to be valued in the market for tax purposes. Support, as defined in the regulation, includes items such as food, shelter, etc., of which the amount will be "the amount of expense incurred by the one furnishing such item." Petitioner in this case has incurred no expense for furnishing the care ordinarily expected of a daughter for an aged mother (and that is all that is here involved) and we hold she cannot count the value of her personal services in computing whether she furnished "over half" of her mother's support.

FISHER, J., DISSENTING: The question here is whether the value of personal service rendered to a dependent is to be considered as support under Internal Revenue Code section 152.

. . . I disagree with the construction the majority places upon the present form of respondent's regulations. The fact that reference to valuing services in determining the amount of support was deliberately deleted by the respondent from his original regulations in no way forecloses the conclusion that such services are proper considerations in determining the support provided a dependent.

To my mind, it is inconsistent in principle to allow the fair market value of lodging furnished an individual (as the regulations clearly do) but not the fair market value of related household services in determining the support provided the same individual. Why not include only the additional "cost" of such lodging?

In addition, I feel that the majority view tends to discriminate in favor of those who can afford to hire the services of others over the not-so-fortunate who can only provide time and effort and are thereby forced personally to provide the needed services.

Question. How should payment of medical expenses and medical insurance premiums enter into computing who provides more than half the support? Payment of medical bills is support. However, if a person is insured (either by private insurance or Medicare), courts have held that payments made by the insurance company do not count as support; only the insurance premiums count. *Turecamo v. Commissioner*, 554 F.2d 564 (2d Cir. 1977). This makes it easier for an aged parent to be the dependent of an adult child. Should Medicaid benefits be considered government support or disregarded, like Medicare? Medicaid consists of government payments for the poor, which (unlike Medicare) are not tied to prior "insurance-like" tax payments. *Archer v. Commissioner*, 73 T.C. 963 (1980).

Williams v. Commissioner, 71 T.C.M. (CCH) 2423 (1996), holds that AFDC and Food Stamps count as government support, making it more difficult for parents to take a dependent's deduction for a child (or to obtain head of household status). Why might government Medicaid benefits be different — that is, less likely to count as a support payment?

[C]—Agency rulemaking

The *Bartsch* case refers to a Regulation. What is a Regulation? A Regulation is usually an interpretation of the statute issued after the public has had an opportunity to comment on a proposed regulation. It is signed by officials in the Treasury with policy responsibility and by the Commissioner of Internal Revenue Service. The procedures used for their promulgation make them the most authoritative agency interpretation of the tax law.

What does it mean to suggest that a Regulation is very authoritative? It means that a court will accord a great deal of weight to a Regulation favoring the government. Other factors adding to that weight are: the contemporaneousness of the Regulation's adoption with passage of the statute; the fact that the Regulation is longstanding; and the existence of specific language in a statutory section authorizing the Regulation's adoption (not just the catch-all authority found in *§ 7805(a))*.

If the Regulation helps the taxpayer, courts will not permit the agency to disavow it retroactively, even if the government could not rely on it to support the government's position. Retroactive revocation is an abuse of agency discretion.

There are other forms of agency interpretation, which you will see cited throughout the course. A private letter ruling is an administrative "declaratory judgment," which the IRS will issue to a taxpayer. If the taxpayer has accurately described the facts and has relied on the ruling to plan future behavior, the agency promises it will not revoke the ruling *as to that taxpayer*. Taxpayers cannot rely on a ruling issued to another taxpayer, although there are occasional cases holding that a taxpayer cannot be denied a ruling received by a competitor. *Farmers' & Merchants' Bank v. United States*, 476 F.2d 406 (4th Cir. 1973).

Revenue Rulings are generally published distillations of the contents of important letter rulings. They are usually issued by the IRS without public participation. The IRS says that taxpayers can rely on Revenue Rulings until revoked. Courts nonetheless say that retroactive revocation of a Revenue Ruling is permitted, but there are hints that retroactivity might be disallowed if the result would be unduly harsh. *Dunn v. United States*, 468 F. Supp. 991, 995 (S.D.N.Y. 1979).

If the government relies on a Revenue Ruling as legal authority, courts usually say that they carry no weight as interpretations of law — they are just the opinion of one of the litigants. *Browne v. Commissioner*, 73 T.C. 723, 731 (1980) (Hall, J., concurring). In fact, the IRS' longstanding adherence to practice contained in a Revenue Ruling is likely to be of some interpretive weight.

In addition, courts deciding tax cases have recently begun to consider whether the Supreme Court's decision in *Chevron U.S.A. Inc. v. Natural Resources Defense Council, Inc.*, 467 U.S. 837 (1984), requires deference to Revenue Rulings comparable to that applicable to Regulations. *Chevron* held that the courts should defer to "reasonable" agency rules if Congress did not resolve the issue. *Chevron* has its clearest application to Regulations, usually issued after notice to the public and an opportunity for public comment. (A recent case, *Hospital Corp. of America v. Commissioner*, 107 T.C. 73 (1996), upheld Treasury Regulations, relying on *Chevron*.) The unanswered question is whether this level of deference applies to Revenue Rulings, which are issued without notice to the public and an opportunity to be heard.

Since no one really knows what *Chevron* means, a tax course may not be the best place to begin speculating. My own view is that the deference accorded Regulations is not appropriate for Revenue Rulings. The process by which agencies make decisions should be relevant to the weight they enjoy in court.

There is a discussion of these issues in Galler, *Judicial Deference to Revenue Rulings: Reconciling Divergent Standards*, 56 Ohio St. L.J. 1037 (1995) (arguing that, with one exception, the courts of appeals thus far have not applied *Chevron* to Revenue Rulings).

[D]—Divorced or separated parents

It is obviously difficult to determine who provides over one half the support for a child of divorced or separated parents. Responding to the fact that about 5% of all lower-level agency disputes involved this issue, Congress passed *§ 152(e)* to reduce controversy. That section gave the dependency deduction to the custodial parent except in certain specified circumstances.

In *Prophit v. Commissioner*, 57 T.C. 507 (1972), *affirmed per curiam*, 470 F.2d 1370 (5th Cir. 1973), a father provided over half the support for a child, who was in the custody of a nonresident alien German mother. There was no dispute over these facts, which would qualify the father for the dependency deduction, in the absence of any special rules applicable to divorced or separated parents. The mother did not in fact claim the deduction and was prohibited from doing so as a nonresident alien. The court held that the reason for the passage of *§ 152(e)* was absent in this case, because there was no controversy between the parents. The father asked the court to consider "the intent of the law and not the 'letter' of it." The court agreed, allowing the father the deduction. It cited the Apostle Paul: "Not of the letter, but of the spirit; for the letter killeth, but the spirit giveth life." The concurring opinion held, more narrowly than the majority, that the taxpayer should win *because* there was only one potential claimant — because the mother was a nonresident alien.

Do you agree with the following dissent?

> TANNENWALD, J., DISSENTING: I think the majority decision flies in the face of section 152(e). That language expressly states that where a child receives over one-half of his support from his parents, who are legally divorced or separated under a decree or written separation agreement, and such child is in the custody of one or both parents "such child shall be treated, for purposes of subsection (a), as receiving over half of his support during the calendar year from the parent having custody for a greater portion of the calendar year," unless the other parent meets certain specified conditions. It is undisputed that petitioner did not satisfy those conditions. I do not think it is possible to deal with this case under section 152(a) without regard to the express language of section 152(e). Granted that the difficulties stemming from conflicting claims between parents for dependency exemptions were the generating force for legislative action, the clear mandate of section 152(e) is not

limited in application to situations where a conflict exists. The fact that the petitioner and respondent have agreed on the amounts of support involved is beside the point. A third party, namely, the other spouse, is usually involved in this type of situation, albeit, in this particular case, the petitioner's former wife was a nonresident alien during the taxable year and therefore not subject to United States tax.

[E]—Statutory interpretation — statutory purpose vs. language

Was the court in *Prophit* correct in disregarding the letter of the law for the spirit? Spirit is presumably another word for "purpose," so it is crucial to define the legislative purpose accurately. The court chose to define purpose in general terms, which was to reduce the number of cases in which there was controversy about who provided support. The statutory mechanism was reduced to the minor status of a means to implement that purpose. But can means and ends be so easily separated? Wasn't the congressional purpose to eliminate disputes by the particular means set forth in *§ 152(e)*?

Perhaps the court thought that Congress had overlooked the particular situation in which the taxpayer found himself. What was that situation? Was it the absence of a dispute between the taxpayer and his spouse about how much support each provided; or was it the special case of one spouse not being allowed to take a personal exemption deduction because she was a nonresident alien? Should the court be freer to apply the spirit of the law if it thinks Congress has overlooked something? Is there any evidence in the statute that the taxpayer's situation was not entirely overlooked?

§ 1.04 MARRIED UNITS

[A]—History of taxing marital units; tax on marriage

Assume that two taxpayers each earn $30,000 salary. Why do their taxes rise if they marry? Compare the rate structures for married couples (*§ 1(a)*) and single individuals (*§ 1(c)*). The lower 15% rate for married couples applies to less than twice the taxable income to which the 15% rate is applied for a single individual. Using 1998 inflation adjusted rate schedules, the single individual 15% tax rate applies to $25,350, or a total of $50,700 for two individuals, but the married couple pays 15% on only the first $42,350. More income is therefore subject to the 28% rate after marriage than before marriage. Notice that married couples cannot avoid this result by filing separate tax returns. Look at the tax rates applicable to them in *§ 1(d)*, which reduces the taxable income subject to the low 15% tax rate. (Another reason for a potential tax on marriage is that the standard deduction for a married couple is less than twice the standard deduction for single individuals).

This result is a product of history. Before 1948, individuals, whether married or not, were taxed on their own income. If a husband and wife each earned $30,000, they paid the same tax as two single individuals with $30,000 income. If a husband earned $60,000, and was married to a wife without income, he paid taxes on $60,000. However, states with Spanish law background (like California) had "community property" laws, which allocated one half of each spouse's earnings to the other; in such states, the marital unit with $60,000 earnings was therefore taxed like two $30,000 single individuals. Because tax rates were progressive, the California married couple was taxed lower than a New York couple with a $60,000/$0 earnings pattern. The Supreme Court recognized state property law for tax purposes. *Poe v. Seaborn*, 282 U.S. 101 (1930).

In 1948, a Republican Congress was in a mood to cut taxes and provided that *all* married couples would be taxed *as though* their income was split in half, with each half subject to the single individual's tax rate. That brought a New York couple's tax down to the California couple's level. It also equalized the tax on married units with the same total income (whether the actual earnings were split $60,000/$0, or $30,000/$30,000).

By 1969, however, one dramatic effect of the split income approach seemed intolerable. A married couple (for example, with $60,000 total income) paid much lower taxes than a single individual with the same $60,000 total income. As marriage was viewed more as an individual preference, the lower tax on married couples seemed to be a tax preference for people who chose a particular life style. Therefore, in 1969, income-splitting was repealed. *§ 1(c) lowered* the tax rates on single individuals. However, a new *§ 1(a)* was passed for married units. It provided them with their own rate structure, based on the tax they would have paid if they had split their income under the *higher* pre-1969 rates.

This "solution" continued to treat all married units with the same total income equally. However, by building the old higher pre-1969 rates on single individuals into the 1969 rates on marital units, two single individuals with approximately equal incomes (for example, $30,000 each) increased their taxes by marrying. Marriage deprived these single individuals of the new lower 1969 tax rates.

Whether marriage will raise total taxes depends on the relative contributions of each spouse to the total income of the marital unit. For example, two individuals with $60,000 and $0 income respectively still lower tax by getting married.

Question. Would you favor repealing *§ 1(a)* to eliminate the tax on marriage and letting a husband and wife file as single individuals under *§ 1(c)*? What are the policy consequences of repealing *§ 1(a)*?

Untaxed housework. Another tax rule has a potential impact on married units. The tax law does not tax the value of services performed for oneself. Carried to an extreme, the prospect of taxing such services seems silly and offensive. Would we tax the value of grooming oneself, walking to work, etc? Why not? Is it hard to value; would detecting and valuing there services intrude the IRS into private life; how would the taxpayer get cash to pay the tax?

Housework presents a special problem. The value of wagework is taxed but the value of housework is not. This means that one spouse can stay home and produce housework tax free, but would have to pay tax on wages earned to pay someone else to do the work. This provides an incentive not to take wagework. The incentive to provide services for oneself always exists, but the social implications are more severe in the case of housework.

Question. Would you favor the following provision: married units with two workers receive a deduction equal to 10% of the lower earning spouse's earnings? Such a provision was repealed by the Tax Reform Act of 1986.

[B]—Defining "marriage" for tax purposes

REV. RUL. 76-255, 1976-2 C.B. 40, 40-41

Advice has been requested concerning the marital status of certain taxpayers for Federal income tax purposes under the circumstances described below. . . .

C and D were married in 1964 and filed joint Federal income tax returns for the years 1964 throughout 1974. In 1975, C and D determined that for Federal income tax purposes it would be advantageous for them to be unmarried so that each of them could file a separate Federal income tax return as an unmarried individual.

On December 30, 1975, C and D secured a divorce under the laws of a foreign jurisdiction. For purposes of this ruling, it is assumed that such divorce was valid. However, at the time of the divorce, they intended to remarry each other and did so in January 1976.

Section 143(a)(1) of the Internal Revenue Code of 1954 [Editor — now *§ 7703*] provides generally that the determination of whether an individual is married shall be made as of the close of the taxable year. . . .

Rev. Rul. 67-442, 1967-2 C.B. 65, provides that the Internal Revenue Service generally will not question for Federal income tax purposes the validity of any divorce decree until a court of competent jurisdiction declares the divorce to be invalid. . . .

[A]lthough C and D were divorced under the laws of the foreign jurisdiction, the divorce was not intended by them to have effect except to enable them to qualify as unmarried individuals who would be eligible to file separate returns. In addition, C and D intended to and did remarry each other early in the succeeding taxable year.

The true nature of a transaction must be considered in light of the plain intent and purpose of the statute. Such transaction should not be given any effect for Federal income tax purposes if it merely serves the purpose of tax avoidance. In determining whether it serves the purpose of tax avoidance all of the surrounding facts and circumstances are to be considered. [The statute does not] contemplate[] a "sham transaction" designed to manipulate for Federal income tax purposes an individual's marital status as of the close of a taxable year.

[Editor — The Ruling concludes that C and D were married for tax purposes as of the close of tax year 1975.]

BOYTER v. COMMISSIONER

74 T.C. 989, 994–1001 (1980),
remanded, 668 F.2d 1382 (4th Cir. 1981)

WILBUR, JUDGE: . . .

[Editor — This case concerns the validity of a divorce obtained for tax purposes.]

We [] agree with the assertion emphatically made by [taxpayer] on brief that "the Tax Court is bound by state law rather than federal law when attempting to construe marital status." Except in a few specific situations, the definition of "husband and wife," or "marriage" is not addressed in the Internal Revenue Code, even though the application of many provisions of the statute turns on the marital status of the taxpayer. It has consistently been held that for Federal income tax purposes, the determination of the marital status of the parties must be made in accordance with the law of the State of their domicile. . . . The rationale for deferring to State law is that domestic relations is "an area that has long been regarded as a virtually exclusive province of the States." . . .

With regard to the provisions for filing a joint return or filing as an unmarried individual, it has been held that State law is determinative on the question of the recognition of common law marriage; the effect of an invalidated Mexican divorce decree; the effect of an interlocutory divorce decree; and whether the taxpayer is legally separated under a decree of separate maintenance. . . . These decisions reflect a consensus that marriage and divorce generally relate to the most intimate and personal of human interaction and are thus better defined by the one entity which has traditionally exercised exclusive regulation and control over these matters.

[Editor — The Tax Court then holds that Maryland courts would not recognize the foreign divorce as effective to terminate the marriage. Hence, petitioners were still married under the tax law. The Court of Appeals reversed the Tax Court decision, holding that the couple was not married under Maryland law. The appellate court was, however, willing to apply the "sham transaction" doctrine to supersede state law. It remanded the case to determine how to apply that doctrine. The case then disappears from the reports, presumably because it was settled.]

Statutory Interpretation — Tax Law and Family Law. Must the word "married" in the tax law have the same meaning as in state family law, as the Tax Court in *Boyter* suggests? Are tax law and family law policies the same?

Consider the following more specific questions: (1) Should a court decide whether two individuals, never married, are living so like a married unit, that they should be taxed as "married?" (2) Should the agency inquire into the marital status for tax purposes of a couple married in name only? The statute is not entirely silent regarding separated married couples. *See § 6013(d)(2); § 7703(a)(2),(b).* (3) Should the agency question whether two single people who marry on December 30 and divorce on January 2 are really married (they want the tax reduction resulting from the fact that one of the individuals has no income)? Is the single-married-single case different from the married-divorced-married case?

One of the significant institutional consequences of not automatically incorporating state family law into the tax law is that the agency administering the tax law has some discretion. Why might you want to deny that discretion? Do your reasons apply to couples who divorce and remarry quickly?

A tempting way to solve "tax avoidance" problems is to say that a taxpayer whose major (or dominant, or significant) purpose is tax avoidance cannot get the benefits otherwise provided by the statute. But that begs the question. The question is whether the statute allows them to do what they did. If it does, they are not avoiding taxes. For example, tax avoidance is no reason to deny an investor the benefit of tax exempt bonds (*§ 103*).

§ 1.05 EARNED INCOME CREDIT *(low income TPs)*

The earned income credit (EIC) (*§ 32*) allows taxpayers with (1) earned income and (2) a "qualifying child" (*§ 32(c)(3)*) to lower their taxes by a percentage of the earned income. It does more. If the credit exceeds taxes otherwise due, the taxpayer gets a payment from the government. The credit is refundable. For example, a taxpayer with only $3,000 of earnings (and therefore no tax after the personal exemption and standard deduction) fills out the tax form and computes the credit as though it had been withheld from wages. The idea is to help lower income earners avoid welfare and to compensate for the burden of social security taxes. There is also a procedure, not much used, for employers to make advance payments of the EIC to employees, rather than rely on end-of-the-year "refunds." *§ 3507(f)* requires the IRS to take appropriate steps to make people aware of the advance payment procedure.

The percentage used to compute the credit varies, depending on whether the taxpayer has one or more than one child. In addition, there is a maximum amount of earned income eligible for the credit. The credits and maximum earnings figures for 1998 (adjusted for inflation) are:

	1 child		More than 1 child	
	%	Max. earnings	%	Max. earnings
1998	34.0	$6,680	40.0	$9,390

ex: if earn le680, can lower that taxable ant. by 34%

The target of the credit is lower-income taxpayers, which not only requires a maximum earnings figure, but also an adjusted gross income threshold, above which the credit begins to disappear by a specified percentage of excess income. The threshold is $12,260 of AGI (or earned income, if greater) — adjusted for inflation. The "phase-out" percentage varies with the number of children and the tax year. With one child, the percentage is 15.98%; with more than one child, the percentage is 21.06%.

The phase-out has the impact of an increased marginal tax rate on lower income earners, counteracting the incentive effects of the credit itself. Marriage between two workers, one of whom has a child, might also be discouraged, if increased total earnings cost the couple the earned income credit.

Problem: Computing the EIC credit. Use tax year 1998 to answer this problem. What is the credit for someone with one child and earnings of $5,000; $6,680; $10,000; $13,260? Assume no other income and no deductible expenses. What is the marginal tax rate on the taxpayer whose income rises from $12,260 to $13,260 (that is, on the last $1,000)? If two taxpayers with $12,260 earnings marry (one of whom has an eligible child from a prior relationship), how much EIC do they lose?

The 1993 tax law introduced one further EIC wrinkle. For the first time, workers without children are eligible — if they are at least age 25 and under age 65, and if they cannot be deducted as another's dependent. The income levels are low, however. Maximum eligible earnings are $4,460, the credit percentage is 7.65%, and the EIC disappears at the rate of 7.65% above $5,570. At what income level would the EIC for workers without children disappear completely?

An additional provision prevents well-off taxpayers from taking advantage of the earned income credit. It denies the credit to individuals with "disqualified income" in excess of an inflation-adjusted threshold. For tax year 1998, the threshold is $2,300. "Disqualified income" is, in general terms, investment income, such as interest and dividends. An important feature of the definition of disqualified income is that it includes tax exempt interest income (*i.e.*, the interest on state and local bonds, discussed in § 6.03, *infra*). *See § 32(i).*

Notice that the income reporting incentives created by the EIC may be perverse. If you have one eligible child, are subject to a 7.65% Social Security tax on earnings, and are eligible for a 34% EIC credit, would you overreport your earnings (for example, state that earnings were $6,000 instead of $5,000)?

There have obviously been considerable compliance problems associated with the earned income credit. The 1997 Tax Act adds several penalty provisions, one of which prohibits claiming the EIC for ten years after a fraudulent EIC claim.

§ 1.06 CHILD TAX CREDIT (§24)

The 1997 tax law added a child tax credit, found in § *24*. You should take this opportunity to note some aspects of the contemporary tax legislative process, which have come in for a lot of criticism.

(1) The credit amount is $400 in tax year 1998; $500 thereafter. Why do you think the amount increases after 1998? The increase means that the impact on the budget deficit is less in the earlier years after passage of the law, allowing Members of Congress to avoid being accused of voting for a rise in the budget deficit in the near future. It also means that, if budget deficits are much larger than expected, the tax breaks can be cut back.

(2) The credit is available for a dependent of the taxpayer, who is a child, a direct descendant of a child, a step-child, or a foster child. The dependent must be under age 17. Why do you think this tax break was preferred to a rate reduction for low and middle income taxpayers?

for whom? (under 17)

Politically, the child tax credit (unlike a rate reduction) can be billed as a benefit for families with children, with strong "conservative" family values overtones. The current political climate is also one in which benefits are carefully targeted to constituent groups and the child tax credit is one example of that phenomenon.

Notice also that targeting benefits accepts tax complexity (in order to define the beneficiaries of the tax break) in preference to tax simplicity. Despite all the political rhetoric about tax simplicity, tax complexity always seems to win out.

(3) The child tax credit is phased out at the rate of $50 for every $1,000 of income (or part thereof) above a threshold. The threshold is $110,000 for married taxpayers filing joint returns and $75,000 for single taxpayers. If there is more than one dependent child eligible for the credit, the phase out applies to the credit for one dependent first and then the next dependent, and so on. *§ 24(b)(1)*. Thus, if there are three dependents of married taxpayers in 1999, the credit phases out at $140,000 of income. This is different from the phase out of personal exemption deductions, where the 2% reduction of the deduction applies to the total personal exemption deductions for each $2500 of "excess" income. § 151(d)(3)(A-B). *What added phantom marginal tax rate does the phase out of the child tax credit produce?*

Notice the potential impact of this phase out rule on the complexity of the tax forms (where tax computations are required). Does the rule have an impact on people who cannot manage tax form complexity?

In addition, take note of where in the income scale this phantom tax rate operates. You have seen some phantom tax rates and will see others in the tax code (*e.g.*, educational and retirement savings tax breaks). Is there any effort to make sure that they do not cumulate at certain income levels to raise effective marginal tax rates too much?

(4) The child tax credit itself is refundable under very limited circumstances. A taxpayer with three or more children can obtain a refund for the child tax credit up to the amount by which social security taxes exceed the refundable EIC. Here is an example. Assume a taxpayer with three or more children with a regular income tax of $500, social security tax of $2000, an EIC of $1200, and a child tax credit of $1500. This taxpayer would first use the child tax credit to offset the $500 of regular income tax, leaving a $1000 unused child tax credit. The social security tax of $2000 exceeds the refundable EIC by $800 ($2000–$1200), so $800 of the $1,000 unused child tax credit would be refunded.

(5) The credit amount and the thresholds are *not* indexed for inflation.

§ 1.07 COMPLEXITY

One complaint about the earned income and child tax credits is an increase in tax complexity. Actually, tax complexity is itself a complex idea.

It is sometimes equated with statutory detail, but that is misleading. The simplest statutory text could increase the *legal* complexity of the tax law by leading to divergent legal authorities and fostering uncertainty. Recall the problem of whether married taxpayers can divorce and remarry soon thereafter to avoid the tax on marriage (divergent Tax Court, Court of Appeals, and IRS authority). In other words, legal complexity does not equate with a detailed text, although it *can* be a byproduct of a text too dense to be understood.

An excessively dense text has its own problems. It often produces jigsaw puzzle *textual* complexity, where it is hard to fit all the statutory pieces together. The rules about refunding the child tax credit are a good example, where the statutory text yields up its secrets only in conjunction with some study aid — such as a committee report or a summary explanation published by a private publisher.

In most public conversations of tax complexity, the reference to complexity is not to legal complexity or the complexity of the statutory text, but to *tax form* complexity. This type of complexity is of greatest concern when it forces taxpayers to hire outside tax return preparers. Both the earned income credit and child tax credit are likely examples of this problem.

All three sources of tax complexity are a concern for small businesses, even though they routinely use tax return preparers, because the expense of return preparation and the risk of litigation are considerably increased by tax complexity. The alternative minimum tax (*see* Chapter 17, *infra*) is a primary source of complaints for small business, arising from legal, textual, and form complexity.

All three types of tax complexity can also increase tax administrative burdens and, therefore, indirectly cause problems for taxpayers, either as a result of administrative errors or excessive agency discretion, as the agency itself struggles to comprehend the law.

Congress is certainly aware of the problem of tax complexity and constantly complains about it, even as it legislates more and more complex rules in response to the political dynamics underlying tax law. (Many recent tax bills have been, on this account, referred to informally as the Lawyers and Accountants Relief Act of [fill in the date].) Those dynamics include: helping taxpayers know exactly what their tax obligations are, such as which former spouse can take the personal exemption deduction for the child (textual complexity driving out legal uncertainty); providing precisely tailored tax breaks (earned income and child tax credits); and selectively closing off tax breaks that taxpayers have uncovered (*see* § 6.04, *infra*, discussing the Industrial Revenue Bond loophole).

The recent Report of the National Commission on Restructuring the IRS (Kerrey-Portman Report), published in 75 Tax Notes 1683 (June 30, 1997), called for Congress to consider a Tax Complexity Analysis for each tax proposal, which would address the following concerns:

(1) did Congress allow for adequate IRS input about administrability;

(2) what are the compliance burdens on taxpayers;

(3) what is the effect on IRS forms and worksheets;

(4) how much time is allowed to the IRS to prepare for administering the new law;

(5) is there a need for rulemaking guidance after passage of the law;

(6) what is the effect of the law on recordkeeping requirements;

(7) what is the number, type, and sophistication of affected taxpayers;

(8) is the IRS given tasks not directly related to revenue raising?

As you reflect on tax complexity discussed in this and later chapters, consider (1) whether Congress gave adequate attention to any of the above sources of complexity; (2) what kind of tax complexity the law causes; and (3) whether the complexity is warranted in achieving the appropriate goals of the income tax law.

CHAPTER 2

WHOSE INCOME IS IT

§ 2.01 INTRODUCTION

Rate differences create an incentive to shift income to different taxpayers to achieve the lowest total tax. A taxpayer wants to do this, however, only if there is a close relationship with the transferee (for example, a family member or wholly owned corporation). Many income shifting efforts therefore occur within the family or between a taxpayer and a controlled corporation. The "kiddie tax" is one complex effort to discourage intra-family income shifting.

This area of the law has special interest for lawyers interested in how tax law is made. Historically, the "law" responding to income shifting was developed first by the courts. The statute (*§ 61*) simply taxed income without saying anything about whose income it was. The seminal case dealing with assignment of income is *Lucas v. Earl*, set forth below. Thereafter, Congress responded with *specific* statutory rules dealing with income shifting in certain areas of the law (for example, setting up family trusts). Still other areas of law are dealt with by detailed Regulations (such as family partnerships).

These various sources of law suggest two questions about the evolution of tax law. First, what is the role of courts in initiating efforts to close potential loopholes? Second, who does a better job of addressing the problem: courts, agency, or legislature?

§ 2.02 PERSONAL SERVICES

LUCAS v. EARL

281 U.S. 111 (1930)

MR. JUSTICE HOLMES delivered the opinion of the Court.

This case presents the question whether the respondent, Earl, could be taxed for the whole of the salary and attorney's fees earned by him in the years 1920 and 1921, or should be taxed for only a half of them in view of a contract with his wife which we shall mention. . . .

By the contract, made in 1901, Earl and his wife agreed "that any property either of us now has or may hereafter acquire . . . in any way, either by earnings (including salaries, fees, etc.), or any rights by contract or otherwise, during the existence of our marriage, or which we or either of us may receive by gift, bequest, devise, or inheritance, and all the proceeds, issues, and profits of any and all such property shall be treated and considered, and hereby is declared to be received, held, taken, and owned by us as joint tenants, and not otherwise, with the right of survivorship." The validity of the contract is not questioned, and we assume it to be unquestionable under the law of the State of California, in which the parties lived. . . .

The Revenue Act of 1918 . . . imposes a tax upon the net income of every individual including "income derived from salaries, wages, or compensation for personal service . . . of whatever kind and in whatever form paid." . . . A very forcible argument is presented to the effect that the statute seeks to tax only income beneficially received, and that taking the question more technically the salary and fees became the joint property of Earl and his wife on the very first instant on which they were received. We well might hesitate upon the latter proposition, because however the matter might stand between husband and wife he was the only party to the contracts by which the salary and fees were earned, and it is somewhat hard to say that the last step in the performance of those contracts could be taken by anyone but himself alone. But this case is not to be decided by attenuated subtleties. It turns on the import and reasonable construction of the taxing act. There is no doubt that the statute could tax salaries to those who earned them and provide that the tax could not be escaped by anticipatory arrangements and contracts however skillfully devised to prevent the salary when paid from vesting even for a second in the man who earned it. That seems to us the import of the statute before us and we think that no distinction can be taken according to the motives leading to the arrangement by which the fruits are attributed to a different tree from that on which they grew.

Judgment reversed.

Questions. How does the Court identify the "import" of the statute? (1) Is the transfer of income from one spouse to the other (this was before joint returns) a tax avoidance "gimmick," a "sham?" (2) Is there something about this income transfer that is especially troublesome? Is it the fact that the taxpayer retains control over whether the income will be produced at all in the future, through the decision to perform personal services?

Impact of attribution to transferor. Mechanically, all *Lucas v. Earl* does is to recast the transaction so that the income collected by the transferee is taxed as though it had first been received by the transferor and then transferred to the transferee. How this recast transaction is taxed depends on the tax rules applicable to the relationship between the various parties. In *Lucas*, the assigned income was salary so the transferor is treated as though he received taxable salary. The transferee is a family member, so the subsequent transfer is a gift to the transferee (gifts are tax free, (*§ 102*), as explained in Chapter 4, *infra*).

Compare Lucas v. Earl to the following *Blair* case.

BLAIR v. COMMISSIONER

300 U.S. 5 (1937)

MR. CHIEF JUSTICE HUGHES delivered the opinion of the Court.

[Editor — The taxpayer was an income beneficiary under a trust. He assigned all of his trust interest to his children prior to the tax years in which the trust income arose, so the income was paid to the children. The issue was whether the assignor or the assignee-children should be taxed on the income. The Court first held that a valid assignment had been made under state law and then discussed its tax consequences, distinguishing *Lucas v. Earl.*]

Our decision[] in *Lucas v. Earl*, 281 U.S. 111 [is] cited. In the *Lucas* Case the question was whether an attorney was taxable for the whole of his salary and fees earned by him in the tax years or only upon one-half by reason of an agreement with his wife by which his earnings were to be received and owned by them jointly. We were of the opinion that the case turned upon the construction of the taxing act. We said that "the statute could tax salaries to those who earned them and provide that the tax could not be escaped by anticipatory arrangements and contracts however skillfully devised to prevent the salary when paid from vesting even for a second in the man who earned it." That was deemed to be the meaning of the statute as to compensation for personal service and the one who earned the income was held to be subject to the tax. . . . [*Lucas* is] not in point. The tax here is not upon earnings which are taxed to the one who earns them. . . .

Key:
Lucas N/A

In the instant case, the tax is upon income as to which, in the general application of the revenue acts, the tax liability attaches to ownership. The Government points to the provisions of the revenue acts imposing upon the beneficiary of a trust the liability for the tax upon the income distributable to the beneficiary. But the term is merely descriptive of the one entitled to the beneficial interest. These provisions cannot be taken to preclude valid assignments of the beneficial interest, or to affect the duty of the trustee to distribute income to the owner of the beneficial interest, whether he was such initially or becomes such by valid assignment. The one who is to receive the income as the owner of the beneficial interest is to pay the tax. If under the law governing the trust the beneficial interest is assignable, and if it has been assigned without reservation, the assignee thus becomes the beneficiary and is entitled to rights and remedies accordingly. We find nothing in the revenue acts which denies him that status.

owner/B is taxed

→ here, children (assignees)

The will creating the trust entitled the petitioner during his life to the net income of the property held in trust. He thus became the owner of an equitable interest in the corpus of the property. By virtue of that interest he was entitled to enforce the trust, to have a breach of trust enjoined and to obtain redress in case of breach. The interest was present property alienable like any other, in the absence of a valid restraint upon alienation. The beneficiary may thus transfer [] his interest []. . . .

We conclude that the assignments were valid, that the assignees thereby became the owners of the specified beneficial interests in the income, and that as to these interests they and not the petitioner were taxable for the tax years in question. The judgment of the Circuit Court of Appeals is reversed and the cause is remanded with direction to affirm the decision of the Board of Tax Appeals.

———

The import of this case is that anyone can assign his entire interest in property (*e.g.*, land, shares of stock, or a bond) and deflect the rent, dividends or interest to the assignee. Why is there a distinction between taxpayers who assign personal service income and those who assign property?

§ 2.03 RETAINED CONTROL OVER CAPITAL

Suppose the taxpayer transfers property (not the right to personal service income), but retains control over the property. This can happen when a taxpayer sets up a trust and retains either (1) management control (by being the trustee or appointing compliant trustees to do their bidding), or (2) distribution control (for example, discretion to decide which child should receive trust income).

Trusts. The Supreme Court originally decided that retention of "too much" control over a trust could result in taxing the trust grantor on trust income. Thereafter, detailed Regulations explained when the grantor could not shift income to the trust or the trust beneficiaries. Finally, the Code was amended to provide very detailed rules specifying when the trust grantor was taxed because of retained control. In this corner of "assignment of income" doctrine, the statutory rules are exclusive. Case law is no longer relevant. *§ 671 (last sentence).*

The use of trusts for tax planning purposes has been substantially reduced by the elegant "solution" of raising the tax rates on trusts. *See § 1(e).* For tax year 1994, the 36% and 39.6% tax rates kick in when taxable income exceeds $5,500 and $7,500 respectively.

Partnerships. Another situation in which retained control over capital might prevent transfer of income to a transferee is the assignment of a partnership income interest to a family member. The Regulations specify the conditions under which the transfer will be effective, including that the transferor not retain too much control over income distribution or over management beyond the reasonable needs of the business. A transfer to a minor child who is not competent to manage his own affairs is generally not effective for tax purposes, unless the child's interests are protected by a judicially-supervised fiduciary. *Treas. Reg. § 1.704-1(e)(1), (2).*

In addition, the transferor of a partnership interest is taxed on a reasonable amount attributable to his personal services. He cannot work for nothing. *§ 704(e)(2).*

Finally, these rules apply only to partnerships in which capital is a material income-producing factor. A partner in a personal service partnership cannot transfer the income to a transferee under the general principles of *Lucas v. Earl.*

§ 2.04 TRANSFERRING INCOME TO A CORPORATION

Suppose a taxpayer is an athlete or movie actor and owns all of the stock of a corporation. The taxpayer-shareholder has a contract with the corporation so that, on paper, the taxpayer-shareholder's services are loaned out by the corporation to the sports team or movie company. Payment for the taxpayer's personal services is made to the corporation. The taxpayer-shareholder receives a salary from her corporation as an employee, which is less than the total personal service income. Who is taxed on the personal service income collected by the corporation?

Several Courts of Appeals have been very reluctant to apply assignment of income doctrine in the corporate-shareholder context to tax the taxpayer-shareholder on the total personal service income. *Foglesong v. Commissioner*, 691 F.2d 848 (7th Cir. 1982), *rev'g* 77 T.C. 1102 (1981); *Sargent v. Commissioner*, 929 F.2d 1252 (8th Cir. 1991), *rev'g* 93 T.C. 572 (1989). In both cases, the Tax Court applied assignment of income doctrine to tax the shareholder-employee on all of the corporation's income, when the shareholder was the employee of the person for whom the services were performed (*e.g.*, a sports team which "borrowed" the taxpayer's services from the taxpayer's corporation). The Courts of Appeals reversed, stressing that a corporation is a separate tax entity, a separation which was contradicted by taxing the shareholder on personal service income deflected to the corporation. Of course, the family member to whom personal service income is transferred is also a separate tax "entity," and yet the transferor is taxed (under *Lucas v. Earl*) on the personal service income.

However, the Tax Court stuck to its guns in *Leavell v. Commissioner*, 104 T.C. 140 (1995). A professional basketball player organized and owned a personal service corporation and agreed to furnish his services to his own corporation. The corporation then executed a contract with an NBA professional basketball team to furnish the player's services to the NBA team. As a condition of executing the player contract, the team required the player to execute a written agreement personally agreeing to perform the individual services called for by the player contract. The team paid the corporation for the player's services, only part of which amount was paid as compensation by the corporation to the player.

The government asserted that the *entire* amount paid to the corporation was the player's personal service income and could not be deflected to the corporation. The Tax Court held that, because the team had the power to control the performance of the services, the player was an employee of the team and could not therefore deflect the personal service income to his corporation, based on the principles of *Lucas v. Earl*. The Tax Court followed its earlier decision in *Sargent*, which had been reversed by the Eighth Circuit.

Why is the employment relationship with the team so important? One reason might be that control over the player, which is implicit in the employment relation with the team, negates control by the player's personal service corporation; and, further, that control by the player's corporation is a prerequisite to the corporation being treated as the income recipient rather than the player. Control by the player's corporation makes the corporation look more like the following situation in which the corporation is clearly the income recipient: a music talent corporation sends out performers to do gigs at various locations during the year and pays the performer a salary, which is less than the corporation collects for lending out the performer's services.

But why should control by the corporation rather than the team negate an inference that the player is the real income earner when the player is the *sole* shareholder who controls the corporation? Perhaps the courts are reluctant to apply the assignment of income doctrine to cases in which a business executive owns his or her own corporation and works for less than the fair market value of the services. The courts are certainly reluctant to insist on the shareholder-executive charging the full fair market value of his services.

But isn't the shareholder-executive situation different from a corporation whose income comes *primarily* from providing the sole shareholder's services? Should a player (or movie performer, etc.) be able to deflect income to his or her own corporation when all the decisions about performing are negotiated between the player and the person to whom the services are provided (such as a team or movie producer), even if the player or movie actor is *not* an employee of the team or movie producer?

The deeper reason for the courts' pro-taxpayer decision may be the double tax on corporate profits. Corporate profits can be provided to shareholders only by suffering both a tax on the corporate profits at the corporate level and again at the shareholder level on dividend distributions. This double tax on corporate profits will usually exceed the tax on personal service income received directly by the shareholder, depending on the corporate and individual tax rates and how long a delay there is before the dividend distribution. Therefore, preventing assignment of income to a corporation might seem unnecessary.

The government has one last string to its bow in *§ 482*, which permits income to be reallocated among businesses to "clearly reflect income." That section has its major impact on relationships between foreign and domestic corporations with common ownership. These corporations fix prices between their respective businesses to deflect income to the country with the lowest tax rate. The Court of Appeals in *Foglesong*, *supra*, held that *§ 482* could not be used to rearrange personal service income between an individual shareholder and a controlled corporation unless the shareholder has a business separate from the corporation. When a shareholder-employee has no business other than performing the services loaned out by his or her corporation, the court held that *§ 482* does not apply.

CHAPTER 3

DEFINING INCOME

§ 3.01 BASIS

[A]—Defining basis

If a taxpayer buys a residence for $60,000 and sells it for $100,000, only $40,000 is included in his gross income. Look at *§ 61(a)(3)* and *§ 1001(a),(c)* and identify what language in these sections determines this result. What statutory language determines how much gross income a taxpayer has if a residence costing $60,000 burns down (rather than being sold) and the owner collects $100,000 insurance? Do not concern yourself with whether the taxpayer can avoid tax on the income by reinvesting the proceeds (*§ 1033* provides this opportunity in some cases), or whether the gain is capital gain. That comes later. Focus solely on the question of computing the amount of gross income. Do not worry about adjustments in basis specified by *§ 1011* and *§ 1016*. There are none in this example.

The function of the $60,000 cost figure in computing the tax base is to prevent imposing tax twice. For example, suppose a taxpayer in the 28% tax bracket earns $83,333 and pays $23,333 tax, and uses the remaining $60,000 to buy a residence. If he later sells the building for $100,000, he should be taxed on $40,000 gain, not $100,000, because $60,000 is a recovery of after tax income invested in the residence. *Basis (or cost) is a record of previously taxed income which should not be taxed again.*

Basis of property received. You have no trouble determining the basis of purchased property — it is the purchase price ("cost," as *§ 1012* says). What is the basis of property *received* in a taxable transaction? For example, suppose the taxpayer receives (rather than purchases) $60,000 worth of land as salary. The basis of property received is its fair market value — $60,000 in this example. The reason is that the taxpayer who receives $60,000 worth of property is in the same position as the taxpayer who buys the property for $60,000 and should, therefore, have the same $60,000 basis, as the following paragraphs explain.

The purchaser. How much income must the taxpayer receive to be able to buy $60,000 worth of property? Assume the taxpayer is in the 28% bracket. She must receive $83,333; tax = .28 times $83,333 = $23,333; subtracting the tax from $83,333 leaves $60,000 to buy the land.

The land recipient. The 28% bracket taxpayer receiving $60,000 of land as salary must pay $16,800 tax [.28 times $60,000 = $16,800]. To pay that tax and still have $60,000 of land left, she must have additional income to pay the tax. How much income does she need to pay $16,800 in tax? The answer is $23,333. A 28% tax on $23,333 = $6,533; after tax she has $16,800.

Therefore, both the land purchaser and land recipient in the 28% tax bracket need $83,333 income to acquire $60,000 worth of land. They should both have the same $60,000 basis, reflecting after tax income invested in the land.

Statutory interpretation — Plain meaning vs. Tax Term of Art. Notice that the statute defines basis as "cost." Ordinary usage of the term "cost" easily fits the purchaser. But the "cost" for the land recipient is not "cost" in any ordinary sense. The statute departs from ordinary usage to implement the statute's underlying structure — basis is after tax income on which no further tax should be paid, whether the taxpayer buys the property or receives it in a taxable event.

[B]—Recovery of basis

Basis is deductible under certain circumstances. For introductory purposes, the following explanation suffices (later chapters discuss some exceptions). The basis of an income-producing asset is deductible when the asset is disposed of. If disposition is by sale or any other disposition which produces gross receipts in excess of basis (*e.g.*, collecting insurance), the deduction of basis from gross receipts is provided for *implicitly* by the reference to gain in *§ 61(a)(3)*. "Gross income" is *explicitly* defined as amount realized minus basis by *§ 1001(a),(b)*. If the disposition produces receipts less than basis (including no receipts), the deduction is a *loss* deduction allowed by *§ 165(a)*. The loss can be by sale, casualty, or abandonment.

The same rules apply to an asset which is not income-producing (such as an asset used for personal purposes, like a home), except that losses are not deductible unless they occur from a casualty. Losses on sale or abandonment of personal use property are not deductible.

Basis of income-producing assets is deductible prior to disposition if the asset is a wasting asset — that is, an asset with a determinable useful life, such as a machine or building. In such cases, the deduction is called a depreciation deduction. The amount depends on the method of deprecation, discussed in Chapter 11. The simplest method is straight line depreciation, which is basis divided by the expected life of the asset. For example: $60 cost; 5-year life; $12 per year straight line depreciation. No depreciation deductions are allowed for personal use property.

Sale of part of the entire property. Suppose a taxpayer owns a ten-acre plot of land and sells an easement permitting the buyer to cross the land to transport goods to a destination. The ten-acre plot has a $60 basis. The sales proceeds for the easement are $10. Does the taxpayer have taxable gain on the sale? What administrative problems do you encounter in answering that question? Suppose the taxpayer sold one-tenth of the land (for example, one acre) for $10. Would your answer in the case of the one-acre sale differ from the easement case? What is the basis of the remaining property after the sale of the easement; the sale of one-acre?

[C]—Inflation *(basis not adjusted)*

Suppose the taxpayer who purchases land for $60,000 sells it in a later year for $120,000 after consumer prices have doubled. If basis records the amount on which the taxpayer should not pay tax again, so that he can buy personal consumption equal to that amount, it is a short step to the conclusion that the basis should be adjusted for inflation. If consumer prices double, the basis should be $120,000. That adjustment will produce no gain on the $120,000 sale and allow the taxpayer to use $120,000 for personal consumption. Because of inflation, $120,000 buys what $60,000 would have bought in the earlier year when the land was bought.

basis can be adjusted for inflation → BUT, is not currently

Our tax system has not so far adjusted basis for inflation, despite proposals to do so. One reason is the lack of symmetry it would create between owners and debtors. If a debtor borrows $60,000 in year 1 and pays it back in year 5 when consumer prices have doubled to $120,000, the debtor arguably has $60,000 of income in year 5. Here is why. The $60,000 paid back in year 5 is the equivalent of $30,000 purchasing power in the earlier year 1 when the taxpayer borrowed $60,000. Borrowing $60,000 in year 1 therefore gave the borrower access to double the amount of personal consumption given up in year 5 when repaying the $60,000 loan. The mechanism for taxing the debtor in year 5 is to increase the debt by the inflation factor (100% in this example — so the loan would be treated as $120,000), and tax the difference between the $120,000 and the amount repaid ($60,000) in year 5. Taxing cancellation of indebtedness is discussed later in this chapter. Reluctance to implement such complexity for debtors is one reason why owners have not been allowed to adjust basis upward for inflation.

§ 3.02 REALIZATION AND TIMING

[A]—Income as "realized" income

The Constitution states that direct taxes must be apportioned among the states according to population. The classic case of a direct tax is a property tax. People living in a state with 90% worth of the country's property but only one-half the population would only pay one-half of a federal property tax. This discourages populous states from voting for a federal property tax. The Supreme Court held that a tax on *income from property* was a direct tax, thereby making it politically impossible to adopt income taxes, even on personal service (non-property) income. The Sixteenth Amendment to the Constitution was then adopted stating that "Congress shall have power to lay and collect taxes on incomes, from whatever source derived, without apportionment. . . ." There was no definition of income.

Eisner v. Macomber, 252 U.S. 189 (1920), supplied a definition. The case dealt with common stock dividends, which are pieces of paper embodying ownership interests in a business carried on in corporate form. The corporation issued one share of common stock as a dividend for every two shares of common stock owned in the corporation. The statute taxed the shareholder on the receipt of the stock dividend. The case held that the tax was unconstitutional, because the stock dividend was not "income." Although the decision rests on constitutional grounds, the language the Court used to define income has had a major impact on how the statute has been written and interpreted after the decision. For example, the terms "derived" and "realized," used in the case, also appear in *§§ 61(a)(2,)(3), 1001(a),(b)*.

The point about statutory interpretation is important because no one thinks the Court's interpretation of the Constitution is still good law. Therefore, Congress could tax unrealized gain if it wanted to. The issues the Court addresses continue to be relevant, however, in deciding whether Congress has imposed tax. "Unrealized" gain is still usually (though not always) excluded from the income tax base because it is not "income," as defined in *§ 61*.

Here are portions of the Court's opinion in *Macomber*.

EISNER v. MACOMBER

252 U.S. 189 (1920)

Mr. Justice Pitney delivered the opinion of the Court.

The fundamental relation of "capital" to "income" has been much discussed by economists, the former being likened to the tree or the land, the latter to the fruit or the crop; the former depicted as a reservoir supplied from springs, the latter as the outlet stream, to be measured by its flow during a period of time. For the present purpose we require only a clear definition of the term "income," as used in common speech, in order to determine its meaning in the amendment, and, having formed also a correct judgment as to the nature of a stock dividend, we shall find it easy to decide the matter at issue.

After examining dictionaries in common use, we find little to add to the succinct definition adopted in two cases arising under the Corporation Tax Act of 1909 — "Income may be defined as the gain derived from capital, from labor, or from both combined," provided it be understood to include profit gained through a sale or conversion of capital assets.

Brief as it is, it indicates the characteristic and distinguishing attribute of income essential for a correct solution of the present controversy. The government, although basing its argument upon the definition as quoted, placed chief emphasis upon the word "gain," which was extended to include a variety of meanings; while the significance of the next three words was either overlooked or misconceived. "*Derived — from — capital*"; "*the gain — derived — from — capital*," etc. Here we have the essential matter: *not* a gain *accruing* to capital; not a *growth* or *increment* of value *in* the investment; but a gain, a profit, something of exchangeable value, *proceeding from* the property, *severed from* the capital, however invested or employed, and *coming in*, being "*derived*" — that is, *received* or *drawn by* the recipient (the taxpayer) for his *separate* use, benefit and disposal — *that* is income derived from property. Nothing else answers the description. The same fundamental conception is clearly set forth in the Sixteenth Amendment — "incomes, *from* whatever *source derived*" — the essential thought being expressed with a conciseness and lucidity entirely in harmony with the form and style of the Constitution.

Can a stock dividend, considering its essential character, be brought within the definition? To answer this, regard must be had to the nature of a corporation and the stockholder's relation to it. We refer, of course, to a corporation such as the one in the case at bar, organized for profit, and having a capital stock divided into shares to which a nominal or par value is attributed. . . .

A "stock dividend" shows that the company's accumulated profits have been capitalized, instead of distributed to the stockholders or retained as surplus available for distribution in money or in kind should opportunity offer. Far from being a realization of profits of the stockholder, it tends rather to postpone such realization, in that the fund represented by the new stock has been transferred from surplus to capital, and no longer is available for actual distribution.

The essential and controlling fact is that the stockholder has received nothing out of the company's assets for his separate use and benefit; on the contrary, every dollar of his original investment, together with whatever accretions and accumulations have resulted from employment of his money and that of the other stockholders in the business of the company, still remains the property of the company, and subject to business risks which may result in wiping out the entire investment. Having regard to the very truth of the matter, to substance and not to form, he has received nothing that answers the definition of income within the meaning of the Sixteenth Amendment. . . .

We have no doubt of the power or duty of a court to look through the form of the corporation and determine the question of the stockholder's right, in order to ascertain whether he has received income taxable by Congress without apportionment. But, looking through the form, we cannot disregard the essential truth disclosed, ignore the substantial difference between corporation and stockholder, treat the entire organization as unreal, look upon stockholders as partners, when they are not such, treat them as having in equity a right to a partition of the corporate assets, when they have none, and indulge the fiction that they have received and realized a share of the profits of the company which in truth they have neither received nor realized. . . .

Conceding that the mere issue of a stock dividend makes the recipient no richer than before, the government nevertheless contends that the new certificates measure the extent to which the gains accumulated by the corporation have made him the richer. There are two insuperable difficulties with this: In the first place, it would depend upon how long he had held the stock whether the stock dividend indicated the extent to which he had been enriched by the operations of the company; unless he had held it throughout such operations the measure would not hold true. Secondly, and more important for present purposes, enrichment through increase in value of capital investment is not income in any proper meaning of the term. . . .

Thus, from every point of view we are brought irresistibly to the conclusion that neither under the Sixteenth Amendment nor otherwise has Congress power to tax without apportionment a true stock dividend made lawfully and in good faith, or the accumulated profits behind it, as income of the stockholder. The Revenue Act of 1916, in so far as it imposes a tax upon the stockholder because of such dividend, contravenes the [] Constitution, and to this extent is invalid, notwithstanding the Sixteenth Amendment.

COMMENTS

No richer than before. The Court in *Macomber* says that the taxpayer who receives the stock dividend is "no richer than before." But tax is often imposed when the taxpayer is no richer than before. Sale of property worth $100 for $100 does not enrich the seller. Prior gain is all that is needed to support the tax.

Indeed, prior gain is not always necessary. If a taxpayer buys stock for $100 and then immediately receives a $20 cash dividend out of corporate profits, the $20 is taxable. *§ 301(a),(b)(1),(c)(1).* The value of the stock probably declines to $80 so the investor has a $20 loss, but that loss is not recognized until sale.

Statute taxing undistributed corporate profits, stock dividends, and unrealized gain. Despite *Macomber*, two statutory provisions tax undistributed corporate profits to the shareholder. In both situations, there are only a small number of shareholders who control the corporation and the shareholders are attempting to avoid taxes through use of foreign corporations. *§§ 551, 951.* In addition, stock dividends which rearrange stock ownership are taxable. *§ 305(b)(2-4).* Finally, several provisions tax unrealized gain or loss. *See, e.g., § 475* (securities dealers taxed on unrealized gain or loss on certain securities); *§ 1256* (unrealized gain or loss taxed on certain option and option-like assets).

Ideas behind "realization." A taxpayer who retains appreciating property does not "realize" gain as the property appreciates. This paradigm suggests the policies requiring realization as a condition for imposing tax. (1) Appreciation generates no cash to pay the tax. (Couldn't the taxpayer borrow on the property?) (2) The taxpayer has not changed his investment. (3) Valuation will be administratively difficult. All three ideas cluster together to make up the theme of realization, but no one idea by itself is sufficient to prevent taxing gain. For example, a taxpayer who exchanges a farm for a residence pays tax, even though it is difficult to value the assets and there is no cash received. Realization does not occur, however, if the taxpayer retains the investment. This suggests that the strongest of the policies which make up the realization requirement is the idea that it is economically undesirable or in some sense unfair to disturb ownership by taxing it, if the taxpayer doesn't want to change ownership.

Statutory response to discrimination between realized and unrealized gain. The realization requirement reverberates throughout the tax law because it creates a sharp distinction between untaxed unrealized gain and taxable realized gain. The economic impact is often referred to as the "lock-in" effect. A taxpayer might not dispose of an asset because realized gain is taxed (that is, the taxpayer is "locked-in"), even though the amount equal to the asset's value could be more efficiently invested elsewhere or the taxpayer might prefer to use that value for personal consumption. The economic implications seem more serious when the taxpayer forgoes an alternative investment.

The tax law responds to the lock-in problem with several provisions, discussed later. First, it sometimes lowers the tax on gain from selling the investment (the capital gains preference). Second, it sometimes defers tax on gain if the taxpayer reinvests the proceeds in certain types of property. None of these rules would be necessary if unrealized gain were taxed annually.

Value of deferral. You should carefully note that the realization requirement provides the taxpayer with tax deferral, not tax exemption. Eventually, it is expected that the taxpayer will realize and pay tax on the deferred gain. Nonetheless, the value of deferral is significant. In effect, the government is lending the taxpayer the deferred tax without interest. The value of that loan to the taxpayer depends on three things: how long the tax is deferred, the tax rate, and the rate of return the taxpayer can obtain by investing the deferred tax.

To illustrate the value of deferral, assume that the taxpayer paid $60 for a share of stock which increases in value to $100 in year 1. The taxpayer is in the 30% bracket (to simplify arithmetic). If there were no deferral on the $40 gain, the government takes $12 tax in year 1 (30% times $40). With deferral of tax on the $40 gain, the taxpayer keeps the full $100.

Now assume that the taxpayer can invest the $100, which includes the $40 gain on which tax is deferred, at a 20% annual rate of return. The stock will rise to $120 in year 2. Now the taxpayer sells the stock, paying a 30% tax (no change in tax rate) on the $40 previously unrealized gain (tax deferral has ended) and on the $20 year 2 appreciation. The total tax on the $60 gain is $18, and the taxpayer retains $102 (120 minus 18). How much better off is the taxpayer as a result of deferring tax on the $40 gain?

You can do the arithmetic mechanically — just assume the $40 gain was taxed in year 1 (tax equals $12, which is 30% times $40), leaving the taxpayer with $88. The $88 appreciates 20% ($17.60) to $105.60 in year 2. A sale in year 2, produces gain of $17.60. (Be sure you see why — what is the basis of the property after the $40 is taxed; subtract that basis from the $105.60 amount realized to get the gain). A 30% tax on $17.60 equals $5.28. That leaves the taxpayer with $100.32 ($105.60 minus $5.28). *So the taxpayer is better off, with deferral, by $1.68 ($102 minus $100.32).*

Is there a way to generalize the $1.68 advantage, without doing all the arithmetic? Sure. If the government allowed the taxpayer to use $40 as an investment for one year without tax, the government has allowed the taxpayer to invest the tax that otherwise would have been paid — that is, $12 (30% times $40). For one year, the taxpayer can invest $12 at 20%, which equals $2.40. But when tax deferral ends, after one year, the taxpayer must pay tax on that $2.40. If the taxpayer is still in the 30% bracket, he keeps 70% times $2.40, which equals $1.68. *So tax deferral gives the taxpayer the after-tax rate of return on the investment of the deferred tax.*

The value of tax deferral can be quantified in another way, with significant policy implications. Focus on the $40 gain which is deferred in the above example. Suppose there is *no* deferral, so the taxpayer has only $28 to invest ($40 minus the 30% tax of $12). Now assume that the taxpayer invests after-tax savings in a bank or stock, just as any saver might. Still assuming a 20% rate of return, the taxpayer earns $5.60 in interest or dividends (20% times $28). The government exempts the investment income. What is the value of the exemption? It is the tax that would have been paid on $5.60; for a taxpayer in the 30% bracket, that is $1.68 (30% times $5.60). *The value of deferring tax on savings equals the exemption of the investment income earned on after-tax savings.*

Notice that these computations assume that the tax rates are the same in all tax years and that the rate of return is the same, regardless of the size of the investment. If tax rates rise after an investment is made, tax deferral may not be the good deal it appears to be. It all depends on how long the deferral lasts and what the rate of return is.

You will encounter numerous examples of tax deferral on savings throughout the course. You should see now why this is so politically popular. Congress would have trouble passing a tax break exempting investment income. But how well does the public understand that deferring tax can provide the equivalent of exempting investment income?

Demise of constitutional realization requirement. It is important to keep in mind that the precise holding of *Eisner v. Macomber* is probably not good law any more. There are probably no constitutional barriers to taxing unrealized appreciated gain and undistributed corporate earnings to the shareholders. One case which is thought to overrule *Eisner v. Macomber* is *Helvering v. Bruun,* 309 U.S. 461 (1940). The taxpayer was a landlord who had leased land to a tenant. The tenant had erected a new building on the premises. On July 1, 1933, the lease was cancelled for default in payment of rent and taxes and the taxpayer gained possession of both the land and building. The government taxed the landlord on the value of the building. The taxpayer argued that "improvements affixed to the soil became part of the realty indistinguishably blended in the capital asset; . . . that they are, therefore, in the same category as improvements added by the [taxpayer] to his land, or accruals of value due to extraneous and adventitious circumstances. Such added value, it is argued, can be considered capital gain only upon the owner's disposition of the asset. The position is that the economic gain consequent upon the enhanced value of the recaptured asset is not gain derived from capital or realized within the meaning of the Sixteenth Amendment and may not, therefore, be taxed without apportionment."

The Court in *Bruun* rejected the taxpayer's argument, as follows (309 U.S. at 468–69):

> . . . Essentially the respondent's position is that the Amendment does not permit the taxation of such gain without apportionment amongst the states. He relies upon what was said in [] the decisions of this court dealing with the taxability of stock dividends to the effect that gain derived from capital must be something of exchangeable value proceeding from property, severed from the capital, however invested or employed, and received by the recipient for his separate use, benefit, and disposal. He emphasizes the necessity that the gain be separate from the capital and separately disposable. These expressions, however, were used to clarify the distinction between an ordinary dividend and a stock dividend. They were meant to show that in the case of a stock dividend, the stockholder's interest in the corporate assets after receipt of the dividend was the same as and inseverable from that which he owned before the dividend was declared. We think they are not controlling here.
>
> While it is true that economic gain is not always taxable as income, it is settled that the realization of gain need not be in cash derived from the sale of an asset. Gain may occur as a result of exchange of property, payment of the taxpayer's indebtedness, relief from a liability, or other profit realized from the completion of a transaction. The fact that the gain is a portion of the value of property received by the taxpayer in the transaction does not negative its realization.
>
> Here, as a result of a business transaction, the respondent received back his land with a new building on it, which added an ascertainable amount

to its value. It is not necessary to recognition of taxable gain that he should be able to sever the improvement begetting the gain from his original capital. If that were necessary, no income could arise from the exchange of property; whereas such gain has always been recognized as realized taxable gain.

KEY: more expansive def'n of "realized" income" → don't need cash or to sever the improvement

Statutory deferral of realized income. Congress decided that the government's victory in *Bruun* should not stand. It adopted §§ 109, 1019. These sections are typical in the following respect. They accept the Court's more expansive definition of "realization" under the statute. They do not amend § 61 to state that the income is not "realized." But the statute *is* amended to exclude realized income from the tax base. Realization remains a core statutory concept (although its contours are expanded), but realized income is not always taxed.

Congress overruled Bruun

Look at § 109 and § 1019 and make sure you understand that they only defer income, not exempt it, even though the statute uses the language of "exclusion." For example, suppose the landlord recovers land with a building worth $20,000 after termination of a lease. The landlord's prior investment in the land is $15,000. He holds the land and building for ten years and then sells them both for $35,000. What is the landlord's taxable gain?

[B]—Losses

Do not assume that the taxpayer always wants an event to be *unrealized* for tax purposes. In *Cottage Savings Association v. Commissioner,* 499 U.S. 554 (1991), the taxpayer was a financial institution which wanted to realize tax-deductible losses by exchanging its interests in one group of residential mortgage loans for a different group of residential mortgage loans. The taxpayer was a savings and loan association (S&L) formerly regulated by the Federal Home Loan Bank Board (FHLBB). Like many S&L's, it held numerous long-term, low-interest mortgages that declined in value when interest rates surged in the late 1970's. If they sold their devalued mortgages to realize tax-deductible losses, FHLBB accounting regulations required them to record those losses on their books. Reporting these losses for

prop. xd to realize tax-ded. losses

banking regulation purposes would have placed many S&L's at risk of closure by the FHLBB.

FHLBB, therefore, relaxed its requirements for the reporting of losses. It determined that S&L's need not report losses associated with mortgages that are exchanged for "substantially identical" mortgages held by other lenders. The FHLBB's acknowledged purpose was to facilitate transactions generating tax losses that would not substantially affect the economic position of the S&L's.

Responding to this opportunity, Cottage Savings transferred "90% participation interests" in 252 mortgages to four S&L's and received "90% participation interests" in 305 mortgages held by these S&L's. All of the loans involved in the transaction were secured by single-family homes, most in the Cincinnati area. The fair market value of the package of participation interests exchanged by each side was approximately $4.5 million. The basis of the participation interests Cottage Savings relinquished in the transaction was approximately $6.9 million. Cottage Savings claimed a deduction for $2,447,091, which represented the difference between the basis of the participation interests that it traded and the fair market value of the participation interests that it received. It did not report this loss to the FHLBB. The Court held that the loss was realized for tax purposes.

COTTAGE SAVINGS ASSOCIATION v. COMMISSIONER

111 S. Ct. 1503 (1991)

JUSTICE MARSHALL delivered the opinion on the Court.

Neither the language nor the history of the Code indicates whether and to what extent property exchanged must differ to count as a "disposition of property" under § 1001(a). Nonetheless, we readily agree with the Commissioner that an exchange of property gives rise to a realization event under § 1001(a) only if the properties exchanged are "materially different." The Commissioner himself has by regulation construed § 1001(a) to embody a material difference requirement:

"Except as otherwise provided . . . the gain or loss realized from the conversion of property into cash, or from the exchange of property for other property differing materially either in kind or in extent, is treated as income or as loss sustained." Treas. Reg. 1.1001-1.

Because Congress has delegated to the Commissioner the power to promulgate "all needful rules and regulations for the enforcement of [the Internal Revenue Code]," 26 U.S.C. § 7805(a), we must defer to his regulatory interpretations of the Code so long as they are reasonable. . . .

Precisely what constitutes a "material difference" for purposes of § 1001(a) of the Code is a more complicated question. The Commissioner argues that properties are "materially different" only if they differ in economic substance. To determine whether the participation interests exchanged in this case were "materially different" in this sense, the Commissioner argues we should look to the attitudes of the parties, the evaluation of the interests by the secondary mortgage market, and the views of the FHLBB. We conclude that § 1001(a) embodies a much less demanding and less complex test. . . .

In three [cases after *Eisner v. Macomber*] we refined Macomber's conception of realization in the context of property exchanges. In each case, the taxpayer owned stock that had appreciated in value since its acquisition. And in each case, the corporation in which the taxpayer held stock had reorganized into a new corporation, with the new corporation assuming the business of the old corporation. While the corporations in [two of the cases] both changed from New Jersey to Delaware corporations, the original and successor corporations in [the third case] both were incorporated in Ohio. In each case, following the reorganization, the stockholders of the old corporation received shares in the new corporation equal to their proportional interest in the old corporation.

The question in these cases was whether the taxpayers realized the accumulated gain in their shares in the old corporation when they received in return for those shares representing an equivalent proportional interest in the new corporations. In [two cases], we held that the transactions were realization events. We reasoned that because a company incorporated in one State has "different rights and powers" from one incorporated in a different State, the taxpayers [] acquired through the transactions property that was "materially different" from what they previously had. In contrast, we held that no realization occurred in [the third case]. By exchanging stock in the predecessor corporation for stock in the newly reorganized corporation [in the same state], the taxpayer did not receive "a thing really different from what he theretofore had.". . .

. . . Taken together, [these cases] stand for the principle that properties are "different" in the sense that is "material" to the Internal Revenue Code so long as their respective possessors enjoy legal entitlements that are different in kind or extent. . . . No more demanding a standard than this is necessary in order to satisfy the administrative purposes underlying the realization requirement in § 1001(a). For, as long as the property entitlements are not identical, their exchange will allow both the Commissioner and the transacting taxpayer easily to fix the appreciated or depreciated values of the property relative to their tax bases. . . .

[T]he complexity of the Commissioner's approach ill serves the goal of administrative convenience that underlies the realization requirement. In order to apply the Commissioner's test in a principled fashion, the Commissioner and the taxpayer must identify the relevant market, establish whether there is a regulatory agency whose views should be taken into account, and then assess how the relevant market participants and the agency would view the transaction. The Commissioner's failure to explain how these inquiries should be conducted further calls into question the workability of his test. . . .

Under our interpretation of § 1001(a), an exchange of property gives rise to a realization event so long as the exchanged properties are "materially different" — that is, so long as they embody legally distinct entitlements. Cottage Savings' transactions at issue here easily satisfy this test. Because the participation interests exchanged by Cottage Savings and the other S&L's derived from loans that were made to different obligors and secured by different homes, the exchanged interests did embody legally distinct entitlements. Consequently, we conclude that Cottage Savings realized its losses at the point of the exchange.

The Commissioner contends that it is anomalous to treat mortgages deemed to be "substantially identical" by the FHLBB as "materially different." The anomaly, however, is merely semantic; mortgages can be substantially identical for [bank regulatory purposes] and still exhibit "differences" that are "material" for purposes of the Internal Revenue Code. Because Cottage Savings received entitlements different from those it gave up, the exchange put both Cottage Savings and the Commissioner in a position to determine the change in the value of Cottage Savings' mortgages relative to their tax bases. Thus, there is no reason not to treat the exchange of these interests as a realization event, regardless of the status of the mortgages [for banking purposes].

The difference between banking regulations and the rules determining tax losses is another example of tax law not automatically incorporating nontax law. Similarly, family law might not necessarily be incorporated into tax law to determine whether someone is married.

§ 3.03 ACCOUNTING METHODS AND TIMING

Realization, technically, determines whether there is "income." The fundamental issue, however, is one of timing — when to report an item as income. The "when" question is also addressed by accounting methods. Even if an item is technically income under *§ 61*, the tax accounting method must be consulted to determine whether it is reported as income in a particular year.

§446

The code section that addresses these issues is *§ 446(a-c)*, but it does not say much. Basically, it authorizes the cash or accrual method, *but only* if the method chosen clearly reflects income. *§ 446(b)*. The following paragraphs give you an introduction to these concepts.

There are two fundamental questions — (1) defining "cash" and "accrual," so that someone using the cash or accrual method knows what to report; and (2) when is a taxpayer allowed to use one or the other method. These paragraphs address the definitional questions, leaving until a later chapter the question of when a taxpayer can or must use a particular accounting method.

Cash method. "Cash" includes more than cash. It includes the fair market value of anything which is the "equivalent of cash." The idea is this — if you earn $10,000 of salary, you should not be able to avoid tax by receiving property worth $10,000 and avoid tax. The property has a taxable cash equivalent. But what is the cash equivalent?

(1) When property is used for personal consumption, its cash equivalent may be influenced by limits on transferability and doubts about the subjective value of the asset to the recipient (as when an employer gives a meal to an employee). (2) When the received property is investment property (such as stock), restrictions on transferability and the potential for forfeiting the property may seriously impair its cash equivalence. (3) There is also doubt about whether a nonnegotiable note (which is "property") should be taxed to a cash method taxpayer, if the note is not likely to sell for anything near its face value. We return to these issues in later chapters.

Accrual method. "Accrual" occurs when all events have occurred to fix the right or liability, except for the passage of time; the amount can be determined with reasonable accuracy; and the promisor is solvent. For example, once the promisee has performed under a contract in year 1, entitling her to $100 in year 2, the right has matured (that is, it is not subject to any conditions), and the amount of the $100 claim accrues in year 1. *Treas. Reg. § 1.451-1(a).* It does not matter that the $100 payment occurs in year 2.

Difference between methods. The discussion highlights the essential difference between cash and accrual taxpayers — a promise not embodied in a note or other instrument of commerce is not itself the equivalent of cash. A cash method taxpayer (unless there is a statutory exception) is therefore able to defer tax on value embodied in a promise, until cash is received. An accrual method taxpayer, however, must accrue a solvent debtor's promise at its face amount. This eliminates the deferral opportunity enjoyed by cash method taxpayers. The accrual method taxpayer, however, is forced to accrue a promise based on its face amount, not its actual value. Thus, a promise to pay $100 results in accrual of $100 income to the promisee, even though sale of the right to collect the $100 might not produce more than $80.

Assignment of income issues. In one situation it is very important for cash method taxpayers to know about accrual accounting rules. The assignment of income rules prevent a cash method taxpayer from shifting accrued income to a transferee. For example, assume that a cash method creditor lends $100,000 at 10% interest payable annually ($10,000 per year) on December 31. In the middle of the next year, the creditor gives the entire bond, with one-half year's accrued interest, to a relative. The $5,000 accrued interest will be taxed to the transfer*or* when it is collected by the relative.

Deductions. Cash and accrual rules also apply to deductions. An accrual method taxpayer accrues a deduction when the obligation to pay is fixed (for example, wage deductions accrue to the employer when an employee has performed personal services). A cash method taxpayer takes a deduction only when cash is paid. "Payment" for deduction purposes, however, is not exactly the same as for receipt purposes. Giving a note, for example, is not "payment" for a cash method taxpayer (even though its receipt is often the equivalent of cash), because that would allow a cash method taxpayer to control the deduction year too easily.

Percentage completion method. There are in fact more accounting methods than cash and accrual. For example, the percentage completion of contract method taxes income from performing a contract (such as building an airplane) while the job is being performed. When one half is completed, one half the anticipated net income from the job is taxed. Until recently, gain on contract performance could be deferred until completion of the contract, but now the percentage completion of contract method must be used, eliminating the opportunity to defer tax until contract completion. *§ 460(a).*

Clearly reflect income. The taxpayer's choice of accounting methods is subject to the overriding requirement that it must clearly reflect income. One example here will suffice. Suppose a cash method taxpayer buys a machine with cash. Can the taxpayer deduct the cost when the cash is paid? Of course not, absent some special tax incentive provision. Income must include both consumption and savings and a deduction for the cost of a long-lived asset would permit a deduction for savings — it would not clearly reflect income.

§ 3.04 ORIGINAL ISSUE DISCOUNT

This section discusses original issue discount. It introduces you to the time value of money — an important and pervasive idea throughout tax law. It also provides an example of forcing cash method taxpayers to report accrued income prior to receipt of cash.

Original issue discount is interest. Normally interest is earned on money loaned to a debtor. For example, if you lend $16.15 to someone at 20% interest (for example, deposit it in a bank), the interest income in the first year is $3.23. The next year, interest is $3.88, assuming you left both the $16.15 and the $3.23 in the bank. Interest is compounding because you get interest on the interest. In ten years, total interest will equal $83.85.

The interest accruing each year on the $16.15 loan is as follows:

Year	Interest	Year	Interest
1	3.23	6	8.04
2	3.88	7	9.65
3	4.65	8	11.57
4	5.58	9	13.89
5	6.70	10	16.67

Suppose a taxpayer does not want to pay tax on the interest until some later date — say, 10 years from now. The taxpayer tries this scheme. She lends $16.15 to a debtor (for example, she buys a corporate bond), and the debtor agrees to pay the creditor $100 in ten years. No interest is paid before then. The difference between the $100 repayment and the $16.15 loan is called original issue discount. It is "original" because it arises when the obligation is originally issued by the debtor. It is "discount" because it is computed by discounting the $100 back to its "present value" in the year of the loan.

The formula for computing present value is:

$$\text{Present value} = \frac{x}{(1 + i)^p}$$

where "x" is the amount paid in the future ($100 in the example), "i" is the interest (or discount) rate (20% in the example), and "p" is the number of time periods during which the interest is paid.

If interest had been earned from a bank in the typical savings deposit, the interest would be taxed annually. The question is whether the loan to a corporation creating original issue discount should be taxed any differently. Obviously, the answer should be "no," if the tax law is to remain neutral between different kinds of investments. The tax law forces the lender to accrue original issue discount periodically as identified in accordance with the above principles, whether or not the lender is a cash method taxpayer. The basic statutory sections are *§§ 1272(a)(1), 1273(a).* For example, assume that the taxpayer lends $1,615 in year 0 in exchange for the borrower's promise to pay $10,000 in year 10. The lender (whether or not a cash or accrual method taxpayer) must report $323 interest income in year 1, etc.

lender must report interest earnings yearly

The above example simplifies current law. The tax law has to make certain decisions — should the interest be computed as though it compounds annually or semi-annually or more often; what should lenders do if the accrual period straddles the end of a tax year (for example interest compounds semi-annually but the loan occurs on October 1, so that the six month period is from October to March). These complexities must be addressed by the tax law but there is no need for you to do so now.

Problem: Original issue discount and the "kiddie" tax. Consider this scheme. Suppose a parent lends $1,615 to a corporation, with $10,000 repayable in 10 years and no stated interest. The original issue discount rules would apply. Could the parent then give away the claim against the corporation to his 4 or 5-year-old child, let the child pay tax (at low rates, presumably) on the original issue discount as it accrues, and then have the child use the $10,000 for a college education when the child collects the $10,000 from the corporate borrower? *See § 63(c)(5), § 151(d)(2), § 1(g).*

More on present value. You will find it useful as you go through the course to apply present value concepts. The following chart sets forth the present value of $1 for different interest rates and future time periods. It in effect specifies how much someone would lend you today in exchange for a promise by you to repay $1 at a specified future date and a specified annual compound interest rate. Notice how little $1, to be received 20 years from now, is worth today when interest rates are 6% or higher. If interest is compounded semi-annually, the present value figures would be different.

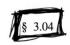

Present Value of $1

Year in Future When Paid	Interest (Discount) Rate 1%	6%	10%	12%	20%	30%
1	.99	.943	.909	.892	.833	.769
5	.951	.747	.62	.567	.401	.269
10	.905	.558	.385	.321	.161	.072
20	.819	.311	.148	.103	.026	.005

§ 3.05 CAPITAL GAINS RATES

We saw earlier that failure to tax unrealized gain created a sharp distinction between unrealized gain and realized gain, encouraging people to hold rather than sell investments. We also observed that *Eisner v. Macomber* conceded that income included "profit gained through the conversion of capital assets." One statutory response to this pattern has been to lower the tax rate on certain realized capital gains. This section introduces the preferential treatment of capital gains; later chapters will revisit the issue.

[A]—Statutory structure

The core example of a capital gain is the gain recognized on the sale of corporate stock, which is not held as inventory by the seller. It is helpful to remember why this is the core case as you try to understand capital gains. The asset is a risky investment whose value has increased due to a favorable change in the future income anticipated from the investment.

The capital gains provisions have the following statutory structure. A capital gain or loss arises on the "sale or exchange of a capital asset." *§ 1222*. This definition has two components: (1) sale or exchange; and (2) capital asset.

The definition of a capital asset appears in *§ 1221*. The statute says that a capital asset means "property," but then excludes certain property from the definition. The most important exclusion is property which is held primarily for sale in the ordinary course of business, such as inventory (*§ 1221(1)*).

§ 1222 distinguishes between long-and short-term capital gains and losses. Long-term capital gains and losses arise on the sale or exchange of capital assets held for *more than one year*. Short-term capital gains and losses arise on the sale or exchange of a capital asset held for one year or less.

The preferential tax rate on capital gains is provided in *§ 1(h)*. More precisely, the preference is for net capital gains, which is net long-term capital gain ("net" means the excess of long-term capital gains over long-term capital losses) over net short-term capital losses (the excess of short-term capital losses over short-term capital gains). *§ 1222(1)*. The idea behind not favoring short-term capital gain is to deny a tax preference for short term speculation.

§ 1(h) makes a further refinement, however, between net capital gain attributable to mid-term capital gain (more than 12 months and not more than 18 months), and "long-term" capital gain (defined for *§ 1(h)* purposes as attributable to capital assets held more than 18 months). "Long-term" gain gets an even lower tax rate than mid-term gain. "Long-term" is in quotes because *§ 1(h)* leaves in place the *§ 1222* definition of a long-term asset as one held more than one year. *§ 1(h)* separates "long-term" gain (more than eighteen months) from mid-term gain through the definition of "adjusted net capital gain." Most people will, however, now label more-than-eighteen-month capital assets as long-term assets, even though that is technically inaccurate. Later problems illustrate how the preference works.

In addition, the 1998 Technical Corrections Act working its way through Congress as of this writing deletes the phrase "mid-term" from *§ 1(h)*. However, people will continue to describe capital assets held more than one year and less than 18 months as mid-term capital assets no matter what Congress says, and I continue that practice.

[B]—History of preferential treatment

Prior to 1921 there was concern about the effect of high progressive tax rates imposed during World War I on the realization of gain accruing over more than one year. The problem was serious for both personal service income earned over a period of time and appreciated gain on capital assets. In both cases, it was feared that the progressive tax rate on accrued income bunched into one year would be higher than the lower rate on the income as it accrued annually. In 1920, the House of Representatives considered allowing taxpayers to spread such income back over the years it was earned or the asset was held, but the provision failed because it appeared too complex.

In 1921, Congress became more concerned with the impact of progressive tax rates on an investor's willingness to shift investment. This impact is known as the lock-in effect. Economically desirable shifts of investments were thought to be discouraged by the difference between taxing sales and not taxing unrealized gain. This resulted in adoption of a tax preference for capital gains for individuals. The mechanism for helping the taxpayer was to limit the tax to 12.5% of the gain, if that produced a lower tax than including the gain in ordinary income. Only assets held for more than two years were eligible for preferential treatment. Corporate capital gains were not preferentially treated, because the top corporate tax on ordinary income was already 12.5%.

This general pattern persisted until 1934. At that time, there was criticism of the capital gains tax rate for two reasons. First, it did not help individual taxpayers in tax brackets below the capital gains rate. Second, it did not differentiate among taxpayers who held capital assets for different periods of time and who were affected differently by the bunching of gain into the year of sale. The statute was therefore amended to tax a declining percentage of capital gain as the asset's holding period lengthened. The declining percentage approach created a bias in favor of holding an asset, however, which was one of the problems which the preferential rates were supposed to alleviate. The declining percentage approach was modified in 1938 and eliminated in 1942.

In 1942, long-term capital gain was defined as gain arising from the sale or exchange of a capital asset held for more than six months. The mechanism for favoring these gains was to allow individuals a deduction of 50% of the gain or to impose a 25% tax on the entire gain, whichever produced a lower tax.

In 1969, the rules were again changed to eliminate the 25% ceiling, except for the first $50,000 of gain. Later, the 25% ceiling was totally eliminated and a deduction became the only preference for an individual's long-term capital gains. By 1986, the deduction was 60% of long-term capital gain. That produced a maximum 20% effective tax rate on an individual's long-term capital gain, because the top marginal tax rate was 50%, and 40% of the gain was taxed.

In 1986, Congress eliminated the preferential tax rate on long-term capital gains for a brief period (the top rate on all income was 28%). Later, when the top individual tax rate was increased to 31%, the capital gains rate was capped at 28%. *§ 1(h).*

In 1993, the top individual tax rates were raised to 36% and 39.6%, but the 28% preferential tax rate on an individual's long-term capital gains was retained. Corporations are not now eligible for a preferential rate on capital gains.

The 1993 tax law also added a special (and complex) rule allowing 50% of an individual's gain on "qualified small business stock" held for more than five years to be excluded from income. § 1202. The gain eligible for this tax break is limited to the greater of $10 million or ten times the stock's basis.

The 1997 Tax Act made further significant reductions in the preferential rate on certain capital gains. The issue was politically contentious, which therefore produced a very complex statute. The pattern of the 1997 law is to retain the current statutory structure defining "net capital gain" in *§ 1222* and to add on additional rules specifying the tax rate. The additional tax rate rules are found in *§ 1(h)*, which provides the maximum capital gains rate on "net capital gain" and "adjusted net capital gain" (which is the new "long-term" more-than-18-month category).

The best way to grasp the new rules is to focus on sales and exchanges after July 28, 1997. The basic pattern is to create two categories of preferentially taxed capital gain — "long-term" capital gain (for property held more than 18 months); and mid-term capital gain (for property held more than 12 months but not more than 18 months). The tax rate on "long-term" capital gain is capped at 20% (except that for people in the 15% bracket, the cap is 10%). The tax rate on mid-term capital gain is still capped at 28% (with no special treatment for taxpayers in the 15% bracket).

The new less-than-28% rates do not apply to "collectibles," defined in *§ 408(m)* (*e.g.*, works of art). These assets, assuming they are capital assets, are still eligible for the preferential 28% rate applicable under pre-1997 law.

A special rule applies to sales/exchanges after December 31, 2000. For "long-term" capital gain (held more than 18 months), the maximum rate is 18% (8% for taxpayers in the 15% bracket), *but only if the asset is held for five years*. Furthermore, the rate reduction to 18% for taxpayers in *higher-than-15% brackets* only applies if the property held for five years was acquired *after* December 31, 2000. A special rule allows taxpayers to elect to pay tax on unrealized gain as though the property were sold on January 1, 2001, and thereby "acquire" the property after December 31, 2000.

(A special transitional rule allows the preferential rate of 20% (10% for taxpayers in the 15% bracket) on property sold after May 6, 1997 and before July 29, 1997, even if it is mid-term property — that is, property held more than 12 months but not more than 18 months.)

The 1997 law does not do anything more for qualified small business stock, in addition to cutting the 28% rate in half. *§ 1202*.

[C]—Capital losses

History. Capital losses have a more complicated history. The basic pattern today (with exceptions) is to limit the deduction of capital losses to capital gains. *§ 1211(a),(b)*. It is tempting to think that this symmetry depends on gains being preferentially taxed, but that is historically inaccurate. Several times, both before 1921 when the tax rate preference was introduced, and for a brief period after 1986 when there was no preferential tax rate on capital gains, the deduction of capital losses was nevertheless still limited to capital gains. Moreover, capital loss limits apply to corporations, whose capital gains are not preferentially taxed.

Rationale. Why should capital losses not be deductible against ordinary income, even when capital gains are taxed at ordinary rates? The reason is that taxpayers have too much control over the timing of capital gains and losses. Assume the taxpayer has two assets, one with an unrealized capital gain and one with an unrealized capital loss equal to the capital gain. The taxpayer has no economic gain or loss. Should the taxpayer be able to realize *just* the capital loss and reduce ordinary income by selling the loss asset? The potential for abuse would be aggravated when progressive tax rates were high in the capital loss year.

Current law. Capital losses are now deductible up to capital gains, plus (in the case of individuals) $3,000 (which may be deducted from ordinary income). They are deductible in computing adjusted gross income; they are not an itemized deduction. *§ 62(a)(3).*

The introduction of several categories of preferentially taxed capital gains raises the question of how net capital losses in one category should offset gains in other categories. The basic pattern is for net losses in the highest tax category to reduce gains in the next highest tax category and so on. Thus, net short-term losses first reduce mid-term gains and, if there are losses left, reduce long-term gains.

Unused capital losses are carried over to other years. An individual's unused capital losses are carried forward forever as whichever category of loss they are (short, mid-, or "long-term"). *§ 1212(b). A corporation's* unused capital losses are carried back three years and forward five years as short-term capital losses. *§ 1212(a).*

[D]—Problems

Assume that the following assets are owned by an individual, are nondepreciable, and are capital assets held for investment. The problems call for the sale of different combinations of these assets. If there is a deductible capital loss, assume the taxpayer has another $70,000 taxable business income.

Problem 1. Sell assets 1, 2 & 3.

Problem 2. Sell assets 2 & 4. Would it matter whether the sale of asset 2 produced ordinary income, rather than short-term capital gain?

Problem 3. Sell assets 2 & 4 in January. What is the tax impact of selling asset 5 in December of the same year?

Problem 4. Sell assets 1, 2, 3, & 6?

	Basis	Sales Price	Holding Period (in months)
Asset 1	$ 80,000	$ 100,000	18 ½
Asset 2	80,000	100,000	4
Asset 3	80,000	100,000	12 ½
Asset 4	90,000	60,000	18 ½
Asset 5	20,000	50,000	18 ½
Asset 6	100,000	70,000	4

[E]—Reasons for preferential rate on capital gains

Two reasons for the capital gains preference have already been noted in discussing the history of the provision — to prevent bunching of past accrued gain in the year of sale and to reduce the lock-in effect.

Bunching past income. Is bunching of past accrued gain a sound reason? If so, why is there no requirement that the taxpayer be in a higher bracket in the year of sale than in the years when the gains accrued? Moreover, gain has sometimes been preferentially taxed even when the asset's holding period was entirely in one tax year (that is, more than six months).

Lock-in. If the lock-in effect is a problem and the Code is intended to encourage shifts of investments by lowering the tax on sale, why isn't there a requirement that the sales proceeds be reinvested? Under current law, sale proceeds producing capital gain can be used for personal purposes.

Inflation. Inflation is sometimes given as a reason for the long-term capital gains preference. The idea is that the gain is not real income. For example, if a taxpayer earns $100 in year 0, pays a $30 tax, and invests the remaining $70, he has paid the tax necessary to entitle him to $70 of consumption whenever he wants to consume. If prices rise 100% by year 5, however, it will take him $140 to buy the same basket of goods in year 5 which he could have bought in year 0 for $70. The capital gains tax break might relieve the taxpayer of some of the burden of an ordinary tax on the $70 gain. But the present rule gives the same benefit to the taxpayer whose investment doubles after two, rather than five years, even though the inflation during the two year period is less than 100%. The tax break is the same regardless of the differential impact of inflation on different assets. Moreover, the present rules give no benefit to the taxpayer who paid $70 in year 0 and then sells for $70 in year 5; or to the creditor who lends $70 in year 0 and collects the $70 debt in depreciated currency in year 5. The correct adjustment for inflation is a basis adjustment for the inflation rate. The $70 investment should result in a $140 basis if there is 100% inflation.

Incentive. Another reason for the capital gains preference is to encourage investments. But why not exempt dividends and interests and other returns on investments, not just the return in the form of capital gains? Perhaps a tax credit for investment would be a more effective incentive to invest. Is there some way to distinguish between high risk venture capital and other investments for preferential rate purposes?

Bunching future income. There is one fairness argument for the capital gains preference. The amount realized is the present value of future income. If the taxpayer waits for the future income, he defers tax. If he sells the asset, the government collects tax for the year of sale. In effect, the taxpayer has helped the government by eliminating tax deferral. Perhaps a lower rate should compensate the taxpayer for paying taxes early.

§ 3.06 GENERAL DEFINITIONS OF INCOME

[A]—Judicial revisions of the "income" definition

We saw earlier that the holding of *Eisner v. Macomber* is no longer considered good constitutional law. In *Glenshaw Glass*, the Court revisited the case law interpretation of the *statutory* term "income." The case considered whether punitive damages were income. The punitive damages arose out an anti-trust lawsuit in which the plaintiff also recovered compensatory damages replacing lost profits. Everyone agreed that the compensatory damages were taxable income.

The Court of Appeals held that the punitive damages did not fall within the *Eisner v. Macomber* definition of income, because they "are not compensatory. They certainly possess no periodicity. They are not derived from capital, from labor or from both combined and assuredly are not profit gained through the sale or conversion of capital assets." The court stated that "the ordinary man regards income as something which comes to him from what he has done, not from something that is done to him. . . . [T]he ordinary man using terms of common speech would not regard punitive damages as 'income'." The Supreme Court reversed, as follows.

COMMISSIONER v. GLENSHAW GLASS CO.

348 U.S. 426 (1955)

MR. CHIEF JUSTICE WARREN delivered the opinion of the Court.

It is conceded by the respondents that there is no constitutional barrier to the imposition of a tax on punitive damages. Our question is one of statutory construction: are these payments comprehended by § 22(a) [Editor — now *§ 61*]?

The sweeping scope of the controverted statute is readily apparent:

SEC. 22. GROSS INCOME.

(a) General definition. "Gross income" includes gains, profits, and income derived from salaries, wages, or compensation for personal service . . . of whatever kind and in whatever form paid, or from professions, vocations, trades, businesses, commerce, or sales, or dealings in property, whether real or personal, growing out of the ownership or use of or interest in such property; also from interest, rent, dividends, securities, or the transaction of any business carried on for gain or profit, *or gains or profits and income derived from any source whatever*. . . . (Emphasis added.)

This Court has frequently stated that this language was used by Congress to exert in this field "the full measure of its taxing power." Respondents contend that punitive damages, characterized as "windfalls" flowing from the culpable conduct of third parties, are not within the scope of the section. But Congress applied no limitations as to the source of taxable receipts, nor restrictive labels as to their nature. And the Court has given a liberal construction to this broad phraseology in recognition of the intention of Congress to tax all gains except those specifically exempted. Thus, the fortuitous gain accruing to a lessor by reason of the forfeiture of a lessee's improvements on the rented property was taxed in *Helvering v. Bruun*, 309 U.S. 461. *Cf. United States v. Kirby Lumber Co.*, 284 U.S. 1. Such decisions demonstrate that we cannot but ascribe content to the catchall provision of § 22(a), "gains or profits and income derived from any source whatever." The importance of that phrase has been too frequently recognized since its first appearance in the Revenue Act of 1913 to say now that it adds nothing to the meaning of "gross income."

Nor can we accept respondents' contention that a narrower reading of § 22(a) is required by the Court's characterization of income in *Eisner v. Macomber*, 252 U.S. 189, 207, as "the gain derived from capital, from labor, or from both combined." The Court was there endeavoring to determine whether the distribution of a corporate stock dividend constituted a realized gain to the shareholder, or changed "only the form, not the essence," of his capital investment. It was held that the taxpayer had "received nothing out of the company's assets for his separate use and benefit." The distribution, therefore, was held not a taxable event. In that context — distinguishing gain from capital — the definition served a useful purpose. But it was not meant to provide a touchstone to all future gross income questions.

Here we have instances of undeniable accessions to wealth, clearly realized, and over which the taxpayers have complete dominion. The mere fact that the payments were extracted from the wrongdoers as punishment for unlawful conduct cannot detract from their character as taxable income to the recipients. Respondents concede, as they must, that the recoveries are taxable to the extent that they compensate for damages actually incurred. It would be an anomaly that could not be justified in the absence of clear congressional intent to say that a recovery for actual damages is taxable but not the additional amount extracted as punishment for the same conduct which caused the injury. And we find no such evidence of intent to exempt these payments.

It is urged that re-enactment of § 22(a) without change since the Board of Tax Appeals held punitive damages nontaxable in *Highland Farms Corp.*, 42 B.T.A. 1314, indicates congressional satisfaction with that holding. Re-enactment — particularly without the slightest affirmative indication that Congress ever had the *Highland Farms* decision before it — is an unreliable indicium at best. Moreover, the Commissioner promptly published his non-acquiescence in this portion of the Highland Farms holding and has, before and since, consistently maintained the position that these receipts are taxable. It therefore cannot be said with certitude that Congress intended to carve an exception out of § 22(a)'s pervasive coverage. Nor does the 1954 Code's legislative history, with its reiteration of the proposition that statutory gross income is "all-inclusive," give support to respondents' position. The definition of gross income has been simplified, but no effect upon its present broad scope was intended. Certainly punitive damages cannot reasonably be classified as gifts, nor do they come under any other exemption provision in the Code. We would do violence to the plain meaning of the statute and restrict a clear legislative attempt to bring the taxing power to bear upon all receipts constitutionally taxable were we to say that the payments in question here are not gross income.

Statutory interpretation. Both the Court of Appeals and the Supreme Court claim to be relying on the ordinary or plain meaning of the statutory text. And yet they reach different results. What exactly do they disagree about?

Legislative reenactment. The Court of Appeals in *Glenshaw*, in holding for the taxpayer, had emphasized congressional reenactment of the identical statutory language after an intervening interpretation of that language by a court. The Supreme Court suggests that mere reenactment without awareness is an unreliable indicator of congressional intent. Would awareness without evidence of approval be enough?

What demonstrates either awareness or approval of an intervening interpretation: a statement by the Senate Finance or House Ways and Means Committee; a statement on the floor of the Senate by a committee member responding to a question about the statute's meaning? How can such statements constitute intent of the legislature?

Income definitions — Sources and uses. It is not unusual for a court to refer to plain or common meaning, but it is also not unusual for the court to add other reasons for the decision. Both decisions in *Glenshaw Glass* elaborate conceptions of income which flesh out the bare statutory language. The Court of Appeals followed the *Eisner v. Macomber* definition of income, stressing gain from particular sources. The Supreme Court stressed "realized accessions to wealth," and "dominion," rejecting limitations on the definition of income which depend on the particular source of income. Think of examples, such as punitive damages, which might come out differently under the two definitions. How about money found and kept by a taxpayer? *Rev. Rul. 61*, 1953-1 C.B. 17. Or gambling winnings?

The following definition of income is usually referred to as the Haig-Simons definition. The quote comes from Simons, *Personal Income Taxation* 50 (1938). How does it differ from the *Glenshaw Glass* and *Eisner v. Macomber* definitions?

> Personal income may be defined as the algebraic sum of (1) the market value of rights exercised in consumption and (2) the change in the value of the store of property rights between the beginning and end of the period in question. In other words, it is merely the result obtained by adding consumption during the period to "wealth" at the end of the period and then subtracting "wealth" at the beginning. The *sine qua non* of income is *gain* as our courts have recognized in their more lucid moments — and gain to someone during a specified time interval. Moreover, this gain may be measured and defined most easily by positing a dual objective

or purpose, consumption and accumulation, each of which may be estimated in a common unit by appeal to market prices.

The point of the Haig-Simons definition is that sources are committed to uses. Any accountant will tell you that. Every credit has a debit. Income sources can be used in two ways. They can be used for personal consumption, such as food, clothing, or vacations; or for savings, such as a deposit in a bank account or purchase of land. That is what the Haig-Simons definition of income, quoted above, explicitly says.

If you think of income as a proxy for the uses to which income is put, a significant legal question in defining income remains, which is whether an item which is allegedly income is really available for consumption or savings. Chapter 7, dealing with employer fringe benefits, discusses this question. From this perspective, *Glenshaw Glass* is an easy case because unrestricted cash (in the form of punitive damages) is available for consumption and savings.

Focusing on uses also helps to explain why the *Eisner v. Macomber* definition might have been so attractive at one time, especially with the "periodicity" gloss mentioned by the Court of Appeals in *Glenshaw Glass.* In an agricultural era, people lived on the periodic gain from rent and crop production, derived from capital and labor. No one would have dreamed of drawing down capital for their own use, and nonperiodic lump sums were regarded as capital which could produce income, contrasted with the income itself. In earlier times, therefore, many people would have felt comfortable saying that some receipts were inherently capital and therefore not income, because they were not available for consumption. This can be restated in the language of *Glenshaw Glass* as follows: even if the taxpayer might have legal and effective dominion over certain resources, social practice did not contemplate exercise of that dominion in all cases. As time passed, however, this pastoral image of the economy became obsolete. People used increases in capital and lump sum receipts for consumption, if they wanted to, and the decision to save or consume became discretionary rather than a more or less automatic practice when certain items were received. Today, we do not associate the availability or lack of availability of wealth for consumption purposes with the source of that wealth. That explains why *Glenshaw Glass* rejects distinctions based on particular sources. Because nothing is inherently capital, it is impossible to say that capital accretion is not income for tax purposes.

[B]—Accession to wealth?

A taxpayer got *erroneous* advice from tax counsel. As a result of the advice, the taxpayer made an election which resulted in a payment of $20,000 more tax than would have been due if no election had been made.

Sometime later, tax counsel paid taxpayer $20,000 to compensate for the error. The payment was *not* taxed because there was no "accession to wealth." *Clark v. Commissioner*, 40 B.T.A. 333 (1939).

Would your answer be different if the compensation had been paid because the taxpayer owed the government an additional $20,000 after tax counsel had erroneously told the taxpayer that some income was exempt? *Priv. Ltr. Rul. 9226032; Priv. Ltr. Rul. 9226033.* An answer to this question is suggested by the following case and private letter ruling.

CONCORD INSTRUMENTS CORP. v. COMMISSIONER

67 T.C.M. (CCH) 3036 (1994)

COLVIN, JUDGE: . . .

[Editor — In an earlier case, the Tax Court held that the taxpayer (Concord) owed back taxes. The taxpayer's lawyer negligently failed to file an appeal. Taxpayer then made a claim against the lawyer's malpractice insurer which was settled for $125,000. In this case, the taxpayer seeks to exclude the $125,000 recovery, based on *Clark*. The court stated:]

Clark v. Commissioner, 40 B.T.A. 333 (1939), is instructive in deciding this case, and is closer to this situation than any other decided case either party has cited. We recognize that in *Clark*, unlike the instant case, there was no dispute that Clark was injured by his counsel's error, and that the amount of the injury was known. In contrast here, there is no certainty whether, or by how much, petitioner was injured by its counsel's conduct. Nevertheless, the fact remains that American Home [the lawyer's insurance company] paid petitioner $ 125,000 to settle the latter's claim against its counsel for malpractice in the handling of the tax case.

Respondent seeks to distinguish *Clark* on the grounds that in *Clark* the attorney's error undisputedly caused the taxpayer to pay more taxes. The essence of respondent's argument is that any error by petitioner's counsel was harmless because petitioner's case was correctly decided by the Tax Court. Under that assumption, any funds petitioner received were an economic benefit and not compensation for injury. . . . Respondent does not argue that American Home paid petitioner the $125,000 for any reason other than petitioner's claim. We conclude that American Home paid the $125,000 because of petitioner's claim. Thus, petitioner's claim and American Home's payment was to compensate petitioner for a loss similar to that in *Clark*.

Question. Suppose there was evidence in *Concord Instruments* that the taxpayer's claim was frivolous and the lawyer and his insurance company settled to avoid the nuisance and bad publicity. Can the government go behind the surface of the taxpayer's claim to recharacterize the recovery, so that it would be a taxable accession to wealth, rather than a tax-free loss recovery? In answering this question, put yourself in the position of a trial judge who must adjudicate such claims. Should you adopt a rule which distinguishes real from frivolous claims?

PRIVATE LETTER RULING 9728052

April 16, 1997

1. This letter is in reply to your letter requesting a ruling that A's receipt of a tax indemnity payment will not be includible in A's gross income.

2. . . . A executed an agreement (the "Agreement") to pay his former spouse annually for [some] years. The Agreement also provides that if the former spouse dies, the payments will be made to her estate. A's attorney informed A that payments under the Agreement would qualify as deductible alimony payments under section 215 of the Internal Revenue Code.

3. The Internal Revenue Service subsequently examined A's federal income tax returns and disallowed the alimony deduction. . . . The payments under the Agreement are not deductible as alimony because A's obligation to make the payments continues after the death of his former spouse. See section 71(b)(1)(D). A is now negotiating with his attorney's malpractice insurer for an indemnification payment. This payment will recompense A for the additional federal income taxes . . . he has paid and the additional federal income taxes he expects to pay over the term of the Agreement arising from the nondeductibility of payments made under the Agreement. . . .

7. The indemnity payment that A will receive as reimbursement for the additional federal income taxes A has paid or will pay are distinguishable from the indemnity payments in *Clark*. . . . In *Clark* . . . the preparers' errors in filing returns . . . caused the taxpayers to pay more than their minimum proper federal income tax liabilities based on the underlying transactions for the years in question. In this case, however, the error of A's attorney related to the underlying transaction, that is, the terms of the Agreement. As a result of that error, A's payments under the Agreement

are properly not deductible. Thus, unlike the situations in *Clark* . . . A is not paying more than his minimum proper federal income tax liability based on A's transactions for the tax years to which the tax reimbursements relate. Therefore, under section 1.61-14(a) the reimbursement of prior and future years federal income taxes that A receives represents a gain that is includible in A's gross income. . . .

9. Accordingly, we conclude that A must include in gross income the indemnity payment A will receive as compensation for additional federal income taxes . . . arising from A's attorney's misrepresentation that payments under the Agreement are deductible under section 215.

[C]—Loans

Loans are not taxable. Why not? The simple answer is that the receipts are offset by debt so the taxpayer has no gain. The receipts are a plus but the debt is an equivalent minus.

Before you assume too readily that the statute does not tax loans, consider the following. Suppose loans were taxed. If they were, then the repayment and interest would have to be deductible, to reflect the fact that the taxpayer has no gain over time. For example, assume a taxpayer wants $100 of personal consumption in year 1. To simplify the arithmetic, assume a 50% tax rate. If loans are taxable, he must borrow $200, to get $100 after tax. Assume further that interest rates are 10% and the loan with interest is paid back after one year. The taxpayer would need $220 gross income to pay back the loan with interest. Taxable income would be zero (220 minus 220 = 0), and the entire $220 would be used to repay the $200 loan and $20 (10%) interest.

If loans were not taxed, the taxpayer has to borrow only $100 in year 1 to get $100 personal consumption. How much gross income does the taxpayer need in year 2 to repay the debt. Because loans were not taxed, repayment is not deductible. The taxpayer needs $200 to get the $100 to repay the loan. What about the interest. She owes $10 interest (10% of $100). How much gross income does she need to get $10 to pay the interest. That depends on whether interest is deductible. In fact, interest on loans for personal purposes may or may not be deductible, depending on the use of the loan (discussed in Chapter 15). At this point, it is enough to know that interest on some personal loans is not deductible. If interest is not deductible, the taxpayer needs $20 gross income to get the $10 after tax to pay the interest, plus $200 gross income to pay back the $100 loan.

In other words, if loans are not taxable *but* interest is not deductible, the taxpayer needs $220 income in year 2 to repay the $100 loan with interest. But that is the same amount she needed if loans were taxable and interest and loan repayments were deductible. Disallowing the interest deduction produced the equivalent of taxing the loan. In both cases the taxpayer needs $220 gross income in year 2 to repay the loan and interest. Why don't taxpayers object to disallowing interest deductions, when they would object vehemently to taxing loans?

[D]—Obligations to repay, but not loans

What happens if someone embezzles income. How can there be any income? There is an obligation to repay which offsets the receipts. Or is there? Put technically, what is the present value of the debt obligation? Put colloquially, what are the chances of repayment?

For some time the Supreme Court did not tax the embezzler. Specifically, it relied on an early case dealing with the taxation of someone whose possession of money was the subject of litigation. The Court established the "claim of right" rule, which stated:

> If a taxpayer receives earnings under a claim of right and without restriction as to its disposition, he has received income . . . , even though it may still be claimed that he is not entitled to retain the money, and even though he may still be adjudged liable to restore its equivalent.

North American Oil Consolidated v. Burnet, 286 U.S. 417 (1932). The Court later viewed "claim of right" as a necessary, not just a sufficient reason to tax. Embezzled funds were therefore not taxable, because the embezzler laid no claim to the income. This holding was reversed in *James v. United States*, 366 U.S. 213 (1961). The Court held that a taxpayer has income "when [the taxpayer] acquires earnings, lawfully or unlawfully, without the consensual recognition, express or implied, of an obligation to repay and without restriction as to their disposition. . . ." Claim of right is now a sufficient but not a necessary condition for having taxable income.

Still, there are borderline cases, of which the following is an example.

GILBERT v. COMMISSIONER

552 F.2d 478 (2d Cir. 1977)

→ *means case*

NOTE: started in tax court

LUMBARD, CIRCUIT JUDGE:

Until June 12, 1962, Gilbert [the taxpayer] was president, principal stockholder, and a director of the E. L. Bruce Company, Inc., a New York corporation which was engaged in the lumber supply business. In 1961 and early 1962 Gilbert acquired on margin substantial personal and beneficial ownership of stock in another lumber supply company, the Celotex Corporation, intending ultimately to bring about a merger of Celotex into Bruce. To this end, he persuaded associates of his to purchase Celotex stock, guaranteeing them against loss, and also induced Bruce itself to purchase a substantial number of Celotex shares. In addition, on March 5, 1962, Gilbert granted Bruce an option to purchase his Celotex shares from him at cost. By the end of May 1962, 56% of Celotex was thus controlled by Gilbert and Bruce, and negotiations for the merger were proceeding; agreement had been reached that three of the directors of Bruce would be placed on the board of Celotex. It is undisputed that this merger would have been in Bruce's interest.

The stock market declined on May 28, 1962, however, and Gilbert was called upon to furnish additional margin for the Celotex shares purchased by him and his associates. Lacking sufficient cash of his own to meet this margin call, Gilbert instructed the secretary of Bruce to use corporate funds to supply the necessary margin. Between May 28 and June 6 a series of checks totalling $1,958,000 were withdrawn from Bruce's accounts and used to meet the margin call. $5,000 was repaid to Bruce on June 5. According to his testimony in the tax court, Gilbert from the outset intended to repay all the money and at all times thought he was acting in the corporation's best interests as well as his own. He promptly informed several other Bruce officers and directors of the withdrawals; however, some were not notified until June 11 or 12.

On about June 1, Gilbert returned to New York from Nevada, where he had been attending to a personal matter. Shortly thereafter he consulted with Shearman, Sterling & Wright, who were outside counsel to Bruce at the time, regarding the withdrawals. They, he, and another Bruce director initiated negotiations to sell many of the Celotex shares to Ruberoid Company as a way of recouping most of Bruce's outlay.

On June 8, Gilbert went to the law offices of Shearman, Sterling & Wright and executed interest-bearing promissory notes to Bruce for $1,953,000 secured by an assignment of most of his property. The notes were callable by Bruce on demand, with presentment and notice of demand waived by

Gilbert. The tax court found that up through June 12 the net value of the assets assigned for security by Gilbert substantially exceeded the amount owed.

After Gilbert informed other members of the Bruce board of directors of his actions, a meeting of the board was scheduled for the morning of June 12. At the meeting the board accepted the note and assignment but refused to ratify Gilbert's unauthorized withdrawals. During the meeting, word came that the board of directors of the Ruberoid Company had rejected the price offered for sale of the Celotex stock. Thereupon, the Bruce board demanded and received Gilbert's resignation and decided to issue a public announcement the next day regarding his unauthorized withdrawals. All further attempts on June 12 to arrange a sale of the Celotex stock fell through and in the evening Gilbert flew to Brazil, where he stayed for several months. On June 13 the market price of Bruce and Celotex stock plummeted, and trading in those shares was suspended by the Securities and Exchanges Commission.

On June 22 the Internal Revenue Service filed tax liens against Gilbert. . . . Several years later Gilbert pled guilty to federal and state charges of having unlawfully withdrawn the funds from Bruce.

The starting point for analysis of this case is *James v. United States*, 366 U.S. 213 (1961), which established that embezzled funds can constitute taxable income to the embezzler. When a taxpayer acquires earnings, lawfully or unlawfully, without the consensual recognition, express or implied, of an obligation to repay and without restriction as to their disposition, "he has received income which he is required to return, even though it may still be claimed that he is not entitled to the money, and even though he may still be adjudged liable to restore its equivalent." *Id.* at 219.

The Commissioner contends that there can never be "consensual recognition . . . of an obligation to repay" in an embezzlement case. He reasons that because the corporation as represented by a majority of the board of directors was unaware of the withdrawals, there cannot have been consensual recognition of the obligation to repay at the time the taxpayer Gilbert acquired the funds. Since the withdrawals were not authorized and the directors refused to treat them as a loan to Gilbert, the Commissioner concludes that Gilbert should be taxed like a thief rather than a borrower.

In a typical embezzlement, the embezzler intends at the outset to abscond with the funds. If he repays the money during the same taxable year, he will not be taxed. As we held in *Buff v. Commissioner*, 496 F.2d 847 (2d Cir. 1974), if he spends the loot instead of repaying, he cannot avoid tax on his embezzlement income simply by signing promissory notes later in the same year.

This is not a typical embezzlement case, however, and we do not interpret James as requiring income realization in every case of unlawful withdrawals by a taxpayer. There are a number of facts that differentiate this case from *Buff* and *James*. When Gilbert withdrew the corporate funds, he recognized his obligation to repay and intended to do so. The funds were to be used not only for his benefit but also for the benefit of the corporation; meeting the margin calls was necessary to maintain the possibility of the highly favorable merger. Although Gilbert undoubtedly realized that he lacked the necessary authorization, he thought he was serving the best interests of the corporation and he expected his decision to be ratified shortly thereafter. That Gilbert at no time intended to retain the corporation's funds is clear from his actions. He immediately informed several of the corporation's officers and directors, and he made a complete accounting to all of them within two weeks. He also disclosed his actions to the corporation's outside counsel, a reputable law firm, and followed its instructions regarding repayment. In signing immediately payable promissory notes secured by most of his assets, Gilbert's clear intent was to ensure that Bruce would obtain full restitution. In addition, he attempted to sell his shares of Celotex stock in order to raise cash to pay Bruce back immediately.

When Gilbert executed the assignment to Bruce of his assets on June 8 and when this assignment for security was accepted by the Bruce board on June 12, the net market value of these assets was substantially more than the amount owed. The Bruce board did not release Gilbert from his underlying obligation to repay, but the assignment was nonetheless valid and Bruce's failure to make an appropriate filing to protect itself against the claims of third parties, such as the IRS, did not relieve Gilbert of the binding effect of the assignment. Since the assignment secured an immediate payable note, Gilbert had as of June 12 granted Bruce full discretion to liquidate any of his assets in order to recoup on the $1,953,000 withdrawal. Thus, Gilbert's net accretion in real wealth on the overall transaction was zero: he had for his own use withdrawn $1,953,000 in corporate funds but he had now granted the corporation control over at least $1,953,000 worth of his assets.

We conclude that where a taxpayer withdraws funds from a corporation which he fully intends to repay and which he expects with reasonable certainty he will be able to repay, where he believes that his withdrawals will be approved by the corporation, and where he makes a prompt assignment of assets sufficient to secure the amount owed, he does not realize income on the withdrawals under the *James* test. When Gilbert acquired the money, there was an express consensual recognition of his obligation to repay: the secretary of the corporation, who signed the checks, the officers and directors to whom Gilbert gave contemporaneous notification, and Gilbert himself were all aware that the transaction was in the nature of a loan. Moreover, the funds were certainly not received by Gilbert "without restriction as to their disposition" as is required for taxability under James; the money was to be used solely for the temporary purpose of meeting certain margin calls and it was so used. For these reasons, we reverse the decision of the tax court.

QUESTIONS

1. How could there be an accession to wealth in *Gilbert*? The taxpayer owed the money he took. Was there the kind of consensual recognition that typically occurs when people borrow money? When did the taxpayer recognize the debt; did the creditor acquiesce in the "loan?" Was the debtor able to pay back the debt?

2. In *Gilbert*, did the debtor think he was helping the creditor; if so, was that expectation plausible? Should that affect the tax result?

3. Compare *Gilbert* to *Buff*. In *Buff* a bookkeeper embezzled $22,000 between January and June, 1965. The crime was discovered in June. The employee confessed and agreed to repay $25 per week out of his paycheck; he also borrowed $1,000 from a bank to make a repayment. In July, 1965, the employee was fired. Is *Buff* a stronger or weaker case for the taxpayer than *Gilbert*? *Buff v. Commissioner*, 58 T.C. 224 (1972) (not tax), *rev'd*, 496 F.2d 847 (2d Cir. 1974) (tax).

4. Why is the government so anxious to tax illegally acquired funds? Why not wait until a later date when repayment is clearly unlikely and impose tax at that time? One answer is that the government has a lien on a taxpayer's property for unpaid taxes and that lien might have priority over the creditor's rights (in *Gilbert* the corporate creditor had failed to protect its security interest). If the government waits too long, the taxpayer's property may be gone.

§ 3.07 DISCHARGE OF INDEBTEDNESS

The following case discusses whether a debtor has income when a debt is forgiven.

bond = debt instrument

UNITED STATES v. KIRBY LUMBER CO.

284 U.S. 1 (1931)

MR. JUSTICE HOLMES delivered the opinion of the court.

In July, 1923, the plaintiff, the Kirby Lumber Company, issued its own bonds for $12,126,800 for which it received their par value. Later in the same year it purchased in the open market some of the same bonds at less than par, the difference of price being $137,521.30. The question is whether this difference is a taxable gain or income of the plaintiff for the year 1923. . . . [G]ross income includes "gains or profits and income derived from any source whatever," and by the Treasury Regulations [] that have been in force through repeated re-enactments, "If the corporation purchases and retires any of such bonds at a price less than the issuing price or face value, the excess of the issuing price or face value over the purchase price is gain or income for the taxable year." We see no reason why the Regulations should not be accepted as a correct statement of the law.

reg.

. Here there was no shrinkage of assets and the taxpayer made a clear gain. As a result of its dealings it made available $137,521.30 assets previously offset by the obligation of bonds now extinct. We see nothing to be gained by the discussion of judicial definitions. The defendant in error has realized within the year an accession to income, if we take words in their plain popular meaning, as they should be taken here. *Burnet v. Sanford & Brooks Co.*, 282 U.S. 359.

Judgment reversed.

① 𝛑/Kirby —issued bonds→ received ←$12 mil. /par value

② 𝛑 ← bought bonds, paid less than par value →

gain = $137,521.30

Basis adjustment. *Kirby*, like *Bruun*, evoked a congressional reaction. Even though there was income under *§ 61*, the taxable event was an inopportune time to impose tax. Debts are often forgiven when taxpayers are in financial trouble and the act of forgiveness provides no cash with which to repay the debt. For this reason, immediately after *Kirby Lumber* was decided, Congress passed the predecessor of *§ 108, § 1017*. These sections provided that certain taxpayers who otherwise had taxable income when a debt was forgiven could elect to reduce the basis of property, thereby deferring the tax on the income that would otherwise be imposed.

The current § 108 is not as generous. The core of the section allows bankrupt or insolvent taxpayers to avoid paying tax when a debt is forgiven, but only at a price. They must reduce various tax benefits in the order specified in *§ 108(b)(2)*, unless they elect to reduce the basis of depreciable property. *§ 108(b)(5)*. Under this provision, insolvent taxpayers cannot exclude from income any more than the amount by which they are insolvent before the forgiveness (*e.g.*, \$100 debt, \$80 assets, \$20 insolvency). *§ 108(a)(3)*.

Prior to the Tax Reform Act of 1986, a solvent taxpayer whose debt was forgiven could reduce the basis of depreciable property used in a trade or business, but that option has been repealed, with two exceptions. *First*, farmers can exclude discharge of indebtedness income and reduce tax benefits, even though they are not insolvent, if the debt is owed to certain types of creditors, and if the debt is related to the farming business. *§ 108(a)(1)(C),(g)*.

Second, an individual who borrows to acquire, construct, or substantially improve business real property (secured by the debt) can elect to exclude forgiven debt from income. The maximum exclusion is (1) the debt prior to the forgiveness, minus (2) the value of the property (reduced by any other debt secured by the property). The taxpayer must reduce basis of depreciable real property in an amount equal to the forgiven debt excluded from income. *§ 108(a)(1)(D),(c), § 1017(b)(3)(F)*. For example, assume a bank lends taxpayer \$100,000 to buy a business building, taking back a first mortgage on the property; the value of the property declines to \$80,000; and the debtor renegotiates the debt to \$70,000 (\$30,000 forgiveness). \$20,000 of the debt forgiveness can be excluded, but basis is reduced from \$100,000 to \$80,000.

Current law also allows a debtor to reduce basis on purchased property if the *seller* forgives all or part of the purchase price, without regard to the debtor's solvency. *§ 108(e)(5)*. This might help the purchaser of a home bought on credit from the seller.

If tax is not deferred by *§ 108*, *Kirby Lumber* applies and the taxpayer has income when the debt is discharged. For example, assume that (as in *Kirby*) a corporate debtor is solvent and buys back bonds for less than the original loan. In that case, the taxpayer would recognize ordinary income when the debt was discharged.

Another example of a forgiven debt that would typically be included in *§ 61* income is the forgiveness of a student loan when the student is solvent. *Rev. Rul. 73–256*, 1973–1 C.B. 56. After this ruling, Congress exempted one category of forgiven student loans. *§ 2117 (a), (c) of the Tax Reform Act of 1976, Pub. L. 94–455, 90 Stat. 1911* (student loans forgiven on condition that the taxpayer work for a certain period of time in certain areas or for certain employers). This exemption was made permanent by *§ 108(f)*. In addition, the 1997 Act expanded the *§ 108(f)* exclusion for forgiven student loans to include forgiveness by universities, if the borrower "serves in occupations with unmet needs or in areas with unmet needs" and is under the direction of a government or exempt organization. A loan forgiveness program for law students who work in an LSO or legal aid office would be covered by this new provision.

Discharge of Debt Other Than By a Creditor. In *Kirby Lumber*, the creditor released the debtor from his obligation. In other situations, a debtor may have a relationship to a third party and the debt is discharged because the third party pays off the creditor. In such cases, the debtor's relationship to the third party determines whether there is taxable income or not; the "discharge of indebtedness" rules are inapplicable. For example, in *Old Colony Trust Co. v. Commissioner*, 279 U.S. 716 (1929), the third party was the debtor's employer. The employer paid salary to the debtor by paying off the debtor's tax obligation. Payment of the tax debt was taxable income to the debtor because it was additional compensation.

In other cases, the third party may have some other relationship with the debtor, so that payment of the debtor's obligation might or might not produce taxable income. If the third party was the debtor's relative, payment of the debt might be a tax exempt gift to the debtor. The third party might owe the taxpayer money because he bought property from the debtor. Payment of the taxpayer's debt might then be additional sales proceeds, taxable as capital gain.

Distinguishing sales proceeds from discharge of indebtedness. In *Gehl v. Commissioner*, 1995 U.S. App. LEXIS 5482 (8th Cir. 1995) (unpublished opinion, reported in case table at 50 F.3d 12), *aff'g* 102 T.C. 784 (1994), an insolvent farmer conveyed property to his creditor in partial discharge of an (approximately) $152,000 debt, for which the farmer was personally liable. The property's basis was about $48,000 and its value about $116,000. After this conveyance, the farmer was still insolvent. The bank also forgave the remainder of the loan (about $36,000). The government argued that this conveyance produced taxable gain to the farmer as a sale of the property in an amount equal to the fair market value of the property minus basis ($68,000 = $116,000 minus $48,000). Both sides agreed that the $36,000 forgiveness was eligible for *§ 108* treatment. The farmer argued that the $68,000 gain on the land was also eligible for *§ 108* treatment, but the court disagreed. The gain on the property was taxable as gain from dealings in property under *§ 61(a)(3)*, not income from discharge of indebtedness. The transaction had to be bifurcated into the gain from the disposition of the property (value over basis) and gain from debt discharge (debt over value), and only the latter was eligible for *§ 108* treatment. The court relied on *Treas. Reg. § 1.1001-2(c) example 8* to support its conclusion.

QUESTIONS

1. If a taxpayer gives property to a relative but requires the donee to pay the gift tax (for which the donor is liable), is the donee's payment of the tax considered sales proceeds to the donor? Some courts had held that the donor was not taxed because she was not "better off after the transfer. . . . She was simply not worse off." *Hirst v. Commissioner*, 572 F.2d 427 (4th Cir. 1978). The Supreme Court disagreed in *Diedrich v. Commissioner*, 457 U.S. 191 (1982), taxing the gift tax paid by the donee as sales proceeds. Is the Court right?

2. Suppose a creditor forgives a debt but only because the creditor owes the debtor money. For example, an employer might lend money to an employee, but later be obligated for wages. The employer-creditor forgives the original loan to the employee as a wage payment. (1) Does the employee have income? (2) What kind of income is it — salary income or discharge of indebtedness income? (3) Does it matter which kind of income it is? *Hint*: suppose the employee is insolvent?

3. Suppose a taxpayer owes $100,000 to a tort plaintiff resulting from a car accident on the taxpayer's vacation, which was the taxpayer's fault. The $100,000 is paid by an insurance company from whom the taxpayer had purchased liability insurance. Does the taxpayer have $100,000 income from this discharge of liability?

§ 3.08 CONSUMPTION

As noted, the *Glenshaw Glass* definition of income invites looking at the definition of income from the point of view of the uses to which income is put (personal consumption and savings). When does a taxpayer have taxable personal consumption? At least some itemized deductions may be permitted on the theory that the expenditures do not provide personal consumption (for example, the medical expense deduction — discussed in a later chapter). Another setting in which the question arises is when a taxpayer receives something other than cash for personal consumption (income in-kind rather than in-cash). This often occurs when an employee receives fringe benefits from an employer, also discussed in a later chapter. Here we look at a benefit received in a non-employment setting — a prize. We want to know whether the subjective benefit enjoyed by a particular taxpayer discounts the taxable benefit below the objective market value of an item.

Prizes. In *Turner v. Commissioner,* 13 T.C.M. (CCH) 462 (1954), the taxpayer won a prize of two nontransferable first-class steamship tickets for a cruise to Buenos Aires for himself and his wife. His income was otherwise quite low and his lifestyle did not include cruises. His wife was from Rio de Janeiro and he was able to turn in the two tickets and $12.50 for four tourist class tickets to Rio for himself, his wife and two children. The taxpayer valued the tickets on the tax return at $520, but the government argued that the retail market value of the tickets, which was $2,220, should be taxed. The court included $1,400 in taxable income.

If the steamship tickets had been transferable for, say, $1,800, would the decision be different? Would transferability for $1,800 eliminate any dispute that the taxpayer should be taxed on $2,220? Suppose a taxpayer receives a new car, with a retail value of $10,000 and a resale value of $8,900. How would you decide what taxable income to report?

Turner is a rare case in which the taxpayer could discount objective retail market value because of lower subjective value. The fact that the court virtually split the difference between taxable value conceded by the taxpayer and retail value suggests that a subjective standard is not administrable. But subjective criteria may still be relevant for rulemaking purposes. Usually, courts, the agency, and the statute take an all or nothing approach to including or excluding an in-kind benefit. In doing this, however, they consider whether taxpayers would derive significant subjective value from the benefit. Subjective value is therefore relevant for framing general rules, even if it is not generally useful on a case-by-case basis.

In *McDonald v. Commissioner*, 66 T.C. 223 (1976), a United States executive in Japan was provided western-style housing by his employer who had rented a house for the employee. Somewhat simplified, the facts were that the employer paid about $1,000 per month to rent the house for the employee. The employee was willing to include $350 per month in income because that was what "a study indicated an average American Businessman with a position and salary comparable to petitioner's would spend for lodgings in the United States." The court included the employer's $1,000 cost in the employee's income. (Note that Congress has come to the rescue of U.S. workers abroad by giving them a deduction for "excessive" housing costs. *§§ 911(a)(2), 911(c)).*

Questions. (1) How does *McDonald* differ from *Turner*? (2) Notice that the taxpayer does not include in income any gain he might enjoy because some things might cost less in a foreign country than in the United States. Do taxpayers who arguably enjoy less than the amount of money spent typically have untaxed offsetting gains?

Compulsive gambler. In *Zarin v. Commissioner*, 92 T.C. 1084 (1989), *rev'd*, 916 F.2d 110 (3d Cir. 1990), a taxpayer, who was a professional engineer, was also a compulsive gambler. In 1980, he ran up a $3,435,000 debt to a gambling establishment in New Jersey named Resorts. He obtained a line of credit by giving his "marker" (like a promissory note) to obtain chips. Currency could not be used to gamble in New Jersey. Resorts had violated state law in various respects, which made its claim against Zarin legally unenforceable. In 1981, a lawsuit to collect the debt was settled for $500,000. The government claimed that the difference between $3,435,000 and $500,000 was discharge of indebtedness income. The 1980 losses could not offset any 1981 gain because *Treas. Reg. § 1.165-10* interprets the rule in *§ 165(d)* (limiting the deduction of gambling losses to gambling gains) to mean that loss deductions can only offset gains arising in the *same* year as the losses.

Zarin involves the following issues: (1) Is there *§ 61* income on the discharge of indebtedness in the first place? If there is no *§ 61* income in the first place, there is no need to rely on *§ 108* to prevent taxation. (2) If there is *§ 61* income, does *§ 108* apply, to provide taxpayer relief?

The Tax Court held against the taxpayer, with a dissent. The Court of Appeals reversed, holding for the taxpayer, with a dissent.

ZARIN v. COMMISSIONER

92 T.C. 1084 (1989)

COHEN, JUDGE: . . .

Petitioner [] relies on the principle that settlement of disputed debts does not give rise to income. [Editor — This is a doctrine originating in the case law, concerned with the definition of *§ 61* income. The idea is that the value received by a borrower cannot be determined until the amount of the debt is undisputed.] Prior to the settlement, the amount of petitioner's gambling debt to Resorts was a liquidated amount. . . . There is no dispute about the amount petitioner received. . . . A genuine dispute does not exist merely because petitioner required Resorts to sue him before making payment of any amount on the debt. The cases cited by petitioner merely require that there be a liquidated debt, *i.e.*, one in which the amount has been determined. In our view, petitioner's arguments concerning his defenses to Resorts' claim which apparently led to Resorts' agreement to discount the debt, are overcome by (1) the stipulation of the parties that, at the time the debt was created, petitioner agreed to and intended to repay the full amount, and (2) our conclusion that he received full value for what he agreed to pay, *i.e.*, over $3 million worth of chips and the benefits received by petitioner as a "valued gambling patron" of Resorts. . . .

Petitioner [next] argues that the settlement with Resorts should be treated as a purchase price adjustment [under § 108(e)(5)] that does not give rise to income from the discharge of indebtedness. . . .

Section 108(e)(5) was enacted "to eliminate disagreements between the Internal Revenue Service and the debtor as to whether, in a particular case to which the provision applies, the debt reductions should be treated as discharge income or a true price adjustment."

For a reduction in the amount of a debt to be treated as a purchase price adjustment under § 108(e)(5), the following conditions must be met: (1) The debt must be that of a purchaser of property to the seller which arose out of the purchase of such property; (2) the taxpayer must be solvent and not in bankruptcy when the debt reduction occurs; and (3) except for § 108(e)(5), the debt reduction would otherwise have resulted in discharge of indebtedness income. . . .

It seems to us that the value received by petitioner in exchange for the credit extended by Resorts does not constitute the type of property to which § 108(e)(5) was intended to or reasonably can be applied. . . .

As indicated above, we are persuaded on the stipulated facts that petitioner received full value for his debt. In arguing that he did not, however, petitioner asserts:

> In exchange for his promise to repay Resorts, Petitioner received chips. . . . These chips may be used only to gamble in the Resorts Casino. Furthermore, the record is void of any assertion that Petitioner's life-style equates to cognizable consideration.

Petitioner purchased the opportunity to gamble as he received chips in exchange for his markers. He did not even use the chips to pay for food, beverage, entertainment or hotel/living accommodations while in Atlantic City, as these services were provided to Petitioner by Resorts on a complimentary basis. Upon receipt of the chips, Petitioner immediately proceeded to gamble with these chips. . . .

. . . [P]etitioner, in entering into the gaming transactions with Resorts, did not receive any item of tangible value. In fact, petitioner received nothing more than the opportunity to bet on which of 36 permutations of the dice would appear on a given roll of the dice. . . .

. . . In support of an argument that "A debt incurred by a casino patron to acquire gambling opportunity is not a typical commercial debt and as such should not be treated as a typical commercial debt," petitioner argues:

> In addition to the character of the gambling debt being different than a typical commercial debt, the Petitioner-Resorts gambling transactions did not occur in the normal commercial debtor-creditor relationship in which a debtor borrows funds from a creditor and uses the loan proceeds elsewhere or uses the funds as purchase money for which he acquires something of value. Petitioner received gambling chips from Resorts. Petitioner received no consideration from Resorts and was, in fact, $500,000 poorer from his transactions, while Resorts parted with nothing.

In support of an argument that "Tax is not imposed on an opportunity to realize income," petitioner asserts:

> Petitioner's receipt of chips on credit represented an opportunity to gamble. The chips, the value of which are not equal to the value of the markers given, cannot be negotiated outside of the issuing casino and may be retained by the casino in satisfaction of the markers if presented by the patron for redemption. Accordingly, the only value represented by the chips is their potential income earning power. . . .

While disagreeing with petitioner's assertion as to the value of what he received, we agree that what he received was something other than normal commercial property. He bargained for and received the opportunity to gamble and incidental services, lodging, entertainment, meals, and transportation. Petitioner's argument that he was purchasing chips ignores the essence of the transaction, as more accurately described in his other arguments here quoted. The "property" argument simply overemphasizes the significance of the chips. As a matter of substance, chips in isolation are not what petitioner purchased.

The "opportunity to gamble" would not in the usual sense of the words be "property" transferred from a seller to a purchaser. The terminology used in § 108(e)(5) is readily understood with respect to tangible property and may apply to some types of intangibles. Abstract concepts of property are not useful, however, in deciding whether what petitioner received is within the contemplation of the section. . . .

Obviously the chips in this case were a medium of exchange within the Resorts casino, and in that sense they were a substitute for cash. . . .

We conclude that petitioner's settlement with Resorts cannot be construed as a "purchase-money debt reduction" arising from the purchase of property within the meaning of § 108(e)(5).

QUESTIONS AND COMMENTS

1. What does the court mean by characterizing the opportunity to gamble as something other than "property?" Aren't stock options an opportunity to gamble which would be "property" within *§ 108(e)(5)*?

2. Why do we care whether the property is "normal commercial property?" Is this a way of saying that the tax law should not favor gamblers?

3. Perhaps the court means that the taxpayer does not come within the spirit of the *§ 108(e)(5)* rule. The typical downward renegotiation of a debt with a seller occurs when the purchased goods are defective (the house had a leaky roof, for example). The reduction of the debt reflects the lack of personal consumption from the original purchase — hence, the price reduction. If the point of taxing debt forgiveness is that the original loan provided the taxpayer with a potential accretion to wealth, which must be taxed when the debt is forgiven, then taxing the discharge of indebtedness is improper if the original loan did not turn out to produce an accession to wealth. The problem with this argument *against* taxing Zarin is that his purchase did not turn sour. He got what he bargained for; he just lost his bets. The problem with this argument *for* taxing Zarin, however, is that the passage of *§ 108(e)(5)* was intended to eliminate the disputes under

prior case law about whether the debt reduction was *§ 61* forgiveness of indebtedness income or a genuine price reduction.

4. How can the chips be of sufficient value to support discharge of indebtedness income but not be "property" within *§ 108(e)(5)*? The dissenting Tax Court judge could not find a reason and applied *§ 108(e)(5)* to help the taxpayer. But perhaps the taxpayer was buying "services" — the casino provided gambling "services" — rather than "property." Would characterizing what the taxpayer bought as "services" end the dispute about whether Zarin should be taxed by depriving the taxpayer of the *§ 108(e)(5)* escape hatch? Why couldn't Zarin still appeal to the old case law involving renegotiation of the price between buyer and seller to determine whether the arrangement was a nontaxable purchase price adjustment or taxable debt forgiveness under *§ 61*?

5. Could the taxpayer argue that he never really expected to pay the full amount of the loan? He knew it would be renegotiated and never really got an accession to wealth, from his point of view, in excess of what he eventually paid. His situation is therefore like a purchaser of defective goods, eligible for the *§ 108(e)(5)* benefit, except that he knew *in advance* that there would be a downward price adjustment.

The Court of Appeals reversed the Tax Court in *Zarin v. Commissioner*, 916 F.2d 110 (3d Cir. 1990), as follows.

COWEN, CIRCUIT JUDGE: . . .

Initially, we find that §§ 108 & 61(a)(12) are inapplicable to the [taxpayer]. Section 61 does not define indebtedness. On the other hand, § 108(d)(1), which repeats and further elaborates on the rule in § 61(a)(12), defines the term as any indebtedness "(A) for which the taxpayer is liable, or [B] subject to which the taxpayer holds property. . . ." [Editor — The court held that a taxpayer was not "liable" for an unenforceable debt, and that the chips were not "property" because they were a "medium of exchange," a "substitute for cash," and only provided "the opportunity to gamble."]

Even were there no relevant legislative pronouncement on which to rely, simple common sense would lead to the conclusion that chips were not property in Zarin's hands. Zarin could not do with the chips as he pleased, nor did the chips have any independent economic value beyond the casino. The chips themselves were of little use to Zarin, other than as a means of facilitating gambling. They could not have been used outside the casino. They could have been used to purchase services and privileges within the casino, including food, drink, entertainment, and lodging, but Zarin would not have utilized them as such, since he received those services from Resorts on a complimentary basis. In short, the chips had no economic substance. . . .

. . . [B]ecause Zarin was not liable on the debt he allegedly owed Resorts, and because Zarin did not hold "property" subject to that debt, the cancellation of indebtedness provisions of the Code do not apply to the settlement between Resorts and Zarin. As such, Zarin can not have income from the discharge of his debt.

Instead of analyzing the transaction at issue as cancelled debt, we believe the proper approach is to view it as disputed debt or contested liability. Under the contested liability doctrine, if a taxpayer, in good faith, disputed the amount of a debt, a subsequent settlement of the dispute would be treated as the amount of debt cognizable for tax purposes. The excess of the original debt over the amount determined to have been due is disregarded for both loss and debt and accounting purposes. Thus, if a taxpayer took out a loan for $10,000, refused in good faith to pay the full $10,000 back, and then reached an agreement with the lender that he would pay back only $7,000 in full satisfaction of the debt, the transaction would be treated as if the initial loan was $7,000. When the taxpayer tenders the $7,000 payment, he will have been deemed to have paid the full amount of the initially disputed debt. Accordingly, there is no tax consequence to the taxpayer upon payment. . . .

The Commissioner argues that . . . the contested liability doctrine only applies when there is a an unliquidated debt; that is, a debt for which the amount cannot be determined. Since Zarin contested his liability based on the unenforceability of the entire debt, and did not dispute the amount of the debt, the Commissioner would have us adopt the reasoning of the Tax Court, which found that Zarin's debt was liquidated, therefore barring the application of . . . the contested liability doctrine.

We reject the Tax Court's rationale. When a debt is unenforceable, it follows that the amount of the debt, and not just the liability thereon, is in dispute. Although a debt may be unenforceable, there still could be some value attached to its worth. This is especially so with regards to gambling debts. In most states, gambling debts are unenforceable. — Nevertheless, they are often collected, at least in part.

In conclusion, we hold that Zarin did not have any income from cancellation of indebtedness for two reasons. First, the Code provisions covering discharge of debt are inapplicable since the definitional requirement in I.R.C. § 108(d)(1) was not met. Second, the settlement of Zarin's gambling debts was a contested liability.

STAPLETON, CIRCUIT JUDGE, dissenting: I respectfully dissent. . . .

Resorts sells for cash the exhilaration and the potential for profit inherent in games of chance. It does so by selling for cash chips that entitle the holder to gamble at its casino. Zarin . . . chose to make this purchase on credit and executed notes evidencing his obligation to repay the funds that were advanced to him by Resorts. As in most purchase money transactions, Resorts skipped the step of giving Zarin cash that he would only return to it in order to pay for the opportunity to gamble. Resorts provided him instead with chips that entitled him to participate in Resorts' games of chance on the same basis as others who had paid cash for that privilege.

[Editor — The dissent then argues that the fact that Resorts advanced credit to Zarin solely to enable him to patronize its casino and that the chips could not be used for other purposes is irrelevant, stating: "When one buys a sofa from the furniture store on credit, the fact that the proprietor would not have advanced the credit for a different purpose does not entitle one to a tax-free gain in the event the debt to the store is extinguished."]

[An argument against this conclusion is] that the $3.4 million benefit sought and received by Zarin is not taxable at all. I find [this] alternative unacceptable as inconsistent with the fundamental principle of the Code that anything of commercial value received by a taxpayer is taxable unless expressly excluded from gross income. . . .

. . . For present purposes, it will suffice to say that where something that would otherwise be includable in gross income is received on credit in a purchase money transaction, there should be no recognition of income so long as the debtor continues to recognize an obligation to repay the debt. On the other hand, income, if not earlier recognized, should be recognized when the debtor no longer recognizes an obligation to repay and the creditor has released the debt or acknowledged its unenforceability.

[Editor — The dissent refused to apply § 108(e)(5) on the ground that it only applies if the taxpayer retains purchased property.]

Comment. We usually accept purchase price as a proxy for valuing taxable personal consumption. Is that assumption valid in the case of a gambler? Does the gambler expect satisfaction equal to the purchase price? Does that depend on how much gambling he does, on the ground that the more he gambles the more total costs are likely to average out and the losses approximate personal consumption? Does it matter whether the gambling is "compulsive?" Who was Zarin: a very rich person who enjoyed dropping over $3 million at the gambling tables; or someone else?

CHAPTER 4

GIFTS

§ 4.01 CASH GIFTS

Look at *§ 102*. It excludes gifts from the donee's income. A typical case is a cash gift from parent to child. The result of this statutory pattern is that the donor pays tax on income necessary to pay the gift, but there is only one tax on that income because the donee is not taxed. What is the rationale for that pattern?

A gift is not periodic income, derived from labor or capital. After *Glenshaw Glass*, however, that should not matter.

Is there another reason for excluding gifts? Should there be two taxes, one on the donor and another on the donee? Are there two items of income when cash flows from person to person? Sometimes there are, as when income is used by a house owner to pay someone to paint the house — in that case, both owner and painter have income. But are there two items of income in the gift case? Isn't the donee (who gets cash) the real recipient of income, rather than the donor (who just has the satisfaction of giving)? This suggests that a gift might produce only one item of income, but why is the don*or* taxed but the donee exempt?

Suppose the donor is a wealthy head of a family. What is the proper tax rate on income shifted around within the family by gift? If you think the donor's rate is the proper rate, you have provided an explanation for the existing pattern of taxing gifts — one tax on the donor, not the donee. In effect, the gift exclusion treats the donor and donee as part of a taxable unit *to the extent of the gift property*. What other examples of treating the family as a taxable unit have you encountered?

Another reason for the gift exclusion is that support payments are not taxed and it is often hard to distinguish gift and support.

§ 4.02 DEFINITION OF GIFT

OSBORNE v. COMMISSIONER

69 T.C.M. (CCH) 1895 (1995)

POWELL, SPECIAL TRRIAL JUDGE: . . .

[Editor — A union, the Air Line Pilots Association International (ALPA), paid strike benefits of $2,400 per month. These payments were financed by assessments against the employees which were deductible in computing the employee's income. The court first discussed the "watershed case [of] *Commissioner v. Duberstein*, 363 U.S. 278 (1960)," which established the test for defining nontaxable gifts. In *Duberstein*, a business associate had given the taxpayer a luxury automobile as thanks for client references. The Court stated that "the mere absence of a legal or moral obligation. . . does not establish that . . . [a voluntarily executed transfer of property, without any consideration or compensation therefor] is a gift." If "the payment proceeds primarily from the constraining force of any moral or legal duty,' or from the incentive of anticipated benefit' of an economic nature, it is not a gift." *Duberstein* established the test of an excludable gift as a transfer that proceeds from a "detached and disinterested generosity," "out of affection, respect, admiration, charity or like impulses." The *Osborne* court then discussed the *Kaiser* case and its application to the ALPA strike benefits, as follows.]

On the same day the opinion in *Duberstein* was handed down, the Court issued its opinion in *United States v. Kaiser*, 363 U.S. 299 (1960). In *Kaiser* the issue was whether certain strike benefits were taxable. The jury had concluded that they were gifts, but the District Court concluded that the benefits paid were not gifts as a matter of law. *Kaiser v. United States*, 15 F. Supp. 865 (E.D. Wis. 1958). The Court of Appeals reversed. *Kaiser v. United States*, 262 F.2d 367 (7th Cir. 1958). The Supreme Court affirmed the judgment of the Court of Appeals for the Seventh Circuit, concluding that there was evidence upon which the jury could have reasonably concluded that the benefits were gifts. However, neither *Duberstein* nor *Kaiser* stands for the proposition that "every trier of the facts . . . [is] free for all future time to disregard guidelines that other trial and appellate courts [have] developed concerning the weight to be given to recurring 'relevant factual elements, with their various combinations.' ". . .

Turning to the question of ALPA's intent, we note initially that neither ALPA's constitution nor the Manual expressly authorizes the awarding of gifts by the union. The officers of a union are bound to "hold its [the union's] money and property solely for the benefit of the organization and its members and to manage, invest, and expend the same in accordance with its constitution and bylaws and any resolutions of the governing bodies adopted thereunder." 29 U.S.C. § 501(a) (1994). The fact that an organization's governing instrument does not authorize the giving of gifts suggests that the organization did not make a gift.

In *Colwell v. Commissioner*, 64 T.C. 584, 587 (1975), this Court discussed a number of other salient factors to be considered in determining whether strike benefits paid by a union are excludable from the recipient's income as a gift. These factors are (1) whether the union was under a moral or legal obligation to make the payments; (2) whether the payments were made upon a consideration of the recipient's financial status and need; (3) whether the benefits continued during the strike regardless of whether the recipient worked elsewhere; (4) whether the recipient was a member of the striking union; (5) whether the payments required the recipient to perform any strike duties such as picketing, and if not, whether or to what extent the recipient was under a moral obligation to participate in such strike activities; and (6) whether any restrictions were placed on the use of the payments, particularly in regard to whether the benefits were restricted to payment of basic necessities such as food and shelter or whether the recipient had unfettered control over use of the funds. An analysis of these factors leads to the conclusion that the amounts paid to the striking pilots were not gifts within the meaning of section 102(a).

While initially ALPA may not have had a legal obligation to pay strike benefits to any striking pilots at the time the strike was called, once the balloting process was completed pursuant to ALPA's operating policy, and strike benefits were authorized, there was at least a moral obligation for ALPA to disburse payments to the striking pilots. . . . ALPA did not look at the individual needs of the pilots. Consequently, it is impossible to distinguish any benefits as being paid out of a detached and disinterested generosity or for other charitable purposes, rather than from a desire to promote the success of the strike. The benefits were set at a level, rather, that ALPA considered acceptable to both striking and nonstriking pilots. . . . Union status . . . had apparently no bearing on the receipt of strike benefits. The Manual provided for the payment of benefits to members as well as nonmembers, in the discretion of the board of directors (with the support of a majority of the membership). Once the benefits were authorized for the striking Eastern pilots, union membership was no longer a consideration. Although in some circumstances union membership may be an important factor, here the distinction is irrelevant.

Petitioners argue that although they participated in strike activities, their receipt of strike benefits was not conditioned on participation. According to the Manual, however, neither pilot could receive benefits unless he was certified . . . as eligible to receive benefits. [A pilot was certified] only if he or she [was] available for and performing any strike activities ALPA asked, not flying for another airline in dispute with ALPA, and not doing any action that would adversely affect the outcome of the dispute. Thus, while payments may not have been conditioned on the performance of specific strike duties, striking pilots had a general duty to back ALPA in its endeavor. It is significant that ALPA sought repayment from those pilots who were not eligible under ALPA policy to receive strike benefits; this further indicates that ALPA's intention in making the payments was not out of charitable impulse.

The striking pilots were unrestricted in the use of the ALPA payments. Payment was not made in the form of vouchers earmarked for basic necessities, as was the case in *United States v. Kaiser*, 363 U.S. 299 (1960). Benefits were paid by check and could have been used for an extended vacation rather than for rent or other basic needs. This reflects upon the union's self-interest in making the payments, as it gives the striking pilots incentive to support the strike.

Petitioners focus on the circumstances that motivated ALPA to strike against Eastern, chronicling the asserted malefactions of Eastern's management. To the extent, however, that this is material, it weighs against petitioners rather than for them. The more egregious the management's behavior, the greater was ALPA's interest in holding a successful strike. ALPA's impulse in funding such a strike could hardly be characterized as detached and disinterested. . . .

It is clear that ALPA had a primary goal of ensuring the economic security of its membership and that strike benefits were paid to that end. In sum, there is no evidence supporting the suggestion that ALPA paid the benefits out of a detached and disinterested generosity.

The government worries a lot about a double tax benefit in the form of excluded gifts being deducted by the payor. *§ 274(b)(1)* attempts to prevent this by disallowing the *payor*'s deduction *if* the payee relies on the gift exclusion to exclude the payment. This is supposed to have the added effect of creating a conflict between payor and payee, because the facts providing a gift exclusion would cost the payor a deduction, and the facts providing the payor a deduction would cost the payee the exclusion. That would not happen, however, in the *Osborne* case because unions are tax exempt and lose nothing if the payments are excludible gifts.

§ 4.03 APPRECIATED PROPERTY

TAFT v. BOWERS

278 U.S. 470 (1929)

MR. JUSTICE MCREYNOLDS delivered the opinion of the Court. . . .

During the calendar years 1921 and 1922 the father of petitioner, Elizabeth C. Taft, gave her certain shares of Nash Motors Company stock, then more valuable than when acquired by him. She sold them during 1923 for more than their market value when the gift was made.

The United States demanded an income tax reckoned upon the difference between cost to the donor and price received by the donee. She paid accordingly and sued to recover the portion imposed because of the advance in value while the donor owned the stock. The right to tax the increase in value after the gift is not denied.

Abstractly stated, this is the problem:

> In 1916 A purchased 100 shares of stock for $1,000, which he held until 1923 when their fair market value had become $2,000. He then gave them to B who sold them during the year 1923 for $5,000. The United States claims that under the Revenue Act of 1921 B must pay income tax upon $4,000, as realized profits. B maintains that only $3,000 — the appreciation during her ownership — can be regarded as income; that the increase during the donor's ownership is not income assessable against her within intendment of the Sixteenth Amendment. . . .

The only question subject to serious controversy is whether Congress had power to authorize the exaction.

It is said that the gift became a capital asset of the donee to the extent of its value when received and, therefore, when disposed of by her no part of that value could be treated as taxable income in her hands. . . .

If, instead of giving the stock to petitioner, the donor had sold it at market value, the excess over the capital he invested (cost) would have been income therefrom and subject to taxation under the Sixteenth Amendment. He would have been obliged to share the realized gain with the United States. He held the stock — the investment — subject to the right of the sovereign to take part of any increase in its value when separated through sale or conversion and reduced to his possession. Could he, contrary to the express will of Congress, by mere gift enable another to hold this stock free from such right, deprive the sovereign of the possibility of taxing the appreciation when actually severed, and convert the entire property into a capital asset of the donee, who invested nothing, as though the latter had purchased at the market price? And after a still further enhancement of the property, could the donee make a second gift with like effect, etc.? We think not.

In truth the stock represented only a single investment of capital — that made by the donor. And when through sale or conversion the increase was separated therefrom, it became income from that investment in the hands of the recipient subject to taxation according to the very words of the Sixteenth Amendment. By requiring the recipient of the entire increase to pay a part into the public treasury, Congress deprived her of no right and subjected her to no hardship. She accepted the gift with knowledge of the statute and, as to the property received, voluntarily assumed the position of her donor. When she sold the stock she actually got the original sum invested, plus the entire appreciation and out of the latter only was she called on to pay the tax demanded.

The provision of the statute under consideration seems entirely appropriate for enforcing a general scheme of lawful taxation. To accept the view urged in behalf of petitioner undoubtedly would defeat, to some extent, the purpose of Congress to take part of all gain derived from capital investments. To prevent that result and insure enforcement of its proper policy, Congress had power to require that for purposes of taxation the donee should accept the position of the donor in respect of the thing received. And in so doing, it acted neither unreasonably nor arbitrarily. . . .

There is nothing in the Constitution which lends support to the theory that gain actually resulting from the increased value of capital can be treated as taxable income in the hands of the recipient only so far as the increase occurred while he owned the property.

The judgment below is affirmed.

In other words, the donee does not realize income at the time of the gift, but the donee is taxed on the property's appreciated gain if and when she realizes it. This is accomplished by transferring the donor's basis to the donee. *§§ 1015(a), 7701(a)(42)(A),(43).*

PROBLEMS: TRANSFERRED BASIS

1. Suppose property with a basis of $1,000 was worth $700 when given by a parent to a child-donee. The donee then sells the property for (a) $600, (b) $800, or (c) $1,100. Be sure to read the portion of *§ 1015(a)* beginning with "except that." What tax avoidance problem does it address?

2. Suppose the parent decides to sell the property in the prior example (basis of $1,000; value and sales price of $700) to recognize the $300 loss. Can she accomplish this by selling to her son, or only by selling to an "outsider?" How is the child taxed if he later sells the property for $600, $800, or $1,100? *See § 267(a)(1),(d).*

§ 4.04 DEATH

Date-of-death-value as basis. Suppose a parent owns property worth $2,000, with a $1,000 basis. That person dies. The child inherits the property and sells it for $5,000. How is the child taxed? *§ 1014(a)(1)* gives the child a date-of-death-value basis in the property. This is usually called a stepped-up basis rule, because property is expected to appreciate. But the date-of-death-value rule applies whether or not the property has gone up or down in value.

What is the reason for the date-of-death-value rule? It does not merely defer gain, but exempts it altogether. If it is meant to compensate for estate tax, why not reduce the income tax by a credit for estate taxes attributable to the gain on the property?

Is it administratively difficult for people to keep track of historical basis? In 1976, the date-of-death-value basis rule was replaced by a transferred basis approach (like an inter vivos gift), but complaints about alleged administrative problems prompted a return to the date-of-death-value basis rule in 1980.

Income in respect of a decedent; §§ 691, 1014(c). There is one important exception to the date-of-death-value basis rule. An item of "income in respect of a decedent" is inherited with a transferred basis from the decedent, just like a gift. Income in respect of a decedent is not defined in the statute, but the idea is very straightforward. Any income which could not be assigned for tax purposes to the donee (under the principles discussed in Chapter 2) is income in respect of a decedent. The right to such income does not receive a basis equal to its value at date of death, but keeps the decedent's pre-death basis.

For example, if a taxpayer dies having earned but not collected $20,000 salary, the $20,000 is fully taxed when collected (assuming, as would normally be the case, that a claim to personal service income has a zero basis). The value of the claim to $20,000 may be only $15,000 at date of death (due to time value of money factors or a financially shaky debtor), but that is irrelevant for income tax purposes. The taxpayer could not have deflected taxation of that income to a donee by a lifetime gift, and it is therefore income in respect of a decedent, which does not enjoy a date-of-death-value basis.

§ 4.05 CARVED OUT INCOME INTEREST

[A]—Gift of carved out income interest, remainder to another

IRWIN v. GAVIT

268 U.S. 161 (1925)

MR. JUSTICE HOLMES delivered the opinion of the Court. . . .

[Editor — The facts of this case can be simplified as follows. A transferor sets up a trust under his will with income to one relative and remainder to another. Under state property law, the owner of the income interest had no property interest in the trust corpus, only the income.]

The statute in Section 2, A, subdivision 1, provides that there shall be levied a tax "upon the entire net income arising or accruing from all sources in the preceding calendar year to every citizen of the United States." If these payments properly may be called income by the common understanding of that word and the statute has failed to hit them it has missed so much of the general purpose that it expresses at the start. Congress intended to use its power to the full extent. By B the net income is to include "gains or profits and income derived from any source whatever, including the income from but not the value of property acquired by gift, bequest, devise or descent." By D trustees are to make "return of the net income of the person for whom they act, subject to this tax," and by D trustees and others, having the control or payment of fixed or determinable gains, etc., of another person who are required to render a return on behalf of another are "authorized to withhold enough to pay the normal tax." The language quoted leaves no doubt in our minds that if a fund were given to trustees for A for life with remainder over, the income received by the trustees and paid over to A would be income of A under the statute. It seems to us hardly less clear that even if there were a specific provision that A should have no interest in the corpus, the payments would be income none the less, within the meaning of the statute and the Constitution, and by popular speech. In the first case it is true that the bequest might be said to be of the corpus for life, in the second it might be said to be of the income. But we think that the provision of the act that exempts bequests assumes the gift of a corpus and contrasts it with the income arising from it, but was not intended to exempt income property so called simply because of a severance between it and the principal fund. . . . The money was income in the hands of the trustees and we know of nothing in the law that prevented its being paid and received as income by the donee.

The courts below went on the ground that the gift to the plaintiff was a bequest and carried no interest in the corpus of the fund. We do not regard those considerations as conclusive. . . . This is a gift from the income of a very large fund, as income. . . . We are of opinion that quarterly payments, which it was hoped would last for fifteen years, from the income of an estate intended for the plaintiff's child, must be regarded as income within the meaning of the Constitution and the law. It is said that the tax laws should be construed favorably for the taxpayers. But that is not a reason for creating a doubt or for exaggerating one when it is no greater than we can bring ourselves to feel in this case.

Judgment reversed.

MR. JUSTICE SUTHERLAND (dissenting).

By the plain terms of the Revenue Act of 1913, the value of property acquired by gift, bequest, devise, or descent is not to be included in net income. Only the income derived from such property is subject to the tax. The question, as it seems to me, is really a very simple one. Money, of course, is property. The money here sought to be taxed as income was paid to respondent under the express provisions of a will. It was a gift by will — a bequest. It, therefore, fell within the precise letter of the statute; and, under well settled principles, judicial inquiry may go no further. The taxpayer is entitled to the rigor of the law. There is no latitude in a taxing statute; you must adhere to the very words.

The property which respondent acquired being a bequest, there is no occasion to ask whether, before being handed over to him, it had been carved from the original corpus of, or from subsequent additions to, the estate. The corpus of the estate was not the legacy which respondent received, but merely the source which gave rise to it. The money here sought to be taxed was not the fruits of a legacy; it was the legacy itself.

With the utmost respect for the judgment of my brethren to the contrary, the opinion just rendered, I think without warrant, searches the field of argument and inference for a meaning which should be found only in the strict letter of the statute.

The Code in *§ 102(b)(2)* now provides the same result as *Irwin v. Gavit.* The income is taxed to the income beneficiary and *§ 273* prevents the owner of an income interest received by gift from taking depreciation deductions for the income interest. The case is still of interest for two reasons: (1) as a statement about statutory interpretation; and (2) as an effort to deal with the problem of carved out income interests.

Statutory interpretation. Holmes and Sutherland disagree about statutory interpretation. Both rely on the text, or at least say they do. Holmes refers to "common understanding" of "income." Sutherland appeals to "plain terms." What does each judge consider to determine the text's meaning? How does each judge deal with interpretive presumptions favoring taxpayers?

Carved out income interest. What is the economic reality of the gift in *Irwin v. Gavit*, where an income interest and remainder are owned by different people? Assume that the total value of the property left to both the income and remainder interests was $100. This is true if interest rates are 20% and the income from the property is $20 per year. At the testator's death, basis equals value. Using the 20% interest and $20 per-year income assumptions, a five-year income interest is worth (approximately) 60% of the total value of the property and the remainder is worth 40%. That means that the income interest has a basis equal to date-of-death value of $60; and the remainder interest's basis is $40.

Do not be troubled by the fact that the property is divided into parts over time. Temporal divisions are as possible as physical divisions. If the inherited property consisted of 10 acres, 6 acres might have a $60 basis and 4 acres a $40 basis. In the example we consider, the division is temporal rather than physical. The following depicts the temporal division.

ANNUAL INCOME = $20; TOTAL BASIS = $100

Five Year, Carved out income interest; Basis = $60	Remainder interest; Basis = $40	⟶

It would appear that, absent a special statutory rule, the owner of the income interest could take depreciation deductions. Recall the earlier example of a depreciable asset with a $60 cost and a five-year life. Straight line depreciation permitted a $12 per year deduction. If the gross income paid to the trust income beneficiary is $20, the annual taxable income would be $8 ($20 minus $12 depreciation); $40 over five years. That seems to be an analytically airtight argument, but it poses a dilemma. If the property had not been given away, there would be $20 income each year; $100 over five years. Where is the other $60 of income?

The answer is this. Look closely at the remainder's interest, worth $40 at the time of death. How much is the remainder's interest worth after five years, when the income interest has expired? Assuming no change in the underlying value of the property (for example, it is land in a stable neighborhood without zoning changes and interest rates do not change), it should be worth $100. You just found the other $60. The $60 accrues gradually over the five-year period as time passes and the remainder's interest gets closer to vesting in possession.

Why not just tax the owner of the remainder interest each year on the appreciation of the $40 investment. After five years, the owner of the income interest will have paid tax on $8 per year (20 minus 12), or a total of $40; and the owner of the remainder interest will pay tax on the other $60. Do you think the remainder will ever report that income? The government usually keeps track of periodic income in the nature of interest by examining information returns filed by debtors, such as banks. The interest-like accession to the remainder's $40 investment will not, however, be reported by any independent party. If the remainder will not report this income, what is the easiest way to make sure the full $20 is taxed each year; $100 over five years. Just tax the owner of the income interest on $20. And that is exactly what the statute now does by taxing the owner of the income interest on all of the gross income ($20) and denying depreciation when the income interest is received by gift (*§ 273*). And that is exactly what the *Irwin* case did by case law, simply disregarding any possibility of a depreciation deduction.

Question. What is the remainder interest's basis after five years passes and he obtains possession of the land?

[B]—Gift of carved out income interest, with retained remainder

HELVERING v. HORST

311 U.S. 112 (1940)

MR. JUSTICE STONE delivered the opinion of the Court.

[Editor — In this case, the income and remainder interests are separated, and the carved out income interest is given away, as in *Irwin v. Gavit*, but the remainder interest is retained.]

The sole question for decision is whether the gift, during the donor's taxable year, of interest coupons detached from the bonds, delivered to the donee and later in the year paid at maturity, is the realization of income taxable to the donor.

In 1934 and 1935 respondent, the owner of negotiable bonds, detached from them negotiable interest coupons shortly before their due date and

Fs:
TP owns negotiable bonds
- detaches interest coupons B4 due date + gives to son; TP retains the bonds

delivered them as a gift to his son who in the same year collected them at maturity. . . .

[Editor — In other words, the donor carved out an income interest, gave it to his children, and retained the remainder interest.]

In the ordinary case the taxpayer who acquires the right to receive income is taxed when he receives it, regardless of the time when his right to receive payment accrued. But the rule that income is not taxable until realized has never been taken to mean that the taxpayer, even on the cash receipts basis, who has fully enjoyed the benefit of the economic gain represented by his right to receive income, can escape taxation because he has not himself received payment of it from his obligor. The rule, founded on administrative convenience, is only one of postponement of the tax to the final event of enjoyment of the income, usually the receipt of it by the taxpayer, and not one of exemption from taxation where the enjoyment is consummated by some event other than the taxpayer's personal receipt of money or property. This may occur when he has made such use or disposition of his power to receive or control the income as to procure in its place other satisfactions which are of economic worth. The question here is, whether because one who in fact receives payment for services or interest payments is taxable only on his receipt of the payments, he can escape all tax by giving away his right to income in advance of payment. . . . If the taxpayer procures payment directly to his creditors of the items of interest or earnings due him, *see Old Colony Trust Co. v. Commissioner*; *United States v. Kirby Lumber Co.*, 284 U.S. 1, or if he sets up a revocable trust with income payable to the objects of his bounty, §§ 166, 167, Revenue Act of 1934 [Editor — Current law *§ 676*], he does not escape taxation because he did not actually receive the money.

Underlying the reasoning in these cases is the thought that income is "realized" by the assignor because he, who owns or controls the source of the income, also controls the disposition of that which he could have received himself and diverts the payment from himself to others as the means of procuring the satisfaction of his wants. The taxpayer has equally enjoyed the fruits of his labor or investment and obtained the satisfaction of his desires whether he collects and uses the income to procure those satisfactions, or whether he disposes of his right to collect it as the means of procuring them.

Although the donor here, by the transfer of the coupons, has precluded any possibility of his collecting them himself he has nevertheless, by his act, procured payment of the interest, as a valuable gift to a member of his family. . . . Even though [the taxpayer] never receives the money he derives money's worth from the disposition of the coupons which he has used as money or money's worth in the procuring of a satisfaction which is procurable only by the expenditure of money or money's worth. The enjoyment of the economic benefit accruing to him by virtue of his acquisition of the coupons is realized as completely as it would have been if he had collected the interest in dollars and expended them for any of the purposes named. . . .

The power to dispose of income is the equivalent of ownership of it. The exercise of that power to procure the payment of income to another is the enjoyment and hence the realization of the income by him who exercises it. We have had no difficulty in applying that proposition where the assignment preceded the rendition of the services, *Lucas v. Earl*. . . . But it is the assignment by which the disposition of income is controlled when the service precedes the assignment and in both cases it is the exercise of the power of disposition of the interest or compensation with the resulting payment to the donee which is the enjoyment by the donor of income derived from them.

This was emphasized in *Blair v. Commissioner*, 300 U.S. 5, on which respondent relies, where the distinction was taken between a gift of income derived from an obligation to pay compensation and a gift of income-producing property. . . . Since the gift was deemed to be a gift of the property the income from it was held to be the income of the owner of the property, who was the donee, not the donor, a refinement which was unnecessary if respondent's contention here is right, but one clearly inapplicable to gifts of interest or wages. . . .

[There is no] adequate basis for distinguishing between the gift of interest coupons here and a gift of salary or commissions. The owner of a negotiable bond and of the investment which it represents, if not the lender, stands in the place of the lender. When, by the gift of the coupons, he has separated his right to interest payments from his investment and procured the payment of the interest to his donee, he has enjoyed the economic benefits of the income in the same manner and to the same extent as though the transfer were of earnings and in both cases the import of the statute is that the fruit is not to be attributed to a different tree from that on which it grew.

COMMENTS

1. ***Horst vs. Blair.*** The *Horst* opinion keeps repeating that the exercise of control by gift is the "realization" of income, but that (of course) is not true. As *Blair* held, a donor of appreciated property is *not* taxed on the income from the property, and, by implication, is not taxed on the gain at the time of a gift. *Blair* can be distinguished from *Horst* on its facts, on the ground that the tree was given away, not just some of the fruit. Well, tax law is not botany. The question is why the gift of a carved out income interest cannot deflect income to a donee, but gift of the entire property can. Nothing in *Horst* really addresses that question, although the decision is still good law — donors cannot deflect income from themselves by giving less than the entire time period they own.

Horst does make sense if you think shifting income around within the family to lower total taxes is improper tax avoidance. But, again, why is that any worse when a carved out income interest is assigned than when the entire property is transferred?

Some of the income from the bond in *Horst* should be taxed to the transferor. Remember our discussion of the carved out income interest and remainder interest in connection with the *Irwin v. Gavit* case. Considering economic reality, *some* of the annual income really does accrue to the remainder interest after an income interest has been carved out. Horst, the transferor, retained the remainder interest, so some of the income from the bond accrues to him and it would be fair to tax him on that limited amount. But not all of the annual income accrues to the transferor with a retained remainder interest. We are still looking for a theory justifying taxation of the transferor on *all* of the annual interest income, when a carved out income interest is given away and a remainder interest retained.

2. **Property vs. personal services.** You have now read three major assignment of income cases: in *Lucas v. Earl*, the transferor could not assign personal service income; in *Horst*, the transferor could not assign property income; in *Blair*, the transferor could assign property income. How should the principles of these cases apply to the following cases? (1) An author who assigns the copyright interest to a relative; *Rev. Rul. 60-227*, 1960-1 C.B. 262 (permitting assignment). (2) Suppose an insurance salesman has a right to "renewal commissions," if people to whom he has sold insurance policies renew the policy, even without any further work by the salesman. Long before the renewals occur, the salesman assigns the future renewal commissions to his child. *Helvering v. Eubank*, 311 U.S. 122 (1940), taxed the salesman on the renewal commissions when they were later paid to the child.

In both cases, personal services are important in generating the income, but (unlike *Lucas v. Earl*) the assignment occurs after the services are performed (no retained control over production of income). Moreover, the assignment occurs long before the income appears to "accrue." Therefore, the rule that accrued income cannot be assigned seems inapplicable. And yet some value seems to have been earned when the assignment occurs. Should that be enough to tax the transferor when the transferee collects the income? Whatever your answer, how can you distinguish the copyright from the renewal commission case? Is a copyright "property"; should that matter for tax law?

3. **Interest free loans.** Suppose a taxpayer lends $200,000 to a child for one year without charging interest. This seems like a good way to avoid *Horst*. The child simply buys a $200,000 bond, collects the interest, and (after one year) sells the bond and returns the $200,000 to the lender. This seemed to work, as far as case law was concerned, to shift the interest income to the child. So the code was amended in *§ 7872* to impute taxable interest to the lender on the interest-free "gift" loan, by *pretending* that the borrower paid interest to the lender at a specified "federal rate." This produces a result similar to *Horst*, in the above example, assuming that the imputed federal interest rate approximates the rate earned by the donee on the bond. However, the interest is (usually) imputed from the debtor to the lender under the statute, whether or not the debtor has any investment income.

Like so many tax statutes, this one has qualifications. First, if the gift loans between creditor and debtor do not aggregate to more than $100,000, the imputed interest cannot exceed the borrower's *actual* investment income. This helps a parent who lends a child money for education. Second, no interest is imputed if gift loans between individuals do not exceed $10,000.

§ 4.06 SPLIT UNITS

[A]—Splitting income?

Suppose a marital unit has split. Should one member of the former unit be able to transfer income *for tax purposes* to the other member from whom he or she is separated? Should the usual rules about assignment of income apply? For example, should a husband be able to assign personal service income or a carved out income interest to a former spouse to discharge an obligation of support? You are likely to answer "yes" to this question, because the separation of husband and wife should make them separate taxable units. Each of them makes their own consumption decisions and they should therefore be recognized as separate for tax purposes.

ass't of income for support
fulfill obligation for support

Admittedly, the assignment of income often discharges an obligation of support. And a taxpayer cannot usually deflect income by assigning it to a creditor. But when I assign income to my creditor, there are often two incomes — mine and the creditors. When the marital unit splits, are there two incomes? If there is only one income, as most people would assume, then the question is whether the income belongs for tax purposes to the payor or payee. The fact that the assignment discharges an obligation does not matter. After all, while married, one spouse may have had an obligation to support the other, but there was only one item of income received by the marital unit. It should not be any different after the marital unit splits — the only question is whose income it should be. And, as noted earlier, you are probably likely to think the income belongs to the payee.

Q:

income belongs to payee ✓

That is exactly what the code provides (and has done so since 1942). The conclusion is so fundamental that there is no need for the payor to assign income in advance to reach that result when the marital unit has split. The payor can periodically collect income, pay it over to the payee, and take a deduction. The payee reports the income. The statutory exclusion and deduction provisions are found in §§ 71(a),(b), 215(a),(b).

PR: DD
PE: income

The payor deduction and payee inclusion approach does not apply, however, if the payment obligation survives the payee's death. § 71(b)(1)(D). In practice, this means that payments made pursuant to many state law marital property splits incident to a divorce (rather than alimony support payments) will not be subject to the deduction-inclusion approach, because the property split obligation usually survives the payee's death.

exception

Like so many ideas in tax law, it is easier to state the general principle, but harder to decide when the principle should apply.

① *First*, when is the unit split? Payments must be made under a "divorce or separation instrument," defined in § 71(b)(1)(A),(2). In addition to a decree of divorce or separate maintenance (where the payor and payee are *not* married for federal tax purposes — § 7703(a)(2)), the definition includes written separation agreements and support or maintenance decrees (where the payor and payee are usually married for tax purposes — but *see* § 7703(b)). Notice that payor and payee can be "split" for purposes of § 71, but still married under § 7703 (and therefore subject to the higher § 1(d) tax rates if they file separately).

"split"?

② *Second*, even if the couple is "split" for tax law purposes under § 71, the payor deduction and payee inclusion is contingent on their not being members of the same household, if they are *not* married for tax purposes. *See* § 71(b)(1)(C). This prevents a couple from divorcing, filing tax returns as single individuals under § 1(c), and avoiding the tax on marriage by splitting their income.

can't be members of same household

Third, only cash payments are subject to the rules shifting income from a payor to payee. *§ 71(b)(1)*. Property transferred between (1) spouses, or (2) former spouses, if incident to a divorce, is treated like a gift, with an exception noted below. *§ 1041*. "Incident to a divorce" is defined in *Treas. Reg. § 1.1041-1T(b)*.

The exception to "gift" treatment is that "loss property" (property worth less than basis at the time of gift) has a transferred basis for both gain *and* loss computations. There is no reduction in basis for computing loss, as there was under *§ 1015(a)*. Presumably, there is no tax avoidance potential from shifting losses around between spouses or split family units.

Fourth, how can you distinguish between a lump sum transfer (which should not be deductible by the payor and taxed to the payee) and periodic payments (which should be)? If a taxpayer gives a former spouse $100,000 in a lump sum, it would distort income to permit that $100,000 to be shifted from the payor to the payee. It makes more sense to tax the payee only on the income derived from the $100,000, such as interest or dividends. Again, the idea is simple but taxpayer ingenuity reaches for tax advantage, requiring a complex statutory response.

Suppose the payor pays a large amount in both years 1 and 2, after the divorce, and declining amounts thereafter. When is "front-loading" more like a lump sum paid in the first year than like periodic payments spread over a long time? The statute's answer is in *§ 71(f)* (too complicated to be reviewed here). Essentially, the cash payments are deducted by the payor and taxed to the payee when made, but front-loading results in the payor taking back the prior deductions into income and the payee deducting previously included income *in a later year*, when it turns out that future payments decline rapidly from a large initial payment. There is an exception if the decline is due to the payee's death or remarriage, or to the payee's right to share in the payor's business income.

Fifth, payments to support children are not deductible. They would not have been deductible if the marriage survived and do not become deductible after a marital split. Frequently, divorce decrees specify that a sum shall be paid to a former spouse, to be reduced when the child reaches a certain age or marries. Is the amount slated for future reduction a nondeductible child support payment? Yes. *See § 71(c)(2)*.

Sixth, the shifting of taxable income from the payor to the payee spouse is elective. *§ 71(b)(1)(B)*. If the payee is in a higher tax bracket than the payor, the parties can elect to make the payment out of the payor's after-tax income and the payee can exclude the payment from income. One tax is imposed on the total income, but the parties can choose the lower of the two individual's tax rates.

[B]—Problem — the case of the Nobel prize

The newpapers recently reported on a divorce agreement between an economist and his spouse that she would receive half of any Nobel Prize to which he became entitled within a specified period of time after the divorce decree. Several years later and some months before the time expired, he won the Nobel Prize. Assume the Prize is $1 million and both former spouses are in the 30% tax bracket. How much does she get and what are the respective tax obligations? Here are some of the state law and tax law possibilities.

(1) The divorce agreement creates interests analogous to splitting a lottery ticket or horse race ticket for both state law and federal tax law purposes — like splitting stock ownership. Consequently, each person owns a 50% chance of winning the prize; each person then owns $500,000 of the prize under state law, and is taxed on that amount under federal tax law.

(2) The property split analogy is inapt under federal tax law either because the prize winner must perform services to win the prize or because the chances of winning are too inchoate. For *tax* purposes, this *might* lead to the conclusion that the economist has $1,000,000 income, and, under assignment of income principles, cannot shift any of that income to his former wife for tax purposes. (For an argument that the assignment of income doctrine might not apply in the husband-wife split situation, so that any payment to the wife would be taxed to her, *see* Michael Asimow, *The Assault on Tax-Free Divorce: Carryover Basis and Assignment of Income*, 44 Tax L. Rev. 65 (1988).)

Even if the husband had to pay tax on the $1 million, payment to the former wife might be deductible under *§§ 71, 215*. But then it might not be — because the former wife's right to payment might survive her death. *§ 71(b)(1)(D)*. Or perhaps the deduction would run afoul of the rules dealing with front-loading large lump sum payments. *§ 71(f)*.

The answer to the *tax* question does not, however, resolve the *state* law question of what the former wife gets. If the arrangement is not a property split for state law purposes, does the divorce agreement provide the wife with one-half of the $1,000,000 prize — that is, $500,000—even if the husband has to pay a $300,000 tax on the $1,000,000; or does the former wife's share under state law get reduced to one-half of the economist's *after-tax* amount, if the husband has to pay tax on $1,000,000 — that is, $350,000 (one-half of $700,000).

It was reported in the newspaper that the divorce agreement arranged for the payee-spouse to get her half, *after* the former husband paid whatever taxes he owed. But, if the tax law is uncertain, how does the former husband know whether to pay $300,000 taxes, and pay his former wife $350,000 (with no further tax on her); or whether to pay his former wife $500,000, and have each person pay tax on $500,000?

Suppose they have an agreement that the former wife gets one-half of the former husband's after-tax prize, but they guess wrong about federal tax law. He pays $300,000 tax and pays her $350,000, but it turns out that the $1 million of income should be split for both state law *and* federal income tax purposes. If they make this mistake, the former wife would have to pay tax on the $350,000 she received and would be entitled to another $150,000 of taxable income from her former husband (a total of $500,000), wouldn't she? Would the husband then file for a $150,000 refund?

Or suppose they guess wrong and he pays her $500,000 but it turns out that he has to pay all of the tax on the $1 million. Would the husband have a cause of action against the former wife to get back $150,000?

As long as the tax law is unclear, is there any way to draft the divorce agreement to avoid these uncertainties? Would applying for a private letter ruling as part of the tax planning incident to the divorce be a solution?

What is the relevance of the following case to this issue? It seems to force the husband to include assigned amounts in income under conventional assignment of income doctrine. In *Smith v. IRS*, 1994 U.S. Dist. LEXIS 13294 (S.D.N.Y 1994), the taxpayer won a lottery in 1985, payable in future annual installments. In 1990, the state court ordered him to pay one-half to his divorced former spouse. Taxpayer argued that the one-half paid to the wife for the *prior* tax year 1987 should *not* have been his income, but the court disagreed. The government agreed that the 1990 court order shifted income to the wife for *future* tax years. But it contended and the court agreed that the 1990 court order did not shift income for pre-1990 years to the wife for federal income tax purposes. The former wife did not own a one-half interest in the property prior to the court order. The payment of the husband's property to the wife did not shift income to the payee-spouse. The court concluded:

> Plaintiff [the former husband] will have suffered an inequity if, but only if, the state court's award to his ex-wife failed to recognize appropriately the plaintiff's after-tax resources. If this occurred, plaintiff's recourse would be to the state court, not the Internal Revenue Service.

See also Kochansky v. Commissioner, 92 F.3d 957 (9th Cir. 1996), affirming on issue of taxing husband, 67 T.C.M. (CCH) 2665 (1994). A husband, who was a lawyer, assigned contingent legal fees to his wife as a property settlement before a divorce. The husband was taxed when the fees were collected by the wife after the divorce. The conventional assignment of income doctrine applied to these fees.

CHAPTER 5

TAXABLE YEAR

§ 5.01 INTRODUCTION

Another major structural provision in an income tax is the taxable period. The government and the taxpayer must close their books periodically, at least provisionally. The usual tax period is one year. *§ 441.* Does that mean that events occurring in one tax year have no impact on the tax treatment of events in another tax year? Do you ever break down the accounting year barrier?

For example, the use of any taxable period is arbitrary and can make two taxpayers with equal total income over a long period look unequal. The obvious case is that of a taxpayer with a business loss in one year (say, $10,000) and a greater gain in the next year (say, $15,000). Total income is $5,000, which is similar to a taxpayer with two $2,500 years. But the former taxpayer will have a total of $15,000 taxable income, if the accounting year barrier is not broken down to account for losses in another tax year.

The obvious solution is to adopt a taxable year provisionally, but make adjustments in later years, much like a wage earner treats tax withholding during a pay period as a tentative tax payment. This chapter is about such adjustments. Some of the rules are from case law, others are statutory. Is there any overall pattern to the rules?

An early Supreme Court case refused to adopt a case law adjustment to the accounting year principle. The taxpayer in *Burnet v. Sanford & Brooks Co.*, 282 U.S. 359 (1931), was performing a river dredging contract. Early years produced losses, and the taxpayer argued against inclusion of later contract profits until they exceeded earlier losses. The later profits arose from proceeds of a breach of warranty lawsuit by the taxpayer-dredger against the other contracting party. The Court of Appeals agreed with the taxpayer, stating that "a return of losses suffered in earlier years" was not income. The Supreme Court disagreed on the ground that profit and loss is specific to particular accounting year periods. The Court said that prior losses were not capital investments, the basis of which must be recovered before there is taxable gain. By implication, the Court refused to analogize prior business losses to costs.

The Court made some very broad and unobjectionable comments about the need for annual accounting to provide the government with taxes at regular intervals. It noted that taxpayers may have income in one year and losses in another, and that this pattern would not preclude taxing the income in profitable years. That broad statement clearly applies to the case of a profitable shoe business in one year and a losing shirt business in another year, but the Court also applied the principle to taxing profits and losses on a single (dredging) contract. The Court therefore failed to treat the profits and losses on a single contract any differently from profits and losses from separate businesses.

§ 5.02 NET OPERATING LOSSES

The statute now overrides *Sanford & Brooks* and allows business losses ("net operating losses") to be carried over to other tax years. *§ 172.* This invites a distinction between business and other income-producing activities which are not businesses. The distinction is murky. A business is an activity carried on with continuity and regularity, to produce a livelihood. Investors in the stock market are rarely in business, unless they are short-term "traders" (people who get most of their income from high-volume sales of stocks and bonds, not dividends and interest). Typical investors, even those who buy and sell short-term, are not "in business." *See Groetzinger v. Commissioner*, 771 F.2d 269 (7th Cir. 1985), *aff'd*, 480 U.S. 23 (1987).

A "business" connection is important not only for identifying what activities are a "business," but also for identifying which expenses are for business. You have already encountered this issue when we discussed the definition of adjusted gross income (*§ 62*); nonemployee "business" expenses were deductible in arriving at AGI (above-the-line expenses). Is the definition of expenses for *§ 62* the same as for *§ 172*? Generally, yes. There is, however, an agency rule that state income taxes on business income are "below-the-line" itemized deductions, even though they arise from the business. *See Rev. Rul. 70-40*, 1970-1 C.B. 50 (relying on a 1944 Senate Finance Committee Report). That ruling, however, treats state income taxes as a business expense for purposes of computing net losses which can be carried over to other years under *§ 172*. Does this distinction make sense? Is the 1944 legislative history dispositive?

The common situation to which *§ 172* applies is illustrated by the following example. Assume that a corporation in year 8 has $100,000 business gross income and $400,000 of related deductions, for a $300,000 net loss. Suppose it has taxable income in years 3, 7, or 12. There is no income or loss in other tax years. Can it ever deduct its $300,000 loss?

The statute allows net operating business losses to be carried back two years and forward twenty years. Taxpayers must first deduct the loss in the earliest carry*back* year and work forward, except that they can waive use of the carryback period and start with the first carryforward year. Quick refunds are paid if a carryback offsets prior taxable income. *§ 6411.*

These carryover periods were adopted by the 1997 Tax Act (effective for tax years beginning after August 5, 1997); the prior rule was back three and forward fifteen years. There are a few exceptions permitting the old three-year carryback period to be used (*e.g.*, losses from Presidentially declared disasters).

There is another operating loss carry*forward* provision, in *§ 186.* It applies to losses from breaches of contract (as in *Sanford & Brooks*), competitive torts, and breaches of fiduciary duty. There is no time limit on these carryovers.

The mechanics of the net operating loss carryover rules reflect their origin in economic policy: encourage new businesses with initial losses; cushion the impact of a recession; encourage risk taking by equating taxable income over multi-tax-year periods. Some of these policies might argue for a refundable tax credit when there are business losses, without regard to whether a taxpayer has income in another tax year. One problem with being too generous to taxpayers with tax losses is that the losses do not always reflect real economic loss. Many provisions, discussed later in the course, allow taxpayers to take deductions in excess of economic loss.

§ 5.03 "TAX BENEFIT" RULE

Despite the strong statements in *Sanford & Brooks* about separate accounting years, the Supreme Court affirmed one case law rule which broke down the accounting year barrier. In *Dobson v. Commissioner*, 320 U.S. 489 (1943), the taxpayer sold stock at a loss and deducted the loss. The loss resulted from fraud in the original stock purchase and the taxpayer sued the person committing the fraud to recover some of her losses. The recovery occurred in a year after the losses were deducted. In the year of the loss deduction, the taxpayer had so many other deductions, that the loss deduction was useless; it provided her with "no tax benefit." She argued that recovery of the item should not be taxed because she received no tax benefit from the deduction. The Court affirmed a Tax Court decision agreeing with the taxpayer. This is known as the "tax benefit" rule, but it might better be called the "no tax benefit" rule.

The *Dobson* Court did not deal very effectively with the *Sanford & Brooks* case. It stated that the losses in *Sanford & Brooks* were "not capital investments, the cost of which . . . must first be restored from the proceeds before there is capital gain taxable as income." The trouble with this statement is that the losses in *Dobson* were not capital investments either; they were losses. Of course, it might make sense to treat the losses *like* capital investments, but it would also have made sense to do that in the dredging contract case as well.

Tax law adjudication. The Court in *Dobson* made some very broad pronouncements about the role of appellate courts in reviewing lower court decisions. It argued that appellate courts should defer to the Tax Court the way they defer to an administrative agency on questions of law, if there was a "rational basis" for the decision.

The Court was motivated by a concern for the trifurcated trial court system and the "fanning out" of the appeals process. Here is a quick overview of that process. A taxpayer has three choices for a judicial trial — the Tax Court, the Federal District Court, and the Court of Federal Claims (previously the Claims Court). The oldest of these is the District Court. As a condition of access, the taxpayer must pay the entire disputed tax for the tax year. She may want to do this to stop interest running, but may not have the cash. One "reward" for paying is the right to a jury trial, not available in any other court.

An alternative, again only by paying the disputed tax in full, is the Court of Federal Claims. This forum (under various names) goes back to the second half of the 19th Century. It is a Washington-based court but the judges travel throughout the country to hear cases.

The Tax Court began in 1924 (as the Board of Tax Appeals), specifically to give the taxpayer a forum to resolve disputes without paying taxes first. The Tax Court is a national court but individual judges travel to local areas to conduct trials. Cases involving important legal issues are reviewed by all 19 Tax Court judges on the written record. Tax Court decisions which are primarily factual, not legal, are not officially published by the government (these are Tax Court Memorandum decisions — T.C.M.), but they are privately published.

Judicial review of lower court decisions from the District Court is the same as for any federal court case — to the Court of Appeals of the taxpayer's residence. The same is true of the Tax Court, which means that the national Tax Court's decisions fan out to divergent Courts of Appeals. The Tax Court conforms to Court of Appeals decisions in the region to which a taxpayer can appeal. *Golsen v. Commissioner*, 54 T.C. 742 (1970). The Tax Court does, however, stick to its own legal views if there is no specific holding in the relevant appellate court.

Appeals from the Court of Federal Claims go to the Court of Appeals for the Federal Circuit, based in Washington, D.C. In the early 1980s this court almost became the single Court of Tax Appeals for the entire nation, ending the multiple appellate court system. Efforts to establish a specialized appellate tax court have consistently failed, allegedly because of enthusiasm for generalist rather than specialist courts. Can you think of any other reason?

This is the judicial system to which the Court reacted in *Dobson*. It wanted to bring some order out of the chaos by elevating the Tax Court to the status of an "expert" court to which special deference was due. The effort did not succeed, however. The statute was amended to conform the standards of appellate review of both the Tax Court and District Courts. *§ 7482(a)*. More fundamentally, the reality of the trifurcated trial system made privileging Tax Court decisions difficult to sustain. One suspects, however, that some courts still defer to the Tax Court's expertise.

The statutory "tax benefit" rule. The *Dobson* decision has been adopted by statute. *§ 111*. You can see how the "tax benefit" rule works from the following example. Assume in year 1 a taxpayer has business losses and also a $1,000 nonbusiness bad debt loss (on a loan made to a corporation). That is, even before the bad debt loss deduction, there is no tax. In year 2, the taxpayer recovers the $1,000 because the debtor suddenly has a reversal of economic fortune. How much of the $1,000 recovery is income in year 2? What would your answer be if the taxpayer's business income in year 1 had been $700 (not a loss). How much of the $1,000 bad debt deduction was useful in lowering the taxpayer's tax in year 1? Disregard personal exemptions and the standard deduction in answering these questions.

Notice carefully the limited scope of the "tax benefit" rule. *First*, it does not lower taxes if the earlier deduction was of some use to the taxpayer. For example, suppose a taxpayer itemized deductions, including $10,000 of state income taxes in year 3, and the deduction lowers taxes by 15%, because the taxpayer is in the 15% bracket. In year 4, her income rises and she is in the 39.6% bracket. She obtains a $2,000 refund of year 3 state income taxes in year 4. She pays 39.6% tax on the $2,000, not 15%. Why? *Second*, assume that the taxpayer was in the high 39.6% bracket in the year of the deduction (year 3), and in the 15% bracket in the tax refund year (year 4). The government cannot force the taxpayer to pay tax equal to 39.6% of the $2,000 refund? Why not?

§ 5.04 "TAX DETRIMENT" RULE

In the examples discussed so far, the taxpayer recovered a loss. What happens if the taxpayer repays income previously received? For example, if the taxpayer was taxed at 39.6% on receipt of income in year 1, but repays the item in year 5 when he is in the 15% bracket, should his tax be reduced by 39.6% or 15% of the repayment? If the tax accounting year barrier is inviolate, the deduction reduces his tax by only 15% of the deductible repayment.

Section 1341 identifies situations in which the accounting year barrier is broken down, allowing the taxpayer to elect (in effect) to take a deduction for the repayment in year 5 (the 15% tax rate year) as though he were still in the 39.6% tax bracket. The election is a one way street *for* the taxpayer. If the taxpayer is in a *higher* bracket in the *repayment* year, the government cannot prevent a deduction at the higher rates.

Are the following repayments eligible for *§ 1341* relief: (1) an embezzler reimburses his victim; (2) repayment by a judge of a lecture fee after newspaper reporters suggested an impropriety in the judge accepting the lecture engagement and the judge was concerned with her reputation; (3) repayment of the price paid for services because a mathematical error overstated the contract price (*Rev. Rul. 68-153*, 1968-1 C.B. 371)? Is there any underlying principle in *§ 1341* which helps you answer borderline cases?

§ 5.05 INCOME AVERAGING

Another example of breaking down the accounting year barrier is income averaging. The prior material in this chapter deals with situations in which there is income in one year and a deduction in another year. Income averaging deals with situations in which there is income in all the relevant years, but the income rises quickly, so that the taxpayer is pushed into a higher bracket. For example, assume that the taxpayer has no income in years 1 and 2, and $90,000 income in year 3. This taxpayer would pay much more in taxes under the current law compared to a situation in which the taxpayer had $30,000 income in years 1, 2 and 3. One method of income averaging treats a taxpayer with a big increase in income over a certain number of years as though the income had been earned in equal yearly increments, rather than all at once. A generally applicable income averaging provision was repealed in 1986 when tax rates were lowered.

The 1997 amendments allow farmers to elect to income average farm income over a three year period. *§ 1301*. The technique is to spread eligible farm income for one year evenly over the prior three years and pay only the tax that would have been due if these one-third amounts had been taxed in the prior three years. Thus, assume a taxpayer with $40,000 income in years 1-3; and $120,000 of income in year 4, $60,000 of which was farm income. This taxpayer could pay tax in year 4 in an amount equal to the tax on $60,000, plus the additional tax that *would have been paid* if $20,000 had been added to income in years 1, 2, and 3. This income averaging election is scheduled to expire after the year 2000.

CHAPTER 6

TAX EXPENDITURES AND THE LEGISLATIVE PROCESS

§ 6.01 DEFINING TAX EXPENDITURES

In addition to raising revenue and distributing tax burdens fairly, the tax law contains numerous provisions intended to encourage certain behavior. These have come to be known as "tax expenditures" because they are similar to direct government appropriations of funds. The idea is that giving up revenue to achieve some objective can be compared to collecting revenue and appropriating government funds to achieve that objective.

The tax expenditure analysis was originally the brainchild of a tax academic, Professor Stanley Surrey. When he became Assistant Secretary of the Treasury for Tax Policy in the 1960s, his ideas about tax expenditures were adopted by the Treasury and later by Congress. Since then, the executive branch has not always agreed with Congress. The published lists of tax expenditures by the Office of Management and Budget (OMB) (in the executive branch) and by the Congressional Budget Office (CBO) differ in certain particulars.

Surrey's definition of tax expenditures, which was embodied in the Budget Act of 1974, states:

> Those revenue losses attributable to provisions of the Federal tax laws which allow a special exclusion, exemption, or deduction from gross income or which provide a special credit, a preferential rate of tax, or a deferral of tax liability.

Surrey & McDaniel, *The Tax Expenditure Concept and the Budget Reform Act of 1974*, 17 B. C. Ind. & Comm. L. Rev. 679 (1976). This definition of tax expenditures assumed that the term "special" referred to a "deviation from the normal tax structure." The conception of a "normal" tax structure began with "widely accepted definitions of income," based on the economist's conception of income as personal consumption plus changes in net wealth. The tax expenditure definition was tempered, however, by the "generally accepted structure of an income tax," thereby excluding unrealized appreciation and imputed income from rental value of homes.

Surrey argued that identification of a tax expenditure was not a judgment about the wisdom of using the tax law to achieve social or economic policy.

Nonetheless, defining an item as a tax expenditure was meant to call attention to the use of the tax law for other than its core purpose of raising revenue fairly. The hope was that potential inefficiencies and unfairness from using the tax law to implement other purposes would be highlighted and, where appropriate, eliminated.

Not everyone could agree on the definition of a tax expenditure. The Reagan Administration was especially concerned about efforts to equate a "normal" tax base with some "ideal." Unable to identify the "ideal," the Reagan Administration had the Office of Management and Budget issue its own tax "subsidy" list (they preferred the term "subsidy" to "expenditure"), which used a slightly different definition. *See* Office of Management and Budget, *The Budget of the United States Government, 1983, Special Analysis G, Tax Expenditures*, 305 (1982). It emphasized as the "norm" the "reference" provisions of the statute, which were "those which deal with the basic structural features of the income tax."

The contrasting CBO and OMB general definitions of tax expenditures did not themselves compel obvious distinctions in application. And indeed there was much agreement. For example, both tax expenditure lists agree that the personal exemption deduction and individual rates below the top rate are not tax expenditures. Both agree that the extra standard deduction for the aged and blind is a tax expenditure. But there were differences. Only CBO, not OMB, treats the corporate tax rates below the top rate as a tax expenditure. OMB argues that no particular rate structure can be identified as a "reference" point and that therefore there are no "departures" which are tax expenditures. Neither list treats the different rate structures for individual and married couples as a tax expenditure.

Professor Bittker had a different objection to the tax expenditure approach. He argued that it encouraged the government to avoid tax rules which would show up adversely on the tax expenditure list, and that this encouraged business and investment tax breaks rather than social welfare tax benefits. For example, lower top tax rates and deferral of tax on unrealized appreciation are not tax expenditures, but tax free fringe benefits for employees are. *See* Bittker, *Accounting for Federal "Tax Subsidies" in the National Budget*, 22 Nat'l. Tax J. 244 (1969).

§ 6.02 EFFICIENCY PROBLEMS AND THE LEGISLATIVE PROCESS

The use of tax law to implement nontax policy raises the same kinds of efficiency questions as any expenditure program. Should the government be encouraging the subsidized activity; is it spending too much money or giving up too much revenue to achieve its goals; are the right people getting the benefit? The principal question raised by tax expenditure analysis concerns whether the political process which produces the tax expenditure is more likely to produce inefficient results than other kinds of government decisions. For example, when the tax law encourages investments by allowing the deduction of savings, is the loss of revenue carefully compared with the benefits that the economy will enjoy? The debate over lower taxes on capital gains is about the same question.

The reason for suspecting that tax expenditures may receive less public and political scrutiny is the assumption that tax committees are an easier target for obtaining government benefits than appropriations committees dealing with specific substantive areas of legislation. First, the public fails to understand the impact of tax breaks, compared to attention given to specific dollar appropriations. Exempting one half of an oil producer's income by excluding some income from the tax base or by raising deductions "feels" different from a $500,000,000 appropriation. Second, tax bills are massive statutes in which a tax break can be well hidden, or used to "purchase" a key supporting vote. Third, political influence operates very strongly through political contributions to tax committee members.

These are, of course, empirical claims which must be verified. Tax committees may in fact be less subject to special interest group pressure than appropriations committees dealing with specific areas of the economy. Tax committees may get campaign contributions from and represent a wide range of interest groups, which might offset each other, resulting in a perceived need to hold the line on tax breaks. By contrast, an appropriations subcommittee may be especially vulnerable to a single constituency. Moreover, publicity about tax expenditures may increase public scrutiny of tax breaks, but appropriations committee work may not be carefully scrutinized, except by the beneficiaries. *See* Zelinsky, *James Madison and Public Choice at Gucci Gulch: A Procedural Defense of Tax Expenditures and Tax Institutions*, 102 Yale L.J. 1165 (1993).

Recent statutory rules about the budget process (in the Gramm-Rudman-Hollings legislation) might also discourage tax expenditures. Any tax decrease must be offset by a tax increase or reduction in entitlement programs, either of which may be very unpopular. More generally, deficit consciousness may transform collusive logrolling activity (which increases all government expenditures), into a competitive political process, which limits all expenditures.

Some observers would favor tax expenditures over direct expenditures precisely because they prefer *less* scrutiny by *administrators*. It is true that any tax expenditure can be designed to have the same bureaucratic monitoring as a direct expenditure (*e.g.*, tax breaks for child care facilities can be conditioned on government approval of the facility), but it is politically less likely. Is less bureaucracy an advantage or a weakness of tax expenditures?

§ 6.03 EFFICIENCY AND PROGRESSIVE RATES

There is another efficiency problem applicable even to the most well thought out tax expenditure. The progressive tax rate system builds in a potential for excessive loss of revenue. The following discussion of tax exempt bonds for core governmental purposes illustrates this potential.

Everyone agrees that the exemption of interest on state and local bonds in *§ 103(a)* is a tax expenditure. The federal government gives up income tax on the interest, which helps state and local governments by lowering interest rates on borrowing. It is not meant to help investors. However, the way interest rates are set results in some of the tax expenditure being enjoyed by high bracket taxpayers. The explanation of this process can be generalized to illustrate a pervasive problem with tax breaks. Whenever someone gets a tax break (such as the investor in tax exempt bonds or the recipient of a tax free fringe benefit), someone who deals with that person will try to capture some of the tax benefit. The state borrower will lower interest rates, or the employer will lower cash wages. Here is how this can happen with tax exempt bonds.

The recipient of interest on a tax exempt bond will accept an interest payment which equals the *after*-tax interest rate on taxable bonds. For example, if the risk associated with a particular borrower requires the borrower to pay 16% taxable interest (a GM bond, for example), how much interest would a state or local government borrower with the same risk have to pay to a taxpayer in the 40% bracket (rounded up from 39.6% to simplify arithmetic)? Interest could fall to 9.6% (60% times 16%), and the tax exempt bond would be as good as a GM bond of equivalent risk.

Why can't the state or local government borrower capture all of the revenue lost by the federal government through tax exemption? Because there are not enough high bracket taxpayers to lend them money. Assume that some 28% bracket taxpayers must be attracted to finance state and local roads and schools. A tax exempt bond paying 9.6% will be shunned by the 28% bracket taxpayer. She can get 11.52% buying a GM bond (72% times 16%). So the government must pay 11.52% tax exempt interest, instead of 9.6%. Some of the tax revenue lost by tax exemption goes to the top 40% bracket taxpayer. What would the tax exempt interest rate be if the government had to attract investment by 31%, but not 28% bracket taxpayers?

What is wrong with the following proposal to eliminate this problem? Every calendar quarter the federal government states that it will pay state and local governments issuing *taxable* bonds a subsidy equal to 29% of the interest. Because the bonds are taxable, the state pays 16% interest but gets back 29% of the interest from the federal government, for a net interest cost to the state or local government of 11.36% (71% times 16%), which is less than the 11.52% in the prior example where interest rates were set to attract the 28% bracket investor. The state or local government is better off, and the windfall for the 40% bracket taxpayer is eliminated (he must pay tax of 40% times the 16% interest on the taxable bond).

§ 6.04 "LOOPHOLES" AND THE POLITICAL PROCESS

Many tax expenditures do attract public attention, but Congress still consciously chooses to enact them. The political process is not always so selfconscious, however. Sometimes a tax break emerges more gradually as a result of tax planning by tax counsel, the acquiescence and even approval of the IRS, and an inattentive legislature. By the time Congress becomes aware of the implications of the tax break, it may be too late. Political forces coalescing around the tax benefit are too powerful for the IRS to interpret the law against the taxpayer, for the Treasury to adopt anti-taxpayer regulations, and even for Congress to revoke the prevailing interpretation. This is what happened to Industrial Revenue Bonds (IRBs).

IRBs are tax exempt bonds in which the debtor is either legally or for all practical purposes a private industry. *§ 103* exempts the interest on state and local bonds. In the usual case, the state or local government borrows money for government purposes (roads, schools, etc.) and finances repayment with taxes. An IRB is different. The government lends its name to the bond and "borrows" the money. The government either re-lends the money to private industry or arranges to construct a facility which is then rented to private industry. The government is either not liable to repay the loan or the lender does not in reality look to the government for repayment. The loan repayment is legally or in reality out of funds paid by the private industry beneficiary of the loan.

How could this arrangement be considered a state or local obligation, especially in the case where the government is not even technically liable. Contrary to the image you may have of an overbearing IRS, the agency actually issued private letter rulings in the 1930s and then published *Rev. Rul. 54-106*, 1954-1 C.B. 28-29, favoring tax exemption of such arrangements. The agency's acquiescence and approval occurred when the amounts involved with IRBs was small. In 1957 only $20 million of such bonds were issued. By 1963 only 23 states even authorized such bonds, although all but three of these had enacted enabling legislation since 1950. Trouble was coming.

The Advisory Commission on Intergovernmental Relations issued a warning in 1963. *See* ACIR, *Industrial Development Bond Financing*

(1963). They saw one group of states pirating business from others (often Southern states attracting Northern business). Moreover, the tax breaks were often wasted, both because they were not really needed to attract the business and because multi-state competition to offer tax exempt IRBs simply lowered the cost of borrowing equally in all states.

Here you have the classic case of a "loophole." That term is sometimes used casually to mean any tax break, but that is misleading. Some tax breaks are consciously adopted. A loophole is different. It is a tax scheme devised by astute tax counsel, which stretches the statute beyond its reasonable meaning. Why doesn't the administrative process adequately address such efforts? Sometimes the administration is unaware of what is happening. Sometimes the authors of letter rulings issued at the lower administrative levels are not alert to the implications of what they are doing. Sometimes the implications are unclear — IRBs started small as efforts to build up rural manufacturing in the South. Over time, the economic implications alter and grow.

By 1969 the Treasury became alarmed. Forty states now authorized such bonds and well over $1 billion were marketed annually. Politically, IRBs were too prominent for the agency to revoke a Revenue Ruling. The Regulation process was therefore invoked. The Treasury adopted a Proposed Regulation that such bonds were *not* an obligation of a state or local government, but the politics of IRBs overwhelmed even the Regulatory process. The Senate Finance Committee proposed an amendment to a pending tax bill *freezing* the tax law on IRBs to accord with the pro-exemption principles of specifically-cited prior Revenue Rulings, including Rev. Rul. 54-106. Some in Congress, often from Northern states and with the backing of labor unions, proposed amendments explicitly withdrawing exemption for IRBs.

The end result was a complex statute allowing interest on some IRBs to be tax exempt (often relating to public purposes like pollution control or airports), while withdrawing exemption for most private industry IRBs. This type of legal evolution is one of the major causes of tax law complexity, as you can see by scanning *§§ 141–47*.

§ 6.05 TAX BREAKS, EQUAL PROTECTION, AND THE POLITICAL PROCESS

Sometimes tax breaks are provided to a narrow group of taxpayers with little pretense of advancing public goals. This can happen as part of regular tax legislation but often occurs in transition provisions when major tax reforms are passed. Law reform disrupts some expectations and industry seeks exceptions from retroactive impact. Only those with political clout, however, get relief from the new law. For example, a real estate developer in New York may get relief from a new tax law ending favorable treatment of real estate investment, but a California developer does not. In the following case, the court held that the selective tax breaks were constitutional. The plaintiffs were not competitors of the taxpayers who benefited from the relief provisions.

TPs not granted the exemptions → holding: selective tax breaks = const'l

APACHE BEND APARTMENTS, LTD. v. UNITED STATES

964 F.2d 1556 (5th Cir. 1992)

GOLDBERG, CIRCUIT JUDGE:

In an effort to dampen the impact of the radical changes brought about by the Tax Reform Act of 1986, Congress provided certain taxpayers exemptions from the new tax laws. In many instances, Congress designed these exemptions, known as "transition rules," to favor only one or a very few taxpayers. The method by which Congress selected those taxpayers that would enjoy the benefit of the transition rules is the subject of this lawsuit.

Tax exmptns.

I: method of selection

Plaintiffs are taxpayers that were not granted any relief under the transition rules. Claiming that they are similarly situated to those taxpayers to whom the transition rules do apply, they brought this lawsuit to challenge the constitutionality of the transition rules under the . . . equal protection component of the Due Process Clause of the United States Constitution. They argued that Congress exhibited favoritism to those taxpayers with strong congressional lobbies, and thus discriminated against those taxpayers, like plaintiffs, that "were not fortunate to have an ear in Congress." Plaintiffs . . . request[ed] the court [to] enjoin the enforcement of the transition rules so that no taxpayer could benefit from them. . . .

claims EPC of DP

request injunction

. . . A transition rule of general application, as opposed to these "rifle shot" transition rules, would have been far more costly in terms of tax revenue, albeit eminently fairer.

general rule more costly

This method of doling out tax breaks raised more than a few eyebrows in Congress. Several members of Congress expressed concern that similarly situated taxpayers were not being treated equally. Others conceded their use of raw political power to obtain transition rules for favored constituents.

Even in this court, the government acknowledges that "political considerations definitely played a significant role in the selection process . . . [and] the focus of the debate was on subjective factors [as opposed to objective factors]."

Plaintiffs contend that no rational basis exists for Congress' classification as between those taxpayers afforded relief under the transition rules and those who were not. They maintain that but for the fact that they did not have "the right people speaking for [them]" in Congress, they are similarly situated to those taxpayers who presently enjoy tax breaks accorded by the transition rules. In plaintiffs' view, this classification — providing benefits only to those taxpayers with connections in Congress and the political savvy to exploit those relationships — amounts to a violation of equal protection. . . .

. . . [T]he legislature has a legitimate governmental purpose in making exceptions from the general application of the Tax Reform Act to protect "substantial reliance interests." . . .

But that does not end our inquiry, for we must evaluate not only the purpose of the legislation, but the purpose and legitimacy of the classifications as well. To do that, we must first identify the classification. Plaintiffs take the position that:

> [w]hile assisting all taxpayers with general transition relief would be a valid and appropriate governmental purpose, the objective of providing selective exemptions to only a few, based upon their access to politicians, is an illegitimate and prohibited objective . . . There can never be a legitimate public purpose served by the arbitrary selection of a favored few from the general applicability of a taxing statute.

Plaintiffs would have us define the "favored" class as those taxpayers with "access to influential members of Congress."

Their argument is not without some foundation. . . . For example, the Chairman of the Senate Finance Committee confessed that

> [i]t would be foolish of me to say that, on occasion, politics did not enter those judgments. If the Speaker of the House requested the chairman of the Ways and Means Committee a transition rule, my hunch is that [he] would give it reasonably high priority in his thinking.
>
> If Senator Dole requested one of me, I would give it reasonably high priority in my thinking.

132 Cong. Rec. S 13,786 (daily ed. Sept. 26, 1986) (statement of Sen. Packwood). [Editor — Dole was Senate Majority Leader and Packwood was Chair of the Senate Finance Committee.] . . .

Moreover, it is quite plain that absent "access to the conference committee which enabled them to obtain a so-called transition rule so their activity could continue to be taxed under the old law," 132 Cong. Rec. S 13,810 (daily ed. Sept. 26, 1986) (statement of Sen. Levin), there was little, if any, chance that a taxpayer would receive transitional relief. As one Senator asked: "[W]hat about those who could not come to Washington and make their case? What about those who could not hire the lobbyists to present their appeal? Where is the fairness to them?" *Id.*

While we recognize that politics played a part in determining to whom the transition rules would apply, we nevertheless believe that, in view of the great deference accorded by the Supreme Court to tax legislation, the classifications contain no constitutional malady. Congress sought to give transitional relief to those taxpayers who petitioned for relief and demonstrated, most convincingly, that they relied substantially on the old tax laws in making major investment decisions. Not every application for transitional relief was granted, however, political clout notwithstanding. Congressional staff members examined more than one thousand requests for rifle shot transition relief before recommending the inclusion of several hundred. As the Senate Finance Committee Chairman explained: . . . [We said] to the staff, "Here are the rules by which transitions are to be selected. Try to avoid violating those rules." . . . Congress could not grant every request for transitional relief, for that would have threatened the success of the Act, which, by design of the President and Congress, was to be revenue neutral, neither raising nor lowering the aggregate level of federal revenue collections.

. . . [A]s far as we can tell from the legislative history, Congress made their decisions based on the merits of the applications for transitional relief made to the Finance Committee. We realize that those taxpayers with political connections had better access to the Committee than others. Nevertheless, nothing suggests that Congress aimed to exclude others or that Congress designed the classifications with such a purpose in mind:

> If the adverse impact on the disfavored class is an apparent aim of the legislature, its impartiality would be suspect. If, however, the adverse impact may reasonably be viewed as an acceptable cost of achieving a larger goal, an impartial lawmaker could rationally decide that that cost should be incurred.

[*United States Railroad Retirement Bd. v.*] *Fritz*, 449 U.S. 166, 181 (1980) (Stevens, J., concurring [in judgment]).

Moreover, it appears that Plaintiffs never sought transitional relief from the Tax Reform Act. That places them in an especially difficult position to challenge the rifle shot rules. They did not ask for, and therefore did not receive, the congressional manna:

Congress cannot be expected to search out on its own those taxpayers whose peculiar circumstances give them strong equitable arguments for special relief from general tax provisions; rather, such taxpayers must come to Congress. . . .

We hold that the classifications made by Congress were not arbitrary. It accorded transitional relief to those deserving taxpayers who applied for such relief and established most convincingly that they relied substantially on the old tax laws in making major investment decisions.

The court's holding was later reversed *en banc* by the Fifth Circuit, 987 F.2d 1174 (5th Cir. 1993), on the ground that the plaintiffs lacked standing. The court noted that "[t]he transition rules apply only to a very, very few taxpayers who requested such relief from Congress. The plaintiffs, claiming to lack political access, did not request such relief. In this lawsuit, they do not seek transition relief for themselves, but ask only that transition relief be denied to the favored taxpayers." In addition, the *en banc* decision emphasized that the "injury of unequal treatment alleged by the plaintiffs is shared in substantially equal measure by a 'disfavored class' that includes all taxpayers who did not receive transition relief." Like myriad taxpayers who did not request transition relief, the plaintiffs have not suffered any direct injury in the sense that they personally asked for and were denied a benefit granted to others. . . . [T]he Supreme Court has made it clear that "when the asserted harm is a 'generalized grievance' shared in substantially equal measure by all or a large class of citizens, that harm alone normally does not warrant 'exercise of jurisdiction.' "

Questions. What does the original Fifth Circuit decision (not the *en banc* decision) suggest that the taxpayer must prove to establish an equal protection claim? (1) Is it sufficient to prove that the taxpayer sought relief from Congress? How would such relief be sought? (2) Must the taxpayer also prove that he/she/it is in all respects like those who got the tax break? (3) What else would you want to prove about those who did get a tax break? (4) Give an example of a fact situation which would support a judgment for the taxpayer under the original *Apache Bend* decision.

§ 6.06 TAX BREAKS, THE POLITICAL PROCESS, AND THE LINE ITEM VETO

The *Apache Bend* case dealt with special transitional tax breaks which are usually part of any major tax bill. Special tax breaks aimed at a limited group of people are not uncommon, either to ease the burden of a new law or simply to help a taxpayer who has complained about a tax provision to a legislator (usually one who is influential on a tax writing committee). A recent law gives the President a "line item veto" over appropriations generally *and* over special tax breaks (called a "limited tax benefit") which help a limited constituency. *Pub. L. 104–130,* 110 Stat. 1200, codified at *2 U.S.C. §. 691 et seq.* (Supp. 1997). Here are some portions of the definition of a "limited tax benefit." *(2 U.S.C. § 691(e)(9)).*

(A) The term "limited tax benefit" means—

(i) any revenue-losing provision which provides a Federal tax deduction, credit, exclusion, or preference to 100 or fewer beneficiaries. . .

(ii) any Federal tax provision which provides temporary or permanent transitional relief for 10 or fewer beneficiaries in any fiscal year from a change to the Internal Revenue Code of 1986.

(B) A provision shall not be treated as described in subparagraph (A)(i) if the effect of that provision is that—

(i) all persons in the same industry or engaged in the same type of activity receive the same treatment;

. . .

(iii) any difference in the treatment of persons is based solely on—

(I) in the case of businesses and associations, the size or form of the business or association involved;

(II) in the case of individuals, general demographic conditions, such as income, marital status, number of dependents, or tax return filing status;

(III) the amount involved;

. . .

(C) A provision shall not be treated as described in subparagraph (A)(ii) if—

(i) it provides for the retention of prior law with respect to all binding contracts or other legally enforceable obligations in existence on a date contemporaneous with congressional action specifying such date; . . .

The Joint Committee on Taxation is required to prepare a statement identifying each limited tax benefit contained in the law, and the

House-Senate Conference Committee decides whether to include the statement in the conference report. If it is included, only those listed items are subject to the line item veto. If the statement is not included, the President is left to determine which items can be vetoed under the standards of the Line Item Veto Act.

President Clinton vetoed three items of the 1997 Tax Act in August, two of which were tax breaks. Seventy nine of the items in the 1997 Tax Act had been listed in the conference report as subject to the line item veto. A challenge to the constitutionality of the line item veto law has been filed. (An earlier case, *Raines v. Byrd*, 956 F.Supp. 25 (D.D.C. 1997), held that the Line Item Veto Act was unconstitutional but the decision was reversed on the grounds that members of Congress lacked standing to make the challenge; 117 S.Ct. 2312 (1997)). The theory against the line item veto is that it allows the President to change the law after it has become effective, which is a legislative function.

The contrary theory, allowing the line item veto, views the Presidential veto as a discretionary power, similar to what Congress has routinely delegated to agencies in modern twentieth century legislation. In that connection, consider the guidelines for a Presidential line item veto (2 U.S.C. § 691(a)): the President should determine that the cancellation of an expenditure or tax break will "(i) reduce the Federal budget deficit; (ii) not impair any essential Government functions; and (iii) not harm the national interest." The President must also notify Congress of the cancellation of spending by special message "within five calendar days (excluding Sundays) after the enactment of the spending law."

PART II

PERSONAL CONSUMPTION AND BUSINESS EXPENSES

CHAPTER 7

INCOME IN-KIND

§ 7.01 MEALS AND LODGING

[A]—Case law background

In *Benaglia v. Commissioner*, 66 B.T.A. 838 (1937), the court held that meals and lodging were not taxable when they were provided to a hotel manager and his wife merely as a convenience to the employer. This case predates adoption of *§ 119* and interprets the definition of *§ 61* income. The court stated that "residence at the hotel was not by way of compensation for [] services, not for his personal convenience, comfort or pleasure, but solely because he could not otherwise perform the services required of him." It did not matter that the expense "relieve[d] him of an expense which he would otherwise bear." Much of the opinion discusses the facts which support the "convenience of the employer" conclusion. The government apparently agreed with the legal test — "convenience of the employer" justified an exclusion — but disagreed with its application in this case. The dissent stressed that the employment contract treated the meals and lodging as compensation. The dissent also disagreed fundamentally with the court's approach. Meals and lodging solely for the employer's convenience are still income because they are necessities the employee would otherwise have to purchase. The employer therefore "enriched" the employee.

Notwithstanding the dissent, the "convenience of the employer" rule persisted and was codified, with added statutory detail, in 1954. *See § 119*. The hope was for greater legal certainty. More precise statutes do not always work out that way, however, because the more precise statute might add new language which is just as hard to interpret as the word "income." Simplicity proves elusive. As the following cases illustrate, the new phrase "business premises" in *§ 119* raised a whole new set of interpretive problems. Before you jump to the conclusion that the new language made matters worse, however, you should compare it with the old. It is possible that the new language is just as difficult to apply as the old but that it significantly reduces the number of situations in which there is a problem applying the law.

The exclusion of meals and lodging provided by the employer should strike you as anomalous — some taxpayers can enjoy meals and lodging tax-free while others finance these expenses out of after tax income. One provision of the tax law might seem to limit this advantage *indirectly*, but it does not. *§ 274(n)* limits the employer's deduction of meals (but not lodging) to 50% of their cost. This will often reduce the amount of tax-free personal consumption for meals that the employee will receive from the employer. But the 1997 Tax Act has repealed the 50% limit on the deduction for meal expenses for an employer who is providing these meals for the convenience of the employer. It did this by amending *§ 132(e)(2)* so that such meals are always treated as *de minimis* fringe benefits under *§ 274(n)(2)(B)* (exempting *de minimis* fringe benefits from the limits on the employer's deduction). *Boyd Gaming Corp. v. Commissioner*, 106 T.C. 343 (1996) had reached the same result under pre-1997 law.

[B]—Business premises

LINDEMAN v. COMMISSIONER

60 T.C. 609 (1973)

[Editor — The employer ran an oceanfront resort hotel in Fort Lauderdale. The employer also owned parking lots and a house across Oakland Park Boulevard, which was the southern boundary of the hotel property. The house, which was on Lot 18, was the residence for the hotel's general manager, the taxpayer in the case.]

These deceptively simple words — "on the business premises" of the employer — have been the subject of extended judicial opinions with varying results. We examine anew the legislative history of § 119 insofar as it bears on the issue presented for decision.

The requirement of § 119 that, to be excludable from gross income, lodging must be furnished and accepted "on the business premises" of the employer was first adopted as part of the 1954 Code. As passed by the House of Representatives, the section used the term "place of employment" rather than "business premises." H. Rept. No. 1337, to accompany H.R. 3300 (Pub. L. No. 591), 83d Cong., 2d Sess., pp. 18, A39 (1954). The Senate changed the term to "business premises," but the accompanying report explained that "Under both bills meals and lodging are to be excluded from the employee's income if they are furnished at the place of employment and the employee is required to meet certain other conditions," S. Rept. No. 1622, to accompany H.R. 8300 (Pub. L. No. 591), 83d Cong., 2d Sess., pp. 19, 190–191 (1954).

The Senate version was adopted with the following explanation in Conf. Rept. No. 2548, 83d Cong., 2d Sess., p. 27 (1954):

The term "business premises of the employer" is intended, in general, to have the same effect as the term "place of employment" in the House bill. For example, lodging furnished in the home to a domestic servant would be considered lodging furnished on the business premises of the employer. Similarly, meals furnished to a cowhand while herding his employer's cattle on leased lands, or on national forest lands used under a permit, would also be regarded as furnished on the business premises of the employer. . . .

As in the case of other exclusions from gross income, this one is subject to abuse, and the statutory language must be construed with this thought in mind. Accordingly, the term "on" in relation to the employer's business premises does not mean "in the vicinity of" or "nearby" or "close to" or "contiguous to" or similar language, but is to be read literally. If the lodging is furnished at a location some distance from the place where the employee works, the lodging is not furnished on his employer's business premises.

In determining what are the employer's "business premises," Congress quite obviously intended a commonsense approach. Read literally, the statutory language ordinarily would not permit any exclusion for lodging furnished a domestic servant, since a servant's lodging is rarely furnished on "the business premises of his employer"; yet the committee report, quoted above, shows a clear intention to allow the exclusion where the servant's lodging is furnished in the employer's home. Similarly, the section, as a condition to the exclusion, does not require that the meals or lodging be furnished at any particular location on the employer's property; thus, the same committee report clearly states that meals provided for a cowhand are excludable even though they are furnished on leased lands or on lands used under a permit.

These illustrations in the committee report, moreover, demonstrate that § 119 does not embody a requirement that the meals or lodging be furnished in the principal structure on the employer's business premises. Thus, the committee report makes it explicitly clear that a cowhand's meals and lodging need not be furnished at the ranch headquarters. And surely the right of a domestic servant to the § 119 exclusion cannot be made to turn on whether his lodging is furnished in the family residence or in servants' quarters located elsewhere on the estate. Indeed, in *Boykin v. Commissioner*, 260 F.2d 249 (C.A. 8, 1958), *aff'g in part and rev'g in part* 29 T.C. 813 (1958), the Commissioner at least implicitly conceded that a physician's living quarters, located on the grounds of a Veterans Administration Hospital, were on his employer's business premises even though he performed none of his employment services in his living quarters. Similarly, the Commissioner has ruled that meals furnished at branch offices of an employer, as well as at a central dining facility, meet the requirements of the section. Rev. Rul. 71-411, 1971-2 C.B. 103.

The issue as to the extent or the boundaries of the business premises in each case is a factual issue, and in resolving that question consideration must be given to the employee's duties as well as the nature of the employer's business. The section 119 exclusion applies where the lodging is furnished at a place where the employee conducts a significant portion of his business. *Commissioner v. Anderson*, 371 F.2d at 67. Or, in the words of this Court in *Gordon S. Dole*, 43 T.C.at 707, "the phrase should be construed to mean either (1) living quarters that constitute an integral part of the business property or (2) premises on which the company carries on some of its business activities."

We think petitioner has shown that the house which his employer furnished him during 1968 and 1969 was part and parcel of the "business premises" of Beach Club Hotel. In reaching this conclusion, we think it apparent that the business premises of the hotel are not limited to 3100 North Ocean Boulevard, where the hotel building is located, but include both parking lots and the house furnished to petitioner.

. . . [T]he nature of the Beach Club Hotel business is such as to require the general manager to live where he is immediately accessible at all hours, and the house on lot 18 meets this need. It is stipulated that:

> In 1963, after a cost study, Beach Hotel Corporation determined it should be more profitable to purchase or rent accommodations for . . . (petitioner) and his family as close to the hotel as possible and have the suite of four rooms he was occupying available to be rented.

Thereupon, [the employer] acquired lot 18, containing the house, and Beach Hotel Corp. leased it to provide housing for petitioner and his family. This was a business decision based on business considerations, and there is no suggestion in the record that it was prompted by any other factors or that it involves an abuse of the section 119 exclusion.

The house is so situated and so used that it is part of the hotel plant. While petitioner's office is located in the business area of the hotel building (as it was while he occupied the suite of rooms as his residence), he is subject to call 24 hours a day, and he is as readily accessible for the frequent calls by direct telephone as he was in the suite located in the hotel building. He often returns to the hotel building several times in an evening. People dealing with him through the direct telephone line have no way of knowing whether he is in the hotel building or his home. Moreover, from the house he can observe the entire south half of the building and can "tell if there is a disturbance of any kind, see if lights are on or off, if the night lights don't come on early enough," and the like.

While petitioner does most of his management work in his office in the hotel building, he also has an office in the house on lot 18. In this latter office in his home, he receives calls from the hotel personnel or guests on the direct telephone line from the hotel while he is not on regular duty. He also uses this office when he is working on new brochures or rate structures and when he is planning a program for future hotel activities, such as "cook-outs, games, picnics on the beach, cocktail parties, and this sort of thing." In addition, he occasionally entertains a guest of the hotel.

In our view, these facts demonstrate that the lodging furnished petitioner is, within the meaning of § 119, "on the business premises of his employer" or, within the meaning of the accompanying committee reports, "at the place of employment." The house in which he lives is an indispensable and inseparable part of the hotel plant, and it is within the perimeter of the hotel property. Since it is part of the premises where petitioner performs the duties required in his job and where his employer carries on its business, we hold that petitioner is entitled to the § 119 exclusion.

Commissioner v. Anderson, 371 F.2d 59 (C.A. 6, 1966), on which respondent relies, is factually distinguishable. In that case, the housing furnished the employee was "two short blocks" from the facility being managed by the taxpayer, and the Court of Appeals did not conclude, as we do here, that the living quarters of the employee-taxpayer were an integral part of the business property. Accordingly, the Court of Appeals held that the requirements of the statute were not met. In the instant case, the premises of the business managed by petitioner include the house in which his lodging was furnished.

Reviewed by the Court.

QUESTIONS

The following questions suggest some of the difficulty in interpreting the phrase "business premises." You will almost certainly find it difficult to apply the "plain meaning" of that phrase. Is there a risk that it will be interpreted in a sterile manner, cut off from the structural principles which underlie the statute? What structural principles would you use — (1) whether the employer's convenience is a dominant factor in making the employee live or eat somewhere; (2) how likely is it that the benefit is what the employee would have selected if he had made a free choice?

Is the taxpayer "on the business premises" in any of the following situations?

1. Meals and lodging are provided by the employer at an Alaskan campsite where an oil pipeline is being constructed. *Treas. Reg. § 1.119-1(f) (Example 7).*

2. A factory manager responsible for labor relations lives in housing owned by the employer about one mile from the factory. The employee must live there to be close enough to get to the factory if labor trouble develops at any time. *Dole v. Commissioner*, 43 T.C. 697 (1965), *aff'd per curiam*, 351 F.2d 308 (1st Cir. 1965). Would it matter if the house was one block from the factory? *Erdelt v. United States*, 715 F. Supp. 278 (D.N.D. 1989), *aff'd without opinion*, 909 F.2d 504 (8th Cir. 1990).
3. A receptionist lives in an apartment above a doctor's office. The receptionist cleans up the office after hours and answers phone calls, and sometimes looks up a file in the office after hours if a patient calls the doctor at home for medical advice. *Nolen v. Commissioner*, 23 T.C.M.(CCH) 595 (1964).
4. A company executive lives in Japan in Western-style housing owned by the employer, in part so that he can entertain company clients. *Compare Adams v. United States*, 585 F.2d 1060 (Ct. Cl. 1978), with *McDonald v. Commissioner*, 66 T.C. 223 (1976).
5. A president of the state university lives in an official residence owned by the university, which is one mile from campus and which is used as an office and to entertain university and state officials. *Rev. Rul. 75-540*, 1975-2 C.B. 53; *Priv. Ltr. Rul. 7823007.* Is the President of the United States taxed on the value of White House lodging?

[C]—Convenience of employer

§ 119 echoes prior case law by requiring that the meals and lodging be for the convenience of the employer. The best argument for excluding benefits provided for the employer's convenience is the lack of choice that often accompanies these benefits. *Treas. Reg. § 1.119-1(a)(2)(i)* states that the presence of a substantial noncompensatory reason satisfies this test. The statute disregards any provision *in the contract* specifying that the meals or lodging are or are not compensatory. *§ 119(b)(1).* Presumably, it is too easy to manipulate the contract to omit reference to such compensation and, in any event, the market place will fix cash wages by taking into account the fringe benefit, regardless of whether the contract specifies that the benefits are compensatory.

If the rationale for exclusion is the likelihood that the benefits would not be freely chosen by the employee, should an employee who is a principal owner of a corporation for which he works ever be allowed to exclude meals and lodging under *§ 119*? *Adolph Coors Co. v. Commissioner*, 27 T.C.M. (CCH) 1351 (1968), permits a principal shareholder who is an employee of his corporation to use *§ 119*. Does that provide a good reason to incorporate?

The Regulations once provided that meals could not be "for the convenience of the employer" if the employee had discretion to buy the meal. Thus, if a company cafeteria served meals for which the employee paid one-half the normal price if he wanted to purchase the meal, the value in excess of the price paid by the employee was taxable. Congress reacted to this IRS position by adopting *§ 119(b)(2)*. This statutory provision does not entirely eliminate the "convenience of the employer" test. It only eliminates one element of the test (the no-employee-discretion element). It is still necessary to prove that there is a good business reason for requiring the employee to eat on the premises. *See, e.g., Treas. Reg. § 1.119-1(f)* (Example 3) (the meal was provided for the employer's convenience where a bank teller's lunch hour was restricted to 30 minutes because that was the peak time for bank business; the employer required the employee to eat on the premises and provided a cafeteria for this purpose).

[D]—Condition of employment

This phrase applies only to housing, not meals. *§ 119(a)(2)*. The Regulations specify that the test is an objective one. How does it differ from the "convenience of the employer" test? *Treas. Reg. § 1.119-1(b)*. Does it make that test somewhat stricter for lodging in some unspecified way, perhaps because housing is a bigger item than food? If not, why is the statute redundant?

[E]—Cash vs. in-kind

SIBLA v. COMMISSIONER

611 F.2d 1260 (9th Cir. 1980)

CURTIS, DISTRICT JUDGE:

During the relevant period [1972 and 1973] the taxpayers were employed as firemen by the Los Angeles Fire Department and were assigned to Fire Station No. 89 in North Hollywood, California. They normally worked 24-hour shifts and were not permitted to leave the fire station on personal business while on duty.

In the late 1950's a desegregation plan was implemented by the Fire Department. Previously segregated posts were consolidated in order to eliminate segregation within a post. The Board of Fire Commissioners adopted rules requiring all firemen at each fire station to participate in a nonexclusionary organized mess at the station house, unless officially excused. The only recognized grounds for nonparticipation was a physical ailment verified by the city's own examining physician.

The Fire Department provided kitchen facilities, but the firemen themselves generally organized the activities themselves. They provided dishes and pots, purchased and prepared the food, assessed members for the cost of the meals and collected the assessments. Meal expenses averaged about $3.00 per man for each 24-hour shift which the taxpayers were required to pay even though they were at times away from the station on fire department business during the mess period. . . .

The Commissioner places heavy reliance upon *Commissioner v. Kowalski*, 434 U.S. 77 (1977), in which the Supreme Court held that "cash meal allowances" were not excludable under § 119. In *Kowalski*, state police troopers employed by the state of New Jersey had included in their gross pay a cash meal allowance. Although the troopers were required to remain on call in their assigned patrol areas during their midshift break, they were not required to eat lunch at any particular location and, indeed, many ate at home. Nor were they required to spend the meal allowance on food. The tax court rejected the deduction, but the court of appeals reversed. The Supreme Court held that cash meal allowance payments were not excludable under § 119, since they are funds over which the taxpayer has complete dominion and they are not meals "furnished by the employer."

Kowalski is of course distinguishable upon the facts. The state troopers could eat any place they wanted, and they had complete dominion over their cash allowances and could spend it as they pleased. In the case before us the fire fighters were required to eat their meals on the employer's premises, and were required to pay for them whether they ate them or not.

The language in the *Kowalski* opinion however presents a more difficult problem. In interpreting § 119, the Court would allow deductions for meals "furnished by the employer in kind" but would disallow the deductions for "cash advances for food." It seems clear throughout the opinion and in the cases the Court discusses that the concept of "cash allowances" assumes an allowance over which the taxpayer has complete dominion. That is, he may eat as little or as much as he wants, or not at all if he wishes, and he may spend any unused portion any way he desires. We do not believe that the Court intended to rule that an allowance otherwise excludable should be denied excludability simply because it was paid in cash. We think the true holding of *Kowalski* can best be demonstrated by the following example. Let us assume that the taxpayers were given scrip for the purpose of paying for their meals. If the scrip were redeemable at any eating establishment in the vicinity or could be exchanged for cash at a bank or elsewhere, there is little doubt in the *Kowalski* factual setting but that the Court would have reached the same result. However, if the scrip were issued in the precise amount of the meal assessment; was redeemable only at the mess; and had to be surrendered whether the fireman ate or not, such an allowance in our view whether paid in scrip or cash would be deductible and we do not read *Kowalski* to the contrary.

In the light of all the circumstances in this case, the meals in question in a very real sense were "furnished in kind by the employer" upon the "business property" by means of a device conceived and established by the employer for its convenience. This being so, the taxpayers should be permitted to exclude from their gross income under the provisions of § 119 the value of these meals notwithstanding the fact that cash has been used as a simple method of implementing the plan.

We hold therefore that taxpayers may . . . exclude [the mess fees] from income under § 119.

KENNEDY, CIRCUIT JUDGE, dissenting:

I respectfully disagree with the majority's holding. . . .

[In *Kowalski*], the Court construed § 119 quite narrowly to meals actually furnished by the employer, rather than meals furnished by the employees in a facility provided by the employer, and I therefore think that the Tax Court's decision should be reversed on the authority of *Kowalski*.

. . . [T]he underlying principle is the idea that forced consumption should in some cases be treated as a transaction that is not dependent on significant elements of personal choice. That is, if the convenience of the employer dictates a certain type of consumption that is likely to be different from that which a taxpayer would normally prefer, this restriction of the taxpayer's preferences is an occasion for an "accession to wealth" over which the taxpayer does not "have complete dominion." *Cf. Commissioner v. Glenshaw Glass Co.*, 348 U.S. 426, 431 (1955) (defining gross income in terms of quoted phrases). It appears from the record that such a restriction on the taxpayers' consumption preferences was not present in this case: the only aspect of the common dining arrangement that suited the employer was its location. The firemen were apparently free to suit their own tastes in the groceries purchased and the food prepared. This freedom points up the critical omission in the majority's hypothetical, which is the failure to specify the amount of the individual taxpayer's participation in either the choice of food or the decision of how much to spend on the meals.

The necessity in cases like these to focus on such minutiae to determine the degree of taxpayer control suggests the hair-splitting artificiality of isolating an otherwise clear type of personal expense which all taxpayers must incur in the ordinary course of living and labeling that expense "business" and therefore nontaxable for a particular, and to that extent special, class of taxpayers. Legislative exceptions such as section 119 should not be broadened beyond their explicit terms by judicial interpretation. . . .

QUESTIONS

1. Are groceries "meals" under the statute? What criteria do you consider to answer that question? *Compare Tougher v. Commissioner*, 51 T.C. 737 (1969), *aff'd per curiam*, 441 F.2d 1148 (9th Cir. 1971) *with Jacob v. United States*, 493 F.2d 1294 (3d Cir. 1974).

2. Look at *§ 119(b)(3)*. If that section had been adopted prior to *Sibla*, would it have affected the decision?

3. Suppose a taxpayer's principal residence burns down and the family lives in a motel and eats at restaurants for a month. The home mortgage, still being paid, is $500 per month. Motel charges are $750 for the month. Food costs are $700, instead of the usual $400. The insurance company pays the taxpayer for their $750 motel and $700 food expenses. Is this insurance reimbursement income? *See § 123*.

§ 7.02 EMPLOYEE FRINGE BENEFITS

Another area of the law that used to be the domain of case law which elaborated on the definition of *§ 61* income has now been taken over by statute. Meals and lodging are only one example of benefits provided by employers to employees. Employers provide a variety of other benefits, such as fancy offices, free flights on airlines, bargain discounts of retail merchandise, use of demonstrator cars, free parking, and free recreational facilities. As a general rule, many, if not most, of these benefits were not reported by the employees as income and employers were not withholding tax from their employees' income. Employers and employees in specific industries came to rely on the exclusion of many of these benefits, even though it was difficult to reconcile that result with the statute. Revenue agents, in the absence of clearer standards than the general language of *§ 61*, were reaching diverse results in different parts of the country, if they were able to detect the benefits at all.

In 1975, the Treasury confronted this chaotic situation by issuing a Discussion Draft of proposed regulations as a trial balloon, but the draft was withdrawn when the political impact of taxing many fringe benefits became apparent. The Treasury did not stop worrying about the matter, however, and Congress decided to prohibit the issuance of regulations dealing with fringe benefits, in the expectation that Congress would address the issue. The expiration date of the prohibition was periodically renewed as Congress found it difficult to resolve the problem. Finally, in 1984, the Code was amended by adopting *§ 132*.

QUESTIONS

How would the following examples be dealt with by the statute? How do you think they would have been treated under pre-*§ 132* law?

1. **"No additional cost."**

a. F, a flight attendant in the employ of A, an airline company, and F's spouse decide to spend their 1984 annual vacation in Europe. A has a policy whereby any of its employees, along with members of their immediate families, may take a number of personal flights annually for a nominal charge. F and F's spouse take advantage of this policy and fly to and from Europe. *§ 132(a)(1), (b),(h)(2),(j)(1).*

b. P is the president of C, a corporation that has its executive offices situated in New York City. P is planning a week-long business trip to Los Angeles and will fly there and back on C's corporate jet. P's spouse intends to accompany P on the round trip flight for personal reasons. *§ 132(a)(1),(b).*

What is the justification for the exclusion of "no additional cost" fringe benefits: the value to the employee should in any event be heavily discounted (as in the *Turner* steamship ticket case); the service would otherwise go to waste and that is bad economic policy; the airline industry had political clout?

2. **Working conditions.**

a. E is an executive employed by C, an advertising company. E feels that the office in which E works is inadequately decorated and C agrees to redecorate the office with more comfortable furniture, live plants and a selection of artwork. The newly redecorated office has made E more comfortable and has created an office environment more conducive to carrying on the ordinary and necessary business activities of the company. *§ 132(a)(3),(d).*

b. S is a salesman employed by A, an automobile dealership. S is supplied with an automobile by A for use as a customer demonstrator during regular business hours. S also uses the automobile both before and after regular business hours for personal errands and for commuting between home and office. *§ 132(a)(3),(j)(3).*

c. F, a financial vice-president employed by A, an automobile manufacturer, is regularly provided with a new automobile for F's personal use. A requires F to file a report describing F's reaction to each automobile.

d. E, an executive employed by M, a multinational corporation, has been promoted to president of S, one of M's foreign subsidiaries. The country in which S is located has been beset by violent terrorist activity. Major targets of such activity are Americans who are employed by American-owned corporations doing business in that country. In order to protect these employees, the American corporations have instituted a number of security measures. For example, a heavily-guarded residential compound has been established within which all American employees and their families must live. Additionally, residents traveling outside the compound are always accompanied by armed security personnel. *§ 132(a)(3),(d).*

3. **Parking.** P, the President of the company, is provided with free parking in the corporate building's indoor parking lot in a big city. No one else enjoys this free privilege. *§§ 132(a)(5); 132(f)(1)(C), (2)(B), 5(C), (7).* As you work through this problem, you will observe that parking fringe benefits can be excluded up to a certain amount. That amount is adjusted for inflation and is $175 for tax year 1998.

4. **Cafeterias.** E, an executive assistant in the employ of B, a bank, works at B's executive offices. B provides, for the use of all executive employees, an on-premises cafeteria which provides meals during regular business hours. The receipts from the cafeteria, on the average, approximately cover the direct costs of providing the meals. *§ 132(e)(2).* Would the fringe benefit in this example be excluded under *§ 119*?

5. **Supper money.** Is "occasional" supper money excluded from income under *§ 132*? For example, A, an assistant manager in the employ of D, a department store, is occasionally required to work overtime to help mark down merchandise for special sales. On those occasions, D pays for the actual cost of A's evening meal at a nearby restaurant. Such payment is pursuant to company policy whereby D will pay the actual, reasonable meal

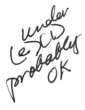

expense of a management-level employee when such an expense is incurred in connection with the performance of services either before or after such an employee's regular business hours. *§ 132(a)(4),(e)(1).*

In view of the following Committee Report, could the government include occasional supper money in income? The Committee Reports related to adoption of *§ 132* stated:

> Treasury Regulations are to be issued to implement the provisions of this bill. Such regulations must be consistent with the language of the bill and with the legislative history (as reflected in part, in the committee reports on the bill). Thus, any example of a fringe benefit which the reports state is excluded under the bill from income and wages must be so treated in the regulations.

The Committee Report further states that occasional supper money is excluded under the de minimis rule. Is the legislative history binding on the IRS?

Is occasional supper money excluded from *§ 61* income in the first place, without relying on *§ 132*? What is the strongest argument you can make to support that position? Does the following Committee Report excerpt prevent a court from considering the *§ 61* argument? The Report states that any "fringe benefit that does not qualify for exclusion under the bill [adopting *§ 132]* . . . or under another specific statutory fringe benefit provision is includable in gross income (under Code sections 61 and 83) for income tax purposes (and withholding) at the excess of its fair market value over any amount paid by the employee for the benefit."

6. **Frequent flyer.** E, an employee of a clothing manufacturer, travels all over the world to sell the employer's product. The employer pays for the travel but the employee can use the frequent flyer miles. At 10,000 miles the employee gets a free upgrade to first class; at 20,000 miles a free domestic ticket; at 100,000 a free international ticket. Is the employee taxed when he accrues 10,000, 20,000, or 100,000 miles; only when he takes advantage of the free benefit; not at all?

7. **Employer discounts.** S, a sales clerk in the employ of D, a retail department store, purchases the following from D at a 20% discount, which covers D's cost: (a) an appliance from the appliance department; (b) an expensive wedding ring from the jewelry department; and (c) auto repair from an auto service center department maintained solely for employees, not the general public. *§ 132(a)(2),(c).*

Are employer discounts analogous to the difference between what some consumers pay and what they would be willing to pay for goods or services? No one seriously argues for imposing tax on the value of that bargain (which is often referred to as "consumer surplus"). Does the exclusion of consumer surplus rest on administrative convenience, which would not explain an exclusion when an employer provides the benefit for which there is a well-established market value?

Valuation. Taxable fringe benefits are taxed at fair market value. But what is the value of a free plane ticket, or free use of a car? There are often many prices at which such services can be purchased. You can get some idea of the complexity of the rules by looking at the following excerpts from the Table of Contents to *Treas. Reg. § 1.61–21*:

(b)(4) fair market value of the availability of an employer-provided vehicle

(b)(5) fair market value of chauffeur services

(b)(6) fair market value of a flight on an employer-provided piloted aircraft

(b)(7) fair market value of the use of an employer-provided aircraft for which the employer does not provide a pilot

(d) automobile lease valuation rule

(e) vehicle cents-per-mile valuation rule

(f) commuting valuation rule

(g) non-commercial flight valuation rule

(h) commercial flight valuation rule

Nondiscrimination rules. Some fringe benefits for employees are subject to nondiscrimination rules, which require that the benefits be provided to a broad range of employees. Of the benefits discussed in this chapter, nondiscrimination rules apply to the "no additional cost," "employee discount," and "*de minimis*" eating facility exclusions. *§ 132(e)(2)(last sentence),(j)(1)*. These rules specify that the benefits must not discriminate in favor of highly compensated employees, defined in *§ 132(j)(6)*. Working condition fringes are not subject to nondiscrimination rules.

If the plan does discriminate in favor of highly compensated employees, only those employees are taxed on the fringe benefit. Other employees continue to receive the benefits tax-free.

§ 7.03 ETHICAL ISSUES

The frequent flyer fringe benefit provides a good opportunity to consider the ethical rules applicable to tax preparers and advisors who tell taxpayers about positions that have some chance (but less than a 50% chance) of success. For example, would it be ethical to advise a client not to report a fringe benefit as income if you think there is only a 20% or one-third chance of winning? Less than 2% of all tax returns are audited, and the risk of audit is even less for most employees because most of their taxes are withheld from their salary. Would it be ethical to consider the likelihood of audit in giving your advice?

[A]—ABA Rules

The 1967 American Bar Association Formal Ethics Opinion 314 states:

> . . . [A] lawyer who is asked to advise his client in the course of the preparation of the client's tax returns may freely urge the statement of positions most favorable to the client just as long as there is a reasonable basis for those positions — [T]he lawyer has no duty to advise that riders be attached to the client's tax return explaining the circumstances surrounding the transaction or the expenditures.

More recently, in 1985, the American Bar Association reconsidered the "reasonable basis" test, stating as follows in Formal Ethics Opinion 85-352:

> The Committee is informed that the standard of "reasonable basis" has been construed by many lawyers to support the use of any colorable claim on a tax return to justify exploitation of the lottery of the tax return audit selection process. . . . This view is not universally held, and the Committee does not believe that the reasonable basis standard, properly interpreted and applied, permits this construction.
>
> However, the Committee is persuaded that as a result of serious controversy over this standard and its persistent criticism by distinguished members of the tax bar, IRS officials and members of Congress, sufficient

doubt has been created regarding the validity of the standard so as to erode its effectiveness as an ethical guideline.

This opinion reconsiders and revises only that part of Opinion 314 that relates to the lawyer's duty in advising a client of positions that can be taken on a tax return. It does not deal with a lawyer's opinion on tax shelter investment offerings, which is specifically addressed by this Committee's Formal Opinion 346 (Revised), and which involves very different considerations, including third party reliance. . . .

Rule 3.1 of the Model Rules, which is in essence a restatement of DR 7-102(A)(2) of the Model Code, states in pertinent part: "A lawyer shall not bring or defend a proceeding, or assert or controvert an issue therein, unless there is a basis for doing so that is not frivolous, which includes a good faith argument for an extension, modification of reversal of existing law." Rule 1.2(d), which applies to representation generally, states: "A lawyer shall not counsel a client to engage, or assist a client, in conduct that the lawyer knows is criminal or fraudulent, but a lawyer may discuss the legal consequences of any proposed course of conduct with a client and may counsel or assist a client to make a good faith effort to determine the validity, scope, meaning or application of the law."

On the basis of these rules and analogous provisions of the Model Code, a lawyer, in representing a client in the course of the preparation of the client's tax return, may advise the statement of positions most favorable to the client if the lawyer has a good faith belief that those positions are warranted in existing law or can be supported by a good faith argument for an extension, modification or reversal of existing law. A lawyer can have a good faith belief in this context even if the lawyer believes the client's position probably will not prevail. (Comment to Rule 3.1; *see also* Model Code EC 7-4). However, good faith requires that there be some realistic possibility of success if the matter is litigated. . . .

Thus, where a lawyer has a good faith belief in the validity of a position in accordance with the standard stated above that a particular transaction does not result in taxable income or that certain expenditures are properly deductible as expenses, the lawyer has no duty to require as a condition of his or her continued representation that riders be attached to the client's tax return explaining the circumstances surrounding the transaction or the expenditures.

In the role of advisor, the lawyer should counsel the client as to whether the position is likely to be sustained by a court if challenged by the IRS, as well as of the potential penalty consequences to the client if the position is taken on the tax return without disclosure. Section 6662 of the Internal Revenue Code imposes a penalty for substantial understatement of tax liability which can be avoided if the facts are adequately disclosed or if there is or was substantial authority for the position taken by the taxpayer. Competent representation of the client would require the lawyer to advise the client fully as to whether there is or was substantial authority for the position taken in the tax return. If the lawyer is unable to conclude that the position is supported by substantial authority, the lawyer should advise the client of the penalty the client may suffer and of the opportunity to avoid such penalty by adequately disclosing the facts in the return or in a statement attached to the return. If after receiving such advice the client decides to risk the penalty by making no disclosure and to take the position initially advised by the lawyer in accordance with the standard stated above, the lawyer has met his or her ethical responsibility with respect to the advice. . . .

In summary, a lawyer may advise reporting a position on a return even where the lawyer believes the position probably will not prevail, there is no "substantial authority" in support of the position, and there will be no disclosure of the position in the return. However, the position to be asserted must be one which the lawyer in good faith believes is warranted in existing law or can be supported by a good faith argument for an extension, modification or reversal of existing law. This requires that there is some realistic possibility of success if the matter is litigated. In addition, in his role as advisor, the lawyer should refer to potential penalties and other legal consequences should the client take the position advised.

[B]—Substantial understatement penalty

No one pretends that it is easy to distinguish between "reasonable basis" and "realistic possibility of success," as it was understood in 1985 when the ABA adopted Formal Ethics Opinion 85–352. One possible clue is the concept of "substantial authority" as it relates to the *§ 6662* 20% "substantial understatement" penalty. For individuals, an understatement is "substantial" if the tax shown on the return is less than that required to be shown by the greater of 10% of the required tax or $5,000.

The substantial understatement penalty is imposed when the taxpayer takes a position for which there is no "*substantial authority*," unless the taxpayer "*adequately discloses*" the position and that position has a "*reasonable basis*." *§ 6662(d)*. (In certain cases, referred to as tax shelters, adequate disclosure is insufficient and the taxpayer must also reasonably believe that his position is "more likely than not" correct.) If "substantial authority" equates with "realistic possibility of success," then "reasonable basis" is a more relaxed standard, as had been suggested prior to the issuance of the 1985 ABA Formal Opinion.

However, the meaning of "substantial authority" has undergone some dilution, which might bring it closer to a "reasonable basis" standard. The

Treasury has complied with a 1989 Committee Report calling for the expansion of the authorities which can provide "substantial authority." Previously, "substantial authority" included cases, Regulations, Revenue Rulings, and authoritative committee reports, but now also includes proposed regulations, post-1976 private letter rulings, and the Blue Book (which is an explanation of the law written after its passage by the staff of the Joint Committee on Taxation). *Treas. Reg. § 1.6662-4(d)(3)(iii).*

[C]—Treasury Rules

In 1994, the Treasury issued ethical rules applicable to those who practice before the Treasury. These rules apply not only to lawyers but also to certified public accountants and those who pass a qualifying examination. They are published in Circular 230, 31 Code of Federal Regulations, § 10. The Treasury published regulations updating its ethical standards "to reflect more closely the standards for return preparers under section 6694 of the Internal Revenue Code of 1986 and professional guidelines." *§ 6694* imposes a penalty on income tax preparers who knew or should have known that an understatement of taxpayer liability did not have a realistic possibility of being sustained on the merits. However, disclosure of a questionable position avoids this penalty *if* the position is not frivolous.

Here are some excerpts from Circular 230, § 10.34. How, if at all, do they differ from the ABA rules? Do they shed any light on the relationship between "realistic possibility of success," "reasonable basis," and "substantial authority"?

Standards for advising with respect to tax return positions and for preparing or signing returns.

(a) Standards of conduct—

(1) Realistic possibility standard. A practitioner may not sign a return as a preparer if the practitioner determines that the return contains a position that does not have a realistic possibility of being sustained on its merits (the realistic possibility standard) unless the position is not frivolous and is adequately disclosed to the Service. A practitioner may not advise a client to take a position on a return, or prepare the portion of a return on which a position is taken, unless—

no one really does this option

(i) The practitioner determines that the position satisfies the realistic possibility standard; or

(ii) The position is not frivolous and the practitioner advises the client of any opportunity to avoid the accuracy-related penalty in section 6662 of the Internal Revenue Code of

1986 by adequately disclosing the position and of the requirements for adequate disclosure.

(2) Advising clients on potential penalties. A practitioner advising a client to take a position on a return, or preparing or signing a return as a preparer, must inform the client of the penalties reasonably likely to apply to the client with respect to the position advised, prepared, or reported. The practitioner also must inform the client of any opportunity to avoid any such penalty by disclosure, if relevant, and of the requirements for adequate disclosure. This paragraph (a)(2) applies even if the practitioner is not subject to a penalty with respect to the position.

(3) Relying on information furnished by clients. [omitted]

(4) Definitions. For purposes of this section:

(i) Realistic possibility. A position is considered to have a realistic possibility of being sustained on its merits if a reasonable and well-informed analysis by a person knowledgeable in the tax law would lead such a person to conclude that the position has approximately a one in three, or greater, likelihood of being sustained on its merits. The authorities described in 26 CFR 1.6662-4(d)(3)(iii), or any successor provision, of the substantial understatement penalty regulations may be taken into account for purposes of this analysis. The possibility that a position will not be challenged by the Service (*e.g.*, because the taxpayer's return may not be audited or because the issue may not be raised on audit) may not be taken into account.

(ii) Frivolous. A position is frivolous if it is patently improper.

The 1994 Treasury rules *seem* to equate substantial authority (under the more relaxed post-1989 standard) with a realistic possibility of success, which is itself equated with a "one-third chance of success." If that is true, what authority supports a "reasonable basis," so that "disclosure *plus* reasonable basis" can avoid the "substantial understatement" penalty?

Note also that the Treasury rules allow the tax preparer to meet the required ethical standards whenever the taxpayer's nonfrivolous position is adequately disclosed. This differs from the ABA standard, where disclosure is not an escape hatch. Why is the ABA so reluctant to encourage disclosure, beyond simply telling the client that disclosure can avoid the substantial understatement penalty?

§ 7.04 INTEREST-FREE LOANS

Suppose an employer gives the employee an interest-free $100,000 loan in year 0, repayable in ten years. Does the employee have income? Look at this loan from the employee's point of view. The employee can deposit a small amount in the bank, earn interest for ten years to have enough to repay the $100,000, and pocket the rest of the $100,000 right now. If the interest rate is 20% per year, $16,150 could be deposited at 20% compounded annually, to produce $100,000 in ten years. The remaining $83,850 could be used by the employee for anything he wants; it was in effect salary. *§§ 7872(b),(c)(1)(B)* taxes this transaction in accordance with its economic reality. The salary element ($83,850) would usually be taxable salary to the employee and deductible by the employer. As time passes, original issue discount would accrue to the employer-lender on the $16,150 loan. The lender would be taxed and the employee-borrower would (probably) deduct annually the amount of that interest.

The problem in the real world is to know what interest rate to impute. The Code settles on a semiannual interest rate on these transactions by reference to "the federal rate." *§ 7872(f)(1)(B),(2); § 1274(d).* That is the rate on federal government bonds which have a maturity comparable to the interest-free loan. This will be a lower rate than would normally be charged. Thus, if the federal rate is 12% per year (6% per six months), the present value of the $100,000 loan is $31,180, computed as follows: 100,000/ $(1+.06)^{20}$. Salary in year 0 is therefore $68,820. Original issue discount is taxed semiannually on a $31,180 loan for ten years. The employer reports interest income and the employee (probably) deducts interest during the ten-year period. The first six months' interest, for example, would be $1,870.

You might think that there is no need to bother with these computations because the employer's deduction for salary is offset by the employer's interest income. Similarly, the employee's salary income is offset by an interest deduction. The easiest thing to do, therefore, would be to pay no attention to the interest element in an interest-free loan. But that would be a mistake. First, the timing of the taxable and deductible items does not occur in the same year, unless it is a one-year loan repayable in the same year. In the example of the 10-year loan, the salary is reported in the year of the loan and interest accrues annually over the following 10-year period. Second, it is not always true that salary and interest are deductible when paid. Salary might be a capital expenditure and interest is not always deductible, as later chapters explain.

§ 7.05 PREPAID CONSUMPTION

Suppose the taxpayer prepays for a consumption item. For example, assume that a prepayment in year 0 entitles the purchaser or designated family member to $1,000 tuition due in two years (in year 2). In effect, the taxpayer is lending money to the payee and would expect a discount in the price sufficient to give him a return on his prepayment at the going interest rate. If that rate is 10%, he would pay (lend) \$826.45 $(1000/1.1)^2$ today (in year 0) and earn 10% interest each year. When he received the service in year 2, he would in effect be collecting in year 2 the \$826.45 loan plus interest, totaling \$1,000, and then pay that \$1,000 for the service. The prepayment technique shortcuts the process, avoiding collection and repayment of the \$1,000. In tabular form, the prepayment is equated with an interest-bearing loan as follows:

Year 0	Year 1	Year 2
-\$826.45 (loan = prepayment)	+ \$82.65 (interest)	+ \$90.91 (interest) + \$826.45 (repay loan) − \$1,000 (pay for tuition)

The lender should pay tax on the interest just as he would if he had deposited the money in a bank. If he was in the 31% bracket, he would not have enough left to pay $1,000 for tuition, but no one in the 31% bracket should be able to get personal consumption of $173.56 (the interest total of $82.65 plus $90.91) by earning just $173.56. You are supposed to earn a greater amount of before-tax income to have $173.56 left. The problem in the above example is that the payor is enjoying a tax free 10% return equal to $173.56, which is the difference between the $1,000 personal consumption in year 2 and the $826.45 prepayment in year 0.

Would the statutory rules dealing with interest earned on loans apply to the above example? The commitment to provide a specified dollar value of future services does contain an interest feature. (1) Does the statute deal with this under *§§ 1272–1274*, which applies to original issue discount? *See § 1273(b).* (2) Is any "interest" feature tax exempt under *§ 103,* if the obligor is a state or local government?

Consolidated Edison of New York v. United States, 10 F.3d 68 (2d Cir. 1993), deals with some of these issues. Is the decision correct? The taxpayer prepaid New York City property taxes to help the City during a financial crisis. In one instance it prepaid $50,000,000, and the City provided Con Edison with a receipt for a tax payment of $50,937,814, calculated to provide an 8% discount. The taxpayer excluded the $937,814 from income on the ground that it was tax exempt *§ 103* interest and deducted the full $50,937,814 as an accrued tax debt. The court held that the $937,814 was income, but was not tax exempt interest. It attached controlling weight to the taxpayer's decision to avoid being a creditor, having refused to lend money explicitly to the City because of bankruptcy concerns. The court distinguished the discount in this case from original issue discount, where the discount is given in exchange for an extension of credit. Here, the court said, the prepayment discount given by the City was not given in exchange for an extension of credit, but as consideration for the taxpayer's agreement to prepay its tax liability. The court also allowed the $50,937,814 to be deducted as accrued taxes under *§ 164(a)(1).*

Suppose that the prepayment entitles the payor to free tuition, not fixed at any specific dollar value, sometime in the future. Here is how the IRS dealt with the Michigan prepaid tuition plan.

PRIVATE LETTER RULING 8825027

March 29, 1988

This is in reply to a ruling request, submitted on behalf of State X on the federal tax consequences of a college tuition prepayment program.

FACTS

State X has enacted legislation providing for a state-created corporation (Trust) to implement and administer a college tuition prepayment program. The program provides a choice of two plans for the prepayment of tuition. The substance of these two plans is described below.

Plan 1

Under the plan, A, an individual, makes a current payment to Trust, and in return, Trust contracts to arrange for four years of educational services at a State X public educational institution, or at a private educational institution within State X, for an irrevocably designated beneficiary, B, when B matriculates. The contract provides, however, that upon the occurrence of certain specified events a cash refund of the up-front payment, less and administrative fee, will be made to C, a person irrevocably designated by A at the time the contract is executed. B and C are related to A and the natural objects of A affection. It is represented that under the law of State X a parent is not under a legal obligation to provide a college education.

A cash refund only will be made if (1) B dies, (2) is denied admission to a State X public educational institution, (3) B certifies that he or she has reached the age of 18 and will not attend a college or university, or (4) the tuition prepayment program administered by Trust is determined to be actuarially unsound. Refunds generally will be paid in four equal, annual installments. No refund will be provided if a beneficiary has completed more than one half the credit hours required by a State X educational institution for a bachelor's degree.

Trust is operated autonomously by a board of directors, and the board's decisions, including those involving investment discretion, may not be overridden by any state agency. The board consists of the Treasurer of State X and eight other persons appointed by the Governor of State X and approved by its legislature. The State X enabling legislation provides that funds collected by Trust are not subject to the claims of the creditors of State X and are not considered the money or common cash of State X. State X may not loan, transfer, or use Trust's funds for any purpose. Trust's funds may only be used for the tuition payment or refund purposes expressly provided in the enabling legislation. Income earned and property held by Trust are exempt from taxation under the laws of State X.

Plan 2

The facts are the same as in Plan 1, except that the plan provides for a cash refund that may be substantially in excess of A's up-front payment. The amount of the excess will be determined by an index tied to the increase in tuition costs of various State X institutions of higher education. The beneficiary may also attend an out-of-state educational institution for which State X will make a payment based on the same index as the refund computation.

ISSUES

1. Is the excess of the fair market value of the educational services (or the cash refund) when received under the contract over the payment for the contract includible in the gross income of the beneficiary, B (or the refund designee, C), under section 61 of the Internal Revenue Code?

2. Is the income of Trust, earned during the administration of the program, excludable from gross income as income earned by an integral part of State X or as income derived from the exercise of an essential governmental function that accrues to a state under section 115 of the Code?

LAW, RATIONALE AND CONCLUSIONS
(Plan 1 and Plan 2)

Issue 1

Section 61 of the Code provides that gross income means all income from whatever source derived. Section 1.61-1 of the Income Tax Regulations, in part, provides that gross income includes income realized in any form, whether in money, property, or services. Gross income can be realized in the form of the receipt of educational services. *See Fulton v. Commissioner*, T.C.M. 1983-17.

Gross income is defined to encompass all "accessions to wealth, clearly realized, and over which the taxpayers have complete dominion." *Commissioner v. Glenshaw Glass Co.*, 348 U.S. 426, 431 (1955), 1955-1 C.B. 207, 209. Property rights will not become gross income subject to taxation until a gain is clearly realized. *Eisner v. Macomber*, 252 U.S. 189 (1920), 3 C.B. 25.

Section 102 of the Code provides that gross income does not include the value of property acquired by gift. A transfer of property is excludable from income by the recipient as a gift if the property is transferred out of a detached and disinterested generosity. *Commissioner v. Duberstein*, 363 U.S. 278 (1960), 1060-2 C.B. 428.

When A executes the contract with Trust and designates B and C, both B and C realize an accession to wealth. Because the contract rights (property) are transferred out of a detached and disinterested generosity, however, the transfer constitutes a gift for income tax purposes and is thus excludable from B's and C's gross income. *See* § 102 and *Duberstein.* Neither A nor B nor C will be considered actually or constructively to be in receipt of income at the time the contract is entered into between A and the Trust.

Although the receipt of property by B and C is excludable from their gross income under § 102, that section has no application to income (including gain) realized from such property subsequent to its receipt. *See* § 1.102-1(a) of the regulations. Thus, to the extent that the fair market value of the educational services received by B, or any cash refund received by C, under the contract exceeds B's or C's basis in the property received by gift from A, either B or C will realize a further accession to wealth and thus gross income. Neither A nor B nor C, however, will be considered actually or constructively to be in receipt of income at any time between the date on which the contract is purchased by A and the date on which either B receives education services or C receives a cash refund. A will not be considered actually or constructively to be in receipt of income when either B receives educational services or C receives a cash refund. Accordingly, A will not realize income as a result of his or her involvement in the program as the purchaser of a contract. (If A designates himself or herself as the beneficiary of the educational services or the cash refund, then the income tax consequences to A will be the same as the consequences to B or C.)

To determine the amount of gross income realized by either B or C, the basis in the property must be determined.

Section 1012 of the Code provides that generally the basis of property shall be the cost of such property.

Section 1015(a) of the code provides that generally the basis of property acquired by gift is the same as it would be in the hands of the donor (a substituted basis).

B's basis in the property is the substituted basis of A, which is A's cost of (payment for) that contract. Because the State X tuition prepayment program is generally designed to provide for educational services over a four-year period, B's basis must be recovered annually over the four-year period during which B receives educational services. *See* § 1.61-6 of the regulations. Thus, when Trust provides educational services for B at the beginning of a school year, B must recognize income to the extent that the fair market value of the educational services to be received for that school year exceeds one quarter of B's basis.

If a refund is received by C, C will realize gross income to the extent that the amount refunded exceeds the allocable portion of C's basis. C's basis in the property is the substituted basis of A. Thus, assuming a one-year tuition installment is refunded to C, then one quarter of C's substituted basis is subtracted from such refund to determine the amount of the refund includible in C's gross income.

Issue 2

Income earned by an integral part of a state or a political subdivision of a state is generally not taxable in the absence of specific statutory authority for taxing such income. *See* Rev. Rul. 87-2, 1987-2 I.R.B. 4, holding that a trust account fund created, supervised, and controlled by a state Supreme Court is an integral part of a state and is therefore not subject to federal income tax.

Trust was created as a corporation to operate independently from State X under an appointed board of directors. Decisions by Trust's board of directors, including those involving investment discretion, may not be overridden by any state agency. Trust's funds are not derived from State X or one of its political subdivisions, and by statute are not subject to the claims of State X creditors and are not considered state money or common cash of the state. State X may not loan, transfer, or use Trust's funds for any purpose. Trust's funds may only be used by Trust for the tuition payment or refund purposes expressly provided in the enabling legislation. These factors indicate that Trust is not an integral part of State X or one of its political subdivisions. Therefore, Trust's income, unless otherwise excluded by statute, is subject to federal income tax.

Section 115(1) of the Code provides, in part, that gross income does not include income derived from the exercise of any essential governmental function that accrues to a state or any political subdivision of a state.

To qualify under § 115, it must be established that the income does not serve private interests such as designated individuals, shareholders of organizations, or persons controlled, directly or indirectly, by such private interests. Thus, even if the income serves a public interest, the requirements of § 115 are not satisfied if the income also serves a private interest that is not incidental to the public interest. The basic principle underlying § 115 is that property (including any income thereon) must be devoted to purposes which are considered beneficial to the community in general, rather than particular individuals.

Trust provides B with a direct economic benefit in the form of education the value of which is expected to be substantially in excess of the up-front payment. Moreover, this benefit is available only to those persons such as B who are beneficiaries of a contract. Thus, the requirements of § 115 are not satisfied and the income of Trust, earned during administration of the program, is not excludable from its gross income. However, payments made under the contract entered into between A and Trust, and any contributions that State X might make to Trust, are excludable from the gross income of Trust.

QUESTIONS AND COMMENTS

1. **Payee university.** Suppose the prepayment for tuition was directly to the service provider (not a trust) — either a state or private university, which agreed to provide free tuition to anyone designated by the prepayor. Is anyone taxed on the investment income earned by the prepaid amount, either annually or when the free tuition is provided?

2. **Payee trust.** In *State of Michigan v. United States*, 40 F.3d 817 (6th Cir. 1994), *rev'g* 802 F. Supp. 120 (D.C. Mich. 1992), the court held that the Michigan Trust in the letter ruling was *not* taxable. This result increases the trust's financial ability to fund its obligations. The income accruing on the investment would not be double-taxed — once when earned by the trust and again when the educational services are provided. This is the same tax result as in situations where the investor makes a prepayment directly to the university for future education services.

The court relied on a principle of law which no one disputed — that no income tax is imposed unless the law imposes tax on the entity in question. The relevant section is *§ 11*, which taxes corporations, and (as the court noted) "this section has never been interpreted as imposing a tax on income earned directly by a state, a political subdivision of a state, or 'an integral part of a State.' " Examples included the following: *Rev. Rul. 71–131*, 1971–1 C. B. 28 (income derived from the operation of liquor stores by the State of Montana is not subject to federal income tax); *Rev. Rul. 87–2*, 1987–1 C. B. 18 (exempting income earned by a Lawyer Trust

Account Fund created by a state supreme court with client funds held by attorneys in a fiduciary capacity, when fund used for public purposes; "Fund is an integral part of the state").

The court adopted a principle of statutory construction "requiring that before a federal tax can be applied to activities carried on directly by the States . . . , the intention of Congress to tax them should be stated expressly and not drawn merely from general wording of the statute applicable ordinarily to private sources of revenue." *State of New York v. United States*, 326 U.S. at 585 (Rutledge, J., concurring). It gave as an example of an express taxing provision *§ 511(a)(2)(B)*, which taxes the unrelated business income "of any college or university which is an agency or instrumentality of any government or any political subdivision thereof, or which is owned or operated by a government or any political subdivision thereof, or by any agency or instrumentality of one or more governments or political subdivisions."

Further litigation about this issue will not occur. A new *§ 529*, adopted in 1996 and amended in 1997, ends the litigation about state educational trusts by explicitly making "qualified state tuition programs," such as the Michigan trust, tax exempt. To qualify, the program must provide a separate accounting for each designated beneficiary and, in general, impose more than a *de minimis* penalty on any refunds which are not used for the beneficiary's education or are not paid on account of the beneficiary's death or disability.

One consequence of this statutory rule is that privately-run trusts are at a tax disadvantage, because they are not tax exempt entities, and would be taxed on the investment income they receive when they invest the prepaid tuition payments.

The 1996 law also explicitly adopts the method of taxing the beneficiary explained in the letter ruling — allocate the basis (that is, cost) over the tuition pay-out period. *§ 529(c)(1),(3)*. This result is specified in the Code by the reference to the method of taxation provided by *§ 72* (which is the method provided for annuities). Annuity taxation is discussed in § 11.01[C], *infra*.

3. **Financial concerns.** Of course, the taxpayer who invests in the Michigan trust is not concerned only with taxes. He is making a financial investment which may be advantageous or not, depending on how high tuition goes up in future years. Even if the tax rules did not favor the investment in the Michigan trust, the *financial* advantage of insuring against rising tuition might be very favorable.

Will the Michigan trust be able to pay tuition or will it go bankrupt? Suppose people stop prepaying tuition five years from now so the trust only has available the investment and income earned thereon to pay future tuition. Can it meet its obligations in year 15? This is the same problem faced by the United States Social Security fund, which relies on new contributions by young workers to pay retirees.

CHAPTER 8

DEDUCTIONS FROM INCOME

§ 8.01 INTRODUCTION

§ 162. The other side of the gross income coin is a deduction. The most important section is *§ 162*, authorizing a deduction for business expenses. If you think income equals personal consumption plus savings, then the deduction for business expenses is an essential feature of the law — business expenses do not provide personal consumption. *§§ 62, 63* deal with whether deductions otherwise allowed are deductible in computing adjusted gross income or taxable income.

§ 212. Another important section is *§ 212(1),(2)*. It was passed after the Supreme Court held that investors were not entitled to business deductions, even though engaged in an income producing activity. *Higgins v. Commissioner,* 312 U.S. 212 (1941). This section expands the kinds of activities taxed on a net income basis.

Itemized deductions. In most cases, a *§ 212* expense is an itemized deduction (replaceable by the standard deduction), and is also subject to the 2% floor on computing deductible itemized deductions. By contrast, most business expenses are "above-the-line," deductible in going from gross to adjusted gross income (except for unreimbursed employee business expenses). Consequently, taxpayers want activities to be business rather than investment activities. *See Groetzinger v. Commissioner*, 480 U.S. 23 (1987) (professional gambler entitled to "above-the-line deductions").

Why are *§ 212* expenses usually treated less generously than business expenses? Are they small and hard to audit? Are they more likely to be personal expenses? *See § 274(h)(7)* (expenses to attend investment seminars are not deductible at all).

The fact that most unreimbursed employee business expenses are itemized deductions creates enormous pressure to finds ways to decide in favor of the employee when the amounts are large. What do you think of the reasoning in *Beatty v. Commissioner*, 106 T.C. 268 (1996)? A sheriff received $31,000 salary and per diem prisoner meal allowances of $110,000. The sheriff could keep any amount of the per diem allowance not spent for prisoner meals. Is the amount spent on prisoner meals (1) a reduction in computing gross income, (2) a deduction in computing adjusted gross income, or (3) an itemized employee business expense deduction? The taxpayer argued that the provision of meals was a separate non-employee trade or business, in which case the prisoner meal expenses were deductible in computing adjusted gross income, reducing the $110,000 per diem allowance included in his gross income. The court took a different route in finding for the taxpayer. Recall that if a taxpayer has a cost in an asset (*e.g.*, a house), that cost is deducted from the gross proceeds of a sale to determine gross income. The same principle applies to a taxpayer who sells inventory — the costs of the inventory (cost of goods sold) is a cost which reduces the gross proceeds from inventory sales to compute gross income. The Tax Court in *Beatty* held that the costs of the meals for prisoners was a cost of goods sold, reducing the $110,000 in computing gross income.

gen. rule

reduce in computing GI → like sale of inventory

Notice that this result avoids opening the flood gates for employees to argue that some of their activities are nonemployee businesses, but still lets a huge expenditure be deducted by the employee. That seems fair, since the itemized deduction status for employee expenses was meant to prevent deductions for small expenses. But how can the court seriously suggest that the meals were "goods sold"? Who bought them?

"Ordinary and necessary." In this chapter we pay no attention to the words "ordinary and necessary" in *§§ 162(a), 212* because (as a later chapter explains) their statutory meaning is not their colloquial meaning and they rarely operate as a limitation on deductions.

Exclusion vs. deduction. The limits on itemized deductions highlight not only the difference between above-the-line and below-the-line deductions, but also the difference between exclusions from income and below-the-line deductions. For example, an exclusion under *§ 119* (meals and lodging for the convenience of the employer) is usually better than including the fringe benefit in income and deducting it as an itemized deduction.

Exclusions raise a broader question than the mechanics of above-and below-the-line deductions. Is it ever sensible to allow an exclusion for benefits provided to a taxpayer (by an employer, for example) under circumstances where the taxpayer is not allowed to take the deduction as a *§ 162* business expense? That question is not about the mechanics of computing deductibility. It is about the underlying conception of income. Is something less deserving of inclusion in the tax base when it is provided as an in-kind benefit?

Sometimes the answer seems to be "yes." The exclusion of part of the cost of the steamship ticket prize in *Turner* rested on the lack of complete dominion (or choice) that accompanies in-kind benefits. Certainly, the price of a freely purchased steamship ticket would not have been partially deductible. And many fringe benefits excluded under *§§ 119 & 132* would not have deductible if purchased by the employee. You should watch throughout this chapter for examples where a deduction might be disallowed (not just replaced by a standard deduction or subject to a 2% floor), but an in-kind benefit for the same item might be excluded. If that happens, ask yourself why. Is it because the benefit is less likely to be *§ 61* income; is the exclusion justified by social policy?

Recall that, in one situation, the statute explicitly conforms exclusion to deductibility — the exclusion of "working condition" fringes under *§ 132(a)(3),(d).*

§ 8.02 DEFINING DEDUCTIBLE BUSINESS EXPENSES

Most deductible business-related expenditures are easy to identify — e.g., salary, rent, and purchase price of raw materials used to make inventory. Some of these outlays might be "costs" rather than "expenses," and their deduction deferred until a later year (*see* Chapter 13), but the business connection is obvious. That connection is not so obvious, however, when the expense might provide personal consumption. The line between business and personal expenses is therefore the focus of this chapter.

[A]—Two Cases

SMITH v. COMMISSIONER

40 B.T.A. 1038 (1939),
aff'd per curiam, 113 F.2d 114 (2d Cir. 1940)

OPPER, JUDGE:

Respondent determined a deficiency of $23.62 in petitioner's 1937 income tax. This was due to the disallowance of a deduction claimed by petitioners, who are husband and wife, for sums spent by the wife in employing nursemaids to care for petitioners' young child, the wife, as well as the husband, being employed. The facts have all been stipulated and are hereby found accordingly.

Petitioners would have us apply the "but for" test. They propose that but for the nurses the wife could not leave her child; but for the freedom so secured she could not pursue her gainful labors; and but for them there would be no income and no tax. This thought evokes an array of interesting possibilities. The fee to the doctor, but for whose healing service the earner of the family income could not leave his sickbed; the cost of the laborer's raiment, for how can the world proceed about its business unclothed; the very home which gives us shelter and rest and the food which provides energy, might all by an extension of the same proposition be construed as necessary to the operation of business and to the creation of income. Yet these are the very essence of those "personal" expenses the deductibility of which is expressly denied.

We are told that the working wife is a new phenomenon. This is relied on to account for the apparent inconsistency that the expenses in issue are now a commonplace, yet have not been the subject of legislation, ruling, or adjudicated controversy. But if that is true it becomes all the more necessary to apply accepted principles to the novel facts. We are not prepared to say that the care of children, like similar aspects of family and household life, is other than a personal concern. The wife's services as custodian of the home and protector of its children are ordinarily rendered without monetary compensation. There results no taxable income from the performance of this service and the correlative expenditure is personal and not susceptible of deduction. Here the wife has chosen to employ others to discharge her domestic function and the services she performs are rendered outside the home. They are a source of actual income and taxable as such. But that does not deprive the same work performed by others of its personal character nor furnish a reason why its cost should be treated as an offset in the guise of a deductible item.

We are not unmindful that, as petitioners suggest, certain disbursements normally personal may become deductible by reason of their intimate connection with an occupation carried on for profit. In this category fall entertainment, and traveling expenses, and the cost of an actor's wardrobe. The line is not always an easy one to draw nor the test simple to apply. But we think its principle is clear. It may for practical purposes be said to constitute a distinction between those activities which, as a matter of common acceptance and universal experience, are "ordinary" or usual as the direct accompaniment of business pursuits, on the one hand; and those which, though they may in some indirect and tenuous degree relate to the circumstances of a profitable occupation, are nevertheless personal in their nature, of a character applicable to human beings generally, and which exist on that plane regardless of the occupation, though not necessarily of the station in life, of the individuals concerned.

In the latter category, we think, fall payments made to servants or others occupied in looking to the personal wants of their employers. And we include in this group nursemaids retained to care for infant children.

Decision will be entered for the respondent.

PEVSNER v. COMMISSIONER *(TP loses)*

628 F.2d 467 (5th Cir. 1980)
rev'g 38 T.C.M. 1210 (1979)

no DD because
pers. exp. → failed
part ② of test
→ objective std.

SAM D. JOHNSON, CIRCUIT JUDGE:

TP = mgr. of YSL store

Since June 1973 Sandra J. Pevsner, taxpayer, has been employed as the manager of the Sakowitz Yves St. Laurent Rive Gauche Boutique located in Dallas, Texas. The boutique sells only women's clothes and accessories designed by Yves St. Laurent (YSL), one of the leading designers of women's apparel. Although the clothing is ready to wear, it is highly fashionable and expensively priced. Some customers of the boutique purchase and wear the YSL apparel for their daily activities and spend as much as $20,000 per year for such apparel.

TP has to wear YSL clothes @ work

As manager of the boutique, the taxpayer is expected by her employer to wear YSL clothes while at work. In her appearance, she is expected to project the image of an exclusive lifestyle and to demonstrate to her customers that she is aware of the YSL current fashion trends as well as trends generally. Because the boutique sells YSL clothes exclusively, taxpayer must be able, when a customer compliments her on her clothes, to say that they are designed by YSL. In addition to wearing YSL apparel while at the boutique, she wears them while commuting to and from work, to fashion shows sponsored by the boutique, and to business luncheons at which she represents the boutique. During 1975, the taxpayer bought, at an employee's discount, the following items: four blouses, three skirts, one pair of slacks, one trench coat, two sweaters, one jacket, one tunic, five scarves, six belts, two pairs of shoes and four necklaces. The total cost of this apparel was $1,381.91. In addition, the sum of $240 was expended for maintenance of these items.

cost of clothes

Although the clothing and accessories purchased by the taxpayer were the type used for general purposes by the regular customers of the boutique, the taxpayer is not a normal purchaser of these clothes. The taxpayer and her husband, who is partially disabled because of a severe heart attack suffered in 1971, lead a simple life and their social activities are very limited and informal. Although taxpayer's employer has no objection to her wearing the apparel away from work, taxpayer stated that she did not wear the clothes during off-work hours because she felt that they were too expensive for her simple everyday lifestyle. Another reason why she did not wear the YSL clothes apart from work was to make them last longer. Taxpayer did admit at trial, however, that a number of the articles were things she could have worn off the job and in which she would have looked "nice." . . .

TP has simple life style → only wore clothes for work

The principal issue on appeal is whether the taxpayer is entitled to deduct as an ordinary and necessary business expense the cost of purchasing and maintaining the YSL clothes and accessories worn by the taxpayer in her employment as the manager of the boutique. This determination requires an examination of the relationship between Section 162(a) of the Internal Revenue Code of 1954, which allows a deduction for ordinary and necessary expenses incurred in the conduct of a trade or business, and Section 262 of the Code, which bars a deduction for all "personal, living, or family expenses." Although many expenses are helpful or essential to one's business activities — such as commuting expenses and the cost of meals while at work — these expenditures are considered inherently personal and are disallowed under Section 262. *See, e.g., United States v. Correll*, 389 U.S. 299 (1967); *Commissioner v. Flowers*, 326 U.S. 465 (1946).

The generally accepted rule governing the deductibility of clothing expenses is that the cost of clothing is deductible as a business expense only if: (1) the clothing is of a type specifically required as a condition of employment, (2) it is not adaptable to general usage as ordinary clothing, and (3) it is not so worn.

In the present case, the Commissioner stipulated that the taxpayer was required by her employer to wear YSL clothing and that she did not wear such apparel apart from work. The Commissioner maintained, however, that a deduction should be denied because the YSL clothes and accessories purchased by the taxpayer were adaptable for general usage as ordinary clothing and she was not prohibited from using them as such. The tax court, in rejecting the Commissioner's argument for the application of an objective test, recognized that the test for deductibility was whether the clothing was "suitable for general or personal wear" but determined that the matter of suitability was to be judged subjectively, in light of the taxpayer's lifestyle. Although the court recognized that the YSL apparel "might be used by some members of society for general purposes," it felt that because the "wearing of YSL apparel outside work would be inconsistent with . . . (taxpayer's) lifestyle," sufficient reason was shown for allowing a deduction for the clothing expenditures. . . .

. . . [T]he Circuits that have addressed the issue have taken an objective, rather than subjective, approach. . . . Under an objective test, no reference is made to the individual taxpayer's lifestyle or personal taste. Instead, adaptability for personal or general use depends upon what is generally accepted for ordinary street wear.

The principal argument in support of an objective test is, of course, administrative necessity. The Commissioner argues that, as a practical matter, it is virtually impossible to determine at what point either price or style makes clothing inconsistent with or inappropriate to a taxpayer's lifestyle. Moreover, the Commissioner argues that the price one pays and the styles one selects are inherently personal choices governed by taste, fashion, and other unmeasurable values. Indeed, the tax court has rejected the argument that a taxpayer's personal taste can dictate whether clothing is appropriate for general use. An objective test, although not perfect, provides a practical administrative approach that allows a taxpayer or revenue agent to look only to objective facts in determining whether clothing required as a condition of employment is adaptable to general use as ordinary streetwear. Conversely, the tax court's reliance on subjective factors provides no concrete guidelines in determining the deductibility of clothing purchased as a condition of employment.

In addition to achieving a practical administrative result, an objective test also tends to promote substantial fairness among the greatest number of taxpayers. As the Commissioner suggests, it apparently would be the tax court's position that two similarly situated YSL boutique managers with identical wardrobes would be subject to disparate tax consequences depending upon the particular manager's lifestyle and "socio-economic level." This result, however, is not consonant with a reasonable interpretation of Sections 162 and 262.

For the reasons stated above, the decision of the tax court upholding the deduction for taxpayer's purchase of YSL clothing is reversed. Consequently, the portion of the tax court's decision upholding the deduction for maintenance costs for the clothing is also reversed.

[B]—"But For" tests

1. If a taxpayer says that "but for" clothes or health she *could* not work, your response is likely to be that the statement is true but that it misses the point. The point is that the taxpayer would have spent the money anyway, whether or not she worked. In the language of the court in *Pevsner*, these expenses are "inherently personal." This is just one version of the "but for" test, however.

2. If the taxpayer offers to prove that "but for" work, she *would* not have incurred the expense, she is making a different argument. The claim is that the work makes the expense necessary, not that the expense is necessary for work. This is what the taxpayer argued in *Pevsner*. So the issue is when can a taxpayer deduct expenses by proving that, "but for" work, she would not make the expenditure.

The Court of Appeals in *Pevsner* adopted an objective test to discourage deduction of work clothing. Is an objective test justified because most taxpayers who buy clothes for work which are adaptable for personal use actually wear them on their own time; or because the extra amount spent on work clothing, which is adaptable for personal use, is usually small (after all, some clothing would have to be purchased whether or not the taxpayer worked)? Would you approve of a rule which allowed the taxpayer to deduct the *extra* cost of work clothing over what clothes for personal use would have cost during working hours, if the taxpayer did not work?

Question. How is the employee taxed (a) if the employer in *Pevsner* had given the clothing to the employee (would *§ 132(a)(3),(d)* apply); (b) if the employer had forbidden her from wearing the clothes off duty; (c) if the employer had taken the clothes back after work each day?

[C]—Origin test

There is yet another argument against the "but for" test, of which the *Smith* case (child care) is probably an example. Even if we admit that extra expenses would not be incurred but for work, shouldn't the origin of the expense in the personal decision by the taxpayer to have children characterize the expense as personal for tax purposes? The child care expenses "originate" with having children, not working. The best known statement of the "origin" test is in the *Gilmore* case, *infra*, where the taxpayer claimed a deduction for legal fees paid to defend against a divorce action brought by his wife. The taxpayer claimed to be protecting his property and livelihood that was put in jeopardy by the divorce action. The deduction was claimed under an earlier 1939 Code version of *§ 212*, which was *§ 23(a)(2)*. Does the origin test developed in *Gilmore* explain the disallowance of child care expenses in *Smith*?

UNITED STATES v. GILMORE

372 U.S. 39 (1963)

MR. JUSTICE HARLAN delivered the opinion of the Court. . . .

At the time of the divorce proceedings, instituted by the wife but in which the husband also cross-claimed for divorce, respondent's property consisted primarily of controlling stock interests in three corporations, each of which was a franchised General Motors automobile dealer. As president and principal managing officer of the three corporations, he received salaries from them aggregating about $66,800 annually, and in recent years his total annual dividends had averaged about $83,000. His total annual income derived from the corporations was thus approximately $150,000. His income from other sources was negligible.

As found by the Court of Claims, the husband's overriding concern in the divorce litigation was to protect these assets against the claims of his wife. Those claims had two aspects: first, that the earnings accumulated and retained by these three corporations during the Gilmores' marriage (representing an aggregate increase in corporate net worth of some $600,000) were the product of respondent's personal services, and not the to that extent

result of accretion in capital values, thus rendering respondent's stockholdings in the enterprises pro tanto community property under California law; second, that to the extent that such stockholdings were community property, the wife, allegedly the innocent party in the divorce proceeding, was entitled under California law to more than a one-half interest in such property.

2
wife gets 50+%

The respondent wished to defeat those claims for two important reasons. First, the loss of his controlling stock interests, particularly in the event of their transfer in substantial part to his hostile wife, might well cost him the loss of his corporate positions, his principal means of livelihood. Second, there was also danger that if he were found guilty of his wife's sensational and reputation-damaging charges of marital infidelity, General Motors Corporation might find it expedient to exercise its right to cancel these dealer franchises.

hubbie to want to defeat claims because ① + ②

The end result of this bitterly fought divorce case was a complete victory for the husband. He, not the wife, was granted a divorce on his cross-claim; the wife's community property claims were denied in their entirety; and she was held entitled to no alimony.

Hub. wins

Respondent's legal expenses in connection with this litigation amounted to $32,537.15 in 1953 and $8,074.21 in 1954 — a total of $40,611.36 for the two taxable years in question. The Commissioner of Internal Revenue found all of these expenditures "personal" or "family" expenses and as such none of them deductible. . . .

his legal fees

I. *are legal fees for divorce here pers'l or bus'n?*

For income tax purposes Congress has seen fit to regard an individual as having two personalities: "one is (as) a seeker after profit who can deduct the expenses incurred in that search; the other is (as) a creature satisfying his needs as a human and those of his family but who cannot deduct such consumption and related expenditures." The Government regards [§ 212] as embodying a category of the expenses embraced in the first of these roles.

→ DDs OK

Initially, it may be observed that the wording of [§ 212] more readily fits the Government's view of the provision than that of the Court of Claims. For in context "conservation of property" seems to refer to operations performed with respect to the property itself, such as safeguarding or upkeep, rather than to a taxpayer's retention of ownership in it. But more illuminating than the mere language of [the statute] is the history of the provision.

Prior to 1942 [the statute] allowed deductions only for expenses incurred "in carrying on any trade or business," the deduction presently authorized by [§ 162]. In *Higgins v. Commissioner*, 312 U.S. 212, this Court gave that provision a narrow construction, holding that the activities of an individual

Higgins

in supervising his own securities investments did not constitute the "carrying on of trade or business," and hence that expenses incurred in connection with such activities were not tax deductible. . . . The Revenue Act of 1942, by adding what is now [§ 212], sought to remedy the inequity inherent in the disallowance of expense deductions in respect of such profit-seeking activities, the income from which was nonetheless taxable.

As noted in *McDonald v. Commissioner*, 323 U.S. 57, 62, the purpose of the 1942 amendment was merely to enlarge "the category of incomes with reference to which expenses were deductible." And committee reports make clear that deductions under the new section were subject to the same limitations and restrictions that are applicable to those allowable under [§ 162]. . . .

A basic restriction upon the availability of a [§ 162] deduction is that the expense item involved must be one that has a business origin. That restriction not only inheres in the language of [the statute] itself, confining such deductions to "expenses . . . incurred . . . in carrying on any trade or business," but also follows from [§ 262], expressly rendering nondeductible "in any case (p)ersonal, living, or family expenses." In light of what has already been said with respect to the advent and thrust of [§ 212], it is clear that the "(p)ersonal . . . or family expenses" restriction of [§ 262] must impose the same limitation upon the reach of [§ 212] — in other words that the only kind of expenses deductible under [§ 212] are those that relate to a "business," that is, profit-seeking, purpose. The pivotal issue in this case then becomes: was this part of respondent's litigation costs a "business" rather than a "personal" or "family" expense?

The answer to this question has already been indicated in prior cases. In *Lykes v. United States*, 343 U.S. 118, the Court rejected the contention that legal expenses incurred in contesting the assessment of a gift tax liability were deductible. The taxpayer argued that if he had been required to pay the original deficiency he would have been forced to liquidate his stockholdings, which were his main source of income, and that his legal expenses were therefore incurred in the "conservation" of income-producing property and hence deductible under [§ 212(2)]. The Court first noted that the "deductibility (of the expenses) turns wholly upon the nature of the activities to which they relate," and then stated:

> Legal expenses do not become deductible merely because they are paid for services which relieve a taxpayer of liability. That argument would carry us too far. It would mean that the expense of defending almost any claim would be deductible by a taxpayer on the ground that such defense was made to help him keep clear of liens whatever income-producing property he might have. For example, it suggests that the expense of defending an action based upon personal injuries caused by a taxpayer's

negligence while driving an automobile for pleasure should be deductible. Section [212] never has been so interpreted by us. . . .

While the threatened deficiency assessment . . . added urgency to petitioner's resistance of it, neither its size nor its urgency determined its character. It related to the tax payable on petitioner's gifts. . . . The expense of contesting the amount of the deficiency was thus at all times attributable to the gifts, as such, and accordingly was not deductible.

If, as suggested, the relative size of each claim, in proportion to the income-producing resources of a defendant, were to be a touchstone of the deductibility of the expense of resisting the claim, substantial uncertainty and inequity would inhere in the rule. . . . It is not a ground for (deduction) that the claim, if justified, will consume income-producing property of the defendant.

In *Kornhauser v. United States*, 276 U.S. 145, this Court considered the deductibility of legal expenses incurred by a taxpayer in defending against a claim by a former business partner that fees paid to the taxpayer were for services rendered during the existence of the partnership. In holding that these expenses were deductible even though the taxpayer was no longer a partner at the time of suit, the Court formulated the rule that "where a suit or action against a taxpayer is directly connected with, or . . . proximately resulted from, his business, the expense incurred is a business expense. . . ." Similarly, in a case involving an expense incurred in satisfying an obligation (though not a litigation expense), it was said that "it is the origin of the liability out of which the expense accrues" or "the kind of transaction out of which the obligation arose . . . which (is) crucial and controlling."

The principle we derive from these cases is that the characterization, as "business" or "personal," of the litigation costs of resisting a claim depends on whether or not the claim *arises in connection with the* taxpayer's profit-seeking activities. It does not depend on the *consequences* that might result to a taxpayer's income-producing property from a failure to defeat the claim, for, as *Lykes* teaches, that "would carry us too far" and would not be compatible with the basic lines of expense deductibility drawn by Congress. Moreover, such a rule would lead to capricious results. If two taxpayers are each sued for an automobile accident while driving for pleasure, deductibility of their litigation costs would turn on the mere circumstance of the character of the assets each happened to possess, that is, whether the judgments against them stood to be satisfied out of income-or non-income-producing property. We should be slow to attribute to Congress a purpose producing such unequal treatment among taxpayers, resting on no rational foundation.

Confirmation of these conclusions is found in the incongruities that would follow from acceptance of the Court of Claims' reasoning in this case. Had this respondent taxpayer conducted his automobile-dealer business as a sole proprietorship, rather than in corporate form, and claimed a deduction under [§ 162], the potential impact of his wife's claims would have been no different than in the present situation. Yet it cannot well be supposed that [§ 162] would have afforded him a deduction, since his expenditures, made in connection with a marital litigation, could hardly be deemed "expenses . . . incurred . . . in carrying on any trade or business." Thus, under the Court of Claims' view expenses may be even less deductible if the taxpayer is carrying on a trade or business instead of some other income-producing activity. But it was manifestly Congress' purpose with respect to deductibility to place all income-producing activities on an equal footing. And it would surely be a surprising result were it now to turn out that a change designed to achieve equality of treatment in fact had served only to reverse the inequality of treatment.

For these reasons, we resolve the conflict among the lower courts on the question before us in favor of the view that the origin and character of the claim with respect to which an expense was incurred, rather than its potential consequences upon the fortunes of the taxpayer, is the controlling basic test of whether the expense was "business" or "personal" and hence whether it is deductible or not under [§ 212]. We find the reasoning underlying the cases taking the "consequences" view unpersuasive.

QUESTIONS

How would the following cases be decided under the origin test?

1. A spouse claims a deduction under *§ 212(1)* for attorney's fees to obtain alimony. *Wild v. Commissioner*, 42 T.C. 706 (1964).

2. A lawyer incurs legal expenses to prevent disbarment based on incompetence to handle money, as evidenced by bouncing checks to buy personal consumption.

3. A dancer accused of being a Communist incurs legal expenses in a libel action to preserve his reputation and permit him to obtain work. *Draper v. Commissioner*, 26 T.C. 201 (1956).

4. An individual employer incurs legal expenses to defend against a charge of sexual harassment in the work place. Are these expenses nondeductible because they have a personal origin? Or does the fact that the activity becomes actionable *because* of the work environment make the expenses deductible? What if the lawsuit alleges both a state law battery and a federal cause of action for gender discrimination in the work place?

§ 8.03 DEPENDENT CARE

Child care expenses have become too important to leave to rules about deducting business expenses. The statute now provides a tax credit for a percentage of expenses to care for a "qualifying individual" (typically a dependent child under age 13 or a disabled dependent relative). Household care expenses are also included if they are in part for care of a qualifying individual. *Treas. Reg. § 1.44A-1(c)(2). See § 21(b)(2)(A).* The expenses to which the credit percentage is applied cannot exceed the lesser of (1) the earnings of the lesser-earning spouse (*§ 21(d)(1)(B)*), or (2) a specific dollar ceiling which varies with the number of children (*§ 21(c)*).

Part-time workers and full-time students can use the credit. Students are presumed to earn income so that they can satisfy the requirement that creditable expenses not exceed earnings of the lesser-earning spouse. *§ 21(d)(2).*

QUESTIONS AND COMMENTS

1. Why does the law provide a credit instead of a deduction?

2. How much credit does the following family receive?

a. The husband earns $15,000. The wife is a full-time student for nine months of the year. The have one child, age 3, whom they support. They pay $3,000 during the nine-month period for a babysitter who also cleans the house during the days when the wife is at school.

b. Would your answer be different: (i) if the wife was not a student but earned $5,000 in part-time afternoon work, and paid the baby sitter $3,000 for working all day; or (ii) if the wife earned $3,000 at a full-time job to pay the babysitter $3,000?

3. Is the credit a tax expenditure or an effort to correct the *Smith* case's denial of a business expense deduction?

4. The taxpayer took her child out of public school and sent him to private school so that she could work. While in public school, the threat of school violence had been so great that the taxpayer had to remain at home so that she could pick up her child from school on short notice. Is the taxpayer allowed a credit for the private school expenses? Should the court use a subjective "but for" test — but for work, she would not incur the expense? Would a "but for" test permit a credit if work were just one motive or only if it were the dominant motive for the private school expenses? *Brown v. Commissioner*, 73 T.C. 156 (1979).

5. If the employer pays for child care or runs a child care center at work, is the value of the child care included in income and a credit taken in accordance with the rules of *§ 21*? *See § 129*, which permits the exclusion from income of benefits provided by an employer-funded child care plan, up to $5,000 per year. If the plan favors highly compensated employees, those employees are not entitled to the *§ 129* exclusion. The excluded benefit reduces the dollar ceiling on employment-related expenses eligible for the child care credit. *§ 21(c)(final paragraph).*

6. **Child care in Canada**. Canada recently revisited the question of deducting child care expenses as a business deduction in *Symes v. Canada,* [1993] 4 S.C.R. 695, [1994] 1 C.T.C. 40. A seven-to-two majority denied a business expense deduction to a law firm partner who employed a nanny to care for her children so that she could work. Much of what the Court said contains interesting parallels to United States law.

The Court expressed a willingness to reconsider an 1891 case which had denied a business expense deduction for the child care expenses. This willingness was based on "a significant social change in the late 1970s and into the 1980s, in terms of the influx of women of child-bearing age into business and into the workplace. This change post-dates the earlier cases dismissing nanny expenses as a legitimate business deduction and therefore it does not necessarily follow that the conditions which prevailed in society at the time of the those earlier decisions will prevail now." The Court went on to state that "[t]he decision to characterize child care expenses as personal expenses was made by judges. As part of our case law, it is susceptible to reexamination in an appropriate case." The Court argued for reexamining the prior decision with a quote from an earlier case affirming that "[j]udges can and should adapt the common law to reflect the changing social, moral and economic fabric of the country." (Is this a strange comment to make? The case concerned statutory interpretation, not the common law.)

On the merits, the Court took note of the Canadian government's "income-producing circle" test, which is reminiscent of Justice Harlan's reference to a "two personality" test in the *Gilmore* case. Under the "circle" test, a distinction is made between nondeductible expenses to approach the income-producing circle (such as clothing and commuting) and those deductible expenses incurred within the circle. The Court considered this test of "limited help," simply restating the personal vs. business dichotomy.

At this point in the opinion, unlike U.S. Tax Court Judge Opper in the 1939 *Smith* case, the Court seemed poised to seriously consider allowing the deduction. But there was more. The Canadian statute contained a detailed rule passed in 1972 allowing child care expenses to be deducted up to a specified limit and varying with the number of children. This provision was reminiscent in its detail of the rules found in the current United States tax credit for child care expenses. *§ 21.* The Court concluded that this specific provision was the exclusive method by which a taxpayer could reduce taxes for child care expenses, leaving no room for application of the general business expense deduction rule.

The two dissenting Justices (the two women on the court) relied heavily on the fact that the specific statutory tax break for child care expenses was passed at an earlier time, before a change in the background values regarding working women, and at a time when child care expenses were still considered personal. The change in background values deprived the specific statutory provision of any negative implication regarding the applicability of the basic statutory authorization of business expense deductions. The dissenters also drew sustenance from the principles of the Canadian Constitutional Charter prohibiting gender discrimination.

§ 8.04 TRAVELING EXPENSES

Traveling expenses test the outer boundaries of the definition of deductible business expenses. The potential for deducting personal expenses should be obvious. Along with entertainment expenses, they present the opportunity for so-called expense account living. Our discussion of traveling expenses first deals with meals and lodging and then transportation expenses.

[A]—Meals and lodging

§ 162(a)(2) and the introductory language to *§ 162* support an elaborate development of cases and rulings dealing with tax deductible expenses for business travelers.

The *Rosenspan* case (*infra*) is an excellent discussion of the current rules and their rationale. Here is an outline of the major factual settings in which the issues arise. Which of the following can deduct meals and lodging at the business destination?

1. The typical business traveler has a home and a permanent business location in one city and travels on business to another city for a week (a convention, for example).

2. The traveler lives in one city and travels to another city, where his principal place of business is located.

3. The temporary worker has a home but no work close to home. He takes jobs some distance from his home, for relatively short periods (a construction worker, for example).

4. The person with no home travels all the time. This is not unheard of — *e.g.*, some traveling salesmen and actors.

ROSENSPAN v. UNITED STATES

438 F.2d 905 (2d Cir. 1971)

FRIENDLY, CIRCUIT JUDGE: . . .

Plaintiff, Robert Rosenspan, was a jewelry salesman who worked on a commission basis, paying his own traveling expenses without reimbursement. In 1962 he was employed by one and in 1964 by two New York City jewelry manufacturers. For some 300 days a year he traveled by automobile through an extensive sales territory in the Middle West, where he would stay at hotels and motels and eat at restaurants. Five or six times a year he would return to New York and spend several days at his employers' offices. There he would perform a variety of services essential to his work — cleaning up his sample case, checking orders, discussing customers' credit problems, recommending changes in stock, attending annual staff meetings, and the like.

Rosenspan had grown [up] in Brooklyn and during his marriage had maintained a family home there. After his wife [died], he used his brother's Brooklyn home as a personal residential address, keeping some clothing and other belongings there, and registering, voting, and filing his income tax returns from that address. The stipulation of facts states that, on his trips to New York City, "out of a desire not to abuse his welcome at his brother's home, he stayed more often" at an inn near the John F. Kennedy Airport. It recites also that "he generally spent his annual vacations in Brooklyn, where his children resided, and made an effort to return to Brooklyn whenever possible," but affords no further indication where he stayed on such visits. . . . Rosenspan does not contend that he had a permanent abode or residence in Brooklyn or anywhere else.

The basis for the Commissioner's disallowance of a deduction for Rosenspan's meals and lodging while in his sales territory was that he had no "home" to be "away from" while traveling. Not denying that this would be true if the language of § 162(a)(2) were given its ordinary meaning, Rosenspan claimed that for tax purposes his home was his "business headquarters," to wit, New York City where his employers maintained their offices, and relied upon the Commissioner's long advocacy of this concept of a "tax home." The Commissioner responded that although in most circumstances "home" means "business headquarters," it should be given its natural meaning of a permanent abode or residence for purposes of the problem here presented. Rosenspan says the Commissioner is thus trying to have it both ways.

The provision of the Internal Revenue Code applicable for 1962 reads:

> § 162. Trade or business expenses.
>
> (a) In general. — There shall be allowed as a deduction all the ordinary and necessary expenses paid or incurred during the taxable year in carrying on any trade or business, including —
>
> (2) traveling expenses (including the entire amount expended for meals and lodging) while away from home in the pursuit of a trade or business;. . . .
>
> . . . .

What is now § 162(a)(2) was brought into the tax structure by § 214 of the Revenue Act of 1921, 42 Stat. 239. Prior to that date, § 214 had permitted the deduction of "ordinary and necessary expenses paid or incurred . . . in carrying on any trade or business," Revenue Act of 1918, 40 Stat. 1066 (1918), without further specification. In a regulation, the Treasury interpreted the statute to allow deduction of "traveling expenses, including railroad fares, and meals and lodging in an amount *in excess of any expenditures ordinarily required for such purposes when at home*," T.D. 3101, 3 C.B. 191 (1920) (emphasis supplied). A formula was provided for determining what expenditures were thus "ordinarily required"; the taxpayer was to compute such items as rent, grocery bills, light, etc. and servant hire for the periods when he was away from home, and divide this by the number of members of his family. Mim. 2688, 4 C.B. 209–11 (1921). The puzzlement of the man without a home was dealt with in a cryptic pronouncement, O.D. 905, 4 C.B. 212 (1921):

> Living expenses paid by a single taxpayer who has no home and is continuously employed on the road may not be deducted in computing net income.

The 1921 amendment, inserting what is now § 162(a)(2)'s allowance of a deduction for the entire amount of qualified meals and lodging, stemmed from a request of the Treasury based on the difficulty of administering the "excess" provision of its regulation. While the taxpayer cites statements of legislators in the 1921 Congress that the amendment would provide "a measure of justice" to commercial travelers, there is nothing to indicate that the members making or hearing these remarks were thinking of the unusual situation of the traveler without a home. There is likewise nothing to indicate that the Treasury sought, or that Congress meant to require, any change in the ruling that disallowed deductions for living expenses in such a case. The objective was to eliminate the need for computing the expenses "ordinarily required" at home by a taxpayer who had one, and the words used were appropriate to that end. If we were to make the unlikely assumption that the problem of the homeless commercial traveler ever entered the legislators' minds, the language they adopted was singularly inept to resolve it in the way for which plaintiff contends. Thus, if the literal words of the statute were decisive, the Government would clearly prevail on the simple ground that a taxpayer cannot be "away from home" unless he has a home from which to be away. Although that is our ultimate conclusion, the Supreme Court has wisely admonished that "More than a dictionary is thus required to understand the provision here involved, and no appeal to the 'plain language' of the section can obviate the need for further statutory construction." We turn, therefore, in the first instance to the Court's decisions.

The initial Supreme Court decision bearing on our problem is *C.I.R. v. Flowers*, 326 U.S. 465 (1946). Flowers, a lawyer, had a "home" in the conventional sense in Jackson, Mississippi, but his principal post of business was at the main office of his employer, the Gulf, Mobile & Ohio Railroad in Mobile, Alabama. Flowers sought to deduct the cost of transportation for his trips to Mobile and the meal and lodging expenses which he incurred in that city. In upholding the Commissioner's disallowance of these deductions, the Court said that "three conditions must thus be satisfied before a traveling expense deduction may be made" under what was substantially the present statute. These were:

> (1) The expense must be a reasonable and necessary traveling expense, as that term is generally understood. This includes such items as

transportation fares and food and lodging expenses incurred while traveling.

(2) The expense must be incurred "while away from home."

(3) The expense must be incurred in pursuit of business. This means that there must be a direct connection between the expenditure and the carrying on of the trade or business of the taxpayer or of his employer. Moreover, such an expenditure must be necessary or appropriate to the development and pursuit of the business or trade.

It noted that "The meaning of the word 'home' . . . with reference to a taxpayer residing in one city and working in another has engendered much difficulty and litigation," with the Tax Court and the administrative officials having "consistently defined it as the equivalent of the taxpayer's place of business" and two courts of appeals having rejected that view and "confined the term to the taxpayer's actual residence." The Court found it "unnecessary here to enter into or to decide this conflict." This was because the Tax Court had properly concluded "that the necessary relationship between the expenditures and the railroad's business was lacking." The railroad's interest was in having Mr. Flowers at its headquarters in Mobile; it "gained nothing" from his decision to continue living in Jackson; hence, the third condition the *Flowers* Court had enunciated as a prerequisite to deductibility was absent. Mr. Justice Rutledge dissented. He did not believe that when Congress used the word "home," it meant "business headquarters," and thought the case presented no other question. The most that Rosenspan can extract from *Flowers* is that it did not decide against his contention that the employer's business headquarters is the employee's tax home.

The Court's next venture into this area was in *Peurifoy v. C.I.R.*, 358 U.S. 59 (1958). That case dealt with three construction workers employed at a site in Kinston, North Carolina, for periods of 20 1/2, 12 1/2, and 8 1/2 months respectively, who maintained permanent residences elsewhere in the state. The Tax Court had allowed them deductions for board and lodging during the employment at Kinston and expenses in regaining their residences when they left, apparently of their own volition and before completion of the project. The Fourth Circuit had reversed. After having granted certiorari "to consider certain questions as to the application of [the 1939 version of section 162(a)(2)] raised by the course of decisions in the lower courts since our decision in *Commissioner v. Flowers*", the Court announced in a per curiam opinion that it had "found it inappropriate to consider such questions." It read *Flowers* as establishing that "a taxpayer is entitled to deduct unreimbursed travel expenses . . . only when they are required by 'the exigencies of business,' a 'general rule' " which the majority seemed to feel would mandate disallowance of the deductions under consideration. However, the Court went on to acknowledge an exception to this rule engrafted by the Tax Court, which would have allowed the claimed deductions if the taxpayer's employment were shown to be "temporary," rather than "indefinite" or "indeterminate." Nevertheless, even within this framework, the majority thought that the Court of Appeals had been justified in holding the Tax Court's finding of temporary employment to be clearly erroneous. Mr. Justice Douglas joined by Justices Black and Whittaker, dissented. Adopting Mr. Justice Rutledge's position in *Flowers*, they disagreed "with the Commissioner's contention that 'home' is synonymous with the situs of the employer's business." While adhering to "the exigencies of business" test announced in *Flowers*, they thought this requirement was satisfied by the fact that, in view of the impracticability of construction workers' moving their homes from job to job, "the expenses incurred were necessary, not to the business of the contractor for whom the taxpayers worked, but for the taxpayers themselves in order to carry on their chosen trade." While the three dissenting Justices thus rejected the Commissioner's identification of "home" with "the situs of the employer's business," the majority did not adopt it and, so far as our problem is concerned, that matter remained in the state of indecision where *Flowers* had left it. . . .

Proper analysis of the problem has been beclouded, and the Government's position in this case has been made more difficult than it need be, by the Commissioner's insistence that "home" means "business headquarters," despite the Supreme Court's having [] declined to endorse this, and its rejection by several courts of appeals. When Congress uses such a non-technical word in a tax statute, presumably it wants administrators and courts to read it in the way that ordinary people would understand, and not "to draw on some unexpressed spirit outside the bounds of the normal meaning of words," *Addison v. Holly Hill Fruit Prods., Inc.*, 322 U.S. 607, 617 (1944). The construction which the Commissioner has long advocated not only violates this principle but is unnecessary for the protection of the revenue that he seeks. That purpose is served, without any such distortion of language, by the third condition laid down in *Flowers*, namely, "that there must be a direct connection between the expenditure and the carrying on of the trade or business of the taxpayer or of his employer" and that "such an expenditure must be necessary or appropriate to the development and pursuit of the business or trade." These requirements were enough to rule out a deduction for Flowers' lodging and meals while in Mobile even if he was "away from home" while there. The deduction would not have been available to his fellow workers living in that city who obtained similar amenities in their homes or even in the very restaurants that Flowers patronized, and Flowers was no more compelled by business to be away from his home while in Mobile than were other employees of the railroad who lived there.

Since the Commissioner's definition of "home" as "business headquarters" will produce the same result as the third *Flowers* condition in the overwhelming bulk of cases arising under 162(a)(2), courts have often fallen into the habit of referring to it as a ground or an alternate ground of decision. . . . But examination of the string of cases cited by plaintiff as endorsing the "business headquarters" test has revealed almost none, . . . which cannot be explained on the basis that the taxpayer had no permanent residence, or was not away from it, or maintained it in a locale apart from where he regularly worked as a matter of personal choice rather than business necessity. This principle likewise affords a satisfactory rationale for the "temporary" employment cases. When an assignment is truly temporary, it would be unreasonable to expect the taxpayer to move his home, and the expenses are thus compelled by the "exigencies of business"; when the assignment is "indefinite" or "indeterminate," the situation is different and, if the taxpayer decides to leave his home where it was, disallowance is appropriate, not because he has acquired a "tax home" in some lodging house or hotel at the worksite but because his failure to move his home was for his personal convenience and not compelled by business necessity. Under the facts here presented, we need not decide whether in the case of a taxpayer who is not self-employed, the "exigencies of business" which compel the traveling expenses away from home refer solely to the business of his employer or to the business of the taxpayer as well. We note only that the latter contention is surely not foreclosed by decisions to date. . . .

Shifting the thrust of analysis from the search for a fictional "tax home" to a questioning of the business necessity for incurring the expense away from the taxpayer's permanent residence thus does not upset the basic structure of the decisions which have dealt with this problem. It merely adopts an approach that better effectuates the congressional intent in establishing the deduction and thus provides a sounder conceptual framework for analysis while following the ordinary meaning of language. We see no basis whatever for believing that when the 1921 Congress eliminated the requirement for determining the excess of the costs of meals and lodging while on the road over what they would have been at home, it meant to disallow a deduction to someone who had the expense of maintaining a home from which business took him away but possessed no business headquarters. By the same token we find it impossible to read the words "away from home" out of the statute, as Rosenspan, in effect, would have us do and allow a deduction to a taxpayer who had no "home," in the ordinary sense. The limitation reflects congressional recognition of the rational distinction between the taxpayer with a permanent residence — whose travel costs represent a duplication of expense or at least an incidence of expense which the existence of his permanent residence demonstrates he would not incur absent business compulsion — and the taxpayer without such a residence. We fail to see how Rosenspan's occasional trips to New York City, assuming for the sake of argument that his "business headquarters" was in New York rather than in his sales territory, differentiate him economically from the homeless traveling salesman without even the modicum of a business headquarters Rosenspan is claimed to have possessed. Yet we approved disallowance of the deduction in such a case many years ago.

It is enough to decide this case that "home" means "home" and Rosenspan had none. He satisfied the first and third conditions of *Flowers*, but not, on our reading of the statute, the second. The judgment dismissing the complaint must therefore be affirmed.

Statutory interpretation — "home". The court in *Rosenspan* opted for the more common everyday meaning of the term "home," rather than giving it a special tax meaning. Would Judge Friendly have rejected the common meaning if that were necessary to implement statutory purpose?

Temporary worker. The government does not always say that "home" means "principal place of business." In *Rev. Rul. 75-432*, 1975-2 C.B. 60, it states this to be the "general rule." However, "in the rare case in which the employee has no identifiable principal place of business, but does maintain a regular place of abode in a real or substantial sense in a particular city from which the taxpayer is sent on temporary assignments, the tax home will be regarded as being the place of abode."

The rule permitting deduction of living expenses at a temporary workplace requires us to define "temporary." In 1992, the statute was amended to specify that a period of employment lasting more than one year was not temporary. *§ 162(a)(next to last sentence).* Suppose the taxpayer works temporarily in a job under a one-year contract, which is then renewed for another three months. Is he temporarily away from home for any or all of the 15-month period?

A taxpayer who works for six months every year away from his residence is not necessarily entitled to a deduction. For example, if the taxpayer takes temporary jobs in the same place every year because he wants to stay permanently as a resident in another location, where he has no job prospects, the deduction will be disallowed because the personal decision where to live is the dominant explanation for the expense. *Tucker v. Commissioner*, 55 T.C. 783 (1971).

The temporary worker may also have trouble establishing a residence back home. What about the case of an actress who signs a six-month contract to act in a New York play? Her home is in Denver with her husband. After the play is a hit, she signs a second six-month contract, but in the meantime her marriage begins to disintegrate and she is about to get a divorce. The work in New York may still be temporary, but her home may now be New York. *Six v. United States*, 450 F.2d 66 (2d Cir. 1971).

Overnight. In *United States v. Correll*, 389 U.S. 299 (1967), the Court upheld a Treasury Regulation limiting the deduction of meals and lodging to cases where the traveler required "sleep or rest." This is usually called the "overnight" rule, because in most cases the requirement is satisfied by staying at the business destination overnight. The Court of Appeals thought that the "plain language of the statute" ("away from home") precluded a temporal requirement. The Supreme Court disagreed, noting that "meals *and* lodging" implied an overnight stay. It also cited some 1954 legislative history affirming the overnight rule. Finally, it appealed to the administrative law principle that "long continued [regulations] without substantial change, applying to unamended or substantially reenacted statutes, are deemed to have received congressional approval and have the effect of law."

Introductory language of *§ 162(a)*. In *Christey v. United States*, 841 F.2d 809 (8th Cir. 1988), the court considered whether policemen could deduct the expenses incurred for restaurant meals while on duty, even though not "away" overnight. The facts were these:

> Steven L. Pillsbury and Karl W. Christey are employed as state troopers by the Minnesota State Highway Patrol. The Patrol is charged by law with enforcing traffic laws, investigating traffic accidents, directing and controlling traffic, providing information and assistance to the public, and cooperating with other law enforcement agencies in apprehending violators of criminal laws. *See* Minn. Stat. § 299D.03, subd. 1 (1986). The normal working day for troopers is between 8 1/2 and 9 hours. Troopers are also subject to call 24 hours a day.
>
> As a requirement of their job, troopers must comply with the rules and regulations contained in the General Orders of the Patrol. These orders address in detail the conduct required of troopers while on duty. General Order R77-20-008 ("the General Order") provides troopers with specific instructions concerning meal breaks while on duty. The General Order requires that troopers "eat their meals in a public restaurant adjacent to

the highway whenever practical" and "report by radio when they eat and . . . advise the telephone number or the code number of the restaurant where they are eating." The restaurant must be open to the public and may not serve liquor. The Order prohibits troopers from eating meals at home during working hours and has been interpreted to prohibit troopers from bringing meals from home and eating in their patrol cars. The Order also details the time at which troopers may eat, the time allowed for a meal, and the number of troopers who may eat together. Failure to adhere to these instructions renders troopers subject to reprimand.

As set forth in the General Order, the principal purpose of these requirements "is to promote public safety and obedience to the law through the physical presence of troopers in uniform and to facilitate, through availability to the public, the reporting of accidents and the dissemination of information with reference to the traffic and motor vehicle laws of the state." The Order also ensures that meal breaks taken by the troopers are designated and staggered in order to maintain maximum coverage of patrol areas with minimal call response time.

There was testimony that during meals troopers are subject to calls for emergencies and other Patrol business to which they must respond immediately. Troopers are also subject to interruptions from the general public who are seeking information about road conditions, weather, traffic laws, and other subjects relating to trooper responsibilities. Thus, troopers are frequently interrupted during their meals and are often unable to finish meals for which they have paid. . . .

The court upheld the deduction, as follows. Does its reliance on the introductory text of *§ 162(a)* suggest pro-taxpayer arguments in any other situations discussed in this chapter?

In support of their contention that meal expenses are nondeductible personal expenses, the government particularly relies on two United States Supreme Court cases. *United States v. Correll*, 389 U.S. 299 (1967), and *Commissioner v. Kowalski*, 434 U.S. 77 (1977). Neither of these cases, however, addresses the issue of whether meal expenses may be deducted as "ordinary and necessary" business expenses under the general provision of § 162(a). *Correll, supra*, concerned the deductibility of meal expenses as "traveling expenses" under § 162(a)(2), while *Kowalski, supra*, concerned the exclusion from gross income under § 119 of a cash meal allowance. Indeed, the Court in *Kowalski* acknowledged that the deductibility of trooper meal expenses under the general provision of § 162(a) was not under consideration.

It is beyond question that the cost of one's meals is ordinarily a personal expense which is nondeductible under § 262. Treas. Reg. § 1.262-1(b)(5)

(1987). However, under certain limited circumstances, such expenses may be deducted under the general provision of § 162(a); "that which may be a personal expense under some circumstances can when circumscribed by company regulations take on the color of a business expense," *Sibla v. Commissioner*, 611 F.2d 1260, 1262 (9th Cir. 1980). . . .

In light of the circumstances of this case, we believe the district court's conclusion that the meal expenses which the taxpayers incurred while on duty in 1981 and 1982 were deductible as ordinary and necessary expenses under § 162(a) is not clearly erroneous. Accordingly, the district court's judgment is affirmed.

Luxury travel. The deduction for traveling expenses encourages taxpayers to live well and deduct the expenses. Taxpayers attend conventions at luxury resorts, stay at the best hotels, and spend lavishly on food. Limitations imposed by employers or by the taxpayer's own financial constraints may have some effect, but the tax law pushes taxpayers towards spending more. When the tax law allowed all meals and lodging to be deducted to avoid the administrative difficulty of separating out normal from extra expenses, it created an incentive to increase the extras. Today many taxpayers rely on the deduction to support a significant tax-free enhancement of their lifestyles.

At this point in the discussion, someone usually mentions the famous example of the prince's aide who lives in the palace, eats at the royal table, and attends opera with the prince, but who hates opera and rich food. H. Simons, *Personal Income Taxation* 53 (1938). How would you respond to a taxpayer who argues against taxing luxury travel expenses because he hates travel? Is a subjective test irrelevant or should you consider the probabilities of subjective enjoyment in framing an objective rule? Most objective legal rules are somewhat unfair because of imprecision in matching the rule's general purpose to specific facts.

Several statutory provisions limit deductions for luxury travel. Special rules apply to foreign conventions outside of North America. *§ 274(h).* The expenses are deductible only if the meeting is directly related to the active conduct of a trade or business and it is as reasonable to meet outside North America as within North America. Certain Caribbean countries are included in North America for these purposes. Cruise ship conventions are also subject to special limitations. *§ 274(h)(2), (5).* Were these rules adopted to implement tax fairness or for other reasons? What lobbying group would have favored these rules?

50% of meal expenses deductible. Only 50% of meal expenses is deductible. *§ 274(n).* The rule is primarily aimed at deductions for business meal entertainment expenses, discussed below, but it applies as well to traveling expense deductions for meals.

exception to the rule

Two permanent businesses. The logic of deducting business travel expenses — that the taxpayer must incur extra expenses away from home — implies that expenses related to business travel at the second of two permanent business locations is deductible. Which location's expenses are deductible in the following example? An Indianapolis corporate lawyer is also a partner in a Miami, Florida firm. He lives in Miami in January, February, and March, practicing law in Florida. The lawyer nets 55% of his total income as a lawyer from the Florida practice, which consists primarily of being a lawyer for estates of deceased former clients. *Markey v. Commissioner*, 490 F.2d 1249 (6th Cir. 1974).

Suppose two spouses work, but in different cities. The husband was just promoted and moved to Chicago from Toledo. The wife will move to Chicago when she can get a job commensurate with her training. She has a Ph.D. in Chemistry. Meanwhile, she is continuing in her old job as an Assistant Professor of Chemistry in Toledo, Ohio. She lives four days a week in Chicago, going to Toledo to meet classes and students for three days per week. *Daly v. Commissioner*, 631 F.2d 351 (4th Cir. 1980), *rev'd on reh'g*, 662 F.2d 253 (1981); *Felton v. Commissioner*, 43 T.C.M. (CCH) 278 (1982), *aff'd*, 723 F.2d 66 (7th Cir. 1983). Are any of this family's meals and lodging expenses deductible?

QUESTIONS

In the following cases, determine whether expenses for meals or lodging are deductible and whether the answer would be different if you define "home" as residence or principal place of business.

1. A professor permanently employed at a New York school visits at another school in California for 10 months. How does this situation differ from the typical business trip? Does the statutory treatment of Members of Congress, limiting the amount of traveling expense deductions, suggest how long-term travelers should be treated? *§ 162(a)(next to last sentence). See also § 162(h)* for a similar but elective approach to state legislators.

a. If the professor brings his family, the expenses allocable to the family are not deductible. *Treas. Reg. § 1.162-2(c).* Contrast this rule with the exclusion for the whole family under *§ 119(a).*

b. Must the professor reduce any deduction to which he is entitled by any rent he receives for renting his residence back home? Is the meal deduction disallowed because the professor shops at the grocery store, incurring no added expense over what he would have incurred at home? *Cass v. Commissioner*, 86 T.C. 1275 (1986); *Michaels v. Commissioner*, 53 T.C. 269 (1969); *Warganz v. Commissioner*, 42 T.C.M. (CCH) 568 (1981).

2. A law student in Cambridge, Massachusetts, is married to a Boston lawyer. After her second year of law school, she takes a temporary summer job clerking for a New York law firm and lives in New York for a two-month period, returning to Boston to complete her third year of law school. Can she deduct the New York expenses? Is her temporary work explained by a personal or business decision? *Hantzis v. Commissioner*, 38 T.C.M. (CCH) 1169 (1979), *rev'd and remanded*, 638 F.2d 248 (1st Cir. 1981).

3. A taxpayer lives in the suburbs and works in the city. One night he has to stay in the city at a hotel because of an unusual business problem that required late-night and early-morning attention. *Coombs v. Commissioner*, 608 F.2d 1269 (9th Cir. 1979).

4. An employee is away from home on business on Friday. To save plane fare, the employee stays overnight on Saturday, incurring an additional $250 hotel and meal expenses. Without the Saturday stay, round trip plane fare is $900; with the Saturday stay it is $500. The employer reimburses the employee for the $250 additional Saturday expense. Does the reimbursement increase the employee's taxable income by $250? *Priv. Ltr. Rul. 9237014*.

[B]—Transportation

Commuting. The term "transportation" refers to the cost of getting from one place to the other, such as plane fare to a business destination or car expenses for a traveling salesman. The IRS has long taken the position that commuting expenses in getting from home to a place of work are not deductible. One way to support this conclusion is to define "home" as principal place of business and decide that the commuter is not away from home. The Supreme Court in *Commissioner v. Flowers*, 326 U.S. 465 (1946), decided that this issue could be resolved by holding that the commuting expense was occasioned by the taxpayer's decision where to live and that commuting was therefore a personal expense without regard to the definition of "home." Is this an application of the origin test, discussed in *Gilmore*?

Do you agree with the conclusion that the gap between work and home is a personal decision? Can a taxpayer realistically live very close to work in the modern city? In *United States v. Tauferner*, 407 F.2d 243 (10th Cir.

1969), the court disallowed a deduction for commuting expenses even though the taxpayer worked for a company testing solid fuel rocket engines at a site located some distance from any residential community because of the danger.

If a deduction were allowed for commuting expenses, who would benefit most — the inner city commuter or the suburbanite?

No home. If a taxpayer is a traveling salesman like Rosenspan, but with no principal place of business and no residence, can he deduct his transportation expenses? Could Correll (who was not "away" overnight) deduct his transportation expenses? These expenses are deductible, even though the taxpayer is not "away from home." What is the statutory authority for this result? *Turner v. Commissioner*, 56 T.C. 27 (1971).

Temporary work. Can a temporary construction worker who travels to the worksite in the morning and back to his home that night deduct commuting expenses? The taxpayer argues that the temporary nature of the job justifies the deduction for the same reason that meals and lodging would be deductible if he was gone overnight. In 1976, the government sought to disallow the deduction, arguing that "commuting is commuting." *Rev. Rul. 76-453*, 1976-2 C.B. 86 (Example 5). Congress then temporarily reinstated the law as it was prior to the ruling. *Public Law 95-427, § 2.*

The latest ruling is *Rev. Rul. 94–47*, 1994–2 C.B. 18. It allows the deduction of commuting expenses in cases in which the temporary work is outside the metropolitan area in which the taxpayer lives. The ruling also allows the deduction (1) if the taxpayer has a regular work location away from the taxpayer's residence and the taxpayer travels to a temporary work location in the same trade or business (an accountant goes to a company's office to audit its books); or (2) if the taxpayer's residence is his principal place of business and the taxpayer travels to another work location in the same trade or business, whether it is temporary or regular (a doctor whose office is in his home and who travels to the hospital).

Two jobs. If a taxpayer travels ten miles to a principal job, another two miles to a second job, and then back home, the cost of traveling two miles between jobs is deductible. *Rev. Rul. 76–453*, 1976–2 C.B. 86 (Example 8). Should this be true if the two-mile trip is directly on the way home so that it does not increase the normal commuting distance?

Carrying tools. If a taxpayer must bring tools to work and transports them in his car, is the expense of getting to work deductible? Does it matter whether he would have driven to work anyway, rather than take the bus? *Fausner v. Commissioner*, 413 U.S. 838 (1973); *Rev. Rul. 75-380*, 1975-2 C.B. 59; *Kallander v. United States*, 526 F.2d 1131 (Ct. Cl. 1975).

Foreign travel. Look at *§ 274(c)*. Roughly speaking, it prevents a taxpayer who spends some time at a foreign business destination on business and some time on vacation from deducting the entire transportation cost, if the entire trip exceeds one week. For example, if the taxpayer spends one week in Paris going to meetings and one week in Paris on vacation, only one-half of the round trip transportation in getting from his home to Paris is deductible. This section provides the kind of allocation formula in separating out the taxable from the nontaxable portion of an expenditure that is so frequently lacking in the fringe benefit area.

The Regulations provide a good example of a difference in taxing employees depending on whether the expenses are reimbursed by the employer or financed by the taxpayer's own funds. *Treas. Reg. § 1.274-4(f)(5)(i)*. When the foreign transportation expenses are reimbursed, the employer is presumed to have so much control over how the money is spent that *§ 274(c)* does not apply, unless the employee is a manager or 10% owner.

If a New York taxpayer spends six weeks in Paris on vacation and one week on business, would any part of the cost of transportation to Paris be deductible under *§ 162(a)*? Remember that *§ 274(c)* limits the deduction of what would otherwise be a deductible business expense in the first place. Thus, one week at a Paris business convention and six weeks vacation at the same place would probably result in disallowing the deduction for round trip transportation between New York and Paris under *§ 162(a)*.

[C]—Moving expenses

Suppose a taxpayer moves to a first job or moves between jobs. Are the moving expenses deductible? Prior to the adoption of *§§ 82, 217*, the taxpayer could take these deductions only by proving that they were business expenses. This would be difficult if it was the first job, for reasons discussed in a later chapter on capital expenditures. In addition, some courts treated unreimbursed expenses as nondeductible personal expenses. The unequal treatment of different taxpayers and the mobility of our society led to allowing the deduction of moving expenses, whether or not for the first job and whether or not reimbursed.

Before tax year 1994, the deduction rules were quite generous, including not only the cost of moving the family and household goods, but also (subject to dollar limits) certain housing search costs and incidental housing sale expenses. As of tax year 1994, deductible moving expenses are limited to moving household goods and the cost of traveling to the new destination (but not meals). In addition, the new principal place of work must be at least 50 miles farther from the taxpayer's former residence than was the prior principal place of work. (If the taxpayer had no prior work, the new principal place of work must be at least 50 miles from the former residence).

The 1994 changes are not all bad. The moving expense deduction is now an above-the-line deduction (since 1986, it had been an itemized deduction, subject to the 2% floor). And employer reimbursements of deductible moving expenses are excludible fringe benefits under *§ 132(a)(6),(g)*; the taxpayer does not have to report them as gross income and take a deduction.

§ 8.05 ENTERTAINMENT EXPENSES

[A]—Substantive rules

Tax-free expense account living may be a more serious problem with entertainment than travel expenses because they are probably more economically wasteful, in addition to permitting tax-free personal consumption. The typical situation is one in which a business taxpayer entertains a client by taking him out for a meal, or to a nightclub, or providing theater tickets.

You might at first wonder how there could be a deduction in the first place, at least for the meals. After all, the taxpayer must eat and is not away from home overnight. The IRS' position is that, technically, the taxpayer could not deduct the portion of her meal which does not exceed normal living expenses. However, the IRS states: "The Service practice has been to apply this rule largely to abuse cases where taxpayers claim deductions for substantial amounts of personal living expenses." *Rev. Rul. 63-144*, 1963-2 C.B. 129. As a practical matter, entertainment expenses are generally deductible in full under *§ 162(a)*.

Consequently, the Code was amended in *§ 274* to place limits on such deductions. The statute is very convoluted, reflecting the sensitive political climate. *§ 274(a)(1)(A)* starts off with a bang, limiting deductions to "directly related" expenses. The idea is that business must actually be conducted during the entertainment period; purchasing business good will is not enough. But then the statute waffles — entertainment expenses "associated with" business are deductible if they precede or follow substantial business discussion. Purchasing good will is therefore sufficient to support a deduction for business meals and night club expenses, if business discussions occur soon before or after. The business meal deduction is also expressly conditioned on the taxpayer or its employee being present — *see § 274(k)(1)(B)*.

In some respects, however, the section has teeth. First, expenses for entertainment facilities are not deductible at all (yachts, hunting lodges, etc.). *§ 274(a)(1)(B)*. Second, only 50% of the expenses for meals and entertainment are deductible. *§ 274(n)(1)*. Third, club dues are not deductible. *§ 274(a)(3)*. There is more fine-tuning (*e.g.* ticket price deductions are limited to face value, not scalper's rates — *see § 274(l)(1))*, but that is enough to give you a flavor of the rules.

[B]—Reimbursements

We have discussed entertainment expenses without paying attention to whether they were reimbursed or not. Many taxpayers incur such expenses without reimbursement — a partner in a business or a sole proprietor (such as a salesman). There is no problem applying the deduction limits to these taxpayers. But suppose you are an employee who incurs entertainment expenses which are reimbursed by the employer. There are two candidates for losing the deduction — the reimbursing employer and the reimbursed employee. Because the expenses seem wasteful and not just disguised personal expenses, it might make sense to disallow the employer's deduction or even tax both employer and employee, rather than just disallow the employee's deduction.

In fact, the *§ 274* limits on entertainment expenses (the directly related, associated with, facility, club dues, and 50% limits) apply to the employer, not the employee, unless the employer decides to report the reimbursements as taxable wages for tax withholding purposes to the federal government. *§§ 274(e)(2),(3), 274(n)(2)(A)*. The employer will almost certainly never treat reimbursements as wages, so the *§ 274* limits normally apply to reimbursing employers, not reimbursed employees.

Be sure you understand that the employee must still satisfy *§ 162* in order to exclude the expenses from his tax base. For example, how would the following transactions be taxed. *Transaction 1.* The employee takes a client from out of town to a nightclub but does not engage in business discussion before or after. The employer reimburses the employee for the $250 expense. Can the employer deduct the expense? Must the employee include the reimbursement in income; if so, can the employee deduct the expense? Does it matter whether the reimbursement is an income and deduction item to the employee or is just excluded from the employee's income in the first place? *Transaction 2.* Would your answer be different if the out of town visitor was not a client but a friend, who plans to reciprocate the entertainment when the taxpayer visits the client's home town?

§ 8.06 RECORDKEEPING

Many taxpayers do not keep good records of expenses. Taxpayers usually have the burden of proof in tax litigation and that might have justified disallowing deductions for unsubstantiated expenses. However, an early case held that some estimate of deductible expenses had to be made once a court was convinced that some were deductible. *Cohan v. Commissioner*,

39 F.2d 540 (2d Cir. 1930). Although the court could severely limit the deduction amount because the taxpayer's records were bad, the prospect of deductibility led taxpayers to make inflated claims as a prelude to advantageous settlement in the audit process.

must keep record to DD amt. of bus. exp.

In response, the statute now conditions deduction of traveling and entertainment expenses on keeping good records regarding their amount, time, place, and business purpose. *§ 274(d).* The precise content of these records are specified in Regulations and numerous Revenue Rulings, and often simplify recordkeeping for smaller expenses.

Application of recordkeeping requirements to reimbursed employees. Reimbursed employees not only can avoid the substantive limits of *§ 274*, but are also not usually required to maintain their own records to substantiate deductible expenses, *if* they make an adequate accounting to their employer. The IRS has discretion to treat reimbursements, per diem, and mileage arrangements as an adequate accounting. *Treas. Reg. § 1.274-5(e)(4),(5),(f).* Employees who own 10% or more of the employer must, however, keep their own records.

Wage withholding from certain reimbursements. The substantive and recordkeeping rules are hard to enforce, especially in the case of reimbursed expenses. *§ 62(c)* is supposed to improve enforcement. It states that failure to account adequately to the employer will result in reimbursements being deductible by an employee, if at all, *only as* itemized deductions. The Committee Report states that this rule requires reimbursements for which there is no adequate accounting to be treated like wages subject to withholding by the employer. This forces the employee to affirmatively prove eligibility for such deductions by deducting them on the employee's return, in addition to overcoming the 2% floor on itemized employee business deductions.

§ 8.07 ESTATE PLANNING AND TAX DETERMINATION EXPENSES

Estate planning and tax determination expenses provide an opportunity to review and expand the discussion of statutory provisions dealing with deductions. Here is a problem to raise the issue. A taxpayer pays a $5,000 bill to her lawyer for "estate planning." The will sets up trusts for children, some of whom are minors and others of whom cannot manage money very well. It also places real estate property in a trust managed by a bank, and other property (stocks and bonds) in a trust managed by relatives. Finally, it minimizes estate taxes, by arranging for the surviving spouse to have certain interests under the trust.

How many different types of expenses can you identify? I can spot three. Are any of the expenses deductible under *§ 212(2)*? Are any of them nondeductible personal expenses, under the "origin" test? Are tax planning (not just tax litigation) expenses deductible under *§ 212(3)*? *See Luman v. Commissioner*, 79 T.C. 846 (1982); *Merian v. Commissioner*, 60 T.C. 187 (1973).

Burden of proof. The taxpayer's route to deducting at least some of the $5,000 is to rely on the *Cohan* case (*see* § 8.06), which allowed the taxpayer to make some estimate of deductible expenses despite having the burden of proof. As of this writing, the House (in H.R. 2676) has passed an amendment in the fall of 1997 to shift the burden of proof to the government. (At least that is the impression given in the popular press.) The actual text of the statute (excerpted below) is more modest, illustrating once again the difference between congressional posturing and statutory reality.

Consider what impact this change in burden of proof would have on cases in which the taxpayer has relied on the *Cohan* case to support a deduction. For example, would it strengthen the taxpayer's chances of success in taking some portion of the $5,000 legal fees as a tax planning expense?

SEC. 7491. BURDEN OF PROOF.

(a) GENERAL RULE. — The secretary shall have the burden of proof in any court proceeding with respect to any factual issue relevant to ascertaining the income tax liability of a taxpayer.

(b) LIMITATIONS. — Subsection (a) shall only apply with respect to an issue if—

(1) The taxpayer asserts a reasonable dispute with respect to such issue,

(2) The taxpayer has fully cooperated with the secretary with respect to such issue, including providing, within a reasonable period of time, access to and inspection of all witnesses, information, and documents within the control of the taxpayer, as reasonably requested by the Secretary, and

(3) [Editor — Omitting partnerships, corporations, and trusts with net worth in excess of $7 million from the new rules shifting the burden of proof to the government.]

(c) SUBSTANTIATION. — Nothing in this section shall be construed to override any requirement of this title to substantiate any item.

Professional ethics. If some of the expenses are deductible tax planning expenses, lawyers are under considerable pressure to help clients allocate their fees to tax planning, to improve client acceptance of high fees. Would you shade your itemized bill to show a larger portion allocable to tax planning? How would you respond to a client's request that you depart from your usual practice of itemizing your bill, so as not to show the percentage allocable to tax planning? Remember that the *Cohan* case permits a court to make some educated guess about the portion of the fee for tax planning, if the bill is not itemized. Rule 1.2(d) of the American Bar Association's *Model Rules of Professional Conduct* states that "A lawyer shall not . . . assist a client in conduct that the lawyer knows is criminal or fraudulent. . . ."

§ 8.08 BUSINESS AS PLEASURE

There is a kind of hybrid activity, often called a "hobby." This is an activity which is not engaged in purely for pleasure or profit. The taxpayer seems to be trying to break-even but not to make money. Typically, a summer vacation home might double as a ranch. In such cases, the net losses from the activity are not deductible. That was the case law, long before it was codified in *§ 183*. That section now adds a pro-taxpayer presumption that an activity is not a "hobby" if it produces *taxable* income for three of five consecutive years, including the tax year.

Does the following situation differ from the typical "vacation-type" hobby?

CHURCHMAN v. COMMISSIONER

68 T.C. 696 (1977)

FORRESTER, JUDGE: . . .

. . . Petitioner Gloria Churchman (hereinafter Gloria or petitioner) is an artist who has been involved in artistic activities for 20 years. She mainly paints but also sculpts, designs, draws, and builds; writes short stories, poems, and songs, performs in films, and has recently made a film. In addition to an undergraduate degree, she has 2 1/2 years of graduate work in psychology and 2 1/2 years of work in art school. She has taught courses at [several schools] as well as given numerous workshops independently of any institution. During the years in issue, petitioner devoted a substantial amount of her time to her artistic activities and she held no other job except as a housewife. Petitioner does her artwork in a home studio which was built for that purpose. . . .

During the 20 years that petitioner has pursued her artistic activities, the income from the sale of her artwork has not exceeded her expenses in any year. Petitioner reported no art-related income whatsoever for the taxable year 1970 and 1971, but she reported $250 of such income for 1972.

[Editor — The IRS denied taxpayer a deduction of net operating losses from this activity.]

IRS:
TP engaged in for profit § 183
NFP → no applies → no DD for expenses

Respondent argues that petitioner's artistic activities are not engaged in for profit so that § 183 applies and the claimed deduction of petitioner's art-related expenses is not allowable. Section 183 allows deductions for ordinary and necessary expenses arising from an activity not engaged in for profit only to the extent of the gross income derived from such activity less the amount of those deductions which are allowable regardless of whether or not the activity is engaged in for profit. Petitioner, on the other hand, argues that her artistic activities were engaged in for profit so that her art-related expenses are deductible in full under §§ 162 and 165.

GI
⊖ amt. of allowable DD's other under other §s

TP:
DD under §162 (not-NFP)

TP's burden:

In order to prevail, petitioner must show that she pursued her artistic activities during the years in question with the objective of making a profit. Petitioner's expectation of profit need not be reasonable, but she must establish that she continued her activities with a bona fide intention [] of making a profit.

Since petitioner has introduced no evidence of net profit derived from her artistic activities for any of the years 1970 through 1975, the § 183(d) presumption cannot help her. Therefore, we must determine whether petitioner's activities were engaged in for profit by reference to all of the facts and circumstances of the instant case, including the relevant factors set forth in § 1.183–2(b), Income Tax Regs., and giving greater weight to objective facts than to the taxpayer's mere statement of her intent.

look at obj. factors to see if TP intended profit

Viewing the record as a whole, we believe that petitioner had a bona fide intention to derive a profit from her artwork. There are admittedly factors in this case which indicate the absence of a profit motive. Petitioner has a history of losses; she has never been dependent upon income from her artistic activities; and there is a significant recreational element inherent in her activities. However, such a history of losses is less persuasive in the art field than it might be in other fields because the archetypal "struggling artist" must first achieve public acclaim before her serious work will command a price sufficient to provide her with a profit. . . .

Fs supporting intent to profit:

While petitioner's artwork involved recreational and personal elements, her work did not stop at the creative stage but went into the marketing phase of the art business where the recreational element is minimal. Petitioner, designed an art gallery and ran it for 1 year, she maintained a mailing list and sent announcements of her shows to persons on such list, she went to galleries in San Francisco and New York attempting to have her work shown, and she published a book. Furthermore, when petitioner saw that her paintings and other works were not selling well, she adopted new techniques, such as making posters and writing books, in an effort to make her work more available and more salable to the public. Although she did not keep a complete set of books pertaining to her artistic activities, petitioner kept all of the receipts for her art expenses and kept a journal recording what she sold and to whom. These facts indicate that petitioner carried on her artistic activities in a businesslike manner for profit.

Moreover, petitioner studied art for 2-1/2 years, she has taught at the college level and in workshops, articles about her have appeared in newspapers and magazines, her work is shown in commercial galleries at least once a year, some of her work has been sold, and she has been given a grant to make a film. Such facts indicate that petitioner has the requisite training to become a successful artist. The fact that petitioner devotes a substantial amount of time to her artistic activities also indicates that she has a profit motive.

she has training to become an artist

It is abundantly clear from her testimony and from the objective evidence that petitioner is a most dedicated artist, craves personal recognition as an artist, and believes that selling her work for a profit represents the attainment of such recognition. Therefore, petitioner intends and expects to make a profit. For § 183 purposes, it seems to us irrelevant whether petitioner intends to make a profit because it symbolizes success in her chosen career or because it is the pathway to material wealth. In either case, the essential fact remains that petitioner does intend to make a profit from her artwork and she sincerely believes that if she continues to paint she will do so.

Petitioner has a relatively large inventory, she has considerable training, she devotes substantial time to her artwork, she has sold some paintings in the past, and is attempting to sell more. It is certainly conceivable, in our view, that she may someday sell enough of her paintings to enable her "to recoup the losses which have meanwhile been sustained in the intervening years." Accordingly, we hold that petitioner's artistic activities were engaged in for profit so that § 183 is inapplicable and petitioner is entitled to deductions for her art-related expenses. . . .

Holding:

QUESTIONS AND COMMENTS

1. Is the test in the hobby loss area subjective (what profits did this taxpayer expect) or objective (what would a reasonable taxpayer expect)?

2. Assume that a taxpayer is engaged in an activity other than for profit, and generates $50,000 gross income and $60,000 expenses. The $10,000

net loss is not deductible. Is the $50,000 fully deductible or is it an itemized deduction; if it is an itemized deduction, is it subject to the 2% floor?

3. A taxpayer may try to camouflage an activity as profit-seeking, not only to turn personal into business expenses, but also to avoid the 2% floor on unreimbursed employee business expenses. In *Beard v. Commissioner*, 69 T.C.M. (CCH) 1768 (1995), a Department of Justice lawyer earned a small amount of fees from private clients but claimed substantially more expenses than fees as business deductions from private lawyering. The expenses were for meals and entertainment of prospective clients, bar association dues, subscriptions to publications (including the Supreme Court reporter), and some home office expenses. The court held that the net losses were not deductible under *§ 183*.

CHAPTER 9

PERSONAL INSURANCE PROTECTION AND PERSONAL LOSSES

Numerous variables affect how personal insurance and personal losses are taxed. The rules are not uniform among different types of insurance and losses and you should consider whether the differences are justified. Here are the variables.

(1) What is the loss insured against? This chapter considers disability (the inability to work); medical expenses; and loss of life. We also discuss insurance for legal costs, which was a tax free fringe benefit until 1993.

(2) There are two potential tax events involving personal losses — (a) when the taxpayer obtains insurance protection; and (b) when the taxpayer suffers the losses and receives cash (or has obligations paid off).

(3) Taxpayers acquire insurance or insurance-like protection in various ways. They can buy it; an employer can buy it for them; their employer can promise to pay them money if a loss occurs; or the government can make a similar promise. The employer or government promise is not technically insurance but often is the economic equivalent. In addition, compensation for losses can be received from tort defendants, not insurance.

We first look at the taxation of insurance (or insurance-like) protection and then at the tax rules when a loss occurs. A detailed discussion of tort recoveries is left to a separate concluding section.

§ 9.01 INSURANCE PROTECTION

[A]—Premiums paid for insurance

Premiums to buy insurance covering personal losses are nondeductible personal expenses, unless the code otherwise provides. The citation is simply *§ 262*, which disallows the deduction of personal expenses. Thus, disability, medical, and life insurance premiums are nondeductible personal expenses, unless the risks against which they insure are business risks. For example, there is no doubt that legal malpractice insurance premiums, including the portion covering legal costs, would be deductible. Would disability insurance premiums be deductible business expenses if only business risks were covered (*e.g.*, only risks from performing hazardous work)? *Rev. Rul. 75-149*, 1975-1 C.B. 65. We assume in the remainder of this chapter that the insurance covers only "personal" risks.

The code does "otherwise provide" a personal insurance deduction in a number of situations. Medical insurance premiums are deductible as medical expenses, except that the 7.5% floor on deductible medical expenses often makes this provision useless. *§ 213(a)*. In addition, a self-employed taxpayer is allowed to deduct a percentage of medical insurance costs as an above-the-line deduction. *§ 162(l)*. That percentage was increased from 25% to 40% by the 1996 tax law, and was scheduled to reach 50% by 2003 and 80% by 2006, over a phase-in period. Then, the 1997 Tax Act raised the percentage again to reach 80% by the year 2003 and 100% by the year 2007.

[B]—Employer-purchased insurance

Taxpayers can often exclude the value of premiums from their income when the employer buys the insurance for the employee-taxpayer. Why does the code do this? First, remember that the employer's promise to pay for losses is not itself taxed (the employees are cash basis taxpayers who do not report the value of promises). Second, the code wants to encourage employers to purchase these socially-desirable benefits (they are "tax expenditures").

As tax expenditures, the exclusion does not always come without conditions. The primary condition consists of "nondiscrimination" rules, which are intended to assure that the insurance protection is not limited to only highly paid employees and employees who own the business. The nondiscrimination rules are not uniform, however, among the tax-free insurance protection discussed in this chapter.

Here is a quick summary of the personal insurance exclusion rules.

Life insurance. Only *term* life insurance protection can be excluded from an employee's income. If the insurance has a cash value to the employee (analogous to a bank account that can be borrowed against or cashed in), there is no exclusion of life insurance protection. In addition, the premium value of no more than $50,000 of term life insurance can be excluded. The exclusion does not apply to high income employees if the plan discriminates in their favor. *§ 79*.

Medical and disability insurance. Medical and disability insurance and insurance-like protection can be excluded from an employee's income. *§ 106*. This covers not only insurance protection but also amounts set aside by an employer in a fund to cover employee losses. This exclusion is not conditioned on nondiscrimination, probably because small businesses appear to have inordinate trouble complying with nondiscrimination rules.

Consequently, high income employees can be the sole beneficiaries of tax-free employer-funded medical and disability insurance protection. (If the only beneficiaries are employees who are also shareholders of a corporation, there is some case law denying the exclusion on the grounds that the plan is for shareholders, not employees. *Larkin v. Commissioner*, 394 F.2d 494 (1st Cir. 1968); *Seidel v. Commissioner*, 30 T.C.M. (CCH) 1021 (1971).)

The 1996 tax law expanded the definition of medical and disability insurance (referred to as accident and health insurance) to include long-term care insurance. *§ 7702B(a)(1)*. The value of the premiums paid by an employer for such insurance is therefore tax free under *§ 106*. The definition of long-term care includes the following: the individual must be chronically ill, which means an inability to perform at least two specified life activities, or require substantial supervision to protect him or her from threats to health or safety due to severe cognitive impairment. *§ 7702B(c)*. Obviously, many elderly will qualify. In addition, the services must be provided pursuant to a plan of care prescribed by a licensed health care practitioner.

Legal insurance. (Former *§ 120*). The value of insurance or insurance-like contributions to a group *prepaid* legal services plan was excludible before 1993. If the group plan discriminated in favor of highly compensated employees, the entire plan was disqualified and all employees were taxed. In addition, a plan was disqualified if more than 25% of the legal insurance benefits were provided to more than 5% owners or their families (a so-called "concentration" rule). There was also a $70 annual cap on the excluded value.

Sunsetting. The rules about legal insurance fringe benefits contained a "sunset" feature — that is, they expired at a certain date. The idea was that the provision would be periodically reviewed to see whether it should be retained. More cynically, sunsetting prevented the tax break from increasing the deficit after the expiration date. As a practical matter, sunsetted tax breaks are usually renewed in a rush at the end of a tax year without much scrutiny. Sometimes the tax year ends before renewal and the tax break is reinstated retroactively. The expiration of the legal insurance fringe benefit after the end of tax year 1992 was somewhat unusual.

Self-employed. Excluding insurance protection from an employee's income is one reason to form a corporation. Owners of a corporation hire themselves as corporate employees and become eligible for tax-free insurance protection. In some cases, a self-employed owner of an unincorporated business can include himself in an insurance plan and deduct the premiums paid for himself as well as for his employees. That was true of legal insurance (*see § 120(d)(1)*). Moreover, as noted earlier, *§ 162(l)* allows self-employed taxpayers to deduct some percentage of medical insurance premiums. There are no similar provisions for disability or life insurance.

Here is a chart summarizing (with some imprecision) the prior discussion. Do the overall results make sense?

TAX DEDUCTIBLE OR TAX FREE PERSONAL INSURANCE —
[ND(HI) = CANNOT DISCRIMINATE FOR HIGH INCOME]

	BUY OWN	EMPLOYER FUNDED	SELF-EMPLOYED BUYS
LIFE	No	Yes [term ins.-ND(HI)]	No
MEDICAL	Yes (over 7.5% AGI)	Yes	Yes (some % of ins.)
DISABILITY	No	Yes	No

Who gets the tax benefit. You might assume that the exclusion of insurance protection from an employee's income helps employees. Don't be too sure. Here is a possible scenario. An employee in the 36% bracket receives medical insurance protection worth $64. The employer knows that the employee would require $100 of before tax wages to get $64 after-tax to buy the insurance. In other words, the before-tax equivalent of the $64 is $100. So the employer lowers the employee's wages by $100, at a $64 cost to the employer. The employer captures the benefit of the $36 exclusion.

What might prevent this from happening? Suppose the employer has a lot of employees in lower tax brackets. Because they have lower income, they do not value insurance at the $64 cost to the employer. They have other needs for the money. By how much could the employer lower *their* wages when he pays $64 per person to buy them insurance? For example, assume one employee in the 15% bracket who values the insurance at $60. The before tax equivalent is only $70.59 (60/(1-.15)). Hence, these employee's wages can only be reduced by $70.59. Can the employer separate employees into different wage pools, lowering some wages by $100 and others by $70.59?

Suppose other employees in the 15% bracket value the insurance at only $50. Now the before tax equivalent is only $58.82, which is less than $64. Why might the employer nonetheless spend $64 for an employee, when the most the employer could save by reducing wages is less than $64? What would you do if you were a 36% bracket taxpayer owning the business who wants tax free insurance, but can get it only by providing nondiscriminatory benefits?

Why would the government encourage employers to spend $64 to acquire benefits which the employee values at only $60 or $50?

§ 9.02 PERSONAL LOSSES

[A]—Background

Now assume that a loss occurs — someone dies; becomes disabled or injured; incurs medical expenses or legal costs.

The tax treatment of personal losses has a long history. After some uncertainty, early agency rulings excluded recoveries for personal injuries, such as physical injuries to the body, or nonphysical personal injuries, such as libel. *S. 1384*, 2 C.B. 71; *Sol. Op. 132*, I-1 C.B. 92. They used some misleading language. One ruling said that "the human body is a kind of capital" and the proceeds compensating for the loss represented "a conversion of the capital lost through the injury." This makes it sound as though the body has a basis equal to the cash recovery, so there is no gain. But the body has no basis.

What fundamental principle(s) about the definition of taxable gain might underlie these rulings? Does any of the following language provide a clue? One ruling justified the absence of taxable gain in the following terms: the invaded right is "personal" and "in no way transferable;" "in the very nature of things there can be no correct estimate of the money value of the invaded rights. The rights on the one hand and the money on the other are incomparable things which cannot be placed on opposite sides of an equation." In discussing money received for surrender of custody of a minor child, one ruling stated that taxing the proceeds would be like treating the child as chattels.

Even this language leaves you wondering. Neither nontransferability nor estimation difficulties necessarily precludes taxing benefits. Is there something else? Does the compensation simply make up for a loss rather than provide gain — *Cf. Clark v. Commissioner*, 40 B.T.A. 333 (1939) (compensation paid by a tax advisor for excess taxes caused by the advisor's negligence is not income to taxpayer)? Is there something inappropriate about taxing amounts received upon a forced sale of a personal right, because it commercializes that which should not be treated as a market commodity?

[B]—Uncompensated losses

One possible implication of excluding compensation for personal injuries from income is that *un*compensated losses should reduce taxable income. If compensation brings someone back to a "zero" baseline, rather than produce taxable gain, an *un*compensated taxpayer has fallen below some baseline norm. Should the tax law recognize the *un*compensated loss by allowing deductions? How would it determine whether such a loss occurred; what dollar figure would it attach to the loss? The tax law does adjust for some personal losses, although it might seem arbitrary. There is an added standard deduction for the blind, *§ 63(f)*, and permanently and totally disabled taxpayers with disability income are eligible for tax credits (*§ 22*) (although the credit is carefully restricted to people with low income). Generally speaking, except for medical expenses discussed below, uncompensated losses for personal injuries do not result in deductions.

Medical expenses. When the personal loss gives rise to medical expenses, the taxpayer can deduct them. The medical expenses fix the amount of the loss accurately. The deduction is limited to amounts over 7.5% of adjusted gross income, and is an "itemized" deduction, but is not subject to the 2% floor on some itemized deductions. Drug expenses are medical expenses if they are for prescribed drugs or insulin. *§ 213(b)*.

Here are some examples of deductible medical expenses. They raise two policy issues:

(1) does the deduction accurately identify personal losses that should reduce taxable gain (are there parallels to the distinction between business and personal expenses);

(2) does the deduction make sense as a tax expenditure — that is, as sound national health care policy?

(1) A hospital bill for a private room is deductible. There is no indication that the IRS will question deductions for somewhat more comfortable or perhaps even luxurious medical facilities. The problem is analogous to first class traveling expenses for business, which are apparently not questioned (despite the parenthetical in *§ 162(a)(2)* prohibiting deduction of lavish traveling expenses).

(2) The Regulations do not permit deduction of expenses to maintain general well being such as a decent diet and exercise. *Treas. Reg. § 1.213-1(e)(1)(ii)*. The point is analogous to disallowing the deduction of food as a business expense even though food is necessary for the taxpayer to be in business. If an everyday expense is abnormally large because of a medical condition, however, the excess is deductible. *Randolph v. Commissioner*, 67 T.C. 481 (1976) (extra cost of health food over normal costs is deductible by a taxpayer whose allergies require eating such food); *Rev. Rul. 62-189*, 1962-2 C.B. 88 (wig deductible when purchased after loss of hair because of a medical problem and a doctor stated that a wigless appearance created a mental health problem); *Murray v. Commissioner*, 43 T.C.M. (CCH) 1377 (1982) (no deduction for health spa costs to lose weight, because there is no special medical problem requiring weight loss); *Rev. Rul. 80-340*, 1980-2

C.B. 81 (deduct cost of adapting TV to receive audio portion visually for a hearing impaired viewer); *Rev. Rul. 70-606*, 1970-2 C.B. 66 (deduct extra cost of adapting car for person in wheelchair).

(3) Luxurious personal expenses are sometimes claimed as medical expenses. Swimming pools are a favorite. There is a preliminary question whether the pool is necessary for medical treatment. *Rev. Rul. 83-33*, 1983-1 C.B. 70 (swimming helped arthritic condition); *Evanoff v. Commissioner*, 44 T.C.M. (CCH) 1394 (1982) (expense questioned because of availability of local community pool). If the pool is medically necessary, the amount spent on the pool might still be too large for the entire cost to be considered a medical expense. Courts vary in their willingness to second guess the amount spent on the pool. The cheapest facility is not required, but it is unclear just how much more can be spent and still be deductible. *Ferris v. Commissioner*, 582 F.2d 1112 (7th Cir. 1978), *rev'g* 36 T.C.M. (CCH) 765 (1977). In any event, the amount of the deduction is reduced by any increase in the residence's value from pool installation. *Treas. Reg. § 1.213-1(e)(1)(iii).*

(4) Private school tuition falls somewhere between luxury items and everyday expenses. If the school's resources for alleviating a mental or physical handicap are a principal reason for spending the tuition, the entire tuition expense is a medical expense. Schools for students with neurologically verifiable learning disabilities are a typical case. *Rev. Rul. 78-340*, 1978-2 C.B. 124. A more difficult case is one where the child has at least average intelligence but still has a learning problem. In *Greisdorf v. Commissioner*, 54 T.C. 1684 (1970), the school was specially established to deal with emotional problems that interfered with learning, the teachers all had psychological training, and education was incidental to the elimination of the students' learning disabilities. The expenses were deductible. But in *Ripple v. Commissioner*, 54 T.C. 1442 (1970), the fact that the school had a remedial reading program for students who had emotional problems did not make it a special school for which tuition was deductible.

(5) Medical expenses arising from particular lifestyle choices are deductible, whatever the lifestyle, *Rev. Rul. 73-325*, 1973-2 C.B. 75 (treatment for alcoholics), unless the expenditure is illegal. *Rev. Rul. 73-201*, 1973-1 C.B. 140 (illegal abortion).

(6) Medical procedures are deductible if they "affect any structure or function of the body," even if nonmedical reasons motivate the expenditure. *Rev. Rul. 73-201*, 1973-2 C.B. 140 (abortion and vasectomy).

Since 1991, the deduction of cosmetic surgery expenses is explicitly disallowed, unless related to congenital abnormality, injury, or disease. *§ 213(d)(9).* Why was it ever deductible? Was the deduction required by the disjunctive "*or* for the purpose of affecting any structure, etc." in *§ 213(d)(1)(A)*? How could you justify a narrower interpretation?

(7) Because the medical expense deduction is subject to a 7.5% floor and is an itemized deduction, taxpayers are often better off if the expense is a business expense. In *Rev. Rul. 71-45*, 1971-1 C.B. 51, a professional singer wanted to deduct the costs of having her throat specially treated by a doctor to keep it in top singing condition. The ruling permitted the deduction only as a medical expense. In *Rev. Rul. 58-382*, 1958-2 C.B. 59, a pilot who was required to have annual physicals to keep his job was allowed a *§ 162* business expense deduction for the physicals, but only a medical expense deduction for any subsequent treatment needed to keep him fit to be a pilot. Are these rulings correct? *See also Denny v. Commissioner*, 33 B.T.A. 738 (1935) (actor lost his teeth while acting and was allowed a business expense deduction for the cost of replacement).

(8) No deduction is allowed if expenses are "compensated for by insurance or otherwise." Suppose a taxpayer collects an unallocated exempt lump sum *§ 104* recovery, which includes compensation for *future* medical expenses. *Rev. Rul. 79-427*, 1979-2 C.B. 120, disallowed a *§ 213* deduction for medical expenses paid after the *§ 104* recovery. However, in *Niles v. United States*, 710 F.2d 1391 (9th Cir. 1983), the court disagreed, in part because allocating the *§ 104* recovery would be very difficult.

(9) The 1996 tax law expanded the list of available deductible medical expenses. First, payments for long-term care, as defined earlier, are itemized medical expense deductions, subject to the 7.5% floor. *§§ 213(d)(1)(C); 7702B(a)(4)*. Premiums for long-term care insurance also qualify as deductible medical expenses, up to specified amounts (inflation-adjusted). *§ 213(d)(1)(D),(10)*.

Second, employees of small businesses and self-employed individuals can deduct contributions to "medical savings accounts" (MSAs) to pay health care costs, as long as the taxpayer also purchases high deductible health insurance. *§ 220*. These deductions for contributions to MSAs reduce AGI; they are not itemized deductions and are not subject to the 7.5% floor. *§ 62(a)(16)*. (In addition, employer contributions to such accounts are not taxed to the employee. *§ 106(b)*). This is a test program available only to the first 750,000 individuals to enroll during the pilot period (1997–2000). It was obviously a political compromise, allowing Congress and the President to begin a program to help finance medical costs without excessive loss of tax revenue. New accounts cannot be set up after 2000, unless Congress renews the program.

In addition, the 1997 Tax Act authorizes medical savings accounts for the first 390,000 of Medicare-eligible individuals (such individuals were not eligible to participate in the MSAs authorized by the 1996 law). *§ 138*.

There is a more general observation to be made about the politics of these changes in the tax rules applicable to medical expenses. Major changes in government subsidies of medical expenses have been politically difficult to pass. Consequently, there has been a downsizing — some would say "tinkering" —with the rules to provide some subsidies through the tax law, without completely overhauling the medical care delivery system.

Question. A taxpayer who lives in New England is advised by her doctor to go to a warm dry climate during certain months of the year to obtain relief from asthma and allergies. Can the taxpayer deduct transportation to get there; or meals or lodging at the destination? She requires no medical treatment at the destination? *See § 213(d)(1)(B),(2). Commissioner v. Bilder*, 369 U.S. 499 (1962).

[C]—Compensated losses

compensation for pers'l loss

If a taxpayer receives compensation for a personal loss, valuation problems disappear. The dollar receipt presumably measures the amount of the loss. Does that mean that the compensation should be excluded from income? Here is the statutory pattern for insurance and employer payments covering loss of life, medical expenses, and disability benefits, and for the now-expired legal cost fringe benefit. Consider whether the rationale for excluding personal injury compensation, discussed at the beginning of this section, can explain the statutory pattern. If there is an exclusion, does it really make up for a personal loss? We leave a detailed discussion of tort damages to the following section.

Loss of life. Life insurance proceeds are tax free if paid on account of the death of the insured, whether the insured buys the insurance or the employer provides it as a tax-free fringe benefit to the employee, and whether it is term insurance or has a cash value. *§ 101(a).* Here is some information about the difference between term and cash value life insurance that helps you decide whether the exclusion of life insurance makes sense. Term insurance is a pure gamble. The insurance company receives a premium each year; the older you are the higher the premium. As in a horse race, there are winners and losers at the end of the year. The "winners" collect; the losers get no money.

With cash value life insurance, the life insurance premiums include both term insurance elements and a savings feature ("cash value"). The savings feature earns interest. You can borrow based on the cash value and can also cash in the policy during your life. When you die, the payment includes a lot of interest which has accrued on the cash value. If you die when you are quite old, is the insurance payment likely to be mostly cash value plus interest, or an amount paid for winning the gamble on the term interest portion of the premium? Is the exclusion from income for the interest element justified?

What if a terminally ill individual draws down life insurance benefits in excess of cost? The 1996 tax law defines tax exempt "death" benefits to include amounts paid to terminally ill individuals, even though the amounts are not paid on account of the death of the insured. *§ 101(g)(1)(A).* A terminally ill individual is one whose physician certifies that death is reasonably expected to occur within 24 months. *§ 101(g)(4)(A).*

In addition, payments under a life insurance contract can be excluded if paid to a chronically ill individual, defined in a manner similar to the new rules dealing with long-term care insurance. *§ 101(g)(1)(B),(3),(4)(B).*

Medical expenses. Medical insurance proceeds are tax free if the insured buys the insurance. *§ 104(a)(3).*

If the employer buys the insurance as a tax-free fringe benefit for the employee, the insurance proceeds are still tax free to the employee. *§ 105(a),(b).* There are no nondiscrimination conditions. However, if the employer pays the employee's medical expenses directly (rather than buying insurance for the employee), exclusion from the employee's income depends on satisfying nondiscrimination rules. *§ 105(h).*

As noted earlier, the 1996 tax law has expanded the category of tax-favored insurance to include long-term care insurance. The proceeds are therefore exempt under *§ 104*, if the insurance is purchased by an individual for his or her own benefit (*§ 7702B(a)(2)*), and under *§ 105*, if purchased by an employer for an employee (*§ 7702B(a)(3)*). However, these exempt amounts are capped at $175 per day (inflation-adjusted), if the insurance contract pays a set amount per diem, unless the individual is terminally ill; amounts over this dollar ceiling *can* be received tax free if they reimburse for *actual* costs. *§ 7702B(d).*

Disability benefits. Disability insurance proceeds are tax free if the insured buys the insurance. *§ 104(a)(3).*

If the employer buys the insurance as a tax-free fringe benefit or pays disability benefits to the employee, the proceeds are tax-free only under the following narrowly defined circumstances: the proceeds must be paid without regard to the time spent out of work and must be for permanent loss or loss of use of a member or function of the body, or permanent disfigurement. *§ 105(a),(c).* An exception is Workers Compensation, which is government-mandated disability insurance funded by employers. Workers Compensation benefits are tax free to the employee in all cases. *§ 104(a)(1).*

Legal costs. Under the now-repealed *§ 120*, compensation for legal costs was tax free if paid pursuant to an employer plan which met the same qualifications exempting the employee on contributions to a group legal services plan. Under current law, no statutory provisions explicitly allow taxpayers to buy legal insurance on their own and exclude the proceeds.

Looking at insurance protection and compensation together. The discussion has looked at insurance protection and compensation for personal losses separately. Was the cost of insurance protection a personal expense? Did the compensation produce "gain?" Maybe you should look at them together. Here is the argument for doing so.

Insurance is a wealth transfer from "losers" to "winners." In that respect it is like a gift. There should be only one tax on the income transfer. If both the insurance protection and the compensation are included in taxable income, more than the total income transfer is taxed. Consider this example. Assume the income transfer occurs without the insurance company charging anything for its services. Ten people buy insurance, for $10 each. One of them suffers a $100 loss, and receives $100. Thus, ten people have paid a total of $100, and one person receives $100. If the insurance protection *and* the compensation is taxed, much more than $100 is taxed.

If there should be only one tax, should it be on the insurance protection or the compensation? The time of loss is likely to be an unpopular time to tax people on the compensation (as with life insurance). In some cases, they may be very strapped for cash (as with medical insurance).

But maybe more that $100 *should* be taxed. If ten people go to bed at night secure in the knowledge that they are protected from serious loss, does security itself produce taxable personal consumption? The nine who suffer no loss have security valued at $90, and the loser has a $100 benefit (or do you subtract the $10 premium from the $100?).

Reconsider the pattern of taxing insurance protection and compensation for personal losses discussed in this chapter. When is there one tax, on either the protection or compensation? When is the value of *both* protection and compensation excluded from income? Does "double exclusion" make sense as social policy, whether or not it makes sense as a definition of taxable "gain?"

QUESTIONS

Although many of the legal issues are answered explicitly by the statute (even though the answers are complicated), there are some situations where the answers are not explicit.

1. Suppose an individual buys legal insurance to cover against *personal* legal expenses. Or, now that *§ 120* has been repealed, suppose that an employer buys such a policy for an employee. Would the insurance *proceeds* be taxable?

2. Suppose an individual buys tax audit insurance, which compensates the taxpayer both for any increase in tax resulting from an audit, and for tax counsel expenses for representation during the audit. Is all or part of the premium deductible; all or part of the insurance proceeds exempt from tax? *A Report on Tax Audit Insurance*, 22 Tax Notes 53 (1984).

3. *Pub. L. No. 104–106*, 110 Stat. 299, authorized the sale of Ready Reserve Mobilization Income Insurance, but this program has now been repealed. It allowed individuals to insure against loss of income from a better paying job if they were mobilized into active duty in the Armed Services during war or national emergency. The law was silent as to tax consequences. Were the premiums deductible; would the insurance compensation paid for lost income have been excludible from income?

§ 9.03 TORT RECOVERIES

As noted earlier, the exclusion of recoveries for personal injuries is rooted in a fundamental conception of gain. The recoveries do not provide "gain" but only compensate for loss. The statute has long contained an explicit rule excluding damages for personal injury. *§ 104(a)(2).* The statutory exclusion has spawned a number of issues.

Physical and nonphysical injury. There had been considerable uncertainty about whether compensation for *non*physical personal injury was excluded from income by the statute. Most courts held that it was; thus, defamation damages were excluded. *Church v. Commissioner*, 80 T.C. 1104 (1983). The injury nonetheless had to be "tort-like," not "contract-like." Payments to a taxpayer for advance waiver of potential personal injury claims were not excludable. A taxpayer, for example, could not exclude payments received in exchange for releasing right of privacy claims potentially arising from a movie production. *Roosevelt v. Commissioner*, 43 T.C. 77 (1964). And proceeds from sale of blood by a taxpayer with a rare blood type were taxable. *United States v. Garber*, 589 F.2d 843 (5th Cir. 1979). Does the tort vs. contract distinction shed any light on the reason for the exclusion in the first place?

There was less certainty about business torts. The government argued against exclusion for business tort recoveries in personal injury cases (*e.g.*, a business libel) on the ground that damages are generally taxed like the replaced income would have been taxed under *Glenshaw Glass*, 348 U.S. 426 (1955). Because business profits were taxable, damages replacing the lost profits were taxable. *Rev. Rul. 85–143*, 1985–2 Cum. Bull. 55. But the courts generally favored the taxpayer (*see Threlkeld v. Commissioner*, 848 F.2d 81 (6th Cir. 1988)), on the ground that (1) *§ 104* is an exception to the rule taxing damages like the income they replace, (2) the replacement of lost wages is exempt under that section in typical negligence cases, even though wages are otherwise taxable, and (3) there is no reason to be less generous to business tort plaintiffs in personal injury cases.

These disputes were mooted by a 1996 amendment, which stated that the exclusion for damages applies only if it is on account of a personal *physical* injury or *physical* sickness. *§ 104(a)(2)*. The impetus for this statutory amendment was the proliferation of tort-like claims under Civil Rights statutes (new statutory torts). In *United States v. Burke*, 504 U.S. 229 (1992), the Court held that a statute providing only back pay money awards in an employment discrimination case did not provide recovery for tort-like injuries. Then, in *Commissioner v. Schleier*, 515 U.S. 323 (1995), the Court narrowed *§ 104(a)(2)* coverage even further. *Schleier*, which involved a civil rights claim for age discrimination, held that the damages had to be "on account of" the personal injury, even if the injury were tort-like. And, further, that back pay damages were not "on account of" the personal injury. The Court bifurcated the impact of the discriminatory act into a personal injury and loss of wages, contrasting it with a physical tort, where the wage loss (including back wages) is the direct result of the personal injury (as in a car accident). The Court did not resolve the tax treatment of *compensatory* damages that *were* causally linked to the personal injury — that is, to the age (or other) discrimination protected against by various civil rights laws. For example, suppose the plaintiff endured pain and suffering from the illegal discharge, or other employers would not hire the plaintiff because they suspected that the discharge from employment reflected badly on employment performance.

As noted, the 1996 statute clearly resolved this issue — against the taxpayer. Moreover, the new limit on exclusion of personal injury awards is not restricted to statutory torts. The fact that the injury is tort-like is no longer sufficient. Thus, recoveries for traditional nonphysical injury torts, such as business libel, are now taxable. The statute adds, explicitly, that emotional distress is not a physical injury. *§ 104(a)(next to last sentence)*. Thus, compensation for physical symptoms caused by emotional distress torts would not be excluded (as in a tort action for negligent infliction of emotional distress); they are on account of a nonphysical injury and are therefore not excluded by the statute.

The new law provides the following exception: it excludes from income any compensation for medical expenses attributable to emotional distress arising from a nonphysical injury (*e.g.*, medical treatment for mental anguish arising after a parent sues for emotional distress caused by witnessing an accident involving his or her child). *§ 104(a)(last sentence).*

The new law also does not change prior law excluding damage recoveries for physical injury, including the exclusion of damages for emotional distress incident to a physical injury. For example, pain and suffering damages incident to a car accident in which the plaintiff was physically injured are excluded. Such damages are on account of a physical injury, not on account of a nonphysical injury.

QUESTIONS

1. Now that nonphysical torts do not support exclusion of compensation from taxable income, it will take some creative lawyering to exclude such damages. Suppose your client has been subject to sex discrimination on the job, which included a touching. This violates federal law, but it may also be a battery under state law. Wouldn't damages for battery still be excluded under *§ 104*? Remember that most cases are settled out of court. How would you draft the settlement agreement to favor your client?

2. There are old rulings excluding compensation from *§ 61* income even without regard to *§ 104. See Priv. Ltr. Rul. 9223046* (payments from the Dutch government to compensate for disability arising while resisting enemy occupying power during WWII); *Rev.Rul. 58–370*, 1958–2 Cum. Bull. 19 (compensation paid by Austrian government for Nazi persecution). Do these rulings survive the recent amendment deleting the exclusion of nonphysical personal injury awards from *§ 104*? Is the personal injury physical? Is the compensation for a loss other than a personal injury in the first place?

Punitive damages. The tax treatment of punitive damages in personal injury cases has been much disputed. Punitive damages are, of course, *§ 61* income. But are they excluded by *§ 104*? A 1989 amendment (*last sentence of § 104(a)*) stated that punitive damages are *not* excluded, if there is no physical injury or physical sickness. It stated that the exclusion from income provided in the statute "shall not apply to any punitive damages in connection with a case not involving physical injury or physical sickness." An earlier draft of the amendment (which did not pass) stated: "paragraph (2) shall not apply to any punitive damages unless such damages are in connection with a case involving physical injury or physical sickness." This drafting history left open the question whether the exclusion *did* apply to punitive damages in connection with a case which *did* involve physical injury.

Subsequent case law and a statutory amendment answered these questions. First, the Supreme Court held that the pre-1996 version of *§ 104(a)(2)* did not exclude punitive damages under any circumstances. *O'Gilvie v. United States*, 117 S. Ct. 452 (1996) (punitive damages where woman died of toxic shock). It relied on the "on account of" language in the *§ 104(a)(2)*, concluding that punitive damages were not received on account of the personal injury. They were imposed to penalize the defendant. This decision built on the decision in *Schleier*, discussed earlier, which dealt with a different issue — the tax treatment of damages to compensate for violations of various civil rights laws.

Second, the Code was amended in 1996 prospectively (*see § 104(a)(2)(first parenthtetical)*) to tax punitive damages (except for punitive damages in wrongful death actions in the rare instance where the state law in effect on September 13, 1995 provides that *only* punitive damages can be recovered).

Pre-judgment interest. An issue that is still important after *Schleier*'s discussion of the "on account of" language in *§ 104(a)(2)* is the tax treatment of pre-judgment interest on personal injury tort awards. The direction of judicial decisions favors inclusion in income. *Kovacs v. Commissioner*, 100 T.C. 124 (1993), *aff'd without published opinion*, 25 F.3d 1048 (6th Cir. 1994), refused to exclude such interest from income. *See also Forest v. Commissioner*, 70 T.C.M. (CCH) 349 (1995) ("Statutory interest imposed on tort judgments . . . must be included in gross income under section 61(a)(4), even under circumstances in which the underlying damages are excludable under section 104(a)(2)"; interest not received "on account of personal injuries"), *aff'd no opinion*, 104 F.3d 348 (1st Cir. 1996); *Brabson v. United States*, 73 F.3d 1040 (10th Cir. 1996) (prejudgment interest compensates for lost time value of money, not for the injury itself).

Wage replacement. Why *does* the statute exclude not only amounts traceable to pain and suffering and medical expenses, but also replacement of lost income in cases of personal physical injury? Why isn't wage replacement taxed like the wages would have been, just as damages replacing business profits would be taxed in a case not involving personal injury (*e.g*, trade mark infringement)?

Evaluate the following arguments for not taxing wage replacement.

(1) *Sorting out settlements.* Most tort claims are settled. If the settlement consisted of both taxable and nontaxable income, fraudulent allocations by

the negotiating parties would occur, and the agency would have considerable difficulty sorting out the correct amounts.

(2) *Undercompensation.* Tort plaintiffs are undercompensated, especially after subtraction of attorney's fees. Tax exclusion indirectly makes up for undercompensation. The risk of undercompensation increases if juries are told that tort recoveries are tax exempt. The federal rule is that juries should be told. *Gulf Offshore Co. v. Mobil Oil Corp.*, 453 U.S. 473, 486–87 (1981).

(3). *Double tax on lump sum awards.* Perhaps we *should* tax wage replacement, but there is a problem if we tax the *lump sum* paid to the taxpayer as compensation in year 0. For example, if the injury to the taxpayer causes $20 lost wages per year for five years (years 1 through 5), payment to the taxpayer of $20 per year in those years should be taxed. But what will be the impact of taxing a lump sum payment in year 0?

To answer that, you must first figure out what the lump sum will be, by discounting the future lost wages to present value. That depends on the interest rate (we assume 20% in the following example). The lump sum will be the amount needed to buy an annuity which will pay the plaintiff $20 per year for five years. The $20 annuity payment will include some of the lump sum investment and some interest earned on that investment. After five years, the investment will be gone. The payments, broken down into annual payments of principal and interest, are as follows (some rounding occurs to force the totals).

$60 INVESTED AT 20% TO PRODUCE 5-YEAR $20 ANNUITY

Year	Principal	Interest	Total
1	8	12	20
2	9.5	10.5	20
3	11.5	8.5	20
4	14	6	20
5	17	3	20
	60	40	100

If we tax the $60 lump sum in year 0, the plaintiff cannot purchase an annuity producing $20 per year. If the plaintiff is in the 28% bracket, taxing the $60 leaves him with only $43.20 to invest. That will produce a five-year annuity of only $14.40 per year. That is not surprising. $14.40 is 72% of $20. By taxing the $60 at a 28% rate, you leave 72% of $60 to invest, so it produces only 72% of what $60 would have produced annually.

Of course, $14.40 is exactly the right amount the plaintiff should end up with every year, if wage replacement were taxed — it is $20 after paying a 28% tax. The trouble is that some of the $14.40 received as an annuity is taxable interest on the $43.20 investment. After taxing the interest, the taxpayer ends up with less than $14.40 per year.

Will exempting the $60 lump sum payment produce the "correct" result — $14.40 per year after tax? No. The exemption is too generous. By exempting the $60 in year 0, rather than just *deferring* tax on the $60, we allow the taxpayer to use the $60 invested in year 0 as deductible basis. Only the 20% interest on the investment is taxed, not the full $20 annual payment. Consequently, the taxpayer who invests the $60 ends up with less than $20 but more than $14.40 in each of the following 5 years.

If we really wanted to equate the plaintiff with someone earning $20 per year, we would let the plaintiff *defer* tax on the $60, if it was invested to produce future annual payments. Then we would tax the $20 annual payments, yielding $14.40 after tax.

There are other ways to modify the generous results under current law and reach the "right" $14.40 answer. *First*, do not pay plaintiff a lump sum. Instead pay the plaintiff annually an amount equal to *after* tax wages (that is, $14.40); then exempt the annual payments.

Second, tax the $60 lump sum. That leaves $43.20 to be invested. Then exempt the interest portion of the annuity when it is collected each year. $14.40 is therefore collected each year without further tax.

What is the impact of *§ 130(a,c)*? It deals with a so-called "structured settlements" in which plaintiffs do not collect a lump sum, but arrange to have the lump sum paid to an insurance company which then makes annual payments to the plaintiff? If the case involves a physical injury or physical sickness, the lump sum is not taxed upon receipt by the insurance company. The periodic payments can then be paid out as a tax free annuity to the plaintiff. (*See* the exemption for "periodic payments" in the *§ 104(a)(2)* parenthetical). Using the prior figures, will the insurance company invest $60 to produce tax free $20 payments or will the bargaining over the settlement lower annual payments to $14.40, or somewhere in between?

Allocation of damage awards. The prior discussion has suggested numerous situations requiring allocation of lump sum awards (including settlements) between taxable and nontaxable amounts — *e.g.*, punitive damages or pre-judgment interest vs. compensatory awards for physical injuries; compensation for state law battery vs. nonphysical federal civil rights injuries. The following case dealt with the allocation issue in a narrow context but has more general implications for allocation. Are there opportunities for fraud in negotiating tort settlements?

In *Delaney v. Commissioner*, 70 T.C.M. (CCH) 353 (1995), *aff'd*, 99 F.3d 20 (1st Cir. 1996), the jury in a tort action returned a verdict in favor of the petitioner in the amount of $287,000, consisting of $175,000 in damages and $112,000 in statutory interest. During the appeal, the suit was settled for $250,000. The government allocated 39% of the settlement to taxable interest, based on the interest percentage in the jury's award. The court made the following general observations about how damage award allocations should be made, obviously leaving a lot to be worked out in future case-by-case litigation.

WELLS, JUDGE: . . .

We have often been asked to decide the proper allocation of the proceeds of a settlement agreement in the context of section 104(a)(2). In cases involving a settlement agreement which contains an express allocation, such allocation is generally the most important factor in deciding whether a payment was made on account of a tortious personal injury for purposes of exclusion under section 104(a)(2). It is well settled that express allocations in a settlement agreement will be respected to the extent that the agreement is entered into by the parties at arm's length and in good faith. . . .

If no lawsuit was instituted by the taxpayer, then we must consider any relevant documents, letters, and testimony. If a lawsuit was filed but not settled, or if a lawsuit was settled but no express allocations were made in the settlement agreement, we must consider the pleadings, jury awards, or any court orders or judgments. If a taxpayer's claims were settled and express allocations are contained in the settlement agreement, we must carefully consider such allocations. As we stated above, however, we are not required to respect the express allocations unless they were negotiated at arm's length between adverse parties. . . .

In the instant case [] the jury verdict identified statutory interest as a specific component of the sum awarded to petitioner. The jury awarded petitioner $ 287,000, which consisted of $ 175,000 in tort damages and $ 112,000 in statutory prejudgment interest. The parties later settled for $ 250,000. Although the stipulation expressly provided that the settlement amount did not include interest, the record in the instant case [] is devoid of evidence that such provision of the stipulation was the product of arm's-length negotiations between the parties. The only evidence in the record is that the parties did not discuss the tax implications of such aspect of the stipulation. Accordingly, we conclude that petitioners have failed to establish that there was no interest component to the settlement.

Based on petitioners' failure to meet their burden of proof, we sustain respondent's determination in the notice of deficiency with respect to the inclusion of $ 97,561 as statutory prejudgment interest.

Deduction of attorneys' fees. Suits for personal injuries will result in attorneys' fees. They give rise to two tax problems. First, expenses related to the production of *tax exempt* income are generally not deductible under *§ 265(a)(1)*, discussed later in § 14.04. This means that attorneys' fees to produce tax exempt awards are not deductible, but the fees allocable to the taxable portion of the award are deductible.

The simplest way to make the allocation is on the basis of the amount of the taxable and nontaxable awards. That is what the government did in *Delaney v. Commissioner*, 70 T.C.M. (CCH) 353 (1995), *aff'd*, 99 F.3d 20 (1st Cir. 1996).

$$\text{Total attorneys' fees} \times \frac{\text{Nonexempt income}}{\text{Total Award}} = \text{Deductible expenses}$$

But is that necessarily the best way to allocate in all cases? Suppose most of the work, based on time spent, was done in connection with recovering the taxable or nontaxable damages; or suppose the really hard work was related to the taxable or nontaxable recovery. Is the dollar amount of recovery just a presumptive figure?

Second, assuming attorneys' fees are deductible, are they deductible in computing AGI or are they itemized deductions? If the damages are for employment discrimination and are taxable, wouldn't the related attorneys' fees be miscellaneous itemized deductions, originating in the trade or business of being an employee, and therefore subject to the 2% floor? Suppose taxable pre-judgment interest and punitive damages are recovered? Are the related attorneys' fees characterized by the underlying cause of action — for example, as employment-related, if the lawsuit concerned the employment relationship? *See Alexander v. IRS*, 72 F.3d 938 (1st Cir. 1996) (taxable damages received for breach of an employment contract; the attorney's fees were deductible as employee business expenses, but only as below-the-line miscellaneous itemized deductions, subject to the 2% floor).

If the lawsuit is *not* employment-related, but has a personal origin (*e.g.*, a car accident on vacation), can the legal expenses be a deductible *§ 212(1)* expense (though still a miscellaneous itemized deduction) to collect nonbusiness income, or does the personal origin of the lawsuit prevent the deduction?

CHAPTER 10

CHARITY

§ 10.01 CHARITABLE DEDUCTIONS

[A]—Rationale

The idea behind the charitable deduction is to allow taxpayers to exclude from their tax base whatever they give to charitable organizations. A nearly complete list of *§ 170(c)* charitable donees includes organizations "organized and operated exclusively for religious, charitable, scientific, literary, or educational purposes," or to foster amateur sports competition, or prevent cruelty to animals. What language in this statutory text includes the following: a hospital; a museum; a legal aid society serving the poor; a public interest law firm litigating issues of public interest where private interests are unlikely to provide effective advocacy (*Rev. Proc. 71-39*, 1971-1 C.B. 575). In addition, tax deductible contributions can be made to the United States and state governments.

The most common justification for the charitable deduction is that the contributions help to defray costs the government would otherwise incur. This is clearly too broad a statement. The government is not likely to directly finance many of the activities covered by *§ 170(c)*. For example, universities are assisted by government funding but it is unlikely that public funding would be at the scale of charitable giving. Moreover, some types of activities would probably not get any government money, such as educational journals, especially those with an ideological slant. Finally, direct government funding of religious groups would violate the Establishment Clause of the Constitution. Perhaps we could reformulate the "substitute for government activity" rationale for charitable deductions by stating that the general activity is one which the government wants to foster, but in a pluralistic society the particular choices should be left to private decisions.

The charitable deduction therefore seems to be a tax expenditure, though one for which eligibility is very loosely defined. The outlays are an expression of the donor's preferences, which are not analogous to those personal expense deductions (such as medical expenses), which arguably do no more than maintain some benchmark standard of living.

Another possible justification for the deduction is that gifts do not provide the donor with taxable personal consumption, because enjoyment of the power and pleasure of giving is not taxable. But why is that enjoyment less taxable than any other use of money? Isn't all enjoyment intangible, however acquired?

What about the donees of the gift? Shouldn't they pay tax and, if so, wouldn't it be a good idea to *disallow* the donor's deduction as a proxy for taxing the donee? The force of this suggestion is diminished, however, when we look at who benefits from charitable giving. Either the poor benefit from the gift (and they should not pay tax on the gift), or the general public benefits from the charitable activities (and it is questionable whether anyone ought to be taxed on such widely dispersed benefits). The donor's deduction should therefore stand or fall on its own merits, uncomplicated by considerations related to the donee.

no inclusion either

[B]—Deductions as the incentive mechanism

Any incentive provision invites the usual questions about whether a deduction is the proper method to encourage the activity. For example, why should the taxpayer in the 36% bracket save 36 cents for every one dollar given, while taxpayers in the 15% bracket save only 15 cents per dollar given? In effect, the 36% bracket taxpayer can give up 64 cents of after tax income and force the government to match it with a 36-cent gift to the charity of his choice, while the 15% bracket taxpayer gives up 85 cents of after tax income to force the government to contribute a 15-cent gift to his favorite charity. But that is always the effect of a deduction in a progressive tax rate structure. If it is meant as an incentive, the question is whether it is needed as an incentive.

why should DD benefit rich?

It is arguable that the well-off need the large benefits of a deduction to encourage them to give. Remember that charitable giving is likely to be low on the taxpayer's list of consumer preferences. The gift precludes other uses of the money, which is compounded if the donor must pay taxes out of other income on the amount of the gift. Lower income taxpayers might not need much of an incentive because they are more likely to give to the charity of their choice, such as a church. Consequently, the upside down effects of a deduction in giving more dollar benefits to higher bracket taxpayers per dollar of expenditure is not necessarily inefficient as social policy, whatever its distributional effects.

[C]—Mechanics

Payment. Technically, a deduction requires a "payment." *§ 170(a)(1).* "Payment" includes out-of-pocket expenses incurred by a taxpayer while helping a charity (transportation to get to a charitable organization's meeting, for example). However, depreciation is not a payment (so use of a car is not a deductible payment). *Rev. Proc. 80-7*, para. 3.02, 1980-1 C.B. 590.

must make a payment to take a DD

Providing personal services without charge is also not a deductible payment — for example, a doctor volunteering some time in a local clinic. *Treas. Reg. § 1.170A-1(g).* The free service provider is not, however, disadvantaged because the value of the services is not included in income. In fact, one rationale for the charitable deduction is that it equates the free service provider (no income, no deduction) with someone who earns money and gives it to charity (income minus deduction).

Percentage limits on deduction. Taxpayers can deduct charitable contributions *to* certain organizations, up to 50% of their adjusted gross income (AGI). These organizations (50% organizations) are listed in *§ 170(b)(1)(A)*, and include churches, schools, hospitals, a governmental unit, and organizations which receive a substantial part of their support from the government or public.

Gifts to other charitable organizations can be deducted up to the lesser of 30% of AGI, or 50% of AGI minus gifts to 50% organizations. *§ 170(b)(1)(B)*. These "30% organizations" may be "private" foundations which engage in charitable activities but do not receive a substantial part of their support from government or the public. These private foundations can be huge — such as the Ford Foundation.

For example, a taxpayer with $100,000 AGI gives $40,000 to a university (a 50% organization), and $20,000 to an educational organization which publishes historical studies (a 30% organization). How much can the donor deduct?

"To" or "for use of". A small statutory wrinkle with potentially large consequences subjects gifts "for the use of" a charity (even for the use of a "50% organization") to the same percentage limits as gifts "to" a "30% organization." A gift in trust for a charity is "for the use of" the charity.

Carryover. Deductions which exceed the percentage ceilings can be carried forward for five years.

Itemized deduction. The charitable deduction is an itemized deduction, not subject to the 2% floor.

Corporations. The above rules apply to individuals. Corporations are subject to different rules. They can deduct 10% of their taxable income as charitable gifts. The AGI and itemized deduction concepts are inapplicable to corporations. *§ 170(b)(2).*

No business deduction for gifts in excess of ceiling. Charitable deductions which exceed the percentage ceiling cannot be deducted as business expenses. *§ 162(b).*

Appreciated property. The deduction for charitable contributions of appreciated property is subject to limits explained later in this chapter.

Procedure to obtain tax exemption. Requesting tax-exempt status from the IRS is usually a condition of becoming a tax-deductible organization. Once on the IRS published list, donors can take deductions for gifts to that organization unless they are aware of circumstances which would result in loss of exemption. Eligibility to receive tax deductible contributions is so important that it is one of the few situations in which disagreement with the IRS can be appealed to a court prior to paying tax or receiving a deficiency notice that tax is due. *§ 7428.*

Working for nothing. Some taxpayers are members of a religious order and take a vow of poverty. They have regular jobs, but they turn over their entire pay checks to the religious order. If a member of an order receives money as the agent of the order, she is not taxed. *Rev. Rul. 77-290*, 1977-2 C.B. 26. That is hardly a startling rule; no agent is taxed on money received for a principal. But when the taxpayer has an employment relationship with a third party, rather than acting as an agent of the religious order, she is the income earner and includes earnings in gross income, even though all income is deflected to the charity. This is an example of the assignment of income rules discussed in an earlier chapter. Examples include: a nurse-practitioner for the federal government (*Schuster v. Commissioner*, 84 T.C. 764 (1985), *aff'd*, 800 F.2d 672 (7th Cir. 1986)); Associate Professor of Religious Studies at Virginia University (*Fogarty v. United States*, 780 F.2d 1005 (Fed. Cir. 1986)); and a lawyer working for a law firm (*Rev. Rul. 77-290*, 1977-2 C.B. 26).

The government cares whether a deductible contribution is first included in the taxpayer's gross income and then deducted, because of the 50%-of-AGI ceiling on charitable deductions. Does the 50% ceiling make sense for a taxpayer who takes a vow of poverty?

§ 10.02 TAX-EXEMPT ORGANIZATIONS

[A]—In general

Tax-exempt organizations are a much broader category than the *§ 170(c)* tax-deductible group. Many of them are listed in *§ 501(c)*. For example, labor unions, business leagues, and social clubs are exempt from income tax. *§ 501(c)(5),(6),(7).* Dues paid to these organizations are not deductible under *§ 170*, however, and can only be deducted if they are business expenses. We are concerned in this chapter primarily with exempt organizations to which deductible contributions can be made. *§ 170(c)* and *§ 501(c)(3)* are virtually identical so people often refer to *§ 501(c)(3)* tax exempt organizations as those to whom tax deductible contributions can be made, even though *§ 170(c)* is the accurate citation.

§ 501(c)(4) provides tax exemption for organizations which promote social welfare, operated primarily to bring about civic betterments and social

improvements. The distinction between *(c)(4)* and *(c)(3)* organizations is murky. *Compare Rev. Rul. 78-68*, 1978-1 C.B. 149 (an organization formed to provide public transportation to isolated areas of town not served by existing city bus systems, thereby enabling low income residents to commute to work, is a *(c)(3)* organization) *with Rev. Rul 78-69*, 1978-1 C.B. 156 (organization providing suburban residents with bus service during rush hours to supplement regular bus service to the city is a *(c)(4)* organization).

[B]—Limits

Profitmaking. There is no general rule prohibiting a donee charitable organization from making profits as long as the profit-making activity does not undermine its charitable objectives. It might undermine that objective if activities were conducted primarily with an eye to making profits, as in the case of a for-profit hospital or a blood bank organized to make money.

There is, however, a separate tax on the unrelated business income of otherwise tax exempt charities, such as a macaroni factory owned by New York University. *§ 511–14.* Museum gift shops, for example, sell some items which are related (reproductions) and others which are not (souvenir items with a museum logo). *See G.C.M. 38949*, discussed in 18 Tax Notes 287 (1983). And, in *Rev. Rul. 78–149*, 1978–1 C.B. 169, a blood bank processed plasma for resale from whole blood acquired for the blood bank's charitable purposes when that blood was nearing the end of its shelf life. This income was "related." However, the sale of plasma would have produced unrelated business income, if the purchase of whole blood was primarily in order to sell the plasma.

A clear case of unrelated business income is advertising revenue in an otherwise exempt publication (such as National Geographic), if the ads are displayed on the basis of the advertiser's ability to pay rather than educating the public in accordance with the magazine's exempt purpose. *United States v. American College of Physicians*, 475 U.S. 834 (1986).

Recent controversy has arisen over whether football bowl sponsorship revenues are unrelated business income (as advertising revenue). Mobil Oil, for example, sponsors a bowl game and has its name prominently displayed on the playing field, scoreboard, and on players uniforms. Public Television also receives contributions and broadcasts acknowledgements which prominently display the donors' names, logos, and brief messages when programs begin. After considerable publicity, the government proposed regulations which virtually give up trying to tax such income as unrelated business income. *See* 58 Fed. Reg. 5687-02 (Jan. 22, 1993). As long as the contribution is not contingent on TV ratings or attendance, there is no comparative information about a competitor's products, and no special treatment of the donor or its officials, the contributions will usually be treated as tax-free "acknowledgement" income rather than taxable unrelated advertising business income.

Then Congress got into the act. The 1997 Tax Act (*§ 513(i)*) specifies that unrelated business income does not include "qualified sponsorship payments," which it defines to mean payments for which there is no arrangement or expectation of "substantial return benefit," other than use or acknowledgement of the payor's name or logo or product lines. Moreover, the payee cannot provide the following:

(1) messages containing qualitative or comparative language, price information, indications of savings or value, an endorsement, or an inducement to purchase, sell, or use the payor's products or services;

(2) any payment conditioned on level of attendance at events, broadcast ratings, or other factors indicating public exposure; and

(3) any payment which entitles the payor to acknowledgement of the payor's name or logo or product lines in regularly scheduled and printed material published by or on behalf of the payee organization, unless it is related to and primarily distributed in connection with a specific event conducted by the payee (such as a program printed in connection with an annual clean air day sponsored by an environmental group).

These rules obviously provide favorable tax treatment for much of what PBS does in its broadcasts to acknowledge gifts.

The House Committee Report also states that granting the payor a license to use the payee's trademark or logo will be treated as separate from the qualified sponsorship transaction in deciding whether there is a tax on unrelated business income.

Unrelated business income is taxed only if it is "regularly carried on." One court held that this requirement prevented taxing advertising revenues from publishing the NCAA basketball program. The tournament lasted only a few weeks and was not serious competition for sports magazines. *NCAA v. Commissioner*, 914 F.2d 1417 (10th Cir. 1990).

The general idea behind taxing unrelated business income is that exempt organizations otherwise have an unfair competitive advantage and that exempt organizations would otherwise have an incentive to buy up for-profit businesses. These are empirical claims about the impact of the tax law which may or may not be true. Congress has held extensive hearings on unrelated business income issues and more legislation may be forthcoming. Congress may, however, neglect a problem at least as serious — whether some exempt organizations should receive tax deductible contributions. Some organizations may no longer need tax deductible status as an incentive to provide goods and services that would otherwise be undersupplied (are hospitals an example?).

For the benefit of an individual. Even if the organization is not organized to make a profit, it is not exempt if the net earnings "inure to the benefit of any private . . . individual." *§ 170(c)(2)(C).* Mail order churches often run afoul of this provision when the founder siphons off too much of the receipts for personal benefit. *See Church of Scientology v. Commissioner*, 823 F.2d 1310 (9th Cir. 1987).

Political activity. The charitable deduction is conditioned on the organization not engaging in certain political activities, to which we return in a later chapter.

[C]—§ 501(c)(3) — Defining "charitable"

BOB JONES UNIVERSITY v. UNITED STATES

461 U.S. 574 (1983)

CHIEF JUSTICE BURGER delivered the opinion of the Court. . . .

I

A

Until 1970, the Internal Revenue Service granted tax-exempt status to private schools, without regard to their racial admissions policies, under § 501(c)(3) of the Internal Revenue Code, and granted charitable deductions for contributions to such schools under § 170 of the Code. . . .

The [IRS'] revised policy on discrimination was formalized in Rev. Rul. 71-447, 1971-2 C.B. 230,

> Both the courts and the Internal Revenue Service have long recognized that the statutory requirement of being "organized and operated exclusively for religious, charitable, . . . or educational purposes" was intended to express the basic common law concept [of "charity"]. . . . All charitable trusts, educational or otherwise, are subject to the requirement that the purpose of the trust may not be illegal or contrary to public policy.

Based on the "national policy to discourage racial discrimination in education," the IRS ruled that "a private school not having a racially nondiscriminatory policy as to students is not 'charitable' within the common law concepts reflected in sections 170 and 501(c)(3) of the Code." *Id.*, at 231.

The application of the IRS construction of these provisions to petitioners, two private schools with racially discriminatory admissions policies, is now before us. . . .

II

A

. . . .

Section 501(c)(3) provides that "[c]orporations . . . organized and operated exclusively for religious, charitable . . . or educational purposes" are entitled to tax exemption. Petitioners argue that the plain language of the statute guarantees them tax-exempt status. They emphasize the absence of any language in the statute expressly requiring all exempt organizations to be "charitable" in the common law sense, and they contend that the disjunctive "or" separating the categories in § 501(c)(3) precludes such a reading. Instead, they argue that if an institution falls within one or more of the specified categories it is automatically entitled to exemption, without regard to whether it also qualifies as "charitable." The Court of Appeals rejected that contention and concluded that petitioners' interpretation of the statute "tears section 501(c)(3) from its roots."

It is a well-established canon of statutory construction that a court should go beyond the literal language of a statute if reliance on that language would defeat the plain purpose of the statute:

> "The general words used in the clause . . . , taken by themselves, and literally construed, without regard to the object in view, would seem to sanction the claim of the plaintiff. But this mode of expounding a statute has never been adopted by any enlightened tribunal — because it is evident that in many cases it would defeat the object which the Legislature intended to accomplish. And it is well settled that, in interpreting a statute, the court will not look merely to a particular clause in which general words may be used, but will take in connection with it the whole statute . . . and the objects and policy of the law. . . ." *Brown v. Duchesne*, 19 How. 183, 194, 15 L.Ed. 595 (1857).

Section 501(c)(3) therefore must be analyzed and construed within the framework of the Internal Revenue Code and against the background of the Congressional purposes. Such an examination reveals unmistakable evidence that, underlying all relevant parts of the Code, is the intent that entitlement to tax exemption depends on meeting certain common law standards of charity — namely, that an institution seeking tax-exempt status must serve a public purpose and not be contrary to established public policy.

This "charitable" concept appears explicitly in § 170 of the Code. That section contains a list of organizations virtually identical to that contained in § 501(c)(3). It is apparent that Congress intended that list to have the same meaning in both sections. In § 170, Congress used the list of organizations in defining the term "charitable contributions." On its face, therefore, § 170 reveals that Congress' intention was to provide tax benefits to organizations serving charitable purposes. The form of § 170 simply makes plain what common sense and history tell us: in enacting both § 170 and § 501(c)(3), Congress sought to provide tax benefits to charitable organizations, to encourage the development of private institutions that serve a useful public purpose or supplement or take the place of public institutions of the same kind.

Tax exemptions for certain institutions thought beneficial to the social order of the country as a whole, or to a particular community, are deeply rooted in our history, as in that of England. The origins of such exemptions lie in the special privileges that have long been extended to charitable trusts. . . .

What little floor debate occurred on the charitable exemption provision of the 1894 Act and similar sections of later statutes leaves no doubt that Congress deemed the specified organizations entitled to tax benefits because they served desirable public purposes. *See, e.g.*, 26 Cong. Rec. 585-586 (1894); *id.*, at 1727. In floor debate on a similar provision in 1917, for example, Senator Hollis articulated the rationale:

> "For every dollar that a man contributes to these public charities, educational, scientific, or otherwise, the public gets 100 percent." 55 *id.*, at 6728 (1917). . . .

In enacting the Revenue Act of 1938, ch. 289, 52 Stat. 447 (1938), Congress expressly reconfirmed this view with respect to the charitable deduction provision:

> "The exemption from taxation of money and property devoted to charitable and other purposes is based on the theory that the Government is compensated for the loss of revenue by its relief from financial burdens which would otherwise have to be met by appropriations from other public funds, and by the benefits resulting from the promotion of the general welfare." H.R. Rep. No. 1860, 75th Cong., 3d Sess. 19 (1938).

A corollary to the public benefit principle is the requirement, long recognized in the law of trusts, that the purpose of a charitable trust may not be illegal or violate established public policy. . . .

When the Government grants exemptions or allows deductions all taxpayers are affected; the very fact of the exemption or deduction for the donor means that other taxpayers can be said to be indirect and vicarious "donors." Charitable exemptions are justified on the basis that the exempt entity confers a public benefit — a benefit which the society or the community may not itself choose or be able to provide, or which supplements and advances the work of public institutions already supported by tax revenues. History buttresses logic to make clear that, to warrant exemption under § 501(c)(3), an institution must fall within a category specified in that section and must demonstrably serve and be in harmony with the public interest. The institution's purpose must not be so at odds with the common community conscience as to undermine any public benefit that might otherwise be conferred.

B

only declare "non-charitable" when offend fund'tal public policy

We are bound to approach these questions with full awareness that determinations of public benefit and public policy are sensitive matters with serious implications for the institutions affected; a declaration that a given institution is not "charitable" should be made only where there can be no doubt that the activity involved is contrary to a fundamental public policy. But there can no longer be any doubt that racial discrimination in education violates deeply and widely accepted views of elementary justice. Prior to 1954, public education in many places still was conducted under the pall of *Plessy v. Ferguson*, 163 U.S. 537 (1896); racial segregation in primary and secondary education prevailed in many parts of the country. This Court's decision in *Brown v. Board of Education*, 347 U.S. 483 (1954), signalled an end to that era. Over the past quarter of a century, every pronouncement of this Court and myriad Acts of Congress and Executive Orders attest a firm national policy to prohibit racial segregation and discrimination in public education.

[Editor — The Court then recounts the various cases, statutes, and executive orders implementing this policy.]

Few social or political issues in our history have been more vigorously debated and more extensively ventilated than the issue of racial discrimination, particularly in education. Given the stress and anguish of the history of efforts to escape from the shackles of the "separate but equal" doctrine of *Plessy v. Ferguson*, it cannot be said that educational institutions that, for whatever reasons, practice racial discrimination, are institutions exercising "beneficial and stabilizing influences in community life," or should be encouraged by having all taxpayers share in their support by way of special tax status.

There can thus be no question that the interpretation of § 170 and § 501(c)(3) announced by the IRS in 1970 was correct. . . . Racially discriminatory educational institutions cannot be viewed as conferring a public benefit within the "charitable" concept discussed earlier, or within the Congressional intent underlying § 170 and § 501(c)(3).

. . . .

D

The actions of Congress since 1970 leave no doubt that the IRS reached the correct conclusion in exercising its authority. It is, of course, not unknown for independent agencies or the Executive Branch to misconstrue the intent of a statute; Congress can and often does correct such misconceptions, if the courts have not done so. Yet for a dozen years Congress has been made aware — acutely aware — of the IRS rulings of 1970 and 1971. As we noted earlier, few issues have been the subject of more vigorous and widespread debate and discussion in and out of Congress than those related to racial segregation in education. Sincere adherents advocating contrary views have ventilated the subject for well over three decades. Failure of Congress to modify the IRS rulings of 1970 and 1971, of which Congress was, by its own studies and by public discourse, constantly reminded; and Congress' awareness of the denial of tax-exempt status for racially discriminatory schools when enacting other and related legislation make out an unusually strong case of legislative acquiescence in and ratification by implication of the 1970 and 1971 rulings.

Ordinarily, and quite appropriately, courts are slow to attribute significance to the failure of Congress to act on particular legislation. We have observed that "unsuccessful attempts at legislation are not the best of guides to legislative intent." Here, however, we do not have an ordinary claim of legislative acquiescence. Only one month after the IRS announced its position in 1970, Congress held its first hearings on this precise issue. Equal Educational Opportunity: *Hearings Before the Senate Select Comm. on Equal Educational Opportunity*, 91st Cong., 2d Sess. 1991 (1970). Exhaustive hearings have been held on the issue at various times since then. These include hearings in February 1982, after we granted review in this case.

Non-action by Congress is not often a useful guide, but the non-action here is significant. During the past 12 years there have been no fewer than 13 bills introduced to overturn the IRS interpretation of § 501(c)(3). Not one of these bills has emerged from any committee, although Congress has enacted numerous other amendments to § 501 during this same period, including an amendment to § 501(c)(3) itself. Tax Reform Act of 1976, Pub. L. 94-455, § 1313(a), 90 Stat. 1520, 1730 (1976). It is hardly conceivable that Congress — and in this setting, any Member of Congress — was not abundantly aware of what was going on. In view of its prolonged and acute awareness of so important an issue, Congress' failure to act on the bills proposed on this subject provides added support for concluding that Congress acquiesced in the IRS rulings of 1970 and 1971.

The evidence of Congressional approval of the policy embodied in Revenue Ruling 71-447 goes well beyond the failure of Congress to act on legislative proposals. Congress affirmatively manifested its acquiescence in the IRS policy when it enacted the present § 501(i) of the Code, Act of October 20, 1976, Pub. L. 94-568, 90 Stat. 2697 (1976). That provision denies tax-exempt status to social clubs whose charters or policy statements

1

Cong. never changed 1970 Rev. Ruling

therefore implicit acceptance

Cong. knew about this issue & refused to change Rev. Ruling

2

Cong. aff'ively manifested its support of Rev. Rul.

provide for "discrimination against any person on the basis of race, color, or religion." Both the House and Senate committee reports on that bill articulated the national policy against granting tax exemptions to racially discriminatory private clubs. S. Rep. No. 1318, 94th Cong., 2d Sess., 8 (1976); H.R. Rep. No. 1353, 94th Cong., 2d Sess., 8 (1976), U.S. Code Cong. & Admin. News 1976, p. 6051.

Even more significant is the fact that both reports focus on this Court's affirmance of *Green v. Connally* [330 F. Supp. 1150 (D.D.C.), *aff'd per curiam*, 404 U.S. 997 (1971)], as having established that "discrimination on account of race is inconsistent with an educational institution's tax exempt status." S. Rep. No. 1318, *supra*, at 7–8 and n. 5; H.R. Rep. No. 1353, *supra*, at 8 and n. 5, U.S. Code Cong. & Admin. News, p. 6058. These references in Congressional committee reports on an enactment denying tax exemptions to racially discriminatory private social clubs cannot be read other than as indicating approval of the standards applied to racially discriminatory private schools by the IRS subsequent to 1970, and specifically of Revenue Ruling 71-447.

Green

[Editor — Portions of the opinion dealing with the taxpayer's free exercise of religion claim are omitted.]

The judgments of the Court of Appeals are, accordingly,

Affirmed.

[D]—Statutory interpretation

Literal language vs. plain purpose. The Court in *Bob Jones* reads a "charitable" limitation into all categories of tax-exempt organizations (that is the statute's "plain purpose"), even though the statute says "charitable *or* educational." What justifies reading a general "charitable" requirement into all of *§ 501(c)(3)*; is it historical context? Does that reading make the specific reference to "charitable" in the *§ 501(c)(3)* list superfluous?

Historical context and evolving meaning. Even if the Court can read into the statute an historical requirement that tax-deductible organizations be "charitable," how can nondiscrimination be one of those requirements? The statute was originally adopted when segregation was the law and practice of the land.

Legislative inaction. How can legislative inaction ratify a prior agency interpretation of a statute? Even if the legislature was aware of the agency's interpretation, inaction does not constitute passage of a law and signature by the President. How can law be made in any other fashion? Moreover, inaction may be the result of a committee bottling up proposals to reject the agency rule, rather than legislative majority approval.

Statutory analogies. The Court cites *§ 501(i)*, which prohibits tax exemption for social clubs discriminating on the basis of race, as evidence of statutory anti-discrimination policy. Why didn't this indicate a *failure* to adopt a similar policy regarding schools and other tax exempt organizations, rather than support for a broad anti-discrimination policy. Moreover, if you look closely at the statutory text, all it does is deal with clubs having written statements favoring discrimination. The statute is silent on discriminatory *practices*, which probably undermines the statute's effectiveness.

Legislative History. The Court also cites Committee Reports supporting the view that schools which practice racial discrimination are not tax-exempt. Is that any way to legislate? Why not just amend the statute to say this explicitly?

What is the Court really doing? Perhaps the Court is really updating a statute to fit contemporary values when there is some support in the historical context for incorporating an evolving concept of charity into the statute. The Court drew on the analogy of the social club provision on the theory that it makes little sense for a legislature to be concerned with social clubs and not school discrimination. Why didn't the Court say this explicitly?

Questions. Are schools exempt if admissions policies limit students to: all male; all female; all African-American?

The Supreme Court has held that it is unconstitutional for an all-male state-supported school (Virginia Military Academy) to deny admission on gender grounds. *United States v. Virginia*, 518 U.S. 515 (1996). Does this mean that gender discrimination is as violative of public policy as race discrimination for purposes of the charitable deduction? An earlier *Technical Advice Memorandum 7744007* held that the "Federal courts have not established that sex discrimination is clearly contrary to public policy" but is instead subject to a "rationality test." Is that what you learned in constitutional law?

Would anyone have standing to force the government to tax someone on the ground that the school should not be tax exempt?

§ 10.03 DEFINING "GIFTS" *§102*

A deduction depends on more than just giving money to a charitable organization. You must also make a gift. If you buy a concert ticket to hear a symphony orchestra, you are purchasing taxable consumption, not making a deductible gift. What kinds of *quid pro quo* will prevent a payment from being a "gift?"

You have already encountered the rules exempting gifts from a donee's income. *§ 102.* We paid no attention at that time to the definition of a gift for purposes of the *§ 102* exclusion. Let's take a look at the *§ 102* gift for a moment and see how it differs from the definition of a charitable gift.

gift excludible from G.I.

The accepted definition of an excludible gift under *§ 102* is a payment made with "detached and disinterested generosity." *Commissioner v. Duberstein,* 363 U.S. 278 (1960). For many years, there was considerable litigation about whether a business could make a gift to an employee or customer. The fact-finder had some freedom to infer that detached and disinterested generosity motivated the payment. At the same time, the payor took a *§ 162* business deduction. The *Duberstein* case required appellate courts to defer to the fact-finder and held that it was possible, however unlikely, that the payor could get a deduction for an excludible gift. That problem has been minimized by *§ 274(b)(1),* which denies a business deduction for most payments which are excludible by the donee only on the ground that they are gifts. This sets up an adverse relationship between the payor and payee, and makes it unlikely that no one will pay tax on the payment.

if so, payor can take a DD?

no §274 (b)(1) busn. DD

gift + (§102) chav. DD (§170)

Despite an occasional case to the contrary, the definition of gift for the *§ 102* exclusion is not the same as the definition for deducting charitable contributions under *§ 170.* Here is why. A payment for business publicity, to build up good will, is not made out of detached and disinterested generosity. But many charitable contributions purchase good will. Corporations contribute to the local symphony, and expect a plaque with their name to be prominently displayed. A "detached and disinterested" test would disallow *§ 170* deductions for such payments and that would discourage a lot of charitable giving.

But what kind of *quid pro quo* will prevent a payment from being a deductible gift. The case of *Singer Co. v. United States,* 449 F.2d 413 (Ct. Cl. 1971), tries to draw the line. Singer sewing machines, given to schools where people learned to sew, were not deductible gifts. The expectation was that the users would become future purchasers. However, gifts of sewing machines to other groups were deductible gifts (for example, to a university theater which used sewing machines to make costumes). Would Mobil Oil's payment to sponsor the Cotton Bowl be a deductible charitable contribution? (Why might Singer or Mobil Oil want a charitable deduction? Couldn't it take a business deduction?)

The following case held that a payment to a religious organization was not a "gift." What does it tell you about the kind of *quid pro quo* which can prevent a deductible gift?

HERNANDEZ v. COMMISSIONER

490 U.S. 680 (1989)

JUSTICE MARSHALL delivered the opinion of the Court.

Section 170 of the Internal Revenue Code of 1954, permits a taxpayer to deduct from gross income the amount of a "charitable contribution." The Code defines that term as a "contribution or gift" to certain eligible donees, including entities organized and operated exclusively for religious purposes. We granted certiorari to determine whether taxpayers may deduct as charitable contributions payments made to branch churches of the Church of Scientology (Church) in order to receive services known as "auditing" and "training." We hold that such payments are not deductible. . . .

Scientologists believe that an immortal spiritual being exists in every person. A person becomes aware of this spiritual dimension through a process known as "auditing." Auditing involves a one-to-one encounter between a participant (known as a "preclear") and a Church official (known as an "auditor"). An electronic device, the E-meter, helps the auditor identify the preclear's areas of spiritual difficulty by measuring skin responses during a question and answer session. Although auditing sessions are conducted one-on-one, the content of each session is not individually tailored. The preclear gains spiritual awareness by progressing through sequential levels of auditing, provided in short blocks of time known as "intensives."

The Church also offers members doctrinal courses known as "training." Participants in these sessions study the tenets of Scientology and seek to attain the qualifications necessary to serve as auditors. Training courses, like auditing sessions, are provided in sequential levels. Scientologists are taught that spiritual gains result from participation in such courses.

The Church charges a "fixed donation," also known as a "price" or a "fixed contribution," for participants to gain access to auditing and training sessions. These charges are set forth in schedules and prices vary with a session's length and level of sophistication. In 1972, for example, the general rates for auditing ranged from $625 for a 12 1/2-hour auditing intensive, the shortest available, to $4,250 for a 100-hour intensive, the longest available. Specialized types of auditing required higher fixed donations: a 12 1/2-hour "Integrity Processing" auditing intensive cost $750; a 12 1/2-hour "Expanded Dianetics" auditing intensive cost $950. This system of mandatory fixed charges is based on a central tenet of Scientology known as the "doctrine of exchange," according to which any time a person receives something he must pay something back. In so doing, a Scientologist maintains "inflow" and "outflow" and avoids spiritual decline.

The proceeds generated from auditing and training sessions are the Church's primary source of income. The Church promotes these sessions not only through newspaper, magazine, and radio advertisements, but also through free lectures, free personality tests, and leaflets. The Church also encourages, and indeed rewards with a 5% discount, advance payment for these sessions. The Church often refunds unused portions of prepaid auditing or training fees, less an administrative charge. . . .

The legislative history of the "contribution or gift" limitation, though sparse, reveals that Congress intended to differentiate between unrequited payments to qualified recipients and payments made to such recipients in return for goods or services. Only the former were deemed deductible. . . . Using payments to hospitals as an example, both [Senate and House] Reports state that the gift characterization should not apply to "a payment by an individual to a hospital *in consideration of* a binding obligation to provide medical treatment for the individual's employees. It would apply only if there were no expectation of any quid pro quo from the hospital. . . ."

In light of this understanding of § 170, it is readily apparent that petitioners' payments to the Church do not qualify as "contribution[s] or gift[s]." As the Tax Court found, these payments were part of a quintessential *quid pro quo* exchange: in return for their money, petitioners received an identifiable benefit, namely, auditing and training sessions. The Church established fixed price schedules for auditing and training sessions in each branch church; it calibrated particular prices to auditing or training sessions of particular lengths and levels of sophistication; it returned a refund if auditing and training services went unperformed; it distributed "account cards" on which persons who had paid money to the Church could monitor what prepaid services they had not yet claimed; and it categorically barred provision of auditing or training sessions for free. Each of these practices reveals the inherently reciprocal nature of the exchange.

Petitioners do not argue that such a structural analysis is inappropriate under § 170, or that the external features of the auditing and training transactions do not strongly suggest a *quid pro quo* exchange. Indeed, the petitioners . . . conceded at trial that they expected to receive specific amounts of auditing and training in return for their payments. Petitioners argue instead that they are entitled to deductions because a *quid pro quo* analysis is inappropriate under § 170 when the benefit a taxpayer receives is purely religious in nature. Along the same lines, petitioners claim that payments made for the right to participate in a religious service should be automatically deductible under § 170.

We cannot accept this statutory argument for several reasons. First, . . . [t]he Code makes no special preference for payments made in the expectation of gaining religious benefits or access to a religious service. . . .

Second, petitioners' deductibility proposal would expand the charitable contribution deduction far beyond what Congress has provided. Numerous forms of payments to eligible donees plausibly could be categorized as providing a religious benefit or as securing access to a religious service. For example, some taxpayers might regard their tuition payments to parochial schools as generating a religious benefit or as securing access to a religious service; such payments, however, have long been held not to be charitable contributions under § 170. Taxpayers might make similar claims about payments for church-sponsored counseling sessions or for medical care at church-affiliated hospitals that otherwise might not be deductible. . . .

Accordingly, we conclude that petitioners' payments to the Church for auditing and training sessions are not "contribution[s] or gift[s]" within the meaning of that statutory expression. . . .

We turn, finally, to petitioners' assertion that disallowing their claimed deduction is at odds with the IRS' longstanding practice of permitting taxpayers to deduct payments made to other religious institutions in connection with certain religious practices. . . .

. . . [P]etitioners . . . make two closely related claims. First, the IRS has accorded payments for auditing and training disparately harsh treatment compared to payments to other churches and synagogues for their religious services: Recognition of a comparable deduction for auditing and training payments is necessary to cure this administrative inconsistency. Second, Congress, in modifying § 170 over the years, has impliedly acquiesced in the deductibility of payments to these other faiths; because payments for auditing and training are indistinguishable from these other payments, they fall within the principle acquiesced in by Congress that payments for religious services are deductible under § 170.

Although the Government demurred at oral argument as to whether the IRS, in fact, permits taxpayers to deduct payments made to purchase services from other churches and synagogues, the Commissioner's periodic revenue rulings have stated the IRS' position rather clearly. A 1970 ruling, still in effect, states: "Pew rents, building fund assessments, and periodic dues paid to a church . . . are all methods of making contributions to the church, and such payments are deductible as charitable contributions within the limitations set out in § 170 of the Code." Rev. Rul. 70-47, 1970-1 C.B. 49. We also assume for purposes of argument that the IRS also allows taxpayers to deduct "specified payments for attendance at High Holy Day services, for tithes, for torah readings and for memorial plaques." *Foley v. Commissioner*, 844 F. 2d, at 94, 96.

The development of the present litigation, however, makes it impossible for us to resolve petitioners' claim that they have received unjustifiably harsh treatment compared to adherents of other religions. . . .

[P]etitioners did not endeavor at trial to adduce from the IRS or other sources any specific evidence about other religious faiths' transactions. The IRS' revenue rulings, which merely state the agency's conclusions as to deductibility and which have apparently never been reviewed by the Tax Court or any other judicial body, also provide no specific facts about the nature of these other faiths' transactions. In the absence of such facts, we simply have no way (other than the wholly illegitimate one of relying on our personal experiences and observations) to appraise accurately whether the IRS' revenue rulings have correctly applied a *quid pro quo* analysis with respect to any or all of the religious practices in question. We do not know, for example, whether any or all of these services are generally provided whether or not the encouraged "mandatory" payment is made.

The IRS' application of the "contribution or gift" standard may be right or wrong with respect to these other faiths, or it may be right with respect to these other faiths, or it may be right with respect to some religious practices and wrong with respect to others. It may also be that some of these payments are appropriately classified as partially deductible "dual payments." With respect to those religions where the structure of transactions involving religious services is established not centrally but by individual congregations, the proper point of reference for a *quid pro quo* analysis might be the individual congregation, not the religion as a whole. Only upon a proper factual record could we make these determinations. Absent such a record, we must reject petitioners' administrative consistency argument.

For the reasons stated herein, the judgments of the Courts of Appeals are hereby Affirmed.

JUSTICE O'CONNOR, with whom JUSTICE SCALIA joins, dissenting. . . .

It must be emphasized that the IRS' position here is *not* based upon the contention that a portion of the knowledge received from auditing or training is of secular, commercial, nonreligious value. Thus, the denial of a deduction in these cases bears no resemblance to the denial of a deduction for religious-school tuition up to the market value of the secularly useful education received. Here the IRS denies deductibility solely on the basis that the exchange is a *quid pro quo*, even though the *quid* is exclusively of spiritual or religious worth. The Government cites no instances in which this has been done before, and there are good reasons why.

When a taxpayer claims as a charitable deduction part of a fixed amount given to a charitable organization in exchange for benefits that have a commercial value, the allowable portion of that claim is computed by subtracting from the total amount paid the value of the physical benefit received. If at a charity sale one purchases for $1,000 a painting whose market value is demonstrably no more than $50, there has been a contribution of $950. The same would be true if one purchases a $1,000 seat at a charitable dinner where the food is worth $50. An identical calculation can be made where the *quid* received is not a painting or a meal, but an intangible such as entertainment, so long as that intangible has some market value established in a noncontributory context. Hence, one who purchases a ticket to a concert, at the going rate for concerts by the particular performers, makes a charitable contribution of zero even if it is announced in advance that all proceeds from the ticket sales will go to charity. The performers may have made a charitable contribution, but the audience has paid the going rate for a show.

It becomes impossible, however, to compute the "contribution" portion of a payment to a charity where what is received in return is not merely an intangible, but an intangible (or, for that matter a tangible) that is not bought and sold except in donative contexts so that the only "market" price against which it can be evaluated is a market price that always includes donations. Suppose, for example, that the charitable organization that traditionally solicits donations on Veteran's Day, in exchange for which it gives the donor an imitation poppy bearing its name, were to establish a flat rule that no one gets a poppy without a donation of at least $10. One would have to say that the "market" rate for such poppies was $10, but it would assuredly not be true that everyone who "bought" a poppy for $10 made no contribution. Similarly, if one buys a $100 seat at a prayer breakfast — receiving as the *quid pro quo* food for both body and soul — it would make no sense to say that no charitable contribution whatever has occurred simply because the "going rate" for all prayer breakfasts (with equivalent bodily food) is $100. The latter may well be true, but that "going rate" *includes* a contribution.

Confronted with this difficulty, and with the constitutional necessity of not making irrational distinctions among taxpayers, and with the even higher standard of equality of treatment among *religions* that the First Amendment imposes, the Government has only two practicable options with regard to distinctively religious *quids pro quo*: to disregard them all, or to tax them all. Over the years it has chosen the former course.

Congress enacted the first charitable contribution exception to income taxation in 1917. War Revenue Act of 1917, ch. 63, § 1201(2), 40 Stat. 330. A mere two years later, in A.R.M. 2, 1 C.B. 150 (1919), the IRS gave its first blessing to the deductions of fixed payments to religious organizations as charitable contributions:

> [T]he distinction of pew rents, assessments, church dues, and the like from basket collections is hardly warranted by the act. The act reads "contributions" and "gifts." It is felt that all of these come within the two terms.
>
> In substance it is believed that these are simply methods of contributing although in form they may vary. Is a basket collection given involuntarily to be distinguished from an envelope system, the latter being regarded as "dues?" From a technical angle, the pew rents may be differentiated, but in practice the so-called "personal accommodation" they may afford is conjectural. It is believed that the real intent is to contribute and not to hire a seat or pew for personal accommodation. In fact, basket contributors sometimes receive the same accommodation informally.

The IRS reaffirmed its position in 1970, ruling that "[p]ew rents, building fund assessments and periodic dues paid to a church . . . are all methods of making contributions to the church and such payments are deductible as charitable contributions." Rev. Rul. 70-47, 1970-1 C.B. 49. Similarly, notwithstanding the "form" of Mass stipends as fixed payments for specific religious services, the IRS has allowed charitable deductions of such payments. *See* Rev. Rul. 78-366, 1978-2 C.B. 241. . . .

There can be no doubt that at least some of the fixed payments which the IRS has treated as charitable deductions, or which the Court assumes the IRS would allow taxpayers to deduct, are as "inherently reciprocal," as the payments for auditing at issue here. In exchange for their payment of pew rents, Christians receive particular seats during worship services. *See Encyclopedic Dictionary of Religion* 2760 (1979). Similarly, in some synagogues attendance at the worship services for Jewish High Holy Days is often predicated upon the purchase of a general admission ticket or a reserved seat ticket. *See* J. Feldman, H. Fruhauf, & M. Schoen, *Temple Management Manual*, Ch. 4, p. 10 (1984). Religious honors such as publicly reading from Scripture are purchased or auctioned periodically in some synagogues of Jews from Morocco and Syria. *See* H. Dobrinsky, *A Treasury of Sephardic Laws and Customs* 164, 175-177 (1986). Mormons must tithe ten percent of their income as a necessary but not sufficient condition to obtaining a "temple recommend," *i.e.*, the right to be admitted into the temple. *See The Book of Mormon*, 3 Nephi 24:7–12 (1921); Reorganized Church of Jesus Christ of Latter Day Saints, *Book of Doctrine and Covenants § 106:1b* (1978); *Corporation of Presiding Bishop v. Amos*, 483 U.S. 327, 330 n. 4 (1987). A Mass stipend — a fixed payment given to a Catholic priest, in consideration of which he is obliged to apply the fruits of the Mass for the intention of the donor — has similar overtones of exchange. According to some Catholic theologians, the nature of the pact between a priest and a donor who pays a Mass stipend is "a bilateral contract known as *do ut facias*. One person agrees to give while the other party agrees to do something in return." 13 *New Catholic Encyclopedia*, Mass Stipend, p. 715 (1967). A finer example of a *quid pro quo* exchange would be hard to formulate. . . .

[Editor — The dissent then responds to the government's argument that a more than incidental personal accommodation is a *quid pro quo* preventing a deduction. The dissent is unable to distinguish the *quid pro quo* provided by the Church of Scientology from that provided by more traditional religions.]

. . . [T]he Government [has not] explained why the benefit received by a Christian who obtains the pew of his or her choice by paying a rental fee, a Jew who gains entrance to High Holy Day services by purchasing a ticket, a Mormon who makes the fixed payment necessary for a temple recommend, or a Catholic who pays a Mass stipend, is incidental to the real benefit conferred on the "general public and members of the faith," while the benefit received by a Scientologist from auditing is a personal accommodation. If the perceived difference lies in the fact that Christians and Jews worship in congregations, whereas Scientologists, in a manner reminiscent of Eastern religions (testimony of Dr. Thomas Love) gain awareness of the "immortal spiritual being" within them in one-to-one sessions with auditors, such a distinction would raise serious Establishment Clause problems. The distinction is no more legitimate if it is based on the fact that congregational worship services "would be said anyway," without the payment of a pew rental or stipend or tithe by a particular adherent. The relevant comparison between Scientology and other religions must be between the Scientologist undergoing auditing or training on one hand and the congregation on the other. . . .

[Editor — Isn't the group nature of the benefits and the fact that they might be provided anyway more relevant than the dissent admits?]

Given the IRS' stance in these cases, it is an understatement to say that with respect to fixed payments for religious services "the line between the taxable and the immune has been drawn by an unsteady hand." *United States v. Allegheny County*, 322 U.S. 174, 176 (1944) (Jackson, J.). . . . Rather, it involves the differential application of a standard based on constitutionally impermissible differences drawn by the Government among religions. As such, it is best characterized as a case of the Government "put[ting] an imprimatur on [all but] one religion." *Gillette v. United States*, 401 U.S. 437, 450 (1971). That the Government may not do.

Congress has reacted to the *Hernandez* decision in a very modest way. The 1993 Act conditions a charitable deduction of $250 or more on taxpayer substantiation by written acknowledgment from the donee organization (subject to waiver by Treasury Regulations). *§ 170(f)(8).* The acknowledgment must state whether the organization has provided goods or services to the donor and include a good faith valuation. Where the goods or services consist solely of an "intangible religious benefit," however, the statement need not include the value.

QUESTIONS

How much, if anything, is deductible in the following situations?

1. Suppose payment is made for a *quid pro quo*, but the payment exceeds the "fair market value." Is some amount deductible or do you assume that

the donor has a high preference for the purchased goods or services, which precludes any deduction? Consider the following examples:

a. Tickets which usually sell for $80 are sold for $200 for an opera sponsored by a charity, proceeds to the Red Cross (which is a *§ 170(c)* organization).

b. In exchange for contributions of at least $25 to a public TV station, the donor gets a free coffee mug or tee shirt with the station logo; for contributions of $100 or more, the donor gets a free carrying bag; all contributors get free program guides unavailable to the general public. *Rev. Proc 90-12*, 1990-1 C.B. 471.

c. Taxpayer contributes $1,000 to the university, which entitles him to purchase football tickets that would otherwise be very difficult to get. Is all or some part of this contribution deductible? *§ 170(l).*

2. A school solicits contributions to support its educational functions from parents of enrolled children. Under what circumstances are the contributions charitable deductions? How do the following facts influence your answer? Do they clearly establish that a deduction is or is not available; do they influence the result one way or the other? *Rev. Rul. 83-104*, 1983-1 C.B. 46.

a. The contribution is a necessary condition of school admission.

b. The school admits a significantly larger percentage of applicants whose parents make contributions.

c. The school is a parochial school run by a church.

i. No tuition is charged. Contributions by parents constitute the bulk of funds needed to run the school, although funds are solicited from church members and nonmembers, and no one whose parents do not contribute is denied admission.

ii. Would your answer change if there was also a significant tuition charge, supplementing parental contributions?

iii. Suppose the church charges tuition to nonmembers but not to church members, whose children attend the church school. Contributions are received from all members, split about 50/50 between parents with children in school and other members.

3. In exchange for a lighter sentence, a drug trafficker pleaded *nolo contendere* and agreed to pay $80,000 to the police department to finance

a sting operation. Is this payment a "gift," which could be a charitable deduction? *Ruddel v. Commissioner*, 71 T.C.M. (CCH) 2419 (1996).

Donor control over gift. Suppose taxpayers belong to the Mormon Church. Pursuant to Church practice, their children became missionaries and the parents transferred funds to the children's personal checking account to support them while they did missionary work. The taxpayers sought a deduction on the ground that the payments were "for the use of" the Church. The Court disagreed, limiting "for the use of" to gifts in trust. *Davis v. United States*, 495 U.S. 472 (1990).

The taxpayers also argued that the expenses were deductible gifts "to" the Church, by analogy to the deduction for out-of-pocket expenses while performing charitable services. Again, the Court disagreed, limiting the out-of-pocket rule to cases where the taxpayer's expenses were incident to their own services, not someone else's (their children's, in this case). The Court's decision was influenced by the potential for tax avoidance if the parents deducted more than was reasonable to enable the children to do missionary work, and by the possibility that the parents and children would both claim a charitable deduction.

Suppose the parents had paid the money directly *to* the Church but the parents (not the Church) had designated their children as the sole beneficiaries. Is that a deductible payment "to" the Church? Can a contributor to a university scholarship fund take a deduction if she names the scholarship beneficiary?

The technical issue in *Davis* concerned the definition of "to" and "for the use of" a charity, but the underlying issue concerned whether payments by parents for children were gifts in the first place. Suppose the parents in *Davis* had paid the money directly to the Church, and the Church (not the parents) had taken the initiative in setting up a special fund to support their children's missionary work. Is that a deductible charitable gift or a nondeductible personal expense? Would the payments be deductible if made by someone other than the parents, such as a resident in the community where the children lived?

Finally, suppose an organization is set up (a) to help one named person obtain an organ transplant, or (b) to help find organ transplants for people generally, one of whom is the child of the founder and controlling officer of the organization. Are these tax deductible organizations? *Parker v. Commissioner*, 52 T.C.M.(CCH) 51 (1986).

§ 10.04 NONCASH GIFTS

[A]—Appreciated property

Absent any special limiting provision, *§ 170(a)(1)* authorizes the deduction of the fair market value of property given to an eligible charity. No gain is recognized to the donor even if property is transferred to discharge a pledge. *Rev. Rul. 55-410*, 1955-1 C.B. 297. Conversely, only the value of depreciated property is deductible and the taxpayer cannot deduct a loss when depreciated property is given to charity. *Withers v. Commissioner*, 69 T.C. 900 (1978).

The taxpayer who gives appreciated property to charity therefore has a "tax shelter," because income not given to charity is sheltered from tax by the deduction of the untaxed appreciated gain. For example, assume that the taxpayer owned property with a cost of $80 and a value of $100. It is fair to permit an $80 deduction because that equals the taxpayer's expenditure for the asset. But why should the untaxed $20 gain, which is tax deferred income, be deducted from other income (such as income from medical or legal fees)? That is inconsistent with the theory behind charitable deductions, which is to exclude otherwise taxable income from the tax base if it is given away, not to shelter other income from tax.

Section 170(e) is a limited response to this problem. When it applies, it reduces the charitable deduction otherwise allowable by the amount of income which would have been taxed if the property had been sold rather than given away.

PROBLEMS

The following problems illustrate the operation of *§ 170(e)*. Assume in all cases that the cost is $80 and the value is $100. Disregard the possibility that *§ 170(e)(3), (4)* might provide an exception to *§ 170(e)* to allow some or all of the entire value of the property to be deducted.

The problems refer to a distinction between ordinary income and long-term capital gain. For this purpose, the definition of long-term capital gain is that provided by *§ 1222* (more than one year), even though, for tax *rate* purposes, the tax code now distinguishes in *§ 1(h)* between "long-term" (greater than 18 months) and mid-term capital gain (greater than twelve but not greater than 18 months).

1. A dealer in stock gives stock to a university. Because the taxpayer is a dealer, the gain on a sale would have been ordinary income, not long-term capital gain.

2. An investor holds a capital asset two years (more than one year is long enough to be eligible for long-term capital gain) and then gives it to a private foundation, other than a private foundation listed in *§ 170(b)(1)(E)*. Does it matter whether the asset is publicly traded stock? *See § 170(e)(5)*.

3. An investor in rare jewels holds them as a capital asset for five years and then gives them to a museum. Suppose the jewels had instead been given to a church.

4. An investor holds stock or land as a capital asset for five years and then gives it to a university.

You should see the fruits of some intense lobbying buried in the technical complexity of *§ 170(e)*. Which lobbying interests prevailed in getting a deduction for the value of appreciated property under certain circumstances?

These lobbying interests were not completely successful. If appreciated capital gain property is given to a "public" charity and the full value is deductible because *§ 170(e)* does not apply, gifts of such appreciated property are deductible only up to 30% of adjusted gross income (not 50%). *§ 170(b)(1)(C)*. However, the 50% ceiling is reinstated if the taxpayer elects to deduct no more than the property's adjusted basis.

The IRS is not bashful about challenging inflated valuation claims by donors. In one case, the court found that the value was 20% of that claimed by the donor. *Skripak v. Commissioner*, 84 T.C. 285 (1985). Special penalties apply if the taxpayer's overvaluation is excessive. *§ 6662(b)(3),(e)(1)(A)*.

[B]—Bargain sale to charity

Suppose a taxpayer, who pays $80 for property now worth $100, sells the asset to the charity for $80. In effect, he has made a $20 gift to the charity. Does he recognize gain on the sale? How much of the $20 gift can he deduct? Absent a special provision, the proceeds of a bargain sale are first allocated to the basis. *Treas. Reg. § 1.1001-1(e).* If that rule applied to a bargain sale to charity, the taxpayer in the above example could eliminate taxable gain ($80 amount realized minus $80 basis), and still deduct $20, if *§ 170(e)* did not apply to the $20 gift.

§§ 170(e)(2), 1011(b) change the way gain is computed on a bargain sale to charity. These sections require the basis to be allocated between the sale and the gift in the same proportion as the value of the sale and the gift. In the above example, the sale and gift are divided in an 80/20 ratio and the $80 basis is therefore allocated $64 to the sale and $16 to the gift. The taxpayer is treated as selling property with a $64 basis for $80, and making a charitable gift of property with a $16 basis and a value of $20.

[C]—Untaxed property given to charity

HAVERLY v. UNITED STATES

513 F.2d 224 (7th Cir. 1975)

Hastings, Senior Circuit Judge:

This case presents for resolution a single question of law which is of first impression: whether the value of unsolicited sample textbooks sent by publishers to a principal of a public elementary school, which he subsequently donated to the school's library and for which he claimed a charitable deduction, constitutes gross income to the principal within the meaning of § 61. . . .

During the years 1967 and 1968 Charles N. Haverly was the principal of [an elementary school] in Chicago, Illinois. In each of these years publishers sent to the taxpayer unsolicited sample copies of textbooks which had a total fair market value at the time of receipt of $400. The samples were given to taxpayer for his personal retention or for whatever disposition he wished to make. The samples were provided, in the hope of receiving favorable consideration, to give taxpayer an opportunity to examine the books and determine whether they were suitable for the instructional unit for which he was responsible. The publishers did not intend that the books serve as compensation.

In 1968 taxpayer donated the books to the Alice L. Barnard Elementary School Library. The parties agreed that the donation entitled the taxpayer to a charitable deduction under 26 U.S.C. § 170, in the amount of $400, the value of the books at the time of the contribution.

The parties further stipulated that the textbooks received from the publishers did not constitute gifts within the meaning of 26 U.S.C. § 102 since their transfer to the taxpayer did not proceed from a detached and disinterested generosity nor out of affection, respect, admiration, charity or like impulses.

Taxpayer's report of his 1968 income did not include the value of the textbooks received, but it did include a charitable deduction for the value of the books donated to the school library. The Internal Revenue Service assessed a deficiency [for 1968] against the taxpayer representing income taxes on the value of the textbooks received. . . .

Section 61(a) [] provides: "Except as otherwise provided in this subtitle, gross income means all income from whatever source derived, including (but not limited to) the following items:". The section thereafter enumerates fifteen items none of which, the government concedes, encompass the receipt of sample textbooks. . . . The only question [] is whether the value of the textbooks received is included within "all income from whatever source derived."

. . . The Supreme Court has [] held that the language of § 61(a) encompasses all "accessions to wealth, clearly realized, and over which the taxpayers have complete dominion." *Commissioner of Internal Revenue v. Glenshaw Glass Co.*, 348 U.S. 426 (1955).

. . . In view of the comprehensive conception of income embodied in the statutory language and the Supreme Court's interpretation of that language, we conclude that when the intent to exercise complete dominion over unsolicited samples is demonstrated by donating those samples to a charitable institution and taking a tax deduction therefor, the value of the samples received constitutes gross income.

The receipt of textbooks is unquestionably an "accession to wealth." Taxpayer recognized the value of the books when he donated them and took a $400 deduction therefor. Possession of the books increased the taxpayer's wealth. Taxpayer's receipt and possession of the books indicate that the income was "clearly realized." Taxpayer admitted that the books were given to him for his personal retention or whatever disposition he saw fit to make of them. Although the receipt of unsolicited samples may sometimes raise the question of whether the taxpayer manifested an intent to accept the property or exercised "complete dominion" over it, there is no question that this element is satisfied by the unequivocal act of taking a charitable deduction for donation of the property.

The district court recognized that the act of claiming a charitable deduction does manifest an intent to accept the property as one's own. It nevertheless declined to label receipt of the property as income because it considered such an act indistinguishable from other acts unrelated to the tax laws which also evidence an intent to accept property as one's own, such as a school principal donating his sample texts to the library without claiming a deduction. We need not resolve the question of the tax consequences of this and other hypothetical cases discussed by the district court and suggested by the taxpayer. To decide the case before us we need only hold, as we do, that when a tax deduction is taken for the donation of unsolicited samples the value of the samples received must be included in the taxpayer's gross income.

This conclusion is consistent with Revenue Ruling 70-498, 1970-2 C.B. 6, in which the Internal Revenue Service held that a newspaper's book reviewer must include in his gross income the value of unsolicited books received from publishers which are donated to a charitable organization and for which a charitable deduction is taken. This ruling was issued to supersede an earlier ruling, Rev. Rul. 70-330, 1970-1 C.B. 14, that mere retention of unsolicited books was sufficient to cause them to be gross income.

The Internal Revenue Service has apparently made an administrative decision to be concerned with the taxation of unsolicited samples only when failure to tax those samples would provide taxpayers with double tax benefits. It is not for the courts to quarrel with an agency's rational allocation of its administrative resources. . . .

Apparently, the tax year in which to include the value of the donated books is the year of the charitable gift. Should it be the year the books were received?

How much income would the donor have in the year of the gift if: (a) the books were worth $300 in 1967 when received and $400 in 1968 when donated; (b) they were worth $400 in 1967 and had declined in value to $300 in 1968?

The *Haverly* case presents a very difficult problem of statutory interpretation. The taxpayer was seeking the same advantage that is enjoyed by investors who give appreciated property to charity and use the untaxed appreciation to shelter other income. Why is the exclusion of the book's value from income in *Haverly* inconsistent with deducting the full value of the books as a gift, *if* exclusion of untaxed appreciation is not inconsistent with deducting the appreciation? By analogy, assume the taxpayer had received a tax exempt gift of $100 cash from a parent and given that cash to charity. In that case, the $100 charitable gift could shelter the donee's other income, even though the donee excluded the $100 from income under *§ 102*. To deny that result would defeat the policy of the statute to exclude parental gifts from income. How is the cash gift, which is given to charity, different from the *Haverly* case?

PART III

SAVINGS

CHAPTER 11

DEPRECIATION

§ 11.01 DEPRECIATION THEORY

[A]—Depreciable assets

An asset is depreciable for tax purposes if: (1) it is used for business or income production; and (2) has a determinable useful life (that is, it will eventually lose its usefulness). The depreciation deduction allocates the deduction of an asset's basis over its useful life, in accordance with some formula. Before you consider possible formulas, be sure you understand why some assets are depreciable.

If a taxpayer pays rent for a business building during its entire useful life, the rent is obviously a deductible business expense. A taxpayer who owns the building should be treated the same way — the periodic cost of the building should be deductible. The owner is like a renter, and the cost of the building is like prepaid rent.

One implication of this analogy is that property held for personal use (a home, for example) is not depreciable. Rent on a home is a nondeductible personal expense, so the investment in the home is not depreciable.

The "determinable useful life" requirement serves a different function. It precludes depreciation of property whose usefulness persists, without time limit. Market value may fluctuate but will not inevitably disappear. Land and corporate stock are examples of nondepreciable assets, even though they are held for income production.

Depreciable assets can be tangible (buildings; machines), or intangible (covenants not to compete), as long as they have a determinable useful life. The term "amortization" is usually used for intangible property instead of depreciation.

Depreciation is not limited to property which physically wastes away. Depreciation is a financial concept dealing with investments, not a physics concept dealing with atoms and molecules. If property is expected to become obsolete in 10 years, it has a 10-year life, even though it physically exists after 10 years.

[B]—Computing depreciation

The depreciation deduction should meet certain theoretical standards. It should "clearly reflect income" by matching deductions against the income generated by the asset. It should not include the asset's anticipated salvage value (*e.g.*, the amount you could get for selling an obsolete computer after 10 years). In practice, these standards are administratively too difficult to meet. The percentage of basis allowed as a depreciation deduction each year is usually fixed by a formula which does not necessarily reflect income clearly in particular cases. And salvage value is often disregarded.

Two other significant policy decisions must be made. (1) Should depreciation be based on historical cost (that is, original basis), or should it take account of inflation? Our tax system does not adjust depreciation basis for inflation. (2) Should depreciation be used to encourage investments as well as attempt to clearly reflect income? Our tax system does use the depreciation deduction to encourage investment.

With that background, here are some examples of two depreciation methods — (1) straight-line and (2) the accelerated method known as double (200%) declining balance. The asset has a $60 cost, a five-year life, and no salvage value. The basis of the asset after the deduction of depreciation is in parentheses after the deduction amount.

Depreciation — $60 cost
(post-depreciation basis in parentheses)

Year	Straight line	Accelerated method — 200% declining balance
1	12 (48)	24 (36)
2	12 (36)	14.40 (21.60)
3	12 (24)	8.64 (12.96)
4	12 (12)	6.48 (6.48)
5	12 (0)	6.48 (0)
	60	60

There are several things to notice about the accelerated method. (1) 200% refers to twice the straight-line rate. Because the asset has a five-year life, the straight-line rate is 20%. Double that is 40%. (2) "Declining balance" refers to the application of the 40% rate to the basis remaining *after* deduction of prior depreciation. (3) When the application of the 40% depreciation rate to the declining basis produces depreciation less than straight line over the remaining life of the asset, switch to straight line (that occurs in years 4 and 5 in the example — 40% times 12.96 would be less than 6.48).

There are other methods of depreciation, based not on useful life, but on what the asset produces, or more precisely, is "expected to produce." One example is the unit of production method, which allocates total basis each year based on the amount produced as a percentage of total anticipated production. If a mine is expected to produce 100,000 tons of ore during its entire life and produces 8,000 tons in a particular year, 8% of the mine's basis is a depreciation deduction. This is often called "cost depletion," rather than depreciation, and is used to recover the basis of investments in natural resources. *§§ 611, 612.* The idea behind cost depletion is the same as depreciation — a reasonable method of deducting basis over the life of the asset.

[C]—Annuities — a simple example of straight-line depreciation

§§ 72

A simple example of straight-line depreciation is the tax treatment of annuities. An annuity is an agreement to pay an annual sum of money to an investor (referred to as an annuitant). Generally, the payor of the annuity is a commercial enterprise, such as a life insurance company.

Consider, for example, a taxpayer who pays $50,000 to a commercial annuity company in exchange for a promise of $5,000 per year for the rest of his life. How much of the $5,000 should be taxed each year? *§ 72* provides the answer. Technically, it provides an "exclusion" of some of the $5,000 from annual income, based on the investment divided by expected income. *§ 72(b).* In this example, the exclusion depends on life expectancy. If the purchaser is expected to live 15 years when the annual $5,000 payments begin, total expected income is expected to equal $75,000. (The Regulations provide sex neutral life expectancy tables; *Treas. Reg § 1.72-9.*) The exclusion is two-thirds of each $5,000 (because $50,000 investment is two thirds of the $75,000 expected income). Notice that this exclusion equals straight-line depreciation of the $50,000 investment over 15 years. Why does the statute refer to an income exclusion rather than a deduction?

How is the $5,000 taxed if the taxpayer lives longer than expected (say, 20 years) or dies early (say, in 10 years)? *§ 72(b)(2),(3).*

[D]—Basis adjustment

When a taxpayer takes a depreciation deduction, some of the basis is deducted. Consequently, the basis must be reduced. When the statute refers to "adjusted basis," the adjustment referred to is often for depreciation deductions. If the rule were otherwise and the basis were not reduced, the same basis could be deducted twice — for example, once through depreciation and again as a recovery of basis if the asset were sold. *See §§ 1011(a), 1016(a)(2).*

reduce basis after DD

[E]—Decelerated depreciation

Straight-line depreciation is always an acceptable depreciation method, if you cannot identify a better depreciation method to clearly reflect income. *See Treas. Reg. § 1.167(b)-1(a).* One argument for this conclusion is that straight-line depreciation would clearly reflect income, on the reasonable assumption that the property produces equal annual income. But that is wrong. Straight-line depreciation does not clearly reflect income when the asset produces equal annual income.

Assume that a $60 investment with a five-year useful life produces $20 income per year, before depreciation. After five years, the property is used up. The $60 is the present value of $20 earned annually over the next five years, assuming a 20% discount rate. What annual depreciation of the $60 investment will produce *net* income (after depreciation) which equals a 20% annual rate of return on the asset's value at the beginning of each year? The following table gives the figures (rounded so that the totals add correctly). Notice that the depreciation is *decelerated* — less than straight line. In the real world the only investors who routinely use this method are banks when they amortize their loans. When a bank makes a five-year $60 loan at 20% interest, its annual net income is reflected by the following chart, using decelerated depreciation. Notice that the net income in the early years is *larger* than it would be using straight-line depreciation. This is, however, very good for the borrower financing purchase of a home, whose interest deduction equals the bank's annual net income on the loan. Larger interest deductions during the early years of repayment are better for the home owner.

Decelerated depreciation
Asset cost = $60; 20% interest rate

Year	Value at beginning of year	Depreciation	Gross Income	Net income
1	60	8	20	12
2	52	9.5	20	10.5
3	42.5	11.5	20	8.5
4	31	14	20	6
5	17	17	20	3
		60	100	40

§ 11.02 DEPRECIATION UNDER THE STATUTE

The discussion has so far focused on possible approaches to depreciation deductions, not current statutory rules. There is a reason for this. The rules change frequently, often to provide economic incentives. Here is a brief summary of recent U.S. "tax depreciation" history. The general authority for deducting depreciation is *§ 167(a)*, but there are many other provisions permitting more generous deductions under certain circumstances.

The amount of the depreciation deduction depends in theory on the answer to three questions. *First*, determine the basis used to compute depreciation. A major issue here is whether to disregard salvage value. *Second*, determine the time over which to depreciate. In the absence of any special provision, the salvage value and useful life depend on the business practice of the particular taxpayer, including consideration of technological obsolescence, not just the physical life of the asset. *Massey Motors, Inc. v. Commissioner*, 364 U.S. 92 (1960). *Third*, determine the rate at which depreciation will be computed.

Because depreciation rules are targeted at particular activities, they vary in accordance with the political judgments of Congress. The rules are very technical but the critical decisions often vary in accordance with the following: whether the property is a building; whether the property is tangible or intangible; whether the property is new or used; and the expected useful life of the property. Not every one of these variables has been important at all times, but each has been relevant in framing depreciation rules at some time or other.

[A]—Before the Tax Reform Act of 1986

[1] Pre-1981

For about a decade before 1981, the useful life of assets was determined by the Asset Depreciation Range system (ADR). This system specified the useful life of classes of assets used in the same business activity, except that assets with common characteristics (like cars) had their own ADR life. The ADR system substantially shortened the useful lives previously employed for depreciation. Taxpayers could elect lives 20% shorter or longer than the ADR life.

When the ADR system was originally proposed by Treasury Regulation, a lawsuit challenging the agency's authority to adopt them was brought by Members of Congress, Common Cause, a business association whose members could not benefit from accelerated depreciation to the same extent as its competitors, and a real estate investor for whom there were no benefits. *Common Cause v. Connally*, Civil Action 1337-71 (D.D.C. 1971). Their standing to bring the lawsuit was doubtful but the issue was mooted when Congress adopted a specific statutory provision authorizing the ADR system. The list of litigants in this lawsuit suggests one of the major features of accelerated depreciation deductions. The benefits are skewed towards industries which are more capital than labor intensive.

The permissible rate of depreciation varied with the type of property. For example, tangible property (other than buildings) with a useful life of at least three years was eligible for 200% declining balance depreciation, if it was not used property. Buildings were not eligible for the 200% rate unless they were new residential realty. Generally, buildings were eligible for a 150% depreciation rate, except that the rates were lower if the buildings were not new.

Pre-1981 law also permitted salvage value of "personal property" to be reduced by 10% of the original cost if the property had at least a three-year useful life. "Personal property" referred primarily to tangible and intangible property other than buildings.

[2] 1981; Adoption of ACRS

The Economic Recovery Act of 1981 introduced the Accelerated Cost Recovery System (ACRS), applicable to depreciable tangible property. In most cases, it significantly increased depreciation deductions for tangible personal and real property, such as machines and buildings. Original cost (not reduced by salvage value) was the basis for depreciation, and both new and used property was eligible for ACRS.

There were five categories of assets, with depreciable useful lives of 3, 5, 10, 15, and 19 years. The category into which an asset fell generally depended on the ADR life which the asset had under the prior ADR system, but the ACRS system shortened the depreciation period. Buildings had a 19-year life, much below the ADR life; low-income housing had a 15-year life.

The ACRS depreciation rates for tangible property, other than buildings, were approximately 150% declining balance. The rules for buildings were a little different. Tables published by the Treasury approximated 175% declining balance over 19 years, except for low income housing, for which the rates approximated 200% declining balance over 15 years.

[B]—Tax Reform Act of 1986, as amended in 1993

Significant revisions of the depreciation rates and recovery periods were made by the Tax Reform Act of 1986. *§ 168(a),(b),(c),(e). Tangible personal* property falls into six recovery periods and depreciation rates — 3-year (200%); 5-year (200%); 7-year (200%); 10-year (200%); 15-year (150%); 20-year (150%). The new ACRS recovery periods are based on the old Asset Depreciation Range class life. Thus, 3-year ACRS property includes property with a 4-year or less ADR class life, except that cars have been moved to the 5-year ACRS category. *§ 168(e)(3)(B).*

Real property was the big loser in the 1986 Act. Residential rental property is eligible for straight-line depreciation over 27.5 years. Other realty, such as commercial real estate, was depreciable over 31.5 years, extended to 39 years by the 1993 Act.

Salvage value is still disregarded and the current rules apply to both new and used property.

The Tax Reform Act of 1986, like prior law, adopts conventions concerning when property is placed in use. Personal property is assumed to be placed in use at the midpoint of the year. However, if more than 40% of the taxpayer's personal property is placed in use in the last three months of the year, the property is assumed to be placed in service in the middle of the quarter in which it was acquired (that is, a mid-quarter convention). For realty, a mid-month, instead of a mid-year, convention is used. *§ 168(d).*

A different "alternative depreciation" system is used for certain property. *§ 168(g).* The alternative system uses straight-line over specified time periods which are longer than under ACRS, generally based on the old ADR useful lives. One type of property subject to these rules is business property which can still be financed by tax-exempt Industrial Revenue Bonds. The idea is that the existing tax exemption for interest on loans incurred to make the investment provides sufficient investment incentives, which should not be augmented by favorable ACRS depreciation methods.

Taxpayers can also opt to use the "alternative depreciation" system. *§ 168(g)(1)(E).*

Before the Tax Reform Act of 1986, lessees who made improvements on property (such as putting up a building) were allowed to use the leasehold period rather than the ACRS period to amortize the cost of the improvements, if the leasehold period was shorter. Lessees are no longer allowed to do this and must depreciate property improvements using ACRS lives.

Tax expenditure? The manipulation of depreciation rules has always been a very attractive political technique because it has the effect of lowering taxes, without explicitly changing the tax rates. For this reason the amount of depreciation in excess of straight-line depreciation has usually been included in the tax expenditure budgets. In a controversial move, the 1983 tax expenditure budget published by the Reagan administration did not include this item. Office of Management and Budget, *The Budget of the United States Government, 1983 Special Analysis G, Tax Expenditures,* 6–7 (1982) contains the following explanation:

> A further illustration of the definition of tax subsidies is provided by the Accelerated Cost Recovery System (ACRS) provisions enacted in the Economic Recovery Tax Act of 1981. Any income tax requires a set of rules for determining how the cost of depreciable assets is recovered. The ACRS provisions now constitute the general income tax rules for that purpose. To see this, one need only ask: If ACRS is "special," what is

the "general" rule in the Internal Revenue Code governing the recovery of cost of depreciable property to which ACRS is an exception? The treatment of ACRS may be contrasted with that of the investment tax credit, which has very similar economic effects for machinery and equipment. The investment credit is considered a tax subsidy because, unlike ACRS, it does not deal with one of the basic structural elements of an income tax. Note further that the fact that the ACRS provisions are clearly a divergence from any measure of economic income is not relevant to the determination that they do not constitute a tax subsidy.

However, OMB later decided to report excess depreciation in its tax expenditure budget under the heading "pre-1983 budget method," making it clear that it did not approve of that method.

[C]—Reasonable method of depreciation

The accelerated methods discussed so far are available without regard to proof that early high depreciation deductions might reflect a reasonable method of depreciation under *§ 167(a)*. Some reasonable methods might, however, result in higher early deductions without regard to ACRS. *§ 168(f)(1)* therefore permits the taxpayer to elect out of ACRS when depreciation is based on a method not tied to the number of years the property will be useful. One example is the unit of production method. Under this method, depreciation in any given year is a percentage of depreciable cost equal to the percentage of total expected production to be derived from the property which is actually realized that year. This method can be used, for example, for equipment related to natural resources exploration.

Another reasonable method of depreciation is the income forecast method. This method is usually used for assets like movies. It allows depreciation by using a fraction in which the numerator is income in a given year and the denominator is total income expected from the asset, or some variation on that theme. The government argued that this method was only available for movie-like assets, but the court disagreed in *ABC Rentals of San Antonio, Inc. v. Commissioner*, 97 F.3d 392 (10th Cir. 1996), *rev'g* 68 T.C.M. (CCH) 1362 (1994). The taxpayer was a rent-to-own business and was allowed to use a fraction with a numerator equal to income and a denominator equal to three times cost.

Congress has responded in the 1997 Tax Act to cases like *ABC Rentals* by disallowing the income forecast method for rent-to-own consumer durables. More precisely, it limited the income forecast method to intangible property, such as copyrights, patents, etc. (but not amortizable section 197 property — discussed below). *§ 167(g)(6)*. The same law added a special three-year depreciation method for "qualified rent-to-own property." *§ 168(e)(3)(A)(iii).*

[D]—Intangibles; *§ 197*

Prior to the 1993 tax law, the depreciation of intangibles was governed by the regular *§ 167(a)* rules. The ACRS method does not apply to intangibles. Many intangibles, such as stock and good will, were not depreciable, because they had no determinable useful life. Other intangible assets, such as copyrights, patents, covenants not to compete, and advantageous contract rights to buy and sell certain assets, were depreciable under any reasonable method (as authorized by *§ 167(a)*), assuming their useful life could be determined.

These rules spawned considerable litigation about whether assets "related" to good will were really depreciable. In 1993, the Supreme Court decided *Newark Morning Ledger Co. v. United States*, 113 S. Ct. 1670 (1993). The taxpayer had purchased a newspaper business and allocated some of the cost to the value of the attachment of at-will subscribers. It argued that this value gradually disappeared and that it was therefore a depreciable asset, unlike good will. The Court agreed, stating:

> Petitioner [] proved to the satisfaction of the District Court that the "paid subscribers" asset was not self-regenerating. . .
>
> "[T]here is no automatic replacement for a subscriber who terminates his or her subscription. Although the total number of subscribers may have or has remained relatively constant, the individual subscribers will not and have not remained the same, and those that may or have discontinued their subscriptions can be or have been replaced only through the substantial efforts of the [taxpayer]." . . .
>
> Petitioner proved as a matter of fact that the value of the "paid subscribers" diminished over an ascertainable period of time.

Congress addressed the problem of depreciating intangibles in 1993 by adopting a uniform 15-year depreciation period for all "section 197 intangibles." These rules, among other things, *permit* previously nondepreciable good will to be depreciated over 15 years, and *require* depreciable "customer-based intangibles," such as the subscriber's attachment to the business in *Newark Morning Ledger*, to be depreciated over 15 years, even if prior law allowed a shorter period. *§ 197(a).*

The new *§ 197* does much more, however, than address the specific problem of good will and customer-based intangibles. It provides broadly for 15-year depreciation for a long list of *§ 197* intangibles. Where the new *§ 197* does not apply, *§ 167(a)* rules usually apply, permitting a reasonable method of depreciation if the property has an ascertainable useful life.

However, some intangibles, excluded from "section 197 intangible" status, have special useful life periods (*e.g.*, computer software has a 36-month life, if it is readily available for purchase by the general public, subject to a nonexclusive license, and has not been substantially modified ("off-the-shelf" software) — *§ 197(e)(3), § 167(f)(1)).*

Here is an incomplete chart of the old and new rules applicable to selected intangibles. *§ 197(d)* contains the list of section 197 intangibles, and *§ 197(c)(2), (e)* contains exceptions. Reference in the chart to "*§ 167 dep.*" means that a reasonable method of depreciation is usually allowed, but *only if* the asset has a determinable useful life.

	Old law	Current law
1. Stock	No dep.	No dep.
2. Good will	No dep.	§ 197-15 year
3. Customer-based intangibles (*e.g.* lists and favorable contracts)	§ 167 dep.	§ 197-15 year
4. Franchise, trade mark, and trade name, *except*	§ 167 dep.	§ 197-15 year
a. Sports franchise	§ 167 dep.	§ 167 dep.
b. Certain periodic, contingent payments	§ 1253(d)(1)	§ 1253(d)(1)
5. Patent, copyright, and covenant not to compete		
(a) if *not* acquired with a business	§ 167 dep.	§ 167 dep.
(b) if acquired with a business	§ 167 dep.	§ 197-15 year

Self-created assets. *§ 197* does not usually apply to *self-created* intangibles (unless there is a related acquisition of business assets), with some exceptions. For example, *§ 197 does apply* to a self-created franchise, trade name or trade mark, whether or not related to a business acquisition. *§ 197(c)(2).* Therefore, capitalized costs relating to the taxpayer's registration or development of a trade name are depreciated over 15 years (even though self-created). But capitalized costs spent by a taxpayer to train employees do not create a section 197 intangible, unless related to a business acquisition.

Favorable loans. *§ 197* does not apply to the premium a taxpayer pays for an existing indebtedness, based on the fact that the interest rate is higher than current market interest rates. *§ 197(e)(5)(B).* That premium is generally depreciable under *§ 171.*

Favorable leases. The new law changes some of the rules applicable to payments for advantageous leases. *See § 167(c)(2).* A favorable lease is one where the obligation under the lease differs from the market rental rate in the absence of a lease. Payments for such a lease would include a premium. Lease premiums paid as part of the acquisition of property subject to a favorable lease (with lease rents *more* than market rents) are now added to the cost of the property subject to the lease (*e.g.*, lease premiums paid when buying a shopping center are part of the shopping center's cost). However, if the lessee acquires a favorable lease (with lease rents *less* than market rents), the prior law still applies (*e.g.* to acquire a lessee interest in using airport gates). *See § 178; § 197(e)(5)(A).*

[E]—Critique of accelerated depreciation as economic incentive

Two major problems have plagued the depreciation system, one of which was partially corrected by the Tax Reform Act of 1986. First, tax incentives were not uniform. Of course, special favoritism for some investment activities might be purposeful, such as for oil exploration or building low income housing. But many tax provisions could not be justified on this ground. Assets with different real economic lives were lumped together in the same useful life category. The five-year life category, for example, might contain assets with real economic lives of five or eight years. Even when the assets in a useful life category had the same economic life, the incentives varied between useful life categories, because the shortening of economic lives was not uniform in each category. For example, even if all five-year ACRS property had an economic eight-year life, and all 19-year ACRS property had an economic 40-year life, the shortening of lives would be more advantageous for the 19-year ACRS category.

Uniform incentives? The Tax Reform Act of 1986 moves in the direction of placing assets with similar economic lives in the same ACRS category and providing similar incentives for assets in all categories. It therefore comes closer to the ideal of providing uniform incentives to all investment. If you wanted to reach that ideal completely, here is how you would do it. The incentive can be quantified in terms of the familiar concept of present value. The full expensing of a deduction is the benchmark. The present value of expensing an outlay is the amount of the outlay. Thus, if $10,000 is spent today and deducted today, the present value of the deduction is $10,000 because the deduction is not postponed. Next, compute the present value of depreciation deductions using "correct" economic depreciation to accurately reflecting income. For this discussion, assume that straight-line depreciation provides the correct economic depreciation method. Thus, if the asset had a ten-year life, you would compute the present value of deductions of $1000 per year over the next ten years. Assume for discussion that the present value is $6000. If Congress wanted to give the taxpayer an incentive equal to one-half of what current expensing would give, it should raise the present value of the future depreciation deductions to $8000.

Inflation. The second problem addressed by accelerated depreciation is inflation. As the cost of replacing assets increases above historical cost, higher depreciation rates might approximate the adjustment to depreciable cost that would be made for inflation. The trouble is that accelerated depreciation rates in the statute are not specifically designed to adjust for inflation. As we saw earlier, the correct method of dealing with inflation is to adjust basis upwards to account for changes in the cost of living. When ACRS was introduced in 1981, inflation was high and the tax benefits of accelerated depreciation approximated what the deductions would be if basis for depreciation had been adjusted for inflation. The solution, however, was fixed by statute without regard to any changes in future inflation rates. Declines in inflation made existing accelerated depreciation extraordinarily favorable, which is one reason the Tax Reform Act of 1986 cut back on depreciation deductions.

The Treasury has proposed dealing with inflation in an analytically straightforward manner, by multiplying the amount of depreciation available under the statutory schedule by the inflation rate. For example, assume that the depreciation deduction without inflation adjustment is $12.00 two years after the initial investment (that is, in year 2). If inflation had gone up after the year of investment by 5% per year, the depreciation deduction in year 2, adjusted for inflation, is $12.00 times 1.05^2 (that is, $13.23).

The Tax Reform Act of 1986 does nothing to deal specifically with inflation, which could be its Achilles heel. If inflation increases again, the pressure to raise depreciation will increase and the tax laws may again provide incentives that will become obsolete if inflation declines. The better approach is to let accelerated depreciation rates directly address the incentive issue and provide separately for inflation adjustments to cost.

[F]—When does depreciation begin

Assume land has been leased to a tenant for 20 years and, in year 5, the tenant constructs a building for $350,000. In year 12, the taxpayer purchases the land with the right to acquire the building at the end of the lease. Total purchase price is $1,250,000. Is any portion of the purchase price depreciable and, if so, when?

[G]—Collector-antique items used in business

In two recent cases the Tax Court and two Courts of Appeals have allowed taxpayer-musicians to depreciate the cost of their musical instruments under the ACRS method (short lives; fast depreciation rate), even though the instruments were the kind of antiques whose collector value guaranteed that their value would not decline below original cost. *Liddle v. Commissioner*, 103 T.C. 285 (1994), *aff'd*, 65 F.3d 329 (3d Cir. 1995);

Simon v. Commissioner, 103 T.C. 247 (1994), *aff'd*, 68 F.3d 41 (2d Cir. 1995). Here are some excerpts from the Court of Appeals decision in *Liddle*. The IRS has nonacquiesced in these decisions; 1996 Action on Decision CC–1996–009.

The courts emphasized the purposes of the 1981 and 1986 changes in depreciation law — to encourage investment and simplify useful life determinations. But do those purposes extend to a case in which value will not decline because of the asset's collector-antique status?

Evaluate the following critique of the opinion. The "wear and tear" and "useful life" requirements for depreciation (which are imposed by *§ 167* and *Treas. Reg. § 1.167(a)–1*) serve the underlying purpose of "clearly reflecting income." When an asset's value will not decline, income cannot be clearly reflected by allowing depreciation and the tax law should be interpreted in light of that principle. It is true that the 1981/1986 laws allowed some departure from a "clearly reflect income" principle by eliminating a lot of the disputes about useful life, but the asset must still be the type of asset which could decline in value, determined without regard to any special tax rules shortening those lives in *§ 168*. Collector-antiques do not satisfy this condition. The court's emphasis on physical "wear and tear" obscures the fact that tax depreciation is concerned with financial rather than physical reality.

There are two possible responses to this critique. First, at least some types of (admittedly) depreciable assets are very unlikely to decline in value because of inflation (*e.g.*, buildings). But collector-antiques are different. It is well known that inflation can prevent decline in value of some assets, and one major purpose of the favorable depreciation rules in *§ 168* was to be an explicit substitute for periodically adjusting the depreciable basis for inflation. Assets which maintain their value because of their special market characteristics as antiques are very different from those which maintain their value due to inflation.

Second, the depreciation rules usually disregard salvage value and, if a court takes account of an asset's retention of value, it is in effect considering salvage value. Again, collector-antiques are different. Salvage value should be disregarded only if the asset is depreciable in the first place. It is one thing to disregard the salvage value of depreciable assets and quite another matter to neglect the reality that "salvage value" is almost certain to equal or exceed original cost in deciding whether the asset is depreciable in the first place.

LIDDLE v. COMMISSIONER

65 F.3d 329 (3d Cir. 1995)

McKee, Circuit Judge: . . .

[Editor — Under the version of *§ 168* applicable to the tax years in this case, *§ 168* applied only if the property was "of a character subject to the allowance for depreciation." Current *§ 168(a)* states that "the depreciation deduction provided by section 167(a) [] shall be determined" as provided in *§ 168.* Does the different wording of current *§ 168* produce a different result? The *Liddle* opinion emphasizes that *§ 168* does not import the "useful life" requirement imposed by *§ 167.* Perhaps the explicit reference in the current version of *§ 168(a)* to *§ 167* would import that requirement (although *Selig v. Commissioner*, 70 T.C.M. (CCH) 1125 (1995) states to the contrary).]

In this appeal from a decision of the United States Tax Court we are asked to decide if a valuable bass violin can be depreciated under the Accelerated Cost Recovery System when used as a tool of trade by a professional musician even though the instrument actually increased in value while the musician owned it. We determine that, under the facts before us, the taxpayer properly depreciated the instrument and therefore affirm the decision of the Tax Court.

I.

Brian Liddle, the taxpayer here, is a very accomplished professional musician. Since completing his studies in bass violin at the Curtis Institute of Music in 1978, he has performed with various professional music organizations, including the Philadelphia Orchestra, the Baltimore Symphony, the Pennsylvania ProMusica and the Performance Organization.

In 1984, after a season with the Philadelphia Orchestra, he purchased a 17th century bass violin made by Francesco Ruggeri (c. 1620–1695), a luthier who was active in Cremona, Italy. Ruggeri studied stringed instrument construction under Nicolo Amati, who also instructed Antonio Stradivari. Ruggeri's other contemporaries include the craftsmen Guadanini and Guarneri. These artisans were members of a group of instrument makers known as the Cremonese School. Liddle paid $ 28,000 for the Ruggeri bass, almost as much as he earned in 1987 working for the Philadelphia Orchestra. The instrument was then in an excellent state of restoration and had no apparent cracks or other damage. Liddle insured the instrument for its then-appraised value of $ 38,000. This instrument was his principal instrument and he used it continuously to earn his living, practicing with it at home as much as seven and one-half hours every day, transporting it locally and out of town for rehearsals, performances and auditions. Liddle purchased the bass because he believed it would serve him throughout his professional career — anticipated to be 30 to 40 years.

Despite the anticipated longevity of this instrument, the rigors of Liddle's profession soon took their toll upon the bass and it began reflecting the normal wear and tear of daily use, including nicks, cracks, and accumulations of resin. At one point, the neck of the instrument began to pull away from the body, cracking the wood such that it could not be played until it was repaired. Liddle had the instrument repaired by renown artisans. However, the repairs did not restore the instrument's "voice" to its previous quality. At trial, an expert testified for Liddle that every bass loses mass from use and from oxidation and ultimately loses its tone, and therefore its value as a performance instrument decreases. Moreover, as common sense would suggest, basses are more likely to become damaged when used as performance instruments than when displayed in a museum. Accordingly, professional musicians who use valuable instruments as their performance instruments are exposed to financial risks that do not threaten collectors who regard such instruments as works of art, and treat them accordingly.

There is a flourishing market among nonmusicians for Cremonese School instruments such as Mr. Liddle's bass. Many collectors seek primarily the "label", *i.e.*, the maker's name on the instrument as verified by the certificate of authenticity. As nonplayers, they do not concern themselves with the physical condition of the instrument; they have their eye only on the market value of the instrument as a collectible. As the quantity of these instruments has declined through loss or destruction over the years, the value of the remaining instruments as collectibles has experienced a corresponding increase.

Eventually, Liddle felt the wear and tear had so deteriorated the tonal quality of his Ruggeri bass that he could no longer use it as a performance instrument. Rather than selling it, however, he traded it for a Domenico Busan 18th century bass in May of 1991. The Busan bass was appraised at $ 65,000 on the date of the exchange, but Liddle acquired it not for its superior value, but because of the greater tonal quality. Liddle and his wife filed a joint tax return for 1987, and claimed a depreciation deduction of $ 3,170 for the Ruggeri bass under the Accelerated Cost Recovery System ("ACRS"), I.R.C. § 168.

II.

The Commissioner originally argued that the ACRS deduction under 168 is inappropriate here because the bass actually appreciated in value. However, the Commissioner has apparently abandoned that theory, presumably because an asset can appreciate in market value and still be subject to a depreciation deduction under tax law. . . .

Here, the Commissioner argues that the Liddles can claim the ACRS deduction only if they can establish that the bass has a determinable useful life. Since Mr. Liddle's bass is already over 300 years old, and still increasing in value, the Commissioner asserts that the Liddles can not establish a determinable useful life and therefore can not take a depreciation deduction. In addition, the Commissioner argues that this instrument is a "work of art" which has an indeterminable useful life and is therefore not depreciable. . . .

[Editor — The court then explains that the 1981 and 1986 changes in the tax rules for depreciation were intended to encourage investment and eliminate disputes about useful life.]

The Commissioner argues that [] § 168 did not eliminate the [prior]§ 167 requirement that tangible personalty used in a trade or business must also have a determinable useful life in order to qualify for the ACRS deduction. She argues that the phrase "of a character subject to the allowance for depreciation" demonstrates that the [] § 167 requirement for a determinable useful life is the threshold criterion for claiming the § 168 ACRS deduction.

Much of the difficulty inherent in this case arises from two related problems. First, Congress left § 167 unmodified when it added § 168; second, § 168 contains no standards for determining when property is "of a character subject to the allowance for depreciation." In the absence of any express standards, logic and common sense would dictate that the phrase must have a reference point to some other section of the Internal Revenue Code. Section 167(a) would appear to be that section. As stated above, that section provides that "there shall be allowed as a depreciation deduction a reasonable allowance for the exhaustion, wear and tear. . . of property used in a trade or business. . . ." The Commissioner assumes that all of the depreciation regulations promulgated under § 167 must, of necessity, be imported into § 168. That importation would include the necessity that a taxpayer demonstrate that the asset have a demonstrable useful life, and (the argument continues) satisfy the phrase "tangible property of a character subject to the allowance for depreciation" in § 168.

However, we do not believe that Congress intended the wholesale importation of § 167 rules and regulations into § 168. Such an interpretation would negate one of the major reasons for enacting the Accelerated Cost Recovery System. Rather, we believe that the phrase "of a character subject to the allowance for depreciation" refers only to that portion of § 167(a) which allows a depreciation deduction for assets which are subject to exhaustion and wear and tear. Clearly, property that is not subject to such exhaustion does not depreciate. Thus, we hold that "property of a character subject to the allowance for depreciation" refers to property that is subject to exhaustion, wear and tear, and obsolescence. However, it does not follow that Congress intended to make the ACRS deduction subject to the § 167 useful life rules, and thereby breathe continued life into a regulatory scheme that was bewildering, and fraught with problems, and required "substantial restructuring."

We previously noted that Congress believed that prior depreciation rules and regulations did not provide the investment stimulus necessary for economic expansion. Further, Congress believed that the actual value of the depreciation deduction declined over the years because of inflationary pressures. In addition, Congress felt that prior depreciation rules governing the determination of useful lives were much too complex and caused unproductive disagreements between taxpayers and the Commissioner. Thus, Congress passed a statute which "de-emphasizes the concept of useful life." Accordingly, we decline the Commissioner's invitation to interpret § 168 in such a manner as to re-emphasize a concept which Congress has sought to "de-emphasize."

The Commissioner argues that de-emphasis of useful life is not synonymous with abrogation of useful life. As a general statement, that is true. However, the position of the Commissioner, if accepted, would reintroduce unproductive disputes over useful life between taxpayers and the Internal Revenue Service. Indeed, such is the plight of Mr. Liddle.

Congress de-emphasized the § 167 useful life rules by creating four short periods of time over which taxpayers can depreciate tangible personalty used in their trade or business. These statutory "recovery periods. . . are generally unrelated to, but shorter than, prior law useful lives." The four recovery periods are, in effect, the statutorily mandated useful lives of tangible personalty used in a trade or business. . . .

Thus, in order for the Liddles to claim an ACRS deduction, they must show that the bass is recovery property as defined in I.R.C. § 168(c)(1). It is not disputed that it is tangible personalty which was placed in service after 1980 and that it was used in Brian Liddle's trade or business. What is disputed is whether the bass is "property of a character subject to the allowance for depreciation." We hold that that phrase means that the Liddles must only show that the bass was subject to exhaustion and wear and tear. The Tax Court found as a fact that the instrument suffered wear and tear during the year in which the deduction was claimed. That finding was not clearly erroneous. Accordingly, the Liddles are entitled to claim the ACRS deduction for the tax year in question.

Similarly, we are not persuaded by the Commissioner's "work of art" theory, although there are similarities between Mr. Liddle's valuable bass, and a work of art. The bass is highly prized by collectors; and, ironically, it actually increases in value with age much like a rare painting. Cases that addressed the availability for depreciation deductions under § 167 clearly establish that works of art and/or collectibles were not depreciable because they lacked a determinable useful life. *See, Associated Obstetricians and Gynecologists, P.C. v. Commissioner*, 762 F.2d 38 (6th Cir. 1985) (works of art displayed on wall in medical office not depreciable); *Hawkins v. Commissioner*, 713 F.2d 347 (8th Cir.) (art displayed in law office not depreciable). *See also, Rev. Rul. 68–232*, 1968–1 C.B. 79 ("depreciation of works of art generally is not allowable" because "[a] valuable and treasured art piece does not have a determinable useful life."). [Editor — Does this mean that an antique desk used by a law firm partner is depreciable, but not the art work on the wall?]

. . . In Brian Liddle's professional hands, his bass viol was a tool of his trade, not a work of art. It was as valuable as the sound it could produce, and not for its looks. Normal wear and tear from Liddle's professional demands took a toll upon the instrument's tonal quality and he, therefore, had every right to avail himself of the depreciation provisions of the Internal Revenue Code as provided by Congress.

III.

Accordingly, for the reasons set forth above, we will affirm the decision of the tax court.

QUESTIONS

The *Liddle* court's discussion of art work displayed in a law office bears examination.

1. The Tax Court opinion in *Liddle* referred to a work of art as a "passive object [] displayed for admiration of its aesthetic qualities." Why does that distinguish art work from the musical instrument, used actively as a tool of the trade? Doesn't displayed art work also deteriorate *eventually* with light and atmospheric exposure? As long as the musical instrument and the art work are used in the business, why should one be depreciable and the other not?

2. Is a work of art different because it *can* be displayed in a museum, as well as be useful in business? But why does that matter as long as the

art work is in fact used in the business? Besides, antique musical instruments are sometimes displayed in museums.

3. Suppose art work costs $100,000 and, after six years, it is removed from the law firm and used for personal enjoyment in a home. Does the change in use result in taxable income? *Cf. § 179(d)(10).* Does thinking about this question suggest a distinction between art work and musical instruments?

4. At the recent auction of assets owned by the estate of Jacqueline Kennedy Onassis, the owner of a well-known cigar magazine paid over $500,000 for a humidor (for keeping cigars) owned by President Kennedy. Would that cost be depreciable if the asset were displayed in the magazine's business headquarters?

§ 11.03 OTHER INVESTMENT INCENTIVES

The statute is filled with numerous rules permitting short-period depreciation (often 60 months), or expensing (a deduction in the year of the expenditure). Expensing is rapid depreciation carried to the extreme of allowing the expenditure to be deducted in full in the year it is incurred.

Sometimes these provisions are tax incentives. But, sometimes, expensing is explicitly permitted, not so much as an incentive, but to simplify administration. As explained in a later chapter, expenditures producing assets with a life beyond the end of the tax year should theoretically be added to basis rather than deducted immediately. However, drawing the line between expenditures which should be added to basis and those which should be expensed is often very difficult. The statute sometimes responds to this administrative difficulty by explicitly permitting expensing.

[A]—Expensing and short-period depreciation

Here is a partial list of some statutory provisions permitting short-period depreciation (often called "amortization") or expensing. What is your best guess as to whether the provision is an incentive or simplifies administration?

Type of expenditure	Statutory section
farmer's soil/water conservation	*§ 175* (expense)
farmer's fertilizer, etc. for land	*§ 180* (expense)
research and development	*§ 174* (expense or 60-month)
remove barriers to handicapped	*§ 190* (expense)
pollution control facility	*§ 169* (60-month)
intangible oil and gas drilling	*§ 263(c)* (expense)
newspaper circulation	*§ 173* (expense)
organization costs of	*§§ 248, 709(b)*

corporation or partnership (60-month)

§ 179 permits a taxpayer to expense up to $18,000 of tangible personal property, rising in steps to $25,000 in 2003. This amount is reduced dollar per dollar as total investment in tangible personal property exceeds $200,000. The amount expensed cannot exceed trade or business income.

[B]—Investment tax credit

At various times in recent decades, the tax law has provided a tax incentive for business investment in the form of an investment tax credit for tangible personal property (not buildings or intangible property). A tax credit is a reduction of *tax*, not income, by some percentage of the investment. A 10% investment tax credit for investing in a $100,000 machine, for example, would reduce tax by $10,000.

The tax law, since the Tax Reform Act of 1986, does not provide a general business investment tax credit. When it was provided, the basic provisions were as follows: (1) a 10% credit, reduced to 6% for short-lived property; (2) investments in *used* property eligible for the credit was subject to a dollar ceiling; (3) one half of the credit reduced basis eligible for depreciation; (4) the credit was limited to $25,000 tax liability plus 75% of tax over $25,000; (5) the credit was not "refundable" if it exceeded tax liability; (6) unused credits could be carried forward to later years.

The tax credit mechanism remains popular, however, for specific types of investments. For example, there is now a credit for housing rehabilitation (*§§ 38(b)(1), 46(1), 47*) and low income housing (*§ 42(a)*). Other credits, such as those for orphan drug clinical testing, research, and job creation, often contain expiration dates which are either periodically renewed or deleted (making the credit permanent). For example, the orphan drug credit (*§ 28*) was extended by the 1996 Act and made permanent by the 1997 Act. The research credit (*§ 41(a)*) was extended through June 30, 1998. A work opportunity credit replaced the targeted job credit as of September 30, 1997 (*§ 51(a)*); it has been extended by the 1997 Tax Act through June 30, 1998. And the 1997 Tax Act adopted a new "Welfare-to-Work" credit for wages paid to long-term family assistance recipients who begin work after 1997 and before May 1, 1999. § *51A*.

The 1996 law introduced a credit for child adoption expenses up to (in general) $5,000 (*§ 23*); this credit phases out when AGI is between $75,000 and $115,000. The new law also provides an exclusion from an employee's income for up to $5,000 of employer-assisted adoption expenses. *§ 137.*

[C]—Multiple incentives

The 1993 tax law adopted multiple incentives for investments in certain regions, including credits, expensing, and/or shorter-period depreciation.

For example, investment in a limited number of urban and rural "Empowerment Zones" selected by HUD and the Agriculture Department, are eligible for (among other benefits) special employment credits and increased expensing under *§ 179. §§ 1391–1397D*. And certain investments on Indian reservations are encouraged by faster depreciation (including a 22-year life for nonresidential realty) and special employment credits. *§§ 45A, 168(j).*

§ 11.04 RECAPTURE OF PRIOR DEPRECIATION DEDUCTION

Basic idea. The basic idea behind statutory "recapture" rules is to reverse the effects of earlier deductions when, in a later year, the deduction turns out to be excessive. The prior deduction is "recaptured" in the later year by turning capital gain into ordinary income. The primary example of deductions that are recaptured are depreciation deductions. For example, if a taxpayer buys an asset for $100, takes $40 depreciation in year 1, and sells the asset for $75 in the year 2, the taxable gain is $15 ($75 minus the $60 basis). (The basis was adjusted downward for depreciation. *§ 1016(a)(2)).* The asset did not decline in value to $60, however, in the amount of the depreciation deduction. It only declined by $25 instead of the $40 reflected in the depreciation deduction. The $15 of excess depreciation must be recaptured as ordinary income.

Recapture and breaking down accounting year barriers. The idea behind recapture of prior deductions as ordinary income is not as unfamiliar as it might seem. The earlier benefit (an ordinary depreciation deduction) justifies reduction of a later benefit (capital gains). The accounting year barrier is broken down to influence tax treatment in a later year, based on events in an earlier tax year. A similar idea underlay the decision in the *Haverly* case, where an earlier benefit (exclusion of a book from gross income) resulted in gross income in a later year when the taxpayer made a charitable contribution and claimed a deduction.

Statutory provisions. The basic recapture provision is *§ 1245*, applicable primarily to assets other than buildings. It works as follows. Suppose a corporate taxpayer pays $20,000 for a business machine and deducts $12,000 depreciation. The basis is adjusted downward to $8,000. *§ 1016(a)(2).* If the taxpayer sells the property for $10,000, the gain is $2,000. How much gain is "recaptured" as ordinary income? All of it. *See § 1245(a)(1).*

If the asset was sold for $25,000 because it had gone up in value, the gain would be $17,000. Of that gain $12,000 would be recaptured as ordinary income (recomputed basis of $20,000 minus $8,000 basis). The remaining $5,000 of gain would probably be capital gain (under *§ 1231*, discussed later).

An additional consequence of converting capital gain to ordinary income is to deny a charitable donor a deduction for the gain that would be ordinary income. For example, if a chemical manufacturer paid $10,000 for a machine, and took $2,000 depreciation, a gift of the asset when it was worth $11,000 would result in only a $9,000 charitable deduction. *§ 170(e)(1)(A).*

There are many other recapture rules in the statute. Earlier in this chapter we mentioned "expensing" provisions. Although expensing is not technically depreciation and therefore not subject to the statutory rules cited above, the statute often provides for recapture of prior expenses if the taxpayer sells an asset created by an expenditure which has been expensed for tax purposes. *§ 1245(a)(2)(C).*

Under current law, none of the gain on real estate is recaptured as ordinary income. The fact that only straight-line depreciation is allowed over a fairly long period of time may be only a partial explanation for this rule. The more favorable rules for buildings may be a tax incentive, or (perhaps) recognition that the gain is more likely to be the result of inflation. Nonetheless, when the 1997 Tax Act lowered capital gains rates below 28%, it added a rule that the tax rate on amounts that would be recapture income on the sale of real estate would be capped at 25%, not a lower preferential rate.

Basis for computing gain. Suppose the taxpayer has a $100 cost for an asset. Proper depreciation is $20, but the taxpayer takes a $25 depreciation deduction. *§ 1016(a)(2)* says that the downward basis adjustment is the greater of the amount allow*ed* or allow*able*. The amount "allowed" is the greater $25 amount, so basis is $75. This means that recapture gain is greater than if the depreciation basis were computed "correctly." This is one aspect of a much broader problem — to what extent is the taxpayer bound in a later year by errors made in a prior year, rather than the government being required to go back to the earlier year to make the correction to income computation in the earlier year?

Suppose the taxpayer deducts only $15, but the correct amount is $20. The statute seems to say that basis is $80, the larger of the amount allowed or allow*able*. The taxpayer who took only $15 depreciation, however, would like to claim an $85 basis, so that a sale for $100 would result in only $15 income, not $20. The government has recently ruled that basis for computing gain when the taxpayer sells the depreciated asset will only be reduced by the lesser amount "allowed" (in the example, basis is $85). *Rev. Proc. 96–31,* 1996–1 C.B. 714 (permitting this result as a change in accounting method)

§ 11.05 BUYER vs. SELLER CONSISTENCY

A buyer obviously wants to allocate more of the purchase price of a business to assets which can be deducted as quickly as possible — that is, depreciable assets with the shortest lives. Sellers are interested in minimizing their taxes by allocating the sales price to preferentially taxed assets, such as capital gains rather than ordinary income.

The sale of intangibles has often been a battleground on which taxpayer allocation has been fought. When the buyer and seller are in adverse positions, the government will usually accept the results of arm's length bargaining. For example, assume a taxpayer sells stock in a corporation and a covenant not to compete. Usually, the stock sale produces preferentially taxed long term capital gain and the covenant sale produces ordinary income. The seller therefore wants as much of the price as possible to be allocated to the stock. The buyer, however, prefers an allocation that favors the covenant, which is depreciable (stock is not depreciable).

Under current law, the buyer's advantage is not as great as it was before a covenant not to compete became a *§ 197* intangible, because the statutory 15-year life is much longer than the real useful life (usually around three years). Still, the buyer prefers to allocate the price to the covenant and the government is therefore likely to accept the buyer-seller allocation. *But see Lemery v. Commissioner*, 52 T.C. 367 (1969), *aff'd per curiam*, 451 F.2d 173 (9th Cir. 1971), where the stock sale produced only *short term* capital gain, which is taxed at ordinary income rates. The seller was therefore indifferent between allocating the purchase price between the stock and the covenant, and the government did not accept the parties' allocation.

§ 1056. In one situation, the statute specifies that the buyer's depreciable cost cannot exceed the sales price *reported* by the seller on the tax return. *§ 1056* states that the buyer's basis for depreciation of sports team player contracts cannot exceed the amount the seller reports on the sale of these contracts. Most of the rest of the purchase price is for a nondepreciable franchise (which has no ascertainable useful life — *§ 197* does not apply to sports franchises). The buyer is usually adverse to the seller because the sale of the player contracts usually results in ordinary income to the seller (it is *§ 1245* recapture income), but the sale of other assets, such as the franchise itself, would produce preferentially taxed capital gain. Thus, the seller wants more sales proceeds allocated to the nondepreciable franchise (preferentially taxed capital gain to the seller), rather than the depreciable player contracts (recapture ordinary income to the seller).

§ 1060. Another section dealing with this problem is *§ 1060*. It forces both the buyer and seller to use a method of reporting the sales price of a business which allocates a significant portion of the purchase price to good will. It also states that a specific agreement between buyer and seller about allocating the purchase price is binding on both parties unless the IRS determines that the allocation is not appropriate.

When *§ 1060* was originally adopted, it prevented the parties from allocating a lot of the purchase price to depreciable cost and inventory cost, both of which decrease the buyer's ordinary income, rather than to nondepreciable good will. Now that the cost of good will is depreciable over 15 years (as a section 197 intangible), the impact of this requirement is reduced but not eliminated. 15-year depreciation will still be an undesirable alternative in many situations.

CHAPTER 12

LOSSES

We have already discussed the recovery of basis through the computation of gain on disposition of an asset (*§ 61*) and through depreciation (*§ 167*). Those basis recovery rules deal with some but not all of the situations in which an asset with a basis can become useless to the taxpayer. For example, what are the tax consequences if an asset is sold at a loss (that is, for less than its basis), or is destroyed by fire when there is no insurance? The loss deduction rules cover such cases.

§ 12.01 REALIZATION

Market fluctuations must be distinguished from realizable taxable events for losses as well as gains. In *United States v. S.S. White Dental Mfg. Co.*, 274 U.S. 398 (1927), the Court dealt with a case in which property had been seized in 1918 by a government with which the United States was at war. There was a chance that some compensation would be recovered after the war, but it was a matter of "grace," not of right, and in any event depended on the hazards of the war in progress. The taxpayer took the deduction in 1918 and the Court agreed. The seizure created a loss "fixed by identifiable events," not mere market fluctuation. In addition, the taxpayer did not have to be "an incorrigible optimist" regarding recovery of the assets or later compensation. The loss therefore resulted from a "closed" transaction — a phrase the Court used as a synonym for "realization."

Realized losses generally result from sale, casualty, or seizure of an asset. They can also result from total obsolescence or abandonment, as long as the taxpayer can fix such a loss by an identifiable event. *Dezendorf v. Commissioner*, 312 F.2d 95 (5th Cir. 1963) (intent to abandon and some act evidencing that intent are required).

A number of cases have addressed whether loss of a monopoly position results in a realized loss — for example, when deregulation of airline routes permits free entry into airline markets. If the air carrier continues to fly the routes, though with fewer flights and with competition, the loss of monopoly position without explicit abandonment of a market is not a realized loss. *Rev. Rul. 84-115*, 1984-2 C.B. 47.

§ 12.02 PERSONAL ASSETS

Should there ever be a deduction for losses of personal assets — that is, assets used for personal purposes, such as a home? Recall the discussion of depreciation, where we agreed that depreciation deductions for personal assets were not allowed because they were the equivalent of rent for personal consumption. If you buy a home for $60,000 and it is destroyed by fire (no insurance) the day after the purchase, what personal consumption have you enjoyed from your investment? None.

The tax law responds to this observation by allowing deductions of personal use property when the loss arises from "fire, storm, shipwreck, or other casualty, or theft." *§ 165(c)(3)*. What is a casualty? The law needs some way to distinguish between the gradual wearing away of the asset, which is the equivalent of nondeductible depreciation, and casualties, in which the loss is not the equivalent of personal consumption. The rulings draw some very fines lines, as the following questions indicate. The general rule is that a casualty occurs only when it is sudden, unexpected, and unusual. *Rev. Rul. 72-592*, 1972 C.B. 101.

QUESTIONS

Which of the following are deductible casualty losses of personal use property? To what extent do the rules accurately distinguish between what should and should not be deductible?

1. Losses due to a hurricane; due to the normal action of waves on the foundation of oceanfront property. *Rev. Rul. 76-134*, 1976-1 C.B. 54.

2. Loss of a water heater which bursts; loss of a rug when the bursting water heater damages the rug. *Rev. Rul. 70-91*, 1970-1 C.B. 37.

3. Damage to a car due to the owner's negligence. *Treas. Reg. § 1.165-7(a)(3)*.

4. Loss of a home in Saigon abandoned before the city fell to the North Vietnamese (*Popa v. Commissioner*, 73 T.C. 130 (1979)); abandoning a car which turns out to be a lemon.

5. Payment to an extortioner who kidnapped a relative. *Rev. Rul. 72-112*, 1972-1 C.B. 60.

6. Loss of ring which falls off while walking; loss of ring when car door slammed on a finger. *Jones v. Commissioner*, 24 T.C. 525 (1955); *White v. Commissioner*, 48 T.C. 430 (1967).

§ 12.03 AMOUNT OF DEDUCTION

[A]—Compensation by insurance

The loss deduction is reduced by insurance compensation. *§ 165(a)*. For example, if the taxpayer paid $100,000 for an asset which is destroyed by fire and the correct amount of the loss deduction was $100,000, insurance proceeds of $80,000 reduce the loss deduction to $20,000.

The prospect of insurance recovery often postpones the deduction until insurance claims are resolved. The taxpayer does not have to wait indefinitely. When the insurance recovery is fixed with some certainty (for example, $65,000), the deduction for the remaining $35,000 is allowed. If it later turns out that the insurance company will pay an additional $15,000, that amount is then included in income. The tax benefit rule (discussed in an earlier chapter) would prevent taxing the $15,000 recovery, however, if the earlier $35,000 loss deduction did not reduce taxes.

Is it fair to postpone the taxpayer's loss deduction while the taxpayer argues with the insurance company? A $100,000 realized loss is postponed because of the prospect of recovering $100,000 at a future date. The present value of that prospect is *less* than $100,000.

[B]—Personal use assets

HELVERING v. OWENS

305 U.S. 468 (1939)

MR. JUSTICE ROBERTS delivered the opinion of the Court.

The courts below have given opposing answers to the question whether the basis for determining the amount of a loss sustained during the taxable year through injury to property not used in a trade or business, and therefore not the subject of an annual depreciation allowance, should be original cost or value immediately before the casualty. To resolve this conflict we granted certiorari . . . .

. . . [T]he facts are that the respondent Donald H. Owens purchased an automobile at a date subsequent to March 1, 1913, and prior to 1934, for $1,825, and used it for pleasure until June 1934 when it was damaged in a collision. The car was not insured. Prior to the accident its fair market value was $225; after that event the fair market value was $190. The respondents filed a joint income tax return for the calendar year 1934 in which they claimed a deduction of $1635, the difference between cost and fair market value after the casualty. The Commissioner reduced the deduction to $35, the difference in market value before and after the collision. . . .

no depreciation DD for personal use

The income tax acts have consistently allowed deduction for exhaustion, wear and tear, or obsolescence only in the case of "property used in the trade or business." The taxpayers in these cases could not, therefore, have claimed any deduction on this account for years prior to that in which the casualty occurred. For this reason they claim they may deduct upon the unadjusted basis, — that is, — cost. As the income tax laws call for accounting on an annual basis; as they provide for deductions for "losses sustained during the taxable year"; as the taxpayer is not allowed annual deductions for depreciation of non-business property; as [§ 165(b)] requires that the deduction shall be on "the adjusted basis provided in [§ 1011]," thus contemplating an adjustment of value consequent on depreciation; and as the property involved was subject to depreciation and of less value in the taxable year, than its original cost, we think [§ 1011(a)] must be read as a limitation upon the amount of the deduction so that it may not exceed cost, and in the case of depreciable non-business property may not exceed the amount of the loss actually sustained in the taxable year, measured by the then depreciated value of the property. The Treasury rulings have not been consistent, but this construction is the one which has finally been adopted.

RULE:

TP loses!

Computing casualty loss deduction. The computation of pre-loss and post-loss values may be difficult, so the Regulations permit using the cost of repairs as a proxy for computing the decline in value, if (1) the repairs are necessary to restore the property to pre-loss condition; (2) the amount spent is not excessive; (3) the repairs do not care for more than the damage suffered; and (4) the value of the property does not exceed pre-loss value as a result of the repairs. *Treas. Reg. § 1.165-7(a)(2)(ii).*

use "cost of repairs" if:

Total losses. The *Owens* case involved a partial loss. Its approach applies to total as well as partial losses of personal use assets. It limits the loss deduction to the difference between pre-and post-casualty value. In the case of a total loss, post-casualty value is $0. *Treas. Reg. § 1.165-7(b)(1).*

if total loss, post-cas. value = $0

Overall limit is basis. The deduction of losses cannot exceed the total basis of the asset prior to the loss. A taxpayer is never allowed to deduct more than basis. *§ 165(b).* The basis reflects the income previously taxed and that is all the taxpayer can deduct. A larger deduction for the excess of value over basis would permit the taxpayer to shelter other income, in addition to the amount of after-tax income invested in the lost asset.

Statutory interpretation. The limitation imposed by *Owens* on the loss deduction for personal use assets makes sense. If a taxpayer cannot deduct depreciation on personal use assets, the decline in value equivalent to personal use should not be deductible as a casualty loss deduction. But what statutory language produces this result? The statute says that adjusted basis is deductible and adjusted basis equals original cost in the case of a personal asset. *Owens* is one of the clearest cases of statutory structure demanding an interpretation that goes beyond what the statute seems to say.

Use of pre-loss value to prevent "depreciation" deduction. Sometimes it does not seem fair to use pre-loss value to limit the deduction of personal use assets, because the decline in value does not really measure the value of prior personal consumption. As soon as you put the ignition key into a new car, for example, the value goes way down. The "purer" rule would be to measure nondeductible depreciation on the asset, reduce its basis to adjust for that depreciation, and use that adjusted basis to measure the deductible casualty loss (rather than using pre-loss value). For example, if the taxpayer bought a car for $20,000 and held it for one-fourth of its useful life, adjusted basis for casualty loss purposes would be $15,000, using straight-line depreciation. A total loss of the car would produce a $15,000 loss deduction, even if the pre-loss value had declined to $12,000. Notice that this approach argues for a change in the law to allow loss deductions on the sale of personal use assets, as well as on casualties, whenever the sales price is less than adjusted basis.

Would you favor the "adjusted basis" approach to computing deductible losses of personal use property, rather than using pre-loss value? Is it worth the administrative bother? Would it understate taxable personal consumption for some people — *e.g.*, those whose lifestyle caused the asset to decline in value below the adjusted basis (such as heavy personal use of a car)?

Deducting personal consumption from using personal assets. In fact, taxpayers can sometimes deduct the value of the personal consumption they enjoy from personal use assets. Here is how. Assume taxpayer pays $100,000 for a residence and lives there for one-half of its useful life. Due to inflation or changes in land use patterns the house is still worth $100,000 when he sells it. How much gross income does he have? Basis is not reduced to account for use of the residence, so there is no gain.

Failure to file insurance claim. Should a casualty loss deduction for personal use assets be contingent on filing an insurance claim? You can imagine a taxpayer deciding not to file out of fear that the policy might be cancelled. Case law held that the taxpayer who did not file a claim was like a taxpayer with no insurance — and was therefore entitled to the deduction. *Hills v. Commissioner*, 76 T.C. 484 (1981), *aff'd*, 691 F.2d 997 (11th Cir. 1982); *Miller v. Commissioner*, 733 F.2d 399 (6th Cir. 1984). The statute was then changed to prohibit the deduction for loss of *personal use* property unless an insured taxpayer filed a timely claim. *§ 165(h)(4)(E).*

Limits on loss deduction of personal use assets. The rules on deducting casualty losses of personal use assets contain additional limitations, which often eliminate its utility. After you compute the amount of the loss deduction in accordance with above rules, further limits apply. First, the first $100 of each casualty loss is not deductible. Second, losses are deductible only if they exceed the sum of casualty gains plus 10% of adjusted gross income. *§ 165(h).* In addition, the deduction is an itemized deduction, but is not subject to the 2% floor.

Government as insurer? Should the government help taxpayers insure against losses by providing a loss deduction when there is no deduction for the insurance premiums themselves? Does the loss deduction provide an incentive (1) against buying insurance; (2) towards purchasing somewhat less sturdy assets? Is the deduction nonetheless fair, notwithstanding its incentive effects?

[C]—Business or income producing assets

A *total* loss of a business or income-producing asset produces a deduction equal to adjusted basis prior to the loss. The taxpayer does not reduce the deduction by pre-loss market value depreciation, because there is no personal consumption. *Treas. Reg. § 1.165-7(b(1)(ii)(last sentence).*

The mechanical rules identifying the amount deductible in case of a partial loss of business or income producing property are the same as for personal use property. *Treas. Reg. § 1.165-7(b(1).* Why is that so? The rule, you will recall, caps the deduction at the difference between value before and value after the loss (but never more than the adjusted basis). If a taxpayer suffers a 50% casualty loss of a business asset, why isn't 50% of the adjusted basis deductible? It is clear that, if one half of the property had been *sold*, one half the basis would be allocated to the sold property. Why the difference between casualty loss and sale? Do you agree with the following case justifying the difference, as follows: "[A] partial sale indicates that there is at least an economic divisibility of the property, and it seems reasonable to apportion the basis [] according to what is kept and what is disposed of. A partial casualty loss indicates no such divisibility for frequently the entire damage must be restored before the whole is to have any productive value." *Alcoma Ass'n. v. United States*, 239 F.2d 365, 370 (5th Cir. 1956).

[D]—Convert from personal to business use

QUESTIONS

1. Suppose a taxpayer owns a home, for which she paid $100,000. The home is later converted to business or income producing use when the building is worth $90,000. Thereafter, the building burns down (no insurance). How much deduction can the taxpayer take?

2. When does a taxpayer convert the property to business or income producing use — by offering it for rent; offering it for sale; actually renting it? The statute refers to losses incurred in "a transaction entered into for profit." *§ 165(c)(1),(2)*. When is that requirement met? Would it matter if the building were rented to a family member, or how much rent was charged? Would it matter how long after abandoning a residence the property was offered for sale? *Compare § 167(a)(2)* which allows depreciation deductions if property is "held for production of income."

[E]—Wagering losses

Can a taxpayer who has gambling losses deduct the losses? The statute says that gambling losses are only deductible up to gambling gains. *§ 165(d)*. The usual explanation is that the net losses are presumed equal to personal enjoyment from gambling. They are personal expenses.

There may be other explanations. First, a net loss deduction might encourage activity which should be discouraged. Second, gamblers might lie about their losses. The rule simplifies administration by reducing the need to check on the veracity of loss claims.

§ 12.04 LIMITS ON DEDUCTION

[A]—Wash sale

If an investor pays $100 for General Motors common stock, sells it for $90, and purchases substantially identical GM common stock for $85 within 30 days of the original sale, he cannot recognize the loss. *§ 1091*. The investor's financial position has not changed enough to justify a loss deduction. What is the seller's basis in the stock he acquires within the 30-day period?

30 day period not long enough

[B]—Sale between related parties

In an early case, the Supreme Court disallowed a loss deduction on a sale between a taxpayer and his wholly owned corporation. *Higgins v. Smith*, 308 U.S. 473 (1940). The Court found so much dominion and control over the asset sold to the corporation, resulting from 100% ownership, that no loss was "sustained."

The statute now specifically disallows a loss deduction on a sale between related parties, as defined in the statute. *§ 267(a)(1),(b)*. Related parties include a corporation and a more than 50% owner; and certain specifically defined relatives. *§ 267(b)(1),(2),(c)(4)*.

CHAPTER 13

CAPITAL EXPENDITURE VS. CURRENT EXPENSE

§ 13.01 INTRODUCTION

Savings, at least in theory, are part of the income tax base. Despite numerous exceptions, this generalization is a valid starting point. The distinction between current expenses and capital expenditures implements the taxation of savings. A capital expenditure *is* savings. The expenditure is therefore added to basis (that is, "capitalized"), rather than being deducted when incurred (that is, rather than being "expensed").

How is the line drawn between current expenses and capital expenditures? The idea is that any expenditure producing value expected to last beyond the end of the taxable year is savings and should be added to basis. Drawing that line can pose formidable administrative difficulties, however. Moreover, the difference between expensing and savings is "just" a matter of timing. If the tax timing differences are small or not necessary to "clearly reflect income," the taxpayer is sometimes allowed to expense a capital expenditure.

Section 13.02 discusses acquisition costs. Section 13.03 distinguishes maintenance expenses from improvements and acquisitions. Section 13.04 considers the tax treatment of education expenditures, which are sometimes current expenses and sometime capital expenditures.

Personal assets. The dominant perspective in this chapter is that of the taxpayer who prefers a current expense to adding an expenditure to basis. The assumption is that it is better to get a deduction now (as an expense) rather than later (through a basis deduction). In fact, that is not always the case. Expenses related to personal use assets are not deductible, but their cost may be (in computing gain on sale or as a casualty loss). Taxpayers therefore prefer to add expenditures to the basis of personal use assets, rather than treat them as expenses.

Sometimes a court does not make clear whether a deduction is denied in the expenditure year because it is a capital expenditure or a personal expense. Recall the Supreme Court *Gilmore* case, applying the origin test to disallow litigation expenditures related to a divorce. A later case permitted Mr. Gilmore to add the expenditures to the basis of the stock he tried to protect from his wife. The court concluded that the denial of the deduction in the expenditure year by the Supreme Court was consistent with adding the expenditure to the stock's basis. *Gilmore v. United States*, 245 F. Supp. 383 (N.D. Cal. 1965). Is the District Court opinion correct?

§ 13.02 ACQUISITION COSTS

When a taxpayer buys land, building, stock, or a car, it is easy to conclude that the expenditure is a capital expenditure. The asset obviously lasts beyond the tax year of purchase and its cost should be added to basis, just like cash in a savings account. It is also easy to slip into the assumption that the tax concept of savings, recorded in basis, correlates with tangible property that you can see and touch. That is a mistake. The tax concept is, fundamentally, a financial accounting concept, which records investments in basis because that is the best way to clearly reflect income. The "assets" acquired with tax savings are not limited to tangible assets.

The section of the statute usually cited as authority for capitalizing expenditures is *§ 263*, which disallows a deduction for amounts paid out for permanent improvements. A much better cite would be *§ 446(b)*, which insists that deductions clearly reflect income.

[A]—Prepaid expenses

COMMISSIONER v. BOYLSTON MARKET ASSOCIATION

131 F.2d 966 (1st Cir. 1942)

MAHONEY, CIRCUIT JUDGE: . . .

We are asked to determine whether a taxpayer who keeps his books and files his returns on a cash basis is limited to the deduction of the insurance premiums actually paid in any year or whether he should deduct for each tax year the pro rata portion of the prepaid insurance applicable to that year.

. . . Advance rentals, payments of bonuses for acquisition and cancellation of leases, and commissions for negotiating leases are all matters which the taxpayer amortizes over the life of the lease. Whether we consider these payments to be the cost of the exhaustible asset, as in the case of advance rentals, or the cost of acquiring the asset, as in the case of bonuses, the payments are prorated primarily because the life of the asset extends beyond the taxable year. To permit the taxpayer to take a full deduction in the year of payment would distort his income. Prepaid insurance presents the same problem and should be solved in the same way. Prepaid insurance for a period of three years may be easily allocated. It is protection for the entire period and the taxpayer may, if he desires, at any time surrender the insurance policy. It thus is clearly an asset having a longer life than a single taxable year. The line to be drawn between capital expenditures and ordinary and necessary business expenses is not always an easy one, but we are satisfied that in treating prepaid insurance as a capital expense we are obtaining some degree of consistency in these matters. . . .

prepaid ins. = cap. exp.
& ∴ can deduct pro rata

Notice that *Boylston* requires prepaid expenses to be capitalized and then depreciated (assuming the asset is depreciable), whether the taxpayer is a cash or accrual method taxpayer.

If the statute explicitly authorizes a deduction, does that provision override the more general capitalization requirement? For example, § 163(a),(h)(1),(2)(D),(3) allows a deduction for home loan interest under certain circumstances discussed in a later chapter. Does that provision permit a deduction for *prepaid* home loan interest in the year paid, when the prepayment covers more than one year's interest obligation? After some litigation, the statute was amended to require prepaid interest to be capitalized and amortized over the loan period. There is an exception, however, for "points" on a home purchase and improvement mortgage (which is the economic equivalent of prepaid interest), if such payments are customary business practice. § 461(g).

[B]—Acquisition-related costs

Expenditures to buy a building are capital expenditures. What if the taxpayer constructs the building?

COMMISSIONER v. IDAHO POWER CO.

418 U.S. 1 (1974)

Mr. Justice Blackmun delivered the opinion of the Court.

[Editor — The taxpayer is a utility. It used cars and trucks to construct assets used to transmit electricity. Cars and trucks are depreciable assets and the taxpayer took depreciation deductions on those assets attributable to the period during which the construction occurred. The Court disallowed the deductions, as follows.]

Our primary concern is with the necessity to treat construction-related depreciation in a manner that comports with accounting and taxation realities. Over a period of time a capital asset is consumed and, correspondingly over that period, its theoretical value and utility are thereby reduced. Depreciation is an accounting device which recognizes that the physical consumption of a capital asset is a true cost, since the asset is being depleted. As the process of consumption continues, and depreciation is claimed and allowed, the asset's adjusted income tax basis is reduced to reflect the distribution of its cost over the accounting periods affected. . . . When the asset is used to further the taxpayer's day-to-day business operations, the periods of benefit usually correlate with the production of income. Thus, to the extent that equipment is used in such operations, a current depreciation deduction is an appropriate offset to gross income currently produced. It is clear, however, that different principles are implicated when the consumption of the asset takes place in the construction of other assets that, in the future, will produce income themselves. In this latter situation, the cost represented by depreciation does not correlate with production of current income. Rather, the cost, although certainly presently incurred, is related to the future and is appropriately allocated as part of the cost of acquiring an income-producing capital asset. . . .

There can be little question that other construction-related expense items, such as tools, materials, and wages paid construction workers, are to be treated as part of the cost of acquisition of a capital asset. The taxpayer does not dispute this. Of course, reasonable wages paid in the carrying on of a trade or business qualify as a deduction from gross income. § 162(a)(1). But when wages are paid in connection with the construction or acquisition of a capital asset, they must be capitalized and are then entitled to be amortized over the life of the capital asset so acquired.

Construction-related depreciation is not unlike expenditures for wages for construction workers. The significant fact is that the exhaustion of construction equipment does not represent the final disposition of the taxpayer's investment in that equipment; rather, the investment in the equipment is assimilated into the cost of the capital asset constructed. Construction-related depreciation on the equipment is not an expense to the taxpayer of its day-to-day business. It is, however, appropriately recognized as a part of the taxpayer's cost or investment in the capital asset. The taxpayer's own accounting procedure reflects this treatment, for on its books the construction-related depreciation was capitalized by a credit to the equipment account and a debit to the capital facility account. By the same token, this capitalization prevents the distortion of income that would otherwise occur if depreciation properly allocable to asset acquisition were deducted from gross income currently realized.

An additional pertinent factor is that capitalization of construction-related depreciation by the taxpayer who does its own construction work maintains tax parity with the taxpayer who has its construction work done by an independent contractor. The depreciation on the contractor's equipment incurred during the performance of the job will be an element of cost charged by the contractor for his construction services, and the entire cost, of course, must be capitalized by the taxpayer having the construction work performed. . . .

The presence of § 263(a)(1) in the Code is of significance. Its literal language denies a deduction for "(a)ny amount paid out" for construction or permanent improvement of facilities. The taxpayer contends, and the Court of Appeals held, that depreciation of construction equipment represents merely a decrease in value and is not an amount "paid out," within the meaning of § 263(a)(1). We disagree.

The purpose of § 263 is to reflect the basic principle that a capital expenditure may not be deducted from current income. It serves to prevent a taxpayer from utilizing currently a deduction properly attributable, through amortization, to later tax years when the capital asset becomes income producing. The regulations state that the capital expenditures to which § 263(a) extends include the "cost of acquisition, construction, or erection of buildings." Treas. Reg. § 1.263(a)-2(a). This manifests an administrative understanding that for purposes of § 263(a)(1), "amount paid out" equates with "cost incurred." The Internal Revenue Service for some time has taken the position that construction-related depreciation is to be capitalized. Rev. Rul. 59-380, 1959-2 C.B. 87; Rev. Rul. 55-252, 1955-1 C.B. 319.

There is no question that the cost of the transportation equipment was "paid out" in the same manner as the cost of supplies, materials, and other equipment, and the wages of construction workers. The taxpayer does not question the capitalization of these other items as elements of the cost of acquiring a capital asset. We see no reason to treat construction-related depreciation differently. In acquiring the transportation equipment, taxpayer "paid out" the equipment's purchase price; depreciation is simply the means of allocating the payment over the various accounting periods affected. As the Tax Court stated in *Brooks v. Commissioner*, 50 T.C., at 935, "depreciation — inasmuch as it represents a using up of capital — is as much an 'expenditure' as the using up of labor or other items of direct cost." . . .

[Editor — The Court notes that depreciation is not a "payment" for purposes of the *§ 170* charitable deduction, but concludes that the charitable deduction rules are irrelevant for the issue of capitalizing costs. Can the term "payment" mean different things in different parts of the same statute?]

We hold that the equipment depreciation allocable to taxpayer's construction of capital facilities is to be capitalized.

Equating builder and purchaser. *Idaho Power* talks about putting the taxpayer who builds its own building on a par with the person who buys the building from a contractor who constructs the building. It accomplishes this result because the depreciation on the equipment used to construct the building would be included in the contractor's costs and therefore in the sale price charged to the taxpayer. However, *Idaho Power* is powerless to completely equate the taxpayer who buys the building from a contractor with a taxpayer who constructs the building. If the taxpayer buys the building for $100,000, it will pay $100,000 out of after tax income, which equals basis. If it builds the building for $90,000, including depreciation in the $90,000 cost, it has a basis of only $90,000. The taxpayer does not include the additional $10,000 of builder profit in income or basis, thereby deferring tax on the $10,000 until the lower depreciation ($90,000 instead of $100,000) results in higher income in later years. The builder-taxpayer is in the same position as one who prepays personal consumption expenses for a vacation at a discount, except that the builder defers rather than excludes the discount from income.

[C]—Uniform capitalization rules

The problem addressed by *Idaho Power* is part of a much broader problem of allocating expenditures to the cost of business property. Cases like *Idaho Power* deal with "direct" costs, which can be readily attributed to a specific asset, whether the taxpayer constructs property for its own use, produces it for sale to another, or buys property for resale.

There are, however, serious accounting problems with allocating "indirect" costs to the construction and production of property for use or sale, and to property purchased for resale. For example, should the salary paid to a manager or a business executive be allocated among various assets constructed, produced, or purchased by the taxpayer? How should interest on corporate loans used to finance construction, production, or purchase of assets be allocated? Generally, these accounting concerns are addressed by accountants, not lawyers. You should know, however, that taxpayers were, for a long time, successfully expensing many of these indirect costs. The statute has now been explicitly amended to require both direct and indirect costs to be allocated to the basis of assets constructed or produced for use or resale, and to assets purchased for resale. *§ 263A*. For example, in *PMT, Inc. v. Commissioner*, 72 T.C.M. (CCH) 5 (1996), 75% of the salary of the corporation's president was capitalized as a direct *§ 263A* inventory cost because he was intimately involved in production design and development of the corporation's inventory.

There are exceptions: for example, *§ 263A* does *not* apply to purchasers for resale with no more than $10 million gross receipts, or to production of intangibles. *§ 263A(b)*.

Of special interest to creative authors and artists is *§ 263A(h)*, which exempts them from the *§ 263A* capitalization requirements. Presumably, the basic accounting rules, requiring capitalization of *direct* costs would still apply (under *Idaho Power*). *See generally Encyclopedia Britannica, Inc. v. Commissioner*, 685 F.2d 212 (7th Cir. 1982) (discussing book publisher and author deductions).

[D]—Start-up costs

RICHMOND TELEVISION CORP. v. UNITED STATES

345 F.2d 901 (4th Cir. 1965)

SOBELOFF, CIRCUIT JUDGE: . . .

The taxpayer was organized in 1952, and among its stated corporate purposes was the operation of a television station. On December 22, 1952, it submitted an application to the FCC for a construction permit to operate Channel 12. . . .

The FCC granted the construction permit on November 30, 1955, and in 1956 it issued a three-year license to the taxpayer which then commenced broadcasting.

[Editor — Prior to receiving the license, taxpayer incurred expenditures to train employees to operate a TV station.]

Although Richmond Television had no receipts from television broadcasting prior to 1956, it undertook, in its original returns for 1952 through 1956, to claim deductions in the aggregate sum of $114,708 for the cost of the training program as well as the cost of obtaining an operating license from the FCC. In 1956, however, after the Internal Revenue Service issued Revenue Ruling 56-520, holding that certain costs incurred in obtaining a television broadcasting license from the FCC were not deductible from gross income, the taxpayer voluntarily capitalized $58,165.79 of the sum previously deducted for its expenses in obtaining the license from the FCC. The remaining $56,552.01 it continued to treat as deductible . . . . These are the items here in dispute. . . .

. . . [T]he Government's position [is] that as a matter of law the sums expended by the taxpayer in training prospective employees in the techniques of television broadcasting in years prior to receipt of the FCC broadcasting license are not ordinary business expenses but capital expenditures. . . .

The taxpayer maintains that these were "ordinary and necessary start-up expenses," and asserts that no case or ruling has ever denied a deduction for such expenses. The taxpayer, however, fails to deal with the point that to qualify for the deduction the expenses must have been incurred in "carrying on . . . (a) trade or business."

The precise question is the deductibility of "pre-opening" expenses incurred between the decision to establish a business and the actual beginning of business operations. During the three-year period under consideration, Richmond Television had indeed been incorporated for the purpose of conducting a television station but it had not yet obtained a license or begun broadcasting. The issue therefore is at what point of time did its business begin, and whether at this doubtful, prefatory stage it was carrying on a business. While decisions are to be found holding that particular taxpayers were or were not engaged in a trade or business, there is little discussion of the question of when, in point of time, a trade or business actually begins. This is usually a factual issue, but the resolution of the issue must have an evidentiary basis. . . .

[Prior case law establishes] that, even though a taxpayer has made a firm decision to enter into business and over a considerable period of time spent money in preparation for entering that business, he still has not "engaged in carrying on any trade or business" within the intendment of § 162(a) until such time as the business has begun to function as a going concern and performed those activities for which it was organized.

Applying this rule, we are of the view that there was no basis in the evidence for a charge permitting the jury to find that the taxpayer was in business during the period in question. We are of the opinion, therefore, that the District Court was in error in failing to hold as a matter of law that Richmond Television was not in business until 1956, when it obtained the license and began broadcasting. Until then there was no certainty that it would obtain a license, or that it would ever go on the air. Since all of the expenditures underlying the disputed deductions were made before the license was issued and broadcasting commenced, they are "pre-operating expenses," not deductible under § 162(a).

If a taxpayer loses a case like *Richmond Television*, it is especially serious because the asset acquired usually has no ascertainable useful life and is therefore not depreciable. The value of a trained workforce is *not* a "section 197 intangible" (*§ 197(d)(1)(C)(i)*), eligible for 15-year depreciation, if it is *self-created. § 197(c)(2).* A great deal therefore turns on defining when the business begins.

Research and development. In one situation, the Code permits expensing of outlays before business has begun. *§ 174* permits expensing of research and experimental costs "in connection with a trade or business." *Snow v. Commissioner*, 416 U.S. 500 (1974), held that this language was broader than "carrying on a trade or business" and permitted preoperating outlays to be expensed. The Court was undoubtedly influenced by the fact that the provision was meant as an economic incentive and that any other interpretation would have favored existing businesses over businesses which were still getting started.

Elective 60-month amortization. *§ 195*, passed after *Richmond Television*, permits the taxpayer to elect to amortize start-up expenditures over 60 months, starting when the business begins. This section applies to investigation expenses to decide whether to enter a business, as well as the start-up expenses of a specific business (as in *Richmond Television*). Will this take some of the pressure off distinguishing start-up from post-start-up expenses? It is still much better to expense than to amortize over 60 months.

[E]—Clearly reflect income — Is capitalizing costs worth the trouble?

One-year rule. If the rationale for capitalizing costs is to clearly reflect income, then it will not always be worth the effort to capitalize every outlay with a savings feature. For example, suppose an asset has a one year useful life, straddling two tax years. The Regulations require expenditures to be capitalized if they create an asset with a useful life extending "substantially beyond the close of the taxable year." *Treas. Reg. § 1.461-1(a)(1)*. Some courts have interpreted this to mean that an expense does not have to be capitalized if its useful life is not more than one calendar year, even if it extends over more than one taxable year. This is the so-called "one-year" rule. *Zaninovich v. Commissioner*, 616 F.2d. 429 (9th Cir. 1980) (one year's rent required to be paid under the lease in December can be deducted when paid), *rev'g* 69 T.C. 605 (1978). In the cited case, the rent was to be paid annually for twenty years. The only difference therefore between deducting the entire rent in the year paid, and allocating 1/12 to the year paid and 11/12 to the next year, occurred in the first and last year of the lease. Still, the "one-year" rule seems to be generally applicable.

Small, recurring expenditures. When expenditures for certain items recur on a frequent basis, the difference between expensing and capitalization-with-depreciation may not be great because taxable income will be similar in either case. This is especially true if expenditures are small. For example, deduction of the annual $1,000 purchase price of assets with a five-year life will, beginning five years after the purchases commence, equal straight-line depreciation.

Depreciation in Year

Purchase	1	2	3	4	5	after year 5
1000	200	200	200	200	200	—
1000		200	200	200	200	etc.
1000			200	200	200	etc.
1000				200	200	etc.
1000					200	etc.
					1000	

The following case discusses when the cost of long-lived assets can be expensed.

CINCINNATI, NEW ORLEANS & TEXAS PACIFIC RAILWAY v. UNITED STATES

424 F.2d 563 (Ct. Cl. 1970)

PER CURIAM:

Plaintiff, The Cincinnati, New Orleans and Texas Pacific Railway Company, during the period in question, operated a railroad as a common carrier in interstate commerce, and as such was subject to the supervision of the Interstate Commerce Commission (ICC). It has consistently reported its income for tax purposes in accordance with the accrual method on a calendar year basis.

In its regulation of rail carriers the ICC has long required that financial statements be prepared in compliance with its "General Instructions of Accounting Classifications." From January 1, 1921 to January 31, 1940, the ICC required that in accounting for purchases of property (other than track) of less than $100, the railroads should charge the expenditure to operating expenses rather than to a capital amount. This procedure is referred to as a "minimum rule."

In 1940 the ICC, after consideration of the economic condition of the railroads, determined that the minimum rule should be raised from $100 to $500. . . .

It is argued that since the items accounted for by the minimum rule admittedly had a useful life longer than one year, they necessarily constitute permanent improvements or betterments, and, therefore, must be capitalized.

In furtherance of this position defendant points out that the capitalization of assets such as furniture, office equipment and other small items is in harmony with a long line of cases deciding this question with respect to specific assets. It is also noted that the Supreme Court has held in Old Colony R.R. Co. v. United States, 284 U.S. 552 (1932), that the accounting rules of regulatory agencies are not binding upon the Commissioner of Internal Revenue. In the same vein, it is defendant's position that under the Internal Revenue Code it is the nature of the property and not its cost which determines its classification as a capital expenditure or as a current operating expense.

Defendant's second major argument is that plaintiff cannot avail itself of the broad statements in § 41 of the Internal Revenue Code of 1939 and [related Regulations], because the minimum rule does not constitute a "method of accounting." [Editor — *§ 41* is the predecessor of *§ 446*.] Furthermore, assuming arguendo that the minimum rule constitutes such a method of accounting, defendant asserts that, "(w)here the treatment of expenditures made to acquire depreciable capital assets is concerned, the method of accounting provisions play no part in the allocation between current and deferred deductions. The capital expenditure and depreciation deduction provisions (§ 24(a)(2)) of the Code establish not only what may be deducted but also the timing of the deduction . . . ." [Editor — *§ 24* is the predecessor of *§ 263*.]

For the following reasons these arguments of the defendant cannot be accepted.

The core of defendant's position that since the items in question admittedly have a useful life in excess of one year, the accounting for them must be in accordance with § 24(a)(2) [Editor — now *§ 263*] which requires the capitalization of "permanent improvements or betterments" and with [related Regulations] which suggests the capitalization of items having a useful life which extends beyond the year in which they are purchased, is twofold. Primarily, it is an argument for an inflexible objective, ipso facto approach to the question of whether an asset is a capital item or one of current expense. That is to say, if an asset has a useful life greater than one year, or if it could be considered by itself to be a "permanent improvement" or "betterment," it must be capitalized automatically without consideration of any other factors. Secondly, defendant's position requires the conclusion that the method of accounting sections of the Code (§ 41 of the 1939 Code and § 446 of the 1954 Code) are subordinate to the capital expenditure and depreciation sections of the Code (§ 24 of the 1939 Code and § 263 of the 1954 Code).

Neither of these underlying precepts is acceptable. The first, the conclusiveness of the one-year rule, simply does not square with basic philosophy concerning asset accounting as reflected in the regulations and in § 41 [Editor — now *§ 446*]. The opening sentence of [that] section permits the use of the taxpayer's regularly employed method of accounting in the computation of net income, as long as that method clearly reflects income. In harmony with this, Treas. Reg. 111, § 29.41-3 recognizes that "no uniform method of accounting can be prescribed for all taxpayers, and the law contemplates that each taxpayer shall adopt such forms and systems of accounting as are in his judgement best suited to his purpose.". . .

Apparently in order to prevent the conclusion that the one year rule is but one test in deciding whether the accounting for an asset is proper, defendant contends that if there is a conflict between the capitalization and depreciation sections and the methods of accounting sections the former must be given preeminence. If this were so, the one-year rule which is an adjunct of the capitalization and depreciation sections would be carried along to a dominant, if not determinative position. This contention is likewise rejected. . . .

TP OK if minimum rule accurately reflects income

$446

We turn now to the ultimate question in this case, does the taxpayer's system of accounting which employs the minimum rule clearly reflect income in taxpayer's circumstances. . . .

The most convincing evidence that the Commissioner has abused his discretion in prohibiting the plaintiff from treating items with a useful life in excess of one year which cost less than $500, not as "permanent improvements or betterments" but as current operating expenditures, is the statistical analysis proffered by the plaintiff which indicates the relationship of the quantum of minimum rule expenses to other substantial income and balance sheet figures. Plaintiff's exhibit 1, which is reproduced in the accompanying findings of fact, is a compilation of significant data for the 17-year period from 1940 to 1956. . . . [Editor — The following numbered paragraphs are from plaintiff's exhibit 1.]

if TP used IRS rule, only minimal change

9. If the plaintiff had reported its income in accordance with the method of accounting insisted upon by the Commissioner and depreciated minimum rule assets over a 15-year period, its income for 1947, 1948 and 1949 would have been increased by $5,400, $3,149 and $15,971 in each respective year. This is 7/100 of 1 percent, 3/100 of 1 percent and 2/10 of 1 percent more than the income computed by the plaintiff in accordance with the minimum rule in each respective year. If a 10-year useful life is employed in making the above comparison both the absolute and relative differences between the different methods are reduced.

10. Stating number 9 above in a somewhat different manner, it is significant that both on a year-to-year basis and on a 17-year overall basis, the disallowed minimum rule expenses are fairly similar to the amount of depreciation that would have been allowed under the defendant's method. Over the 17-year period plaintiff expensed $229,810 of minimum rule items. If it had employed the defendant's method and a 10-year useful life, plaintiff would have been entitled to total ratable depreciation deductions of $175,806 for items covered by the minimum rule. If the useful life employed had been 15 years, total ratable depreciation deductions of $157,599 would have been allowed. When compared with the total operating expense, total depreciation deductions claimed, or the total net income of the plaintiff, the differences between the depreciation deductions computed under plaintiff's and defendant's methods are so minute as to become unfathomable. This observation is accentuated when it is realized that had plaintiff employed the Commissioner's method, substantial additional clerical expense would have been incurred, thus reducing the already small difference between net income as computed under each of the parties' respective methods.

11. A final observation discernible from plaintiff's exhibit is that the plaintiff's method of accounting for small items does not always lead to

less taxable income; there are years where it is clear that the minimum rule has generated a lower deduction than would have been proper under the ratable depreciation method. It would seem that over the long run the total amounts deductible would be similar and the main question involved is the timing of the deduction. . . .

. . . Where the burden on both taxpayers and Service to account for each item of property separately is great, and the likelihood of distortion of income is nil or minimal, the Code is not so rigid and so impracticable that it demands that nevertheless all items be accounted for individually, no matter what the trouble or the onus. . . .

For the reasons stated, it is concluded that the Commissioner of Internal Revenue has abused his discretion under §§ 24 and 41 of the Internal Revenue Code of 1939 [Editor — now *§§ 263, 446*] in disallowing the use of the minimum expense rule, and therefore, plaintiff is entitled to recover.

[F]—"Recapturing" prior expenses

Suppose a taxpayer can expense a capital expenditure because adding the cost to basis is not worth the trouble, as in the *Cincinnati* case. If the taxpayer later sells the expensed property, is the gain ordinary income to the extent of the prior deduction? An earlier chapter dealt with the "recapture" of *depreciation* deductions when the sales price did not decline as much as the depreciation deductions. *See § 1245*. But expensing is not technically "depreciation." *§ 1245 does* apply explicitly to a few expensing situations, including *§ 179* expensing for small businesses (*§ 1245(a)(2)(C)*), but not to expensing generally. No explicit statutory rule recaptures the expensed deduction in *Cincinnati*.

Should case law convert what would otherwise be capital gain to ordinary income, when a taxpayer sells previously expensed property? You have encountered this problem before. The broad issue is whether events in an earlier year should influence taxability in a later year. One example was the "tax benefit" rule, which *helped* the taxpayer by excluding from income the recovery of items whose deduction did not previously reduce tax. Now the shoe is on the other foot. Because the cost of the asset was previously expensed and therefore reduced ordinary income, the government wants to recharacterize capital gain on the sale of the asset as ordinary income. We know that the government cannot tax recoveries of income at high rates in a low rate year, just because the recovery is related to deductions taken in an earlier high rate year. The case law does not permit the accounting year barrier to be broken down just to account for tax rate differentials in different years. But is the "capital gain-prior *ordinary* deduction" problem different?

The Supreme Court struggled with this issue in *Hillsboro National Bank v. Commissioner*, 460 U.S. 370 (1983). It discussed the "tax benefit" rule as a "judicially developed principle that allays some of the inflexibilities of the annual accounting system. . . . The purpose of the rule is . . . to approximate the results produced by a tax system based on transactional rather than annual accounting." It adopted the following test for applying the transactional approach:

> The basic purpose of the tax benefit rule is to achieve rough transactional parity in tax, and to protect the Government and the taxpayer from the adverse effects of reporting a transaction on the basis of assumptions that an event in a subsequent year proves to have been erroneous. Such an event, unforeseen at the time of an earlier deduction, may in many cases require the application of the tax benefit rule. We do not, however, agree that this consequence invariably follows. Not every unforeseen event will require the taxpayer to report income in the amount of his earlier deduction. On the contrary, the tax benefit rule will "cancel out" an earlier deduction only when a careful examination shows that the later event is indeed fundamentally inconsistent with the premise on which the deduction was initially based. That is, if that event had occurred within the same taxable year, it would have foreclosed the deduction. In some cases, a subsequent recovery by the taxpayer will be the only event that would be fundamentally inconsistent with the provision granting the deduction. In such a case, only actual recovery by the taxpayer would justify application of the tax benefit rule. For example, if a calendar-year taxpayer made a rental payment on December 15 for a 30-day lease deductible in the current year under § 162(a)(3), the tax benefit rule would not require the recognition of income if the leased premises were destroyed by fire on January 10. The resulting inability of the taxpayer to occupy the building would be an event not fundamentally inconsistent with his prior deduction as an ordinary and necessary business expense under § 162(a). The loss is attributable to the business and therefore is consistent with the deduction of the rental payment as an ordinary and necessary business expense. On the other hand, had the premises not burned and, in January, the taxpayer decided to use them to house his family rather than to continue the operation of his business, he would have converted the leasehold to personal use. This would be an event fundamentally inconsistent with the business use on which the deduction was based. In the case of the fire, only if the lessor — by virtue of some provision in the lease — had refunded the rental payment would the taxpayer be required under the tax benefit rule to recognize income on the subsequent destruction of the building. In other words, the subsequent recovery of the previously deducted rental payment would be the only event inconsistent with the provision allowing the deduction. It therefore

is evident that the tax benefit rule must be applied on a case-by-case basis. A court must consider the facts and circumstances of each case in the light of the purpose and function of the provisions granting the deductions.

If (as the Court says) the conversion of an asset to personal use results in recapture of the prior ordinary deduction, then sales proceeds from disposing of an asset should produce ordinary income to the extent of the prior deduction. A sale for value is obviously "fundamentally inconsistent" with a prior deduction. Would a gift to a relative be inconsistent, thereby triggering recapture of the prior deduction as ordinary income in the year of the gift?

Suppose the right to expense was intended by the statute as a special incentive, as when *§ 174* permits research costs to be expensed. Should sale of the business include recapture of all or part of those expenses as ordinary income? *Rev. Rul. 85-186*, 1985-2 C.B. 84.

Prior erroneous deduction. The "tax benefit" rule in *Hillsboro* is different from the tax benefit rule discussed in § 5.03, *supra*. In the prior discussion the tax benefit rule helped the taxpayer, excluding from income the recovery of an item previously deducted without any tax reduction. The version of the tax benefit rule in this chapter hurts a taxpayer—it includes in ordinary income the recovery of an item for which a prior deduction has been taken even though the tax rules would *not* otherwise provide for ordinary income. But what if the prior deduction was improper?

In *Hughes & Luce v. Commissioner*, 70 F.3d 16 (5th Cir. 1995), the taxpayer was a law firm which had deducted advances on behalf of clients in connection with litigation (such as court costs and filing fees). In a later year, it recovered these advances when they collected fees from their clients. The court held that the earlier deductions were improper on the ground that the advances were loans. But the deduction *had* been taken and the Fifth Circuit decision included the amount collected later as reimbursements in the law firm's taxable income, based on the tax benefit rule.

The Tax Court (68 T.C.M. (CCH) 1169 (1994)), had reached the same result but refused to apply the "anti-taxpayer" tax benefit rule on the ground that it was inapplicable whenever the prior deduction was erroneous (the "erroneous deduction" exception). The court argued that the proper course for the government to take was to make a correction in the earlier year, when the deduction was taken; if the statute of limitations had run, that was the government's responsibility. The Tax Court did, however, rule against the taxpayer on the basis of a "duty of consistency" (or quasi-estoppel) principle. That principle, the Tax Court asserted, applies in the following circumstances:

> The duty of consistency applies when: (1) The taxpayer made a representation or reported an item for Federal income tax purposes in one year, (2) the Commissioner acquiesced in or relied on that representation or report for that year, and (3) the taxpayer attempts to change that representation or report in a subsequent year, after the period of limitations has expired with respect to the year of the representation or report, and the change is detrimental to the Commissioner. When the duty of consistency applies, the Commissioner may proceed as if the representation or report on which she relied continues to be true, although, in fact, it is not. Simply put, the taxpayer is estopped from taking a position to the contrary.

The government prefers the "tax benefit" approach, however, because it does not require proving that any of the quasi-estoppel circumstances exist. The Tax Court states that the second requirement is met — *i.e.*, respondent acquiesced in or relied on a representation or report by the taxpayer — when a taxpayer files a return that contains an inadequately disclosed item and respondent accepts the return and allows the period of limitations to expire without an audit of the return. To avoid the second of the quasi-estoppel conditions, the taxpayer must provide respondent with sufficient facts to supply her with actual or constructive knowledge of a possible mistake in the reporting of the erroneously disclosed item.

§ 13.03 MAINTENANCE EXPENSES vs. IMPROVEMENTS AND ACQUISITIONS

[A]—"Future benefits"

Treas. Reg. § 1.263(a)-1(b) states that capital expenditures "include amounts paid or incurred (1) to add to the value, or substantially prolong the useful life, of property owned by the taxpayer, such as plant or equipment, or (2) to adapt property to a new or different use." The following cases try to apply this standard to expenditures which acquire intangible value for a business.

INDOPCO, INC. v. COMMISSIONER

503 U.S. 79 (1992)

JUSTICE BLACKMUN delivered the opinion of the Court.

[Editor — A corporation was a target of a friendly takeover. The taxpayer, Indopco, Inc. (formerly named National Starch and Chemical Corporation) manufactures and sells adhesives, starches, and specialty chemical products. Representatives of Unilever United States, Inc., expressed interest in acquiring National Starch, which was one of its suppliers, through a friendly transaction. National Starch was a large publicly held corporation with over 6,563,000 common shares held by approximately 3700 shareholders. Frank and Anna Greenwall were the corporation's largest shareholders and owned approximately 14.5% of the common stock. The Greenwalls indicated that they would transfer their shares to Unilever only if a tax-free transaction could be arranged, which was done. National Starch's directors were told by Debevoise, Plimpton, Lyons & Gates, National Starch's counsel, that under Delaware law they had a fiduciary duty to ensure that the proposed transaction would be fair to the shareholders. National Starch thereupon engaged the investment banking firm of Morgan Stanley & Co., Inc., to evaluate its shares, to render a fairness opinion, and generally to assist in the event of the emergence of a hostile tender offer.

The tax issue was whether payments to Debevoise and Morgan Stanley related to the takeover, amounting to about $2,500,000, were capital expenditures. The Court dealt explicitly with its earlier decision in *Commissioner v. Lincoln Savings and Loan Ass'n.*, 403 U.S. 345 (1981).]

National Starch contends that the decision in *Lincoln Savings* announced an exclusive test for identifying capital expenditures, a test in which "creation or enhancement of an asset" is a prerequisite to capitalization, and deductibility under § 162(a) is the rule rather than the exception. We do not agree, for we conclude that National Starch has overread *Lincoln Savings*.

In *Lincoln Savings*, we were asked to decide whether certain premiums, required by federal statute to be paid by a savings and loan association to the Federal Savings and Loan Insurance Corporation (FSLIC), were ordinary and necessary expenses under § 162(a), as Lincoln Savings argued and the Court of Appeals had held, or capital expenditures under § 263, as the Commissioner contended. We found that the "additional" premiums, the purpose of which was to provide FSLIC with a secondary reserve fund in which each insured institution retained a pro rata interest recoverable in certain situations, "serv[e] to create or enhance for Lincoln what is essentially a separate and distinct additional asset." "[A]s an inevitable consequence," we concluded, "the payment is capital in nature and not an expense, let alone an ordinary expense, deductible under § 162(a)."

Lincoln Savings stands for the simple proposition that a taxpayer's expenditure that "serves to create or enhance . . . a separate and distinct" asset should be capitalized under § 263. It by no means follows, however, that only expenditures that create or enhance separate and distinct assets are to be capitalized under § 263. We had no occasion in *Lincoln Savings* to consider the tax treatment of expenditures that, unlike the additional premiums at issue there, did not create or enhance a specific asset, and thus the case cannot be read to preclude capitalization in other circumstances. In short, *Lincoln Savings* holds that the creation of a separate and distinct asset well may be a sufficient but not a necessary condition to classification as a capital expenditure.

Nor does our statement in *Lincoln Savings* that "the presence of an ensuing benefit that may have some future aspect is not controlling" prohibit reliance on future benefit as a means of distinguishing an ordinary business expense from a capital expenditure. Although the mere presence of an incidental future benefit — "some future aspect" — may not warrant capitalization, a taxpayer's realization of benefits beyond the year in which the expenditure is incurred is undeniably important in determining whether the appropriate tax treatment is immediate deduction or capitalization. *Central Texas Savings & Loan Assn. v. United States*, 731 F.2d 1181, 1183 (CA5 1984) ("While the period of the benefits may not be controlling in all cases, it nonetheless remains a prominent, if not predominant, characteristic of a capital item."). Indeed, the text of the Code's capitalization provision, § 263(a)(1), which refers to "permanent improvements or betterments," itself envisions an inquiry into the duration and extent of the benefits realized by the taxpayer.

In applying the foregoing principles to the specific expenditures at issue in this case, we conclude that National Starch has not demonstrated that the investment banking, legal, and other costs it incurred in connection with Unilever's acquisition of its shares are deductible as ordinary and necessary business expenses under § 162(a).

Although petitioner attempts to dismiss the benefits that accrued to National Starch from the Unilever acquisition as "entirely speculative" or "merely incidental," the Tax Court's and the Court of Appeals' findings that the transaction produced significant benefits to National Starch that extended beyond the tax year in question are amply supported by the record. For example, in commenting on the merger with Unilever, National Starch's 1978 "Progress Report" observed that the company would "benefit greatly from the availability of Unilever's enormous resources, especially in the area of basic technology." . . .

In addition to these anticipated resource-related benefits, National Starch obtained benefits through its transformation from a publicly held, freestanding corporation into a wholly owned subsidiary of Unilever. . . .

Courts long have recognized that expenses such as these, " 'incurred for the purpose of changing the corporate structure for the benefit of future operations are not ordinary and necessary business expenses.' " Deductions for professional expenses thus have been disallowed in a wide variety of cases concerning changes in corporate structure. . . .

The expenses that National Starch incurred in Unilever's friendly takeover do not qualify for deduction as "ordinary and necessary" business expenses under § 162(a). The fact that the expenditures do not create or enhance a separate and distinct additional asset is not controlling; the acquisition-related expenses bear the indicia of capital expenditures and are to be treated as such.

[Editor — These costs are *not* "section 197 intangibles" and therefore cannot be depreciated over 15 years. *§ 197(e)(8)*.]

Business expansion costs. The general question which *INDOPCO* addresses is how to treat expenditures which produce intangible assets with speculative future value. A major battleground has been business expansion costs. In *NCNB Corp. v. United States*, 684 F.2d 285 (4th Cir. 1982) (*en* *banc*), *rev'g* 651 F.2d 942 (4th Cir. 1981), the taxpayer-bank wanted to expand throughout North Carolina. The facts are stated as follows in the original three-judge opinion.

> The taxpayer in the instant case is a "full service" national bank offering a wide range of banking services to its customers. To further its goal of providing banking services throughout North Carolina, taxpayer has pursued for several years an expansion program involving over a dozen mergers with other banks, reconstruction of some of its existing facilities, and the establishment of new facilities ("branching"). Because taxpayer is a national bank, it must obtain the approval of the Comptroller of the Currency to establish a new branch or to retain and operate the existing branch of a bank with which it consolidates.
>
> Varied are the costs incurred in the many aspects of taxpayer's expansion program, ranging from selecting an area of the state for expansion, to planning future branches in that area, to turning such general plans into a concrete course of action, to obtaining the approval of the Comptroller of the Currency. During the tax years in question, four of taxpayer's applications for approval were protested and were later approved only after an evidentiary hearing held by the Regional Administrator of the Office of the Comptroller. In one instance, the protest resulted in extensive litigation, in which taxpayer ultimately was successful. The costs involved in the expansion program were both internal (*e.g.,* salaries, supplies, depreciation, amortization) and external (*e.g.,* fees paid to the Comptroller, attorneys' fees, amounts paid to outside consultants for marketing studies).
>
> As part of its long-range planning, the bank produced or purchased marketing studies of large metropolitan areas, reports which it called "Metro Studies." In addition to setting out long-and short-range recommendations regarding future branches, Metro Studies contained information which was used in planning future branches, data which were needed for applications to the Comptroller, and material which was relevant to action which might be taken in connection with existing branches. The District Court, in reaching its decision in taxpayer's favor on grounds independent of when anticipated revenues would match expenditures for Metro Studies, made no finding with respect to the useful life of the Metro Studies. Nevertheless, the record clearly implies that theirs was a multi-year utility, the value not being entirely restricted to nor exhausted within the single year of expenditure. Neither the parties nor the court made any allocation of that extended utility among (a) continued monitoring of the operations of existing branches, (b) planning for new branches, and (c) bringing those new branches into existence.

A second stage of planning produced what taxpayer calls "feasibility studies." The reports focused on specific locations for potential branches. To help management decide whether or not to open a new branch in the particular location, a feasibility study estimated additional income to be anticipated from a branch in the location, net of the further costs associated with opening a branch there. As with the Metro Studies, the court made no finding as to the duration of useful life. Correspondingly, there was no finding as to whether the feasibility studies, in part at least, played any role in the production of current income.

In concluding that at least some of the above expenses should be capitalized, the three-judge court (later reversed *en banc*) anticipated at least some of the reasoning in the later Supreme Court *INDOPCO* decision, as follows:

In addition to arguing for a special-purpose accounting system, taxpayer contends that regardless of accounting principles a current deduction must be allowed for any expenditure which does not produce a "capital asset" as defined by I.R.C. § 1221, which does not relate to a new trade or business, and which does not procure for taxpayer some independent property interest. The argument runs that, without at least one of these properties, it may not be capitalized, but must be expensed. Although any one or more of three factors when present may be sufficient to require that an expenditure be capitalized, none of them, individually or together, must necessarily be present to make capitalization appropriate. Even in their absence, if an expenditure is part of the cost of producing future rather than current income, expensing the expenditure when incurred will not "clearly reflect income," and a deduction may be barred by the Commissioner. I.R.C. § 446(b). . . .

A similar analysis applies to the suggestion that an enterprise should carry forward even those costs lasting for more than a year only when they are associated with property interests. Where such an expenditure is in fact so associated, an appropriate part of it must be carried forward. That is the holding of *Commissioner v. Lincoln Savings & Loan Association*, 403 U.S. 345, 354, (1971) (presence of such an interest called "controlling"). The case did not suggest a need for the presence of a property interest (or, a fortiori, for the presence of corporeality or salability or realizable value) before capitalization may be required. That one was there made the result all the more obvious. But the case does not hold that, in the absence of a property interest, the opposite result was compelled.

The Court of Appeals' *en banc* reversal contained the following observations. Are they inconsistent with the Supreme Court's *INDOPCO* decision? Is there some way to justify the deduction in the *Briarcliff* decision, discussed in the following opinion, without allowing NCNB a deduction for its expansion costs?

> It is important to recognize that all of these expenses were connected with NCNB's developing and operating a statewide network of branch banking facilities. In order to maintain its position in the industry, NCNB found it necessary to continually explore the market for its varied services and facilities. It is a long recognized principle of tax law that expenditures for the protection of an existing investment, the continuation of an existing business, or the preservation of existing income from loss or diminution are ordinary and necessary business expenses within the meaning of IRC § 162. *Briarcliff Candy Corp. v. Commissioner of Internal Revenue*, 475 F.2d 775, 787 (2nd Cir. 1973).
>
> The Second Circuit's *Briarcliff* opinion is of particular interest in the case before us. *Briarcliff* involved a candy company which had sold its products primarily through a chain of company owned stores in urban centers. Demographic changes forced the company to seek markets for its products in suburban areas. When company owned suburban stores failed to attract satisfactory business, the company decided to develop a network of franchised dealers. The company, in preparing its income tax returns, treated the costs of developing the network, such as sales calls and advertisements in trade magazines, as deductible expenses. The Commissioner disallowed the deductions, however, reasoning that these promotional expenses were distinct from the operating expenses of the franchise division. The Commissioner said the expenses were actually capital in nature because they were incurred in obtaining 159 dealer contracts. The contracts were said to constitute the capital assets of the franchise division. The Second Circuit, citing *Lincoln Savings & Loan*, rejected the Commissioner's argument that the expenditures were capital in nature because benefits from them extended into future years. The court said the expenditures would be capital only if they served to create or enhance a separate and distinct additional asset. Turning to the issue of whether the contracts were such assets, the court stated that an expenditure is a "capital asset" only if "at the time it is furnished to the company, it has an ascertainable and measurable value — that is, a value in money or a fair market value." Noting that there is no special statutory definition of "capital asset" for IRC §§ 162 and 263, the court said the term must be taken in its "usual and customary business sense as items of ownership of a permanent or fixed nature which are convertible into cash." The Second Circuit concluded that the contracts were not capital assets and thus expenses incurred in obtaining them were not capital costs. The *Briarcliff* reasoning is applicable in the instant case because NCNB, like the *Briarcliff* taxpayer, was expanding its business into new territories.

> We do not, however, hold as determinative the fact that the branch banks could not be turned into cash. But that is a factor to consider in determining whether they were "separate and distinct additional asset(s)" within the meaning of *Lincoln Savings & Loan*. The costs NCNB incurred in exploring such expansion are analogous to the costs in *Briarcliff* for developing the franchise network. Particularly relevant is the Second Circuit's rejection of the Commissioner's argument that the possible long term benefits of such expenditures mandated their capitalization. . . .
>
> In conclusion, we emphasize that NCNB's business is operating a statewide network of branch banks. In order to maintain this network, NCNB must continually evaluate its market position through various means that utilize both internal and external resources. It has every right to keep abreast of demographic trends and the like in its necessary allocation of resources as well as in ascertaining where the public demand for its services exists. The bank must regularly take actions such as the opening and closing of branches so as to maintain profitability and a sound financial position. Where these actions result in the creation or retirement of separate and identifiable assets such as buildings and equipment, then the taxpayer must make adjustments to its capital accounts. But where these expenditures do not create or enhance separate and identifiable assets, they are properly considered "ordinary and necessary." IRC § 162(a).

Remember that the *purchase* price of new opportunities to expand a business, such as a price paid to another company for its good will or for exclusive distribution rights, would almost certainly be a capital expenditure. *Manhattan Co. of Virginia, Inc. v. Commissioner*, 50 T.C. 78 (1968). If the taxpayer can expense the outlays it incurs to develop these assets, there is a tax difference between developing and purchasing such assets. That distinction is what the Court wanted to avoid in *Idaho Power*, dealing with capitalization of depreciation expenses related to constructing an asset.

POST-INDOPCO DEVELOPMENTS

It is obvious that the INDOPCO decision has worried a lot of taxpayers because there has been a rash of Revenue Rulings in which the government has tried to ease taxpayer concern. Here are four more pro-taxpayer rulings (are they too generous to taxpayers?).

Advertising costs. *Rev. Rul. 92–80,* 1992–2 Cum. Bull. 57

Does the Supreme Court's decision in *INDOPCO, Inc, v. Commissioner*, 503 U.S. 79 (1992), affect the treatment of advertising costs as business expenses which are generally deductible under section 162 of the Internal Revenue Code?

Section 162(a) of the Code allows a deduction for all the ordinary and necessary expenses paid or incurred during the taxable year in carrying on any trade or business. Section 1.162-1(a) of the Income Tax Regulations expressly provides that "advertising and other selling expenses" are among the items included in deductible business expenses under section 162 of the Code. Section 1.162-20(a)(2) of the regulations provides, in part, that expenditures for institutional or goodwill advertising which keeps the taxpayer's name before the public are generally deductible as ordinary and necessary business expenses provided the expenditures are related to the patronage the taxpayer might reasonably expect in the future. . . .

The *INDOPCO* decision does not affect the treatment of advertising costs under section 162(a) of the Code. These costs are generally deductible under that section even though advertising may have some future effect on business activities, as in the case of institutional or goodwill advertising. Only in the unusual circumstance where advertising is directed towards obtaining future benefits significantly beyond those traditionally associated with ordinary product advertising or with institutional or goodwill advertising, must the costs of that advertising be capitalized. *See, e.g., Cleveland Electric Illuminating Co. v. United States*, 7 Cl. Ct. 220 (1975) (capitalization of advertising costs incurred to allay public opposition to the granting of a license to construct a nuclear power plant).

Severance pay. *Rev. Rul. 94–77*, 1994–2 C.B. 19

Does the Supreme Court's [*INDOPCO*] decision affect the treatment of severance payments, made by a taxpayer to its employees, as business expenses which are generally deductible under § 162 of the Internal Revenue Code?. . .

The *INDOPCO* decision clarifies that the creation or enhancement of a separate and distinct asset is not a prerequisite to capitalization. That clarification does not, however, change the fundamental legal principles for determining whether a particular expenditure may be deducted or must be capitalized. With respect to expenditures that produce benefits both in the current year and in future years, the determination of whether such expenditures must be capitalized requires a careful examination of all the facts. Although the mere presence of some future benefit may not warrant capitalization, a taxpayer's realization of future benefits is undeniably important in determining whether an expenditure is immediately deductible or must be capitalized.

. . . [A]lthough severance payments made by a taxpayer to its employees in connection with a business down-sizing may produce some future benefits, such as reducing operating costs and increasing operating efficiencies, these payments principally relate to previously rendered services of those employees. Therefore, such severance payments are generally deductible as business expenses under § 162 and § 1.162–10.

Energy conservation expenditures. *Rev. Rul. 95–32*, 1995–1 C.B. 5

In this ruling, the IRS applied the severance payment ruling favorably for the taxpayer. The case involved expenditures incurred by a public utility for the implementation and operation of energy conservation programs. The utility pays contractors to install low-cost water heating and lighting systems in its customers' houses and to make energy-saving structural improvements to its customers' houses; and incurs employee compensation costs by helping its industrial customers design efficient manufacturing processes. It makes these expenditures without obligating any of its customers participating in these programs to purchase power in the future; and it does not retain title to any of the property purchased in connection with these programs. For financial and regulatory accounting purposes, the public utility capitalizes these costs. The ruling states:

> [The] expenditures are not capital expenditures within the meaning of § 263. No asset is created or acquired and retained [] as a result of [the] expenditures. Moreover, although [the] expenditures may reduce future operating and capital costs, these kinds of benefits, without more, do not require capitalization of these expenditures. *See, e.g.*, Rev. Rul. 94–77 (severance payments made to employees in connection with a business downsizing are deductible even though they may reduce future operating costs and increase operating efficiencies). In addition, the treatment of an expenditure for ratemaking or rate base purposes is not determinative of its treatment for federal income tax purposes.

Training costs. *Rev. Rul. 96–62*, 1996–2 C.B. 9

The *INDOPCO* decision does not affect the treatment of training costs under § 162. Amounts paid or incurred for training, including the costs of trainers and routine updates of training materials, are generally deductible as business expenses under that section even though they may have some future benefit. *See, e.g.*, *Century Electric Illuminating Co. v. United States*, 7 Cl. Ct. 220 (1985) (deduction for costs of training employees to operate new equipment in an existing business); Rev. Rul. 58–238, 1958–1 C.B. 90, 91 (deduction for costs of training employees that relate to the regular conduct of the employer's business). Training costs must be capitalized only in the unusual circumstance where the training is intended primarily to obtain future benefits significantly beyond those traditionally associated with training provided in the ordinary course of a taxpayer's trade or business. *See, e.g.*, *Cleveland Electric*, 7 Cl. Ct. at 227–29 (capitalization of costs for training employees of an electric utility to operate a new nuclear power plant, which were akin to start-up costs of a new business).

Hostile takeovers. There has also been litigation over expenditures related to hostile takeovers (*INDOPCO* involved a friendly takeover)—that is, management does not enthusiastically embrace the offer. In *A.E. Staley Mfg. Co. v. Commissioner*, 105 T.C. 166 (1995), management did not welcome outside offers for corporate stock. The corporation paid investment bankers for advice about whether the offers were high enough. The bankers said that the first two offers were too low, but that a third offer was fair. The taxpayer's board of directors thereupon recommended that the shareholders accept the third offer and it was accepted.

The court disallowed deduction of the payments to the investment bankers, noting that there *was* a change in corporate structure; that, eventually, the corporate management recommended the merger; and that there were significant benefits to the corporation beyond the year of merger. Consequently, the initial hostility in the takeover bid did not preclude a capital expenditure. The court also rejected the argument that some of the payments were deductible because they related to the first two offers, which were abandoned. It conceded that costs for abandoned projects *are* deductible at the time of abandonment, but could not identify any portion of the fees paid to the investment bankers as attributable to an abandoned project.

The court distinguished *United States v. Federated Dept. Stores*, 171 Bankr. 603 (S.D.Ohio 1994), where the court allowed a deduction of "break-up" fees paid to "white knights" to fend off a hostile merger. "Break-up" fees are paid in the following circumstances. Management dislikes a merger offer—that is, the proposed merger is hostile. Management solicits someone else (a "white knight") to make a better merger offer but promises to pay a break-up fee to the white knight if the merger with the white knight does *not* occur.

The Tax Court decision in *Staley* was reversed in 119 F.3d 482 (7th Cir. 1997), on the ground that "[i]t is clear that [the taxpayer] was engaged in the process of defending its business from attack. . . . The totality of the Tax Court's factual findings makes clear that [taxpayer] was defending against an unwanted acquisition in an effort to maintain and protect an established business. [Taxpayer] hired the investment bankers and incurred their fees while resisting an acquisition. . . . Of course, it is the nature of the services performed by the investment bankers that determines the proper tax treatment of the costs of those services. [The taxpayer's] major defensive strategy was to engage in a capital transaction that would prevent the. . . acquisition. . . . The investment bankers. . . provided advice to [taxpayer] with respect to a number of alternatives, which included a recapitalization, a leveraged buy-out, . . . a spin-off, a public offering, and an offer to buy [the potential acquirer] ("pac-man" defense). . . ."

The Court of Appeals observed that "[n]one of these tasks served to facilitate the. . . acquisition. Instead, objectively assessed, the tasks performed by the investment bankers frustrated the occurrence of the merger that eventually took place. Moreover, in substance, most of the services the investment bankers performed consisted of failed attempts to engage in alternative capital transactions."

The court concluded "that the bulk of costs at issue in this case related to [the taxpayer's] defense of its business and its corporate policy and is therefore deductible under sec. 162(a). Those costs properly allocable to the efforts to engage in an alternate transaction are also deductible under sec. 165. . . . [M]ost of the fees paid to the investment bankers were not 'of value in more than one taxable year.' The main efforts of the investment bankers were directed towards defeating a hostile tender offer by exploring alternate capital transactions. These efforts failed; the investment bankers' services in this regard bore no fruit. As a result, unlike the taxpayer in *INDOPCO*, [taxpayer] did not obtain a long-term benefit as a result of making these expenditures. . . . The majority of investment banker fees in this case will reap no revenues to match; those fees are an immediate loss in the year incurred. To require capitalization under the facts of this case would result in an overstated net income for the year. . . ."

Consequently: "[T]he fees associated with the preparation of the evaluation of [taxpayer's] stock and with the few hours of facilitative work performed by the investment bankers at the time of the merger must be capitalized. However, the other fees may be deducted. . . . We therefore remand for the Tax Court to allocate a sum of the fees for capitalization to the facilitative activities of the investment bankers and printer performed in preparing the evaluation of [taxpayer's] stock and in facilitating the merger at the time of its consummation. . . . Given the fee arrangement in this case, we understand. . . that allocation may not be a simple task. Businesses in the future would do well to structure their agreements in a fashion more amenable to the requirements of the Tax Code as we have delineated today. Of course, the Commissioner could facilitate greatly the collection of the revenues by issuing precise regulations addressing this recurring problem in American corporate life."

The Court of Appeals decision is clearly more sympathetic to a deduction than the Tax Court's opinion when there is a threat of a hostile takeover but the takeover eventually occurs. And yet both courts admit that, with the proper proof, some amounts can be allocated to deductible outlays which provide no benefit to the taxpayer.

In addition, the Tax Court appears to agree that, if the merger *never* occurs, the taxpayer would be able to deduct the expenditures. The case would then be very much like those discussed in the next section, dealing with unexpected maintenance costs.

QUESTIONS

1. Should job search costs (*e.g.*, travel costs or an employment agency fee) be deductible and, if so, when? *Rev. Rul. 75-120*, 1975-1 C.B. 55 held the following: (a) job search costs in a successful or unsuccessful search to obtain new employment in the *same* trade or business are deductible expenses; and (b) there is never a deduction if the job sought was in a *new* trade or business, whether or not the search was successful. Is the Revenue Ruling correct?

2. Is a third-year law student taxed on reimbursements received from a law firm for interview travel costs? Would *§ 132(a)(3),(d)* (working conditions) apply? Are the reimbursements *§ 61* income?

Relationship of expensing and depreciation. There should be a relationship between expensing outlays to maintain an asset and depreciating that asset. The shorter the depreciable life, the more expenditures to maintain that asset are likely to lengthen its tax life, which *should* make them capital expenditures. Current tax rules do not, however, seem concerned with this relationship. Depreciable lives are shortened for tax purposes, but "repair" expenses are deductible even though they extend the asset's life beyond the depreciable period.

These comments have special relevance to our discussion of intangibles. A taxpayer who expenses advertising or business expansion costs may also be depreciating the purchase price of the asset with respect to which the expansion costs are incurred. This possibility is increased after the passage of *§ 197*, permitting the purchase price of previously nondepreciable good will to be depreciated over 15 years. In one respect, however, *§ 197* reduces the tension between expensing and depreciation rules. Prior to its passage, the Supreme Court held that certain customer-based intangibles (such as the subscription lists acquired in a business purchase) were depreciable if the buyer could prove the price allocable to the asset and its useful life. *Newark Morning Ledger Co. v. United States*, 113 S. Ct. 1670 (1993). In such cases, the depreciable life was often quite short (maybe five years) and yet the taxpayer was almost certainly expensing the advertizing and business expansion costs to extend that life beyond five years. *§ 197* extends the depreciable life to 15 years.

See also Technical Advice Memorandum (TAM) 9618004, in which the IRS argued that the cost of a major overhaul of an airplane engine, required by the Federal Aviation Administration as a condition of flying, was a capital expenditure. These overhauls were performed about every four years. The useful life for tax depreciation was seven years. As long as these overhauls were performed, the "real" useful life was about twenty two years. This lengthening of useful life was a major factor in disallowing the deduction. Does reliance on the life-lengthening factor to require capitalization of the expenditures defeat the tax incentive purpose of the shorter useful lives? Perhaps twenty two years was not only longer than tax lives but also longer than the useful life for financial accounting purposes?

[B]—Unexpected maintenance

MT. MORRIS DRIVE-IN THEATRE CO. v. COMMISSIONER

25 T.C. 272 (1955), aff'd per curiam, 238 F.2d 85 (6th Cir. 1956)

KERN, JUDGE:

When petitioner purchased, in 1947, the land which it intended to use for a drive-in theatre, its president was thoroughly familiar with the topography of this land which was such that when the covering vegetation was removed and graveled ramps were constructed and used by its patrons, the flow of natural precipitation on the lands of abutting property owners would be materially accelerated. Some provision should have been made to solve this drainage problem in order to avoid annoyance and harassment to its neighbors. If petitioner had included in its original construction plans an expenditure for a proper drainage system no one could doubt that such an expenditure would have been capital in nature.

Within a year after petitioner had finished its inadequate construction of the drive-in theatre, the need of a proper drainage system was forcibly called to its attention by one of the neighboring property owners, and under the threat of a lawsuit filed approximately a year after the theatre was constructed, the drainage system was built by petitioner who now seeks to deduct its cost as an ordinary and necessary business expenses, or as a loss.

Holding

We agree with respondent that the cost to petitioner of acquiring and constructing a drainage system in connection with its drive-in theatre was a capital expenditure.

Here was no sudden catastrophic loss caused by a "physical fault" undetected by the taxpayer in spite of due precautions taken by it at the time of its original construction work as in *American Bemberg Corporation*, 10 T.C. 361; no unforeseeable external factor as in *Midland Empire Packing Co.*, 14 T.C. 635; and no change in the cultivation of farm property caused by improvements in technique and made many years after the property in question was put to productive use as in *J. H. Collingwood*, 20 T.C. 937. In the instant case it was obvious at the time when the drive-in theatre was constructed, that a drainage system would be required to properly dispose of the natural precipitation normally to be expected, and that until this was accomplished, petitioner's capital investment was incomplete. In addition, it should be emphasized that here there was no mere restoration or rearrangement of the original capital asset, but there was the acquisition and construction of a capital asset which petitioner had not previously had, namely, a new drainage system.

That this drainage system was acquired and constructed and that payments therefor were made in compromise of a lawsuit is not determinative of whether such payments were ordinary and necessary business expenses or capital expenditures. "The decisive test is still the character of the transaction which gives rise to the payment." *Hales-Mullaly v. Commissioner*, 131 F.2d 509, 511, 512.

In our opinion the character of the transaction in the instant case indicates that the transaction was a capital expenditure.

Reviewed by the Court.

RAUM, J., concurring:

The expenditure herein was plainly capital in nature, and, as the majority opinion points out, if provision had been made in the original plans for the construction of a drainage system there could hardly be any question that its cost would have been treated as a capital outlay. The character of the expenditure is not changed merely because it is made at a subsequent time, and I think it wholly irrelevant whether the necessity for the drainage system could have been foreseen, or whether the payment therefor was made as a result of the pressure of a law suit.

COMMENTS AND QUESTIONS

1. **Improvements.** Why aren't the drainage system expenses nondeductible improvement expenditures, as specified in *Treas. Reg. § 1.263(a)-1(b)*? It is difficult to analyze the expenditure which prevents a drastic decline in business as an improvement. For example, would you consider the legal expenses to defend against disbarment an improvement cost?

2. **Acquisition of capital asset.** Why isn't the expenditure for the drainage system an acquisition cost? First, as the court notes, if the taxpayer had planned to incur the drainage system expenditure when he originally acquired the land, the expenditure would be capitalized as part of the original acquisition cost of the land. The trouble is that the expenditure was not part of the original acquisition plan.

Second, why isn't the expenditure a cost to acquire a separate asset — the drainage system. In fact, the court does say: "In addition . . . there was the acquisition and construction of a capital asset which petitioner had not previously had." That is too simplistic. Many deductible maintenance (or repair) expenses acquire long-lived assets. The cost of a door knob would certainly be treated as a deductible maintenance expense, related to the larger asset (the building), rather than a capital expenditure to acquire a long-lived door knob. What is the difference for tax purposes between door nobs and a drainage system? Does it matter that one expense is large and nonrecurring and the other is one of many small recurring expenditures?

3. **Foreseeability and loss deductions.** What do you think of the following rationale for deducting some large nonrecurring expenditures? If there is an *unforeseeable* threat to a business, the taxpayer may have to incur large nonrecurring expenditures to head off the threat. These threats are very much like the sudden events that should result in a partial loss deduction. But how much is that loss deduction? It is not easy to determine. The deduction for the cost of heading off an unforeseeable threat might

be understood as a convenient substitute for computing a loss deduction. The "unforeseeability" principle could explain the *Mt. Morris* decision, in which the court placed a lot of emphasis on foreseeability in denying a deduction.

If heading off unforeseen threats is a principled reason for allowing a deduction, how should the following cases be decided?

a. *Treas. Reg. § 1.263(a)-2(c)* states that the cost of defending or perfecting title to property is a capital expenditure. Even unanticipated costs to defend title are added to the property's basis. Does that make sense?

b. Taxpayer purchased a farm with an earthen dam in 1967. The dam had been built in the late 1950s. Water began to seep through the dam after its acquisition by taxpayer. After unsuccessful attempts to stop the seepage, the water was drained and $50,000 was spent to replace the soil in the dam and seal it. Is the $50,000 deductible? *Evans v. Commissioner*, 557 F.2d 1095 (5th Cir. 1977); *Oberman v. Manufacturing Co. v. Commissioner*, 47 T.C. 471 (1967).

c. Taxpayer's business is threatened by an ordinance prohibiting operation of the business. Are legal fees incurred to successfully challenge the validity of the ordinance deductible? *Rev. Rul. 78-389*, 1978-2 C.B. 126.

4. **Environmental clean-up**

In *Rev. Rul 94–38*, 1994–1 C.B. 35, the government dealt with environmental clean-up costs. The taxpayer incurred costs to clean up land and to treat groundwater that the *taxpayer itself* had contaminated with hazardous waste. There was no doubt that the cost of constructing groundwater treatment facilities were capital expenditures. But what about the clean-up costs that did not result in permanent structures? The ruling allowed the deduction, as follows:

> . . .X's soil remediation expenditures and ongoing groundwater treatment expenditures (*i.e.*, the groundwater treatment expenditures other than the expenditures to construct the groundwater treatment facilities) do not produce permanent improvements to X's land within the scope of § 263(a)(1) or otherwise provide significant future benefits. Under the facts of this ruling, the appropriate test for determining whether the expenditures increase the value of property is to compare the status of the asset after the expenditure with the status of that asset before the condition arose that necessitated the expenditure (*i.e.*, before the land was contaminated by X's hazardous waste). X's soil remediation and ongoing groundwater treatment expenditures do not result in improvements that increase the value of X's property because X has merely restored its soil

and groundwater to their approximate condition before they were contaminated by X's manufacturing operations.

No other aspect of § 263 requires capitalization of X's ongoing soil remediation or ongoing groundwater treatment expenditures. These expenditures do not prolong the useful life of the land, nor do they adapt the land to a new or different use. Moreover, since the land is not subject to an allowance for depreciation, amortization, or depletion, the amounts expended to restore the land to its original condition are not subject to capitalization under § 263(a)(2). Accordingly, the expenses incurred by X for the soil remediation and ongoing groundwater treatment do not constitute capital expenditures under § 263.

In *Private Letter Ruling 9541005* (Sept. 27, 1995), the taxpayer acquired contaminated land for $1. The issue was whether clean-up costs were deductible or had to be capitalized. Now the government insisted on capitalization, stating:

> Revenue Ruling 94–38 does not apply to the Taxpayer's situation. The ruling applies only if a taxpayer's environmental remediation expenditures restore the contaminated property to what was its uncontaminated condition at the time it was acquired by the taxpayer. This determination is made by "comparing the status of the asset after the expenditure with the status of that asset before the condition arose that necessitated the expenditure (*i.e.*, before the land was contaminated by the taxpayer's hazardous waste)."

QUESTIONS

1. In *Priv. Ltr. Rul. 9541005*, should the fact that the taxpayer paid only $1 for the property matter?

2. Why does it matter whether the taxpayer is restoring the land to a condition before the taxpayer contaminated it? Suppose that the taxpayer acquired the land for a substantial price and did not (and could not reasonably) have foreseen the existence of the contamination when acquiring the asset; or that, even if the contamination was foreseen or foreseeable, the taxpayer could not have reasonably foreseen the legal and financial implications of a clean-up? Why not allow expensing of clean-up costs even if the taxpayer was not responsible for the contamination?

3. How should public policy considerations influence the answer to these questions? Should a deduction be *more* available if the taxpayer itself contaminated the land?

4. **1997 Tax Act.** A new *§ 198* allows taxpayers to elect to currently deduct "qualified cleanup costs," if the expenditures would otherwise be capitalized costs. The expenditure must be paid or incurred to abate or control "hazardous substances" at a "qualified contamination site." A site qualifies if it is within a "targeted area" and there has been a release or threat of release of any hazardous substance. State officials must designate target areas with hazardous substances, using definitions of these terms set out in the income tax code.

The qualified expenditures include depreciation costs allocable to the cleanup operation under the principles in the *Idaho Power* case; but they do not include the cost of demolishing structures.

The legislative history states that this new law is not meant to create any inference about whether cleanup costs are or are not currently deductible as expenses under current law.

§ 198 is not all good news. If it allows a deduction for an expenditure which would otherwise be added to cost, the expenditure is treated as *§ 1245* property (the "recapture" provision). Any gain on sale of property whose cost was expensed because of *§ 198* is subject to the recapture rules. If the expenditure had been an expense under normal tax accounting rules, there would be no recapture.

This election to deduct cleanup costs expires after December 31, 2000.

§ 13.04 EDUCATION EXPENDITURES

[A]—Trade or business expenses?

The deduction for education expenditures is analyzed using the principles discussed in this and an earlier chapter, distinguishing current expenses from capital expenditures and personal from business expenses. The following case deals with a taxpayer who tried to improve her work status by investing in education.

TONER v. COMMISSIONER (TP loses; educat'l exp. not DDible)

71 T.C. 772 (1977) (Tax Court excerpts below)
rev'd, 623 F.2d 315 (3d Cir. 1980)

SIMPSON, JUDGE: . . .

During the year 1973, Mrs. Toner was employed as a lay teacher at St. Clement's Catholic Elementary School (St. Clement's), a school operated under the auspices of the Philadelphia archdiocese. . . .

Mrs. Toner had graduated from high school and had completed 2 full years of college when she began teaching at St. Clement's in 1971. The usual educational background of a beginning lay teacher at St. Clement's was a high school education, and none of the other lay teachers at St. Clement's had a college degree when Mrs. Toner began teaching there. The number of Catholic elementary school teachers who had bachelor's degrees when they began teaching varied from parish to parish, but no parish in the Philadelphia archdiocese required a bachelor's degree of its beginning elementary teachers. On the other hand, virtually all the teachers in the Catholic high schools in the archdiocese were required to have a college degree when they were hired. The State of Pennsylvania imposed no educational requirements for teachers hired by the Philadelphia archdiocese. However, the State generally did require that a nonvocational teacher in a public school or in a nonreligious private school possess a bachelor's degree. Salaries for teachers in the Catholic elementary schools in the Philadelphia area were significantly lower than those in the public schools.

Upon commencing employment at a Catholic elementary school in the Philadelphia archdiocese, a lay teacher was required to sign an agreement that she take a minimum of 6 college credits per year until such time as she obtained her college degree. Mrs. Toner signed such an agreement. The purpose of such agreement was to assure that a teacher would keep abreast of current practices in the teaching profession. The teacher was required to sign this agreement annually until such time as she obtained a college degree. However, aside from the requirement that she sign such agreement, a teacher was not required to obtain a degree. A teacher who already had her bachelor's degree or State certification did not have to sign such agreement. No other educational requirements were imposed on teachers at St. Clement's, although teachers there were advised to take some theology courses, in keeping with the religious nature of the school. A teacher with a bachelor's degree received a higher salary than a teacher with similar experience but without a degree.

The functions of a teacher at St. Clement's were to train her students in Christian principles and to teach formal classes in subjects such as religion, social studies, math, and English. The religious purpose of the education was also carried over to the teaching of secular subjects. Mrs. Toner's functions were the same as those of all other teachers at St. Clement's and included preparing the children for their liturgy at mass, teaching prayers, and preparing the students for confirmation and religious ceremonies. Her responsibility for religious instruction was the same as that of the teachers who belonged to the religious order. Mrs. Toner was accorded full faculty status equal to that of other faculty members at St. Clement's, and she served on faculty committees and had an equal voice in faculty affairs. She was also covered by the lay employees' retirement plan operated by the archdiocese of Philadelphia.

Since she was a child in grade school, Mrs. Toner expected to go to college; she was interested in the areas of medicine and teaching. After graduation from high school, she entered Villanova University as a full-time student in 1968. She began in the nursing school but soon transferred to the general humanities program. In September 1970, she enrolled in Villanova's night school and changed her major to education, with a specialty in English. She obtained her bachelor's degree in September 1973. Villanova had a State-approved program for teacher certification, and upon graduation, Mrs. Toner received a State teaching certificate issued by the Pennsylvania Board of Education. She has never applied for a teaching position in the public schools. She continued to teach at St. Clement's until December 1976, shortly before the birth of her first child.

In 1973, Mrs. Toner took 15 credits at Villanova consisting of the following courses: Education 263, The Problem Child; Education 298, Student Teaching; English 224, Major American Writers II; and Psychology 225, Psychology of Motivation. On her Federal income tax return for 1973, she deducted her expenses for tuition, student teaching, transportation, textbooks, and other related amounts for a total of $906.28. In his notice of deficiency, the Commissioner disallowed the entire amount on the grounds that the expenses were incurred to meet the minimum educational requirement for qualification in her employment and were not deductible.

We must decide whether the petitioner is entitled to deduct the educational expenses paid by her in 1973. She maintains that when she began teaching at St. Clement's, she already satisfied the minimum educational requirement of her employer, that the educational courses taken by her in 1973 were to maintain and improve her skills as a teacher, and that she is entitled to deduct the expenses incurred for such education. The Commissioner concedes that the minimum educational requirement of St. Clement's, the petitioner's employer, was graduation from high school, that the petitioner had met such educational requirement when she was employed, and that the education pursued by her in 1973 did in fact maintain or improve her skills as a teacher. Nevertheless, the Commissioner contends that her educational expenses were personal and not deductible because her education was pursued to enable her to achieve her lifelong objective of completing a college education and because such education enabled her to satisfy the minimum educational requirement generally applicable to members of the teaching profession. We need not decide whether a teacher's education to obtain a bachelor's degree is always to be treated as meeting the minimum educational requirements of the profession, but we are satisfied that in this case, the expenses of the education are not deductible.

Section 162(a), I.R.C. 1954, allows a deduction for all the ordinary and necessary expenses of carrying on a trade or business. On the other hand, section 262 expressly disallows a deduction for all personal expenses. Section 1.162-5, Income Tax Regs., sets forth criteria for distinguishing those educational expenses which are deductible as business expenses under section 162(a) from those educational expenses which are personal and not deductible. In part, such section provides:

Sec. 1.162-5 Expenses for education.

(a) *General rule.* Expenditures made by an individual for education (including research undertaken as part of his educational program) which are not expenditures of a type described in paragraph (b)(2) or (3) of this section are deductible as ordinary and necessary business expenses (even though the education may lead to a degree) if the education —

(1) Maintains or improves skills required by the individual in his employment or other trade or business, or

(2) Meets the express requirements of the individual's employer, or the requirements of applicable law or regulations, imposed as a condition to the retention by the individual of an established employment relationship, status, or rate of compensation.

(b) *Nondeductible educational expenditures* —

(1) *In general.* Educational expenditures described in subparagraphs (2) and (3) of this paragraph are personal expenditures or constitute an inseparable aggregate of personal and capital expenditures and, therefore, are not deductible as ordinary and necessary business expenses even though the education may maintain or improve skills required by the individual in his employment or other trade or business or may meet the express requirements of the individual's employer or of applicable law or regulations.

(2) *Minimum educational requirements.*

(i) The first category of nondeductible educational expenses within the scope of subparagraph (1) of this paragraph are expenditures made by an individual for education which is required of him in order to meet the minimum educational requirements for qualification in his employment or other trade or business. The minimum education necessary to qualify for a position or other trade or business must be determined from a consideration of such factors as the requirements of the employer, the applicable law and regulations, and the standards of the profession, trade, or business involved. . . .

(ii) The minimum educational requirements for qualification of a particular individual in a position in an educational institution is the

> minimum level of education (in terms of aggregate college hours or degree) which under the applicable laws or regulations, in effect at the time this individual is first employed in such position, is normally required of an individual initially being employed in such a position. . . .
>
> (3) *Qualification for new trade or business.*
>
> (i) The second category of nondeductible educational expenses within the scope of subparagraph (1) of this paragraph are expenditures made by an individual for education which is part of a program of study being pursued by him which will lead to qualifying him in a new trade or business. . . .

Such criteria have been consistently approved and used by the courts in deciding whether educational expenses are deductible. . . .

In this case, we are particularly concerned with the meaning of § 1.162-5(b)(2), Income Tax Regs., relating to the minimum educational requirement. By its terms, the provision applies to education which meets the minimum educational requirement "for qualification in his employment *or other trade or business*." (Emphasis added.) In determining what is the minimum requirement, the regulations also suggest that we look at both "the requirements of the employer" and "the standards of the profession, trade, or business involved." Thus, the provision clearly applies either to education which meets the minimum requirement of the taxpayer's employer *or* to education which meets the minimum requirement of another trade or business.

In connection with the construction of § 1.162-5, Income Tax Regs., we declared in *Garwood v. Commissioner*, 62 T.C. 699, 702 (1974), "The thrust of the regulations is to distinguish between educational expenses that are ordinary and necessary expenses of a trade or business and those that are personal and capital expenditures." . . .

Without the bachelor's degree, the petitioner could teach only in the Catholic elementary schools. However, as a result of the educational program which she completed in 1973, she secured her bachelor's degree, and with that degree, she could also teach in the Catholic high schools. Moreover, with her degree, she was certified by the State as a teacher, thereby qualifying her to teach in the public schools and in private nonreligious schools. Although we have no evidence that she ever planned to teach in other schools, she was qualified if she ever wished to do so. In summary, although the petitioner had met the minimum educational requirement for the position as a Catholic elementary school teacher, the completion of her college education enabled her to meet the minimum educational requirement of another trade or business; that is, she was fully qualified to accept a teaching position in schools generally. . . .

how Ct. reads (b)(2):

by getting college degree, TP met minimum req'ts to teach in high school + public schools

In deciding whether the education qualifies a teacher for a new trade or business, § 1.162-5(b)(3)(i), Income Tax Regs., states: "For this purpose, all teaching and related duties shall be considered to involve the same general type of work." However, such provision does not assist the petitioner in this case. In *Diaz v. Commissioner*, [70 T.C. 1067 (1978)], the taxpayer, who had not yet completed her college education, was working as an associate teacher while continuing her college education. The Court considered § 1.162-5(b) (3)(i), Income Tax Regs., but held that such provision was applicable only to those teachers who had already met the minimum educational requirement for becoming a teacher. Here, the petitioner was qualified to teach in the Catholic elementary schools only; she had not met the minimum educational requirement for teacher certification and could not teach in the schools generally. On the facts of this case, we hold that the petitioner's educational expenses are not deductible because her education enabled her to satisfy the minimum educational requirement generally applicable in the teaching profession.

STERRETT, J., concurring: . . .

The majority, in making reference to § 1.162-5(b)(2), Income Tax Regs., seems to be saying that that subparagraph requires disallowance of educational expenses incurred in order to meet the minimum educational requirements necessary for qualification in *another* trade or business, with the implication that such trade or business is a new trade or business. If that subparagraph actually so provided, subparagraph (3) of that regulation would be redundant. In my view, subparagraph (2) in fact refers to any present trade or business of the taxpayer other than his employment.

It is § 1.162-5(b)(3), Income Tax Regs., that disqualifies the petitioner herein from deducting her educational expenses.

CHABOT, J., concurring:

I concur in the result in this case . . . . As set forth hereinbelow, I would reach the result by a different route.

During the taxable year before us, petitioner was employed as a nonvocational teacher in a Catholic elementary school under the auspices of the Philadelphia Archdiocese in Philadelphia, Pa. State law generally required a nonvocational teacher in a public school or in a nonreligious private school to possess a bachelor's degree, but did not impose any educational requirements for teachers hired by the Philadelphia Archdiocese.

Either the Pennsylvania nonvocational elementary school teachers in public and nonreligious private schools are generally in the same trade or business as petitioner and we proceed under § 1.162-5(b)(2), Income Tax Regs., or they are generally in a different trade or business from petitioner and we proceed under § 1.162-5(b)(3), Income Tax Regs.

Same trade or business. — If they are in the same trade or business, then (under the regulations) the expenditures are not deductible if the education was required of petitioner in order to meet the minimum educational requirements for qualification in that trade or business (§ 1.162-5(b)(2)(i), Income Tax Regs.), i. e., the minimum level of education which is normally required of an individual initially being employed in an elementary school teaching position (§ 1.162-5(b)(2)(ii), Income Tax Regs.). Since a bachelor's degree normally is required of elementary school teachers in Pennsylvania, and petitioner's educational expenditures were for courses which led to an acceptable bachelor's degree, it follows that under the same-trade-or-business alternative, petitioner is not entitled to deduct the expenditures here at issue.

New trade or business. — If nonvocational elementary school teaching in public or nonreligious private schools is a new trade or business, then (under the regulations) the expenditures are not deductible if the education is part of a program of study being pursued by petitioner which will lead to qualifying her in that trade or business (§ 1.162-5(b)(3)(i), Income Tax Regs.). . . .

Conclusion. — The same result appears to follow whether we conclude that the boundary of petitioner's trade or business includes or excludes teaching in Pennsylvania public or nonreligious private schools. . . .

GOFFE, J., dissenting: I respectfully dissent.

[T]he majority attempts to distinguish *Laurano v. Commissioner,* 69 T.C. 723 (1978), by pointing out that "the taxpayer was already a fully certified teacher, and she was seeking to deduct the expenses of some additional education." The taxpayer there was a teacher certified to teach in Toronto, Canada, and during the taxable year before the Court was teaching in a parochial school in New Jersey. She took three courses at Kean College, none of which the diocese required her to take but one of which was required for certification in New Jersey; another directly related to the curriculum which she was teaching; and the third she hoped to use in the future in specialized teaching. The Commissioner relied upon (b)(2) of the regulations but we held for the taxpayer by emphasizing the following quoted language from (b)(2): "Once an individual has met the minimum educational requirements for qualification in his employment or other trade or business (as in effect when he enters the employment or trade or business), he shall be treated as continuing to meet those requirements even though they are changed." (§ 1.162-5(b)(2), Income Tax Regs.) That language applies with equal force here. Petitioner fully met the educational requirements of her teaching post at St. Clement's. The Commissioner there also relied upon (b)(3), arguing that because the taxpayer was seeking certification in New Jersey she was taking the courses to qualify for a new trade or business.

We held that because the teaching duties in Canada and New Jersey involved the same general type of work, the taxpayer had previously met the educational requirements for qualification in her employment. I fail to see the distinction between qualifying to teach in a different school, whether it be in Canada or New Jersey, parochial or public, provided the duties involve the same general type of work. The majority does not hold nor does respondent argue that the duties were different in the Pennsylvania public schools than in the Pennsylvania parochial schools. The Commissioner acquiesced in that decision. The effect of the majority opinion is to overrule Laurano which should not be done, especially in light of the Commissioner's acquiescence. . . .

FEATHERSTON, FAY, IRWIN, QUEALY, HALL, and WILES agree with this dissenting opinion.

The *Toner* case illustrates the following general problem. Taxpayers often qualify to get started in a business but need more training to get ahead. Sometimes it is easy to say that the taxpayer has not yet met the minimum qualifications because the job is not permanent. That is how courts usually dispose of graduate assistants who try to deduct Ph.D. costs. *Jungreis v. Commissioner*, 55 T.C. 581 (1970). Toner, however, had crossed the line regarding permanence. The Third Circuit's reversal of the Tax Court *Toner* decision admitted that a deduction might be "somewhat of an anomaly," but noted that the Regulations treated all teaching as the same line of work and that qualifying for public and nonreligious private school teaching was therefore not a new trade or business.

SHARON v. COMMISSIONER

66 T.C. 515 (1976)
aff'd per curiam, 591 F.2d 1273 (9th Cir. 1978)

Simpson, Judge: . . .

3. *License to Practice Law in California*

[Editor — The following excerpt deals with the deductibility of bar review course expenditures.]

It is clear that the amount the petitioner paid for the bar review course was an expenditure "made by an individual for education" within the meaning of § 1.162-5(a) of the Income Tax Regulations. Although the petitioner was authorized to practice law in some jurisdictions when he took the California bar review course, such course was nevertheless educational in the same sense as the first bar review course. The deductibility of such educational expenses is governed by the rules of § 1.162-5 of the regulations. . . .

Educational expenses which are incurred to meet the minimum educational requirements for qualification in a taxpayer's trade or business or which qualify him for a new trade or business are "personal expenditures or constitute an inseparable aggregate of personal and capital expenditures." § 1.162-5(b), Income Tax Regs. We find that the bar review course helped to qualify the petitioner for a new trade or business so that its costs are personal expenses.

We have previously adopted a "commonsense approach" in determining whether an educational expenditure qualifies a taxpayer for a "new trade or business." If the education qualified the taxpayer to perform significantly different tasks and activities than he could perform prior to the education, then the education qualifies him for a new trade or business. Thus, we have held that a professor of social work is in a different trade or business than a social caseworker. A licensed public accountant is in a different trade or business than a certified public accountant. A registered pharmacist is in a different trade or business than an intern pharmacist, even though an intern performs many of the same tasks as a registered pharmacist, but under supervision.

Before taking the bar review course and passing the attorney's bar examination, the petitioner was an attorney licensed to practice law in New York. As an attorney for the Regional Counsel, he could represent the Commissioner in this Court. However, he could not appear in either the State courts of California, the Federal District Courts located there, nor otherwise act as an attorney outside the scope of his employment with the

IRS. See Cal. Bus. & Prof. Code § 6125 (West 1974); 20 Op. Cal. Atty. Gen. 291 (1952). If he had done so, he would have been guilty of a misdemeanor. Cal. Bus. & Prof. Code § 6126 (West 1974). Yet, after receiving his license to practice law in California, he became a member of the State bar with all its accompanying privileges and obligations. He could appear and represent clients in all the courts of California. By comparing the tasks and activities that the petitioner was qualified to perform prior to receiving his license to practice in California with the tasks and activities he was able to perform after receiving such license, it is clear that he has qualified for a new trade or business. Consequently, the expenses of his bar review course were personal and are not includable in the cost of his license to practice law in California.

It is true that even before he became a member of the bar of California, the petitioner was engaged in the business of practicing law. However, in applying the provisions of § 1.162-5 of the regulations to determine whether educational expenses are personal or business in nature, it is not enough to find that the petitioner was already engaged in some business — we must ascertain the particular business in which he was previously engaged and whether the education qualified him to engage in a different business. Before taking the bar review course and becoming a member of the bar of California, the petitioner could not generally engage in the practice of law in that State, but the bar review course helped to qualify him to engage in such business. . . .

Sharon also discussed other expenses to become a member of the California bar — bar exam and court admission fees. They were amortizable over the taxpayer's life expectancy. These deductions are probably small, but the same principle supports amortization of physicians' fees to acquire hospital privileges. *Walters v. Commissioner*, 383 F.2d 922 (6th Cir. 1967).

must be in trade or business
BAL incurring educ'l exp. to get
the D̶

Prebusiness expenses. If a taxpayer has not yet entered a trade or business, education expenses are not deductible, even if they would be deductible for someone in a trade or business. Thus, a taxpayer who has completed a J.D. degree and then immediately obtains an LL.M. degree, before joining a law firm, cannot deduct the cost of the LL.M. degree. *Randik v. Commissioner,* 35 T.C.M. (CCH) 195 (1976) (the fact that the taxpayer did some remunerative legal work while at law school did not make a difference).

In *Ruehmann v. Commissioner,* 30 T.C.M. (CCH) 675 (1971), however, the taxpayer studied law for three years in a state where two years of law school were sufficient to permit practice of law. He worked at a law firm between the second and third year of law school and again during the Christmas break of the third year. The firm made him an offer of permanent work during the third year. He worked with the firm in the summer after the third year and then studied for an LL.M. degree. He was permitted to deduct the cost of the LL.M. degree. The cost of the third year of law school was not deductible, because it was customary for law students to complete three years of law school before practice, and the J.D. was therefore a minimum qualification for being a lawyer.

Do the prebusiness education expense cases suggest why Ms. Hantzis could not deduct her traveling expenses related to a summer job away from home between the second and third year of law school? *See* § 8.04[A], *supra.* Her expenses originated as a result of her being in the preparatory stage of her career.

Amortization. Why can't a taxpayer amortize the cost of college, law school, or the bar review course?

Employer fringe benefit. Suppose an employer pays for an employee's education under circumstances that would not qualify as an employee deduction because it qualifies the employee for a new trade or business. The employee should in that case include the value in taxable income. It is not a working condition fringe benefit. (*See § 132(d)* — be sure you understand why.) Such on-the-job-training may be good for the economy, however — for example, a secretary training to be a paralegal. Moreover, as a practical matter, it is hard to know what is a new trade or business. To ease administrative problems and to encourage such training, *§ 127* was passed, excluding employer educational assistance program benefits from an employee's income. This tax free fringe benefit is limited to situations where the benefit does not discriminate in favor of highly compensated employees and the employer does not incur more than 5% of the expenditures for more-than-5% owners. The excluded amount is also capped —

presently, at $5,250. This is one of those tax breaks that is scheduled to expire but is continually renewed.

[B]—Scholarships

Scholarship income is excluded for degree candidates. *See § 117(a).* Only amounts used for tuition, fees, books, supplies, and equipment are excluded. *§ 117(b).* Amounts for food and lodging were excluded before 1986 but no longer. The idea behind repealing the living expense exclusion was that taxpayers with low incomes used for normal living expenses should rely on the personal exemption and standard deductions to lower their taxes. Students were no different from other lower income taxpayers.

Services required as a condition of scholarship. The exclusion of scholarship income is withdrawn if the scholarship is a payment for services required as a condition for receiving the scholarship. *§ 117(c).* The "no payment for services" rule is not easy to apply. It generally does not hurt recipients of college scholarships (what about athletic scholarships?), because they are not required to do any work to get the scholarship. Graduate students who work as teaching and research assistants are vulnerable, however, as discussed below.

Private Letter Ruling 9526020 (April 3, 1995) dealt with a scholarship conditioned on the "recipient agree[ing] to practice on a full-time basis in a public service, not-for-profit, or lower-income sector of the legal profession for a specified period of time following completion of legal training. The areas of acceptable service [we]re within the selection option of the grantee, but [we]re restricted by compensation limitations intended to have the effect of requiring recipients to perform work of a public nature or benefit. Recipients [we]re not required to work for, or as directed by [the law school]." The ruling notes that "scholarships that represent payment for services are not excludable under current law, [but that] not all grants that are subject to conditions or limitations represent payment for services." It then concludes that this scholarship does "not represent compensation for services within the meaning of section 117(c) of the Code. The service commitment imposed upon participants [] does not constitute the requirement of a substantial quid pro quo from the recipients; on the contrary, the grants are relatively disinterested grants of the [law school], designed to accomplish public rather than private or proprietary purposes. Recipients are free to take nearly any position of their choosing, anywhere, subject only to the compensation limitations prescribed. The service commitment is essentially a de minimis limitation designed to assure that [the] graduates practice in all income sectors of the legal profession, including public, lower-paying, and otherwise underserved areas or capacities, a public purpose for which the. . . scholarship program has been established by [the law school]. Any benefit inuring to the University-grantor appears remote, insubstantial, and inconsequential for purposes of section 117(c)."

Qualified tuition reduction. Another subsection excludes from gross income the value of tuition reduction provided to employees of educational institutions, primarily under two circumstances. *§ 117(d)*. *First*, it excludes the tuition reduction for family members of school employees (such as professors) who attend the employer's school or another school with whom the employer has a reciprocal relationship. It is a fringe benefit which often benefits the teacher of this course with children in school. *Second*, the exclusion also applies to tuition reduction for the school's employees, not just the employee's family. This often helps university staff members who can take courses at reduced tuition. Does this help the graduate student doing teaching and research in exchange for a tuition reduction?

A closer look at the graduate student. An initial observation, adverse to the graduate student, is that *§ 117(d)* applies only to education below the graduate level (*see* the parentheses in *(d)(2)*). The counter observation, favorable to the graduate student, refers to *§ 117(d)(4)*, which permits graduate students who are teaching or research assistants to rely on the *§ 117(d)* exclusion. But you are not home free. The *§ 117(d)* exclusion for qualified tuition reduction is itself limited by the rule in *§ 117(c)*, which taxes scholarships *and* tuition reduction if the student is required to work as a condition of receiving the scholarship or tuition reduction. This leaves something of a puzzle. The tax break for graduate level tuition reduction requires that the graduate student be an employee performing teaching or research services. But tuition reduction *conditioned* on performing services is *not* excluded from income. How can the graduate student perform teaching or research services and still receive a tax free tuition reduction? Would tuition reduction be tax free in any of the following cases?

(1) The graduate student receives a $2,000 stipend for being a teaching assistant. She also receives a tuition reduction; instead of $5,000 tuition, she pays $1,000.

(2) All graduate students must teach as a condition of getting a degree. Some or all graduate students also get tuition reductions.

(3) The tuition reduction to the working graduate student is not technically conditioned on working. Like many athletes, they can quit and still get the tuition break for the rest of the year.

[C]—Education tax subsidies

The nondeductibility of education expenses sometimes leads to the observation that the income tax law disfavors investment in human capital. But that may not be true. In addition to excluding scholarship income, the difference between tuition and the school's cost of education is not taxable income to the student.

Moreover, the code contains a host of provisions favoring education, though many are quite scatter-shot. Some of those previously discussed include:

(1) Exclusion of scholarship income. *See* § 13.04[B].

(2) Parent's dependent deduction can be available for children who are students even though they earn more than the exemption amount. *See* § 1.03.

(3) Section 127 exclusion of employer educational assistance fringe benefit. *See* § 13.04[A].

(4) Education loan forgiveness is not income if the student takes certain jobs. *See* § 3.07.

(5) Qualified state tuition programs. *See* § 7.04.

In addition, *see* § 135 (gain on Treasury Bonds excluded if proceeds used for "qualified education expenses"). And interest on certain student loans is discussed in § 15.01[c], *infra.*

The 1997 Tax Act has added many provisions to subsidize higher education. You should ask critically whether these subsidies will have a major impact. They certainly allow Members of Congress to tell their constituents how helpful they have been in favoring education, but the incentive and distributional impacts of these tax expenditures is questionable. Do they increase educational expenditures that the society should be subsidizing; who gets the tax breaks? Notice also that these are among the many provisions in which politically popular targeted tax breaks are provided at the sacrifice of tax simplicity. Despite rhetoric to the contrary, tax complexity always seems to triumph over tax simplicity. The reason for the complexity is that the following issues (among others) must be addressed:

(1) make sure that only deserving expenditures get the tax break (*e.g.*, tuition only or also room and board, etc.);

(2) inflation adjustments;

(3) phase-outs so higher income taxpayers do not get the benefit.

[1]—Hope Scholarship and Lifetime Learning credits; *§ 25A*

The 1997 law adopts a Hope scholarship credit (Hope) and a Lifetime learning credit (Lifetime). The Lifetime credit is not available for any expenditures with respect to a student for whom the Hope credit is claimed in that same year.

Rules applicable to both credits. Both credits are elective and they are not refundable. The credits cannot be claimed based on expenditures for which another tax break is allowed (*e.g.*, the exclusion of scholarships and the employer educational assistance fringe benefit) or for which a deduction is taken (*e.g.*, as a business expense).

Both credits are computed based on tuition (but not books, or room and board). In general, the education must be provided at an "eligible educational institutions" (generally, degree and certificate granting institutions, including some vocational institutions).

Both credits are available for the education expenditures of the taxpayer, the taxpayer's spouse, and the taxpayer's dependents. However, no credit is allowed to an individual for whom a dependent's deduction is "allowed" under *§ 151* to another taxpayer (*e.g.*, a child of a parent). In such cases, the tuition paid by the dependent is treated as paid by the other taxpayer.

The total of the Hope and Lifetime tax breaks in any one year phases out as income rises above a threshold, which is $40,000 for a single taxpayer and $80,000 for a married couple filing jointly. The threshold is adjusted gross income, with certain modifications. The rate of phase-out is the excess income (modified AGI minus the threshold) divided by $10,000 (for single taxpayer), and divided by $20,000 (for married couple filing jointly). Thus, a single taxpayer with modified AGI of $50,000 would have no credit; a married couple filing jointly would have no credit with modified AGI of $100,000. The thresholds are inflation-adjusted after 2001 (note the back-loading of the inflation adjustments).

If a married couple has $20,000 income over the $80,000 threshold, how much is the phantom tax rate due to the phase-out of the credit? You do not know the answer to this question unless you know how much credit is available in the "excess income" year. Thus, does $20,000 of excess income cost the taxpayer $1,000, $1,500, or $2,500 in tax breaks?

Hope credit. The Hope credit covers the first two years of the student's post-secondary education, beginning after December 31, 1997. There is a maximum of $1,500 per student per year, computed at 100% of the first $1,000 and 50% of the next $1,000 of expenditures. These figures are inflation-adjusted after the year 2001. The student must carry at least one-half of a full-time course workload.

Lifetime credit. The Lifetime credit applies to educational expenditures paid after June 30, 1998. It equals 20% of up to $5,000 per year ($10,000 beginning in 2003 — again, notice the backloading of tax breaks). The credit percentage is multiplied by the *total* expenditures which the taxpayer incurs for qualified students (the Hope credit is per student). The dollar figures are not inflation-adjusted. The Lifetime credit is available (1) for an unlimited number of years of study, (2) applies to undergraduate and graduate schooling, and (3) does not require meeting half-time course workload requirements *if* the education improves job skills.

Example. A taxpayer has three children and incurs the following costs in the same year. Child 1 is attending the first year of junior college; taxpayer pays $4,000 tuition. Child 2 and Child 3 are in the third year of a four-year program (twins); taxpayer pays $3,500 tuition each ($7,000 total). A $1,500 Hope credit is available for the first child's tuition. No Lifetime credit is available for the first child's tuition this year, because you cannot take both credits for the same student. A $1,000 Lifetime credit is available for the second and third child's tuition; 20% times a maximum of $5,000 (before the year 2003).

[2]—Educational individual retirement accounts (Education IRAs); *§ 530*

A second tax break for education allows taxpayers to set aside amounts which can accumulate income tax-free and distribute both the amount set aside and the income tax-free at some future date for educational purposes to designated beneficiaries. There is no deduction for the amount set aside. The amounts must be used exclusively for paying the "qualified higher education expenses" of a designated beneficiary. No contribution qualifies if made after the beneficiary reaches age eighteen.

The maximum amount which can be set aside under this program is $500 per year per child; this amount is not indexed for inflation.

Qualified higher education expenses are defined under the same rules applicable to Hope/Lifetime credits, except that (1) room and board are qualified expenses; and (2) there is no requirement of half-time attendance (except for room and board). In addition, contributions to a qualified state tuition program for the beneficiary are qualified higher education expenses.

The $500 amount is phased out as income rises above a threshold, which is modified AGI (single taxpayers, $95,000; married filing jointly, $150,000). The rate of phase-out is the excess income (modified AGI minus the threshold) divided by $15,000 (for single taxpayer), and divided by $10,000 (for married couple filing jointly). Thus, a single taxpayer with modified AGI of $110,000 and a married couple filing jointly with modified AGI of $160,000 could not set aside any amount as an educational IRA. Do you detect any effort to prevent the phantom tax rates resulting from phased-out benefits from cumulating? Compare the thresholds at which personal exemptions, and the Hope and Lifetime credits begin to disappear.

Distributions from education IRAs are excluded from income when made to beneficiaries for certain education expenses. If the distribution does not exceed "qualified higher education expenses," it is all tax free. The problem is to figure out what to do if the distributions are more than qualified education expenses. The basic mechanism is to treat distributions in the same manner as distributions from an annuity, which are part-capital, part-income. The part that is capital is always tax-free, as a gift to the beneficiary. The part that is income is tax-free if used for qualified higher education expenses. The capital-income allocation is based on the ratio of contributions to the total account balance at the time of distribution; for example, $15,000 of contributions and a $25,000 account balance results in a 60/40 capital/income ratio. Now assume a $2,000 distribution, which is $1200 capital and $800 income. Assume, further, that there are only $1500 of qualified education expenses. In that case three-fourths (1500/2000) of the $800 income (that is, $600) is tax-free, but $200 is taxable. There is also a 10% penalty on taxable distributions, which is waived under certain circumstances (such as the death or disability of the beneficiary).

Distributions in excess of education expenses can be rolled over into an education IRA without tax consequences, if made for a family member of the beneficiary within 60 days of the distribution.

The exclusion is not available for any year in which a *§ 25A* credit (Hope or Lifetime education credit) is elected with respect to education expenditures of the beneficiary.

PART IV

LIMITS ON DEDUCTIONS

Parts II and III of this course discussed the basic structural provisions of the tax law permitting a deduction for certain expenses and losses. This Part is about limits on these deductions. The limits usually arise from two considerations. First, public policy considerations sometimes favor disallowing the deduction (the deduction of fines, for example). These policy limits are the converse of tax expenditures because they increase rather than decrease taxes. Second, sometimes the structural principles only *appear* to be well served by allowing a deduction. Supplemental rules are therefore required to prevent the deduction (for example, no deduction for expenses to produce tax exempt income).

Sometimes, the rules reflect a combination of public policy concerns and doubts about whether underlying structural principles would be furthered by a deduction (for example, limiting the deduction of wasteful entertainment expenses with personal consumption overtones).

Chapter 14 discusses policy and structural principles which limit deductions.

The remainder of Part IV deals with specific limits on certain deductions. Chapter 15 considers limits on the interest deduction. Chapter 16 discusses the inclusion of borrowed money in basis and the limitations on deductions that this rule has spawned. Chapter 17 discusses the alternative minimum tax, most (though not all) of which is concerned with eliminating the advantage of deductions under the regular tax.

CHAPTER 14

PUBLIC POLICY AND STRUCTURAL PRINCIPLES

§ 14.01 ORDINARY, NECESSARY, REASONABLE, LAVISH

[A]—"Ordinary and necessary"

We considered *§ 162* without paying much attention to the requirement that the expenses be "ordinary and necessary." That was not an oversight. The words do not mean much. As the Court said in *Commissioner v. Tellier*, 383 U.S. 687 (1966):

> . . . Our decisions have consistently construed the term "necessary" as imposing only the minimal requirement that the expense be "appropriate and helpful" for "the development of the (taxpayer's) business." *Welch v. Helvering*, 290 U.S. 111, 113. The principal function of the term "ordinary" in § 162(a) is to clarify the distinction, often difficult, between those expenses that are currently deductible and those that are in the nature of capital expenditures, which, if deductible at all, must be amortized over the useful life of the asset. *Welch v. Helvering*, *supra*, 290 U.S., at 113–116.

Statutory interpretation. There is an interpretive maxim that statutory texts do not contain surplusage. As an admonition to good drafting, this makes sense. As a guide to statutory meaning, it is questionable. The word "ordinary" is surplusage as a requirement for capitalizing expenditures.

The *Welch* case, cited in *Tellier*, has proved somewhat troublesome. It says that "ordinary" invokes the difference between current expenses and capital expenditures and that "necessary" means "appropriate and helpful," but it also says some other things which have proved distracting. Here is Justice Cardozo's opinion.

WELCH v. HELVERING

290 U.S. 111 (1933)

MR. JUSTICE CARDOZO delivered the opinion of the Court.

The question to be determined is whether payments by a taxpayer, who is in business as a commission agent, are allowable deductions in the computation of his income if made to the creditors of a bankrupt corporation in an endeavor to strengthen his own standing and credit.

In 1922 petitioner was the secretary of the E. L. Welch Company, a Minnesota corporation, engaged in the grain business. The company was adjudged an involuntary bankrupt, and had a discharge from its debts. Thereafter the petitioner made a contract with the Kellogg Company to purchase grain for it on a commission. In order to re-establish his relations with customers whom he had known when acting for the Welch Company and to solidify his credit and standing, he decided to pay the debts of the Welch business so far as he was able. In fulfillment of that resolve, he made payments of substantial amounts during five successive years. . . .

We may assume that the payments to creditors of the Welch Company were necessary for the development of the petitioner's business, at least in the sense that they were appropriate and helpful. He certainly thought they were, and we should be slow to override his judgment. But the problem is not solved when the payments are characterized as necessary. Many necessary payments are charges upon capital. There is need to determine whether they are both necessary and ordinary. Now, what is ordinary, though there must always be a strain of constancy within it, is none the less a variable affected by time and place and circumstance. Ordinary in this context does not mean that the payments must be habitual or normal in the sense that the same taxpayer will have to make them often. A lawsuit affecting the safety of a business may happen once in a lifetime. The counsel fees may be so heavy that repetition is unlikely. None the less, the expense is an ordinary one because we know from experience that payments for such a purpose, whether the amount is large or small, are the common and accepted means of defense against attack. The situation is unique in the life of the individual affected, but not in the life of the group, the community, of which he is a part. At such times there are norms of conduct that help to stabilize our judgment, and make it certain and objective. The instance is not erratic, but is brought within a known type.

The line of demarcation is now visible between the case that is here and the one supposed for illustration. We try to classify this act as ordinary or the opposite, and the norms of conduct fail us. No longer can we have recourse to any fund of business experience, to any known business practice.

Men do at times pay the debts of others without legal obligation or the lighter obligation imposed by the usages of trade or by neighborly amenities, but they do not do so ordinarily, not even though the result might be to heighten their reputation for generosity and opulence. Indeed, if language is to be read in its natural and common meaning, we should have to say that payment in such circumstances, instead of being ordinary is in a high degree extraordinary. There is nothing ordinary in the stimulus evoking it, and none in the response. Here, indeed, as so often in other branches of the law, the decisive distinctions are those of degree and not of kind. One struggles in vain for any verbal formula that will supply a ready touchstone. The standard set up by the statute is not a rule of law; it is rather a way of life. Life in all its fullness must supply the answer to the riddle.

The Commissioner of Internal Revenue resorted to that standard in assessing the petitioner's income, and found that the payments in controversy came closer to capital outlays than to ordinary and necessary expenses in the operation of a business. His ruling has the support of a presumption of correctness, and the petitioner has the burden of proving it to be wrong. Unless we can say from facts within our knowledge that these are ordinary and necessary expenses according to the ways of conduct and the forms of speech prevailing in the business world, the tax must be confirmed. But nothing told us by this record or within the sphere of our judicial notice permits us to give that extension to what is ordinary and necessary. Indeed, to do so would open the door to many bizarre analogies. One man has a family name that is clouded by thefts committed by an ancestor. To add to this own standing he repays the stolen money, wiping off, it may be, his income for the year. The payments figure in his tax return as ordinary expenses. Another man conceives the notion that he will be able to practice his vocation with greater ease and profit if he has an opportunity to enrich his culture. Forthwith the price of his education becomes an expense of the business, reducing the income subject to taxation. There is little difference between these expenses and those in controversy here. Reputation and learning are akin to capital assets, like the good will of an old partnership. For many, they are the only tools with which to hew a pathway to success. The money spent in acquiring them is well and wisely spent. It is not an ordinary expense of the operation of a business. . . .

Cases after *Welch* had trouble deciding whether unusual expenditures were deductible. For example, in *Friedman v. Delaney*, 171 F.2d 269 (1st Cir. 1948), a lawyer paid a client's bankruptcy debt because he had assured creditors that his client would be able to pay his debts. The court denied the deduction, stating that the taxpayer's payment originated in a "gratuitous assurance," and a "voluntary underwriting of the obligation of another." It concluded: "the emphasis placed by the [taxpayer] upon his moral obligation to keep his professional word should not obscure the fact that the transaction on his part was voluntary from the beginning;" and it is "no part of a lawyer's business to take on a personal obligation to make payments which should come from his client." All this is somewhat puzzling, because it does not focus on whether the lawyer's reputation-related payment was a deductible current expense or a capital expenditure. The "voluntariness" of the payment looms as a dispositive fact, without any explanation of why that should be so.

Later decisions have downplayed any implication that a voluntary or unusual expense is, on that account, not deductible. The real problem is deciding whether reputation-related expenses are current or capital. The cases are not easy, because expenditures related to intangible assets (like reputation) always present difficult problems. But the framework is the conventional one of current expense vs. capital expenditure analysis, unencumbered by additional criteria limiting deductions. The following Revenue Ruling is a more up-to-date discussion of reputation-related expenses.

REV. RUL. 76-203, 1976-1 C.B. 45

The taxpayer is a furniture moving and storage company. During the taxable year a fire totally destroyed its warehouse, which contained household goods of many of the taxpayer's customers. Although some of the customers are insured under personal policies and some are insured under the taxpayer's general insurance policy, other customers have no insurance coverage. The taxpayer is in the process of rebuilding its warehouse, and is continuing its operations in temporary quarters. Some of the taxpayer's customers were unhappy over their losses and complained that they were not sufficiently informed about their insurance options. To preserve its goodwill among its customers, and to protect its business reputation, the taxpayer plans to make at least partial monetary restitutions to the uninsured customers. . . .

In *Dunn & McCarthy, Inc. v. Commissioner*, 139 F.2d 242 (2d Cir. 1943), the court held that a corporation's payment of personal debts owed by the corporation's insolvent deceased president, and due its salesmen, qualified as an ordinary and necessary business expense because such payment was paid to conserve its goodwill among its salesmen and customers. In its opinion, the court emphasized the payment was an outlay to retain existing goodwill rather than an outlay to acquire goodwill for a new business. . . .

In the present case, the sole purpose of the planned monetary restitutions by the taxpayer to its uninsured customers is to preserve the taxpayer's goodwill among its customers and to protect its business reputation.

Accordingly, the amounts to be expended by the taxpayer to preserve its goodwill and to protect its business reputation under the above circumstances, are ordinary and necessary business expenses that are deductible under § 162(a) of the Code.

See also Jenkins v. Commissioner, 47 T.C.M. 238 (1983) (country music singer can deduct voluntary payments to investors in his defunct entertainment business, intended to preserve his business reputation); *Pepper v. Commissioner*, 36 T.C. 886 (1961) (lawyer can deduct payments to creditors of defrauding client when the lawyer had helped arrange the loans without knowing about the fraud).

Do not conclude that the government can never succeed in disallowing a deduction if the business connection is too tenuous. In *Love Box Co., Inc. v. Commissioner,* 842 F.2d 1213 (10th Cir. 1988), the taxpayer paid a well-known free enterprise advocate to give seminars about economic history and comparative economics to employees, customers, and the general public. Most of those attending were neither employees nor customers. With a dissent, the court held that the business connection was too tenuous to justify the deduction, either as education for employees or promotional/goodwill as to others. Was this a personal expense?

[B]—Excessive compensation

[i] Reasonable salary; *§ 162(a)(1)*

Statutory Interpretation — Legislative History and Statutory Language. *§ 162(a)(1)* allows a deduction for "a reasonable allowance for salaries or other compensation for personal services actually rendered." There is evidence in the legislative history of this section that it was never meant to limit deductions, but was instead meant to *allow* deductions. It was passed when there was a tax on excess profits. Under the excess profits tax, owners of an unincorporated business who did not draw down salary would have their profits overstated (and therefore subject to tax) if some provision was not made to reduce profits by the value of the services. Griswold, *New Light on "A Reasonable Allowance"for Services*, 59 Harv. L. Rev. 286(1945).

Knowing this legislative history might call attention to an ambiguity in the wording of *§ 162(a)(1)* that would otherwise escape attention. Why, for example, would a section limiting a deduction refer to a reasonable "*allowance for* salaries" rather than a reasonable "*payment of* salary"?

Employees and owners. Whatever the history, the section on reasonable salaries is now a limit on deductions. In effect, this is one area where an expense must be more than just "appropriate and helpful." The issue arises most often when an employee has contracted for a percentage of profits and the business later flourishes. If the original contract for the profit percentage was a "free bargain," the profit payment will not be questioned, even though it exceeds the reasonable salary which would be paid if the salary were negotiated in the later payment year. If the original bargain was not "free" (as evidenced by family pressure on the payor to help a relative, for example), the deductible amount will depend on the reasonable value of services in the year of payment. *Harolds Club v. Commissioner*, 340 F.2d 861 (9th Cir. 1965).

In one situation, it might seem rational to limit the deduction of salary to a reasonable amount. Shareholders of a corporation want to take out corporate income as salary rather than profits, because profit distributions (that is, dividends) are not deductible by the corporation. However, any unreasonable salary paid to a corporate owner would be recharacterized as a nondeductible dividend, even without *§ 162(a)(1)*. A dividend is simply not an "expense." This must be the correct interpretation of the statute or else an unreasonable rental payment or other excessive price paid to a shareholder would be deductible by the corporation, even though it was a disguised dividend. *See Safway Steel Scaffolds Co. v. United States*, 590 F.2d 1360 (5th Cir. 1979) (excessive rent to shareholder-lessor was dividend).

[ii] Excess executive pay in publicly held corporation; *§ 162(m)*

The 1993 tax law added another limit on the deduction of salary. Publicly held corporations cannot deduct more than $1 million of compensation paid to any of five corporate officials — the chief executive officer and (in most cases) the four highest paid officers. *§ 162(m)*. There are two exceptions — (1) commissions based on income generated directly by the officer's performance; and (2) amounts payable on account of meeting performance goals (such as stock price, market share, sales, or earnings), if the goals are determined by a committee of outside directors and approved by shareholder vote.

[C]—Lavish or Extravagant

Several statutory provisions disallow the deduction of "lavish or extravagant" meals, lodging, or entertainment. *§ 162(a)(2)* (meals and lodging while traveling); *§ 274(k)(1)(A)* (business meals). These phrases may be as ineffective in limiting deductions as the word "necessary" in the introductory language of *§ 162(a)*. However, the Committee Reports to the Tax Reform Act of 1986 state that the reference in *§ 274(k)(1)(A)* was added, "thereby emphasizing an intent that this standard is to be enforced by the Internal Revenue Service and the courts."

In addition, a host of specific rules prevent deduction of business expenses which seem extravagant and wasteful, and which may provide personal consumption. *See, e.g., § 274(h)* (certain cruise ships and foreign conventions), *§ 274(l)* (limit deduction to face value of entertainment tickets), *§ 274(m)* (luxury water transportation), *§ 274(n)* (50% of meals and entertainment), *§ 280F* (limit on luxury automobile depreciation).

§ 14.02 ILLEGAL ACTIVITY

[A]—"Tax fines"

You have read about tax expenditures — tax provisions explicitly designed to encourage activities which Congress considers desirable. Now we consider the use of the tax law to discourage undesirable activities by disallowing deductions that would otherwise be allowed. If the analogy between tax expenditures and direct subsidies is apt, then disallowing deductions to achieve nontax policy should invite comparison between the use of the tax law to discourage the activity and the use of civil or criminal fines imposed by an agency or court charged with implementing that policy.

If we conceptualize disallowance of a deduction as a "tax fine," we are naturally led to ask whether tax fines make any sense in comparison with civil or criminal penalties. First, the tax fine varies with the tax rate, rather than with the rules relevant under the state or federal law imposing penalties on undesirable behavior.

Second, it is not always clear that permitting the deduction has any effect on behavior. (Would you justify disallowing the deduction merely as an expression of public displeasure?)

Third, if the decision about whether to limit deductions is left to case law development, we are asking courts which decide tax cases to pass on the strength or weakness of the public policy served by disallowing the deduction. The courts might not be good at making that judgment.

[B]—Expenses — case law

In *Commissioner v. Tellier*, 383 U.S. 687 (1966), the taxpayer incurred legal expenses in the unsuccessful defense of a criminal prosecution originating in the securities business. The deduction was challenged on public policy grounds. The Court expressed a grudging acceptance of the public policy limitation on deductions, but found no policy against legal expenses in criminal cases. The Court stated:

> We start with the proposition that the federal income tax is a tax on net income, not a sanction against wrongdoing. That principle has been firmly imbedded in the tax statute from the beginning. One familiar facet of the principle is the truism that the statute does not concern itself with the lawfulness of the income that it taxes. Income from a criminal enterprise is taxed at a rate no higher and no lower than income from more conventional sources. . . .
>
> The application of this principle is reflected in several decisions of this Court. As recently as *Commissioner v. Sullivan*, 356 U.S. 27, we sustained the allowance of a deduction for rent and wages paid by the operators of a gambling enterprise, even though both the business itself and the specific rent and wage payments there in question were illegal under state law. In rejecting the Commissioner's contention that the illegality of the enterprise required disallowance of the deduction, we held that, were we to "enforce as federal policy the rule espoused by the Commissioner in

this case, we would come close to making this type of business taxable on the basis of its gross receipts, while all other business would be taxable on the basis of net income. If that choice is to be made, Congress should do it." In *Lilly v. Commissioner*, 343 U.S. 90, the Court upheld deductions claimed by opticians for amounts paid to doctors who prescribed the eyeglasses that the opticians sold, although the Court was careful to disavow "approval of the business ethics or public policy involved in the payments. . . ." And in *Commissioner v. Heininger*, 320 U.S. 467, a case akin to the one before us, the Court upheld deductions claimed by a dentist for lawyer's fees and other expenses incurred in unsuccessfully defending against an administrative fraud order issued by the Postmaster General.

. . . The Court has [] given effect to a precise and longstanding Treasury Regulation prohibiting the deduction of a specified category of expenditures; an example is lobbying expenses, whose nondeductibility was supported by considerations not here present. *Textile Mills Securities Corp. v. Commissioner*, 314 U.S. 326; *Cammarano v. United States*, 358 U.S. 498. But where Congress has been wholly silent, it is only in extremely limited circumstances that the Court has countenanced exceptions to the general principle reflected in the *Sullivan*, *Lilly* and *Heininger* decisions. Only where the allowance of a deduction would "frustrate sharply defined national or state policies proscribing particular types of conduct" have we upheld its disallowance. *Commissioner v. Heininger*, 320 U.S., at 473. Further, the "policies frustrated must be national or state policies evidenced by some governmental declaration of them." *Lilly v. Commissioner*, 343 U.S., at 97. Finally, the "test of nondeductibility always is the severity and immediacy of the frustration resulting from allowance of the deduction." *Tank Truck Rentals v. Commissioner*, 356 U.S. 30, 35. In that case, . . . we upheld the disallowance of deductions claimed by taxpayers for fines and penalties imposed upon them for violating state penal statutes; to allow a deduction in those circumstances would have directly and substantially diluted the actual punishment imposed.

The present case falls far outside that sharply limited and carefully defined category. No public policy is offended when a man faced with serious criminal charges employs a lawyer to help in his defense. That is not "proscribed conduct." It is his constitutional right. In an adversary system of criminal justice, it is a basic of our public policy that a defendant in a criminal case have counsel to represent him.

Congress has authorized the imposition of severe punishment upon those found guilty of the serious criminal offenses with which the respondent was charged and of which he was convicted. But we can find no warrant for attaching to that punishment an additional financial burden that Congress has neither expressly nor implicitly directed. To deny a deduction for expenses incurred in the unsuccessful defense of a criminal prosecution would impose such a burden in a measure dependent not on the seriousness of the offense or the actual sentence imposed by the court, but on the cost of the defense and the defendant's particular tax bracket. We decline to distort the income tax laws to serve a purpose for which they were neither intended nor designed by Congress.

[C]—1969 Legislation

Judicial impatience with disallowing a deduction on public policy grounds spilled over into Congress in 1969, when *§ 162* was amended to adopt *§ 162(c),(f),(g)*. The Senate Finance Committee Report for the 1969 Act stated that the "provision for the denial of the deduction of payments in these situations which are deemed to violate public policy is intended to be all inclusive. Public policy, in other circumstances, generally is not sufficiently clearly defined to justify the disallowance of deductions." *S. Rept. No. 91-552*, 91st Cong., 1st Sess. (1969), *reprinted in* 1969 U.S.C.C.A.N. 2027, 2311.

In its present form, *§ 162(c),(f),(g)* accomplishes the following.

Illegal payments, etc. *§ 162(c)* is a catch-all for a variety of illegal payments. Illegal bribes and illegal kickbacks paid to government officials and government employees are not deductible, except that payments to foreign officials and foreign employees are not deductible only if the payments are illegal under the Foreign Corrupt Practices Act of 1977. *§ 162(c)(1)*. Bribes and kickbacks (even if not illegal) are not deductible when made to suppliers of services in connection with Medicaid and Medicare. *§ 162(c)(3)*.

Illegal bribes and illegal kickbacks (not already covered by *§ 162(c)(1)*), and other illegal payments, are also not deductible, *if* they would subject the taxpayer to a criminal penalty or loss of license or privilege to engage in business. *§ 162(c)(2)*. The "other illegal payment" rule is subject to an interesting qualification in the case of payments which are illegal under State law. The state law must be "generally enforced." Desuetude is therefore a legally relevant consideration in determining whether an expense is so contrary to state public policy that it should not be deductible. *§ 162(c)(2)*. *Treas. Reg. § 1.162-18(b)(3)* states that a law is generally enforced unless it is never enforced or enforced only when the defendants are infamous or the violations are extraordinarily flagrant. Is this regulation a valid interpretation of the statute?

Recall the discussion of the *Sullivan* case in *Tellier*, *supra*, which held that illegal rent and wage payments were deductible by a gambler. The decision predates adoption of *§ 162(c)*. Would the payments in *Sullivan* be deductible under current law?

Under all of the provisions of *§ 162(c)*, the government has the burden of proof on the question of illegality. Usually, under the income tax law, the taxpayer has the burden of proof.

In *Rev. Rul. 74-323*, 1974-2 C.B. 40, a taxpayer had incurred advertising expenses but the advertisement violated the law against sex discrimination. Because there was no criminal penalty or loss of a license or privilege to do business for violating the law, the expenses were deductible.

Fines and similar penalties. *§ 162(f)* disallows the deduction of fines or similar penalties paid to a government. The Regulations include civil as well as criminal fines in the nondeductible category, but compensatory damages are deductible. *Treas. Reg. § 1.162-21(b).*

It is not always easy to identify a fine. A "fine or similar penalty" has a "punitive, as opposed to remedial, meaning." *Jerry Rossman Corp. v. Commissioner*, 175 F.2d 711 (2d Cir. 1949). But how do you draw the line between punitive and remedial? After all, both criminal penalties and remedial tort liability share a deterrent objective. Legislative intent is often considered relevant in drawing the line, but legislative intent is no easier to divine on this question than on any other. Courts often look at the legislative history, but may also rely on their own model of what constitutes a punitive rather than a remedial payment — such as the method of computing the payments.

One setting in which judges have grappled with this issue is a statute which provides for "liquidated damages," or some other fixed amount of compensation. We have already encountered this problem when discussing the *exclusion* of damages under *§ 104(a)*. In *Commissioner v. Schleier*, 515 U.S. 323 (1995) (discussed in § 9.03, *supra*), the Court concluded that the liquidated damages provisions of the civil rights statute were punitive, which militated against characterizing these amounts as "on account of" personal injury. The same issue arises on the deduction side.

In *Hawronsky v. Commissioner*, 105 T.C. 94 (1995), the court held that the liquidated damages provisions of the statute were punitive "fines" rather than compensatory payments. The taxpayer had received a tax-exempt scholarship from the Indian Health Services Scholarship Program to attend medical school. The statute regulating the scholarship program required the taxpayer to sign a contract agreeing to serve in the Indian Health Service for four years. Failure to serve this term resulted (under the statute) in treble damages paid to the Department of Health and Human Services (HHS).

After completing about one year and eight months of the required four years of service with the Indian Health Service, taxpayer quit and paid

$275,326.86 as treble damages to HHS. Taxpayer claimed a deduction for this amount as a business expense. Taxpayer argued that the treble damages payment was compensatory and not punitive, relying on District Court cases which applied contract principles to characterize the treble damages provision as liquidated damages. The court held that those cases were unpersuasive because they were decided before two Courts of Appeals held that *statutory intent* and not contract principles governed the parties' obligations under the Indian Health Service statute, and that Congress intended the treble damages under this statute to be an enforceable civil penalty.

The court also noted that the treble damages had no demonstrated relationship to the Government's actual damages from the loss of petitioner's services, taking into account the costs of finding a doctor to practice in an underserved area.

One implication of this case is that the characterization of liquidated damages can vary from statute to statute. If that is true, it makes it difficult to know whether such damages are or are not nondeductible fines under *§ 162(f)* (and, also, whether they are excludible personal injury damages under *§ 104*). *See also Colt Indus., Inc. v. United States*, 880 F.2d 1311 (Fed. Cir. 1989) (legislative history showed an intent to punish).

In two rulings, the IRS could not find a legislative intent to punish. In *Rev. Rul 80–334*, 1980–2 Cum. Bull. 61, a taxpayer which engaged in the sale of petroleum products was allowed to deduct court-ordered payments to prior customers and to the Treasury for oil price violations when the taxpayer's violation was unintentional. As part of the consent order requiring the payments, the Department of Energy agreed that civil or criminal penalties would be inappropriate. And in *Rev. Rul. 88–46*, 1988–1 Cum. Bull. 530, payments labeled as "performance penalties" were not fines because the legislative history showed that they were imposed to equalize the costs on those whose violations of environmental standards would otherwise give them a competitive advantage. Do these agency rulings suggest a government policy to make environmental "fines" deductible in order to encourage settlement of disputes?

Other cases appear to broaden the inquiry beyond specific evidence of legislative intent. In *True v. United States*, 894 F.2d 1197 (10th Cir. 1990), *rev'g* 603 F. Supp. 1370 (D. Wyo. 1985), the method of computing the payment was important. The court disallowed the deduction, distinguishing between deductible compensatory/remedial payments to the government and nondeductible punitive/retributive payments, under the Federal Water Pollution Control Act. The payments in this case were nondeductible, in part because the amounts were determined by reference to the size of the payor's business and the effect on the payor continuing business, both of which bore no relation to compensating an injured party.

Settlements. Payments "in settlement of the taxpayer's actual or potential liability for a fine or penalty" are fines. *Treas. Reg. § 1.162-21(b)(1)(iii).* In *Allied-Signal, Inc. v. Commissioner*, 63 T.C.M. (CCH) 2672 (1992), there was a lawsuit to determine if the taxpayer had to pay a fine for environmental pollution. The case was settled before there was a finding of taxpayer responsibility. The settlement called for a payment by the taxpayer to a *§ 501(c)(4)* organization which helped clean up the environment. Payments to this organization were not tax deductible charitable contributions, but could be *§ 162(a)* expenses. The taxpayer insisted that the payments were voluntary and therefore not fines or settlements in lieu of fines. The court disallowed the deduction on the ground that they were fines, placing little weight on the "voluntariness" of the payment.

Payment "to." The fact that the payment is not technically made "to" the government is not dispositive. In *Waldman v. Commissioner*, 88 T.C. 1384 (1987), *aff'd*, 850 F.2d 611 (9th Cir. 1988), the court held that restitution paid to victims by order of the court to avoid execution of a sentence was a nondeductible fine. *See also Rev. Rul. 79-148*, 1979-1 C.B. 93 (the court ordered the taxpayer to pay money to a charity in lieu of a fine; the payment was not a deductible charitable gift because it was paid under compulsion, and was disallowed as a business deduction because of *§ 162(f)*).

Punitive damages. Can punitive damages in a breach of contract action be deducted? *Rev. Rul. 80-211*, 1980 C.B. 27 permitted the deduction. What justifies that result? Are the payments "to" the plaintiff, not the government? Suppose the government is the plaintiff? Do the following cases have any relevance to answering this question: *Browning-Ferris Indus. of Vermont, Inc. v. Kelco*, 492 U.S. 257 (1989) (Court held that punitive damages in civil action are not generally subject to the U.S. Constitution's prohibition of "excessive fines," but did not decide whether this rule applies when the government prosecutes a case or shares in the award); *Austin v. United States*, 113 S. Ct. 2801 (1993) ("excessive fine" prohibition applies to Government-imposed civil forfeiture of property used in illegal drug business because civil sanction is not just remedial but also punitive — that is, retributive or deterrent)?

Treble damages. In civil anti-trust cases, a losing defendant must pay three times actual damages. *§ 162(g)* disallows a deduction for the two-thirds portion of the treble damages, if the taxpayer has been convicted or pleads guilty or nolo contendere in a criminal proceeding. What effect might this have on the taxpayer's willingness to plead guilty?

[D]—Costs — defining "gross income"

The discussion so far has focused primarily on *§ 162* expense deductions, which are deductible in reducing *§ 61* gross income to taxable income. What happens if the expenditure which the taxpayer wants to deduct is a cost, which reduces amount realized (that is, gross receipts) to gross income?

The courts have had some difficulty deciding how to apply the "public policy" doctrine to costs, which are used to compute gross income. The very definition of income seems to be implicated when cost and gross receipts are netted to produce gross income. This makes the courts somewhat reluctant to disallow the deduction of costs. But why? If cost is nothing but an expenditure which should be added to basis for future deduction, the difference between an expense and a cost lies only in the timing of a deduction. How can the public policy doctrine have greater vitality when the deduction is claimed at the time the expenditure is made, rather than when the deduction is deferred?

Courts divide on this issue. The cases involve payments by taxpayers which are in excess of price control ceilings imposed during wartime. In *Pedone v. United States*, 151 F. Supp. 288 (Ct. Cl. 1957), and *Weather-Seal Mfg. Co. v. Commissioner*, 16 T.C. 1312 (1951), *aff'd per curiam*, 199 F.2d 376 (6th Cir. 1952), the court held that excessive wages which would be part of deductible costs of goods sold could *not* be included in cost. *But see Commissioner v. Weisman*, 197 F.2d 221 (1st Cir. 1952) (excessive cost of materials used to manufacture inventory is included in deductible cost of goods sold); *Sullenger v. Commissioner*, 11 T.C. 1076 (1948) (same, except taxpayer bought meat for resale).

The current Regulations purport to give an answer to this question. *Treas. Reg. § 1.471-3 (last sentence)* states that outlays of a type for which a deduction would be disallowed under *§ 162(c),(f),(g)* cannot be added to cost.

[E]—Costs — losses

MAZZEI v. COMMISSIONER

61 T.C. 497 (1974)

QUEALY, JUDGE:

[Editor — Blick, a friend of petitioner's, was told about a scheme to reproduce money. Two men, Collins and Joe, showed Blick a black box, into which they placed a $10 bill and two pieces of white paper. The box was plugged in, turned on, and after 10 minutes, out came what appeared to be a new $10 bill. Collins told Blick they needed more paper to make more money. Blick told all this to petitioner, who received a similar demonstration and was told that more paper was needed. Petitioner was told to show up with $20,000 in $100 bills. Petitioner did this with Blick. Collins began placing the money in water and then in between two pieces of white paper. At this point, petitioner was told that the black box was broken and two men, impersonating police officers, staged a raid. Petitioner ran away and told the police. They all returned to the apartment, finding Blick alone.]

On his Federal income tax return for the calendar year 1965, petitioner claimed a theft loss in the amount of $20,000 and took a deduction therefor in the amount of $19,900.

In his statutory notice of deficiency, respondent disallowed the deduction for the loss under § 165(c)(2) or (3) on the ground[] . . . that allowance of the deduction would be contrary to public policy.

Petitioner contends that the fact that he incurred a loss is substantiated by the evidence and that such loss is deductible under § 165(c)(2) or § 165(c)(3). Respondent contends . . . [that] a deduction for such loss would not be allowed under [either section] on the grounds that allowance of such a deduction would be contrary to public policy. . . .

[Editor — The court relied on the *Richey* case, which disallowed a deduction to a conspirator in a counterfeiting scheme when his co-conspirators stole $15,000 of the money he had provided for use in the scheme. *Richey* held that a loss deduction "would constitute an immediate and severe frustration of the clearly defined policy against counterfeiting obligations of the United States."]

Petitioner would distinguish the *Richey* case on the grounds that there the taxpayer was involved in an actual scheme to duplicate money where the process was actually begun, only to have the taxpayer swindled when his cohorts made off with his money, whereas in the instant case there never was any real plan to counterfeit money, it being impossible to duplicate currency with the black box. Petitioner contends that, from the inception, the only actual illegal scheme was the scheme to relieve petitioner of his money, and petitioner was a victim and not a perpetrator of the scheme.

In our opinion, the fact that the petitioner was victimized in what he thought was a plan or conspiracy to produce counterfeit currency does not make his participation in what he considered to be a criminal act any less violative of a clearly declared public policy. Not only was the result sought by the petitioner contrary to such policy, but the conspiracy itself constituted a violation of law. The petitioner conspired with his co-victim to commit a criminal act, namely, the counterfeiting of United States currency and his theft loss was directly related to that act. If there was a transaction entered into for profit, as petitioner argues, it was a conspiracy to counterfeit. . . .

We also do not feel constrained to follow *Edwards v. Bromberg*, 232 F.2d 107 (C.A. 5, 1956), wherein the court allowed a deduction for a loss incurred by the taxpayer when money, which he thought was being bet on a "fixed" race, was stolen from him. The taxpayer never intended to participate in "fixing" the race.

The ultimate question for decision in this case is whether considerations of public policy should enter into the allowance of a theft loss under § 165(c)(3). Where there is a "theft" — and the loss by the petitioner of his money would certainly qualify as such — the statute imposes no limitation on the deductibility of the loss. Nevertheless, in *Luther M. Richey, Jr.*, *supra*, this Court held that the deduction of an admitted theft was properly disallowed on grounds of public policy in a factual situation which we find indistinguishable. We would follow that case.

STERRETT, J. I respectfully dissent. . . .

. . . The Senate Finance Committee report for the 1969 Tax Reform Act states "The provision for the denial of the deduction for payments in these situations which are deemed to violate public policy is intended to be all inclusive. Public policy, in other circumstances, generally is not sufficiently clearly defined to justify the disallowance of deductions." S. Rept. No. 91-552, 91st Cong., 1st Sess. (1969), 1969-3 C.B. 597. . . .

While the above statements have direct effect under section 162, where most of the public policy decisions have arisen, it does seem to call for judicial restraint in other areas where Congress has not specifically limited deductions. . . .

The majority seems to indicate that a deduction can be denied where there is any relationship between the loss or expense and the illegal activity, a position specifically rejected by *Sullivan*. Such reasoning does not readily lend itself to being "sharply limited" or "carefully defined." Had petitioner contracted pneumonia on his New York excursion, would the majority also deny him a medical expense deduction?

Or assume that customers on the premises of the bookmaking establishment involved in *Sullivan* were robbed by an outside intruder. Would the majority deny them a theft loss because they were engaged in an illegal activity? Or would the majority have this Court of special jurisdiction add to its assigned duties of interpreting the Internal Revenue Code the task of grading criminal activity, a task for which we obviously have no particular expertise. The authority for undertaking such additional duties remains obscure to me and would also be, I suspect, obscure to Congress.

Congress has authorized the imposition of severe punishment upon those found guilty of counterfeiting United States currency. It is designed to repress such criminal conduct. In the interest of uniform application of the Internal Revenue Code, where the frustration of State or national policy is neither severe nor immediate, we must not be tempted to impose a "clean hands doctrine" as a prerequisite to deductibility. To hold otherwise, especially in light of the broad brush-stroke of public policy applied by the majority opinion, makes the taxing statute an unwarranted instrument of further punishment.

Forrester, Featherston, Hall, and Wiles, JJ., agree with this dissent.

QUESTIONS

1. Taxpayer violated state law by selling liquor to a retailer at a discount. The discount was provided by selling 13 bottles for the regulated price applicable to 12 bottles. Can the taxpayer deduct the cost attributable to the thirteenth bottle? *Max Sobel Wholesale Liquors v. Commissioner*, 69 T.C. 477 (1977), *aff'd.*, 630 F.2d 670 (9th Cir. 1980).

2. *§ 280E* disallows deductions for illegal drug dealers. Are they taxed on gross receipts or gross income? The Senate Committee Report says that gross income is taxed. *S. Rep. No. 97-494*, Vol. 1, p. I-309 (1982).

3. Can investors in low-income housing take advantage of the *§ 42* credit if they discriminate against tenants on the basis of race?

4. Does the discussion in this chapter shed any light on whether policy considerations should be relevant in determining whether a charitable organization should be tax exempt? *See Bob Jones University*, § 10.02[C], *supra*.

5. Recently, the question of dependency status in gay relationships has become very important because exclusion of employer-funded insurance fringe benefits is available for both the employee and his or her dependents. *Treas. Reg. 1.106-1.* (Head of household status may also be available, if the taxpayer has a dependent. *§ 2(b)(1)(A)(ii).*) When Congress adopted *§ 152(b)(5)* in 1958, the committee report stated that it was aimed at preventing dependency deductions for "common law" spouses where such relationships were unrecognized under state law. *H.R. No. 775*, 85th Cong., 1st Sess. (1957), 1958–3 C.B. 811, 817–18. But the statutory test is broader than the specific example in the legislative history; the legal issue is whether the relationship violates local law.

In that spirit, cases have denied dependency deductions in cases of adultery (*Ochs v. Commissioner*, 52 T.C.M. (CCH) 1218 (1986)), and "open and notorious cohabitation" (*Peacock v. Commissioner*, 37 T.C.M. (CCH)

177 (1978)). In the Tax Court's opinion in *Ensminger v. Commissioner*, 36 T.C.M. (CCH) 934 (1977), the court made much of the fact that taxpayers had the burden of proof and had introduced no evidence to contradict the government's claim that "lascivious cohabitation" (meaning "habitual sexual intercourse") had occurred. The court also noted that the statute had not fallen into disuse because cases applying it had surfaced in the state appellate courts as recently as 1970.

Recent letter rulings have not squarely confronted *§ 152(b)(5)* in the context of gay relationships. *Private Letter Ruling 9231062* (May 7, 1992), dealing with an accident and health plan fringe benefit, took account of a city's "domestic partner" law and stated: "The existence of a local law that affirmatively recognizes unmarried cohabitation may address the legality of the relationship. . . ." The implication is that the "domestic partner" law would overcome other laws dealing with lascivious cohabitation or sodomy. Of course, as the ruling noted, the support test must still be met.

Private Letter Ruling 9603011 (Oct. 18, 1995) is even more opaque. A company adopted an accident and health plan benefit which could include "domestic partners," as defined under the plan. There was no reference to a government law or ordinance recognizing domestic partners. ("For an individual to qualify as a Domestic Partner under the Plan, the Domestic Partner and the Qualified Employee must execute an affidavit evidencing their intention to be domestic partners as defined in the Plan.") The ruling repeats the *§ 152(b)(5)* requirement regarding legality under local law, and then states that domestic partners can be covered as dependents if they meet that requirement.

What would be the impact on this issue of a state law which allowed same-sex marriages? Would that establish the absence of state policy against such relationships and prevent § 152(b)(5) from denying a deduction, even if the gay partners were not married? Or does it condone these relationships only in the case of marriage?

What is the impact of the new law in which Congress has refused to recognize same-sex marriages (*e.g.*, for filing joint returns under *§ 1(a)*)? The Defense of Marriage Act, *Pub. L. No. 104–199*, 104th Cong., 2d Sess., 110 Stat. 2419, provides a definition of marriage and spouse in *1 U.S.C. § 7*, as follows:

> In determining the meaning of any Act of Congress, or of any ruling, regulation, or interpretation of the various administrative bureaus and agencies of the United States, the word "marriage" means only a legal union between one man and one woman as husband and wife, and the word "spouse" refers only to a person of the opposite sex who is a husband or a wife.

But this federal law does not say anything about the impact of local law and the definition of dependents under *§ 152(b)(5)*.

6. Can a taxpayer deduct a legal kickback — for example, a payment made by a record producer to a disc jockey (assuming it is legal)? *Raymond Bertolini Trucking Co. v. Commissioner*, 45 T.C.M. (CCH) 44 (1982), *rev'd*, 736 F.2d 1120 (6th Cir. 1984); *Car-Ron Asphalt Paving Co. Commissioner*, 758 F.2d 1132 (6th Cir. 1985). Are these ordinary and necessary expenses?

7. Suppose a lawyer advances court costs for the client and the amounts are deductible. This assumption *may* be incorrect — the advances may be loans — but in *Boccardo v. Commissioner*, 56 F.3d 1016 (9th Cir. 1995), the court held that they were deductible expenses when there was no explicit client obligation to repay. But there was another issue. These advances might have violated the rules of professional responsibility, adopted by the California Supreme Court. If they did, would they be nondeductible "illegal payments"? Is the Supreme Court rule a "state law"? Is it "a state law that is generally enforced, which subjects the payor to a criminal penalty or the loss of a license"?

§ 14.03 POLITICAL EXPENDITURES

[A]—Nondeductible business expenses

Many political expenditures are incurred for income-producing purposes. These include the cost of getting elected, of lobbying legislators to obtain passage of a statute favorable to business, and of grass-roots lobbying to get public support for such statutes. In 1918, Treasury Regulations stated that corporations could not deduct lobbying expenses and this rule was extended to individuals in 1938. The Supreme Court upheld the Regulations in *Cammarano v. United States*, 358 U.S. 498 (1959). The expense of getting elected and reelected is also not deductible. *McDonald v. Commissioner*, 323 U.S. 57 (1944).

What theory might support disallowing these deductions? Political expenses are not against public policy but their deduction may be. One argument for this result is that the deduction favors higher bracket taxpayers over those in lower brackets and over those for whom the expenditure is personal and therefore nondeductible. When the deduction is disallowed, everyone pays the same after-tax amount for political expenses. But how does a deduction favor the higher bracket business taxpayer? Consider two taxpayers. One is an environmentalist, seeking the personal goals of clean air. The other is a corporation, seeking profits. Both value the results of lobbying at $100,000. If the corporation's $100,000 profit is taxable, why would it spend more than $100,000 on the lobbying effort, even if the expenses were deductible? If it is in the 35% bracket, the after-tax benefits of $100,000 income are only $65,000. The after-tax cost of spending a deductible $100,000 for lobbying is also $65,000. It will therefore not spend any more than $100,000 to lobby, which is also the maximum the environmentalist will spend.

There might be another reason for disallowing the deduction for political expenses. The well-off in higher brackets and corporations are already in a better position to spend discretionary income. A lot of people with lower incomes cannot value a political benefit at $100,000 because of their income level. Moreover, the well-off might be better organized and be able to buy more for $100,000 than the less well-off. A deduction for the well-off solidifies these advantages. These concerns suggest, however, that disallowing deductions may be a very limited and ineffective way to reduce the effect of money on politics.

Tax rules about political expenditures seem to be little more than tinkering with a very fundamental problem, which can only be addressed by more substantial steps, such as public financing of elections or spending limits. More substantial steps, however, raise serious questions about the relationship of government to political activity, not the least of which is their constitutionality. *Buckley v. Valeo*, 424 U.S. 1 (1976) (ceilings on independent expenditures for political purposes is an unconstitutional violation of free speech).

Whatever the force of the reasoning for disallowing the deduction of political expenses, the rule exists and has spawned a number of problems.

[B]—Getting elected vs. staying in office

REV. RUL. 71-470, 1971-2 C.B. 121

Advice has been requested whether the amounts paid by a taxpayer under the circumstances described below are deductible under § 162 of the Internal Revenue Code of 1954 as ordinary and necessary business expenses.

The taxpayer was elected to a public office, but shortly after he entered office, a special election was held wherein the voters were asked to vote whether he should be recalled from that office.

The taxpayer waged an active campaign in his defense, and successfully defeated the recall. He incurred and paid expenses in his campaign against recall. . . .

In *Michael F. McDonald v. Commissioner*, 323, U.S. 57 (1944), the Supreme Court of the United States held that the campaign expenditures of a taxpayer seeking election as a judge were not incurred in carrying on the taxpayer's business of "judging." The Court held that such expenditures were neither losses incurred in a transaction entered into for profit nor expenses incurred for the production or collection of income. However, the taxpayer in the instant case was not a candidate for public office, and was not seeking a new term. He was merely defending his position for his current term, and the Supreme Court of the United States has held that the ordinary and necessary expenses of defending one's business are deductible. *Commissioner v. S. B. Heininger*, 320 U.S. 467 (1943).

Accordingly, the amounts paid by the taxpayer in this case in defending his position as an elected public official are deductible as ordinary and necessary business expenses under section 162 of the Code.

COMMENTS AND QUESTIONS

1. You should find the distinction between retaining office (the facts of the Ruling) and seeking election (*McDonald*) very troublesome. The taxpayer in *McDonald* lost an election to fill the judicial position he already held and, under normal tax principles, would therefore have been allowed a deduction. *McDonald* is usually thought to stand for the proposition that normal tax principles do *not* apply to political election expenses. *Cf. Levy v. Commissioner*, 535 F.2d 47 (Ct. Cl. 1976) (taxpayer cannot add cost of getting elected to basis and depreciate the basis). Why then should "retaining office" expenses be deductible as ordinary and necessary expenses, as held in *Rev. Rul. 71-470*? Is such a deduction less likely to "corrupt" politics with money? Is the Ruling limited to recall cases?

2. A taxpayer unsuccessfully sought reelection as president of a large union. Are his expenses deductible? *Carey v. Commissioner*, 56 T.C. 477 (1971), *aff'd per curiam*, 460 F.2d 1259 (4th Cir. 1972).

3. President Ford nominated New York Governor Rockefeller to be Vice President. Could Rockefeller deduct expenses related to the nomination process? *Rockefeller v. Commissioner*, 83 T.C. 368 (1984), *aff'd*, 762 F.2d 264 (2d Cir. 1985).

4. Are legal expenses to defend against a criminal charge of vote-buying deductible? *Rev. Rul. 86-3*, 1986-1 C.B. 81.

Here is another case involving deductions of political expenses. How do the expenses differ from those incurred by the judge in *McDonald*, who was seeking election?

DIGGS v. COMMISSIONER

715 F.2d 245 (6th Cir. 1983)

NATHANIEL R. JONES, CIRCUIT JUDGE:

. . . The expenses which an officeholder incurs [] in connection with his personal political goals or with the political goals of a party have been held to be nondeductible. We recognize that the trend of recent tax court decisions may be to allow deductions for expenses incurred in seeking new employment. But we follow more recent tax court and appellate court decisions in rejecting the analogy between seeking new employment and seeking new political office. . . . The fact that expenses incurred in seeking employment may be deductible, therefore, does not undermine the nondeductibility of expenses incurred in connection with political self-aggrandizement or political party aggrandizement.

Although we conclude that personal and party aggrandizement is not sufficiently connected with the trade or business of being a Congressman to qualify for a § 162(a)(2) deduction, we do not deny that some activities are indeed so closely related to the trade or business of being a Congressman as to qualify for such a deduction. . . .

There is no question that a member of Congress may have deductible expenses of his or her trade or business as a member. We are certainly not prepared to say, for example, that the efforts of congressional representatives to learn of the concerns facing their constituents are activities outside the scope of their trade or business. To this effect, the Tax Court has held recently that a legislator's trade or business includes discussion of the issues with constituents. . . . The healthy pursuit of that trade or business [] requires that a congressional representative become educated in the concerns of constituents. That education necessarily includes ascertaining and assessing the particular needs and interests of those constituents. Through this educational process, a congressman more fully represents and advances before the House of Representatives the interests of his or her constituents. The "educational" expenses incurred by a congressman in ascertaining and assessing the interests of constituents may be less formal than those educational expenses typically afforded a § 162 deduction, but they are nonetheless directly related to the trade or business of a congressman.

We are led by the clear import of the case law in this area, therefore, to conclude that the expenses incurred by a legislator in connection with the duty to ascertain, assess and advance the interests of constituents are deductible, while expenses incurred by a congressman in connection with personal and party aggrandizement are not deductible.

B. Application of the Proper Legal Standard

(1) National Black Political Conference

In 1972, Congressman Diggs attended ten meetings of the BPC. The first of these meetings was held in Michigan, the state from which Diggs was elected and in which he ran for reelection in 1972. The conference's assembly was held in Gary, Indiana on March 10 through 13, 1972. The remaining eight meetings were held in Illinois, Ohio, New York and Nevada. The purpose of these BPC meetings was "to make an assessment of the concerns of black citizens in the United States and to develop a national black agenda regarding those concerns." Congressman Diggs testified that the national black agenda was used as a basis for legislation by the congressional black caucus. The agenda was presented to the platform committees of both the Democratic and the Republican National Conventions of 1972. The BPC clearly desired its agenda to be a part of a national platform, regardless of which party succeeded in the election. The objective was to commit both parties to minority legislative goals, rather than to support either party in the general election.

These minority legislative goals are largely the goals of Congressman Diggs' constituency, the great majority of which are black. In his role as the senior black member of the House of Representatives, and as the representative of a predominantly black district, Congressman Diggs' participation in the formulation of a nonpartisan minority legislative agenda was certainly connected with his trade or business as a legislator. At the BPC meetings, Congressman Diggs ascertained the problems faced by his constituents, identified those solutions that are legitimately pursued through the legislative process, informed his colleagues about those concerns and solutions, and received guidance and alliance from those colleagues toward effectuating legislative action on behalf of his constituents. We cannot say that such activities by Congressman Diggs on behalf of his constituents did not indirectly increase the possibility of his reelection. But neither are we prepared to say that every action by a Congressman on behalf of constituents is motivated solely by the drive toward personal or party aggrandizement. In this case, where Congressman Diggs' attendance at BPC meetings was so directly connected with ascertaining, assessing and advancing the interests of his constituents independent of party affiliation, we hold that the expenses incurred in that attendance are sufficiently related to the trade or business of a legislator to be deductible under § 162(a).

(2) The Democratic National Convention

Diggs played a significant role at the Democratic National Convention as a voting delegate. Attendance at the Democratic National Convention as a delegate, of course, does not necessarily preclude a deduction. In Revenue Ruling 59-316, 1959, the Commissioner stated that:

> An individual who can bring his cause within the provisions of Section 162(a) of the Code by making a factual showing that he attended the convention in connection with his own business interests and is, therefore, entitled to a business expense deduction is not deprived of the deduction in the event he should be elected or appointed a delegate . . .

Diggs' attendance at the DNC as a delegate, however, was not so directly connected to advancing the interests of his constituents as it was to advancing his own political goals and the goals of his party. . . .

The party's platform is carried to the polls on the shoulders of the party's presidential and vice-presidential nominees. That platform, however, is also buttressed by the party's nominees for other national offices. As the Democratic Party's candidate for reelection to the House of Representatives in 1972, Diggs was one such national officeholder responsible for advancing the party's platform.

Diggs' attendance at the DNC was thus inextricably connected to his own election goals and to the election goals of the Democratic Party. National attention and the media focused on the Democratic Party's effort to achieve those goals for itself and its officeholders. Diggs participated in that effort. His attendance at the DNC thrust his own reelection campaign and political career into national attention. Clearly, his attendance was more directly related to his own personal political goals and to the goals of his party than it was to the goals of his constituents. We conclude, therefore, that the expenses that Diggs incurred while attending the Democratic National Convention were not so directly connected with his trade or business as a legislator as to qualify for a § 162 deduction.

[C]—Lobbying

In 1962, Congress decided that some *legislative* lobbying expenses should be deductible, if they were otherwise deductible expenses. Then, the 1993 tax law reversed course. *First*, it explicitly reinstated the pre-1962 prohibition on the deduction of expenses for legislative lobbying. *§ 162(e)(1)(A)*. *Second*, it codified the nondeductibility of expenses for grass roots lobbying and for participating in a campaign for or against a candidate. *§ 162(e)(1)(B),(C)*.

Third, it added to the list of nondeductible lobbying expenses amounts paid to communicate with the President, Vice President and certain specified high executive officials in an attempt to influence *their official actions*.

Previously, all "executive" lobbying expenses were deductible. *§ 162(e)(1)(D),(5).*

The rules about lobbying expenses related to executive officials and other administrators are now quite complex. (i) Payments to *all* such officials to influence their participation in the legislative process are not deductible under the *§ 162(e)(1)(A)* prohibition. (ii) Payments to the President, Vice President, and certain high officials to influence *their official actions* are not deductible, as noted above. (iii) Payments to other executive and administrative officials to influence their *official administrative (not legislative) actions* continue to be subject to the regular deduction rules and are not disallowed by *§ 162(e)(1).*

The statute explicitly *dis*allows a business deduction for the percentage of dues paid to tax exempt organizations (such as trade associations and unions), which the organization notifies the taxpayer are allocable to nondeductible political expenses. *§ 162(e)(3).* The dues are nonetheless deductible if the organization pays a "proxy" tax on its political expenses in lieu of providing notice to the dues-paying members. *§ 6033(e)(2).*

The pre-1993 rules permitting a deduction for business-related legislative lobbying survive in one situation. The statute still allows a deduction for expenses directly connected to appearances and communications with a local council or similar body regarding legislation or proposed legislation of direct interest to the taxpayer and for communications with organizations of which the taxpayer is a member regarding such legislation. *§ 162(e)(2).* The reason is that local legislation is often hard to distinguish from administrative rulemaking, and expenses to seek administrative rules are usually deductible.

Lobbyists themselves can take business deductions for engaging in the business of lobbying. *§ 162(e)(5)(A).* Payments to the lobbyist for such activities are subject to the *§ 162(e)(1)* rules disallowing deductions.

What is legislative lobbying? The statute disallows deductions for influencing legislation, defined as "any attempt to influence any legislation through communication with any member or employee of a legislative body. . . *162(e)(1),(4)(A).* Recent regulations (*Treas. Reg. § 1.162–29*) adopt an expansive definition of "influencing legislation." They define "influencing legislation" to mean "[a]ny attempt to influence any legislation through a lobbying communication" and define "lobbying communication" to be a communication which "[r]efers to specific legislation and reflects a view on that legislation." *Treas. Reg. § 1.162-29(b)(1,3)*. The Regulation defines "specific legislation" to include "a specific legislative proposal that has not been introduced in a legislative body." *Treas. Reg. § 1.162-29(b)(5).*

In accordance with common practice, the Treasury issued proposed regulations for public commentary before issuing final regulations. And then, when the final regulations were published, the government provided an explanation of why it did or did not adopt the public's suggestions. Here are some excerpts from the government's explanation accompanying the final regulations and from the regulations themselves.

T.D. 8602, 60 FED. REG. 37568

July 21, 1995

The proposed regulations provide that a lobbying communication is any communication that (1) refers to specific legislation and reflects a view on that legislation, or (2) clarifies, amplifies, modifies, or provides support for views reflected in a prior lobbying communication. The proposed regulations provide that the term specific legislation includes both legislation that has already been introduced in a legislative body and a specific legislative proposal that the taxpayer either supports or opposes.

Several commentators stated that the phrase "reflects a view" should be defined to mean an explicit statement of support or opposition to legislative action. Some commentators also suggested that the regulations should make clear that a taxpayer is not reflecting a view on specific legislation if it presents a balanced analysis of the merits and defects of the legislation.

The final regulations do not adopt either of these recommendations. A taxpayer can reflect a view on specific legislation without specifically stating that it supports or opposes that legislation. Thus, as illustrated in section 1.162-29(b)(2), Example 8, a taxpayer reflects a view on specific legislation even if the taxpayer does not explicitly state its support for, or opposition to, action by a legislative body. Moreover, a taxpayer's balanced or technical analysis of legislation reflects a view on some aspect of the legislation and, thus, is a lobbying communication.

The proposed regulations do not contain a definition of the term "specific legislative proposal," but do contain several examples to illustrate the scope of the term. For instance, in Example 5 of section 1.162-29(b)(2) of the proposed regulations, a taxpayer prepares a paper indicating that increased savings and local investment will spur the state economy. The taxpayer forwards a summary of the paper to legislators with a cover letter that states, in part:

> You must take action to improve the availability of new capital in the state.

The example concludes that the taxpayer has not made a lobbying communication because neither the summary nor the cover letter refers to a specific legislative proposal.

In Example 6 of that section, a taxpayer prepares a paper concerning the benefits of lowering the capital gains tax rate. The taxpayer forwards a summary of the paper to its representative in Congress with a cover letter that states, in part:

> I urge you to support a reduction in the capital gains tax rate.

The example concludes that the taxpayer has made a lobbying communication because the communication refers to and reflects a view on a specific legislative proposal.

Numerous commentators stated that they do not perceive a distinction between the two examples. In addition, certain commentators requested that the term "specific legislative proposal" be defined.

Whether a communication refers to a specific legislative proposal may vary with the context. The communication in Example 5 is not sufficiently specific to be a specific legislative proposal, and no other facts and circumstances indicate the existence of a specific legislative proposal to which the communication refers. [Editor — Suppose there was a bill reducing tax on capital gains up for a vote the day after the legislator received this communication?] In Example 6, however, support is limited to a proposal for reduction of a particular tax rate. Although commentators suggested a number of definitions of the term "specific legislative proposal," none was entirely satisfactory in capturing the full range of communications referred to in section 162(e)(4)(A). Thus, the final regulations do not adopt these suggestions.

[D]—Charitable deductions

A complete picture of the impact of the tax law on political expenditures requires considering the rules dealing with charitable deductions. If expenditures which are not deductible business expenses *are* charitable deductions, the policy against deducting political expenditures would obviously be circumvented. The business deduction rules broke down into three major categories — election-related, legislative lobbying, and grass roots lobbying — and the same distinctions will be followed in discussing charitable deductions.

Election-related. *§ 170(c)(2)(D)* prohibits charitable deductions to organizations which participate in a campaign for or against a candidate.

Lobbying. Most tax-deductible organizations listed in *§ 170(c)* cannot engage in "substantial" lobbying (*see* the cross-reference in *§ 170(c)(2)(D)* to *§ 501(c)(3)*), and retain tax-deductibility status. The statutory phrase for "lobbying" is "attempting to influence legislation."

The "substantiality" test for lobbying produced a lot of criticism because a fixed dollar amount which was substantial for one organization might be insubstantial for another. Moreover, the government was reluctant to invoke the test because it was an all-or-nothing penalty. Too much political lobbying cost the organization its status as a tax-deductible organization. The statute was therefore amended to permit (but not require) public charities to elect to be subject to a 25% excise tax on "excess" expenditures to influence legislation. A separate rule taxes excess grass roots lobbying in particular. "Excess" lobbying expenditures are those which exceed a certain percentage of the organization's total expenditures. The percentage declines as the total expenditures by the organization increase, so that a smaller organization can spend a larger percentage of its total expenditures on political activity without incurring an excise tax. *§ 4911.*

If the charity elects to be subject to the excise tax, the "substantiality" test is not applied to determine whether the organization loses its tax-deductible status. Instead, that status is denied because of lobbying activities only if the lobbying expenditures exceed 150% of the amount above which an excise tax is imposed during a consecutive four-year period. *§ 501(h)*; *Treas. Reg. § 1.501(h)-3(b),(c)(7).*

Private foundations continue to be subject to the uncertainties of the "substantiality" test and are, in addition, subject to an excise tax on certain political expenditures. *§ 4945(d)(1),(2), § 4945(e).*

Churches cannot elect to be subject to the excise tax on excess lobbying expenditures. *§ 501(h)(3)(B),(5)(A).* Why not?

Charitable deductions for political expenditures? Do these rules about charitable deductions potentially allow taxpayers to deduct political expenditures, even though they would not be deductible business expenses? There must be some tax avoidance potential because the 1993 tax law prohibits a charitable deduction if a principal purpose of the contribution is to avoid taxes by obtaining a deduction for activities which would not have been deductible under *§ 162(e)(1)*, if the taxpayer had incurred the expenditures directly. *§ 170(f)(9).*

Can you think of ways that a charitable deduction might indirectly permit the deduction of political expenditures, absent the *§ 170(f)(9)* prohibition? Suppose a charitable organization incurs (i) legislative lobbying expenses, but not in excessive amounts, or (ii) lobbies high executive officials to influence their action.

Exemption for veterans' organization. Not every organization listed in *§ 170(c)* is prohibited from engaging in political activity. There is an exception for veterans organizations. *See § 170(c)(3).* In *Regan v. Taxation With Representation*, 461 U.S. 540 (1983), the Court upheld the special rule favoring lobbying by veterans' organizations, making the following points. First, Congress can legitimately favor veterans. Second, there is no indication that any other group was denied tax exemption for political activity because of its unpopular ideas.

Third, other groups could set up a separate *§ 501(c)(4)* tax exempt organization to carry on lobbying without losing *§ 501(c)(3)* status for its other activities. For example, it is a common practice for *§ 501(c)(3)/§ 170(c)* organizations to maintain separate sister organizations which lobby — *e.g.*, the NAACP and NAACP, Inc. Fund. Favorable *§ 501(c)(3)* tax-deductible status was not therefore conditioned on abandoning its First Amendment right to lobby through another related group.

Government discretion to identify "political" activity. Is there a risk that the government's discretion in identifying "impermissible" political behavior will discourage unobjectionable activity? In *Big Mama Rag, Inc. v. United States*, 631 F.2d 1030 (D.C. Cir. 1980), the court dealt with the Regulations requiring "advocacy" groups to present a "full and fair exposition of the pertinent facts," as a condition to receiving deductible contributions. Otherwise their actions would violate the prohibition on political activity. The court held that the definition of "advocacy" and a "full and fair exposition" were both so vague as to be unconstitutional. For example, there was a "full and fair exposition" if the organization allowed "an individual or the public to form an independent opinion or conclusion," but "mere presentation of unsupported opinion" did not meet the required standard. *Treas. Reg. § 1.501(c)(3)-1(d)(3).*

After the *Big Mama Rag* case, the IRS issued *Rev. Proc. 86–43*, 1986–2 C.B. 729, which explained in detail how the IRS would determine whether an advocacy group was too "political" for contributions to be charitable deductions. In *The Nationalist Movement v. Commissioner*, 102 T.C. 558 (1994), the court held that the Revenue Procedure "is not unconstitutionally vague or overbroad on its face, nor is it unconstitutional as applied. Its provisions are sufficiently understandable, specific, and objective both to preclude chilling of expression protected under the First Amendment and to minimize arbitrary or discriminatory application by the IRS. The revenue procedure focuses on the method rather than the content of the presentation. In contrast, it was the potential for discriminatory denials of tax exemption based on speech content that caused the Court of Appeals for the District of Columbia Circuit to hold that "the vagueness of the 'full and fair exposition' standard violates the First Amendment [in *Big Mama Rag., Inc. v. United States*]. Petitioner has not persuaded us that either the purpose or the effect of the revenue procedure is to suppress disfavored ideas."

Notice the dates of the *Big Mama Rag* and *Nationalist Movement* cases. Does the difference in the decisions suggest a shift away from suspicion of the government, as the Vietnam War fades from memory?

See also Rev. Rul. 72-512, 1972-2 C.B. 246; *Rev. Rul. 72-513*, 1972-2 C.B. 24, where the agency dealt with the effect on a university's tax-deductible status of certain activity. In one case, a political science class permitted two weeks of political campaigning by the students as part of the course syllabus. In the other, the school newspaper engaged in political editorializing adopted by its editorial board without university interference. In both instances, the tax-deductible status was not jeopardized by these political activities, but there were rumors that the IRS had raised an eyebrow at such activities before finally publishing the favorable rulings. You will recall that these rulings occurred during the Vietnam War. *See Center on Corp. Public Responsibility, Inc. v. Shultz*, 368 F. Supp. 863, 867 (D.D.C. 1973).

Defining "grass roots" lobbying. Consider whether the definition of "grass roots" lobbying is the same for *§ 162* and *§ 170*. Recent Regulations seem lenient to the taxpayer in the charitable deduction context. *Treas. Reg. § 56.4911-2(b)(2)*; *see* 48 Tax Notes 1305 (1990). "Grass roots lobbying," in the charity context, must express a view about specific legislation (including legislative proposals) and encourage action by the recipient of the communication. Thus, an advertisement taking a position on proposed legislation increasing the tax on social security benefits, without encouraging action, would *not* be grass roots lobbying. Encouraging action is defined as one of the following four steps: telling people to contact legislators; giving a legislator's address or phone contact; providing a petition, tear-off card or the like to reach a legislator; or identifying the recipient's representative or legislators who are opposed, undecided, or hold membership on a relevant committee.

Nonpartisan positions (which contain a full and fair exposition of facts to enable an independent conclusion) are not grass roots lobbying, even if they advocate a position on specific legislation, as long as none of the first three methods of encouraging action are used (identifying certain legislators is allowed for nonpartisan positions). *Treas. Reg. § 56.4911-2(c)(1)*.

There is also a rebuttable presumption that advertising about the general subject of legislation in the mass media two weeks before a vote on highly publicized legislation will, under certain circumstances, be grass roots lobbying.

The definition of "grass roots" lobbying under *§ 162* seems less favorable to the taxpayer than under the rules applicable to charities. *Prop. Reg. § 1.162-20(c)(4)(iii) (example 2)* states that a newspaper ad calling for state tax incentives is grass roots lobbying, because the ad is aimed at individuals in their capacity as voters, even though the ad does *not* encourage action by the reader or listener.

[E]—Taxing political recipients and organizations

Gifts to political campaign. Gifts to a politician or her campaign are not taxable to the recipient unless converted to personal (nonpolitical) use. *Rev. Rul. 75-103*, 1975-1 C.B. 17. This rule developed as a gloss on the definition of *§ 61* income. Surely, the gifts are not excluded under *§ 102*; there is not enough "detached and disinterested generosity." But the result makes sense, doesn't it? One tax is imposed on the contributions — on the donor, as in the case of intrafamily gifts.

Taxpayers who transfer appreciated property to a political organization must pay tax on the appreciation at the time of the contribution. *§ 84*. This differs from the intrafamily gift, where the donee is taxed on appreciated gain.

Taxing political organizations. Political organizations are not taxed on contributions they receive, as long as the contributions are devoted to the political selection process. The organizations are taxed, however, on income from investing contributions (such as interest or dividends). *§ 527*. A recent Senate bill proposed taxing political organizations on campaign contributions if they refused to abide by campaign spending limits. Is that proposal constitutional?

[F]—Payments relating to House of Representatives reprimand

Suppose the Speaker of the House is reprimanded by the House for having improperly used a class taught at a tax exempt university for political campaign purposes and not having properly divulged information about this activity to congressional investigators. In this connection, the Speaker agrees to pay the government $300,000. This amount is designated in the settlement with the House (perhaps on advice of tax counsel) as a payment which compensates the government for its investigation costs.

Assume first that the Speaker pays this amount out of his own resources. (1) Is it a nondeductible fine? (2) Even if it is not a fine, does its *origin* in campaign activity render it nondeductible under the same principle which disallows deductions for campaign expenditures?

Assume now that these payments are made by the Speaker's campaign organization. These organizations do not pay tax (nor is the candidate taxed) on contributions to the campaign organization as long as they are used in the political selection process. If they were used for the candidate's personal purposes (*e.g.*, for a vacation), he or she would have to pay tax on such amounts. Would payment of the $300,000 amount by the campaign organization be taxable to the Speaker? (1) Doesn't the same argument which *disallows* the deduction if the amount comes out of the Speaker's own pocket (that it is campaign related) prevent taxing the Speaker if it is paid by the campaign organization, on the ground that it is related to the political selection process? (2) If the amount is considered a "fine," do the public policy implications make it taxable to the Speaker, even though paid by the campaign organization?

§ 14.04 EXPENSES TO PRODUCE TAX-EXEMPT INCOME

[A]—General principle

An otherwise deductible expense is often not deductible if it is incurred to produce tax exempt income. This rule makes sense on the theory that the real purpose of the income exemption is to exclude the *net* income produced by the exempt activity from the tax base. If expenses to produce tax exempt income were deductible, the exemption would also permit a taxpayer to shelter nonexempt income from tax. For example, if the taxpayer spent $20 to earn $100 of tax-exempt income, and also had $20 of wages, his taxable income should be $20, not zero. Disallowing the expense deduction assures that result.

The most common example of tax-exempt income is interest on state and local bonds (*§ 103*), but there are other examples: *e.g.*, certain foreign personal service income (*§ 911*); a portion of scholarships (*§ 117*); recoveries for personal injuries (*§ 104(a)(2)*); parsonage allowances (*§ 107*).

The most important section dealing with expenses related to tax exempt income is *§ 265*. *§ 265(a)(1)* prohibits all deductions "allocable" to all categories of exempt income, *except* exempt interest. Under that section, if an expense is "allocable to both a class of nonexempt income and a class of exempt income, a reasonable proportion thereof determined in the light of all the facts and circumstances in each case shall be allocated to each." *Treas. Reg. § 1.265-1(c)*. For example, in *Rev. Rul. 85-98*, 1985-2 C.B. 51, litigation expenses were deductible only to the extent allocable to taxable punitive damages, not personal injury recoveries exempt under *§ 104*.

When the exempt income is interest, however, *§ 265(a)(1)* only forbids the deduction of *§ 212* expenses. The major impact of this exception is that the deduction of business expenses is not prohibited by *§ 265(a)(1)* when they are incurred to produce tax-exempt interest income. Banks obviously benefit from this provision.

There is, however, another provision dealing with tax-exempt interest income. *§ 265(a)(2)* prohibits the deduction of *interest* expenses to earn tax-exempt interest. The application of *§ 265(a)(2)* is discussed in the next chapter.

Question. Does the following decision make any sense and, if not, how would you write a judicial opinion to reach a contrary result? A taxpayer buys a depreciable interest in an intangible asset, specifically a life estate interest in a trust. The trust pays out tax-exempt interest. The taxpayer claims depreciation deductions under *§ 167(a)(2)*, because a life estate is a depreciable asset, and the depreciation expense is related to the production of income. The government argued that the depreciation expense was essentially a *§ 212* expense to produce tax-exempt interest, whose deduction was disallowed by *§ 265(a)(1)*. *Manufacturers Hanover Trust Co. v. Commissioner*, 431 F.2d 664 (2d Cir. 1970) held for the taxpayer and allowed the deduction.

§ 264(a)(1). Life insurance premiums paid by a business to cover the lives of key employees, with the proceeds payable to the business (not the employee's family), would be deductible expenses under *§ 162*. The insurance proceeds are, however, tax exempt under *§ 101*. To prevent the double benefit, *§ 264(a)(1)* disallows the deduction of such premiums.

[B]—Exempt reimbursements

MANOCCHIO v. COMMISSIONER

78 T.C. 989 (1982)

DAWSON, JUDGE:

Petitioner is a veteran of the U.S. Air Force. During 1977, he was employed as an airline pilot with Hughes Air West. He attended flight-training classes approved by the Veterans' Administration (VA) at National Jet Industries in Santa Ana, Calif., from June 5, 1977, to June 9, 1977, and again from August 24, 1977, to August 25, 1977. The classes cost a total of $4,162 and maintained and improved skills required in petitioner's trade or business.

As a veteran, petitioner was eligible for an educational assistance allowance from the VA pursuant to 38 U.S.C. § 1677 (1976), equal to 90 percent of the costs incurred. The VA required a certification of completed training each month signed by both a school official and the petitioner before it would release payment checks. Consequently, at the end of each month in which petitioner received qualified instruction, National Jet Industries mailed a certification of flight training to the VA showing the total amount billed to his account. The VA then mailed petitioner a check for 90 percent of the amount specified, which he then endorsed over to the flight school. He paid the remaining 10 percent by personal check.

During 1977, petitioner received $3,742.88 from the VA as a direct reimbursement of his flight-training expenses. On his 1977 Federal income tax return, he excluded the VA payments from income pursuant to 38 U.S.C. § 3101(a) (1976). He also claimed a deduction of [$4,162]. . . .

It is respondent's position that the portion of the flight-training expenses reimbursed by the VA is allocable to a class of tax-exempt income and, therefore, nondeductible under § 265. . . .

1. Applicability of Section 265

We agree with respondent that § 265 bars the deduction of the reimbursed expenses. . . . Under this provision, an amount cannot be deducted if it is "allocable to" a class of tax-exempt income other than interest. . . . [T]he reimbursement received by petitioner clearly qualifies as a class of exempt income for purposes of § 265. The only issue, then, is whether the educational costs are allocable to the reimbursement.

Petitioner argues that the expenses are not allocable to the reimbursement, but rather to the income derived from his employment as a pilot. More specifically, his position is that § 265(1) was intended to apply only to expenses incurred in the production of exempt income, and should not be construed to apply to expenses which were merely paid out of exempt income. In support, he quotes from the committee reports accompanying § 24(a)(5) of the Revenue Act of 1934, ch. 277, 48 Stat. 680, 691 (the predecessor of § 265), which indicate that the purpose of the statute is to disallow deductions allocable "to the production" of exempt income.

Unquestionably, a principal target of the legislation was expenses incurred in connection with an ongoing trade or business or investment activity, the conduct of which generates exempt income. The committee reports give as examples expenses incurred in earning interest on State securities, salaries by State employees, and income from leases of State school property. Nevertheless, we do not infer from these examples that Congress intended to limit the application of the statute to such situations and preclude its application under the circumstances presented in this case. The words it selected to describe the necessary relationship between the expense and exempt income — "allocable to" — do not carry an inherently restrictive connotation. Certainly, if Congress had wanted to confine the reach of the statute to the standard situations referred to in the committee reports, it could have easily done so by using more precise definitional language. It did not take a narrow approach, however, and we think the language employed is broad enough, particularly when construed in light of the policy behind the statute, to embrace the reimbursement situation where, but for the expense, there would simply be no exempt income. The right to reimbursement for the flight-training expenses arises only when the VA receives a certification from the flight school, signed by both the veteran and a school official, of the actual training received by the veteran during the month and the cost of such training. The training allowance is then computed at 90 percent of the certified cost. Thus, there is a fundamental nexus between the reimbursement income and the expense which, in our opinion, falls within the scope of any reasonable interpretation of the "allocable to" requirement.

We agree with petitioner that if the income derived from his employment as a commercial pilot were tax-exempt, and his educational expenses were not reimbursed by the VA, the flight-training deduction would be allocable to such income for purposes of § 265(1). We do not agree, however, that the deduction is permanently locked into his employment income where the expenses are also subject to exempt reimbursement. In that situation, we think the proximate one-for-one relationship between the reimbursement and the deduction overrides the underlying relationship between the deduction and the employment income, leaving the deduction "directly allocable," as that term is used in § 1.265-1(c), Income Tax Regs., solely to the reimbursement and to no other class of income. . . .

. . . Although it is true that petitioner is left in the identical situation, from the standpoint of tax consequences, as if he had received a taxable reimbursement, in which case section 265 would not bar his deduction, there will obviously be instances where the veteran's flight-training expenses will be nondeductible irrespective of section 265. For example, the expenses might not satisfy the conditions for deductibility imposed by § 1.162-5, Income Tax Regs., or, assuming they do, the veteran might not have sufficient itemized deductions to take advantage of the deduction. In either of these situations, he would realize additional taxable income in the absence of the exemption provision.

In short, there is nothing in the legislative history of the relevant veterans' provisions to suggest that Congress intended for a veteran to have both an exemption and a tax deduction where his reimbursed flight-training expenses otherwise qualify as deductible business-related education. On the other hand, the legislative purpose behind § 265 is abundantly clear: Congress sought to prevent taxpayers from reaping a double tax benefit by using expenses attributable to tax-exempt income to offset other sources of taxable income. This is precisely what petitioner is attempting to do here, and in our judgment, the application of § 265(1) to disallow the reimbursed portion of the flight-training expense deduction is both reasonable and equitable.

The problem this case raises is whether the exemption of the reimbursement from income is meant to allow the taxpayer both an exclusion of the reimbursement and a deduction of the expense. Before you conclude too quickly that the answer must be "no," remember that a gift from a parent could be used to incur deductible business expenses. To deny the deduction would deny the exclusion of the gift. The same reasoning applies to tax-exempt interest income used to finance otherwise deductible expenses.

Thus, a taxpayer with $100 exempt interest income, $100 wages, and $100 of deductible expenses related to wages, has $100 available for personal consumption, none of which should be taxable. If the $100 deduction were disallowed, taxable income would be $100 and the exemption for interest would, in effect, be denied.

Why isn't an exempt reimbursement for veterans' education like an exempt gift or exempt interest income? The court must be concluding that it would stretch legislative intent too far in the case of veterans' benefits to provide both an exclusion and a deduction. It interprets the exclusion of in-kind educational benefits to be an assurance of a tax-free educational benefit for all recipients, whether or not the expenses would be deductible if incurred out of the taxpayer's own pocket.

It is a little strained to reach that result through *§ 265(a)(1)*, however, because that section does not appear to prohibit deductions of an expenditure based on the fact that the expenditure is financed by tax-exempt in-kind benefits earmarked for the expenditure. The focus of *§ 265(a)(1)* is on the exempt nature of the income, in connection with which the taxpayer incurs a separate expenditure, like attorney's fees to collect tax-exempt personal injury recoveries. Still, perhaps an interpretation of *§ 265(a)(1)* to disallow a double benefit is not too strained, if the result is satisfactory. The deeper question is where the court gets its understanding of legislative intent. The court in *Manocchio* says there was nothing in the legislative history to suggest allowing a double benefit (exclusion and deduction), but was there anything in the legislative history to deny it?

This appears to be another *Haverly*-type problem (which involved charitable gifts funded by tax-exempt income), where the issue was whether to combine an exclusion from tax with a later deduction. There is no way to resolve this issue without asking whether the double benefit makes sense as a matter of statutory interpretation.

[C]—"Allocable" to exempt income

HUGHES v. COMMISSIONER

65 T.C. 566 (1975)

STERRETT, JUDGE: . . .

[Editor — In this case, the taxpayer earned foreign personal services income, which was exempt under § 911. The issue was whether some of the petitioner's moving expenses, otherwise deductible under § 217, must be disallowed because they are "properly allocable to or chargeable against" exempt income, earned at the new foreign principal place of employment.]

Petitioner's primary argument is that his moving expenses are deductible in full because they are personal rather than business expenses, and as such they are not "properly allocable to or chargeable against" his income exempted from tax under § 911(a). Petitioner in support of his position points to several elements included in the moving expense deduction which he claims are purely personal. Respondent's answer is that, although petitioner's moving expenses meet the requirements of § 217, the deduction is subject to the allocation provisions of § 911(a).

Before their deductibility was authorized by statute, moving expenses were considered by this Court to be nondeductible personal expenses. Section 217 now provides for their deductibility but only when they are incurred in connection with the commencement of work at a new principal place of employment. § 217. Such expenses then to be deductible must have a definite relationship to the production of gross income. It is in those situations where the relationship does not exist that moving expenses are purely personal and nondeductible.

We believe that this analysis is supported by the legislative history that accompanied the adoption of § 217. Before the enactment of § 217, an existing employee reimbursed for his moving expenses was not required to include such sum in his gross income because such expenses were considered to have been incurred "in the interest of the employer." The Congress believed that this discriminated against new employees and employees who were not reimbursed. One of the purposes of § 217 then was to equalize this latter group with those employees who were reimbursed. This appears to be a recognition that moving expenses could be incurred in the "interest of the employee" and his trade or business. . . .

Furthermore, Congress placed moving expenses in the category of items deductible from gross income to reach adjusted gross income, giving further evidence of their view that such an expense is income-related.

[Editor — From 1986 to 1993, moving expenses were itemized deductions. If the case had come up then, should the result have been different?]

Dawson, C.J., dissenting:

. . . Underlying [§ 217] was a congressional desire to remove a deterrent to labor mobility, moving expenses, which would in turn assist in reducing local structural unemployment. H. Rept. No. 749, 88th Cong., 1st Sess. (1963), 1964-1 C.B. (Part 2) 125, 183. Congress, not wanting to allow such a deduction to any taxpayer electing to move, limited this personal expense deduction to those moving for the purpose of living near their place of employment. . . .

. . . I think § 217 provides qualifying taxpayers with a deduction for personal expenses which are not related to the income from a trade or business, despite the language in § 217 which conditions its benefits on postmove employment. This language was included only to limit the section's coverage to taxpayers who are a part of the work force after their move. The overriding concern of Congress was to remove a hindrance to labor mobility. This conclusion does nothing to contravene the operation of § 911, which was enacted to promote foreign trade by encouraging American businessmen to venture overseas and sell American-made products. Any removal of a hindrance to mobility should complement § 911.

. . .

§ 14.05 DISALLOWING DEDUCTION INSTEAD OF TAXING INCOME RECIPIENT

Is a deduction for a payment ever disallowed as an *indirect* way of taxing the pay*ee*? Sometimes an income recipient is so unlikely to report income and the agency so despairs of enforcing the law that the statute disallows the payor's deduction. The employer's loss of a deduction for certain employer reimbursed entertainment expenses (*§ 274(e)(3)*) can be explained on this ground.

Excess employee achievement awards are another example. No deduction is allowed for the cost of these awards if they exceed a certain ceiling. *§ 274(j)*. Awards which exceed that ceiling are also includible in the employee's income, *§ 74(c)*, but the employee is not likely to report excess awards. The statute therefore disallows the employer-payor's deduction.

The intuition behind this approach is as follows.

(1) Assume that the payor is in the 30% tax bracket and has set aside $100 for a business purpose, as long as the payment is deductible. This $100 costs the payor $70 *after*-tax.

(2). If the $100 payment is taxable to the payee, who is also in the 30% bracket, the payee will have $70 after tax.

(3) Now assume that the payee will not report the income, pocketing the full $100.

(4) If you disallow the payor's deduction, what economic decision will the payor make. That same $100, which previously had a $70 after tax cost to the payor, now costs the payor $100 *after*-tax because there is no deduction. Consequently, the payor will pay only $70 to the payee.

(5) Now, the government can let the payee conceal the income. The government has its $30 (no payor deduction) and the payee has only $70 *after* (not paying) tax.

There is only one thing wrong with this scenario. The payor may be in a lower tax bracket than the payee, in which case disallowing the payor's deduction will not make up for the payee's not paying tax. Similarly, tax exempt employers are not hurt when deductions are disallowed.

Deductible "gifts"? Here is another more complex example. A wholesaler who sells home appliances wants to show its gratitude to a longtime retail purchaser. To that end, it makes a "gift" of a large sum of money around Christmas to the retailer. The money is probably not a gift excluded under *§ 102* (no detached and disinterested generosity), but the recipient is unlikely to report it. If detected, the recipient will claim it is a gift.

§ 274(b)(1) disallows a deduction for payments excluded from the recipient's income solely on the ground that it is a gift. The donor and donee are now in a bind. If the donee does not report the income, claiming it is a gift, that undermines the don*or*'s deduction. If the donor takes the deduction, it must justify its claim on the ground that the payment was not a gift, which undermines the don*ee*'s exclusion. Armed with *§ 274(b)* and (optimistically?) with knowledge of the payment, the government will tax both parties (disallow the deduction and include the money in the payee's income) and let them fight it out.

Question. Would you favor using this approach (that is, disallowing a payor's deduction) for other likely-to-be-excluded income? What about an employee's use of employer-financed frequent flyer awards? What deductible employer payment would you disallow?

CHAPTER 15

LIMITING THE INTEREST DEDUCTION

§ 15.01 PERSONAL LOANS

[A]—Background

§ 163(a) states that interest is deductible. This provision was included in the original Income Tax Act of 1913 without explanation in the legislative history. The subsection's scope is very broad. It applies to interest on loans for personal use, whether for current consumption (like a vacation) or for personal assets (like a home or car), and for income-producing purposes, even if the loan is used to make a capital expenditure. Over the years limitations have been placed on the interest deduction. We have already encountered one — requiring most prepaid interest to be capitalized and later amortized (*§ 461(g)*).

The deduction of interest on loans incurred for personal purposes is usually said to be a tax expenditure, but there is a counter argument. Interest is unavailable to the taxpayer for consumption or savings. Admittedly, the interest payment enables the taxpayer to get the loan and thereby to accelerate personal consumption. But accelerating the date of personal consumption is not itself personal consumption. Indeed, if it were, loans themselves would be taxable. It is sufficient to tax the income earned at a later date to repay the loan.

[B]—Loans to buy personal assets

The above comments justifying the deduction of personal interest usually leave people unconvinced, but that is probably because there is another reason to be concerned about the interest deduction. The loan is often used to acquire personal use assets, like a home, which produces tax-exempt income in the form of the property's rental value. The interest expense is equal to some portion of that exempt income and the uneasiness about the interest deduction arises from uneasiness about this exemption. The following paragraphs explain this problem.

Renter. The taxpayer who rents his home does so out of *after-tax* income. The rent covers the landlord's costs, including: depreciation on the building, interest on any loan the landlord incurred for construction or acquisition of the building, and profit for the landlord. Assume that the rental amount is $10,000.

Home owners who do *not* borrow. Someone who has the wealth to invest in a home enjoys a return on the investment, much like a landlord. Assume that the rental value of the home is $10,000, to parallel the renter. That enjoyment is personal consumption, but is any of it included in income? Most of it is not. Some of the $10,000 is taxed indirectly, because it includes nondeductible depreciation (assume it is $4,000). What about the $10,000 rental value in excess of depreciation — $6,000 in the example? The investor does not have to include that amount in income. It is "imputed income," which is not considered "realized" *§ 61* income. Some of the $10,000 rental value is therefore not taxed.

Home owners who *do* borrow. Now assume that the investor borrows some of the money to buy the home, producing the same total $10,000 rental value. In addition to the $4,000 depreciation, the owner pays $4,500 interest. If you decide that the rental value ought to be taxed to the maximum amount possible, you could disallow the interest deduction. Then at least $8,500 of the $10,000 rental value would be taxed ($4,000 depreciation, plus $4,500 interest; the $1,500 "profit" would *not* be taxed). If you think renters get a bum deal in the tax law, because they finance personal consumption out of after-tax income, you can get closer to equal treatment of renters and borrowers by disallowing the deduction of interest incurred to finance the purchase of personal use assets.

Dilemma. Disallowing the interest deduction brings borrowers closer to renters, but introduces another inequity into the tax law. The wealthy investor who does not borrow, and the borrower who has paid off the loan, do not pay tax on the rental value in excess of depreciation. There is nothing you can do about this dilemma, unless you give renters a deduction for a portion of rent, and let borrowers deduct the interest. Barring that, you must choose which inequity to accept. Current law, as you will see, allows a deduction for most home loan interest, allowing the borrower to more closely approximate the nonborrowing investor. As we become a nation of renters, this may change and we may disallow the interest deduction to bring the borrower closer to the renter.

[C]—Tax Reform Act of 1986

Prior to the Tax Reform Act of 1986, interest on personal loans was deductible. That has changed. Now only interest on *some* personal loans is deductible. *§ 163(h)*. Notice that the statutory definition of nondeductible personal interest is *all* interest, except that specifically listed. This means, for example, that interest on federal income tax underpayments is *not* deductible.

Qualified residence interest. *§ 163(h)(2)(D)* allows a deduction for "qualified residence interest." The definition applies to certain loans related to the principal residence and one other residence, if the debt is secured by the residence. This means that vacation home loans, dear to the real estate industry, can qualify. They are, however, a potential target for elimination; a move to prevent boats from being a residence failed in 1988.

There are two categories of eligible loans. (1) Acquisition indebtedness covers acquiring, constructing, or substantially improving the residence. Eligible acquisition indebtedness cannot exceed $1 million. The acquisition debt on which the interest is deductible is reduced as the loan is paid off. (2) Interest on home equity indebtedness is the other category of qualified residence interest. It equals the value of a qualified residence minus unpaid acquisition indebtedness. The home equity loan can be used for any purpose, including a personal purpose. The maximum amount of home equity loans on which interest is deductible is $100,000. *§ 163(h)(3),(4).*

For example, assume a purchaser buys a home for $500,000, with a $400,000 debt, and pays off $50,000 of the debt. The value of the home goes up to $575,000. The interest on the acquisition loan (which is $350,000 after paying off $50,000 of debt) is deductible. Home equity equals $575,000 minus $350,000, or $225,000, but is subject to the $100,000 ceiling. The taxpayer could therefore borrow up to $100,000 secured by a second mortgage on the home to buy a car for personal use, and deduct the interest.

Qualified residence interest is an itemized deduction, not subject to the 2% floor on miscellaneous deductions.

Question. Can a child borrow money from a parent, pledging the home as security for the loan, and deduct the interest?

Student loans. The 1997 Tax Act adds another tax break for education — an above-the-line deduction for interest on certain "qualified" higher education loans. *§ 221.*

The deduction is available on loans to pay for the "qualified" education expenses of the taxpayer, the taxpayer's spouse, or the taxpayer's dependent. Qualified expenses are defined more broadly than for the Hope and Lifetime credits (*see* § 13.04[C], *supra*); they include tuition, room and board, and books and supplies. The expenses must be paid within a reasonable time before or after the debt is incurred.

The maximum interest deduction is $1,000, rising in increments to $2,500 by 2001. Notice the "backloading" of the revenue loss in the 1997 Tax Act, so as to reduce the chances of increasing the budget deficit until later years. Only the first 60 months of interest payments are eligible for the deduction.

The deduction is phased-out (adding yet another phantom tax rate) as adjusted gross income (with modifications) rises above a threshold ($40,000 for a single taxpayer and $60,000 for a married couple filing a joint return). The phase-out formula reduces the otherwise deductible amount by:

$$\frac{\text{AGI minus threshold amount}}{\$15{,}000} \times \text{ the deductible amount (\$1000 in 1998)}$$

What is the phantom rate produced by this phase-out formula?

§ 15.02 INTEREST EXPENSE TO EARN TAX-EXEMPT INTEREST

Taxpayers often borrow to invest in many types of tax-exempt activities, not just to acquire personal use assets. One such purpose is to "purchase or carry" tax-exempt bonds. *§ 265(a)(2)* addresses these situations. The first problem is "tracing" — is the loan traceable to the purchasing or carrying of tax-exempt bonds? The second problem, assuming that the loan is so traced, is to decide how much interest should be disallowed. *Rev. Proc. 72-18*, *infra*, deals with both these issues. The rules discussed in the Revenue Procedure are applied *before* the rules dealing with personal interest under *§ 163(h)*. In other words, first you decide if the deduction of any interest is disallowed under *§ 265(a)(2)*. If *§ 265(a)(2)* does not disallow the deduction, then go to *§ 163(h)* to see whether that section disallows the deduction.

[A]—*§ 265(a)(2)*

§ 265(a)(2) prevents the deduction of "interest on indebtedness incurred or continued to carry or purchase obligations the interest on which is wholly tax-exempt." This requires tracing the loan proceeds to the tax-exempt bonds.

The effect of *§ 265(a)(2)* is to discriminate between borrowers and investors who use their own funds. The investor who uses his own funds can sell a taxable investment (*e.g.*, stock), giving up the taxable dividend, and buy a tax-exempt bond, thereby avoiding tax. The borrower, who pays interest, also forgoes use of a taxable dividend (in the amount equal to the interest payment). But the borrower does not avoid tax, because the interest to acquire the tax-exempt bond is not deductible. *Denman v. Slayton*, 282 U.S. 514 (1931), held that such discrimination was constitutional.

REV. PROC. 72-18, 1972-1 C.B. 740

SECTION 1. PURPOSE.

The purpose of this Revenue Procedure is to set forth guidelines for taxpayers and field offices of the Internal Revenue Service for the application of section 265(2) of the Internal Revenue Code of 1954 [Editor — now *§ 265(a)(2)*] to certain taxpayers holding state and local obligations the interest on which is wholly exempt from Federal income tax. . . .

SEC. 3. GENERAL RULES.

.01 Section 265(2) of the Code is only applicable where the indebtedness is incurred or continued for the purpose of purchasing or carrying tax-exempt securities. Accordingly, the application of section 265(2) of the Code requires a determination, based on all the facts and circumstances, as to the taxpayer's purpose in incurring or continuing each item of indebtedness. Such purpose may, however, be established either by direct evidence or by circumstantial evidence.

.02 Direct evidence of a purpose to purchase tax-exempt obligations exists where the proceeds of indebtedness are used for, and are directly traceable to, the purchase of tax-exempt obligations. Section 265(2) does not apply, however, where proceeds of a bona fide business indebtedness are temporarily invested in tax-exempt obligations. . . .

.03 Direct evidence of a purpose to carry tax-exempt obligations exists where tax-exempt obligations are used as collateral for indebtedness. "[O]ne who borrows to buy tax-exempts and one who borrows against tax-exempts already owned are in virtually the same economic position. Section 265(2) makes no distinction between them." *Wisconsin Cheeseman v. United States*, 338 F.2d 420, at 422 (1968).

.04 In the absence of direct evidence linking indebtedness with the purchase or carrying of tax-exempt obligations as illustrated in paragraphs.02 and.03 above, section 265(2) of the Code will apply only if the totality of facts and circumstances supports a reasonable inference that the purpose to purchase or carry tax-exempt obligations exists. Stated alternatively, section 265(2) will apply only where the totality of facts and circumstances establishes a "sufficiently direct relationship" between the borrowing and the investment in tax-exempt obligations. *See Wisconsin Cheeseman*, 388 F.2d 420, at 422. The guidelines set forth in section[] 4 . . . shall be applied to determine whether such a relationship exists.

.05 Generally, where a taxpayer's investment in tax-exempt obligations is insubstantial, the purpose to purchase or carry tax-exempt obligations will not ordinarily be inferred in the absence of direct evidence as set forth in sections 3.02 and 3.03. In the case of an individual, investment in tax-exempt obligations shall be presumed insubstantial only where during the taxable year the average amount of the tax-exempt obligations (valued at their adjusted basis) does not exceed 2 percent of the average adjusted basis of his portfolio investments (as defined in section 4.04) and any assets held in the active conduct of a trade or business. . . .

SEC. 4. GUIDELINES FOR INDIVIDUALS.

.01 In the absence of direct evidence of the purpose to purchase or carry tax-exempt obligations (as set forth in sections 3.02 and 3.03), the rules set forth in this section shall apply.

.02 An individual taxpayer may incur a variety of indebtedness of a personal nature, ranging from short-term credit for purchases of goods and services for personal consumption to a mortgage incurred to purchase or improve a residence or other real property which is held for personal use. Generally, section 265(2) of the Code will not apply to indebtedness of this type, because the purpose to purchase or carry tax-exempt obligations cannot reasonably be inferred where a personal purpose unrelated to the tax-exempt obligations ordinarily dominates the transaction. For example, section 265(2) of the Code generally will not apply to an individual who holds salable municipal bonds and takes out a mortgage to buy a residence instead of selling his municipal bonds to finance the purchase price. Under such circumstances the purpose of incurring the indebtedness is so directly related to the personal purpose of acquiring a residence that no sufficiently direct relationship between the borrowing and the investment in tax-exempt obligations may reasonably be inferred.

.03 The purpose to purchase or carry tax-exempt obligations generally does not exist with respect to indebtedness incurred or continued by an individual in connection with the active conduct of trade or business (other than a dealer in tax-exempt obligations) unless it is determined that the borrowing was in excess of business needs. However, there is a rebuttable presumption that the purpose to carry tax-exempt obligations exists where the taxpayer reasonably could have foreseen at the time of purchasing the tax-exempt obligations that indebtedness probably would have to be incurred to meet future economic needs of the business of an ordinary, recurrent variety. *See Wisconsin Cheeseman v. United States*, 388 F.2d 420, at 422. The presumption may be rebutted, however, if the taxpayer demonstrates that business reasons, unrelated to the purchase or carrying of tax-exempt obligations, dominated the transaction.

.04 Generally, a purpose to carry tax-exempt obligations will be inferred, unless rebutted by other evidence, wherever the taxpayer has outstanding indebtedness which is not directly connected with personal expenditures (*see* section 4.02) and is not incurred or continued in connection with the active conduct of a trade or business (*see* section 4.03) and the taxpayer owns tax-exempt obligations. This inference will be made even though the indebtedness is ostensibly incurred or continued to purchase or carry other portfolio investments.

Portfolio investment for the purposes of this Revenue Procedure includes transactions entered into for profit (including investment in real estate) which are not connected with the active conduct of a trade or business. Purchase and sale of securities shall not constitute the active conduct of a trade or business unless the taxpayer is a dealer in securities within the meaning of section 1.471-5 of the Income Tax Regulations. A substantial ownership interest in a corporation will not be considered a portfolio investment. For example, where a taxpayer owns at least 80 percent of the voting stock of a corporation that is engaged in the active conduct of a trade or business, the investment in such controlling interest shall not be considered to be a portfolio investment.

A sufficiently direct relationship between the incurring or continuing of indebtedness and the purchasing or carrying of tax-exempt obligations will generally exist where indebtedness is incurred to finance portfolio investment because the choice of whether to finance a new portfolio investment through borrowing or through the liquidation of an existing investment in tax-exempt obligations typically involves a purpose either to maximize profit or to maintain a diversified portfolio. This purpose necessarily involves a decision, whether articulated by the taxpayer or not, to incur (or continue) the indebtedness, at least in part, to purchase or carry the existing investment in tax-exempt obligations.

A taxpayer may rebut the presumption that section 265(2) of the Code applies in the above circumstances by establishing that he could not have liquidated his holdings of tax-exempt obligations in order to avoid incurring indebtedness. The presumption may be overcome where, for example, liquidation is not possible because the tax-exempt obligations cannot be sold. The presumption would not be rebutted, however, by a showing that the tax-exempt obligations could only have been liquidated with difficulty or at a loss; or that the taxpayer owned other investment assets such as common stock that could have been liquidated; or that an investment advisor recommended that a prudent man should maintain a particular percentage of assets in tax-exempt obligations. Similarly, the presumption would not be rebutted by a showing that liquidating the holdings of tax-exempt obligations would not have produced sufficient cash to equal the amount borrowed.

The provisions of this paragraph may be illustrated by the following example:

> Taxpayer A, an individual, owns common stock listed on a national securities exchange, having an adjusted basis of $200,000; he owns rental property having an adjusted basis of $200,000; he has cash of $10,000; and he owns readily marketable municipal bonds having an adjusted basis of $41,000. A borrows $100,000 to invest in a limited partnership interest in a real estate syndicate and pays $8,000 interest on the loan which he claims as an interest deduction for the taxable year. Under these facts and circumstances, there is a presumption that the $100,000 indebtedness which is incurred to finance A's portfolio investment is also incurred to carry A's existing investment in tax-exempt bonds since there are no additional facts or circumstances to rebut the presumption. Accordingly, a portion of the $8,000 interest payment will be disallowed under section 265(2) of the Code. See section 7 concerning the amount to be disallowed.

SEC. 7. PROCEDURES.

.01 When there is direct evidence under sections 3.02 and 3.03 establishing a purpose to purchase or carry tax-exempt obligations (either because tax-exempt obligations were used as collateral for indebtedness or the proceeds of indebtedness were directly traceable to the holding of particular tax-exempt obligations) no part of the interest paid or incurred on such indebtedness may be deducted. However, if only a fractional part of the indebtedness is directly traceable to the holding of particular tax-exempt obligations, the same fractional part of the interest paid or incurred on such indebtedness will be disallowed. For example, if A borrows $100,000 from a bank and invests $75,000 of the proceeds in tax-exempt obligations, 75 percent of the interest paid on the bank borrowing would be disallowed as a deduction.

.02 In any other case where interest is to be disallowed in accordance with this Revenue Procedure, an allocable portion of the interest on such indebtedness will be disallowed. The amount of interest on such indebtedness to be disallowed shall be determined by multiplying the total interest on such indebtedness by a fraction, the numerator of which is the average amount during the taxable year of the taxpayer's tax-exempt obligations (valued at their adjusted basis) and the denominator of which is the average amount during the taxable year of the taxpayer's total assets (valued at their adjusted basis) minus the amount of any indebtedness the interest on which is not subject to disallowance to any extent under this Revenue Procedure.

QUESTIONS AND COMMENTS

1. On June 1 and June 20 your client buys $20,000 worth of tax-exempt bonds. On June 10, he takes out a $20,000 home mortgage loan. Is the interest on the loan deductible? *Mariorenzi v. Commissioner*, 490 F.2d 92 (1st Cir. 1974).

2. *Rev. Proc. 72-18* suggests the difficulty of tracing loans to particular asset acquisitions. The problem is that taxpayers can often choose whether to keep one asset (asset A) and borrow to buy another (asset B), *or* sell asset A and use the cash to buy asset B. Given these options, it is hard to say which asset (A or B) the taxpayer is financing with the loan — the purchase of asset B or the retention of asset A. This difficulty is sometimes used as an argument for allowing all interest to be deducted.

But is it really so difficult to devise a system to trace interest deductions to particular assets? Consider the following possibilities, using tax-exempt bonds as an example. (Regardless of what system you use, omit assets which are very hard to sell, unless they have been purchased with or pledged as security for the loan.) (1) All interest would be allocated between investments in tax-exempt bonds and all other assets, based on their adjusted basis. *Rev. Proc. 72-18* uses such an allocation formula to determine nondeductible interest, but only *after* the loan has first been traced to carrying tax-exempt bonds. (2) Use a stacking procedure which assumes that interest is first allocated either (a) to tax-exempt bonds, or (b) to assets producing other income.

[B]—Critique of disallowing interest deduction

Interest is a peculiar kind of expense. It is the cost of capital and taxpayers can incur this cost either by disposing of an investment, thereby foregoing investment income, or by borrowing. There is nothing to stop a taxpayer in the 36% bracket, who earns 10% taxable interest (yielding 6.4% after tax), from selling his investment and buying a tax-exempt bond (yielding 6.9% before and after tax), ending up with *no* taxable income. Why can't he borrow at 10% interest (keeping the taxable investment earning 10%), and invest in the 6.9% tax-exempt bond, and *still* end up with *no* taxable income?

You can describe a taxpayer who makes either of these investment decisions as engaged in arbitrage. A taxpayer engaged in arbitrage gives up a return in one market, where he gets a lower after-tax return, and obtains a better after-tax return in another market. There are several reasons to discourage arbitrage, but they might not be very persuasive in the context of tax-exempt bonds.

Shifting investments to obtain a tax-exempt return might be economically undesirable, because: (1) it might not create any new investment but only move investments around; (2) the exemption might encourage investment in activities with low real economic returns, but high after tax returns; (3) it might encourage only well off high bracket investors to make the investment, and they are not necessarily the persons who know the most about good investing.

The trouble with these arguments is that they all seem to undercut the underlying congressional decision to allow tax-exempt interest on state and local bonds in the first place. Of course the exemption does not encourage new investment. It was supposed to encourage shifting investment to state and local government bonds. Moreover, the possibility that the economic returns to the tax-exempt investment are low is another way of questioning whether the governmental activities financed by the bonds are necessarily desirable. Congress seems to have decided that they are. Finally, it is true that the well off control the investment decision, but those with wealth always control investment decisions. And they are probably pretty good at making the kind of investments which *§ 103* encourages. In sum, all of these arguments against the interest deduction on loans to invest in tax-exempt bonds seem to be attacks on the exemption itself. Does *§ 265(a)(2)* persist because we are in fact uneasy about taxpayers borrowing to buy tax-exempt Industrial Revenue Bonds (*see* § 6.03, *supra*), some of which are still afforded tax-exemption even though they are not the traditional type of tax-exempt bond?

Recall that the code only looks unkindly on shifting investments by borrowing to buy tax-exempt bonds, not by selling a taxable investment to buy a tax-exempt bond. Are there any special problems arising from the fact that the taxpayer is borrowing? A borrower might be encouraged to take too many risks, holding on to other investments (like stocks), while investing in tax-exempt bonds. But that is probably not a strong objection, at least if the borrower risks losing his other investments if the debt is not repaid (because he is personally liable for the debt or pledges non-tax-exempt investments as security).

In a later chapter we will consider the problem of tax shelters more closely, where taxpayers borrow to invest in what are in effect tax-exempt (or partially tax-exempt) investments. The borrowing is often "nonrecourse," which means that the taxpayer is not personally liable to repay the loan except out of the asset purchased with the borrowed funds. In that context, the economic efficiency concerns about arbitrage by borrowing to invest in tax preferred investments might be much stronger than in the case of borrowing to invest in tax-exempt bonds.

§ 15.03 LOANS FOR INVESTMENT PURPOSES

Statutory provisions. The taxpayer who borrows to make an investment must worry not only about *§ 265(a)(2)*, if he owns tax exempt bonds at the time of the loan, but also about *§ 163(d)*, whether or not he owns tax-exempt bonds. *§ 163(d)* limits the deduction of investment interest. The *§ 163(d)* limits are applied *after* applying *§ 265(a)(2)*. Therefore, a taxpayer who has some investment interest not disallowed under *§ 265(a)(2)* must then contend with *§ 163(d)*.

Here is an example, where there are *no* tax-exempt bonds. A taxpayer borrows $100,000 to invest in appreciating investment property (land or speculative stock). The property will not produce much income until many years later, probably when the asset is sold. All the appreciated gain is "unrealized" income. The gain may even be untaxed if the investor dies and there is a date-of-death-value basis. Rather than add the interest to the basis of specific assets, *§ 163(d)* disallows the deduction of investment interest, *to the extent it exceeds investment income*.

Investment income, from which investment interest can be deducted, includes net income from dividends and interest. Before the 1993 Act, investment income also included the net gain from disposition of investment assets. At that time, the preferential tax rate on long term capital gains was 28% and the top individual tax rate was 31%, not too much of a difference. Therefore, deducting investment interest in an amount equal to preferentially taxed capital gain was not too much of a tax break. The 1993 tax law, however, increased the gap between the top individual rate (39.6%) and the preferential capital gains rate (28% — now less than 28%). Consequently, preferentially taxed capital gain is *no longer* considered investment income, except to the extent the taxpayer elects to report that gain as ordinary income. *§ 163(d)(4)(B)*. For example, assume the taxpayer incurs $20,000 investment interest and has $5,000 dividend income and $15,000 preferentially taxed long term capital gain. $15,000 of the investment interest cannot be deducted.

The excess of investment interest over investment income can be carried forward to future years and be deducted from later investment income, if any. *§ 163(d)(2)*.

The impact of these rules is that a taxpayer can shelter existing investment income by paying interest on loans to make new investments, even if those new investments do not produce current investment income. The taxpayer who is hurt by these rules is one who has inadequate investment income, but who borrows to invest in appreciating property, hoping to shelter non-investment income with the interest. In effect, the statute makes a stacking decision, allocating all investment interest first to taxable investment income.

The investment interest deduction is an itemized deduction, which is not subject to the 2% floor on miscellaneous itemized deductions.

Tracing. The investment interest deduction limitations apply only to loans "properly allocable to property held for investment." *§ 163(d)(3)(A)*. In other words, the interest is disallowed only after the loan is "traced" to investment purposes. What tracing rules apply under *§ 163(d)*? Is it the complex approach set forth in *Rev. Proc. 72-18*, applicable to carrying tax-exempt bonds, or is it a more direct "tracing" approach, requiring an actual tracing of borrowed funds to purchasing an investment?

Temporary Regulations (*Temp. Reg. § 1.163-8T(a)(3)*) define investment interest for *§ 163(d)* by reference to the *use* to which the loan is put. This means, for example, that pledging investment stock as security for a loan used to buy a personal car generates personal, not investment interest. The fact that investment property was pledged as security does not link the loan with "carrying" investment property under *§ 163(d)*. This contrasts with the rules dealing with "carrying" tax-exempt bonds. If tax-exempt bonds had been pledged as security for a loan, the interest would be traced to carrying the tax-exempt bonds, not to the use to which the loan proceeds were put.

Question. *§ 163(d)* only applies to individuals. Why doesn't it apply to corporate borrowers? By contrast, *§ 265(a)(2)* applies to all taxpayers, both individuals and corporations.

Carryover limits? How should the rules governing carryover of undeducted investment interest apply in the following situation? Suppose a taxpayer has $25,000 investment interest, no investment income, and taxable income of $20,000 earnings in a particular year. Can he carry forward $20,000 or $25,000 of unused investment interest under *§ 163(d)*? Before adoption of *§ 163(d)*, the taxpayer could deduct investment interest from earnings, but could not carry over the unused $5,000 deduction to another year. The general rules on carrying over net losses to another year do not allow the excess of investment interest over taxable income to be carried forward, because the excess is not a business net operating loss (*see § 172*). Now that *§ 163(d)* prevents the deduction of investment interest against noninvestment income, but permits a carry forward of undeducted investment interest to future years, does the carry forward include the full $25,000 in this example, or only the $20,000 (equal to the earned income)?

After litigating this issue in numerous cases (*see, e.g, Beyer v. Commissioner*, 916 F.2d 153 (4th Cir. 1990), *rev'g* 92 T.C. 1304 (1989)), the IRS threw in the towel regarding the carryover of investment interest in excess of taxable income. *Rev. Rul. 95–16*, 1995–1 C.B. 9. The IRS noted that four federal appellate courts and the United States Tax Court (in a 1993 opinion reviewed by the court) had rejected the Service position. Consequently, in the above example, $25,000 of undeducted investment interest can be carried forward.

Do not think this was an entirely altruistic move on the government's part. In *Allbritton v. Commissioner*, 37 F.3d 183 (5th Cir. 1994), the court had awarded litigation costs to the taxpayer in accordance with *§ 7430*. The court stated:

> The government's assertion of deficiencies in the Taxpayers' income taxes, and its appeal based on the same statutory interpretation previously rejected by the Fourth Circuit, the Federal Circuit, and several district courts constitutes "circuit-shopping" at the Taxpayers' expense in the hopes of creating a circuit conflict. Under 26 U.S.C. § 7430, a taxpayer who establishes that "the position of the United States in the proceeding was not substantially justified" may recover the reasonable costs of litigation. The Commissioner's repeated losses on the identical issue establish beyond serious question that the government's actions in assessing the deficiencies, litigating again an issue so consistently lost, and appealing the grant of the Taxpayers' motion for summary judgment, were not "justified to a degree that could satisfy a reasonable person."
>
> We have previously ruled that, while the Commissioner is free by law to relitigate prior lost issues in other circuits, he does so at the risk of incurring the obligation to reimburse the taxpayer. Therefore, in continuing to litigate this issue despite constant jurisprudence to the contrary, the Commissioner is not substantially justified and should bear all reasonable costs of Taxpayers' litigation.

Global vs. schedular tax. The carryover of the disallowed investment interest deduction highlights a feature of the tax law that is becoming more prominent. It treats investment activities as a category of income different from business income. We no longer have what has been called a "global" income tax, in the sense that all income is treated alike, with net losses from one activity reducing gains from unrelated activities, *if* they occur in the same tax year. Now net losses from *certain* activities are "quarantined," and can only be carried over to reduce income from the same activity in another year. The term "schedular" is sometimes used to describe such a tax system, in which different types of income are subject to different tax rules (that is, taxed in accordance with different "schedules").

§ 15.04 ECONOMIC REALITY

[A]—Case law limits

The following case discusses a case law limitation on the interest deduction, based on the economic reality of the underlying transaction. It is important to remember that these case law rules apply to all investors, whether corporations or individuals, but that some statutory limits (such as *§ 163(d)*) do not apply to corporations.

163(d) N/A to corps.

GOLDSTEIN v. COMMISSIONER

TP loses

364 F.2d 734 (2d Cir. 1966)

WATERMAN, CIRCUIT JUDGE: . . .

During the latter part of 1958 petitioner received the good news that she held a winning Irish Sweepstakes ticket and would shortly receive $140,218.75. This windfall significantly improved petitioner's financial situation, for she was a housewife approximately 70 years old and her husband was a retired garment worker who received a $780 pension each year. In 1958 the couple's only income, aside from this pension and the unexpected Sweepstakes proceeds, was $124.75, which represented interest on several small savings bank accounts. The petitioner received the Sweepstakes proceeds in December 1958 and she deposited the money in a New York bank. She included this amount as gross income in the joint return she and her husband filed for 1958 on the cash receipts and disbursements basis.

Petitioner's son, Bernard Goldstein, was a certified public accountant, practicing in New York in 1958. In November of that year Bernard either volunteered or was enlisted to assist petitioner in investing the Sweepstakes proceeds, and in minimizing the 1958 tax consequences to petitioner of the sudden increase in her income for that year. A series of consultations between Bernard and an attorney resulted in the adoption of a plan, which, as implemented, can be summarized as follows: During the latter part of December 1958 petitioner contacted several brokerage houses that bought

plan

and sold securities for clients and also arranged collateral loans. With the assistance of one of these brokerage houses, Garvin, Bantel & Co., petitioner borrowed $465,000 from the First National Bank of Jersey City. With the money thus acquired, and the active assistance of Garvin, Bantel, petitioner purchased $500,000 face amount of United States Treasury 1 1/2% notes, due to mature on October 1, 1962. Petitioner promptly pledged the Treasury notes so purchased as collateral to secure the loan with the Jersey City Bank. At approximately the same time in 1958 Bernard secured for petitioner a $480,000 loan from the Royal State Bank of New York. With the assistance of the Royal State Bank petitioner purchased a second block of $500,000 face amount of United States Treasury 1 1/2% notes, due to mature on October 1, 1961. Again the notes were pledged as collateral with this bank to secure the loan. Bernard testified that the petitioner purchased the Treasury notes because he believed "the time was ripe" to invest in this kind of government obligation. Also, pursuant to the prearranged plan, petitioner prepaid to the First National Bank of Jersey City and to the Royal State Bank the interest that would be due on the loans she had received if they remained outstanding for 1 1/2 to 2 1/2 years. These interest prepayments, made in late December of 1958, totaled $81,396.61. Petitioner then claimed this sum as a Section 163(a) deduction on the 1958 income tax return she filed jointly with her husband.

After reviewing these transactions in detail the Tax Court held the $81,396.61 was not deductible as "interest paid or accrued" on "indebtedness" under Section 163(a). In large part this holding rested on the court's conclusion that both loan transactions were "shams" that created "no genuine indebtedness." To support this conclusion the court stressed that, even though petitioner was borrowing approximately one half million dollars from each bank, the banks had agreed to the loans without any of their officers or employees having met petitioner or having investigated her financial position. The court noted that in each of the loan transactions petitioner was not required to commit any of her funds toward the purchase of the Treasury notes in their principal amount. And at several points the court appears to have attached great weight to the fact that most of the relevant transactions were apparently conducted by Garvin, Bantel and the Jersey City Bank, or by Bernard and the Royal State Bank, without petitioner's close supervision. Taking all these factors together, the Tax Court decided that, in fact, each transaction was ". . . an investment by the bank in Treasury obligations; wherein the bank, in consideration for prepayment to it of 'interest' by a customer . . . would carry such Treasury notes in the customer's name as purported collateral for the 'loan.' " The court went on to say that ". . . if it is necessary to characterize the customer's payment, we would say that it was a fee to the bank for providing the 'facade' of a loan transaction."

There is a certain force to the foregoing analysis. Quite clearly the First National Bank of Jersey City and the Royal State Bank of New York preferred to engage in the transactions they engaged in here rather than invest funds directly in Treasury notes because petitioner's loans bore interest at an appreciably higher rate than that yielded by the government obligations. This fact, combined with the impeccable property pledged as security for the loans, may have induced these banks to enter into these transactions without all the panoply that the court indicates usually accompanies loan transactions of such size. Indeed, while on its face purporting to be a debtor-creditor transaction between a taxpayer and a bank, in fact there can be a situation where the bank itself is, in effect, directly investing in the securities purportedly pledged by taxpayer as collateral to taxpayer's obligation; in such a transaction the taxpayer truly can be said to have paid a certain sum to the bank in return for the "facade" of a loan transaction. For Section 163(a) purposes such transactions are properly described as "shams" creating no "genuine indebtedness" and no deduction for the payment of "interest" to the bank should be allowed.

In our view, however, the facts of the two loan arrangements now before us fail in several significant respects to establish that these transactions were clearly shams. We agree with the dissent below that the record indicates these loan arrangements were ". . . regular and, moreover, indistinguishable from any other legitimate loan transaction contracted for the purchase of Government securities." In the first place, the Jersey City Bank and the Royal State Bank were independent financial institutions; it cannot be said that their sole function was to finance transactions such as those before us. Second, the two loan transactions here did not within a few days return all the parties to the position from which they had started. Here the Royal State Bank loan remained outstanding, and, significantly, that Bank retained the Treasury obligations pledged as security until June 10, 1960, at which time petitioner instructed the bank to sell the notes, apply the proceeds to the loan, and credit any remaining balance to her account. The facts relating to the Jersey City Bank loan are slightly different: this loan was closed in June 1959 when the brokerage house of Gruntal & Co. was substituted for the Jersey City Bank as creditor. Gruntal received and retained the 1962 Treasury 1 1/2's originally pledged as security for the loan until December 1, 1959 when, pursuant to instructions from petitioner and her advisors, these notes were sold, and $500,000 face amount of United States Treasury 2 1/2% bonds were purchased to replace them as security. Petitioner's account with Gruntal was not finally closed until June 13, 1960 when the last of these substituted bonds were sold, the petitioner's note was marked fully paid, and the balance was credited to petitioner. Third, the independent financial institutions from which petitioner borrowed the funds she needed to acquire the Treasury obligations possessed significant control over the future of their respective loan arrangements: for example, the petitioner's promissory note to the Jersey City Bank explicitly gave either party the right to accelerate the maturity of the note after 30 days, and it was the Jersey City Bank's utilization of this clause that necessitated recourse to Gruntal; the Royal State Bank had the right at any time to demand that petitioner increase her collateral or liquidate the loan, and on several occasions it made such a demand. Fourth, the notes signed by petitioner in favor of both banks were signed with recourse. If either of the independent lending institutions here involved had lost money on these transactions because of the depreciation of the collateral pledged to secure the loans we are certain that, upon petitioner's default of payment, they would have without hesitation proceeded against petitioner to recover their losses. Moreover, all things being equal, the banks' chances of judgments in their favor would have been excellent. In view of this combination of facts we think it was error for the Tax Court to conclude that these two transactions were "shams" which created no genuine indebtedness. Were this the only ground on which the decision reached below could be supported we would be compelled to reverse. . . .

One ground advanced by the Tax Court seems capable of reasoned development to support the result reached in this case by that court. The Tax Court found as an ultimate fact that petitioner's purpose in entering into the Jersey City Bank and Royal State Bank transactions "was not to derive any economic gain or to improve here beneficial interest; but was solely an attempt to obtain an interest deduction as an offset to her sweepstake winnings." This finding of ultimate fact was based in part on a set of computations made by Bernard Goldstein shortly after the Jersey City Bank and Royal State Bank loan transactions had been concluded. These computations were introduced by the Commissioner below and they indicated that petitioner and her financial advisors then estimated that the transactions would produce an economic loss in excess of $18,500 inasmuch as petitioner was out of pocket the 4% interest she had prepaid and could expect to receive 1 1/2% interest on the Treasury obligations she had just purchased plus a modest capital gain when the obligations were sold. This computation also reflected Bernard's realization that if the plan was successful this economic loss would be more than offset by the substantial reduction in petitioner's 1958 income tax liability due to the large deduction for interest "paid or accrued" taken in that year. The memorandum drawn up by Bernard is set out in full in the opinion of the Tax Court. In fact, petitioner sustained a $25,091.01 economic loss on these transactions for some of the Treasury obligations were ultimately sold for less than the price that had been originally anticipated by petitioner's advisors.

Before the Tax Court, and before us, petitioner has argued that she realistically anticipated an economic gain on the loan transactions due to anticipated appreciation in the value of the Treasury obligations, and that this gain would more than offset the loss that was bound to result because of the unfavorable interest rate differential. In support of this position, Bernard testified, and documentary evidence was introduced, to the effect that in December 1958 the market for Treasury obligations was unreasonably depressed, and that many investors at that time were favorably disposed toward their purchase. In short, petitioner argued that she intended a sophisticated, speculative, sortie into the market for government securities.

In holding that petitioner's sole purpose in entering into the Jersey City Bank and Royal State Bank transactions was to obtain an interest deduction, the Tax Court rejected this explanation of her purpose in entering into these transactions. For several reasons we hold that this rejection was proper. First, petitioner's evidence tending to establish that she anticipated an economic profit on these transactions due to a rising market for Treasury obligations is flatly contradicted by the computations made by Bernard contemporaneously with the commencement of these transactions and introduced by the Commissioner at trial. These computations almost conclusively establish that petitioner and her advisors from the outset anticipated an economic loss. Petitioner's answer to this damaging evidence is that the set of Bernard's computations introduced by the Commissioner was only one of several arithmetic projections made at the same time by Bernard, and that Bernard intended the computations introduced by the Commissioner to represent the worst that could befall the plan if prices for government obligations continued to decline. . . . [Editor — The court goes on to conclude that petitioner and her advisors could not have entertained a reasonable hope of economic profit.]

For all of the above reasons the Tax Court was justified in concluding that petitioner entered into the Jersey City Bank and Royal State Bank transactions without any realistic expectation of economic profit and "solely" in order to secure a large interest deduction in 1958 which could be deducted from her sweepstakes winnings in that year. This conclusion points the way to affirmance in the present case.

We hold, for reasons set forth hereinafter, that Section 163(a) of the 1954 Internal Revenue Code does not permit a deduction for interest paid or accrued in loan arrangements, like those now before us, that cannot with reason be said to have purpose, substance, or utility apart from their anticipated tax consequences. Although it is by no means certain that Congress constitutionally could tax gross income, it is frequently stated that deductions from "gross income" are a matter of "legislative grace." There is at least this much truth in this oft-repeated maxim: a close question whether a particular Code provision authorizes the deduction of a certain item is best resolved by reference to the underlying Congressional purpose of the deduction provision in question.

Admittedly, the underlying purpose of Section 163(a) permitting the deduction of "all interest paid or accrued within the taxable year on indebtedness" is difficult to articulate because this provision is extremely broad: There is no requirement that deductible interest serve a business purpose, that it be ordinary and necessary, or even that it be reasonable. Nevertheless, it is fair to say that Section 163(a) is not entirely unlimited in its application and that such limits as there are stem from the Section's underlying notion that if an individual or corporation desires to engage in purposive activity, there is no reason why a taxpayer who borrows for that purpose should fare worse from an income tax standpoint than one who finances the venture with capital that otherwise would have been yielding income.

In order fully to implement this Congressional policy of encouraging purposive activity to be financed through borrowing, Section 163(a) should be construed to permit the deductibility of interest when a taxpayer has borrowed funds and incurred an obligation to pay interest in order to engage in what with reason can be termed purposive activity, even though he decided to borrow in order to gain an interest deduction rather than to finance the activity in some other way. In other words, the interest deduction should be permitted whenever it can be said that the taxpayer's desire to secure an interest deduction is only one of mixed motives that prompts the taxpayer to borrow funds; or, put a third way, the deduction is proper if there is some substance to the loan arrangement beyond the taxpayer's desire to secure the deduction. After all, we are frequently told that a taxpayer has the right to decrease the amount of what otherwise would be his taxes, or altogether avoid them, by any means the law permits. *E.g., Gregory v. Helvering*, 293 U.S. 465 (1935). On the other hand, and notwithstanding Section 163(a)'s broad scope this provision should not be construed to permit an interest deduction when it objectively appears that a taxpayer has borrowed funds in order to engage in a transaction that has no substance or purpose aside from the taxpayer's desire to obtain the tax benefit of an interest deduction: and a good example of such purposeless activity is the borrowing of funds at 4% in order to purchase property that returns less than 2% and holds out no prospect of appreciation sufficient to counter the unfavorable interest rate differential. Certainly the statutory provision's underlying purpose, as we understand it, does not require that a deduction be allowed in such a case. Indeed, to allow a deduction for interest paid on funds borrowed for no purposive reason, other than the securing of a deduction from income, would frustrate Section 163(a)'s purpose; allowing it would encourage transactions that have no economic utility and that would not be engaged in but for the system of taxes imposed by Congress. When it enacted Section 163(a) Congress could not have intended to permit a taxpayer to reduce his taxes by means of an interest deduction that arose from a transaction that had no substance, utility, or purpose beyond the tax deduction. . . .

[T]he Supreme Court cautions us . . . that in cases like the present "the question for determination is whether what was done, apart from the tax motive, was the thing which the statute intended." We here decide that Section 163(a) does not "intend" that taxpayers should be permitted deductions for interest paid on debts that were entered into solely in order to obtain a deduction. It follows therefore from the foregoing, and from the Tax Court's finding as a matter of "ultimate" fact that petitioner entered into the Jersey City Bank and Royal State Bank transactions without any expectation of profit and without any other purpose except to obtain an interest deduction, and that the Tax Court's disallowance of the deductions in this case must be affirmed.

[B]—Statutory interpretation; Tax avoidance

This case is helpful in defining the issue of tax avoidance as one of statutory interpretation. The case holds, as a matter of statutory interpretation, that the interest deduction is permitted only if the loan is incurred in a transaction which could produce an economic profit (or is it a subjective test — a transaction which the taxpayer thought could produce an economic profit?).

Less helpful is the court's statement that congressional intent is relevant. The court says that "Congress could not have intended to permit a taxpayer" a deduction in this case. The fact is that Congress probably had no specific intent about this type of transaction.

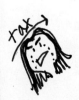

The general principle in *Goldstein* is difficult to apply, however, because it is not always clear how much of a profit motive is necessary and whether Congress intended tax benefits, even for tax-motivated transactions. In *Fox v. Commissioner*, 82 T.C. 1001, 1014–27 (1984), the court held that *§ 165(c)(2)* (dealing with loss deductions in transactions "entered into for profit") required a "primary profit" motive. The statutory test under *§ 165(c)(2)* is a different (and stricter) requirement than the "case law" *Goldstein* test, but in the process of applying *§ 165(c)(2)*, the court made a statement that is relevant to all tests based on potential economic profit. The court stated that it would relax the profit requirement "for those essentially tax-motivated transactions which are unmistakably within the contemplation of congressional intent." The court listed as examples of such congressionally sanctioned transactions an investment in tax-exempt securities and purchases motivated by accelerated depreciation, the investment tax credit, and the interest deduction.

Now you should see why the problem of tax avoidance is so difficult. How does a court decide which transactions with negligible economic purposes, apart from tax breaks, should be recognized for tax purposes? Which tax breaks does the code want you to exploit, even if there are low pre-tax economic profits?

Out of pocket loss. A taxpayer like Goldstein is still out of pocket the difference between the interest expense and the gross income from the investment. Is that difference deductible under *§ 165(c)(2)* as a loss in an income producing transaction? *Knetsch v. United States*, 348 F.2d 932 (Ct. Cl. 1965).

In some cases in which an interest expense exceeds the return on the investment, the person who persuaded the taxpayer to make the investment lied to the taxpayer. He falsely stated that property had actually been purchased for the taxpayer with the borrowed funds. In such a case, can the taxpayer deduct the out of pocket investment as an embezzlement or theft loss? *Nichols v. Commissioner*, 43 T.C. 842 (1965).

§ 15.05 DEDUCTING INTEREST ON INCOME TAX DEFICIENCIES

If the taxpayer can prove that an income tax deficiency is related to business income, is the interest owed on that tax deficiency deductible as *business* interest? Even before the 1986 law limiting the deduction of personal interest, the characterization of interest on tax deficiencies was important. Although the interest could be deducted as an itemized deduction under the old pre-1986 *§ 163*, a *business* deduction was better for a number of reasons — (1) it reduced adjusted gross income, rather than being just an itemized deduction; and (2) it increased net operating loss carryovers to other years. After the 1986 amendments, business deduction status is even more important for interest on income tax deficiencies. If the interest is not a business deduction, it is not deductible at all, because it is nondeductible personal interest.

The dispute over whether tax-related expenses are business-related is not limited to interest, but also concerns state income taxes and tax-related litigation expenses. The following discussion of the deductibility of state income taxes, litigation expenses related to income taxes, and interest on income tax deficiencies, is based on case law and the IRS position in *Rev. Rul. 70–40*, 1970–1 C.B. 50, and *Rev. Rul. 92–29*, 1992–1 C.B. 20. It gives you some background for reading the *Redlark* case, *infra*, in which the Tax

Court permitted a business deduction for interest on income tax deficiencies related to the determination of business income.

State income taxes. These were and still are deductible as itemized expenses. *§ 164(a)(3).* Case law and IRS rulings, relying on *clear legislative history*, held that these taxes were *never* business expenses for purposes of computing adjusted gross income (AGI) even though they might be related to business income. However, in the absence of clear legislative history, case law and the IRS agreed that these taxes, if related to business income, could increase a net operating loss (NOL) carryover to other years.

Litigation expenses related to income taxes. Case law has held that litigation expenses related to income taxes were business expenses if the tax dispute was related to business income, for purposes of computing *both* AGI and the NOL. The IRS conceded only that they could be business expenses for the NOL carryover, but not for determining AGI.

Interest on income tax deficiencies. Before 1986, case law treated interest on income tax deficiencies, if related to taxes on business income, as a business expense for both the AGI and NOL computations. Again, the IRS conceded on the NOL, but not on the AGI issue. Then came the new *§ 163(h)*, disallowing most personal interest. As the following Tax Court decision in the *Redlark* case explains, there was some explicit legislative history which suggested that interest on income tax deficiencies was not deductible at all, even if the tax related to business income, and the Regulations explicitly denied the deduction. *Redlark*, which allowed the deduction, is therefore as much about whether courts should defer to Treasury Regulations and legislative history, as about the specific substantive tax issue. The case of *Miller v. United States*, 65 F.3d 687 (1995), upheld the Regulations and disallowed the deduction, as did the Ninth Circuit in reversing the Tax Court's *Redlark* decision. *Redlark v. Commisioner,* 1998 WL 164767 (9th Cir. 1998). The *Redlark* case is discussed in Popkin, *The Taxpayer's Third Personality: Comments on Redlark v. Commissioner*, 72 Ind. L.J. 41 (1996).

SUMMARY CHART

Deductibility of expenses, assuming related to business income

	AGI	NOL
State income taxes	No	Yes
Tax litigation expenses	Yes - cases No - IRS	Yes
Interest on tax deficiences	Cases disagree No - IRS	Yes

REDLARK V. COMMISSIONER

106 T.C. 31 (1996),

rev'd, 1998 WL 164767 (9th Cir. 1998)

TANNENWALD, J.: . . .

[Editor — The dispute concerned errors made when an unincorporated business converted from an accrual to a cash method of accounting. Interest was paid on back federal income taxes in 1989 and 1990. The court acknowledged that it was not always easy to determine how much of the back taxes and the associated interest was allocable to business income, but assumed that a correct allocation had been made in this case. The court also noted that the relevant language of *§ 163(h)(2)(A)* when adopted in 1986 referred to interest on indebtedness "incurred or continued in connection with the conduct of a trade or business," and that a 1988 amendment referred to interest "properly allocable to a trade or business." But the court affirmed that the 1988 amendment was intended to conform the definition of personal interest to the language of the investment interest limitation in *§ 163(d)* and not to make any substantive change in the law.

The court first recounts the pre-1986 cases which allowed interest and litigation expenses to be deducted in computing both adjusted gross income and net operating losses and then states as follows.]

With the foregoing [case law] as background, we address the critical issue before us, namely, the effect of section 163(h)(2)(A) and section 1.163-8T, Temporary Income Tax Regs., 52 Fed. Reg. 24999 (July 2, 1987), and section 1.163-9T(b)(2)(i)(A), Temporary Income Tax Regs., which specifically denies the deduction herein claimed. This case is one of first impression in this Court on this issue. . . .

Initially, we note that temporary regulations are accorded the same weight as final regulations. The regulations involved herein were promulgated pursuant to the general authority granted to the Secretary of the Treasury by section 7805(a) and not pursuant to specific legislative authority; they are therefore interpretative. An interpretative regulation is owed "less deference than a regulation issued under a specific grant of authority to define a statutory term or prescribe a method of executing a statutory provision." *United States v. Vogel Fertilizer Co.*, 455 U.S. 16, 24 (1982) (quoting *Rowan Cos. v. United States*, 452 U.S. 247, 253 (1981)). An interpretative regulation will be upheld if it is found to "implement the congressional mandate in some reasonable manner. " *United States v. Vogel Fertilizer Co.*, 455 U.S. at 24 (quoting *United States v. Correll*, 389 U.S. 299, 307 (1967)).

Recently, the Supreme Court summarized the standard of review as follows:

> Under the formulation now familiar, when we confront an expert administrator's statutory exposition, we inquire first whether "the intent of Congress is clear" as to "the precise question at issue." *Chevron U.S.A. Inc. v. Natural Resources Defense Council, Inc.*, 467 U.S. 837, 842 (1984). If so, "that is the end of the matter." Ibid. But "if the statute is silent or ambiguous with respect to the specific issue, the question for the court is whether the agency's answer is based on a permissible construction of the statute." Id., at 843. If the administrator's reading fills a gap or defines a term in a way that is reasonable in light of the legislature's revealed design, we give the administrator's judgment "controlling weight." Id., at 844. . . .

Against the foregoing background, we consider the regulatory framework and legislative history that relate to the deductibility of interest on income tax deficiencies. Section 1.163-9T(b)(1)(i), Temporary Income Tax Regs., 52 Fed. Reg. 48409 (Dec. 22, 1987), specifically references section 1.163-8T, Temporary Income Tax Regs., by providing that interest is not personal interest if it is "paid or accrued on indebtedness properly allocable (within the meaning of § 1.163-8T) to the conduct of a trade or business". Additionally, paragraph (b)(3) of section 1.163-9T, Temporary Income Tax Regs., 52 Fed. Reg. 48410, further references section 1.163-8T, Temporary Income Tax Regs., "for rules for determining the allocation of interest expense to various activities. . . ."

Section 1.163-8T, Temporary Income Tax Regs., establishes an allocation method based on the expenditure, *i.e.*, the use, of the debt proceeds. It provides in paragraph (c)(1):

> (c) Allocation of debt and interest expense—(1) Allocation in accordance with use of proceeds. Debt is allocated to expenditures in accordance with the use of the debt proceeds and, . . . debt proceeds and related interest expense are allocated solely by reference to the use of such proceeds, and the allocation is not affected by the use of an interest in any property to secure the repayment of such debt or interest. . . . [52 Fed. Reg. 25000 (July 2, 1987).]

On this basis, it can be argued that the proceeds of an individual's income tax indebtedness cannot be considered as expended in a trade or business. From this it would follow that section 1.163-9T(b)(2)(i)(A), Temporary Income Tax Regs., which treats interest on income tax deficiencies as personal interest, simply represents a specific example of the application of the expenditure method of allocation of indebtedness set forth in section 1.163-8T, Temporary Income Tax Regs., and is therefore valid.

The question to be resolved is whether section 7805(a) provides a sufficient basis to justify the application of the expenditure method of allocation set forth in section 1.163-8T(c), Temporary Income Tax Regs., to the factual situation involved herein. Whatever the merits of such method of allocation may be in other contexts, we do not think that the Secretary of the Treasury should be entitled to use the authority conferred by section 7805(a) to construct a formula which excludes an entire category of interest expense in disregard of a business connection such as exists herein. Such a result discriminates against the individual who operates his or her business as a proprietorship instead of in corporate form where the limitations on the deduction of "personal interest" would not apply. We are not persuaded that we should view the category of income tax deficiencies as simply an incidental example, which unfortunately falls within the broad spectrum of indebtedness to which the application of the expenditure method of allocation would be appropriately applied, a situation which, in and of itself, might not be sufficient to invalidate the regulation. . . .

Moreover, we are not convinced that the reach of section 1.163-8T, Temporary Income Tax Regs., necessarily provides a sufficient basis for validating, under all circumstances, the specific provision of section 1.163-9T, Temporary Income Tax Regs. Thus, section 1.163-8T(b)(5), Temporary Income Tax Regs., 52 Fed. Reg. 25000 (July 2, 1987), defines personal expenditure to mean "an expenditure that is not a business expenditure" and section 1.163-8T(c)(3)(ii), Temporary Income Tax Regs., 52 Fed. Reg. 25001 (July 2, 1987), provides:

> (ii) Debt assumptions not involving cash disbursements. If a taxpayer incurs or assumes a debt in consideration for the sale or use of property, for services, or for any other purpose, or takes property subject to a debt, and no debt proceeds are disbursed to the taxpayer, the debt is treated

for purposes of this section as if the taxpayer used an amount of the debt proceeds equal to the balance of the debt outstanding at such time to make an expenditure for such property, services, or other purpose.

Under this provision, it would appear permissible to analyze the elements of the income tax indebtedness to determine whether its imputed expenditure is properly allocable to business activity. Indeed, such an interpretation would be consistent with the overall legislative purpose in enacting section 163(h), namely to end the deduction for interest incurred to fund consumption expenditures. To conclude that an income tax deficiency is ipso facto a consumption expenditure begs the issue. Thus, aside from our conclusion that the regulatory provisions contained in section 1.163-8T, Temporary Income Tax Regs., are unreasonable as applied to the facts herein, it is possible to conclude that the provisions are sufficiently elliptical so that the validity of section 1.163-9T, Temporary Income Tax Regs., can, in any event, be appropriately independently determined. Accordingly, we turn our attention to that task.

Section 1.163-9T(b)(2)(i)(A), Temporary Income Tax Regs., provides:

> (2) Interest relating to taxes—(i) In general. Except as provided in paragraph (b)(2)(iii) of this section, personal interest includes interest—
>
> (A) Paid on underpayments of individual Federal, State or local income taxes . . . regardless of the source of the income generating the tax liability;

The only legislative history of section 163(h) which directly addresses the issue involved herein is the conference committee report which states:

> Under the conference agreement, personal interest is not deductible. Personal interest is any interest, other than interest incurred or continued in connection with the conduct of a trade or business (other than the trade or business of performing services as an employee), investment interest, or interest taken into account in computing the taxpayer's income or loss from passive activities for the year. Personal interest also generally includes interest on tax deficiencies. [H. Conf. Rept. 99–841 at II-154 (1986), 1986–3 C.B. (Vol. 4) 1, 154.]

The General Explanation of the Tax Reform Act of 1986 [issued by the Joint Committee on Taxation Staff in the "Blue Book" after passage of the law] elaborates on this statement by providing as follows:

> Personal interest also includes interest on underpayments of individual Federal, State or local income taxes notwithstanding that all or a portion of the income may have arisen in a trade or business, because such taxes are not considered derived from the conduct of a trade or business. . . .

We first address the language of the conference committee report. Respondent argues that the word "generally" was intended only to permit deduction of interest on past-due business taxes, such as sales and excise taxes which the regulations specifically exclude from the definition of personal interest. See § 1.163-9T(b)(2)(iii)(A), Temporary Income Tax Regs., 52 Fed. Reg. 48409 (Dec. 22, 1987). On this basis, respondent concludes that section 1.163-9T(b)(2)(i)(A), Temporary Income Tax Regs., is reasonable and that additional proof of reasonableness is provided by the statement in the Joint Committee Staff Explanation. . . .

We think [the] respondent overlook[s] the use of the word "deficiencies" in the sentence in the conference committee report. That word has had a long-established and well-known meaning. It has been described as a "term of art[,]" represented by statutory definition as "the amount by which the income, gift, or estate tax due under the law exceeds the amount of such tax shown on the return." Moreover, in cases too numerous to cite, the word "deficiency" has been treated as embodying such a definition and has consequently acquired a fixed and settled meaning. Such being the case, we have every reason to assume that the conference committee used the word in that sense.

In short, we think that when the conference committee used the phrase "tax deficiencies," it was referring to amounts due by way of income, estate, and gift taxes. In this context, the word "generally" in the conference committee report takes on a significant meaning. It signals that not all interest relating to income tax, etc., deficiencies are included in "personal interest." The logical explanation for what is excluded by "generally" is such interest that constitutes an ordinary and necessary business expense and is therefore "allocable to an indebtedness of a trade or business" within the meaning of the exception clause of section 163(h)(2)(A). To adopt respondent's position would require us to substitute the word "always" for "generally" and to expand the interpretation of the word "deficiencies" beyond its accepted meaning to encompass taxes other than income, etc., taxes in order to account for the use of the word "generally." By way of contrast, our interpretation accepts the established meaning of "deficiencies" and gives effect to "generally" without modification. . . .

Nor can respondent's position be salvaged by the Joint Committee Staff Explanation. Such a document is not part of the legislative history although it is entitled to respect. Livingston, "What's Blue and White and Not Quite as Good as a Committee Report: General Explanations and the Role of 'Subsequent' Tax Legislative History," 11 Amer. J. Tax Policy 91 (1994). Where there is no corroboration in the actual legislative history, we shall not hesitate to disregard the General Explanation as far as congressional intent is concerned. [S]ee also Livingston, supra at 93 ("The Blue Book is on especially weak ground when it adopts anti-taxpayer positions not taken in the committee reports."). Given the clear thrust of the conference committee report, the General Explanation is without foundation and must fall by the wayside. To conclude otherwise would elevate it to a status and accord it a deference to which it is simply not entitled. [Editor — In a footnote, the court states: In this connection, we also note that the Tax Reform Act of 1986, Pub. L. 99–514, 100 Stat. 2085, was enacted on Oct. 22, 1986, during the 99th Congress, whereas the General Explanation was published on May 4, 1987, during the 100th Congress. Thus, the General Explanation is not even entitled to the respect it might otherwise be accorded if it had been prepared for the Congress which enacted § 163(h).]

One final comment. Suppose that the only income reported on the return of petitioners had been Schedule C [business] income . . . and that the entire deficiency related to the type of errors that the courts have previously concluded were expected to occur in the ordinary course of business. It would constitute an unrealistic application of our tax laws to conclude that the interest on such deficiency is not attributable to an indebtedness properly allocable to a trade or business under section 163(h)(2)(A), in the absence of clear legislative intent that such a result is required. Yet, such is the inescapable consequence of adopting respondent's position.

In light of the foregoing, and with all due respect to the Court of Appeals for the Eighth Circuit [in *Miller v. United States*, 65 F.3d 687 (1995)], we hold that, as applied to the circumstances involved herein, section 1.163-9T(b)(2)(i)(A), Temporary Income Tax Regs., constitutes an impermissible reading of the statute and is therefore unreasonable. Accordingly, we further hold that the interest involved herein is interest "on indebtedness properly allocable to a trade or business" and therefore excluded from personal interest under section 163(h)(2). . . .

Reviewed by the Court. Swift, Jacobs, Wright, Parr, Wells, Chiechi, and Vasquez, JJ., agree with this majority opinion. Foley, J., concurs in the result only.

Halpern, J., dissenting: . . .

[The majority's holding] departs from the Supreme Court's teachings in *Chevron, U.S.A., Inc. v. Natural Resources Defense Council, Inc.*, 467 U.S. 837, 842–844 (1984). I believe that application of those decisions leads to the conclusion that the temporary regulations at issue are valid, which leads to a decision for respondent.

Section 163(h) was added to the Code by the Tax Reform Act of 1986, Pub. L. 99–514, § 511(b), 100 Stat. 2085, 2246. In the case of individual taxpayers, section 163(h)(1) disallows a deduction for all personal interest paid or accrued during the taxable year. Section 163(h)(2) then provides that all interest is personal interest unless that interest falls into one of the five exceptions listed in paragraph (2). The only relevant exception for our purposes is contained in subparagraph (A), which provides that the term "personal interest" does not include "interest paid or accrued on indebtedness properly allocable to a trade or business." § 163(h)(2)(A).

The term "properly allocable" is ambiguous, because Congress has not indicated the method by which, or the assumptions under which, taxpayers, the Service, and the courts are to decide whether a particular indebtedness is "properly allocable" to a trade or business. Clearly, there is more than one way to allocate interest. Compare, for example, the asset based apportionment method found in section 265(b)(2) with the tracing method outlined in section 1.163-8T(a)(3), Temporary Income Tax Regs., 52 Fed. Reg. 24999 (July 2, 1987). More importantly, the statute is silent with respect to the specific issue at hand— whether interest with respect to an individual's Federal income tax liability is deductible. . . .

[Editor — Judge Halpern then argues that Temporary Income Tax Reg. § 1.163-8T is valid, based (in part) on the fact that it is reasonable to treat payment of income taxes on business income as personal consumption and, therefore, to treat the interest on a debt incurred for that purpose as personal interest.]

Prior to the War Revenue Act, ch. 63, 40 Stat. 300 (1917), Federal income taxes were deductible. *See, e.g.,* § 5(a) of the Revenue Act of 1916, ch. 463, 39 Stat. 756, 759; Seidman, Seidman's Legislative History of Federal Income Tax Laws 1938–1861, 943–944 (1938) (re: 1917 Act). Before 1917, Federal income taxes allocable to a business reasonably could be considered a cost of that business, and both any deficiency interest allocable to such taxes and any interest on indebtedness incurred to pay such taxes likewise could be considered a cost of business. Congress, however, has not allowed a deduction for Federal income taxes since such deduction was eliminated by the War Revenue Act, ch. 63, § 1201(1), 40 Stat. 300, 330 (1917). By not allowing a deduction, Congress has signaled that money expended for Federal income taxes constitutes a consumption expenditure, and not a cost of earning income.

Congress' present treatment of Federal income taxes is reasonable. Plainly, an expenditure made for Federal income taxes is not an expenditure made in consideration of any specific property or service received by the taxpayer. The payment of Federal income taxes is a civic duty, not a matter of business contract or investment advantage. All taxpayers, as well as others (citizens and noncitizens) receive benefits on account of the funding of the Federal Government. The payment of Federal income taxes reduces a taxpayer's wealth otherwise available for consumption. Thus, Federal income tax payments exhibit characteristics not common to business (or investment) expenditures. Justice Holmes made a point that serves nicely to emphasize the nonbusiness aspect to tax payments: "Taxes are what we pay for civilized society." *Compania General de Tabacos de Filipinas v. Collector of Internal Revenue*, 275 U.S. 87, 100 (1927) (Holmes, J., dissenting).

If Federal income taxes constitute consumption, and not a trade, business, or investment expense, then, under a tracing rule, such as the rule of section 1.163-8T, Temporary Income Tax Regs., the inescapable, and reasonable, conclusion is that any deficiency interest, or interest on a borrowing to pay income taxes, is personal interest. The taxpayer's purpose for borrowing the money, or the reason the deficiency arose (*e.g.*, "my accountant made a mistake!") simply is irrelevant. Though that approach may appear wooden, it is unambiguous.

The rule found in section 1.163-9T(b)(2)(I)(A), Temporary Income Tax Regs., and invalidated by the majority, is nothing more than a fact-specific application of section 1.163-8T, Temporary Income Tax Regs. It is specific to the fact that Federal taxes are reasonably considered a nondeductible, personal expenditure. Section 1.163-8T, Temporary Income Tax Regs., is a valid regulation and must be given "controlling weight." Accordingly, section 1.163-9T(b)(2)(A), Temporary Income Tax Regs., also is valid.

[Editor — As for the inconsistency between corporate deduction of the interest and denying individuals the deduction, Judge Halpern states: "[T]he majority does not explain why Congress may not discriminate between individuals doing business as proprietorships and in corporate form. Granted, section 163(h) applies only to individuals. Congress has been of two minds as to the deductibility of Federal income taxes, and perhaps the distinction reflects some residual ambiguity. Perhaps Congress views corporate deficiency interest as properly an investment expense of shareholders. We do not know. In any event, the majority has not convinced me that the inconsistency is unconstitutional."]

CHAPTER 16

LOANS, BASIS, AND TAX OWNERSHIP

§ 16.01 LOANS AND BASIS

[A]—Debt included in basis

When can debt be included in a taxpayer's basis? For example, if a taxpayer buys a building with a $50,000 loan, is the building's basis $50,000?

Basis is usually the amount invested out of after-tax income. The tax issue raised by loans is whether a taxpayer is entitled to include debt in basis, even though the out of pocket investment will occur in the future. In effect, the taxpayer wants to accrue the debt and include it in basis before the debt is paid.

We have already seen that borrowing is not taxed at the time of the loan. You can think of the borrower's obligation as offsetting the receipt of the loan proceeds, thus preventing any increase in net wealth. The expectation of loan repayment arguably justifies the offset.

A corollary of this approach is that borrowed money which is used to purchase property is included in the property's basis. If the $50,000 loan used to buy a building were not included in basis (that is, if basis were zero), then when the taxpayer sold the building before repaying the loan, the taxpayer would have $50,000 gross income. In effect, the taxpayer would be taxed on the loan proceeds prior to the time of repayment. But that would be inconsistent with the fundamental rule postponing taxation until the loan is repaid out of after-tax income.

The full implications of this conclusion can only be appreciated by considering the use of borrowed money to make investments in depreciable and expensed property. Taxpayers can combine early deduction rules for investments with exclusion of loan proceeds from income, with startling results.

The *Crane* case, *infra*, is usually cited as the seminal authority for including debt in basis. Technically, the case held that inherited property has a basis equal to its gross value, including debt to which the property is subject. "Debt to which the property is subject" refers to situations in which the property is security for the debt but the debtor is *not* personally liable (often referred to as *nonrecourse* debt). The case was soon extended to property acquired by *purchase* with borrowed money. *Mayerson v. Commissioner*, 47 T.C. 340 (1966). Consequently, unpaid debt is included in basis, both when the taxpayer is personally liable and when the debt is nonrecourse.

CRANE v. COMMISSIONER

331 U.S. 1 (1947)

MR. CHIEF JUSTICE VINSON delivered the opinion of the Court.

The question here is how a taxpayer who acquires depreciable property subject to an unassumed mortgage, holds it for a period, and finally sells it still so encumbered, must compute her taxable gain. . . .

[Editor — Assume the following facts. Taxpayer inherited depreciable property worth $100,000, subject to a $100,000 debt (that is, the property was security for the debt). The owner was not personally liable. She treated the property as though it had a $100,000 basis and took $60,000 depreciation deductions over several years. She never paid off any of the debt. When she sold the property, the property's value had increased to $103,000, but she received only $3,000 cash, because the property was still encumbered by a $100,000 debt.

She argued that the basis of the sold property was zero, and that she had a $3,000 gain on the sale. She claimed that the original basis at inheritance was zero, because the net value (considering the $100,000 debt) was zero. She admitted that her claim of a zero basis was inconsistent with her prior depreciation deductions. The remedy for that, she said, was to go back to earlier tax years and disallow the depreciation. The government responded that the original basis was $100,000, including the debt, and that the amount realized at the time of the sale included unpaid debt.

These issues arose under an earlier version of the code with different section numbers. The code references are deleted from the case but the statutory text is the same as under current law in all important respects, regarding the definition of "amount realized," "basis," and "adjusted basis."]

The 1938 Act defines the gain from "the sale or other disposition of property" as "the excess of the amount realized therefrom over the adjusted basis. . . ." It proceeds to define "the amount realized from the sale or other disposition of property" as "the sum of any money received plus the fair market value of the property (other than money) received." Further, [] the "adjusted basis for determining the gain or loss from the sale or other disposition of property" is declared to be "the basis [] adjusted . . . for exhaustion, wear and tear, obsolescence, amortization . . . to the extent allowed (but not less than the amount allowable). . . ." The basis . . . "if the property was acquired by . . . devise . . . or by the decedent's estate from the decedent," is "the fair market value of such property at the time of such acquisition."

Logically, the first step under this scheme is to determine the unadjusted basis of the property, and the dispute in this case is as to the construction to be given the term "property." If "property," as used in that provision, means the same thing as "equity," it would necessarily follow that the basis of petitioner's property was zero, as she contends. If, on the contrary, it means the land and building themselves, or the owner's legal rights in them, undiminished by the mortgage, the basis was [$100,000].

We think that the reasons for favoring one of the latter constructions are of overwhelming weight. In the first place, the words of statutes — including revenue acts — should be interpreted where possible in their ordinary, everyday senses. The only relevant definitions of "property" to be found in the principal standard dictionaries are the two favored by the Commissioner, *i.e.*, either that "property" is the physical thing which is a subject of ownership, or that it is the aggregate of the owner's rights to control and dispose of that thing. "Equity" is not given as a synonym, nor do either of the foregoing definitions suggest that it could be correctly so used. Indeed, "equity" is defined as "the value of a property . . . above the total of the liens. . . ." The contradistinction could hardly be more pointed. Strong countervailing considerations would be required to support a contention that Congress, in using the word "property," meant "equity," or that we should impute to it the intent to convey that meaning.

In the second place, the Commissioner's position has the approval of [] administrative construction. . . . With respect to the valuation of property under that section, [the Regulations] provided that "the value of property as of the date of the death of the decedent as appraised for the purpose of the federal estate tax . . . shall be deemed to be its fair market value. . . ." As the quoted provision of the Regulations has been in effect since 1918, and as the relevant statutory provision has been repeatedly reenacted since then in substantially the same form, the former may itself now be considered to have the force of law. . . .

A further reason why the word "property" [] should not be construed to mean "equity" is the bearing such construction would have on the allowance of deductions for depreciation and on the collateral adjustments of basis.

[The statute] permits deduction from gross income of "a reasonable allowance for the exhaustion, wear and tear of property. . . ." [It] declare[s] that the "basis upon which depletion exhaustion, wear and tear . . . are to be allowed" is the basis "for the purpose of determining the gain upon the sale" of the property, which is the basis "adjusted . . . for exhaustion, wear and tear . . . to the extent allowed (but not less than the amount allowable). . . ."

Under these provisions, if the mortgagor's equity were the basis, it would also be the original basis from which depreciation allowances are deducted. If it is, and if the amount of the annual allowances were to be computed on that value, as would then seem to be required, they will represent only a fraction of the cost of the corresponding physical exhaustion, and any recoupment by the mortgagor of the remainder of that cost can be effected only by the reduction of his taxable gain in the year of sale. If, however, the amount of the annual allowances were to be computed on the value of the property, and then deducted from an equity basis, we would in some instances have to accept deductions from a minus basis or deny deductions altogether. The Commissioner also argues that taking the mortgagor's equity as the basis would require the basis to be changed with each payment on the mortgage, and that the attendant problem of repeatedly recomputing basis and annual allowances would be a tremendous accounting burden on both the Commissioner and the taxpayer. Moreover, the mortgagor would acquire control over the timing of his depreciation allowances.

Thus it appears that the applicable provisions of the Act expressly preclude an equity basis, and the use of it is contrary to certain implicit principles of income tax depreciation, and entails very great administrative difficulties. It may be added that the Treasury has never furnished a guide through the maze of problems that arise in connection with depreciating an equity basis, but, on the contrary, has consistently permitted the amount of depreciation allowances to be computed on the full value of the property, and subtracted from it as a basis. Surely, Congress' long-continued acceptance of this situation gives it full legislative endorsement.

We conclude that the proper basis is the value of the property, undiminished by mortgages thereon, and that the correct basis here was [$100,000]. The next step is to ascertain what [basis] adjustments are required. As the depreciation rate was stipulated, the only question at this point is whether the Commissioner was warranted in making any depreciation adjustments whatsoever.

[The statute] provides that "proper adjustment in respect of the property *shall in all cases be made* . . . for exhaustion, wear and tear . . . to the

prop. = $100K basis

(2) what adjustments?

extent allowed (but not less than the amount allowable). . . ." (Emphasis supplied.) The Tax Court found on adequate evidence that the apartment house was property of a kind subject to physical exhaustion, that it was used in taxpayer's trade or business, and consequently that the taxpayer would have been entitled to a depreciation allowance, except that, in the opinion of that Court, the basis of the property was zero, and it was thought that depreciation could not be taken on a zero basis. As we have just decided that the correct basis of the property was not zero, but [$100,000] we avoid this difficulty, and conclude that an adjustment should be made as the Commissioner determined.

Petitioner urges to the contrary that she was not entitled to depreciation deductions, whatever the basis of the property, because the law allows them only to one who actually bears the capital loss, and here the loss was not hers but the mortgagee's. We do not see, however, that she has established her factual premise. There was no finding of the Tax Court to that effect, nor to the effect that the value of the property was ever less than the amount of the lien. Nor was there evidence in the record, or any indication that petitioner could produce evidence, that this was so. The facts that the value of the property was only equal to the lien in 1932 and that during the next six and one-half years the physical condition of the building deteriorated and the amount of the lien increased, are entirely inconclusive, particularly in the light of the buyer's willingness in 1938 to take subject to the increased lien and pay a substantial amount of cash to boot. Whatever may be the rule as to allowing depreciation to a mortgagor on property in his possession which is subject to an unassumed mortgage and clearly worth less than the lien, we are not faced with that problem and see no reason to decide it now.

At last we come to the problem of determining the "amount realized" on the 1938 sale. [The statute], it will be recalled, defines the "amount realized" from "the sale . . . of property" as "the sum of any money received plus the fair market value of the property (other than money) received," and [the statute] defines the gain on "the sale of property" as the excess of the amount realized over the basis. Quite obviously, the word "property," used here with reference to a sale, must mean "property" in the same ordinary sense intended by the use of the word with reference to acquisition and depreciation, both for certain of the reasons stated heretofore [], and also because the functional relation of the two sections requires that the word mean the same in one section that it does in the other. If the "property" to be valued on the date of acquisition is the property free of liens, the "property" to be priced on a subsequent sale must be the same thing.

Starting from this point, we could not accept petitioner's contention that the [$3,000] net cash was all she realized on the sale except on the absurdity that she sold a [valuable] property for roughly one per cent of its value, and took a 99 per cent loss. Actually, petitioner does not urge this. She argues, conversely, that because only [$3,000] was realized on the sale, the "property" sold must have been the equity only, and that consequently we are forced to accept her contention as to the meaning of "property" [for computing basis]. We adhere, however, to what we have already said on the meaning of "property," and we find that the absurdity is avoided by our conclusion that the amount of the mortgage is properly included in the "amount realized" on the sale.

Petitioner concedes that if she had been personally liable on the mortgage and the purchaser had either paid or assumed it, the amount so paid or assumed would be considered a part of the "amount realized." The cases so deciding have already repudiated the notion that there must be an actual receipt by the seller himself of "money" or "other property," in their narrowest senses. It was thought to be decisive that one section of the Act must be construed so as not to defeat the intention of another or to frustrate the Act as a whole, and that the taxpayer was the "beneficiary" of the payment in "as real and substantial (a sense) as if the money had been paid it and then paid over by it to its creditors."

Both these points apply to this case. The first has been mentioned already. As for the second, we think that a mortgagor, not personally liable on the debt, who sells the property subject to the mortgage for additional consideration, realizes a benefit in the amount of the mortgage as well as the boot.[37] If a purchaser pays boot, it is immaterial as to our problem whether the mortgagor is also to receive money from the purchaser to discharge the mortgage prior to sale, or whether he is merely to transfer subject to the mortgage — it may make a difference to the purchaser and to the mortgagee, but not to the mortgagor. Or put in another way, we are no more concerned with whether the mortgagor is, strictly speaking, a debtor on the mortgage, than we are with whether the benefit to him is, strictly speaking, a receipt of money or property. We are rather concerned with the reality that an owner of property, mortgaged at a figure less than that at which the property will sell, must and will treat the conditions of the mortgage exactly as if they were his personal obligations. If he transfers subject to the mortgage, the benefit to him is as real and substantial as if the mortgage were discharged, or as if a personal debt in an equal amount had been assumed by another.

Therefore we conclude that the Commissioner was right in determining that petitioner realized [$103,000] on the sale of this property. . . .

[37] Obviously, if the value of the property is less than the amount of the mortgage, a mortgagor who is not personally liable cannot realize a benefit equal to the mortgage. Consequently, a different problem might be encountered where a mortgagor abandoned the property or transferred it subject to the mortgage without receiving boot. That is not this case.

Petitioner contends that the result we have reached taxes her on what is not income within the meaning of the Sixteenth Amendment. If this is because only the direct receipt of cash is thought to be income in the constitutional sense, her contention is wholly without merit. If it is because the entire transaction is thought to have been "by all dictates of common-sense . . . a ruinous disaster," as it was termed in her brief, we disagree with her premise. She was entitled to depreciation deductions for a period of nearly seven years, and she actually took them in almost the allowable amount. The crux of this case, really, is whether the law permits her to exclude allowable deductions from consideration in computing gain. We have already showed that, if it does, the taxpayer can enjoy a double deduction, in effect, on the same loss of assets. The Sixteenth Amendment does not require that result any more than does the Act itself.

[B]—Comments

Changing basis? What was the Court in *Crane* worried about when it stated:

> The Commissioner also argues that taking the mortgagor's equity as the basis would require the basis to be changed with each payment on the mortgage, and that the attendant problem of repeatedly recomputing basis and annual allowances would be a tremendous accounting burden on both the Commissioner and the taxpayer. Moreover, the mortgagor would acquire control over the timing of his depreciation allowances.

Consider this example: The taxpayer pays $5,000 down in year 1 and promises to pay $185,000 for a building with a 19-year depreciable life. It then pays $3,000 of the debt in year 1. What complications arise if the taxpayer cannot use $190,000 as the basis for depreciation? Would you depreciate the $8,000 out-of-pocket investment in year 1 over 19 years? If $4,000 more principal on the debt were paid in year 2, would that be another investment, depreciable over 19 (or 18) years?

Isn't there an easy way to solve the problem of changing basis? Just compute depreciation using the $190,000 basis, but cap the deduction at the actual out-of-pocket investment. In the example, $10,000 straight-line depreciation in the first year would be capped at $8,000 ($5,000 down plus $3,000 debt paid). The unused $2,000 deduction would be carried forward to the next year, so a total of $12,000 potential depreciation would be allowed, if that much debt were paid.

Amount realized when basis includes debt. Be sure you understand why the amount realized must include unpaid debt. Using the above example, how much debt does the taxpayer still owe after one year? The answer is $182,000 (only $3,000 of the $185,000 debt is paid). How much of the purchase price of the building has been deducted — $10,000. That

$10,000 includes the $8,000 the taxpayer paid ($5,000 down plus $3,000 debt paid). The taxpayer has gotten a $10,000 deduction, for an $8,000 out-of-pocket investment.

What is wrong with this $10,000 deduction? After all, the taxpayer can deduct unpaid debt. But we allow the deduction of unpaid debt *because* the debt is going to be paid in the future. Once the taxpayer disposes of the property, what chance is there that the debt will be paid by the taxpayer. The answer is "none," if the taxpayer is not personally liable and, very little, even if he is personally liable. The taxpayer will therefore enjoy a $10,000 deduction but only pay $8,000. That is like borrowing $10,000 and paying back only $8,000.

What to do? Do the same thing that the tax law did in the case of debt forgiveness, discussed in an earlier chapter. Tax the $2,000 as income. The mechanical rule, which includes unpaid debt in amount realized, will always have that effect. For example, assume the property is worth $182,000. Because the debt equals value, no one will pay additional cash for the property. A transfer of the property for which the debt was security would result in $182,000 amount realized. The basis of the property is $180,000 ($190,000 minus the $10,000 depreciation deduction). The gain is therefore $2,000.

Realizable taxable event. The need for this rule is sufficiently strong that the tax law treats events as taxable dispositions which would not otherwise be taxable. For example, the transfer of property as a gift is not usually a taxable event. A gift of property subject to a debt is, however, a taxable event — the amount realized equals the unpaid debt. A gift to a child or a charity can therefore produce taxable gain to the donor.

Abandonment of property is also a realizable taxable event. This might sound fanciful. Why abandon property? Assume that the investment of $190,000 in the prior example was an investment in a partnership which has not been very productive. After some years the property is worth $130,000 but the unpaid debt is still quite high — say, $150,000. The partners are not personally liable and do not want to continue paying off the debt. The partnership therefore abandons the property to the creditor-bank. Unpaid debt minus basis is taxable gain.

Another example where taxing gain is more obviously necessary is the taxpayer with appreciated property who borrows cash, pledging the property as security. For example, assume a taxpayer owns stock with a $50,000 basis but a much higher value. He then borrows $150,000 cash, pledging the stock as security. The cash is available in this case for any purpose, not just to buy the property (it is not a purchase-money debt). When the property declines in value to $130,000, still subject to the $150,000 debt, the taxpayer abandons the property to the bank, at which time there is $150,000 amount realized and $100,000 taxable gain. *Woodsam Associates, Inc. v. Commissioner*, 198 F.2d 357 (2d Cir. 1952).

Property value less than unpaid debt. For some time, there was doubt about whether there was taxable gain when the value of the property was less than nonrecourse debt at the time of gift or abandonment. *See* footnote 37 in *Crane*. This footnote was based on a failure to understand the similarity between a discharge of indebtedness and the case of disposing of property on which deductions exceed out-of-pocket investment. The Court revisited this issue in *Commissioner v. Tufts,* 461 U.S. 300 (1983), and got it right. Amount realized includes unpaid debt regardless of the value of the property at the time the property is disposed of.

As a practical matter the government still has trouble finding the taxpayer who gives or abandons property which has declined in value. The law is clear but taxpayers often "forget" to report the gain, especially when no cash changes hands.

Discharge of indebtedness vs. sales income. There is one final issue to consider. When the taxpayer disposes of property secured by unpaid debt, should the income be gain from the sale or exchange of the property, or should it be discharge of indebtedness income under *§ 108*? Which is better for the taxpayer or government — discharge of indebtedness income (remember the possibility of *§ 108* elections to defer tax), or sale or exchange treatment (remember the difference between capital gains and ordinary "recapture" income; and the possibility that there might be a loss on the sale or exchange, which might not be deductible)?

The taxation of the disposition of property can be explained by this example. Assume an unpaid debt of $182,000; the value of the asset is $179,000 and basis is $180,000. *See Treas. Reg. 1.1001–2(a).*

(1) *If the taxpayer is not personally liable on the debt (nonrecourse debt),* the unpaid debt is an amount realized on a sale of the asset and all gain is from sale of the property ($2,000 in this example), not forgiveness of indebtedness income. *Rev. Rul. 76–111*, 1976–1 C.B. 214.

(2) *If the taxpayer is personally liable (recourse debt)*, the answer is more complex.

(a) *Release of property to creditor.* In the usual case, the property is released to the creditor (whether through foreclosure sale or otherwise) and the debt is forgiven. In that case, any gain resulting from the excess of unpaid debt over the value of the property is discharge of indebtedness income ($3,000 in the prior example — debt of $182,000 minus $179,000 of value). Then compute gain or loss from the sale of the asset, based on the difference between the value and basis (a loss of $1,000 in the example

— $180,000 basis minus $179,000 value). The net result is $2,000 gain ($3,000 discharge of indebtedness income minus a $1,000 loss, assuming the loss is deductible).

Is there any reason why the recourse and nonrecourse examples should be treated differently? The Court in *Commissioner v. Tufts*, 461 U.S. 300 (1983), acknowledged that the nonrecourse loan case should be treated like the personal liability case, but acquiesced in the government's treatment of the entire gain as gain on the sale of the asset ($2,000 in the example) when the debt is nonrecourse.

What happens if the debtor remains personally liable after the creditor takes the property? Does that postpone discharge of indebtedness income ($3,000 in the example)? The government says "no." *But see Aizawa v. Commissioner*, 99 T.C. 197 (1992), *aff'd in unpublished opinion*, 29 F.3d 630 (9th Cir. 1994). In *Aizawa*, the court held that, if the debtor remained personally liable after release of the property to the creditor, the discharge of indebtedness income based on the difference between the debt and the value of the property is held in suspense to see if the debtor will pay the debt in the future. This means that the taxpayer, in the example, takes a $1,000 loss and waits to see if he must report $3,000 of discharge of indebtedness income in the future. What chance is there that the debtor will report the discharge of indebtedness income, if the debt is not repaid? *See* Wolfman, *Foreclosure Sales and Recourse Debt*, 78 Tax Notes 221 (1998) (criticizing *Aizawa* decision).

If the debtor-taxpayer remains personally liable and has already reported the $3,000 as discharge of indebtedness income, what happens if the debtor *does* pay the $3,000 in the future? Does the taxpayer have a $3,000 loss deduction? Is it a capital loss (assuming the asset was a capital asset)?

(b) *Third party debt assumption.* If the property is sold to a third party who assumes the debt, the assumed debt is included in the amount realized on the sale, whether or not the seller remains personally liable; in the prior example, assumption of the $182,000 debt produces a $2,000 gain. What is the answer if the buyer assumes only $179,000 of the debt and the seller remains liable for the full $182,000?

§ 16.02 CRITIQUE OF INCLUDING BORROWED FUNDS IN BASIS

[A]—Tax exempt bond analogy

A taxpayer who deducts investments financed with loans gets the best of two worlds. The investment is eligible for the tax breaks which reduce the tax on savings (such as accelerated depreciation, expensing, or an investment tax credit). At the same time the interest is deductible. Recall the earlier discussion which explained how deductions for savings (of which accelerated depreciation is an example), is like taxing the savings but exempting the income earned on after-tax savings. In effect, some portion of the investment is analogous to buying tax exempt bonds. And yet interest on the loan to acquire that investment is deductible, a result that is denied in the tax exempt bond situation.

You can understand this point by the following example. First, assume a taxpayer who invests $500, at a 10% rate of return, for one year. The $500 is expensed for tax purposes even though it has value beyond the year. In year 2, the taxpayer collects $550. The tax rate in all years is 28%. The after tax income in year 2 is $396 (72% times $550). Notice that this is the equivalent of taxing the $500 in year 1, investing $360 after-tax, and keeping the 10% return of $36 tax free.

Now assume that the taxpayer made this investment by borrowing $360 of its purchase price, with a 10% interest charge. Still, the entire $500 deduction is allowed, producing the equivalent of a $360 investment earning 10% tax free. But the interest on the $360 loan to produce this "exempt" income is deductible!

[B]—Tax shelter computations

[i] Explanation

A more mechanical but more complete way of looking at the tax advantages of including debt in basis is to compute the rate of return that the taxpayer gets on his out-of-pocket investment when he borrows. For example, if a taxpayer invests $20,000 out-of-pocket and borrows $80,000 to invest a total of $100,000 in a business, his real concern is whether the return on the $20,000 in future years produces a good rate of return. The following summary of factors will help you understand how that rate of return would be computed. It explains what goes into a tax shelter. You should pay close attention to whether the factors are tax rules or financial facts which exist independent of the tax rules. It is too common to focus on the desirable tax results without paying attention to the financial facts which might make the investment unwise, despite the tax advantages. Factors 1–5 deal with annual cash flows. Factors 6–7 deal with disposing of the property.

First, what is the gross income from the venture? This is a financial fact.

Second, what cash payments must be made each year? This is also a financial fact. The taxpayer might have expenses unrelated to debt, such as maintenance costs for the property. In a lease transaction, however, the tenant is often responsible for these costs. The investor is likely to be a lawyer or doctor who never sees the property and does not want responsibility for managing it. The most significant payments by the taxpayer are for principal and interest on the debt. The period over which the debt will be paid determines how much principal and interest will be paid each year. If the payments in the early years are mostly interest (something that will look good to the taxpayer because the interest is deductible), the taxpayer must remember that he may have to raise money in the future to repay the debt. Sometimes all the payments in the early years are interest and the principal must be repaid in one year in the future (a balloon payment). Frequently, the debt and interest payments equal the gross income.

Third, the tax deductions and credits must be computed for every year of the investment. If the investment is eligible for an investment credit, that usually has the effect of reducing the amount of out-of-pocket investment the taxpayer must incur. It may also reduce basis. The rate at which basis can be deducted must also be computed. This requires determining depreciation and amortization rates and deciding whether outlays can be expensed rather than capitalized. Every legal question you have encountered involving depreciation and amortization rates and the distinction between capital expenditures and current expenses becomes important at this point. To the extent that the tax deductions exceed the income from the venture, the sheltering effect comes into play and the taxpayer increases cash flow in the form of reduced taxes on other income.

In the early years of the venture there will be net operating losses for tax purposes. Most debts are paid off in level payments, with the interest being a large portion of the payment in the early years. Thus, repayment of an $80,000 debt will consist of a very small amount of debt repayment in the early years, with most of the payment being interest. However, the basis for depreciation deductions will include the full $80,000, and will be much more than the principal payments on the debt. Interest plus depreciation deductions will therefore exceed the gross income from the venture.

Fourth, the tax rate must be estimated. The value of the shelter usually depends on net losses offsetting other income, the value of which is a function of the tax rate.

Fifth, in the later years, the tax deductions will decline, as the depreciation is used up, and the taxable income from the venture becomes positive. The point in time when this occurs is usually called the crossover point. At that time the taxpayer must pay tax, often resulting in a negative cash flow. The debt payments are probably continuing unabated and the taxpayer must consider how to get the money to pay the tax. One way to deal with this possibility is to subtract from the earlier positive cash flow a sum of money (a sinking fund) and put it in a bank where it will accumulate interest sufficient to pay off the obligations that might arise in the future. For financial planning purposes, this sum of money is generally treated as a reduction of the positive cash flows in the early years of the tax shelter and reduces the net cash flow in those years.

Sixth, the taxpayer must think about the possibility that he will want to get out of the venture, often at the crossover point. In this connection, he must consider how easily he can sell the property. He must also consider what the value of the property is likely to be. Both of these facts are financial facts, not tax facts. If the value is high enough, he might sell the property and get cash over and above any unpaid debt. If the property has gone down in value, the taxpayer must worry about whether the debt is recourse or nonrecourse. If it is recourse, he must find the money to repay the debt unless the buyer will assume the debt. If the debt is nonrecourse, however, he can walk away from the property and let the creditor worry about collecting the debt out of the value of the property. It is too common for investors in tax shelters not to worry about the future, because they are blinded by the sheltering effects of the early deductions. In fact, the economic projections for a tax shelter may assume optimistic future values, without which the investment would be unwise.

Seventh, the tax consequences of disposition must also be considered. Any disposition (including a gift) triggers realization of unpaid debt as an amount realized. The government suspects that many taxpayers never report this amount. The tax treatment of the gain is also important. If recapture rules apply, converting capital gain to ordinary income, a great deal of the gain will be ordinary income.

[ii] Example

The above text explaining tax shelters can be illustrated by the following example.

Financial facts. We assume that residential rental real estate is purchased in year 0 for $20,000 down and an $80,000 nonrecourse 30-year loan, paying 10% interest. Debt payments and rent begin in year 1. The annual payments on the mortgage are $8,486.33, part interest, part principal. Annual rent is $10,607.92. This rent gives the taxpayer a real financial 10% rate of return on the $100,000 investment over 30 years, assuming that real financial depreciation (not tax depreciation) occurs on a decelerated depreciation basis. (The present value of year 30 rent is 607.92 (10607.92/ 1.1^{30}); real depreciation in year 1 is therefore 607.92 and net income is 10000.) We further assume that the taxpayer sells the asset after 5 years, and that the asset has sufficient value over unpaid debt for the taxpayer to collect $20,000 cash. This assumption is made to provide easy comparison between the rates of return for the tax shelter investor and for the investor who puts $20,000 into a bank account for five years; in each case the investor invests $20,000, which he gets back after a five-year period.

Tax facts. The taxpayer can deduct the interest and depreciate the $100,000 purchase price over a 27.5-year period ($100,000 divided by 27.5 = 3,636.36 per year — assume a full year's depreciation in the first year). Capital gains are taxed at 25%. The taxpayer is in the 39.6% tax bracket. One would expect therefore that the after-tax return on the $20,000 investment for a taxpayer in the 39.6% bracket would be 6.04%, given the 10% before tax rate of return. The taxpayer, however, does better than that. Why?

(A) CASH FLOW WITHOUT TAX *BEFORE* SALE

YEAR	RENT	INTEREST	PRINCIPAL	TOTAL PAYMENTS	NET $ FLOW
1	10607.92	8000.00	486.33	8486.33	2121.59
2	10607.92	7951.36	534.97	8486.33	2121.59
3	10607.92	7897.86	588.47	8486.33	2121.59
4	10607.92	7839.02	647.31	8486.33	2121.59
5	10607.92	7774.28	712.05	8486.33	2121.59
			2969.13		

Cash flow *after* sale. The sale in year 5 increases net cash flow IN YEAR 5 by $20,000, for a year 5 total of $22,121.59.

(B) TAX COMPUTATION BEFORE SALE

YEAR	RENT	INTEREST	DEPREC.	TOTAL DEDUCT.	TAXABLE INCOME	TAX REFUND
1	10607.92	8000.00	3636.36	11636.36	(1028.44)	407.26
2	10607.92	7951.36	3636.36	11587.72	(979.80)	388.00
3	10607.92	7897.86	3636.36	11534.22	(926.30)	336.81
4	10607.92	7839.02	3636.36	11474.38	(867.46)	343.51
5	10607.92	7774.28	3636.36	11410.64	(802.72)	317.88

(C) COMPUTATION OF TAX ON SALE

The sale in year 5 would produce gain, computed as follows:

1. AMOUNT REALIZED = UNPAID DEBT PLUS CASH.

The unpaid debt is the original $80,000 debt minus $2,969.13 of principal paid, which equals $77,030.87. Cash received equals $20,000. Amount realized is therefore $97,030.87.

2. BASIS = ORIGINAL COST MINUS DEPRECIATION.

The original cost is $100,000. Depreciation (5 times $3,636.36) equals $18,181.80. Basis is therefore $81,818.20.

3. GAIN = AMOUNT REALIZED MINUS BASIS = $15,212.67 ($97,030.87 MINUS $81,818.20).

4. TAX ON CAPITAL GAIN = $3,803.17 (.25 TIMES $15,212.67).

The overall year 5 tax is therefore a *payment* (not a refund) of $3,485.29 ($3,803.17 MINUS the $317.88 "refund").

(D) CASH FLOW WITH TAXES

YEAR	NET CASH FLOW WITHOUT TAXES	TAX REFUND (+) OR PAYMENT (-)	TOTAL CASH FLOW
1	2121.59	+ 407.26	2528.85
2	2121.59	+ 388.00	2509.59
3	2121.59	+ 366.81	2488.40
4	2121.59	+ 343.51	2465.10
5	22,121.59	- 3485.29	18,636.30

The total cash flow produces an after-tax rate of return on the original $20,000 of 9.29%, rather than 6.04%. You can see this by thinking of the annual cash flow as money you can draw down from a bank at a 9.29% interest rate (that is, $1,858 per year; 9.29% times $20,000). You may think the rate of return is higher than that, looking at annual total cash flows, but remember that you must not take all of the annual cash flow each year because you must save some money to pay taxes in year 5 (a sinking fund) and have $20,000 left.

You should use this problem to understand what tax law changes would increase or decrease the after tax rate of return. What effect would the following changes in the law have: (1) slower depreciation (*e.g.*, 39 years for commercial realty, as of May, 13, 1993; previously 31.5 years), expensing, or a tax credit (*e.g.*, low-income housing); (2) a higher tax bracket; (3) ending the preferential tax on capital gains at the time of disposition; (4) higher asset value after five years?

[C]—Policy concerns specific to tax shelter borrowing

There are several reasons why borrowing to make tax shelter investments might pose more serious policy concerns than borrowing for other activities.

(1) The investments might not be economically desirable. Congress probably adopted many of the tax incentives, such as accelerated depreciation and credits, without expecting borrowers to package the tax breaks to produce unexpectedly large total benefits for low economic return activities.

(2) High-bracket borrowers might buy up property from those who cannot use the tax breaks. They do this because they are able to use the deductions and credits to offset not only the income from the activity financed with loans but also other income. They can, in other words, shelter other income, such as personal service and investment income with tax losses from the activity. This may cause a shift of ownership to urban dwellers, such as lawyers, doctors, and others who know little about the business in which they invest, such as farming.

(3) The investor is not taking much risk. Remember the analogy in the discussion of tax-exempt bonds between borrowing and shifting an investment from stock to tax-exempt bonds. The analogy seemed apt because the borrower had to contemplate the possibility of using the stock to pay off the loan. Tax shelter borrowing is often nonrecourse, however, so the creditor can foreclose only on property used as security, not other investments which the taxpayer may own. This is likely to produce a lot of excess speculation in property with low economic returns.

(4) Another way to think about the tax shelter is that the ability to shelter income with the deductible loan allows the individual taxpayer to use the

tax sheltered money for personal consumption purposes. In effect the taxpayer is borrowing for personal consumption. It is true that taxpayers can usually borrow for personal consumption without current tax, but the typical consumer loan is usually short-term. The time gap between *tax shelter* borrowing and repayment might be quite large. Moreover, a lot of consumer interest is not deductible anymore and it would be anomalous to allow consumer interest to be deductible through a tax shelter vehicle. Borrowing through the use of nonrecourse loans might therefore not be the kind of borrowing that the tax law wants to encourage.

These criticisms have not led Congress to prevent debt (not even nonrecourse debt) from being included in basis, but they have provided political support for modifications in the law applicable to investments generally — the slowing down of depreciation, cutting back on expensing, requiring certain costs to be capitalized. It also provided a justification for lowering the top tax rate to 31% in the 1980s. It remains to be seen what effect the adoption of a top 39.6% tax rate in 1993 will have on tax shelter investing.

Congress has, however, responded to the tax shelter problem in two ways — limiting the deductibility of net losses (i) created by nonrecourse debt, and (ii) when the taxpayer does not materially participate in the business activity. These legislative provisions are discussed in § 16.05, *infra*. But first we turn our attention to several judicial doctrines (*not* explicit statutory rules) which directly limit the inclusion of debt in basis.

§ 16.03 DEBT NOT INCLUDED IN BASIS

The *Crane* case assumed that the taxpayer had a real financial commitment equal to the debt. Even if the debtor was not personally liable, the opportunity to acquire equity in the property, eventually ripening into full ownership, would result in payment of the debt. There was no hint in *Crane* that the debt was artificially inflated to exceed the value of the property. Nor was the debt contingent. Inflated or contingent debt provides insufficient likelihood of payment to justify inclusion in basis, as this section explains.

[A]—Contingent debt

"Contingent debt" is not included in basis, even after *Crane*. "[N]o amount is to be included in cost with respect to those obligations which are so contingent and indefinite that they are not susceptible to present valuation, until such time as they become fixed and absolute and capable of determination with reasonable accuracy." *Rev. Rul. 55-675*, 1955-2 C.B. 567. In *Gibson Products Co. v. United States*, 460 F. Supp. 1109 (N.D. Tex. 1978), *aff'd*, 637 F.2d 1041 (5th Cir. 1981), the court summarized the cases dealing with contingent debt, as follows: "These cases hold that an obligation, which is too contingent and speculative, should not be included in cost basis, irrespective of the possible application of the *Crane* doctrine. In a sense, the nature of the inquiry is similar to the all-events test used for accrual tax accounting purposes, although none of the above-cited cases make reference to that test." *See also Redford v. Commissioner*, 28 T.C. 773 (1957) (purchaser agreed to pay the lesser of $25,000 or one-half of the profits from the resale of the purchased land; the obligation could not be included in basis).

[B]—Value less than nonrecourse debt

ESTATE OF FRANKLIN v. COMMISSIONER

544 F.2d 1045 (9th Cir. 1976)

SNEED, CIRCUIT JUDGE: . . .

This case involves another effort on the part of the Commissioner to curb the use of real estate tax shelters. In this instance he seeks to disallow deductions for the taxpayers' distributive share of losses reported by a limited partnership with respect to its acquisition of a motel and related property. These "losses" have their origin in deductions for depreciation and interest claimed with respect to the motel and related property. These deductions were disallowed by the Commissioner on the ground either that the acquisition was a sham or that the entire acquisition transaction was in substance the purchase by the partnership of an option to acquire the motel and related property on January 15, 1979. The Tax Court held that the transaction constituted an option exercisable in 1979 and disallowed the taxpayers' deductions. We affirm this disallowance although our approach differs somewhat from that of the Tax Court.

The interest and depreciation deductions were taken by Twenty-Fourth Property Associates (hereinafter referred to as Associates), a California limited partnership of which Charles T. Franklin and seven other doctors were the limited partners. The deductions flowed from the purported "purchase" by Associates of the Thunderbird Inn, an Arizona motel, from Wayne L. Romney and Joan E. Romney (hereinafter referred to as the Romneys) on November 15, 1968.

Under a document entitled "Sales Agreement," the Romneys agreed to "sell" the Thunderbird Inn to Associates for $1,224,000. The property would be paid for over a period of ten years, with interest on any unpaid balance of seven and one-half percent per annum. "Prepaid interest" in the amount of $75,000 was payable immediately; monthly principal and interest installments of $9,045.36 would be paid for approximately the first ten years, with Associates required to make a balloon payment at the end of the ten years of the difference between the remaining purchase price, forecast as $975,000, and any mortgages then outstanding against the property.

The purchase obligation of Associates to the Romneys was nonrecourse; the Romneys' only remedy in the event of default would be forfeiture of the partnership's interest. The sales agreement was recorded in the local county. A warranty deed was placed in an escrow account, along with a quitclaim deed from Associates to the Romneys, both documents to be delivered either to Associates upon full payment of the purchase price, or to the Romneys upon default.

The sale was combined with a leaseback of the property by Associates to the Romneys; Associates therefore never took physical possession. The lease payments were designed to approximate closely the principal and interest payments with the consequence that with the exception of the $75,000 prepaid interest payment no cash would cross between Associates and Romneys until the balloon payment. The lease was on a net basis; thus, the Romneys were responsible for all of the typical expenses of owning the motel property including all utility costs, taxes, assessments, rents, charges, and levies of "every name, nature and kind whatsoever." The Romneys also were to continue to be responsible for the first and second mortgages until the final purchase installment was made; the Romneys could, and indeed did, place additional mortgages on the property without the permission of Associates. Finally, the Romneys were allowed to propose new capital improvements which Associates would be required to either build themselves or allow the Romneys to construct with compensating modifications in rent or purchase price.

In holding that the transaction between Associates and the Romneys more nearly resembled an option than a sale, the Tax Court emphasized that Associates had the power at the end of ten years to walk away from the transaction and merely lose its $75,000 "prepaid interest payment." It also pointed out that a deed was never recorded and that the "benefits and burdens of ownership" appeared to remain with the Romneys. Thus, the sale was combined with a leaseback in which no cash would pass; the Romneys remained responsible under the mortgages, which they could increase; and the Romneys could make capital improvements. The Tax Court further justified its "option" characterization by reference to the nonrecourse nature of the purchase money debt and the nice balance between the rental and purchase money payments.

Our emphasis is different from that of the Tax Court. We believe the characteristics set out above can exist in a situation in which the sale imposes upon the purchaser a genuine indebtedness within the meaning of § 167(a), Internal Revenue Code of 1954, which will support both interest and depreciation deductions. . . .

In none of [the cases establishing a genuine indebtedness], however, did the taxpayer fail to demonstrate that the purchase price was at least approximately equivalent to the fair market value of the property. Just such a failure occurred here. The Tax Court explicitly found that on the basis of the facts before it the value of the property could not be estimated.[3] In our view this defect in the taxpayers' proof is fatal. [Editor — The seller in this case was the creditor. That is why the debt exceeded the value of the property. A third-party lender, such as a bank, is unlikely to lend more than value.]

Reason supports our perception. An acquisition such as that of Associates if at a price approximately equal to the fair market value of the property under ordinary circumstances would rather quickly yield an equity in the property which the purchaser could not prudently abandon. This is the stuff of substance. It meshes with the form of the transaction and constitutes a sale.

No such meshing occurs when the purchase price exceeds a demonstrably reasonable estimate of the fair market value. Payments on the principal of the purchase price yield no equity so long as the unpaid balance of the purchase price exceeds the then existing fair market value. Under these circumstances the purchaser by abandoning the transaction can lose no more than a mere chance to acquire an equity in the future should the value of the acquired property increase. While this chance undoubtedly influenced the Tax Court's determination that the transaction before us constitutes an option, we need only point out that its existence fails to supply the substance necessary to justify treating the transaction as a sale ab initio. It is not necessary to the disposition of this case to decide the tax consequences of a transaction such as that before us if in a subsequent year the fair market

---

[3] The Tax Court found that appellants had "not shown that the purported sales price of $1,224,000 (or any other price) had any relationship to the actual market value of the motel property. . . ." Petitioners spent a substantial amount of time at trial attempting to establish that, whatever the actual market value of the property, Associates acted in the good faith *belief* that the market value of the property approximated the selling price. However, this evidence only goes to the issue of sham and does not supply substance to this transaction. . . .

value of the property increases to an extent that permits the purchaser to acquire an equity.[4]

Authority also supports our perception. It is fundamental that "depreciation is not predicated upon ownership of property *but rather upon an investment in property*." In the transaction before us and during the taxable years in question the purchase price payments by Associates have not been shown to constitute an *investment in the property*. Depreciation was properly disallowed. Only the Romneys had an investment in the property.

Authority also supports disallowance of the interest deductions. This is said even though it has long been recognized that the absence of personal liability for the purchase money debt secured by a mortgage on the acquired property does not deprive the debt of its character as a bona fide debt obligation able to support an interest deduction. However, this is no longer true when it appears that the debt has economic significance only if the property substantially appreciates in value prior to the date at which a very large portion of the purchase price is to be discharged. Under these circumstances the purchaser has not secured "the use or forbearance of money." Nor has the seller advanced money or forborne its use. Prior to the date at which the balloon payment on the purchase price is required, and assuming no substantial increase in the fair market value of the property, the absence of personal liability on the debt reduces the transaction in economic terms to a mere chance that a genuine debt obligation may arise. This is not enough to justify an interest deduction. To justify the deduction the debt must exist; potential existence will not do. For debt to exist, the purchaser, in the absence of personal liability, must confront a situation in which it is presently reasonable from an economic point of view for him to make a capital investment in the amount of the unpaid purchase price. Associates during the taxable years in question, confronted no such situation. *Compare Crane v. Commissioner*, 331 U.S. 1 (1947).

Our focus on the relationship of the fair market value of the property to the unpaid purchase price should not be read as premised upon the belief that a sale is not a sale if the purchaser pays too much. Bad bargains from the buyer's point of view — as well as sensible bargains from buyer's, but exceptionally good from the seller's point of view — do not thereby cease to be sales. We intend our holding and explanation thereof to be understood as limited to transactions substantially similar to that now before us.

---

[4] These consequences would include a determination of the proper basis of the acquired property at the date the increments to the purchaser's equity commenced.

COMMENTS AND QUESTIONS

1. *Estate of Franklin* does not technically decide whether some value less than the nonrecourse debt could be included in basis when the asset is purchased. In *Pleasant Summit Land Corp. v. Commissioner*, 863 F.2d 263 (3d Cir. 1988), the court held that the value of the property could be included in basis, where the nonrecourse debt exceeded value. The court reasoned that the taxpayer would be likely to pay off *that amount* to prevent the creditor from foreclosing. The government objected that this created significant valuation problems. And, indeed, most courts have disagreed with *Pleasant Summit* and have not allowed the taxpayer to include in basis any of the unpaid debt in an *Estate of Franklin* situation — that is, whenever unpaid nonrecourse debt is much greater than the purchased asset's value. *See Bergstrom v. U.S.*, 37 Fed. Cl. 164 (*Ct. Fed. Cl. 1996*).

Evaluate the following critique of *Pleasant Summit*. *First*, if the taxpayer wants the property, he would be willing to pay its value. But does he want it? If not, we cannot be confident that even the property's value will be paid. Taxpayers who state nonrecourse debt far in excess of value are after the tax breaks, not the property. Often, there is a balloon payment obligation (the debt is due only after ten or twenty years). This is very different from nonrecourse buyers whose debt is *less* than value in a typical commercial purchase; these buyers want the property and will pay the debt. *Second*, it is hard to know what the value is. Why should the taxpayer be allowed to create difficult valuation problems for the government when the debt is much greater than value?

In *Pleasant Summit*, the nonrecourse debt was created in connection with the acquisition of the asset. Suppose the taxpayer is a creditor-bank which acquires the property in a foreclosure proceeding, subject to a preexisting large nonrecourse debt, which exceeds the property's value. In that case, should the bank be allowed to include up to the value of the property in basis?

2. If basis does *not* include nonrecourse debt or value at the time of purchase, what if value later exceeds unpaid debt — *e.g.*, either because debt is paid or value increases? Do you suddenly include the remaining unpaid debt in basis for the future?

3. If basis does not include debt or value, because debt far exceeds value, how should the taxpayer treat the annual debt payments that are in fact made? In *Estate of Franklin*, the borrower leased the property back to the seller for rent, and the buyer-borrower's "debt" and "interest" payments equalled the rent received. It was a washout. Shouldn't the tax law recognize these events as a washout by permitting a deduction of the "debt" and "interest" payments from the rent?

Suppose the buyer-borrower does not lease the property back to the seller, but actually makes "debt" and "interest" payments to the seller. Should these payments be deductible by the buyer? On what theory — are they the seller's share of profits from the property; are they depreciation? *Cf. Holden Fuel Oil Co. v. Commissioner*, 479 F.2d 613, 616 (6th Cir. 1973).

§ 16.04 TAX OWNERSHIP

You have read the Court of Appeals decision in *Estate of Franklin*, which emphasized that the unpaid debt far exceeded the asset's value. The Tax Court had relied on a different theory — that the taxpayer was not the tax owner of the property. The taxpayer was instead like the holder of an option to buy the property. If the taxpayer thought the investment was a good one, the "debt" would be paid and the property would belong to the taxpayer. The material in this section discusses the concept of "tax ownership." The inquiry is related to the question asked frequently in this course — when is a state law relationship recognized for tax purposes (*e.g.*, what does "marriage" mean in the tax law?).

The discussion involves sale-leasebacks used to finance construction of buildings. The cast of characters includes an outside party who is the lender (often an insurance company). The two key players are the buyer and seller of the property. The buyer borrows money to buy the property and then leases the property to the seller — hence the phrase "sale-leaseback." Or at least that is how the parties want the transaction to be viewed for tax purposes.

In fact, the "buyer" may have little to gain from the transaction, other than tax breaks. The seller is very much like a borrower who obtains a loan to finance the construction. When the "seller" becomes a tenant, by taking back a lease from the buyer, the rent is like the principal and interest on the loan. The issue in these cases is whether the "seller" should be treated as the borrower, rather than the buyer.

The seller-tenant would probably have preferred to borrow directly and own the property. The seller-tenant is, however, unable to use the tax breaks (such as accelerated depreciation), or at least cannot use them as advantageously as the "buyer." The seller-tenant may already have net operating losses or be in a lower tax bracket than the buyer. So a "middleman" becomes the buyer, uses the tax breaks, and compensates the "seller-tenant" in some way — often through a lower rent charge.

FRANK LYON CO. v. UNITED STATES

435 U.S. 561 (1978)

MR. JUSTICE BLACKMUN delivered the opinion of the Court.

[Editor — Here is an abbreviated statement of the facts. Lyon is a closely held corporation. Worthen is a bank. Frank Lyon is a majority shareholder in Lyon and serves on Worthen's board of directors. Federal regulations did not allow Worthen to invest directly in a new bank building. The deal to construct the building took shape in accordance with the State Bank Department's requirement that Worthen have an option to buy the building at the end of the fifteenth year of the lease and the Federal Reserve Board's requirement that the building be owned by an independent third party. It was arranged for Worthen to construct and Lyon to acquire the building and lease it to Worthen on a net lease basis. In a net lease, the tenant is responsible for all expenses related to the property such as insurance, taxes, and repairs. City Bank, first, and then New York Life Insurance Company would lend Lyon $7,140,000 to construct and acquire the building. Lyon also paid $500,000 of its own funds to implement this plan. Lyon originally offered Worthen a reduced rental obligation but eventually it was agreed that the rent would be higher than this offer but that Lyon would pay more interest to Worthen on an unrelated loan from Worthen to Lyon.

The primary term of the lease was 25 years. Rental payments from Worthen equaled the debt and interest due to the New York Life Insurance Company. Lyon was personally liable on the $7,140,000 debt. After 25 years Worthen could renew the lease for 8 five-year terms, at $300,000 rent per year. The land on which the building sat was owned by Worthen and was rented to Lyon for 75 years, which was 10 years longer than the building lease period could run if all options to renew were exercised. The rent for the land (called "ground rent") was negligible for the first 25 years but substantial thereafter, except that it declined to $10,000 for the last 10 years. The net payments to Lyon resulting from any lease renewals after the first 25 years (equal to the building rent minus ground rent) were calculated to approximate payment to Lyon of its $500,000 plus 6% compound interest. Worthen had options to buy the building at 11, 15, 20 and 25 years after entry into the lease, with the price set to assure payment of the insurance company's loan and Lyon's $500,000 with 6% compound interest. The District Court found as a fact that the option prices were the negotiated estimate by the parties of the fair market value of the building at the option dates and that they were reasonable.]

. . . [T]he Government takes the position that the Worthen-Lyon transaction in its entirety should be regarded as a sham. The agreement as a whole, it is said, was only an elaborate financing scheme designed to provide economic benefits to Worthen and a guaranteed return to Lyon. The latter was but a conduit used to forward the mortgage payments, made under the guise of rent paid by Worthen to Lyon, on to New York Life as mortgagee. This, the Government claims, is the true substance of the transaction as viewed under the microscope of the tax laws. Although the arrangement was cast in sale-and-leaseback form, in substance it was only a financing transaction, and the terms of the repurchase options and lease renewals so indicate. It is said that Worthen could reacquire the building simply by satisfying the mortgage debt and paying Lyon its $500,000 advance plus interest, regardless of the fair market value of the building at the time; similarly, when the mortgage was paid off, Worthen could extend the lease at drastically reduced bargain rentals that likewise bore no relation to fair rental value but were simply calculated to pay Lyon its $500,000 plus interest over the extended term. Lyon's return on the arrangement in no event could exceed 6% compound interest (although the Government conceded it might well be less). Furthermore, the favorable option and lease renewal terms made it highly unlikely that Worthen would abandon the building after it in effect had "paid off" the mortgage. The Government implies that the arrangement was one of convenience which, if accepted on its face, would enable Worthen to deduct its payments to Lyon as rent and would allow Lyon to claim a deduction for depreciation, based on the cost of construction ultimately borne by Worthen, which Lyon could offset against other income, and to deduct mortgage interest that roughly would offset the inclusion of Worthen's rental payments in Lyon's income. If, however, the Government argues, the arrangement was only a financing transaction under which Worthen was the owner of the building, Worthen's payments would be deductible only to the extent that they represented mortgage interest, and Worthen would be entitled to claim depreciation; Lyon would not be entitled to deductions for either mortgage interest or depreciation and it would not have to include Worthen's "rent" payments in its income because its function with respect to those payments was that of a conduit between Worthen and New York Life. . . .

It is true, of course, that the transaction took shape according to Worthen's needs. As the Government points out, Worthen throughout the negotiations regarded the respective proposals of the independent investors in terms of its own cost of funds. It is also true that both Worthen and the prospective investors compared the various proposals in terms of the return anticipated on the investor's equity. But all this is natural for parties contemplating entering into a transaction of this kind. Worthen needed a building for its banking operations and other purposes and necessarily had to know what its cost would be. The investors were in business to employ their funds in the most remunerative way possible. And, as the Court has said in the past, a transaction must be given its effect in accord with what actually occurred and not in accord with what might have occurred.

There is no simple device available to peel away the form of this transaction and to reveal its substance. The effects of the transaction on all the parties were obviously different from those that would have resulted had Worthen been able simply to make a mortgage agreement with New York Life and to receive a $500,000 loan from Lyon. . . .

[M]ost significantly, it was Lyon alone, and not Worthen, who was liable on the notes, first to City Bank, and then to New York Life. Despite the facts that Worthen had agreed to pay rent and that this rent equaled the amounts due from Lyon to New York Life, should anything go awry in the later years of the lease, Lyon was primarily liable. No matter how the transaction could have been devised otherwise, it remains a fact that as the agreements were placed in final form, the obligation on the notes fell squarely on Lyon. Lyon, an ongoing enterprise, exposed its very business well-being to this real and substantial risk.

The effect of this liability on Lyon is not just the abstract possibility that something will go wrong and that Worthen will not be able to make its payments. Lyon has disclosed this liability on its balance sheet for all the world to see. Its financial position was affected substantially by the presence of this long-term debt, despite the offsetting presence of the building as an asset. To the extent that Lyon has used its capital in this transaction, it is less able to obtain financing for other business needs. . . .

Other factors also reveal that the transaction cannot be viewed as anything more than a mortgage agreement between Worthen and New York Life and a loan from Lyon to Worthen. There is no legal obligation between Lyon and Worthen representing the $500,000 "loan" extended under the Government's theory. And the assumed 6% return on this putative loan — required by the audit to be recognized in the taxable year in question — will be realized only when and if Worthen exercises its options.

[Editor — The government treated the $500,000 as a loan by Lyon accruing original issue discount during the 11-year period prior to the first date on which Worthen could exercise an acquisition option. The discount was computed on the assumption that the option price equalled the redemption price of the loan.]

The Court of Appeals acknowledged that the rents alone, due after the primary term of the lease and after the mortgage has been paid, do not provide the simple 6% return which, the Government urges, Lyon is guaranteed. Thus, if Worthen chooses not to exercise its options, Lyon is gambling that the rental value of the building during the last 10 years of the ground lease, during which the ground rent is minimal, will be sufficient to recoup its investment before it must negotiate again with Worthen regarding the ground lease. There are simply too many contingencies, including variations in the value of real estate, in the cost of money, and in the capital structure of Worthen, to permit the conclusion that the parties intended to enter into the transaction as structured in the audit and according to which the Government now urges they be taxed.

It is not inappropriate to note that the Government is likely to lose little revenue, if any, as a result of the shape given the transaction by the parties. No deduction was created that is not either matched by an item of income or that would not have been available to one of the parties if the transaction had been arranged differently. . . .

We recognize that the Government's position, and that taken by the Court of Appeals, is not without superficial appeal. One, indeed, may theorize that Frank Lyon's presence on the Worthen board of directors; Lyon's departure from its principal corporate activity into this unusual venture; the parallel between the payments under the building lease and the amounts due from Lyon on the New York Life mortgage; . . . the nature and presence of the several options available to Worthen; and the tax benefits, such as the use of double declining balance depreciation, that accrue to Lyon during the initial years of the arrangement, form the basis of an argument that Worthen should be regarded as the owner of the building and as the recipient of nothing more from Lyon than a $500,000 loan.

We however, as did the District Court, find this theorizing incompatible with the substance and economic realities of the transaction: . . . Worthen's undercapitalization; Worthen's consequent inability, as a matter of legal restraint, to carry its building plans into effect by a conventional mortgage and other borrowing; the additional barriers imposed by the state and federal regulators; the suggestion, forthcoming from the state regulator, that Worthen possess an option to purchase; the requirement, from the federal regulator, that the building be owned by an independent third party; the presence of several finance organizations seriously interested in participating in the transaction and in the resolution of Worthen's problem; the submission of formal proposals by several of those organizations; the bargaining process and period that ensued; the competitiveness of the bidding; the bona fide character of the negotiations; the three-party aspect of the transaction; Lyon's substantiality and its independence from Worthen; the fact that diversification was Lyon's principal motivation; Lyon's being liable alone on the successive notes to City Bank and New York Life; the reasonableness, as the District Court found, of the rentals and of the option prices; the substantiality of the purchase prices; Lyon's not being engaged generally in the business of financing; the presence of all building depreciation risks on Lyon; the risk borne by Lyon, that Worthen might default or fail, as other banks have failed; the facts that Worthen could "walk away" from the relationship at the end of the 25-year primary term, and probably would do so if the option price were more than the then-current worth of the building to Worthen; the inescapable fact that if the building lease were not extended, Lyon would be the full owner of the building, free to do with it as it chose; Lyon's liability for the substantial ground rent if Worthen decides not to exercise any of its options to extend; the absence of any understanding between Lyon and Worthen that Worthen would exercise any of the purchase options; the nonfamily and nonprivate nature of the entire transaction; and the absence of any differential in tax rates and of special tax circumstances for one of the parties — all convince us that Lyon has far the better of the case.[18]

In so concluding, we emphasize that we are not condoning manipulation by a taxpayer through arbitrary labels and dealings that have no economic significance. Such, however, has not happened in this case.

In short, we hold that where, as here, there is a genuine multiple-party transaction with economic substance which is compelled or encouraged by business or regulatory realities, is imbued with tax-independent considerations, and is not shaped solely by tax-avoidance features that have meaningless labels attached, the Government should honor the allocation of rights and duties effectuated by the parties. Expressed another way, so long as the lessor retains significant and genuine attributes of the traditional lessor status, the form of the transaction adopted by the parties governs for tax purposes. What those attributes are in any particular case will necessarily depend upon its facts. It suffices to say that, as here, a sale-and-leaseback, in and of itself, does not necessarily operate to deny a taxpayer's claim for deductions.

The judgment of the Court of Appeals, accordingly, is reversed.

MR. JUSTICE STEVENS, dissenting.

In my judgment the controlling issue in this case is the economic relationship between Worthen and petitioner, and matters such as the number of parties, their reasons for structuring the transaction in a particular way, and the tax benefits which may result, are largely irrelevant. The question whether a leasehold has been created should be answered by

[18] Thus, the facts of this case stand in contrast to many others in which the form of the transaction actually created tax advantages that, for one reason or another, could not have been enjoyed had the transaction taken another form. *See, e.g., Sun Oil Co. v. Commissioner of Internal Revenue*, 562 F.2d 258 (CA 3 1977) (sale-and-leaseback of land between taxpayer and tax-exempt trust enabled the taxpayer to amortize, through its rental deductions, the cost of acquiring land not otherwise depreciable). Indeed, the arrangements in this case can hardly be labeled as tax-avoidance techniques in light of the other arrangements being promoted at the time.

examining the character and value of the purported lessor's reversionary estate.

For a 25-year period Worthen has the power to acquire full ownership of the bank building by simply repaying the amounts, plus interest, advanced by the New York Life Insurance Company and petitioner. During that period, the economic relationship among the parties parallels exactly the normal relationship between an owner and two lenders, one secured by a first mortgage and the other by a second mortgage. If Worthen repays both loans, it will have unencumbered ownership of the property. What the character of this relationship suggests is confirmed by the economic value that the parties themselves have placed on the reversionary interest.

All rental payments made during the original 25-year term are credited against the option repurchase price, which is exactly equal to the unamortized cost of the financing. The value of the repurchase option is thus limited to the cost of the financing, and Worthen's power to exercise the option is cost free. Conversely, petitioner, the nominal owner of the reversionary estate, is not entitled to receive any value for the surrender of its supposed rights of ownership. Nor does it have any power to control Worthen's exercise of the option.

"It is fundamental that 'depreciation is not predicated upon ownership of property *but rather upon an investment in property*.' No such investment exists when payments of the purchase price in accordance with the design of the parties yield no equity to the purchaser." *Estate of Franklin v. Commissioner*, 544 F.2d 1045, 1049 (CA 9 1976) (citations omitted; emphasis in original). Here, the petitioner has, in effect, been guaranteed that it will receive its original $500,000 plus accrued interest. But that is all. It incurs neither the risk of depreciation, nor the benefit of possible appreciation. Under the terms of the sale-leaseback, it will stand in no better or worse position after the 11th year of the lease — when Worthen can first exercise its option to repurchase — whether the property has appreciated or depreciated. And this remains true throughout the rest of the 25-year period.

Petitioner has assumed only two significant risks. First, like any other lender, it assumed the risk of Worthen's insolvency. Second, it assumed the risk that Worthen might not exercise its option to purchase at or before the end of the original 25-year term.[6] If Worthen should exercise that right

[6] The possibility that Worthen might not exercise its option is a risk for petitioner because in that event petitioner's advance would be amortized during the ensuing renewal lease terms, totaling 40 years. Yet there is a possibility that Worthen would choose not to renew for the full 40 years or that the burdens of owning a building and paying a ground rental of $10,000 during the years 2034 through 2044 would exceed the benefits of ownership.

not to repay, perhaps it would then be appropriate to characterize petitioner as the owner and Worthen as the lessee. But speculation as to what might happen in 25 years cannot justify the present characterization of petitioner as the owner of the building. Until Worthen has made a commitment either to exercise or not to exercise its option,[7] I think the Government is correct in its view that petitioner is not the owner of the building for tax purposes. At present, since Worthen has the unrestricted right to control the residual value of the property for a price which does not exceed the cost of its unamortized financing, I would hold, as a matter of law, that it is the owner.

I therefore respectfully dissent.

HILTON v. COMMISSIONER

74 T.C. 305 (1980)
aff'd per curiam, 671 F.2d 316 (9th Cir. 1982)

NIMS, JUDGE:

[Editor — It has not been easy to apply *Frank Lyon*. In *Hilton*, a department store was constructed with insurance company financing. The store was sold to several limited partnerships, which leased the store back to the Broadway company, which ran the store.

The taxpayers were partners who had invested $334,000 in the partnerships. Under partnership tax law, tax losses are passed through to partners. All of the partners' investment was used to pay the tax shelter promoters. The lease was a net lease. The lessee's rent during the first 30-year term was sufficient to pay 90% of the insurance company's nonrecourse construction loan. The remaining 10% was due at the end of the first 30 year term (hence the description "balloon payment"). Thereafter the lease could be

[7] In this case, the lessee is not "economically compelled" to exercise its option. Indeed, it may be more advantageous for Worthen to let its option lapse since the present value of the renewal leases is somewhat less than the price of the option to repurchase. *See Brief for United States* 40 n. 26. But whether or not Worthen is likely to exercise the option, as long as it retains its unrestricted cost-free power to do so, it must be considered the owner of the building.

In effect, Worthen has an option to "put" the building to petitioner if it drops in value below $500,000 plus interest. Even if the "put" appears likely because of bargain lease rates after the primary terms, that would not justify the present characterization of petitioner as the owner of the building.

renewed for terms of 23, 23, and 22 years. Rent under the first renewal term would more than cover any refinancing of the balloon payment.

The taxpayer's expert witness was unable to substantiate his claim that the department store would have a substantial residual value at the end of the various lease terms. It was also very likely that the tenant would renew the lease for one term (extending the 30-year term for another 23 years) because of the low rents. The court found that the taxpayers "would not at any time find it imprudent from an economic point of view to abandon the property."]

. . . [T]he central issue in this case is the bona fides of the sale-leaseback. This is essentially an exercise in substance versus form, and as earlier stated by the Supreme Court, "In the field of taxation, administrators of the law, and the courts, are concerned with substance and realities, and formal written documents are not rigidly binding." Notwithstanding the approval of the sale-leaseback in the *Frank Lyon* case, we do not understand the teaching of the Supreme Court's decision in that case to be that we are to accept *every* putative sale-leaseback transaction at face value, but rather that our precept is to determine whether there is, in the words of the Supreme Court, "a genuine multiple-party transaction with economic substance which is compelled or encouraged by business or regulatory realities, is imbued with tax-independent considerations, and is not shaped solely by tax-avoidance features that have meaningless labels attached." *Frank Lyon Co. v. United States*, 435 U.S. 561, 583–584.

We also recognize, as the Supreme Court made clear in *Frank Lyon*, that a sale-leaseback, in and of itself, does not necessarily operate to deny a taxpayer's claim for deductions. In this connection, implicit in the Supreme Court's opinion is the acceptance of the proposition (a position here argued in the brief amicus curiae) that the seller-lessee's financing requirements may be a valid business purpose to support a sale-leaseback transaction for tax purposes.

To recapitulate the foregoing, the transaction before us will not stand or fall merely because it involved a sale-leaseback mandated by Broadway's financing requirements, but rather must be tested to determine whether it (the transaction) (1) is genuinely multiple-party, (2) with economic substance, (3) compelled or encouraged by business realities (no "regulatory" realities are claimed), and (4) is imbued with tax-independent considerations which are not shaped solely by tax-avoidance features. *Frank Lyon Co. v. United States*, *supra*.

One key element of the above test is the phrase "genuinely multiple-party" for obviously, when looked at only from the viewpoint of Broadway, as seller-lessee, the transaction had economic substance and was encouraged by business realities. Petitioners have claimed in their brief and we have no reason to gainsay them that, had conventional mortgage financing been used, the insurance companies would have lent only 75 percent of the value of the property. The insurance companies, furthermore, had limitations on the total amounts and proportions of their funds that could be committed to direct real estate mortgages. Under the sale-leaseback approach Broadway was, in effect, able to finance 100 percent of the acquisition cost of the property. . . .

Similarly, Broadway had limitations in its loan and credit agreements with its banks which put a ceiling on the total amount of debt it could incur and also limited the total value of its property which could be mortgaged. At the same time, Broadway expected to be able to deduct as rent, during the initial 30-year term of the lease, an amount equal to 90 percent of the principal amortization and 100 percent of the interest costs of the underlying mortgage on the property. The mortgage contained a 10-percent balloon at the end of the 30-year term.

It is thus apparent that, viewed broadly from the vantage point of Broadway and the insurance companies, the sale-leaseback transaction followed what is essentially a widely used and acceptable business practice embracing substantial business as well as tax purposes and which had significant economic, nontaxable substance. In this context, we do not deem the existence of a net lease, a nonrecourse mortgage or rent during the initial lease term geared to the cost of interest and mortgage amortization to be, in and of themselves, much more than neutral commercial realities. Furthermore, the fact that the transaction was put together by an "orchestrator" (to use petitioner's term) would not alone prove fatal to the buyer-lessor's cause provided the result is economically meaningful on both sides of the equation. For even before the enactment of the at-risk rules of section 465 [Editor — *§ 465* is discussed later in this chapter], equipment-leveraged leases, often "packaged" by brokers, were acceptable to the Commissioner where substantial nontax economic interests were acquired by the buyer-lessor. Rev. Proc. 75-21, 1975-1 C.B. 715.

Overall, considering the involvement of Broadway and the insurance companies, there was at least a two-party aspect to the transaction. We explore subsequently herein, whether the facts, as they did in *Frank Lyon*, disclose a genuine three-party aspect.

But what Broadway sees is a reflection from only one polygon of the prism. In the *Frank Lyon* case, the Supreme Court appraised not only the substance of the seller-lessee's interest, but also that of the buyer-lessor and the legal and economic substance of the contractual relationship between the two.

We, therefore, turn now to a consideration of the substance of the buyer-lessor's (*i.e.,* the petitioners') interest, and here the substantiality of that interest, aside from tax considerations, is far less apparent. We must thus inquire: does the buyer-lessor's interest have substantial legal and economic significance aside from tax considerations, or is that interest simply the purchased tax byproduct of Broadway's economically impelled arrangement with the insurance companies? . . .

Under the *Frank Lyon* test, petitioners must show not only that their participation in the sale-leaseback was not motivated or shaped solely by tax avoidance features that have meaningless labels attached, but also that there is economic substance to the transaction independent of the apparent tax shelter potential. Another way of stating the test is suggested by the Ninth Circuit's opinion in *Estate of Franklin v. Commissioner*, 544 F.2d 1045 (9th Cir. 1976), *affg.* 64 T.C. 752 (1975), to wit: Could the buyer-lessor's method of payment for the property be expected at the outset to rather quickly yield an equity which buyer-lessor could not prudently abandon? An affirmative answer would produce, in the words of the Circuit Court, "the stuff of substance. It meshes with the form of the transaction and constitutes a sale." Consequently, if the test is not met, the buyer-lessor will not have made an investment in the property, regardless of the form of ownership. And it is fundamental that depreciation is not predicated upon ownership of property but rather upon an investment in property. *Estate of Franklin v. Commissioner*, *supra* at 1049.

We recognize that the result in *Estate of Franklin* was predicated upon a finding that the purchase price of the property in question exceeded a demonstrably reasonable estimate of the fair market value. Nevertheless, we consider the imprudent abandonment test to be equally applicable to other fact patterns. For example, we find it appropriate to inquire, as we do in the instant case, whether the foreseeable value of the property *to the buyer-lessor* would ever make abandonment imprudent. This then requires an examination of the economics of the buyer-lessor's position to determine whether there has been, in fact, an investment in the property. . . .

[T]he potential sources of economic gain for the petitioners [come] under the following categories:

(1) Net income or losses;

(2) Net proceeds resulting from: (a) mortgage refinancing; (b) condemnation; or (c) sale. . . .

. . . [W]e first address the following question: At what point, at what time, and under what conditions could it be presumed there would be net income to distribute, and in what amounts? Under the lease and deed of trust, all rent payments due under the lease for the first 30 years are to be used to service the mortgage notes, so no cash flow will be available to petitioners during the 30-year period. The lease rental is sufficient to amortize 90 percent of the principal amount of the mortgage notes, leaving $313,750 due in 1998.

At the end of the initial term of the lease, petitioners will have the option of either making capital contributions to cover the balloon payment or refinancing the balloon. Since there would be little incentive to do the former, in light of the rent provisions in the lease for subsequent option periods and the probability (as discussed supra) that Broadway would continue its occupancy for 23 years (at least beyond 1998), it must be assumed that, if possible, refinancing will be sought.

Assuming refinancing at 5 1/8-percent interest (the rate in the original mortgage) over the 23-year period of the first lease extension, the annual financing cost would be approximately $23,000, to be paid out of the fixed rental of $47,062.50; thus leaving a total pre-tax cash flow for division among and distribution to all of the petitioners of approximately $23,000 per annum. It goes without saying that the opportunity to earn $23,000 annually, commencing 30 years from the inception of the transaction, would not in and of itself appear to justify the $334,000 original investment by the petitioners in the . . . partnerships.

The foregoing analysis assumes, of course, that Broadway would exercise its renewal option for the first 23-year period. Given the extremely favorable terms on which Broadway could renew, however, the only conceivable reason why it (or any corporate successor) would not renew would be that the property had lost its economic viability, in which event the property would also be worthless to the petitioners. . . .

We are, in summary, persuaded that an objective economic analysis of this transaction from the point of view of the buyer-lessor, and therefore the petitioners, should focus on the value of the cash flow derived from the rental payments and that little or no weight should be placed on the speculative possibility that the property will have a substantial residual value at such time, if ever, that Broadway abandons the lease. The low rents and almost nominal cash flow leave little room for doubt that, apart from tax benefits, the value of the interest acquired by the petitioners is substantially less than the amount they paid for it. In terms discussed above, the buyer-lessor would not at any time find it imprudent from an economic point of view to abandon the property. *Estate of Franklin v. Commissioner*, 544 F.2d 1045 (9th Cir. 1976), *affg.* 64 T.C. 752 (1975). There is thus no justification for the petitioners' participation in this transaction apart from its tax consequences.

Having so analyzed petitioners' lack of potential for economic gain, we must nevertheless confront the question of how petitioners' position differs, if it does, from that of the buyer-lessor in the *Frank Lyon* case. . . .

Among the facts in the *Frank Lyon* case which distinguish it significantly from those in the case before us are the following:

(1) The rent during the initial lease term was sufficient to completely amortize the underlying mortgage principal, whereas in the case before us, the rent will amortize only 90 percent of the note principal, leaving a sizable balloon at the end.

(2) The rent in *Frank Lyon* was fair rental value for the property and after the initial lease term was substantial and free and clear to the buyer-lessor. In the case before us, the rent is not based on fair rental value. In the first renewal option period, the rent is relatively insignificant and, if applied to amortize the refinanced balloon, will provide an insignificant, if any, cash flow to petitioners.

(3) The buyer-lessor in *Frank Lyon* paid $500,000 of its own funds to the seller-lessee; in the case before us none of petitioners' funds went to Broadway.

(4) In *Frank Lyon*, the buyer-lessor stood to realize a substantial gain in the event the seller-lessee exercised its repurchase option; in the case before us, the petitioners cannot dispose of the property at a profit.

(5) In *Frank Lyon*, the buyer-lessor was a substantial corporate entity which participated actively in negotiating the terms and conditions of the sale and leaseback, while in the instant case the entire "deal" was packaged as a financing transaction by the orchestrator, Cushman, and then marketed by him and his colleagues as a tax shelter. While, as we have indicated previously, this factor, alone, might not be fatal to petitioners' cause, considered in concert with the other negative factors outlined above, it lends no credence to any contention that there is here present any "genuine multi-party transaction with economic substance," as mandated by the Supreme Court in *Frank Lyon*.

(6) The fact that the buyer-lessor in *Frank Lyon* was personally liable on the mortgage was, of course, a significant factor supporting the bona fides of the sale-leaseback transaction in that case. Nevertheless, we regard personal liability on the mortgage as atypical in modern real estate transactions and, consequently, we consider the absence of personal liability as a neutral factor in the case before us.

In summary, after considering all of the facts and circumstances in the case before us, we find that the petitioners have failed to show a genuine multiparty transaction with economic substance, compelled or encouraged by business realities and imbued with tax-independent considerations and not shaped solely by tax-avoidance features that have meaningless labels attached. . . .

Critique of sale-leasebacks as tax expenditures. You should be accustomed by now to taxpayers shifting around tax breaks through economic bargaining. For example, much of the benefit of tax exempt bond interest accrues to the state and local government debtor, not the taxpayer whose interest is exempt. Perhaps parties to sale-leaseback transactions shift tax breaks with favorable public policy results. Buildings get built which would not otherwise be built and renters enjoy lower rents. There is some reason to doubt whether sale-leasebacks produce such favorable consequences. First, some of the investment by middlemen-lessors goes to pay tax shelter promoters. Second, the renter does not capture all of the tax breaks through lower rent. The middleman keeps some of the tax benefits. A Joint Committee on Taxation study found that 21.5% of the tax benefits went to the middleman-lessor.

You might also be concerned about the following feature of sale-leasebacks. Who are the middlemen who get some of the tax breaks? Does their enjoyment of the tax benefits raise serious tax equity concerns? If you are concerned with problems related to sale-leasebacks but want to encourage taxpayers unable to use tax breaks to make investments without the middleman, why not do the following? Allow taxpayers to convert net operating business losses to a refundable tax credit right away. Do not wait for taxpayers to have offsetting gains in later years. Thus, a $100,000 net operating loss in year 1 would produce a refundable tax credit in year 1 equal to the top tax bracket times $100,000. That would eliminate the taxpayers' incentive to seek indirect ways to capture unusable tax breaks in the form of lower rent paid to tax shelter investors.

§ 16.05 STATUTORY LIMITS ON A TAX OWNER'S TAX BENEFITS

The materials in the prior sections show how hard it is for courts to deal with tax shelter problems. Unless economic potential, regardless of taxes, is virtually nonexistent, the transaction is not likely to be recast to deny tax breaks or tax ownership to the apparent owner. The statute has therefore been modified to limit the use of tax benefits under certain circumstances.

The major provisions deny deduction of *net losses* when there is either insufficient financial commitment or insufficient participation in the business by the taxpayer. Remember that these rules apply only after the case law determines that the taxpayer is entitled to deductions in the first place.

[A]—Limiting deductible net losses to financial stake

There are several keys to achieving a tax shelter. One is to include debt in basis. Another is to use net losses from a business to offset other income, such as personal service income. Doctors and lawyers often invested in tax shelters to reduce tax on professional fees. *§ 465* is the statute's direct response to this problem, adopted in 1976 and applied to real estate in 1986. As you go through the discussion, ask yourself whether the taxpayers in *Frank Lyon Co.*, *Hilton*, or *Estate of Franklin* would be caught by *§ 465*.

The best way to understand *§ 465* is to keep in mind the issues to which it is addressed. (1) *What taxpayers* are affected? (2) *What activities* are affected? (3) *What deductions are disallowed*: (a) deductions attributable to all debt or only *nonrecourse* debt; (b) all deductions, including those which offset income from the business financed by the debt, or, less broadly, only the deduction of *net losses* from that business? Think of *§ 465* as a series of forks in the road that give answers to these questions.

(1) *What taxpayers* are affected? *§ 465* affects individuals, partnerships, and corporations with five or fewer shareholders owning more than 50% of the stock. Other corporations, including publicly held corporations, do not worry about *§ 465*.

(2) *What activities* are affected? With two exceptions, all activities are covered. (Before 1986, real estate was *not* covered.) The exceptions are for corporations with five or fewer shareholders owning more than 50% of the stock. These corporations are *not* covered, *if* the activity is equipment leasing (a computer, for example), or it is an "active business," with, among other things, at least three non-owner employees. *§ 465(c)(4),(7)*.

(3) *What deductions are disallowed?* The target of the section is nonrecourse debt (with a major exception) which produces net losses, capable of reducing taxable income. The section does not prevent deductions from income arising from the specific activity in which the debt is incurred. That produces the following rules. *§ 465(a)(1),(b)(1),(2)*.

(a) *At-risk limitations.* First, net losses from the debt-financed activity are deductible only to the extent the taxpayer is "at risk." What does "at risk" mean? (1) It refers to out-of-pocket investment and debt for which the taxpayer is personally liable. (2) In addition, nonrecourse loans secured by real estate are treated as "at risk," if the lender is a typical business lender (like a bank), or a party related to the borrower if the loan is like that a commercial lender would make. This is an obvious benefit for real estate investment. *§ 465(b)(6).*

(b) *Only net losses affected.* Second, the at-risk limitation only applies to net losses, not deductions offsetting net income from the debt-financed activity itself.

The following example illustrates these rules. Assume an individual taxpayer pays $10,000 down and borrows nonrecourse $180,000, to buy a business machine.

The *financial* facts are:

Receipts			
	rent =	$19,000	
Expenditures			
	interest =		$18,000
	debt principal repayment =		2,000

The *tax* facts are:

Gross income			
	rent =	$19,000	
Deductions			
	interest =		$18,000
	depreciation =		27,000
			45,000
Net tax loss =			(26,000)

Imagine yourself as a tax policymaker confronted with the above example. Your *first* thought might be that $12,000 of the depreciation deduction ($27,000) should be deductible, because it is supported by the $12,000 out-of-pocket investment ($10,000 down and a $2,000 debt payment), but that the remaining $15,000 of depreciation should not be deducted, because it is supported only by nonrecourse debt. That might seem a bit harsh, however. In this example, the business income without depreciation is $1,000 (rent minus interest). You might therefore decide to take a *second* approach and let the nonrecourse debt support a deduction of basis equal to the net income from the investment financed by the nonrecourse debt, and only disallow the deduction of net losses from the business attributable to the nonrecourse debt.

The statute takes this *second* approach. It only addresses the problem of net losses and specifies that only $12,000 of the $26,000 net loss is deductible, offsetting the taxpayer's other income. The remaining $14,000 of net losses is not deductible, but is carried forward to later years. The nonrecourse debt is available to support a deduction against the $1,000 net income from the activity. In later years, the previously undeducted net loss of $14,000 is deductible when the taxpayer pays off the nonrecourse debt or when the taxpayer includes the unpaid debt in income (under the *Crane* and *Tufts* cases, *supra*).

The "at-risk" rules are a typical tax reform statute. Rather than alter the general rules about when basis includes debt, the statute limits the impact of those rules with complex and finely tuned provisions, which make very difficult reading.

[B]—Limiting deductible net losses if losses are "passive"

After *§ 465* was adopted, Congress continued to worry about the deduction of net business losses by certain taxpayers who were able to negotiate the *§ 465* maze. Consequently, *§ 469* was adopted in 1986. The taxpayer first applies *§ 465* to see if some or all net losses are still deductible. If they are, the taxpayer considers whether *§ 469* applies.

General idea. The general idea, not always worked out precisely in the statutory text, is that net losses from business should be available only if the taxpayer "materially participates" in the business. Even an at risk investment is insufficient. The statutory term for a net loss arising from a business activity in which the taxpayer does not "materially participate" is a "passive activity loss."

rule:

More specifically, the statute generally prevents passive activity losses from offsetting investment income, personal service income, and business income, except that a net loss from a passive activity can offset gain from another passive activity. For example, assume that a taxpayer covered by the passive activity rules has a $100,000 loss from a passive activity, $40,000 gain from a passive activity, and $80,000 personal service income. $60,000 of passive activity losses are disallowed. The passive activity rules are therefore like the investment interest rules — all passive activity losses and gains are lumped together the way investment interest and investment income are lumped together, and the overall losses from these activities are disallowed.

If passive activity losses are disallowed, they are carried forward to a later year and may end up being deducted in the future.

Who is covered by passive activity loss rules? Individuals, including partners, are covered by the passive activity loss rules. Corporations are *not* covered, with some exceptions. *First*, a corporation principally engaged in earning personal service income attributable to an owner's services is usually covered. *Second*, a corporation with five or fewer shareholders owning more than 50% of the stock cannot use passive activity losses to offset investment income, but can use passive activity losses to offset business income which does not arise from passive activities. Thus, a small family corporation could deduct passive losses from its "nonpassive" business income, but not from dividends and interest on its investments.

These rules leave most large corporations untouched. They can use net losses from passive activities to offset any income. Should General Electric be allowed to use passive losses to offset its income from sale of electric light bulbs or from interest and dividends?

Defining passive activity. The statute defines "material participation" to mean "regular, continuous, and substantial" involvement in the operations of the activity. That is some, but not much, help. Regulations provide an elaborate definition. *Treas. Reg. § 1.469-5T.* Limited partners usually lack "material participation."

Because the test is so difficult to administer, the statute treats some activities as automatically "passive." Rental activity is in that category. Then the statute gives back a little of what it took away. *First*, net losses from *real estate* rental activity will be deductible if an individual (but not a partnership) "actively" participates in the business — but only up to $25,000 per year (a boon which disappears as incomes rise over $100,000).

Second, the 1993 tax law added another exception for real estate rental activities. A taxpayer is not subject to the passive activity loss rules on real estate rental activity, if: (i) more than one half of the personal services the taxpayer performs during the year is in the real estate business in which the taxpayer materially participates; and (ii) the taxpayer performs more than 750 hours of services during the year in real property trades or businesses in which the taxpayer materially participates.

These rules will strike you as exceedingly complex and dry, but a lot of people care about them. In one State of the Union message, President Bush advocated repeal of the passive activity loss rules — to considerable applause. One can only wonder what the TV audience thought.

Defining "passive income" to absorb "passive losses." *§ 469* is just one more example of the point-counterpoint between taxpayers attempting to obtain an advantage, met with a legislative response, followed by a taxpayer response, and so forth. Taxpayers took net loss deductions, to which Congress responded, first with *§ 465* and then *§ 469*. Taxpayers sought ways to absorb passive losses with passive income, but Regulations denied passive income status to certain types of income, followed by litigation over the validity of the Regulation, as in the following case.

SCHAEFER V. COMMISSIONER

105 T.C. 227 (1995)

RAUM, JUDGE: . . .

Under the provisions of section 469 a taxpayer's right to make use of passive activity losses in any year is limited to the amount of the taxpayer's passive activity income for that year. § 469(a), (d)(1). While it has been stated that "issues arising under section 469 typically focus on whether a loss is to be properly characterized as a 'passive' loss so that the taxpayer may utilize the loss to offset what the taxpayer and respondent agree is passive income," the issue here [] is whether the taxpayer's income is passive so that it may be offset by the taxpayer's passive losses.

Section 1.469-2T(c)(7)(iv), Temporary Income Tax Regs., 53 Fed. Reg. 5686, 5716 (Feb. 25, 1988), provides that passive activity gross income does not include "Gross income of an individual from a covenant by such individual not to compete." The result of this provision is that income from a covenant not to compete may not be offset by passive losses. § 469(a), (d)(1). Petitioner argues that this regulation is invalid. We hold otherwise.

We begin by noting that a temporary regulation is entitled to the same weight as a final regulation. . . . Treasury regulations are entitled to a high degree of deference from the courts. A Treasury regulation must be upheld if it "implement[s] the congressional mandate in some reasonable manner." Put differently, Treasury regulations "must be sustained unless unreasonable and plainly inconsistent with the revenue statutes." Indeed, the Supreme Court has stated that the issue is not how the Court itself might construe the statute in the first instance, "but whether there is any reasonable basis for the resolution embodied in the Commissioner's Regulation." Our conclusion, hereinafter reached, is that [the Temporary Regulation] fairly implements the congressional purpose underlying section 469 and is a valid regulation. . . .

[C]ertain types of income are specifically excluded from the computation of passive income. These include so-called portfolio income, namely, interest, dividends, annuities, or royalties, as well as gain attributable to the disposition of property, and earned income; § 469(e). Further, the Secretary is specifically instructed to issue regulations "which provide that certain items of gross income will not be taken into account in determining income or loss from any activity," § 469(l)(2). Congress included these exceptions because these income sources "generally are positive income sources that do not bear deductible expenses to the same extent as passive investments. Since taxpayers commonly can rely upon salary and portfolio income to be positive . . . they are susceptible to sheltering by means of investments in activities that predictably give rise to tax losses," Staff of the Joint Comm. on Taxation, General Explanation of the Tax Reform Act of 1986, at 215 (J. Comm. Print 1987). It is with this understanding of the purpose behind section 469, and the specific types of income Congress meant to ensure were not sheltered by losses from passive activities, that we examine [the Temporary Regulations]. . . .

[Editor — The court then discusses a long line of cases holding that payments for a covenant not to compete are ordinary income, not capital gain, because they are a substitute for personal service income.] These cases are cited to show the long history of viewing payments under a covenant not to compete as similar to types of income specifically excluded from passive income by Congress itself under section 469(e)(3). In view of this history, the regulation at issue cannot be held unreasonable or contrary to Congress's intent. . . .

TP's arg't: Petitioner argues that compensation under a covenant not to compete is the polar opposite of earned income, because the point of a covenant not to compete is that services will not be rendered. . . .

Petitioner's point is superficially persuasive, but reflection will disclose that it is fallacious. It is fallacious because petitioner assumes that "services actually rendered" must involve some positive action, rather than affirmatively refraining from doing something. And it is that personal deliberate failure to act that the purchaser has bargained for in this case. Such personal refraining to engage in competition traditionally has been equated in the tax law with the rendition of personal services. . . . At most, the interpretation of the statutory language, "personal services actually rendered," is open to differing interpretations — precisely the kind of situation that is appropriate for a regulation to resolve.

[C]—Vacation homes

Vacation homes work like this. A taxpayer invests in a second home, but only lives there part of the year, renting it out for some portion of the remaining period. Any expenses allocable to the personal use part of the year should, of course, not be deductible, except for interest and taxes that are deductible regardless of personal use. The net losses attributable to the rental period could, however, be substantial. Are they in effect personal expenses, tolerated by the taxpayer as an expense of taking vacations (like "hobby" losses)?

The statute responds with one clear rule. Net losses on vacation homes are not deductible if the taxpayer lives there more than the greater of two weeks or 10% of the time the property is rented. Two weeks is the operative planning period because of rental uncertainties. § *280A(a),(b),(d),(e)*. If the taxpayer lives in the vacation home for "too long," expenses related to the rental period are deductible up to the rental income (computed after deduction of interest and taxes attributable to the rent), but net losses are not deductible. These net losses can*not* be carried over to another year — they are, in effect, nondeductible personal expenses.

Taxpayers who are covered by these rules will want to attribute as little interest and taxes as possible to the rental income, so that there is more income to absorb other deductions (such as depreciation). Remember that home interest and taxes *not* attributable to rental income are usually deductible anyway as personal expenses. Is the denominator for allocating interest and taxes the entire year or only the number of days the property is used for business and pleasure. The taxpayer wants to use the entire year (a large denominator means less interest and taxes attributed to the rental period). *McKinney v. Commissioner*, 732 F.2d 414 (10th Cir. 1983), agrees with the taxpayer.

[D]—Profit-making purpose? — *§ 183*

If a taxpayer successfully avoids the limits on deducting net losses discussed in the prior paragraphs, the government has one more string to its bow. If the government can prove that the taxpayer never really expects to make an economic profit, it can invoke *§ 183* to disallow the net losses. Although *§ 183* is aimed primarily at hobby losses, where the taxpayer's purpose is personal, the statutory text is written broadly to apply whenever the taxpayer lacks an income producing purpose. It has therefore provided the government with a statutory basis to prevent net losses from tax shelters from being deducted against other income. *Brannen v. Commissioner*, 78 T.C. 471 (1982), *aff'd*, 722 F.2d 695 (11th Cir. 1984); *Estate of Baron v. Commissioner*, 798 F.2d 65 (2d Cir. 1986).

This has raised concerns among some investors who respond to tax incentives and engage in activity without hope of economic profit apart from the tax benefit from deducting net losses. *See Rev. Rul. 79-300*, 1979-2 C.B. 113 (investors in low-income housing, who regularly suffer economic losses computed without regard to the tax breaks targeted on these investments, are not denied a deduction for the net losses).

§ 16.06 NONSUBSTANTIVE LAW ATTACKS ON TAX SHELTERS

[A]—Penalties

The substantive law uncertainties regarding tax shelters led many taxpayers to take their chances, given the low risk of audit. The statute has responded with several provisions, backed up by penalties for noncompliance, aimed at people who deal with tax shelter investors: (1) Tax shelter organizers must register tax shelters and make available their customer lists to the government — *§§ 6111–6112*; *6707–6708*; (2) Creditors must report receipt or abandonment of property to pay debts, so that unpaid debt will not go unreported — *§ 6050J*. (3) Promoting tax shelters by making or furnishing a statement which the provider knows or should know is false or by making gross valuation overstatements is subject to penalty. *§ 6700*.

In addition, taxpayers who make tax shelter investments must worry not only about the usual fraud and negligence penalties, but also about a 20% penalty on substantial understatements of tax. *§ 6662(b)(2),(d)*. In the case of non-tax shelter items, this penalty is avoided if there is "adequate disclosure" or if the taxpayer's position is supported by "substantial authority." For a tax shelter, disclosure is unavailing, and, in addition to showing substantial authority, the taxpayer must reasonably believe that his position was more likely than not to prevail.

[B]—Ethical rules

Additionally, the American Bar Association adopted ethical rules specifically aimed at lawyers who counsel about tax shelters. These rules recognize that the lawyer's role extends beyond responsibility to the client to include care about the impact of his or her actions on the general public, when the public is likely to rely on the lawyer. In this respect, a lawyer is treated like an accountant whose audits are available to the general public.

A.B.A. FORMAL ETHICS OPINION 346 (1982)

An opinion by a lawyer analyzing the tax effects of a tax shelter investment is frequently of substantial importance in a tax shelter offering. The promoter of the offering may depend upon the recommendations of the lawyer in structuring the venture and often publishes the opinion with the offering materials or uses the lawyer's name in connection with sales promotion efforts. The offerees may be expected to rely upon the tax shelter opinion in determining whether to invest in the venture. It is often uneconomic for the individual offeree to pay for a separate tax analysis of the offering because of the relatively small sum each offeree may invest.

Because the successful marketing of tax shelters frequently involves tax opinions issued by lawyers, concerns have been expressed by the organized bar, regulatory agencies and others over the need to articulate ethical standards applicable to a lawyer who issues an opinion which the lawyer knows will be included among the tax shelter offering materials and relied upon by offerees. . . .

A "tax shelter opinion," as the term is used in this Opinion, is advice by a lawyer concerning the federal tax law applicable to a tax shelter if the advice is referred to either in offering materials or in connection with sales promotion efforts directed to persons other than the client who engages the lawyer to give the advice. The term includes the tax aspects or tax risks portion of the offering materials prepared by the lawyer whether or not a separate opinion letter is issued. . . .

Disciplinary Standards

A false opinion is one which ignores or minimizes serious legal risks or misstates the facts or the law, knowingly or through gross incompetence. The lawyer who gives a false opinion, including one which is intentionally or recklessly misleading, violates the Disciplinary Rules of the Model Code of Professional Responsibility. Quite clearly, the lawyer exceeds the duty to represent the client zealously within the bounds of the law. See DR 7-101. Knowingly misstating facts or law violates DR 7-102(A)(5) and is "conduct involving dishonesty, fraud, deceit, or misrepresentation," a violation of DR 1-102(A)(4). The lawyer also violates DR 7-102(A)(7) by counseling or assisting the offeror "in conduct that the lawyer knows to be illegal or fraudulent." In addition, the lawyer's conduct may involve the concealment or knowing nondisclosure of matters which the lawyer is required by law to reveal, a violation of DR 7-102(A)(3).

The lawyer who accepts as true the facts which the promoter tells him, when the lawyer should know that a further inquiry would disclose that these facts are untrue, also gives a false opinion. . . . Recklessly and consciously disregarding information strongly indicating that material facts expressed in the tax shelter opinion are false or misleading involves dishonesty as does assisting the offeror in conduct the lawyer knows to be fraudulent. Such conduct violates DR 1-102(A)(4) and DR 7-102(A). We equate the minimum extent of the knowledge required for the lawyer's conduct to have violated these Disciplinary Rules with the knowledge required to sustain a Rule 10b-5 recovery [in securities law]. . . .

Ethical Considerations . . .

Lawyer as Advisor. EC 7-22 says "a litigant or his lawyer may, in good faith and within the framework of the law, take steps to test the correctness of a ruling of a tribunal." See also EC 7-25. Principles similar to these are applied where the lawyer represents a client in adversarial proceedings before the Internal Revenue Service. In that case the lawyer has duties not to mislead the Service by any misstatement, not to further any misrepresentations made by the client, and to deal candidly and fairly. ABA Formal Opinion 314 (1965).

The lawyer rendering a tax shelter opinion which he knows will be relied upon by third persons, however, functions more as an advisor than as an advocate. See EC 7-3, distinguishing these roles. Since the Model Code was adopted in 1969, the differing functions of the advisor and advocate have become more widely recognized.

The Proposed Model Rules specifically recognize the ethical considerations applicable where a lawyer undertakes an evaluation for the use of third persons other than a client. These third persons have an interest in the integrity of the evaluation. The legal duty of the lawyer therefore "goes beyond the obligations a lawyer normally has to third persons." Because third persons may rely on the advice of the lawyer who gives a tax shelter opinion, the principles announced in ABA Formal Opinion 314 have little, if any, applicability.

Establishing lawyer's relationship. The lawyer should establish the terms of the relationship with the offeror-client at the time the lawyer is engaged to work on the tax shelter offering. This includes making it clear that the lawyer requires from the client a full disclosure of the structure and intended operations of the venture and complete access to all relevant information.

Making factual inquiry. ABA Formal Opinion 335 (1974) establishes guidelines which a lawyer should follow when furnishing an assumed facts opinion in connection with the sale of unregistered securities. The same guidelines describe the extent to which a lawyer should verify the facts presented to him as the basis for a tax shelter opinion:

> [T]he lawyer should, in the first instance, make inquiry of his client as to the relevant facts and receive answers. If any of the alleged facts, or the alleged facts taken as a whole, are incomplete in a material respect; or are suspect; or are inconsistent; or either on their face or on the basis of other known facts are open to question, the lawyer should make further inquiry. The extent of this inquiry will depend in each case upon the circumstances; for example, it would be less where the lawyer's past relationship with the client is sufficient to give him a basis for trusting the client's probity than where the client has recently engaged the lawyer, and less where the lawyer's inquiries are answered fully than when there appears a reluctance to disclose information.
>
> Where the lawyer concludes that further inquiry of a reasonable nature would not give him sufficient confidence as to all the relevant facts, or for any other reason he does not make the appropriate further inquiries, he should refuse to give an opinion. However, assuming that the alleged facts are not incomplete in a material respect, or suspect, or in any way inherently inconsistent, or on their face or on the basis of other known facts open to question, the lawyer may properly assume that the facts as related to him by his client, and checked by him by reviewing such appropriate documents as are available, are accurate. . . .

> The essence of this opinion . . . is that, while a lawyer should make adequate preparation including inquiry into the relevant facts that is consistent with the above guidelines, and while he should not accept as true that which he should not reasonably believe to be true, he does not have the responsibility to "audit" the affairs of his client or to assume, without reasonable cause, that a client's statement of the facts cannot be relied upon. ABA Formal Opinion 335 at 3, 5–6.

For instance, where essential underlying information, such as an appraisal or financial projection, makes little common sense, or where the reputation or expertise of the person who has prepared the appraisal or projection is dubious, further inquiry clearly is required. Indeed, failure to make further inquiry may result in a false opinion. See supra, Disciplinary Standards. If further inquiry reveals that the appraisal or projection is reasonably well supported and complete, the lawyer is justified in relying upon the material facts which the underlying information supports.

Relating law to facts. In discussing the legal issues in a tax shelter opinion, the lawyer should relate the law to the actual facts to the extent the facts are ascertainable when the offering materials are being circulated. A lawyer should not issue a tax shelter opinion which disclaims responsibility for inquiring as to the accuracy of the facts, fails to analyze the critical facts or discusses purely hypothetical facts. It is proper, however, to assume facts which are not currently ascertainable, such as the method of conducting future operations of the venture, so long as the factual assumptions are clearly identified as such in the offering materials, and are reasonable and complete. . . .

Material tax issues. A "material" tax issue for purposes of this Opinion is any income or excise tax issue relating to the tax shelter that would have a significant effect in sheltering from federal taxes income from other sources by providing deductions in excess of the income from the tax shelter investment in any year or tax credits which will offset tax liabilities in excess of the tax attributable to the tax shelter investment in any year. The determination of what is material is to be made in good faith by the lawyer based on the information which is available at the time the offering materials are being circulated.

The lawyer should satisfy himself that either he or another competent professional has considered all material tax issues. In addition, the tax shelter opinion should fully and fairly address each material tax issue respecting which there is a reasonable possibility that the Internal Revenue Service will challenge the tax effect proposed in the offering materials. . . .

Opinion as to outcome — material tax issues. Since the term "opinion" connotes a lawyer's conclusion as to the likely outcome of an issue if challenged and litigated, the lawyer should, if possible, state the lawyer's opinion of the probable outcome on the merits of each material tax issue. However, if the lawyer determines in good faith that it is not possible to make a judgment as to the outcome of a material tax issue, the lawyer should so state and give the reasons for this conclusion.

A tax shelter opinion may question the validity of a Revenue Ruling or the reasoning in a lower court opinion which the lawyer believes is wrong. But there must also be a complete explanation to the offerees, including what position the Service is likely to take on the issue and a summary of why this position is considered to be wrong. The opinion also should set forth the risks of an adversarial proceeding if one is likely to occur.

Over-all evaluation of realization of tax benefits. The clear disclosure of the tax risks in the offering materials should include an opinion by the lawyer or by another professional providing an overall evaluation of the extent to which the tax benefits, in the aggregate, which are a significant feature of the investment to the typical investor are likely to be realized as contemplated by the offering materials. In making this evaluation, the lawyer should state that the significant tax benefits, in the aggregate, probably will be realized or probably will not be realized, or that the probabilities of realization and nonrealization of the significant tax benefits are evenly divided.

In rare instances the lawyer may conclude in good faith that it is not possible to make a judgment of the extent to which the significant tax benefits are likely to be realized. This impossibility may occur where, for example, the most significant tax benefits are predicated upon a newly enacted Code provision when there are no regulations and the legislative history is obscure. In these circumstances, the lawyer should fully explain why the judgment cannot be made and assure full disclosure in the offering materials of the assumptions and risks which the investors must evaluate.

The Committee does not accept the view that it is always ethically improper to issue an opinion which concludes that the significant tax benefits in the aggregate probably will not be realized. However, full disclosure requires that the negative conclusion be clearly stated and prominently noted in the offering materials. . . .

If the lawyer disagrees with the client over the extent of disclosure made in the offering materials . . . and the disagreement cannot be resolved, the lawyer should withdraw from the employment and not issue an opinion.

CHAPTER 17

ALTERNATIVE MINIMUM TAX

§ 17.01 THE GENERAL IDEA

Congress is aware of the criticism of many of the tax benefits discussed in prior chapters. Some have been repealed, but many remain, with the potential for lowering the effective tax rate. The problem first came dramatically to the public's attention when the Treasury published data showing that many rich taxpayers paid no tax at all. The alternative minimum tax was therefore adopted. Technically, *§ 55* imposes an alternative minimum tax on an amount equal to the "tentative minimum tax" minus the "regular tax."

The alternative minimum tax has the same general attributes as the regular tax — its own tax base, personal exemptions, and tax rates. The tax rates are lower than the regular rates found in *§ 1 (individuals), § 11 (corporations)*. The general idea is to define a broader more inclusive tax base than is found under the regular tax and make sure that some minimum tax is paid on that amount. In effect, Congress has identified those tax expenditures which should not enable taxpayers to avoid paying tax at the minimum rate. However, the tax expenditures so characterized are not the complete list that appears in either the executive or congressional branch's tax expenditure budgets. Political factors still shape definition of the alternative minimum tax base.

Political factors also influence who is subject to the Alternative Minimum Tax. Small businesses were successful in the 1997 Tax Act in gaining an exemption from the alternative minimum tax for "small corporations." A small corporation is one which has no more than $5,000,000 average gross receipts for the three tax years ending with the first tax year beginning after December 31, 1996. Once eligible, the corporation usually retains small corporation status as long as the prior gross receipt three year average does not exceed $7,500,000.

§ 17.02 MECHANICS

[A]—Tax rates

The alternative minimum tax rate for individuals is 26% on the first $175,000 of alternative minimum taxable income, and 28% on income over that amount. A graduated rate structure was an innovation in 1993; before then the rate was a flat 24%. The alternative minimum tax rate on corporations is 20% (this was unchanged in 1993). *§ 55(b((1).*

[B]—Tax Base

Here is a small sampling of how the alternative minimum tax base differs from the regular tax base.

Individuals and corporations. "Alternative minimum taxable income" is regular taxable income, with adjustments and additions. *§ 55(b)(2).* Most of the adjustments add back regular tax deductions, which is why the alternative minimum tax is in this part of the book (dealing with limits on deductions).

For purposes of the alternative minimum tax, the 200% declining balance method under the regular tax is modified so that taxpayers use a 150% rate. Beginning in tax year 1999, the depreciation period for the alternative minimum tax is the same as for the regular tax (previously, the longer "alternative depreciation" periods provided *§ 168(g)* had to be used). *§ 56(a)(1)(A).* For example, buildings will no longer have to use the 40-year life provided by *§ 168(g).*

Sometimes expensing under the regular tax is replaced by three-or ten-year amortization under the alternative minimum tax. *§ 56(b)(2)(A).*

The alternative minimum tax is really a parallel tax universe to the regular tax. Thus, slower depreciation produces a higher basis under the alternative minimum tax than under the regular tax. Computation of gain under the alternative minimum tax will therefore be different than under the regular tax. For example, if real estate costing $300,000 is entitled to $30,000 depreciation under the regular tax, its adjusted basis is $270,000. Under the alternative minimum tax, slower depreciation (assume only $20,000), results in an adjusted basis for the alternative minimum tax of $280,000. Sale of the asset for $350,000 produces less gain under the alternative minimum tax than under the regular tax ($70,000, rather than $80,000).

A complete list of adjustments and additions common to individuals and corporations appears in *§§ 56(a), 57.* In addition to the rules modifying depreciation and expensing, a few adjustments add back exempt income; *see § 57(a)(5)* (interest on most "private activity" bonds is not exempt under the alternative minimum tax).

The pattern here should be obvious. Various items have long been targeted for "tax reform" elimination, but the political will to do so is lacking. As a compromise, these tax benefits are eliminated under the alternative minimum tax, but not the regular tax.

Until recently, the long-term capital gain which is deductible on certain gifts of appreciated property to charity was a tax preference item under the alternative minimum tax, but not after the 1993 tax law. Consequently, the full value of art work and stock (not just the basis) is usually deductible in computing alternative minimum taxable income. Museums and universities are obvious beneficiaries of this rule.

Individuals. The alternative minimum tax permits only certain itemized deductions which are allowed under the regular tax. *§ 56(b)(1).* These include casualty, charitable, and medical expenses (but only in excess of 10% of adjusted gross income, not 7.5%). State income and property taxes are *not* deductible. Employee business expense deductions which are *itemized* deductions (subject to the 2% floor) are also not deductible. Loss of employee business expense deductions is one way that lower income taxpayers might find themselves subject to the alternative minimum tax.

Personal home interest deductions are also more narrowly defined for the alternative minimum tax. The loan must be used to acquire, construct, or rehabilitate the residence. The opportunity afforded under the regular tax to deduct interest on a home equity loan is not permitted under the alternative minimum tax. *§ 56(b)(1)(C),(e).*

Corporations. The alternative minimum tax base for corporations is increased by 75% of the excess of a modified version of earnings and profits over what would otherwise be the tax base for the alternative minimum tax. The earnings and profits figure is something like what accountants would compute as the economic profits of the business. It *includes* tax exempt bond income. *§ 56(c)(1),(g).*

Net operating loss carryovers. Only 90% of the net operating loss computed under the alternative minimum tax can be carried over to another tax year.

Credits. The discussion has so far focused on how the alternative minimum tax deals with deductions and exclusions which reduce the regular tax. Tax credits, however, can reduce the regular tax. How does the alternative minimum tax deal with tax credits? The general pattern is that tax credits do not reduce the alternative minimum tax. Mechanically, the code achieves this result by setting a ceiling on regular tax credits equal to the regular tax (without reduction by credits) minus the tentative minimum tax. *See §§ 26(a),(b)(1), 28(d)(2), 29(b)(6), 30(b)(3), 38(c).* For example, assume a taxpayer with a potential tax credit of $20; regular tax without the credit of $100; and tentative minimum tax of $95. Only $5 of the potential tax credit is allowed under the regular tax (with the remainder carried over to other years in accordance with the credit's carryover rules).

The 1993 tax law permits one credit to reduce part of the alternative minimum tax. The employment tax credit related to "empowerment zones" can offset 25% of the alternative minimum tax. *§ 38(c)(2)(A).*

The increasing number of credits (*e.g.*, child tax credits; Hope and Lifetime education credits) may also subject more people to the alternative minimum tax, as the regular tax is reduced by credits not available under the alternative minimum tax. A similar impact can arise from the lowering of the tax rate on capital gains. One recent estimate suggests that there will be a ten-fold increase in the number of taxpayers covered by the alternative minimum tax between 1997 and 2006.

[C]—Exemptions

After computing the alternative minimum tax base, the taxpayer deducts an exempt amount — $45,000 for married couples and $33,750 for single individuals. These amounts are phased out at the rate of 25 cents per dollar of alternative minimum taxable income above $150,000 for a married couple ($112,500 for a single individual). Corporations receive a $40,000 exemption, phased out at 25 cents per dollar of income over $150,000. *§ 55(d).*

Comment on phase-out and marginal rates. The phase-out of the personal exemption raises the marginal tax rates on married couples with incomes between $150,000 and $330,000. The phase-out is at the rate of 25 cents per dollar of "excess" income over $150,000, so $180,000 "excess" income wipes out the $45,000 exemption (180000/4 = 45000). The marginal tax rate on income between $150,000 and $330,000 is therefore higher than the stated rate. Do you see why? The clue is that $1 dollar of income raises taxable income by $1.25. For a taxpayer in the 28% bracket, that increases tax by 35 cents (28% times $1.25), which is 35% of $1 dollar of additional income.

[D]—Tax planning.

Can you generalize about when an individual taxpayer should start worrying about the alternative minimum tax? Only very tentatively.

We can say something about people with very high incomes, for whom the $45,000 personal exemption has been phased out. Look at the top alternative minimum tax rate for individuals — 28%. The regular rate is 39.6%, which is about 40% higher than 28% (39.6 – 28 = 11.6; and 11.6/28 is about.40). This suggests that, if the adjustments and additions to regular taxable income are about 40% of regular taxable income, an alternative minimum tax might be due. Do you see why? 28% times $1.40 (39.2 cents) is just about 39.6% times $1 (39.6 cents).

Generalizations are more difficult for people whose income is not so high. Two factors tug in opposite directions. First, at lower income levels, the *average* regular tax rate is often much less than 39.6%, so it takes *less* than a 40% increase in the regular tax base before 28% (or perhaps the lesser 26%) alternative minimum tax rate will produce a tax equal to the regular tax. This makes the alternative minimum tax *more* likely. Second, at lower income levels, the personal exemption (or at least some of it) will still be available under the alternative minimum tax, making the alternative minimum tax *less* likely.

In some cases, taxpayers with fairly low incomes might be subject to the alternative minimum tax. Consider a married employee with $35,000 regular taxable income, subject to a 15% tax rate (regular tax = $5,250). Assume that the alternative minimum taxable income is double that amount, or $70,000. This is not as unlikely as it sounds. The personal exemption deductions under the regular tax must be added back to compute alternative minimum taxable income and the taxpayer could have been a professor on sabbatical with large employee business expenses not deductible under the alternative minimum tax. The $70,000 is reduced by the $45,000 personal exemption to $25,000, but 26% times $25,000 is $6,500. That produces an alternative minimum tax of $1,250 (6500 - 5250).

In *Ruggiero v. Commisisoner*, 24 T.C.M. 662 (1997), a professor received a $60,000 fellowship but was denied sabbatical leave by his university. He then negotiated a leave with full pay in exchange for paying the university $30,000 of his fellowship. But the $30,000 was a below-the-line itemized employee business expense deduction which was not deductible in computing the alternative minimum tax base. Consequently, an alternative minimum tax was due.

[E]—Impact of inflation

Inflation could make many more future taxpayers subject to the alternative minimum tax, assuming taxable incomes rise along with inflation, for two reasons. First, the alternative minimum tax personal exemption and the related phase-out threshold are not adjusted upward for inflation (although the 1993 tax law increased the deduction — from $40,000 to $45,000 for married taxpayers). Second, the *regular* tax rate brackets, personal exemption, and related phase-out *expand* with inflation, so that regular taxes as a percentage of income do *not* increase with inflation.

For example, consider a married couple with $150,000 of alternative minimum taxable income before subtracting the $45,000 personal exemption. This produces a tentative minimum tax of $27,300 (26% times 105,000). If this couple had $113,000 of *regular* taxable income in 1994, there is no alternative minimum tax because the regular tax would be a bit more than the $27,300 tentative minimum tax ($27,334.50, which is 24.19% of taxable income).

If inflation doubles the taxable income for *both* the regular tax and alternative minimum tax (a plausible but not necessary result), the couple has $300,000 alternative minimum taxable income, and $226,000 regular taxable income. The alternative minimum tax personal exemption declines to $7,500, so alternative minimum taxable income is $292,500. The current 26%-28% rate structure produces a $78,400 tentative minimum tax. Because the regular tax brackets expand due to inflation, the regular tax is still 24.19% of $226,000, or $54,669.40 — much less than $78,400 — and an alternative minimum tax is due.

[F]—The problem of deferral tax preferences

The interaction of the alternative minimum and regular taxes creates a potential for double taxation of the same item when the alternative minimum tax results from disallowing tax deferral available under the regular tax. The problem is illustrated by the following extreme example. Assume $500 of income taxable under both the regular and alternative minimum tax in both years 1 and 2. Assume also a $100 expenditure in year 1, which is expensed under the regular income tax in year 1, but cannot be deducted at all in year 1 under the alternative minimum tax. The expenditure is, however, deductible in full in year 2 under the alternative minimum tax.

Year		Regular tax	Alternative minimum tax
1	Gross income =	500	500
	Deduction =	100	0
		400	500
2	Gross income =	500	500
	Deduction =	0	100
		500	400

The excess of the alternative minimum tax base over the regular tax base in year 1 is $100, and that same $100 is subject to regular tax in year 2.

The technical solution to this problem is to isolate how much of an alternative minimum tax the taxpayer has to pay in year 1 as a result of *deferral* tax preferences (such as having to add back some fast depreciation or expensing). That additional alternative minimum tax is carried forward as a credit to later years and reduces the excess of the regular tax over the tentative minimum tax in a later year. Using the above figures, assume that the year 1 alternative minimum tax resulting from adding back the $100 deduction was $26 (assuming a 26% rate). Assume further that in year 2, the regular tax on $500 now exceeds the tentative minimum tax on $400 by $39.60. The credit reduces the regular tax by $26 and only $13.60 regular tax is due in year 2, *attributable to the $100*. That produces a total of $39.60 tax over *both* years on the $100 ($26 in year 1, and $13.60 in year 2), which is the regular tax rate.

The complication raised by this solution is to limit the credit to the year 1 alternative minimum tax attributable to *deferral* tax breaks. Some taxpayers may have alternative minimum tax due to other disallowed tax breaks, such as losing an interest deduction. Thus, assume that the above taxpayer had an alternative minimum tax base in year 1 of $550 (more than the $500 in the above example), because $50 of home equity interest was attributable to a loan used to buy a personal car. The interest deduction is a *non*deferral tax break. The excess of the alternative minimum tax over the regular tax attributable to the nondeferral tax break is *not* available as a credit in future years.

[G]—Impact on incentives

One of the consequences of having parallel tax universes is that the incentive effects of deductions under the regular tax will be eliminated for someone subject to the alternative minimum tax, *if* the deduction is unavailable under the alternative minimum tax.

If the deduction is available under the alternative minimum tax, what is the incentive effect of the deduction for someone subject to the alternative minimum tax? The tax benefit of a deduction is often less under the alternative minimum tax, because the tax rate is less (only 26% or 28%). However, the *marginal* alternative minimum tax rate may be similar to the regular tax rate, because disappearing personal exemptions create a 35% marginal tax rate "bubble" — from $150,000 to $330,000 of alternative minimum taxable income for a married taxpayer. A marginal alternative minimum tax rate of 35% is close to the top 36% and 39.6% regular marginal tax rates under *§ 1.*

PART V

TAXING APPRECIATED GAIN

Unrealized gain is not taxed. That has spawned a variety of rules to reduce the disparity between realized and unrealized gain.

Chapter 18 discusses situations in which gain is realized but not "recognized."

Chapter 19 discusses capital gains. Primary emphasis is on the history and structure of the long term capital gains preference; the definition of "capital assets"; and the special status of assets used in the business.

Chapter 20 deals with the special problem of carved out income interests, as when a taxpayer sells an income interest and retains the remainder.

Chapter 21 discusses deferred payments. We are especially concerned with the installment method; combining capital gains and deferral; and hidden original issue discount in deferred payments.

CHAPTER 18

NONRECOGNITION OF REALIZED GAIN

§ 18.01 INTRODUCTION

One of the basic structural principles in the tax law is the requirement that gain be realized before it can be included in *§ 61* income. One important consequence of this rule is that appreciated gain is not taxed until some event other than mere appreciation. This creates a sharp distinction between retention of an asset and its sale for cash or exchange for another asset. This is often called a lock-in effect, because the tax burden on sale locks in the taxpayer's investment. One way to eliminate this effect would be to permit a nontaxable sale or exchange to occur, if the taxpayer replaced the sold property within some period of time after the sale occurred. Gain would technically be realized under *§ 61,* but not recognized. Taxable gain would be deferred until such time as the taxpayer withdrew his investment from the qualified replacement property. The tax law has a number of provisions like the general rule just proposed, but they are hedged about with many conditions. This chapter deals with the mechanics of these provisions and reviews some of the definitional problems encountered in determining which transactions are eligible.

§ 18.02 NONRECOGNITION — MECHANICS

There are many tax provisions which explicitly defer tax on realized gain. The statute usually states that gain is not "recognized."

Work out the following problems under *§ 1031(a),(b),(d)* to see how tax deferred exchanges are treated. Assume that *§ 1031,* dealing with "like-kind" exchanges, applies. The same general pattern prevails in other tax deferred nonrecognition transactions, including the rules dealing with (1) corporate organizations and reorganizations (*§§ 351, 354*), and (2) reinvestment of the proceeds of an involuntary conversion in property which is similar or related in kind or use to the converted property (*§ 1033*).

PROBLEMS

It may help you to understand the mechanics of *§ 1031* if you remember (1) that a sale of property with a $40,000 basis for $60,000 cash cannot produce more than $20,000 recognized gain, and (2) that cash always has a basis equal to its face amount.

1. The taxpayer transfers Property A with a basis of $40,000 and a value of $60,000. The taxpayer receives in exchange like-kind Property B worth $60,000. What gain, if any, is realized; what gain is recognized; and what is the taxpayer's basis in Property B?

2. How would your answer change if Property B (a) was worth $50,000 and the taxpayer also received $10,000 cash; or (b) Property B was worth $35,000 and the taxpayer received $25,000 cash?

3. Now change the example so that the value of Property A is $30,000 (there is a loss on the exchange); basis is still $40,000. The taxpayer receives Property B, worth $25,000 and $5,000 cash.

4. Suppose the taxpayer owns Property A with a basis of $40,000, a gross value of $70,000, subject to a $10,000 debt. That property is exchanged for like-kind Property B worth $60,000. Does the taxpayer recognize any gain? What if the Property B received by the taxpayer had a $90,000 gross value, subject to a $30,000 debt? *Treas. Reg. § 1.1031(d)-2(example 2).*

§ 18.03 LIKE-KIND EXCHANGES

One major example of a nonrecognition transaction is a like-kind exchange, provided for by *§ 1031.*

[A]—Statutory coverage

To be eligible, a taxpayer must exchange property held for investment or for productive use in a trade or business, for like-kind property held for investment or for productive use in a trade or business. Property held for personal use (such as a residence) is therefore ineligible for tax deferral under *§ 1031(a)(1).*

Property held primarily for sale (such as inventory) is also not eligible. *§ 1031(a)(2)(A).* However, unproductive realty held for future use or for realization of increment in value is held for investment, not primarily for sale. *Treas. Reg. § 1.1031(a)-1(b).*

Certain investment interests, such as stock and debt, are excluded from *§ 1031.* Partnership interests are also excluded, even though exchange of the underlying business property might have qualified. *§ 1031(a)(2)(B),(D).* The exclusion of partnerships was adopted in 1984, in part to discourage the exchange of tax shelter partnership interests, but its scope is not limited to tax shelters.

QUESTIONS

1. Suppose Taxpayer A exchanges a farm used for business for a building in a rural area used and owned by Taxpayer B as a personal residence. Taxpayer A will convert B's former residence to a farm. Is either A or B eligible for like-kind exchange treatment under *§ 1031?*

2. The reasons for deferring tax on like-kind exchanges and on stock dividends (discussed in *Eisner v. Macomber*) are sometimes said to be similar — there is no cash received on the exchange, valuation is very difficult, and the taxpayer has not really changed his investment. Do these policies really explain tax deferral on like-kind exchanges? Can you have a tax deferred exchange and still receive cash; if you get cash, do you have to know the value of the assets exchanged? As for the "no change of investment rationale," consider the following examples.

[B]—Administrative rules

What is like-kind property? The Regulations state, using vague language, that like-kind refers to the "nature or character of the property and not to its grade or quality . . ." *Treas. Reg. § 1.1031(a)-1(b).*

If property is of like-kind: (a) property held for business use can be exchanged for property held for investment use and vice versa. *Treas. Reg. § 1.1031(a)-1(a)*; (b) new property can be exchanged for used property. *Treas. Reg. § 1.1031(a)-1(c)*; and (c) a lease of at least thirty years is "like" a fee interest. *Rev. Rul. 78-72,* 1978-1 C.B. 258; *Treas. Reg. § 1.1031(a)-1(c).*

Realty. The Regulations put some flesh on the definition of like-kind property in a way that is quite generous to real estate. Thus, "the fact that any real estate involved is improved or unimproved is not material, for that fact relates only to the grade or quality of the property and not its kind or class." *Treas. Reg. § 1.1031(a)-1(b).* And, if taxpayer A owns farm land and buildings used for business purposes and taxpayer B owns land and a building used for business in the city, they can swap properties, and both are eligible for *§ 1031. Treas. Reg. 1.1031(a)-1(c).*

Personalty.

(1) Proposed Regulations set forth rules about whether personal property is of a "like class," in which case it is considered "like kind." *Prop. Treas. Reg. 1.1031(a)-2.* Although failure to be of "like class" creates no negative inference about whether the assets are like kind, the "like class" safe havens may operate to limit what a tax *planner* will consider "like kind."

(2) Specific rules apply to intangible property — for example, copyrights on different novels are of like-kind, but not copyrights on a song

and a novel; good will of different businesses is not of like-kind. *Treas. Reg. 1.1031(a)-2(c).*

(3) Coins can be held for different purposes — such as, currency, collector's items, bullion for the value of their metal, or for industrial use. Each use differs from the other so that only an exchange within each category can qualify for a like-kind exchange. *Rev. Rul. 79-143*, 1979-1 C.B. 264 (numismatic-type gold coins are not like bullion-type gold coins); *Rev. Rul. 82-166*, 1982-2 C.B. 190 (gold and silver bullion held for investment are not like kind, because silver is essentially an industrial commodity).

[C]—Sale vs. Exchange

§ 1031 sharply distinguishes between (a) a sale for cash followed by reinvestment of the proceeds in like-kind property and (b) an exchange of like-kind property. This produces a tax planning problem when the taxpayer wants like-kind property but wants cash from the buyer if such property cannot be found. The following case illustrates how taxpayers have tried to deal with the problem and the government's response.

CARLTON v. UNITED STATES

385 F.2d 238 (5th Cir. 1967)

GEWIN, CIRCUIT JUDGE:

The facts of the case are fully stipulated. During the year 1959 and for several years prior thereto the appellants [Carlton] had been engaged in the ranching business. In connection with that business they owned a tract of land in Saint Lucie County, Florida, (ranch property) having a basis of $8,918.91. On October 18, 1958, they executed a contract with General Development Corporation (General) which gave General an option to acquire the ranch property for $250.00 an acre. General paid the appellants $50,000 deposit which was to be credited to the total purchase price should General exercise its option. The contract also provided that the appellant could require General, by notifying it in writing, to acquire such other land as designated by the appellants for the purpose of exchange in lieu of a cash payment or mortgage. General's obligation to supply funds for any down payment which might be needed to bind any contracts to purchase other land for exchange was not to exceed the $50,000 advanced at the time the option was executed. In the event such an exchange could not be effected, General was to pay for the ranch property by cash and a mortgage securing the balance of the purchase price. From the outset of negotiations with General, the appellants desired to continue ranching operations and intended to exchange the ranch property for other property suitable for ranching. They also desired an exchange as opposed to a sale in order to obtain the tax benefits incident to an exchange under § 1031. At all times General desired simply to purchase the ranch property.

Following the execution of the option contract with General, Thad Carlton (Carlton) found two suitable parcels of land, one in Gladen County, Florida (Lyons), and one in Hendry County, Florida (Fernandez). He conducted all the negotiations for the acquisition of these lands and paid the deposit for each by a cashiers check issued by his bank. The total deposit on both pieces of property did not exceed the fifty thousand dollars paid by General. When the negotiations to acquire the Lyons and Fernandez properties were complete, Carlton notified General in writing that he would require it to purchase these lands for the purpose of exchanging them for his ranch property, and the actual agreements of sale were executed by General. On May 11, 1959 General exercised its option to acquire the ranch property and arrangements were made to close the entire transaction around August 1, 1959. The closing of the several transactions actually occurred on August 3rd and 4th and in closing the appellants deviated from the original plan which resulted in the tax problem here in issue.

In order to avoid unnecessary duplication in title transfer, a procedure was adopted whereby title to the Lyons and Fernandez properties would be conveyed directly to the appellants instead of to General and then to the appellants. To accomplish this result, General, on August 3rd, assigned to the appellants its contracts to purchase the two pieces of property and paid the appellants, by check, the total amount it would have been required to pay if it had actually first purchased the Lyons and Fernandez property in its own name and then conveyed the land to the appellants. Later that same day Carlton took the assignment of the contracts to purchase and purchased the Lyons property, using his personal check to close the sale. On August 4 he purchased the Fernandez property in a similar manner. At the time Carlton issued these checks, the balance in his checking account was too small to cover them, but he deposited the check received from General when the transaction with it was closed to meet these outstanding checks. This check was the balance of the cash purchase price and was in addition to the $50,000.00 paid when the option was executed.

The district court held that on the basis of these facts the transfers constituted a sale and repurchase. The court concluded that because General never acquired the legal title to the Lyons and Fernandez property, it could not have exchanged those properties for the ranch property. Rather, the court found that the appellants sold the ranch property to General and applied the cash thereby acquired to the purchase of the Lyons and Fernandez properties. The court also noted that Carlton was the active party in arranging the acquisition of the Lyons and Fernandez tracts and that he was personally liable on the notes and mortgages involved in such acquisitions. . . .

Both parties agree that had the appellants followed the original plan, whereby General would have acquired the legal title to the Lyons and Fernandez properties and then transferred the title to such properties to the appellants for their ranch property, the appellants would have been entitled to postpone the recognition of the gain pursuant to § 1031. However, instead of receiving the title to the Lyons and Fernandez properties from General for their ranch property, the appellants received cash and an assignment of General's contract rights to those properties. Thus, the ultimate question becomes whether the receipt of cash by the appellants upon transferring their ranch property to General transformed the intended exchange into a sale. The Government asserts that it does, and under the facts and in the circumstances of this case, we agree.

Section 1031 was designed to postpone the recognition of gain or loss where property used in a business is exchanged for other property in the course of the continuing operation of a business. In those circumstances, the taxpayer has not received any gain or suffered any loss in a general and economic sense. Nor has the exchange of property resulted in the termination of one venture and assumption of another. The business venture operated before the exchange continues after the exchange without any real economic change or alteration, and without realization of any cash or readily liquefiable asset. The statute specifically limits the nonrecognition of gain or loss to exchanges of property, and it is well settled that a sale and repurchase do not qualify for nonrecognition treatment under the section. Thus, even though the appellants continued their ranching business after the transaction here in question, that does not control the tax consequences of the transfers. Rather, it is essential that the transfers constituted an exchange and not a sale and repurchase if the tax benefits of § 1031 are to be applicable.

The appellants contend that the entire transaction must be viewed as a whole in determining whether a sale or an exchange has occurred. They argue that the transfer of the ranch property to General for the cash and assignments was part of a single unitary plan designed and intended to effect an exchange of their ranch property for other property suitable for ranching. Thus, they conclude, the transfers of property should be construed to be an exchange.

While it is true that the incidence of taxation is to be determined by viewing the entire transaction as a whole, that rule does not permit us to close our eyes to the realities of the transaction and merely look at the beginning and end of a transaction without observing the steps taken to reach that end. The requirement is that the transaction be viewed in its entirety in order to determine its reality and substance, for it is the substance of the transaction which decides the incidence of taxation. In the instant case, while elaborate plans were laid to exchange property, the substance of the transaction was that the appellants received cash for the deed to their ranch property and not another parcel of land. The very essence of an exchange is the transfer of property between owners, while the mark of a sale is the receipt of cash for the property. Where, as here, there is an immediate repurchase of other property with the proceeds of the sale, that distinction between a sale and exchange is crucial. Further, General was never in a position to exchange properties with the appellants because it never acquired the legal title to either the Lyons or the Fernandez property. Indeed, General was not personally obligated on either the notes or mortgages involved in these transaction. Thus it never had any property of like kind to exchange. Finally, it can not be said that General paid for the Lyons and Fernandez properties and merely had the properties deeded directly to the appellants. The money received from General by the appellants for the ranch property was not earmarked by General to be used in purchasing the Lyons or Fernandez properties. It was unrestricted and could be used by the appellants as they pleased. The fact that they did use it to pay for the Lyons and Fernandez properties does not alter the fact that their use of the money was unfettered and unrestrained. It is an inescapable fact that the money received by appellants from General was money paid to them for a conveyance of their land. As a result, the separate transaction between General and the appellants must be construed to be a sale, and the transactions between the appellants and Lyons and Fernandez as a purchase of other property.

The appellants' intention and desire to execute an exchange does not alter the reality and substance of the situation. It is well established that the intention of a taxpayer to avail himself of the advantages of a particular provision of the tax laws does not determine the tax consequences of his action, but what was actually done is determinative of the tax treatment. Thus, the intention of the appellants to effect an exchange does not convert the transfer of property for cash into an exchange. . . .

Therefore, we are compelled to conclude that the transfer of the ranch property to General constituted a sale, and rendered the nonrecognition of gain provisions of 1031 inapplicable. Considering how close the appellants came to satisfying the requirements of that section and the stipulation that an exchange was intended, this result is obviously harsh. But there is no equity in tax law, and such must the result be if the limitation in 1031 to exchanges is to have any meaning.

The judgment of the district court is Affirmed.

Suppose the taxpayer in *Carlton* had found the like-kind property by contacting a third party and arranged to have it transferred directly to the taxpayer, without General taking title. General paid the third party for the like-kind property with cash. Is that a like-kind exchange? *Rev. Rul. 90-34*, 1990-1 C.B. 154.

Statutory Interpretation — Statutory purpose, "Equity of the Statute." The decision in *Carlton* makes one remarkable statement at the end of the opinion. The judge says that tax law has no "equity." What does that mean? It has nothing to do with whether the tax law is or is not harsh. In statutory interpretation lingo, the "equity" of a statute refers to its purpose. So understood, the court's statement that tax law has no "equity" is much too simplistic. Recall the *Owens* case, in which statutory purpose was used to overcome the literal language dealing with personal loss deductions.

The lack of "equity" in tax law might mean that form prevails over substance. That, too, is simplistic. Sometimes form is substance and that is why it prevails. Thus, in *§ 1031,* a sale for cash is the "substance" of the transaction even though it is a formal step, adopted as part of a plan to repurchase like-kind property with the cash. All "form vs. substance" distinctions suffer from the same ambiguity. Form prevails over substance *when* that implements the statutory purpose. Judicial statements about statutory "substance" are always legal conclusions. The question in all cases is what does the statute mean. If *§ 1031* forbids receipt of cash, then receipt of cash is not an irrelevant formal step, to be disregarded in the interest of some broader statutory substance.

[D]—Deferred receipt of like-kind property

In *Starker v. United States*, 602 F.2d 1341 (9th Cir. 1979), the taxpayer entered into a "land exchange agreement" to convey 1843 acres of timberland in Oregon to the buyer. The buyer agreed to transfer other like-kind realty to the taxpayer within five years after the timberland was received, or to pay cash. The buyer added a 6% "growth factor" for each year it failed to convey land to the taxpayer. The buyer did in fact convey property to the taxpayer in the tax year after the timberland transfer. The government argued that simultaneity of exchange is a formal requirement of *§ 1031.*

The court declined to require simultaneity, but the 6% growth factor was taxable interest.

§ 1031(a)(3) reverses the *Starker* decision and requires that the like-kind property must be identified and transferred to the taxpayer within a specified period of time. The committee reports express concern with the indefinite deferral that *Starker* might permit. What is wrong with indefinite deferral of the gain?

[E]—Losses

§ 1031 defers recognition of losses as well as gains. This leads taxpayers to try to avoid like-kind exchanges by receiving cash. Sale-leaseback arrangements are a common feature in cases where the taxpayer tries to recognize a loss. For example, assume the taxpayer owns property with a $4,000,000 basis, which is now worth $2,400,000. It sells the property for cash, to recognize the loss, and leases it back for 30 years. In such cases, the government argues that the primary purpose of *§ 1031* is to eliminate valuation problems and that any reciprocal exchange of like-kind property (here it is a fee interest for a 30-year lease) therefore falls within the nonrecognition provisions. *Century Electric Co. v. Commissioner*, 192 F.2d 155 (8th Cir. 1951), agreed with the government and denied a loss deduction.

Other cases support the taxpayer. *Leslie Co. v. Commissioner*, 539 F.2d 943 (3d Cir 1976); *Jordan Marsh Co. v. Commissioner*, 269 F.2d 453 (2d Cir. 1959). In *Leslie*, for example, the court emphasized that the rent paid when the seller leased the property back was fair rental value, so that the taxpayer gave up a fee interest and received no property interest in return, other than the $2,400,000 cash. If the rents were below market value, then the taxpayer might be receiving a property interest in the form of a bargain-rental 30-year leasehold, in addition to the cash. Courts finding for the taxpayer stress that the primary purpose of *§ 1031* is to eliminate recognition (either gain or loss) of paper gains and losses on property exchanges. A taxpayer receiving $2,400,000 for property whose value equals that amount does not have any *paper* gain or loss on a property exchange. *Leslie* states that if the statute "intended to obviate the necessity of making difficult valuations, one would have expected them to provide for nonrecognition of gains and losses in all exchanges, whether the property received in exchanges were 'of like kind' or not of a like kind."

Sale or loan. Receipt of cash is not necessarily a sale. Borrowers as well as sellers get cash. Sale-leasebacks are recast as loans when the seller-tenant is more like a borrower. That would be true if the seller-tenant is very likely to own the property after the lease term or the buyer-lessor is not likely to make any ownership profits. For example, suppose the "tenant" has an option to buy the property after the 30-year lease expires for $1; or to renew the lease at a bargain rental, for most of the property's useful life.

§ 18.04 OTHER NONRECOGNITION PROVISIONS

As noted, *§ 1031* is just one of many tax deferral provisions. In other situations where the statute allows tax deferral, a taxpayer can sometimes receive all cash, as long as the cash is reinvested in certain property. In some cases, gain is deferred but not loss. Here are a few examples. What justifies the statutory rule permitting receipt of all cash? Why might gain but not loss be deferred?

[A]—Sale of principal residence

Before the 1997 Tax Act, *§ 1034* allowed taxpayers to sell a principal residence and reinvest the proceeds on a tax deferred basis, recognizing only the gain up to the amount of unreinvested sales proceeds. In addition, the old *§ 121 exempted* up to $125,000 of otherwise recognized gain on the sale of a principal residence by a taxpayer age 55 or older; this was a one-time exclusion.

The 1997 Tax Act repeals *§ 1034* and greatly broadens the scope of *§ 121*. It increases the exempt amount to $250,000 ($500,000 for a married couple filing a joint return). The exclusion applies regardless of the taxpayer's age. And the exclusion is no longer a one-time tax break; every sale is eligible as long as there is a two-year gap between sales.

To obtain the exclusion, the home must have been owned and occupied as the principal residence in two of the five years prior to the sale. There are special rules allowing some portion of the gain to be excluded if the sale is due to unforeseen circumstances which prevent satisfaction of the time limit requirements. This two-out-of-five-year rule should minimize the nagging problem of deciding whether the taxpayer who rents out the residence for a period of time while looking for a buyer has maintained the abode as a principal residence.

The exclusion does *not* apply to any depreciation adjustments provided by *§ 1250(b)(3)* on the residence after May 6, 1997. Thus, if the taxpayer rents out the property and takes $10,000 depreciation, gain will not be exempt up to that $10,000 amount.

[B]—*§ 1033*

A typical *§ 1033* transaction is the reinvestment of insurance proceeds in a new factory to replace a factory which burns down, or reinvestment in new land to replace condemned land.

Tax deferral under *§ 1033* generally applies in more narrow circumstances than *§ 1031* (except that it is not limited to business and investment property). *§ 1033* applies only to *in*voluntary conversions, not voluntary transfers. And, the replacement property must be "similar or related in service or use" to the lost property, which is narrower than like-kind.

The idea behind *§ 1033* seems to be that it is unfair to tax someone who reinvests in virtually the same asset after an involuntary conversion. The reinvestment shows that the taxpayer didn't want to sell at all.

§ 1033 is more of a taxpayer relief provision than *§ 1031.* If the taxpayer had a loss in involuntarily converted property, losses *are* recognized even if the taxpayer reinvests cash proceeds incident to the conversion. In addition, tax deferral of gain after money is reinvested in "similar" property is optional with the taxpayer. By contrast, *§ 1031* is mandatory and losses are not recognized. *§ 1031(c).*

The difference between *§ 1031* and *§ 1033* is illustrated by *Private Letter Ruling 9723032* (March 10, 1997). The issue was whether a motel was similar or related in service or use to an apartment building destroyed by fire so that the realized gain from the insurance proceeds attributable to the apartment building could be deferred under *§ 1033(a).* The ruling denied tax deferral based on the fact that the taxpayer changed his relationship from a lessor of apartments to an operator of a motel, which substantially altered his relationship to the properties. As a lessor of apartment units, the essence of the taxpayer's investment was the generation of fixed, periodic rental income. Although the taxpayer provided certain services typical of a landlord, he was not required to be on the premises on a daily basis. As a landlord, the taxpayer was insulated from the day-to-day operating responsibilities and activities that are demanded by the operation of the motel. In contrast, the business of operating the motel required daily oversight. Taxpayer was responsible for furnishing the rooms, cleaning the rooms, and washing the linens, services which were not required as an apartment building landlord. By changing from an owner-lessor of property to an owner-operator, taxpayer's relationship to the properties changed substantially and the property was not similar or related in service or use. By contrast, the exchange of the apartment for the motel property would be a like-kind exchange under *§ 1031.*

Notice *§ 1033(g).* If business or investment realty is condemned, qualified replacement property includes both "like-kind" *and* "similar" property. Why isn't the same concession made for insurance proceeds, if the realty burns down?

See also § 1033(h), added by the 1993 tax law. This subsection provides a special rule for the involuntary conversion of a principal residence and its contents, damaged by presidentially declared disasters. First, no gain is recognized on receipt of insurance proceeds for "unscheduled" property (usually routine personal contents of the house, other than antiques, jewelry, etc., which are specially listed for insurance purposes). Second, the insurance proceeds for the residence and scheduled property are treated as received for a *single* item of property. Third, the replacement period is four years. What does this new provision do for the taxpayer that the prior law did not do?

The effective date of the new *§ 1033(h)* is September 1, 1991. It was not part of the tax bill which passed either the House or Senate, but first appeared in the legislation during the conference committee proceedings to resolve House-Senate differences. What might explain the unusual retroactivity provision and conference proceedings?

[C]—Miscellaneous

Tax deferral is a handy policy tool.

(1) *§§ 1081-1083* allows tax deferral on exchanges of stocks and securities to obey orders of the Securities and Exchange Commission.

(2) *§ 1043* allows public officials who must divest themselves of property when they take office to defer gain on the sales proceeds if they reinvest within 60 days in "permitted" property (generally U.S. obligations or diversified investment funds).

(3) *§ 1044* (adopted by the 1993 tax law) permits certain taxpayers who sell publicly traded stock to defer a limited amount of gain, if the sales proceeds are reinvested in a specialized small business investment company.

CHAPTER 19

CAPITAL GAINS AND LOSSES—DEFINITION

In § 3.05, *supra*, we discussed the tax preference for certain capital gains. You may want to review that discussion now. The essential prerequisites for capital gains were "sale or exchange" of a "capital asset." To obtain the lower tax rate, the asset had to be held for more than one year; more than 18 months was even better; and more than five years will be even better after December 31, 2000.

In this chapter we look closely at the definitions of the key terms — primarily "capital asset," but also "sale or exchange."

§ 19.01 PRIMARILY FOR SALE IN THE ORDINARY COURSE OF BUSINESS

The primary distinction between capital gain and ordinary income is that between the gain attributable to property which produces income and the periodic income produced by that property. This distinction is implemented by the exclusion of items from the definition of a "capital asset" as provided in *§ 1221(1),* which is applied in the following case.

BIEDENHARN REALTY CO. v. UNITED STATES

526 F.2d 409 (5th Cir. 1976)

GOLDBERG, CIRCUIT JUDGE:

The taxpayer-plaintiff, Biedenharn Realty Company, Inc. (Biedenharn), filed suit against the United States in May, 1971, claiming a refund for the tax years 1964, 1965, and 1966. . . . In its present action, plaintiff asserts that the whole real estate profit represents gain from the sale of capital assets and consequently that the Government is indebted to taxpayer for $32,006.86 in overpaid taxes. Reviewing the facts of this case in the light of our previous holdings and the directions set forth in this opinion, we reject plaintiff's claim and in so doing reverse the opinion of the District Court.

I.

. . . [W]e believe it useful to set out in plentiful detail the case's background and circumstances as best they can be ascertained.

A. The Realty Company. Joseph Biedenharn organized the Biedenharn Realty Company in 1923 as a vehicle for holding and managing the Biedenharn family's numerous investments. The original stockholders were all family members. The investment company controls, among other interests, valuable commercial properties, a substantial stock portfolio, a motel, warehouses, a shopping center, residential real property, and farm property.

B. Taxpayer's Real Property Sales — The Hardtimes Plantation. Taxpayer's suit most directly involves its ownership and sale of lots from the 973 acre tract located near Monroe, Louisiana, known as the Hardtimes Plantation. The plaintiff purchased the estate in 1935 for $50,000.00. B. W. Biedenharn, the Realty Company's president, testified that taxpayer acquired Hardtimes as a "good buy" for the purpose of farming and as a future investment. The plaintiff farmed the land for several years. Thereafter, Biedenharn rented part of the acreage to a farmer who Mr. Biedenharn suggested may presently be engaged in farming operations.

1. The Three Basic Subdivisions. Between 1939 and 1966, taxpayer carved three basic subdivisions from Hardtimes — Biedenharn Estates, Bayou DeSiard Country Club Addition, and Oak Park Addition — covering approximately 185 acres. During these years, Biedenharn sold 208 subdivided Hardtimes lots in 158 sales, making a profit in excess of $800,000.00. These three basic subdivisions are the source of the contested 37 sales of 38 lots. Their development and disposition are more fully discussed below.

(a) Biedenharn Estates Unit 1, including 41.9 acres, was platted in 1938. Between 1939 and 1956, taxpayer apparently sold 21 lots in 9 sales. Unit 2, containing 8.91 acres, was sold in 9 transactions between 1960 and 1965 and involved 10 lots.

(b) Bayou DeSiard Country Club Addition, covering 61 acres, was subdivided in 1951, with remaining lots resubdivided in 1964. Approximately 73 lots were purchased in 64 sales from 1951 to 1966.

(c) Oak Park Units 1 and 2 encompassed 75 acres. After subdivision in 1955 and resubdivision in 1960, plaintiff sold approximately 104 lots in 76 sales. . . .

[Editor — The court then describes the sale of lots from non-Hardtimes property.] Unfortunately, the record does not unambiguously reveal the number of sales as opposed to the number of lots involved in these dispositions. Although some doubt exists as to the actual sales totals, even the most conservative reading of the figures convinces us of the frequency and abundance of the non-Hardtimes sales. For example, from 1925 to 1958, Biedenharn consummated from its subdivided Owens tract a minimum of 125, but perhaps upwards of 300, sales (338 lots). Eighteen sales accounted for 20 lots sold between 1923 and 1958 from Biedenharn's Cornwall property. Taxpayer's disposition from 1927 to 1960 of its Corey and Cabeen property resulted in at least 50 sales. Plaintiff made 14 sales from its Thomas Street lots between 1937 and 1955. Moreover, Biedenharn has sold over 20 other properties, a few of them piecemeal, since 1923. . . .

D. Real Property Improvements. Before selling the Hardtimes lots, Biedenharn improved the land, adding in most instances streets, drainage, water, sewerage, and electricity. The total cost of bettering the Plantation acreage exceeded $200,000 and included $9,519.17 for Biedenharn Estates Unit 2, $56,879.12 for Bayou DeSiard County Club Addition, and $141,579.25 for the Oak Park Addition.

E. Sale of the Hardtimes Subdivisions. Bernard Biedenharn testified that at the time of the Hardtimes purchase, no one foresaw that the land would be sold as residential property in the future. Accordingly, the District Court found, and we do not disagree, that Biedenharn bought Hardtimes for investment. Later, as the City of Monroe expanded northward, the Plantation became valuable residential property. The Realty Company staked off the Bayou DeSiard subdivision so that prospective purchasers could see what the lots "looked like." As demand increased, taxpayer opened the Oak Park and Biedenharn Estates Unit 2 subdivisions and resubdivided the Bayou DeSiard section. Taxpayer handled all Biedenharn Estates and Bayou DeSiard sales. Independent realtors disposed of many of the Oak Park lots. Mr. Herbert Rosenhein, a local broker, sold Oak Park Unit 1 lots. Gilbert Faulk, a real estate agent, sold from Oak Park Unit 2. Of the 37 sales consummated between 1964 and 1966, Henry Biedenharn handled at least nine transactions (Biedenharn Estates (2) and Bayou DeSiard (7)) while "independent realtors" effected some, if not all, of the other 28 transactions (Oak Park Unit 2.). Taxpayer delegated significant responsibilities to these brokers. In its dealings with Faulk, Biedenharn set the prices, general credit terms, and signed the deeds. Details, including specific credit decisions and advertising, devolved to Faulk, who utilized on-site signs and newspapers to publicize the lots.

In contrast to these broker induced dispositions, plaintiff's non-brokered sales resulted after unsolicited individuals approached Realty Company employees with inquiries about prospective purchases. At no time did the plaintiff hire its own real state salesmen or engage in formal advertising. Apparently, the lands' prime location and plaintiff's subdivision activities constituted sufficient notice to interested persons of the availability of Hardtimes lots. Henry Biedenharn testified:

> (O)nce we started improving and putting roads and streets in people would call us up and ask you about buying a lot and we would sell a lot if they wanted it.

The Realty Company does not maintain a separate place of business but instead offices at the Biedenharn family's Ouachita Coca-Cola bottling plant. A telephone, listed in plaintiff's name, rings at the Coca-Cola building. Biedenharn has four employees: a camp caretaker, a tenant farmer, a bookkeeper and a manager. The manager, Henry Biedenharn, Jr., devotes approximately 10% of his time to the Realty Company, mostly collecting rents and overseeing the maintenance of various properties. The bookkeeper also works only part-time for plaintiff. Having set out these facts, we now discuss the relevant legal standard for resolving this controversy.

II.

The determination of gain as capital or ordinary is controlled by the language of the Internal Revenue Code. The Code defines capital asset, the profitable sale or exchange of which generally results in capital gains, as "property held by the taxpayer." 26 U.S.C. § 1221. Many exceptions limit the enormous breadth of this congressional description and consequently remove large numbers of transactions from the privileged realm of capital gains. In this case, we confront the question whether or not Biedenharn's real estate sales should be taxed at ordinary rates because they fall within the exception covering "property held by the taxpayer primarily for sale to customers in the ordinary course of his trade or business." 26 U.S.C. § 1221(1).[20]

The problem we struggle with here is not novel. We have become accustomed to the frequency with which taxpayers litigate this troublesome question. Chief Judge Brown appropriately described the real estate capital gains-ordinary income issue as "old, familiar, recurring, vexing and ofttimes elusive." The difficulty in large part stems from ad-hoc application of the numerous permissible criteria set forth in our multitudinous prior opinions. Over the past 40 years, this case by case approach with its concentration on the facts of each suit has resulted in a collection of decisions not always reconcilable. . . .

Assuredly, we would much prefer one or two clearly defined, easily employed tests which lead to predictable, perhaps automatic, conclusions.

[20] Neither party contends, nor do we find, that Internal Revenue Code § 1237, guaranteeing capital gains treatment to subdividing taxpayers in certain instances, is applicable to the facts of this suit.

However, the nature of the congressional "capital asset" definition and the myriad situations to which we must apply that standard make impossible any easy escape from the task before us. No one set of criteria is applicable to all economic structures. Moreover, within a collection of tests, individual factors have varying weights and magnitudes, depending on the facts of the case. The relationship among the factors and their mutual interaction is altered as each criteria increases or diminishes in strength, sometimes changing the controversy's outcome. As such, there can be no mathematical formula capable of finding the X of capital gains or ordinary income in this complicated field.

Yet our inability to proffer a panaceatic guide to the perplexed with respect to this subject does not preclude our setting forth some general, albeit inexact, guidelines for the resolution of many of the § 1221(1) cases we confront. This opinion does not purport to reconcile all past precedents or assure conflictfree future decisions. Nor do we hereby obviate the need for ad-hoc adjustments when confronted with close cases and changing factual circumstances. Instead, with the hope of clarifying a few of the area's mysteries, we more precisely define and suggest points of emphasis for the major Winthrop delineated factors[22] as they appear in the instant controversy. In so doing, we devote particular attention to the Court's recent opinions in order that our analysis will reflect, insofar as possible, the Circuit's present trends.

III.

We begin our task by evaluating in the light of Biedenharn's facts the main Winthrop factors — substantiality and frequency of sales, improvements, solicitation and advertising efforts, and brokers' activities — as well as a few miscellaneous contentions. A separate section follows discussing the keenly contested role of prior investment intent. Finally, we consider the significance of the Supreme Court's decision in *Malat v. Riddell*.

A. *Frequency and Substantiality of Sales*

---

[22] In United States v. Winthrop, 5 Cir. 1969, 417 F.2d 905, 910, the Court enumerated the following factors:

> (1) the nature and purpose of the acquisition of the property and the duration of the ownership; (2) the extent and nature of the taxpayer's efforts to sell the property; (3) the number, extent, continuity and substantiality of the sales; (4) the extent of subdividing, developing, and advertising to increase sales; (5) the use of a business office for the sale of the property; (6) the character and degree of supervision or control exercised by the taxpayer over any representative selling the property; and (7) the time and effort the taxpayer habitually devoted to the sales.

The numbering indicates no hierarchy of importance.

Scrutinizing closely the record and briefs, we find that plaintiff's real property sales activities compel an ordinary income conclusion.[25] In arriving at this result, we examine first the most important of Winthrop's factors — the frequency and substantiality of taxpayer's sales. Although frequency and substantiality of sales are not usually conclusive, they occupy the preeminent ground in our analysis. The recent trend of Fifth Circuit decisions indicates that when dispositions of subdivided property extend over a long period of time and are especially numerous, the likelihood of capital gains is very slight indeed. Conversely, when sales are few and isolated, the taxpayer's claim to capital gain is accorded greater deference.

On the present facts, taxpayer could not claim "isolated" sales or a passive and gradual liquidation. Although only three years and 37 sales (38 lots) are in controversy here, taxpayer's pre-1964 sales from the Hardtimes acreage as well as similar dispositions from other properties are probative of the existence of sales "in the ordinary course of his trade or business." [] Biedenharn sold property, usually a substantial number of lots, in every year, save one, from 1923 to 1966. . . .

The frequency and substantiality of Biedenharn's sales go not only to its holding purpose and the existence of a trade or business but also support our finding of the ordinariness with which the Realty Company disposed of its lots. These sales easily meet the criteria of normalcy set forth in Winthrop. . . .

B. *Improvements*

Although we place greatest emphasis on the frequency and substantiality of sales over an extended time period, our decision in this instance is aided by the presence of taxpayer activity — particularly improvements—in the other Winthrop areas. Biedenharn vigorously improved its subdivisions, generally adding streets, drainage, sewerage, and utilities. . . .

C. *Solicitation and Advertising Efforts*

Substantial, frequent sales and improvements such as we have encountered in this case will usually conclude the capital gains issue against taxpayer. Thus, on the basis of our analysis to this point, we would have little hesitation in finding that taxpayer held "primarily for sale" in the "ordinary course of (his) trade or business." "(T)he flexing of commercial muscles with frequency and continuity, design and effect" of which Winthrop spoke, is here a reality. This reality is further buttressed by Biedenharn's sales efforts, including those carried on through brokers.

---

25 Our power to review the District Court's ultimate legal determination that taxpayer did not hold property "primarily for sale to customers in the ordinary course of his trade or business" is plenary and not limited by the clearly erroneous rule. See United States v. Winthrop, 5 Cir. 1969, 417 F.2d 905, 910.

Minimizing the importance of its own sales activities, taxpayer points repeatedly to its steady avoidance of advertising or other solicitation of customers. Plaintiff directs our attention to stipulations detailing the population growth of Monroe and testimony outlining the economic forces which made Hardtimes Plantation attractive residential property and presumably eliminated the need for sales exertions. We have no quarrel with plaintiff's description of this familiar process of suburban expansion, but we cannot accept the legal inferences which taxpayer would have us draw.

The Circuit's recent decisions . . . implicitly recognize that even one inarguably in the real estate business need not engage in promotional exertions in the face of a favorable market. As such, we do not always require a showing of active solicitation where "business . . . (is) good, indeed brisk," and where other Winthrop factors make obvious taxpayer's ordinary trade or business status. Plainly, this represents a sensible approach. In cases such as Biedenharn, the sale of a few lots and the construction of the first homes, albeit not, as in Winthrop, by the taxpayer, as well as the building of roads, addition of utilities, and staking off of the other subdivided parcels constitute a highly visible form of advertising. Prospective home buyers drive by the advantageously located property, see the development activities, and are as surely put on notice of the availability of lots as if the owner had erected large signs announcing "residential property for sale." We do not by this evaluation automatically neutralize advertising or solicitation as a factor in our analysis. This form of inherent notice is not present in all land sales, especially where the property is not so valuably located, is not subdivided into small lots, and is not improved. Moreover, inherent notice represents only one band of the solicitation spectrum. Media utilization and personal initiatives remain material components of this criterion. When present, they call for greater Government oriented emphasis on Winthrop's solicitation factor.

D. *Brokerage Activities*

In evaluating Biedenharn's solicitation activities, we need not confine ourselves to the [] Winthrop theory of brisk sales without organizational efforts. Unlike in [] Winthrop where no one undertook overt solicitation efforts, the Realty Company hired brokers who, using media and on site advertising, worked vigorously on taxpayer's behalf. We do not believe that the employment of brokers should shield plaintiff from ordinary income treatment. Their activities should at least in discounted form be attributed to Biedenharn. . . . In [some cases], the taxpayer turned the entire property over to brokers, who, having been granted total responsibility, made all decisions including the setting of sales prices. In comparison, Biedenharn determined original prices and general credit policy. Moreover, the Realty Company did not make all the sales in question through brokers . . . .

IV.

The District Court found that "(t)axpayer is merely liquidating over a long period of time a substantial investment in the most advantageous method possible." In this view, the original investment intent is crucial, for it preserves the capital gains character of the transaction even in the face of normal real estate sales activities.

The Government asserts that Biedenharn Realty Company did not merely "liquidate" an investment but instead entered the real estate business in an effort to dispose of what was formerly investment property. Claiming that Biedenharn's activities would result in ordinary income if the Hardtimes Plantation had been purchased with the intent to divide and resell the property, and finding no reason why a different prior intent should influence this outcome,[38] the Government concludes that original investment purpose is irrelevant. Instead, the Government would have us focus exclusively on taxpayer's intent and the level of sales activity during the period commencing with subdivision and improvement and lasting through final sales. Under this theory, every individual who improves and frequently sells substantial numbers of land parcels would receive ordinary income.[39]

While the facts of this case dictate our agreement with the Internal Revenue Service's ultimate conclusion of taxpayer liability, they do not require our acquiescence in the Government's entreated total elimination of Winthrop's first criterion, "the nature and purpose of the acquisition." Undoubtedly, in most subdivided-improvement situations, an investment purpose of antecedent origin will not survive into a present era of intense retail selling. The antiquated purpose, when overborne by later, but substantial and frequent selling activity, will not prevent ordinary income from being visited upon the taxpayer. Generally, investment purpose has no built-in perpetuity nor a guarantee of capital gains forever more. Precedents, however, in certain circumstances have permitted landowners with earlier investment intent to sell subdivided property and remain subject to capital gains treatment. . . .

We reject the Government's sweeping contention that prior investment intent is always irrelevant. There will be instances where an initial

---

[38] The Government emphasizes the "unfairness" of two taxpayers engaging in equal sales efforts with respect to similar tracts of land but receiving different tax treatment because of divergent initial motives.

[39] The Government suggests that taxpayer can avoid ordinary income treatment by selling the undivided, unimproved tract to a controlled corporation which would then develop the land. However, this approach would in many instances create attribution problems with the Government arguing that the controlled corporation's sales are actually those of the taxpayer. Furthermore, we are not prepared to tell taxpayers that in all cases a single bulk sale provides the only road to capital gains.

investment purpose endures in controlling fashion notwithstanding continuing sales activity. We doubt that this aperture, where an active subdivider and improver receives capital gains, is very wide; yet we believe it exists. We would most generally find such an opening where the change from investment holding to sales activity results from unanticipated, externally induced factors which make impossible the continued pre-existing use of the realty. *Barrios Estate v. Commissioner,* 5 Cir. 1959, 265 F.2d 517, is such a case. There the taxpayer farmed the land until drainage problems created by the newly completed intercoastal canal rendered the property agriculturally unfit. The Court found that taxpayer was "dispossessed of the farming operation through no act of her own." Similarly, Acts of God, condemnation of part of one's property, new and unfavorable zoning regulations, or other events forcing alteration of taxpayer's plans create situations making possible subdivision and improvement as a part of a capital gains disposition.[40]

. . . [W]e caution that although permitting a land owner substantial sales flexibility where there is a forced change from original investment purpose, we do not absolutely shield the constrained taxpayer from ordinary income. That taxpayer is not granted carte blanche to undertake intensely all aspects of a full blown real estate business. Instead, in cases of forced change of purpose, we will continue to utilize the Winthrop analysis discussed earlier but will place unusually strong taxpayer-favored emphasis on Winthrop's first factor.

Clearly, under the facts in this case, the distinction just elaborated undermines Biedenharn's reliance on original investment purpose. Taxpayer's change of purpose was entirely voluntary and therefore does not fall within the protected area. Moreover, taxpayer's original investment intent, even if considered a factor sharply supporting capital gains treatment, is so overwhelmed by the other Winthrop factors discussed supra, that that element can have no decisive effect. However wide the capital gains passageway through which a subdivider with former investment intent could squeeze, the Biedenharn Realty Company will never fit.

---

[40] A Boston University Law Review article canvassing factors inducing involuntary changes of purpose in subdivided realty cases enumerates among others the following: a pressing need for funds in general, illness or old age or both, the necessity for liquidating a partnership on the death of a partner, the threat of condemnation, and municipal zoning restrictions. Levin, Capital Gains or Income Tax on Real Estate Sales, 37 B.U.L.Rev. 165, 194–95 (1957). Although we might not accept all of these events as sufficient to cause an outcome favorable to taxpayer, they are suggestive of the sort of change of purpose provoking events delineated above as worthy of special consideration.

V.

The District Court, citing *Malat v. Riddell*, 1966, 383 U.S. 569, stated that "the lots were not held . . . primarily for sale as that phrase was interpreted . . . in Malat . . . ." Finding that Biedenharn's primary purpose became holding for sale and consequently that Malat in no way alters our analysis here, we disagree with the District Court's conclusion. Malat was a brief per curiam in which the Supreme Court decided only that as used in Internal Revenue Code § 1221(1) the word "primarily" means "principally," "of first importance." The Supreme Court, remanding the case, did not analyze the facts or resolve the controversy which involved a real estate dealer who had purchased land and held it at the time of sale with the dual intention of developing it as rental property or selling it, depending on whichever proved to be the more profitable. In contrast, having substantially abandoned its investment and farming[43] intent, Biedenharn was cloaked primarily in the garb of sales purpose when it disposed of the 38 lots here in controversy. With this change, the Realty Company lost the opportunity of coming within any dual purpose analysis.

We do not hereby condemn to ordinary income a taxpayer merely because, as is usually true, his principal intent at the exact moment of disposition is sales. Rather, we refuse capital gains treatment in those instances where over time there has been such a thoroughgoing change of purpose, as to make untenable a claim either of twin intent or continued primacy of investment purpose.

VI.

Having surveyed the Hardtimes terrain, we find no escape from ordinary income. The frequency and substantiality of sales over an extended time, the significant improvement of the basic subdivisions, the acquisition of additional properties, the use of brokers, and other less important factors persuasively combine to doom taxpayer's cause. Applying Winthrop's criteria, this case clearly falls within the ordinary income category delineated in that decision. . . .

We cannot write black letter law for all realty subdividers and for all times, but we do caution in words of red that once an investment does not mean always an investment. A simon-pure investor forty years ago could

[43] The District Court found that Biedenharn "is still farming a large part of the land . . . ." 356 F.Supp. at 1336. The record suggests neither that Biedernharn as opposed to a lessee currently farms on the Hardtimes Plantation nor that the magnitude of that lessee's farming operations is substantial. More importantly, the District Court did not find and the plaintiff does not assert that Biedenharn simultaneously held the subdivided land for sale and for farming either before or at the time of disposition. Taxpayer claims no dual purpose.

by his subsequent activities become a seller in the ordinary course four decades later. The period of Biedenharn's passivity is in the distant past; and the taxpayer has since undertaken the role of real estate protagonist. The Hardtimes Plantation in its day may have been one thing, but as the plantation was developed and sold, Hardtimes became by the very fact of change and activity a different holding than it had been at its inception. No longer could resort to initial purpose preserve taxpayer's once upon a time opportunity for favored treatment. The opinion of the District Court is reversed.

Why is original investment purpose relevant? *Biedenharn* obviously downplays the relevance of this factor but is reluctant to give it up. Does it have anything to do with the fair treatment of an investor who holds property for a long time, during which it rises in value, and who then sells the asset in the ordinary course of business? Would it be fair to allocate the gain between capital gain (based on value when the shift to selling in the ordinary course of business occurs) and ordinary income? *§ 1237* achieves that result in a limited way under limited circumstances. *See also* footnote 39 in *Biedenharn.*

Biedenharn states that the taxpayer was primarily selling, not investing or holding with a dual investment/sale purpose. On reflection, that is a puzzling way to explain the distinction between capital gain and ordinary income. After all, many investors (including the core capital gain example of the stock investor) hold primarily for sale, but receive capital gains. When the court in *Biedenharn* refers to investing, it probably means both (1) holding an asset to produce periodic income, as when property is farmed or leased; and (2) holding an asset for sale, but not in the ordinary course of business. That would explain why most of the opinion, denying capital gain, is about how the taxpayer sold, not whether sale was the primary motive.

This suggests a further question. Why can't property held to produce income (such as rent) also be held primarily for sale in the ordinary course of business? The following case deals with that issue.

———

INTERNATIONAL SHOE MACHINE CORP. v. UNITED STATES

Sales are part of OCofB4 ∴ income from sales is "ordinary" & not capital

491 F.2d 157 (1st Cir. 1974)

COFFIN, CHIEF JUDGE: . . .

Income from leasing

It is undisputed that during the years in question, 1964 through 1966, appellant's main source of income derived from the leases of its shoe machinery equipment, rather than from their sales. The revenue from sales of the leased machinery comprised, respectively, only 7 percent, 2 percent, and 2 percent of appellant's gross revenues. In fact, because the appellant preferred the more profitable route of leasing its machines, it never developed a sales force, never solicited purchases, set prices high to make purchasing unattractive, and even attempted to dissuade customers from purchasing them.

Yet the district court found that, beginning in 1964, when the investment tax credit made it more attractive for shoe manufacturers to buy shoe machinery rather than to lease it, the selling of machinery became an accepted and predictable, albeit small, part of appellant's business. Since appellant's chief competitor was selling leased shoe machines, it was necessary for appellant to offer its customers the same option. During the years in issue, appellant never declined to quote a price, nor did it ever decline to make a sale if the customer was persistent. Unlike previous years, purchase inquiries were referred to the appellant's vice president for sales, normally charged with selling new, nonleased machines, whereupon a price was negotiated. A schedule was prepared, indicating the sales price of leased machines, based upon the number of years that the machines had been leased. In total, 271 machines were sold to customers who, at the time of the sales, had been leasing the machines for at least six months. . . .

FS: supporting "sale"

In support of its contention that "primarily" refers to a contrast between sales and leases, appellant relies upon *Malat v. Riddell,* 383 U.S. 596 (1966). There, the taxpayer purchased a parcel of land, with the alleged intention of developing an apartment project. When the taxpayer confronted zoning restrictions, he decided to terminate the venture, and sold his interest in the property, claiming a capital gain. The lower courts found, however, that

Malat

the taxpayer had had a "dual purpose" in acquiring the land, a "substantial" one of which was to sell if that were to prove more profitable than development. Therefore, since the taxpayer had failed to establish that the property was not held primarily for sale to customers in the ordinary course of his business, his gain was treated as ordinary income. The Supreme Court vacated and remanded the case, stating that the lower courts had applied an incorrect legal standard when they defined "primarily" as merely "substantially" rather than using it in its ordinary, everyday sense of "first importance" or "principally". . . .

We cannot agree that *Malat* is dispositive. Even if "primarily" is defined as "of first importance" or "principally," the word may still invoke a contrast between sales made in the "ordinary course of . . . business" and those made as liquidations of inventory, rather than between leases and sales. *Malat* itself concerned the dual purposes of developing an apartment complex on the land and selling the land. Although these two possible sources of income might be characterized as income from "lease" or "sale," a more meaningful distinction could be made between on-going income generated in the ordinary course of business and income from the termination and sale of the venture. . . .

The real question, therefore, concerns whether or not the income from the sales of appellant's shoe machinery should have been characterized as having been generated in the "ordinary course of . . . business." Appellant contests the conclusion of the district court that selling was "an accepted and predictable part of the business" by pointing out that sales were made only as a last resort, after attempts to dissuade the customer from purchasing had failed. We think that the district court was correct in its finding. While sales were made only as a last resort, it seems clear the after 1964 such sales were expected to occur, on an occasional basis, and policies and procedures were developed for handling them. Purchase inquiries were referred to the vice president for sales, a price schedule was drawn up, and discounts were offered to good customers. Appellant may not have desired such sales. It is likely that appellant would never have developed a sales policy for its leased machines had it not been forced to do so by the pressure of competition. But it was justifiable to find that such occasional sales were indeed "accepted and predictable."

Even "accepted and predictable" sales might not, however, occur in the "ordinary course of . . . business." For example, a final liquidation of inventory, although accepted and predictable, would normally be eligible for capital gains treatment. Appellant's final contention, therefore, is that the sales in question represented the liquidation of an investment. Appellant points out that the machines were leased for an average of eight and one half years before they were sold, during which time depreciation was taken on them and repairs were made. Thus, appellant seeks to bring itself within the scope of the "rental-obsolescence" decisions, which hold that the sale of rental equipment, no longer useful for renting, is taxable at capital gains rates.

In the "rental obsolescence" decisions, however, equipment was sold only after its rental income-producing potential had ended and "such sales were . . . the natural conclusion of a vehicle rental business cycle." Moreover, the equipment was specifically manufactured to fit the requirements of lessees; it was sold only when lessees no longer found the equipment useful. In the present case, however, the shoe manufacturing equipment was sold, not as a final disposition of property that had ceased to produce rental income for the appellant but, rather as property that still retained a rental income producing potential for the appellant. Had appellant chosen not to sell the shoe machinery, the machinery would have continued to generate ordinary income in the form of lease revenue. Thus, the sale of such machinery, for a price which included the present value of that future ordinary income, cannot be considered the liquidation of an investment outside the scope of the "ordinary course of . . . business."

The actual decision in *International Shoe* should seem relatively unimportant because the asset was tangible personal property subject to depreciation and the recapture rules would turn the gain into ordinary income, except in the unlikely case of the gain exceeding prior depreciation. Under current law, however, gain on the sale of buildings does not produce recaptured ordinary income (and gain on land never does), so the decision is still important in identifying when gain on the sale of previously rented property is capital gain or ordinary income.

§ 19.02 *§ 1231*

Look at *§ 1221(2)*. It excludes certain assets used in the trade or business from the definition of a capital asset. An example is a factory and the land on which it sits. But isn't the gain on these assets as deserving of preferential capital gain treatment as the typical investment in stock? Or should the business function of the asset prevent preferential tax treatment?

Until 1938, the gain on such assets was capital gain. Consequently, losses were capital losses, which meant that their deduction was limited. During the Depression, the loss limitation became a problem for businesses which wanted to dispose of their old business assets. The businesses claimed that they were discouraged from selling the assets by the loss limitation. Moreover, the losses were thought to be the functional equivalent of depreciation deductions which had not been taken but should have been taken. To respond to these concerns, certain business assets were removed from the capital asset definition. The losses were now ordinary. But that also meant that the gain was ordinary. By 1942, gains were common because values went up during the war.

The current statutory pattern, adopted in 1942, is found in *§ 1231*. It is illustrated by the following problems. The statute treats net losses from *§ 1231* transactions as ordinary losses, but net gains as long-term capital gains. A net *§ 1231* gain goes into the *§ 1222* calculation pot, to be added to other capital gains and netted with capital losses under *§ 1222*.

PROBLEMS

Assume all transactions occur in the same tax year unless otherwise specified; that the factory has been held more than one year; and that there is no recapture of prior depreciation deductions as ordinary income. How much capital gain or ordinary loss does the taxpayer have in each of the following problems?

	Asset	Cost	Proceeds	Transaction
1.	Factory	80	100	Sale
2.	Factory	100	70	Condemned under eminent domain
3.	Factory	100	55	Fire loss, covered by $55 insurance
4.	Factory	40	70	Fire loss, with $70 insurance reinvested in similar factory

Problem 1. Transactions 1 & 2. This illustrates the core example of a *§ 1231* transaction, which is the sale or compulsory or involuntary conversion of property used in the business and held for more than one year.

Problem 2. Transactions 1 & 3. This illustrates the operation of *§ 1231(a)(4)(C)*. The purpose of this provision is to treat taxpayers who deduct insurance premiums for business casualty insurance like taxpayers who do not insure (or who underinsure) business property, but suffer losses.

Problem 3. Transactions 1, 3 & 4. This problem should remind you that *§ 1231* (and *§ 1221*) do not create recognized gain or loss, but only operate on otherwise recognizable gains or losses.

Problem 4. Transaction 2 followed four years later by transaction 1. This problem addresses the taxpayer's opportunity to control the timing of losses to their advantage. *§ 1231(c)* reduces that opportunity.

§ 19.03 SALE OF ENTIRE BUSINESS

The distinction among sales of inventory, *§ 1231* assets, and certain investment property should now be apparent. When a taxpayer owns stock in a corporation which owns various properties, however, the differences are homogenized and the taxpayer simply sells stock, which is usually a capital asset.

But when a taxpayer runs an unincorporated business (a sole proprietorship, for example), sale of the business is treated as a sale of each item of business property. *Williams v. McGowan,* 152 F.2d 570 (2d Cir. 1945). Sales proceeds must therefore be allocated among the items sold.

Partnership interests are hybrids. Sale of a partnership interest is usually sale of a capital asset, except to the extent that the proceeds are attributable to inventory which has appreciated substantially, and unrealized receivables. *§§ 741, 751.*

§ 19.04 CAPITAL vs. ORDINARY LOSSES

[A]—"Integral part of the business"?

Can stocks or bonds ever be ordinary rather than capital assets? Sure. If a taxpayer holds them for sale primarily in the ordinary course of business, they are not capital assets. Are there other cases?

Here is a hypothetical. A taxpayer needs raw materials to produce a product. To secure a steady supply, the taxpayer buys stock or bonds in a supplier. Variations on this theme are purchases of stock or bonds in a buyer of business output to assure steady sales.

Corn

Some interpretations of a Supreme Court case, *Corn Products Refining Co. v. Commissioner,* 350 U.S. 46 (1955), seemed to support ordinary asset treatment on such stocks and bonds. The taxpayer in that case manufactured products made from grain corn. It had limited storage capacity, only three weeks supply. So, to secure a steady supply of corn, it purchased options to acquire corn. If corn was scarce, the value of the options increased; if corn was plentiful, the value of the option declined. The taxpayer sold the unexercised options each year if they were not needed, sometimes realizing gain and sometimes loss. In *Corn Products,* gains far exceeded losses, so the taxpayer argued that they were capital gains.

The Supreme Court disagreed with the taxpayer, holding that the sales produced ordinary gain and loss. However, it used some language that later came back to haunt the government in cases like the earlier stock and bond examples, when the taxpayer had a loss on the investment. The Court buttressed its "ordinary income" holding in *Corn Products* with the observation that the options were "an integral part of its business designed to protect its manufacturing operation against a price increase in its principal raw material and to assure a ready supply for future manufacturing requirements." That seemed to describe stocks and bonds purchased in supplier-corporations to protect a source of supply, or, inferentially, in buyer-corporations to protect sales volume. In the following case, dealing with stock, the Court corrected mistaken implications derived from the prior *Corn Products* decision.

ARKANSAS BEST CORP. v. C.I.R.

TP loses: loss = capital

485 U.S. 212 (1988)

JUSTICE MARSHALL delivered the opinion of the court. . . .

The issue presented in this case is whether capital stock held by petitioner Arkansas Best Corporation (Arkansas Best) is a "capital asset" as defined in § 1221 of the Internal Revenue Code regardless of whether the stock was purchased and held for a business purpose or for an investment purpose.

I

Arkansas Best is a diversified holding company. In 1968 it acquired approximately 65% of the stock of the National Bank of Commerce (Bank) in Dallas, Texas. Between 1969 and 1974, Arkansas Best more than tripled the number of shares it owned in the Bank, although its percentage interest in the Bank remained relatively stable. These acquisitions were prompted principally by the Bank's need for added capital. Until 1972, the Bank appeared to be prosperous and growing, and the added capital was necessary to accommodate this growth. As the Dallas real estate market declined, however, so too did the financial health of the Bank, which had a heavy concentration of loans in the local real estate industry. In 1972, federal examiners classified the Bank as a problem bank. The infusion of capital after 1972 was prompted by the loan portfolio problems of the bank.

Petitioner sold the bulk of its Bank stock on June 30, 1975, leaving it with only a 14.7% stake in the Bank. On its federal income tax return for 1975, petitioner claimed a deduction for an ordinary loss of $9,995,688 resulting from the sale of the stock. The Commissioner of Internal Revenue disallowed the deduction, finding that the loss from the sale of stock was a capital loss, rather than an ordinary loss, and that it therefore was subject to the capital loss limitations in the Internal Revenue Code.

Arkansas Best challenged the Commissioner's determination in the United States Tax Court. The Tax Court, relying on cases interpreting *Corn Products Refining Co. v. Commissioner,* 350 U.S. 46 (1955), held that stock purchased with a substantial investment purpose is a capital asset which, when sold, gives rise to a capital gain or loss, whereas stock purchased and held for a business purpose, without any substantial investment motive, is an ordinary asset whose sale gives rise to ordinary gains or losses. The court characterized Arkansas Best's acquisitions through 1972 as occurring during the Bank's " 'growth' phase," and found that these acquisitions "were motivated primarily by investment purpose and only incidentally by some business purpose." The stock acquired during this period therefore constituted a capital asset, which gave rise to a capital loss when sold in 1975. The court determined, however, that the acquisitions after 1972 occurred during the Bank's " 'problem' phase," and, except for certain minor exceptions, "were made exclusively for business purposes and subsequently held for the same reasons." These acquisitions, the court found, were designed to preserve petitioner's business reputation, because without the added capital the Bank probably would have failed. The loss realized on the sale of this stock was thus held to be an ordinary loss. . . .

II

Section 1221 of the Internal Revenue Code defines "capital asset" broadly, as "property held by the taxpayer (whether or not connected with his trade or business)," and then excludes five specific classes of property from capital-asset status. . . . Arkansas Best acknowledges that the Bank stock falls within the literal definition of capital asset in § 1221, and is outside of the statutory exclusions. It asserts, however, that this determination does not end the inquiry. Petitioner argues that in *Corn Products Refining Co. v. Commissioner, supra,* this Court rejected a literal reading of § 1221, and concluded that assets acquired and sold for ordinary business purposes rather than for investment purposes should be given ordinary-asset treatment. Petitioner's reading of *Corn Products* finds much support in the academic literature and in the courts. Unfortunately for petitioner, this broad reading finds no support in the language of § 1221.

In essence, petitioner argues that "property held by the taxpayer (whether or not connected with his trade or business)" does not include property that is acquired and held for a business purpose. In petitioner's view an asset's status as "property" thus turns on the motivation behind its acquisition. This motive test, however, is not only nowhere mentioned in § 1221, but it is also in direct conflict with the parenthetical phrase "whether or not connected with his trade or business." The broad definition of the term "capital asset" explicitly makes irrelevant any consideration of the property's connection with the taxpayer's business, whereas petitioner's rule would make this factor dispositive.

In a related argument, petitioner contends that the five exceptions listed in § 1221 for certain kinds of property are illustrative, rather than exhaustive, and that courts are therefore free to fashion additional exceptions in order to further the general purposes of the capital-asset provisions. The language of the statute refutes petitioner's construction. Section 1221 provides that "capital asset" means "property held by the taxpayer[,] . . . but does not include" the five classes of property listed as exceptions. We believe this locution signifies that the listed exceptions are exclusive. The body of § 1221 established a general definition of the term "capital asset," and the phrase "does not include" takes out of that broad definition only the classes of property that are specifically mentioned. . . .

Petitioner's reading of the statute is also in tension with the exceptions listed in § 1221. These exclusions would be largely superfluous if assets acquired primarily or exclusively for business purposes were not capital assets. Inventory, real or depreciable property used in the taxpayer's trade or business, and accounts or notes receivable acquired in the ordinary course of business, would undoubtedly satisfy such a business-motive test. Yet these exceptions were created by Congress in separate enactments spanning 30 years. Without any express direction from Congress, we are unwilling to read § 1221 in a manner that makes surplusage of these statutory exclusions.

In the end, petitioner places all reliance on its reading of *Corn Products Refining Co. v. Commissioner,* 350 U.S. 46 (1955) — a reading we believe is too expansive. In *Corn Products*, the Court considered whether income arising from a taxpayer's dealings in corn futures was entitled to capital-gains treatment. The taxpayer was a company that converted corn into starches, sugars, and other products. After droughts in the 1930's caused sharp increases in corn prices, the company began a program of buying corn futures to assure itself an adequate supply of corn and protect against price increases. The company "would take delivery on such contracts as it found necessary to its manufacturing operations and sell the remainder in early summer if no shortage was imminent. If shortages appeared, however, it sold futures only as it bought spot corn for grinding." The Court characterized the company's dealing in corn futures as "hedging." As explained by the Court of Appeals in *Corn Products*, "[h]edging is a method of dealing in commodity futures whereby a person or business protects itself against price fluctuations at the time of delivery of the product which it sells or buys." In evaluating the company's claim that the sales of corn futures resulted in capital gains and losses, this Court stated:

> "Nor can we find support for petitioner's contention that hedging is not within the exclusions of [§ 1221]. Admittedly, petitioner's corn futures do not come within the literal language of the exclusions set out in that section. They were not stock in trade, actual inventory, property held for sale to customers or depreciable property used in a trade or business. But the capital-asset provision of [§ 1221] must not be so broadly applied as to defeat rather than further the purpose of Congress. Congress intended that profits and losses arising from the everyday operation of a business be considered as ordinary income or loss. . . . Since this section is an exception from the normal tax requirements of the Internal Revenue Code, the definition of a capital asset must be narrowly applied and its exclusions, interpreted broadly." 350 U.S., at 51–52 (citations omitted).

The Court went on to note that hedging transactions consistently had been considered to give rise to ordinary gains and losses, and then concluded that the corn futures were subject to ordinary-asset treatment.

The Court in *Corn Products* proffered the oft-quoted rule of construction that the definition of capital asset must be narrowly applied and its exclusions interpreted broadly, but it did not state explicitly whether the holding was based on a narrow reading of the phrase "property held by the taxpayer," or on a broad reading of the inventory exclusion of § 1221. In light of the stark language of § 1221, however, we believe that *Corn Products* is properly interpreted as involving an application of § 1221's inventory exception. Such a reading is consistent both with the Court's reasoning in that case and with § 1221. The Court stated in *Corn Products* that the company's futures transactions were "an integral part of its business designed to protect its manufacturing operations against a price increase in its principal raw material and to assure a ready supply for future manufacturing requirements." 350 U.S., at 50. The company bought, sold, and took delivery under the futures contracts as required by the company's manufacturing needs. As Professor Bittker notes, under these circumstances, the futures can "easily be viewed as surrogates for the raw material itself." 2 B. Bittker, *Federal Taxation of Income, Estates and Gifts* § 51.10.3, p. 51–62 (1981). The Court of Appeals for the Second Circuit in *Corn Products* clearly took this approach. That court stated that when commodity futures are "utilized solely for the purpose of stabilizing inventory cost[,] . . . [they] cannot reasonably be separated from the inventory items," and concluded that "property used in hedging transactions properly comes with the exclusions of [§ 1221]." 215 F.2d, at 516. This Court indicated its acceptance of the Second Circuit's reasoning when it began the central paragraph of its opinion, "Nor can we find support for petitioner's contention that hedging is not within the exclusions [§ 1221]." 350 U.S., at 51. . . . This discussion, read in light of the Second Circuit's holding and the plain language of § 1221, convinces us that although the corn futures were not "actual inventory," their use as an integral part of the taxpayer's inventory-purchase system led the Court to treat them as substitutes for the corn inventory such that they came within a broad reading of "property of a kind which would properly be included in the inventory of the taxpayer" in § 1221.

Petitioner argues that by focusing attention on whether the asset was acquired and sold as an integral part of the taxpayer's everyday business operations, the Court in *Corn Products* intended to create a general exemption from capital-asset status for assets acquired for business purposes. We believe petitioner misunderstands the relevance of the Court's inquiry. A business connection, although irrelevant to the initial determination of whether an item is a capital asset, is relevant in determining the applicability of certain of the statutory exceptions, including the inventory exception. The close connection between the futures transactions and the taxpayer's business in *Corn Products* was crucial to whether the corn futures could be considered surrogates for the stored inventory of raw corn. For if the futures dealings were not part of the company's inventory-purchase system, and instead amounted simply to speculation in corn futures, they could not be considered substitutes for the company's corn inventory, and would fall outside even a broad reading of the inventory exclusion. We conclude that *Corn Products* is properly interpreted as standing for the narrow proposition that hedging transactions that are an integral part of a business' inventory-purchase system fall within the inventory exclusion of § 1221. Arkansas Best, which is not a dealer in securities, has never suggested that the Bank stock falls within the inventory exclusion. *Corn Products* thus has no application to this case.

It is also important to note that the business-motive test advocated by petitioner is subject to the same kind of abuse that the Court condemned in *Corn Products*. The Court explained in *Corn Products* that unless hedging transactions were subject to ordinary gain and loss treatment, taxpayers engaged in such transactions could "transmute ordinary income into capital gain at will." The hedger could garner capital-asset treatment by selling the future and purchasing the commodity on the spot market, or ordinary-asset treatment by taking delivery under the future contract. In a similar vein, if capital stock purchased and held for a business purpose is an ordinary asset, whereas the same stock purchased and held with an investment motive is a capital asset, a taxpayer such as Arkansas Best could have significant influence over whether the asset would receive capital or ordinary treatment. Because stock is most ordinarily viewed as a capital asset, the Internal Revenue Service would be hard pressed to challenge a taxpayer's claim that stock was therefore a capital gain. If the same stock is sold at a loss, however, the taxpayer may be able to garner ordinary-loss treatment by emphasizing the business purpose behind the stock's acquisition. . . .

III

We conclude that a taxpayer's motivation in purchasing an asset is irrelevant to the question whether the asset is "property held by a taxpayer (whether or not connected with his business)" and is thus within § 1221's general definition of "capital asset." Because the capital stock held by petitioner falls within the broad definition of the term "capital asset" in § 1221 and is outside the classes of property excluded from capital-asset status, the loss arising from the sale of the stock is a capital loss. *Corn Products Refining Co. v. Commissioner, supra,* which we interpret as involving a broad reading of the inventory exclusion of § 1221, has no application in the present context. Accordingly, the judgment of the Court of Appeals is affirmed.

[B]—Bad debts

Worthless debts produce capital loss, if the debt is a capital asset, and if *§ 165(g)* treats worthlessness as a sale or exchange.

But *§ 165(g)* does not apply to debt without interest coupons or not in registered form, such as loans to a corporation on open account payable on demand. What is the tax treatment of worthless debts not covered by *§ 165(g)?* To answer that question, turn to *§ 166.* For corporations, the deduction is ordinary. *§ 166(a).* For individuals, there is a distinction between business and nonbusiness bad debts. *§ 166(d).* Business bad debts are ordinary losses; nonbusiness bad debts are short term capital losses. The following case discusses how to establish a "business" bad debt.

UNITED STATES v. GENERES

405 U.S. 93 (1972)

MR. JUSTICE BLACKMUN delivered the opinion of the Court. . .

[Editor — The taxpayer and Kelly, his son-in-law, each owned 44% of the corporation's stock. Other members of the family owned the rest. Taxpayer was president of the corporation and earned $12,000 per year. Kelly was executive vice president and earned $15,000 per year. The taxpayer worked six to eight hours per week in this job and also had another job as president of a bank, earning $19,000 per year. His total gross income averaged about $40,000 per year. His original investment in the stock of the corporation was $38,900 and he also loaned the corporation almost $160,000.

The corporation was engaged in the construction business. To obtain performance bonds, the taxpayer agreed to indemnify the company issuing these bonds. When the corporation was unable to complete two projects, the taxpayer had to pay about $162,000 to discharge his indemnity agreement. Because he was unable to recover this amount from the corporation, he deducted it as a business bad debt loss under *§ 166*.]

The fact responsible for the litigation is the taxpayer's dual status relative to the corporation. Generes was both a shareholder and an employee. These interests are not the same, and their differences occasion different tax consequences. In tax jargon, Generes' status as a shareholder was a nonbusiness interest. It was capital in nature and it was composed initially of tax-paid dollars. Its rewards were expectative and would flow, not from personal effort, but from investment earnings and appreciation. On the other hand, Generes' status as an employee was a business interest. Its nature centered in personal effort and labor, and salary for that endeavor would be received. The salary would consist of pre-tax dollars.

Thus, for tax purposes it becomes important and, indeed, necessary to determine the character of the debt that went bad and became uncollectible. Did the debt center on the taxpayer's business interest in the corporation or on his nonbusiness interest? If it was the former, the taxpayer deserves to prevail here. . . .

We conclude that in determining whether a bad debt has a "proximate" relation to the taxpayer's trade or business, as the Regulations specify, and thus qualifies as a business bad debt, the proper measure is that of dominant motivation, and that only significant motivation is not sufficient. We reach this conclusion for a number of reasons: . . .

B. Application of the significant-motivation standard would [undermine the conclusion] that a shareholder's mere activity in a corporation's affairs is not a trade or business. . . . [B]oth motives — that of protecting the investment and that of protecting the salary — are inevitably involved, and an inquiry whether employee status provides a significant motivation will always produce an affirmative answer and result in a judgment for the taxpayer.

C. The dominant-motivation standard has the attribute of workability. It provides a guideline of certainty for the trier of fact. The trier then may compare the risk against the potential reward and give proper emphasis to the objective rather than to the subjective. As has just been noted, an employee-shareholder, in making or guaranteeing a loan to his corporation, usually acts with two motivations, the one to protect his investment and the other to protect his employment. By making the dominant motivation the measure, the logical tax consequence ensues and prevents the mere presence of a business motive, however small and however insignificant, from controlling the tax result at the taxpayer's convenience. This is of particular importance in a tax system that is so largely dependent on voluntary compliance. . . .

G. The Regulations' use of the word "proximate" perhaps is not the most fortunate, for it naturally tempts one to think in tort terms. The temptation, however, is best rejected, and we reject it here. In tort law factors of duty, of foreseeability, of secondary cause, and of plural liability are under consideration, and the concept of proximate cause has been developed as an appropriate application and measure of these factors. It has little place in tax law where plural aspects are not usual, where an item either is or is not a deduction, or either is or is not a business bad debt, and where certainty is desirable. . . .

[Editor — The Court went on to conclude that the indemnity agreement could not reasonably be ascribed to a dominant business motivation to preserve the taxpayer's salary.]

[C]—Transactional approach

In an earlier chapter, we considered whether the events in one tax year should affect how later events are taxed — that is, break down the accounting year barrier. Here is another example, prompted by a repayment of money originally taxed as capital gains. How does *Arrowsmith* differ from a case in which a taxpayer receives income in a low tax bracket year and deducts a repayment in a later high tax bracket year?

ARROWSMITH v. COMMISSIONER

344 U.S. 6 (1952)

MR. JUSTICE BLACK delivered the opinion of the Court.

This is an income tax controversy growing out of the following facts as shown by findings of the Tax Court. In 1937 two taxpayers, petitioners here, decided to liquidate and divide the proceeds of a corporation in which they had equal stock ownership. Partial distributions made in 1937, 1938, and 1939 were followed by a final one in 1940. Petitioners reported the profits obtained from this transaction, classifying them as capital gains. They thereby paid less income tax than would have been required had the income been attributed to ordinary business transactions for profit. About the propriety of these 1937-1940 returns, there is no dispute. But in 1944 a judgment was rendered against the old corporation and against Frederick R. Bauer, individually. The two taxpayers were required to and did pay the judgment for the corporation, of whose assets they were transferees. Classifying the loss as an ordinary business one, each took a tax deduction for 100% of the amount paid. Treatment of the loss as a capital one would have allowed deduction of a much smaller amount. The Commissioner viewed the 1944 payment as part of the original liquidation transaction requiring classification as a capital loss, just as the taxpayers had treated the original dividends as capital gains. Disagreeing with the Commissioner the Tax Court classified the 1944 payment as an ordinary business loss. Disagreeing with the Tax Court the Court of Appeals reversed, treating the loss as "capital." . . .

[I.R.C. § 1222] treats losses from sales or exchanges of capital assets as "capital losses" and I.R.C. [§ 331] requires that liquidation distributions be treated as exchanges. The losses here fall squarely within the definition of "capital losses" contained in these sections. Taxpayers were required to pay the judgment because of liability imposed on them as transferees of liquidation distribution assets. And it is plain that their liability as transferees was not based on any ordinary business transaction of theirs apart from the liquidation proceedings. It is not even denied that had this judgment been paid after liquidation, but during the year 1940, the losses would have been properly treated as capital ones. For payment during 1940 would simply have reduced the amount of capital gains taxpayers received during that year.

It is contended, however, that this payment which would have been a capital transaction in 1940 was transformed into an ordinary business transaction in 1944 because of the well-established principle that each taxable year is a separate unit for tax accounting purposes. But this principle is not breached by considering all the 1937-1944 liquidation transaction events in order properly to classify the nature of the 1944 loss for tax purposes. Such an examination is not an attempt to reopen and readjust the 1937 to 1940 tax returns, an action that would be inconsistent with the annual tax accounting principle. . . .

Mr. Justice Jackson, whom Mr. Justice Frankfurter joins, dissenting. . . .

This Court simplifies the choice to one of reading the English language, and declares that the losses here come "squarely within" the definition of capital losses contained within two sections of the Internal Revenue Code. What seems so clear to this Court was not seen at all by the Tax Court, in this case or in earlier consideration of the same issue; nor was it grasped by the Court of Appeals for the Third Circuit.

I find little aid in the choice of alternatives from arguments based on equities. One enables the taxpayer to deduct the amount of the judgment against his ordinary income which might be taxed as high as 87%, while if the liability had been assessed against the corporation prior to liquidation it would have reduced his capital gain which was taxable at only 25% (now 26%). The consequence may readily be characterized as a windfall (regarding a windfall as anything that is left to a taxpayer after the collector has finished with him).

On the other hand, adoption of the contrary alternative may penalize the taxpayer because of two factors: (1) since capital losses are deductible only against capital gains, plus $1,000, a taxpayer having no net capital gains in the ensuing five years would have no opportunity to deduct anything beyond $5,000; and (2) had the liability been discharged by the corporation, a portion of it would probably in effect have been paid by the Government, since the corporation could have taken it as a deduction, while here the total liability comes out of the pockets of the stockholders.

Solicitude for the revenues is a plausible but treacherous basis upon which to decide a particular tax case. A victory may have implications which in future cases will cost the Treasury more than a defeat. This might be such a case, for anything I know. Suppose that subsequent to liquidation it is found that a corporation has undisclosed claims instead of liabilities and that under applicable state law they may be prosecuted for the benefit of the stockholders. The logic of the Court's decision here, if adhered to, would result in a lesser return to the Government than if the recoveries were considered ordinary income. Would it be so clear that this is a capital loss if the shoe were on the other foot?

Where the statute is so indecisive and the importance of a particular holding lies in its rational and harmonious relation to the general scheme of the tax law, I think great deference is due the twice-expressed judgment of the Tax Court. In spite of the gelding of *Dobson v. Commissioner*, 320 U.S. 489, by the recent [1948] revision of the Judicial Code [Editor — now found in *§ 7482(a)*], I still think the Tax Court is a more competent and steady influence toward a systematic body of tax law than our sporadic omnipotence in a field beset with invisible boomerangs. I should reverse, in reliance upon the Tax Court's judgment more, perhaps, than my own.

QUESTIONS

1. Does *Arrowsmith* make sense? If the capital loss deduction limitation is intended to prevent taxpayers from choosing when losses are recognized, does that concern apply in an *Arrowsmith* situation?

2. Would the *Arrowsmith* principle apply if capital gains were not eligible for a preferential tax rate?

3. When is a repayment so closely linked to a prior receipt that *Arrowsmith* applies? Section 16(b) of the Securities Act of 1934 specifies that certain corporate shareholders must turn over profits from dealing in the corporation's stock to the corporation, if a purchase and sale of the stock occur within six months of each other. The corporate President buys stock for $80,000 and sells it one year later for $140,000 to another individual. He then buys it back two months after that, for $120,000 ($20,000 less than the sales price). He argues that the Securities Act does not apply but, to avoid bad publicity, he pays the $20,000 to the company. Should the $20,000 be a capital loss, an ordinary loss, or (perhaps) added to the basis of the stock bought for $120,000? *Brown v. Commissioner*, 529 F.2d 609 (10th Cir. 1976); *Cummings v. Commissioner*, 506 F.2d 449 (2d Cir. 1974). To decide this question, should the court consider the public policy implications of allowing an ordinary loss?

4. Oil producers can sometimes deduct a percentage of their gross income in computing taxable income (the percentage depletion allowance), even though it exceeds regular depreciation deductions. Assume the deduction is 20% of oil gross income, in effect taxing only 80 cents per dollar received. If the taxpayer has to pay back $1 of prior oil income, can it deduct $1 or only 80 cents? Does *Arrowsmith* apply to reduce the deduction to 80 cents? *United States v. Skelly Oil Co.*, 394 U.S. 678 (1969).

§ 19.05 CASE LAW LIMITS ON CAPITAL GAINS

The statutory language defining a "capital asset" is very expansive — all "property" is a capital asset, subject to exceptions. *§ 1221 (introductory language)*. Courts have not been bashful, however, about interpreting the definition narrowly to make sure that capital gains preferences are not applied beyond their rationale. That does not mean the courts always get it right, as the prior discussion of the history of the *Corn Products* doctrine suggests. This section evaluates some other judicial attempts at defining capital assets.

[A]—Original issue discount

Original issue discount was discussed earlier in the course. The statute now explicitly requires lenders to accrue interest attributable to most original issue discount. Before that statute was passed, however, the Supreme Court held (in *Midland-Ross*) that gain attributable to this discount was ordinary income. Because the principles developed in this case have broader application, beyond the confines of original issue discount, we read excerpts from the case. Also, be sure you understand why the decision did not eliminate the need for an explicit statutory rule dealing with original issue discount.

—

UNITED STATES v. MIDLAND-ROSS CORP.

381 U.S. 54 (1965)

MR. JUSTICE BRENNAN delivered the opinion of the Court. . . .

The more favorable capital gains treatment applie[s] only to gain on "the sale or exchange of a capital asset." Although original issue discount becomes property when the obligation falls due or is liquidated prior to maturity and [the statute] defined a capital asset as "property held by the taxpayer," we have held that

> "not everything which can be called property in the ordinary sense and which is outside the statutory exclusions qualifies as a capital asset. This Court has long held that the term 'capital asset' is to be construed narrowly in accordance with the purpose of Congress to afford capital-gains treatment only in situations typically involving the realization of appreciation in value accrued over a substantial period of time, and thus to ameliorate the hardship of taxation of the entire gain in one year."

. . . .

Earned original issue discount serves the same function as stated interest, concededly ordinary income and not a capital asset; it is simply "compensation for the use or forbearance of money." Unlike the typical case of capital appreciation, the earning of discount to maturity is predictable and measurable, and is "essentially a substitute for . . . payments which [the statute] expressly characterizes as gross income [; thus] it must be regarded as ordinary income, and it is immaterial that for some purposes the contract creating the right to such payments may be treated as 'property' or 'capital.' " The $6 earned on a one-year note for $106 issued for $100 is precisely like the $6 earned on a one-year loan of $100 at 6% stated interest. The application of general principles would indicate, therefore, that earned original issue discount, like stated interest, should be taxed under [what is now *§ 61*] as ordinary income.[4]

The concept of discount or premium as altering the effective rate of interest is not to be rejected as an "esoteric concept derived from subtle and theoretic analysis." For, despite some expressions indicating a contrary view, this Court has often recognized the economic function of discount as interest. . . . For example, accrued bond interest on stated interest bonds sold between interest dates has long been taxable to the seller of the bonds. *See* I.T. 3175, 1938-1 Cum. Bull. 200. But on "flat" sales of defaulted notes at prices in excess of face amount, with no attribution of interest arrearages in the sale price, the requirement of allocation to treat a portion of the proceeds as ordinary income dates only from 1954. *Fisher v. Commissioner*, 209 F.2d 513 (C.A.6th Cir.); *see Jaglom v. Commissioner*, 303 F.2d 847, (C.A.2d Cir.). The propriety of such allocation in the present case is even more evident; unlike defaulted bond interest, there is no suggestion that full payment of the original issue discount will not be made at maturity.

Some of the reasoning in the case is questionable even though the result is sound. When a taxpayer disposes of a claim which has accrued original issue discount, there is potential hardship from taxing the entire gain in one year. Remember that this case was decided before original issue discount was accrued to the lender each year, so all of the interest-like income was taxed in one year, at the time of disposition. The real reason

[4] . . . Since no argument is made that the gain on the sale of each note varied significantly from the portion of the original issue discount earned during the holding period, we do not reach the question of the tax treatment under the 1939 Code of "market discount" arising from post-issue purchases at prices varying from issue price plus a ratable portion of the original issue discount, or of the tax treatment of gains properly attributable to fluctuations in the interest rate and market price of obligations as distinguished from the anticipated increase resulting from mere passage of time.

for denying capital gain is that the income is "predictable and measurable," attributable to the "mere passage of time" (*see* footnote 4). It is too much like interest. That is not what the capital gains tax preference rewards. The capital gains preference rewards investors who take risks regarding future income, such as whether a company will earn profits in the future. When profit prospects increase, the investor has gain, which is capital gain.

Market discount. Market discount arises when interest fluctuates after a loan is made. For example, a $100 loan earning 10% interest is worth $100, if market interest rates are 10%. If market interest rates rise to 12%, the investor can only sell the claim for less than $100 (say, $80). (Who would invest $100 to earn a 10% rate of interest when interest rates are 12%?) The difference between the buyer's $80 investment and the $100 face amount of the claim is market discount.

The statute now taxes market discount as ordinary income when the claim is disposed of. The amount of market discount is the ratable portion of the total market discount ($20 in the example), based on the number of days the investor owned the claim (a straight line method). This is different from the compound interest method used to tax original issue discount. For example, assume that the bond in the example has 10 years to go before collection after its purchase for $80, and is sold for $95 five years later (one half of the ten year period). The sale produces $10 of ordinary income and $5 of capital gain. In lieu of this approach, the $80 investor can elect to use the compound interest computation method instead of straight line; and the investor can also elect to accrue the interest annually, rather than wait for disposition of the claim. *§§ 1276(a)(1),(b)(2), 1278(b).*

[B]—Already earned income

Capital gain does not include periodic income accrued to property, like rent or interest. *I.T. 3175,* 1938-1 Cum. Bull. 200. Otherwise, a taxpayer could just delay collection of rent or interest, and convert it to capital gain by selling the claim to the accrued income. That is true even if you sell the rented land or building along with the right to the accrued rent, or the bond with accrued interest. (In that case, you must allocate the sales price between the property, which is often a capital asset producing capital gain, and the right to the accrued income, the sale of which produces ordinary income.)

The underlying idea is that the capital gains preference should reduce the tax burden only when the taxpayer realizes the present value of future income by selling property. In effect, the taxpayer has collapsed into the year of the sale the future income which would otherwise have been taxed in later years. The government gets its money early, so it seems fair to lower the tax rate. Moreover, if the tax is not lowered, the taxpayer is reluctant to sell and accelerate tax on the income, rather than wait for future collection.

For example, assume a taxpayer has invested $80 in land on January 1. The land soon turns out to be much more valuable as rental property because rental values go way up. The land is therefore now worth $200. The taxpayer rents the property for $20 per year. Two years after the purchase, on December 20, almost an entire year's rent has accrued but is not yet collected. Assume the taxpayer sells the land (worth $200) and the accrued rent for $219.95. The capital gain is the difference between the value of the land ($200) and the original cost ($80), equal to $120. The sales price attributable to the accrued rental income produces $19.95 ordinary income.

There are borderline cases. For example, if past accrued interest income might not be collected, because the debtor has been defaulting on interest payments, should the original lender get capital gain even on the sales price attributable to the accrued interest? *Jaglom v. Commissioner,* 303 F.2d 847 (2d Cir. 1962) forced the lender to allocate some of the sales price to ordinary income (attributable to accrued interest). However, the purchaser of such a risky investment (not the original lender) who later sells the claim, including the right to accrued defaulted interest, gets capital gain on the entire gain. *Rev. Rul. 60-284,* 1960-2 Cum. Bull. 464.

[C]—Contract rights

Another case law qualification to the definition of a capital asset appears in the following case, dealing with sales of contract rights.

BISBEE-BALDWIN CORP. v. TOMLINSON

320 F.2d 929 (5th Cir. 1963)

WISDOM, CIRCUIT JUDGE: . . .

The facts are not in dispute.

Bisbee-Baldwin, the taxpayer, is in the mortgage banking business. Most of its loans are secured by mortgages on residential property in Jacksonville, Florida. After making a loan, the company invariably assigns the mortgage to an institutional investor. The essential profit-making element is the investor's agreement to employ the mortgage company as its agent to service the mortgages. The company receives no profit on the assignment of a mortgage but earns an annual commission of one-half of one per cent of the principal outstanding balance of the mortgages serviced. The servicing activities generate other business. For example, the company often writes fire insurance on the property mortgaged, acts as real estate broker when the property is sold, and serves as property manager when a mortgage

TP: mortgage lender

is foreclosed. Escrow deposits by the mortgagors enhance its credit standing, a substantial benefit since the company must borrow large sums from the banks in the operation of its affairs. Thus the success of the mortgage servicing business depends upon the amount of mortgage indebtedness it services.

The taxpayer had no right to assign the servicing agreement and could not demand any payment from a successor servicing agent if the investor transferred its business to another company. The taxpayer was not the exclusive agent for any investor, even in the Jacksonville area serviced by it. Each investor had the right to enter into similar agreements with other servicing agents, and the taxpayer had the right to assign and service mortgages for other investors.

During the fiscal year ending April 30, 1957, various investors cancelled servicing agreements with the taxpayer, and gave the business to other agents. When an investor cancels such an agreement without cause, it is customary for the investor to pay a termination fee equal to one per cent of the principal balance of the mortgages then being serviced by the mortgage company. In this case, several of the taxpayer's agreements with investors expressly provided for such a termination fee. The taxpayer received net termination fees of $206,454.63. The investors paid this sum to Bisbee-Baldwin, but were reimbursed by the new servicing agents for the amount of the termination fees paid to the taxpayer. In substance, therefore, the mortgage servicing was transferred from Bisbee-Baldwin to other agents for, as the district court found, the cancellations would not have taken place had the successor mortgage servicing agents not agreed to reimburse the investors in the amount of the termination fees. . . .

The question is, what do the mortgage servicing rights under the contracts represent. If they represent the right to earn future income in the form of commissions for services rendered, then the sum received for the cancellation of the contracts and the transfer of rights is ordinary income. . . .

The line between contractual rights representing capital assets and those representing the right to receive future income is far from clear. Judge Friendly, for the Second Circuit, after an extremely able, thorough survey of all the relevant cases, reached the following conclusion:

> One common characteristic of the group held to come within the capital gain provision is that the taxpayer had either what might be called an "estate" in (*Golonsky*, *McCue*, *Metropolitan*), or an "encumbrance" in (*Ray*), or an option to acquire an interest in (*Dorman*), property which, if itself held, would be a capital asset. In all these cases the taxpayer had something more than an opportunity, afforded by contract, to obtain periodic receipts of income, by dealing with another (*Starr*, *Leh*, *General*

> *Artists*, *Pittston*), or by rendering services (*Holt*), or by virtue of ownership of a larger "estate" (*Hort*, *P. G. Lake*). *Commissioner v. Ferrer*, 2nd Cir.1962, 304 F.2d 125, 130–131.

In Judge Friendly's analysis, . . . some components of the "bundle" of contractual rights held by a taxpayer are capital assets while others represent a substitute for future income. Thus in Ferrer the taxpayer's "lease" of a play and his power, incident to the lease, to prevent a disposition of motion picture, radio, and television rights until after a certain date were capital assets. However, that part of the taxpayer's compensation for his contractual rights representing his right to forty per cent of the proceeds from the motion picture was taxable as ordinary income. We agree with this analysis. . . .

[Editor — The taxpayer in *Ferrer* held these contractual rights in a literary property, which eventually became the movie, Moulin Rouge. Although his lease of the play entitled him to produce a play based on the literary property, he never produced a play based on these rights. Instead he released all of his rights back to the original author.]

Applying these principles to the factual situation before us, we find that the basic rights Bisbee-Baldwin sold were the annual servicing commissions on the principal balance outstanding on the mortgages. Indeed the termination fee of one per cent of the mortgages serviced by the taxpayer was equivalent to two years gross income in commissions and was, to our minds, a substitute for the income which would have been earned by Bisbee-Baldwin had the contracts not been transferred. . . .

Still, some parts of the "bundle" of contractual rights transferred by Bisbee-Baldwin were capital assets. The mortgage correspondent relationships have value in addition to the rights to servicing commissions. It acts as a "feeder" for related businesses, such as insurance and real estate, frequently engaged in by mortgage bankers. The monthly escrow deposits made by the mortgagors considerably enhance the servicing agent's credit standing. Moreover, . . . there is a sale of "good will." The mortgage portfolio of the mortgage banker tends to increase each year as both the mortgagors and the investors look to the mortgaging servicing agent for further funds and further outlets for investment. The taxpayer's extensive files and equipment are in the nature of capital assets. (Most of these were retained by the taxpayer.) These items are closely related to the everyday business operations of the taxpayer. They are not so integrally related, however, as to be insusceptible of separate valuation.

We summarize. Essentially, the contract was a management contract for the employment of personal services. The consideration received for the right to earn future servicing commissions must be regarded as a substitute for such future ordinary income. This important part of the bundle of rights sold or exchanged can be separated from the other parts and should be taxed for what it is — not for what it is not. . . .

[Editor — The court remanded to the District Court to allocate the purchase price between sale of capital and ordinary assets.]

Personal services contracts. In *Bisbee-Baldwin* itself, the taxpayer's relationship was at will; there was no binding contract to provide services. Perhaps that should matter, but it doesn't. *Bisbee-Baldwin* is one of a larger group of cases denying capital gain on proceeds from disposition of personal service contracts. *See, e.g., Foxe v. Commissioner,* 53 T.C. 21 (1969); *Furrer v. Commissioner,* 566 F.2d 1115 (9th Cir. 1977); *Foote v. Commissioner,* 81 T.C. 930 (1983), *aff'd,* 751 F.2d 1257 (5th Cir. 1985). *But see Jones v. Corbyn,* 186 F.2d 450 (10th Cir. 1950) (capital gains on release of lifetime general insurance agency contract).

Sale of contract rights. *Bisbee-Baldwin* is also one of a larger group of cases which denies capital gains when the taxpayer disposes of any contract right, not just for personal services. The quote in *Bisbee-Baldwin* from the *Ferrer* case is a good summary: "An opportunity, afforded by contract, to obtain periodic receipts of income, by dealing with another," is not a capital asset. Typical cases denying capital gain involve sale of the right to purchase raw materials (*Commercial Solvents Corp. v. United States,* 427 F.2d 749 (Ct. Cl. 1970)) or to sell products to a particular customer (*Commissioner v. Starr Bros., Inc.,* 204 F.2d 673 (2d Cir. 1953)).

Why not capital gain? Why shouldn't the sale of a contract right produce capital gain? Is it because the right sold is a right to future income? But isn't the sale of stock also a sale of a right to future income? Is it because the taxpayer has no out-of-pocket investment in the contract?

Using the out-of-pocket investment theory might help to explain some of the statutory and case law rules dealing with eligibility for the capital gains preference, such as the following: (1) *§ 1221(3)* (copyright owned by copyright creator is not a capital asset); (2) *United States v. Garber,* 589 F.2d 843 (5th Cir. 1979) (sale of blood does not produce capital gain); (3) taxpayer's release of distributorship is a sale or exchange, if the taxpayer has a significant investment in the distributorship (*§ 1241*).

Why is good will a capital asset? *Bisbee-Baldwin* also states the general rule that good will is a capital asset. Why should that be true, at least if the taxpayer has no independent investment in the good will and the expenditures to create good will have been deducted? To be sure, it is a property interest under state law, not a contract right. But why should state law characterization as "property" be dispositive for tax law?

QUESTIONS

1. Taxpayer is a theater producer who owns the right to produce a play based on a book and to a percentage of future movie profits if a movie is ever made based on the book. The producer does in fact invest in the play, which is produced. He later sells his claim to movie profits. Does that sale produce capital gain? *Martin v. Commissioner,* 50 T.C. 341 (1968).

2. Taxpayer was a professor who sued for denial of tenure. Are the damages capital gains? *Foote v. Commissioner,* 81 T.C. 930 (1983).

§ 19.06 SOME STATUTORY ISSUES

[A]—Holding period

It seems easy enough to determine the holding period for determining eligibility for preferential rates on capital gains — just compare the purchase and sale dates. But what if the taxpayer has given the property to a relative or has disposed of the property in a nonrecognition transaction (*e.g., § 1031*). In these situations, there is a "substituted" basis ("transferred" in the gift case and "exchanged" in the nonrecognition case). In the gift case, the donor's holding period is tacked on to the donee's holding period. In the nonrecognition case, the taxpayer's holding period of the property given up is tacked on to the holding period of the replacement property (*e.g.*, property received in a like-kind exchange).

If a taxpayer buys an option to acquire property, the option period is not (usually) tacked on to the holding period of the property purchased by exercising the option. The purchase price for the property is a significant new investment and receives its own holding period. *Weir v. Commissioner*, 10 T.C. 996 (1948), *aff'd*, 173 F.2d 222 (3d Cir. 1949). The 1997 Tax Act provides an exception to this rule. It allows taxpayers to include the option period for purposes of determining whether the five year holding period is satisfied, in order to obtain the 18% preferential rate applicable to certain capital gains recognized after the year 2000.

[B]—Realization on short sale

Suppose a taxpayer has held stock for four months — *e.g.*, since August 31, 1992 — and fears a decline in market value. He wants to freeze his gain, so he enters into the following arrangement on December 31, 1992.

He finds someone interested in buying the stock and receives the sales price of the stock from the prospective buyer, but does not actually deliver the stock now. He agrees to deliver the stock nine months from now, on September 30, 1993. This is referred to as a "short sale." If the price of the stock goes up, the taxpayer can deliver the old stock to the buyer. However, the seller has insulated himself from downward fluctuations in the market as of December 31, 1992.

Before the 1997 Tax Act, the Code addressed this problem by treating the holding period as coming to an end when the risk of decline terminated — after four months, on December 31, 1992. This produced short term capital gain when the property was eventually delivered on September 30, 1993. *§ 1233(b)* (applying, in general, to stock, securities, and commodities futures).

The 1997 Tax Act treats a short sale of stock and securities as a realizable taxable event, when the stock to be delivered is the same or substantially identical to the stock owned at the time of the sale, *and* the taxpayer has an unrealized gain in the stock he owns. Thus, in the prior example, taxpayer realizes short term capital gain on December 31, 1992. Under prior law, the short sale did not produce realized gain until the delivery of the stock to the buyer (on September 30, 1993). *§ 1259.*

[C]—"Sale or exchange"

Capital gains arise only if there is a sale or exchange. *§ 1222.* There can be gain or loss, however, even if there is no sale or exchange. For example, suppose the taxpayer has an $8,000 basis in a building which burns down and he collects $10,000 of insurance. Or suppose an investor buys a claim against a financially strapped debtor for $8,000, when the amount owed is $10,000; the debtor's fortunes improve and $10,000 is collected. *Hudson v. Commissioner,* 20 T.C. 734 (1953), *aff'd sub. nom, Ogilvie v. Commissioner,* 216 F.2d 748 (6th Cir. 1954). In each case, the collection of the $10,000 liquidates the taxpayer's investment (there is a disposition), but the money is not (technically) received in a sale or exchange. Unless a specific section of the Code treats the event as a sale or exchange (as many do), the gain is ordinary income.

The same question arises on the loss side. If a taxpayer with an $8,000 basis in good will abandons the business because it has no prospect of showing profit, the abandonment results in an ordinary loss deduction because there is no sale or exchange. *Rev. Rul. 57-503,* 1957-2 Cum. Bull. 139.

There are many Code sections treating collection and worthlessness of an investment as a sale or exchange, but they do not cover every situation. Gain on collection of most debt will be treated as a sale or exchange

(*§ 1271(a)(1),(b)(1)*). Collection of insurance proceeds, *§ 1231,* and liquidation of a corporation, *§ 331*, are usually treated as a sale or exchange. Losses from the worthlessness of securities held as a capital asset produce a capital loss. *§ 165(g).*

There are two arguments which might justify at least some of the statutory provisions treating dispositions as sales or exchanges. First, it is arguable that any liquidation of an investment deserves capital gains treatment. This argument stresses encouraging investment as the rationale for the preferential taxation of capital gains. As long as the taxpayer has taken risks making an investment, capital gains should be permitted when the investment is cashed in. This attitude emerges in some cases interpreting "sale or exchange" broadly to include some events which might fall outside the definition. Thus, in *Commissioner v. Ferrer,* 304 F.2d 125 (2d Cir. 1962), the taxpayer released back to the author of a play the rights to produce the play which the taxpayer had previously acquired. The court held that the release was a sale or exchange, refusing to become entangled in a definitional distinction between a sale to a third party and a release back to the author. *§ 1234A* reaches the same result under current law.

Second, it seems hard to distinguish a loss from abandoning worthless property from loss on a sale just prior to the abandonment. Unless the law treats these events the same, there is an artificial distinction between sellers, who get capital losses, and others, who would get ordinary losses.

CHAPTER 20

CARVED OUT INCOME INTERESTS

§ 20.01 THE PROBLEM

The problem addressed by this chapter arises whenever there is a "carve out" of an income (often referred to as a "term") interest from a remainder interest. Before you worry why this causes a problem, be sure you understand what is meant by a carved out income interest.

You are familiar with dividing property physically — 60% of the land to one person and 40% to another. Property can also be divided temporally. For example, assume that property is worth $100 because it will produce $20 per year forever before tax (*e.g.*, rent from land), when the before tax discount rate is 20%. This asset could be divided into two parts — a five-year income interest and a remainder interest, which vests in possession when the five years expire. Based on the income and interest rate assumptions just made, the present value of the five-year income interest is just about $60. (Discount $20 per year, using a 20% discount rate. The present value is just a few cents below $60 but we round up to $60.) The remainder interest is therefore worth $40 — it has to be worth $100 minus the value of the income interest. A carved out income interest is simply the temporal carving out of an income interest, leaving the remainder interest and income interests in different ownership.

To understand the tax avoidance potential from a carved out income interest, you must understand what happens *before* a carve out. Assume that the example above involves nondepreciable property, such as land or stock. It produces $20 income per year. *The benchmark for tax analysis is that $20 should be reported each year as taxable income.* When a carve out occurs, the $20 may not be reported annually. To see why, consider one type of carve out — the sale of a five-year income interest and retention of the remainder by the seller. The sale of the income interest is for $60, and the seller retains a remainder worth $40. First, we look at the buyer and then at the seller who retains the remainder interest. Assume also that the entire asset has a $100 basis, equal to its value.

The buyer. The buyer has bought a depreciable five-year asset for $60. How much income will the buyer report each year (using straight line depreciation)?

Buyer of Income Interest

Year	Gross Income	Depreciation	Net Income
1	20	12	8
2	20	12	8
3	20	12	8
4	20	12	8
5	20	12	8
	100	60	40

Something has gone wrong. There is only $8 taxable income per year and a $40 total for five years. Before the sale, there was $20 per year and $100 total for five years. Where is the missing $60 income over five years?

The seller. Now look at the seller, who sold a carved out income interest worth $60. Based on what we have learned so far, the gain on the sale of the income interest is taxed. But the income interest was worth 60% of the total asset and the basis of the entire asset was $100. The seller therefore has a $60 basis in the income interest. $60 sales proceeds minus $60 basis = $0. *No gain.*

But the remaining $60 of income has not disappeared. Look at the owner of the remainder interest, who is the seller. What is the value of the retained remainder at the time of sale — $40 ($100 minus the $60 sales price of the carved out income interest). What happens to that value over the next five years? Before you try to answer that question, answer this one — what is the property worth to the owner of the remainder interest *after* five years, assuming interest rates stay the same and the property's expected income continues to be $20 per year? Be sure you understand that the answer *must be* $100. Well, if you have property worth $40 today, which will be worth $100 in five years, you have $60 gain. There it is. The "missing" $60 gain accrues to the retained remainder interest.

Based on the assumptions in the example, how much income accrues to the remainder owner each year. As time passes, the value of the remainder increases annually by 20%, as follows (after rounding to the nearest half dollar)*

* These figures can also be derived by discounting back the $100 to be received in the future to earlier years. After one year has passed, the owner of the remainder interest has four years to wait until possession. The present value of the future $100 claim is therefore $100/(1+.20)^4$ which is $48 (allowing for rounding). That means an increase in value from $40 to $48, or $8 in the first year. Similar arithmetic produces the value and annual gain figures after two, three, four, and five years have passed. The annual gain is the same figure you would get by putting $40 in the bank and getting 20% interest per year, compounded annually.

Year	Value accruing to remainder
1	$ 8
2	9.5
3	11.5
4	14
5	17
	60.00

So there really *is* a total of $100 income over the five years earned by the owners of both income and remainder interests. No alchemy caused some income to disappear. What kind of income accrues to the remainder interest? Isn't it ordinary income, based on *Midland-Ross'* discussion of original issue discount. It seems to be income which is "predictable and measurable," arising due to the "mere passage of time." In what respects is this analogy to original issue discount not correct?

What chance is there that the remainder's $60 income will be reported? And, *when*, if ever, will the owner of the remainder interest report the $60 gain? Will he report it as ordinary income or capital gain? Do you see the dilemma? How can we assure taxation of the remainder's $60 income? In the rest of this Chapter we consider case law and statutory solutions to this problem in a variety of situations involving a carved out income interest. Note that a carve out can occur in many ways. Here are the most likely variations.

(1) *Sell term/retain remainder.* A taxpayer could sell a term interest and keep the remainder, as in the prior example.

(2) *Gift of term/gift of remainder.* A term and remainder interest could both be given away, either inter vivos or through inheritance, to a spouse and child of a deceased. *See Irwin v. Gavit*, § 4.05[A], *supra.*

(3) *Buy term/buy remainder.* Two people could buy term and remainder interests from an owner.

(4) *Retain term/give or sell remainder.* A term interest could be retained, but the remainder interest given away or sold.

You will find that the *case law* has addressed some of these situations effectively, that *statutory* provisions have been adopted to deal with some situations, and that sometimes no satisfactory solution has been reached.

§ 20.02 THE SOLUTIONS

[A]—Sale of income interest — retained remainder

A lot of case law dealt with the *sale* of a carved out income interest, with retained remainder. Here is some of what the courts typically said. They were very bold in their willingness to use a theory about the underlying structure of the code to interpret the meaning of the capital gains provisions. But did they get the theory right?

In *Commissioner v. Gillette Motor Transport Co.*, 364 U.S. 130 (1960), the government seized taxpayer's property for one year (1945) because it was needed during WWII. There was, in other words, a forced sale of a carved out income interest. The Court denied capital gains, as follows:

> While a capital asset is defined [] as "property held by the taxpayer," it is evident that not everything which can be called property in the ordinary sense and which is outside the statutory exclusions qualifies as a capital asset. This Court has long held that the term "capital asset" is to be construed narrowly in accordance with the purpose of Congress to afford capital-gains treatment only in situations typically involving the realization of appreciation in value accrued over a substantial period of time, and thus to ameliorate the hardship of taxation of the entire gain in one year. *Burnet v. Harmel*, 287 U.S. 103, 106. . . .

In *Commissioner v. P. G. Lake, Inc.*, 356 U.S. 260 (1958), the taxpayer sold three years of income from oil property. The Court denied capital gains:

> The purpose of [the capital gains provision] was "to relieve the taxpayer from . . . excessive tax burdens on gains resulting from a conversion of capital investments, and to remove the deterrent effect of those burdens on such conversions." *See Burnet v. Harmel*, 287 U.S. 103, 106. And this exception has always been narrowly construed so as to protect the revenue against artful devices.
>
> We do not see here any conversion of a capital investment. The lump sum consideration seems essentially a substitute for what would otherwise be received at a future time as ordinary income. The pay-out of these particular assigned oil payment rights could be ascertained with considerable accuracy. Such are the stipulations, findings, or clear inferences. In the O'Connor case, the pay-out of the assigned oil payment right was so assured that the purchaser obtained a $9,990,350 purchase money loan at 3 1/2 percent interest without any security other than a deed of trust of the $10,000,000 oil payment right, he receiving 4 percent from the taxpayer. Only a fraction of the oil or sulphur rights were transferred, the balance being retained. . . . [C]ash was received which was equal to the amount of the income to accrue during the term of the assignment, the assignee being compensated by interest on his advance. The substance of what was assigned was the right to receive future income. The substance of what was received was the present value of income which the recipient would otherwise obtain in the future. In short, consideration was paid for the right to receive future income, not for an increase in the value of the income-producing property.

The language of *P.G.Lake* has given commentators fits because it states that sales proceeds are ordinary income if they are a substitute for future ordinary income. But capital gains *are* a substitute for future income. Capital gains is attributable to the present value of future income.

The *Gillette* case is also misleading. Selling one year's income can produce a bunching of gain into one year. If the taxpayer had bought the property in 1938 and in 1945 sold the right to year 1945 income, surely that right to one year's income would have gone up in value gradually as a result of wartime inflation and recovery from the Depression.

The actual holding of these cases, as opposed to the theory stated by the Court, may be quite sensible. They deny capital gains to the seller of the carved out income interest, but also do much more. They also deny the seller of the carved out income interest any use of the basis attributable to the term interest. *Shafer v. United States*, 204 F. Supp. 473 (D. Ohio 1962), *aff'd*, 312 F.2d 747 (6th Cir. 1963). Consequently, reverting to our earlier example of the sale of a five-year interest, the seller would have $60 ordinary income under the *Gillette* and *P.G.Lake* rules (Amount realized = $60; Basis = 0). That means that the seller of the carved out income interest has $60 ordinary income at the time of sale and the buyer has $8 annual income for five years.

In chart form, that produces the following result, assuming the sale occurs on January 1, year 1, and the annual income is earned in years 1–5.

Year	Buyer of Income Interest	Owner of Retained Remainder Interest	Total
1	8	$60	68
2	8	—	8
3	8	—	8
4	8	—	8
5	8	—	8
	40	60	100

Not a bad result. A total of $100 is reported, which is the correct total. However, it is a little unfair to the taxpayer. Now the income is reported *earlier* than if there had been no sale. $60 is accelerated as ordinary income to year 1. In effect, the case law taxes the $60 accruing to the retained remainder in year 1. Can you devise a solution to the potential for tax avoidance that is not unfair, either under case law or by amending the statute? (Notice that the seller who is taxed under *Gillette* and *P.G.Lake* is the same person who has income accruing to the remainder interest — the seller *is* the owner of the retained remainder.)

Missing basis? We have found the missing income, but now there is a missing basis problem. What happens to the basis that the seller of the carved out income interest could not use? Remember that the cases dealt with the sale of the income interest. The courts did not *have* to decide what happens to the basis. Presumably it does not disappear, but is given to the remainder interest. Thus, assuming the seller's basis in the income interest is $60, the remainder interest has a $100 basis after the sale of the carved out income interest.

QUESTIONS AND COMMENTS

1. Does the *Gillette* and *P. G. Lake* approach have a place in the law even if capital gains are not preferentially taxed? Sure. In the example, the property did not even have a gain. Its value was $100 and so was the basis. The problem is really about preventing tax avoidance on $60 of income.

2. **Sale as loan.** Suppose the "sale" for $60 in the prior example had been recast as a $60 loan. The so-called "seller" of the income interest would be treated as the continued owner of the *entire* property, who borrowed $60. During each of the five years after the "purchase," the so-called "buyer" would get $20, but not as a buyer. The $20 would be treated as a loan repayment. That means that the so-called "seller" reports the $20 income as owner of the property and deducts the interest portion of the $20 which the buyer receives. The buyer reports the interest portion of the $20 as income, but not the portion attributable to the loan repayment.

Look at the tax result of loan treatment during the five-year loan period in the following chart. That is a sensible result, isn't it, taxing the "buyer" and the "seller" annually on some of the $20 income?

Year	Seller-Borrower			Buyer-Lender
	Gross income	Interest Deduction	Taxable Income	Interest Income
1	20	12	8	12
2	20	10.50	9.50	10.50
3	20	8.50	11.50	8.50
4	20	6	14	6
5	20	3	17	3
			60	40

In fact, in the *P. G. Lake* situation itself, where the taxpayer sold a carved out income interest in oil, the statute now treats the sale as a loan. *§ 636.* In addition, there is case law treating sales of carved out income interests as loans when the "buyer" is virtually guaranteed payment of the "purchase price" plus interest. *Mapco Inc. v. United States*, 556 F.2d 1107 (Ct. Cl. 1977) (amount paid to "buyer" equals sales price plus interest and the "seller" agrees to make best efforts to maintain oil revenue from which payments will be made). In other cases involving sale of a carved out income interest, the *P.G.Lake* and *Gillette* case law still applies, taxing the sales proceeds as ordinary income. *Stranahan's Estate v. Commissioner*, 472 F.2d 867 (6th Cir. 1973).

[B]—Income and Remainder Interests Acquired By Gift

Armed with this understanding of the underlying problem and a critique of the case law applicable to the sale/retention case, examine the rules applicable to other carve out situations and critique the results.

Assume that someone dies leaving land to two individuals — L inherits a life estate and R inherits the remainder interest. The total value and basis of both L and R at death is $100. Under current law the basis is allocated between L and R in accordance with life expectancy and an assumed interest rate. *Treas. Reg. § 1.1014-5(a)*; *§ 20.2031-7(f)(Table B)*. The Regulations specify that the basis is adjusted as L gets older — L's basis goes down and R's goes up.

Assuming that the life estate is 60% of the total value at the time of death, the basis would be allocated $60 to L and $40 to R. As L gets older, L's basis decreases below $60 and R's basis increases over $40. The basis adjustment reflects value changes occurring with the passage of time. When L dies, R's basis will be $100.

Now, consider how L and R would be taxed (just as we did in the sale/retention case), if there were no special statutory rules. L owns a depreciating asset. The underlying land is not depreciable, but the life estate is. Assuming a five-year life expectancy (parallelling the prior sale/retention example), L reports only $8 per year taxable income. The same problem of disappearing income encountered in the sale/retention case recurs.

The statute has a specific solution to this problem. L loses the depreciation deduction. *§ 273*. People who receive term interests by gift or inheritance cannot depreciate their basis. (This was the case law rule adopted by *Irwin v. Gavit*, § 4.04[A], *supra*.) Consequently, assuming $20 income per year, the full $20 is taxed each year to L. There is no "missing" income. There is no need to tax the owner of the remainder interest on the annual increase in the value of his interest. Because L and R are probably in the same family, it is not offensive to tax L on the entire $20, even the portion accruing to R.

Sale of income interest. What happens if L sells the income interest which he has inherited for $60 the day after the inheritance. Without any special statutory provision, the seller has a $60 basis which reduces the gain to $0. In *McAllister v. Commissioner*, 157 F.2d 235 (2d Cir. 1946), the court held that L *could* use the $60 basis to compute gain. (If there had been gain, it was capital gain.)

Now the problem of missing income recurs as a result of the sale. The buyer from L for $60 has a depreciable asset, reporting only $8 income per year. R, the remainder owner, has an asset worth $40 at the time of death which gradually increases in value to $100, but that gain is unlikely to be taxed.

Here is how the statute responds. *§ 1001(e)* denies L (the seller) the right to use the $60 basis at the time of sale, just as L could not take depreciation deductions. The seller therefore reports $60 *capital gain* at the time of sale. As in the *Gillette* and *P. G. Lake* cases, $60 is taxed at the time of sale, and $8 is taxed annually thereafter. However, the $60 is capital gain. That makes good sense, however, lowering the tax in exchange for accelerating income.

Why give L and R a basis? You may be wondering why the Regulations go through the bother of assigning a basis to L and R, and then taking away L's basis. Look at *§ 1001(e)(3)* and consider this example. L and R get together and sell both their interests — L to B1 and R to B2. L and R can now use their basis to compute gain. The statute says so. But now the "problem" recurs. B1 depreciates his $60 basis and B2 is unlikely to report the gain accruing to the remainder interest for which he paid $40. The following paragraphs discuss whether the law responds to this tax avoidance potential.

[C]—Other carve out situations

We earlier noted that carve outs are not limited to sale/retention or gift/gift situations. For example, (1) the term and remainder could be bought by two people (B1 and B2, as above); or (2) an owner might retain the term interest and give or sell the remainder. Does the case law or statute deal adequately with such cases?

§ 167(e). The carve out problem must have worried the Treasury and Congress, because in 1989, Congress passed *§ 167(e)*. It prohibits the owner of the carved out income interest from taking depreciation deductions, if the income and remainder owners are "related." "Related" is defined in the statute to include spouses, ancestors, and lineal descendants, and two corporations where one owns more than 50% of the other. The statute makes this new section inapplicable when *§ 273* already applies, because it is superfluous. The new *§ 167(e)* would apply, however, if L sold his interest to B1 and R sold his interest to B2, who was B1's child.

The new *§ 167(e)* would also apply to the following case. A corporation owns land. It gives away a remainder interest in the land to a 100% owned subsidiary corporation, retaining an income interest for a 40 year term. The transferor corporation tries to depreciate the income interest. There is one case prohibiting the depreciation deduction. *Lomas Sante Fe, Inc. v.*

Commissioner, 74 T.C. 662 (1980), *aff'd*, 693 F.2d 71 (9th Cir. 1982). However, the government no longer has to rely on case law. *§ 167(e)* prevents depreciation.

What happens to the basis which is not depreciated because of *§ 167(e)?* As in the gift/gift case, the remainder owner's basis usually increases gradually as the income interest wastes away. At the end of the term, the remainder's basis will equal the basis of the entire property when the property was split into income and remainder interests. The remainder's basis does not increase, however, if the income owner is a tax exempt organization. Do you see why?

QUESTIONS

The statute and case law you have read do not specifically address every carve out problem. Assume, as before, a 5-year income interest worth $60, and a remainder worth $40. (1) Suppose B1 and B2 buy the income and remainder interest from L and R respectively, who had originally inherited the property interests. B1 and B2 are *un*related. (2) Or suppose corporation X sells the remainder interest to Y for $40, an unrelated investor, and keeps a 5-year income interest, with a value and basis of $60.

1. Can the owner of the income interest in either case depreciate its cost?

2. If the owner of the income interest cannot take depreciation deductions, what happens to the unused basis; does the remainder owner get it?

3. If the remainder interest was bought for $40, and after five years the property is sold for $100 when the income interest expires, how is the remainder's gain taxed?

The following case deals with the gain on sale of the remainder interest — as in question 3 above. It taxes at least some of the gain as ordinary income. What is the strongest argument you can make against that result? *Hint* — what deductions could the income interest owner take?

JONES v. COMMISSIONER

330 F.2d 302 (3d Cir. 1964)

PER CURIAM.

Taxpayer, inter alia, purchases remainder interests in trusts. In the two interests before us in this review, as is his practice, after the deaths of the life tenants but prior to the distribution of the estate remainders of the trusts, he transferred his interests therein. His motivation is to obtain capital gains treatment for income tax purposes. The Tax Court held that the taxpayer could not transmute gain which would be ordinary income to him into capital gain by the device of a sale, notwithstanding that the sale was the bona fide sale of a capital asset. The Commissioner argues for the sustaining of the decision on the theory that the taxpayer's gain upon the sales of the remainders represents an increase in value attributable to interest income, in the form of an interest discount in his original purchase price for the remainders. We are impressed with this and in connection therewith consider it necessary to remand the case to the Tax Court for further proceedings to determine what part, if any, of the gain received upon the taxpayer's sale of the remainders was in fact the realization of interest discount and, if the latter is established, to make an allocation of the proceeds between its ordinary income and capital gain components.

The decision will be vacated and the case remanded to the Tax Court for further proceedings in line with this opinion.

[D]—*§ 1286*

In one situation, the Code specifically allocates annual income between the owners of a carved out income and remainder interest. This situation is referred to by the statute as a "stripped bond." The statute applies to most debt where there is a separation in ownership between the income and remainder interest. It applies whether the separation occurs by sale or gift.

The following example illustrates the operation of the section. A taxpayer pays $100 for a $100 bond, earning 10% interest ($10 per year). On December 31, 1993, the owner gives away the following year's income from the bond. The basis in the income and remainder interest is $9.09 and $90.91 respectively. When the donee of the income interest collects $10 in 1994, he has $.91 income (10 minus 9.09 basis). The remainder accrues income in 1994 equal to $9.09 (100 -90.91). The donor and donee have a total of $10 income, split between them.

Notice that *§ 1286* overrides the specific result in *Horst* (§ 4.05[B], *supra*), which involved a gift of a carved out income interest in a bond, with a retained remainder. The general principle of *Horst* is not overridden, however, because gifts of a carved out income interest in property other than a bond (land, for example) still cannot deflect any income to the donee.

§ 20.03 SELLING "LESS THAN ALL"

You have read a lot of cases in which the courts try to apply the theory underlying the capital gains rules without following the literal meaning of the statutory text. Here is one last case which you can use to review the basic principles. The Court, again, will deny capital gains treatment. Does the result make sense?

HORT v. COMMISSIONER

313 U.S. 28 (1941)

MR. JUSTICE MURPHY delivered the opinion of the Court.

We must determine whether the amount petitioner received as consideration for cancellation of a lease of realty in New York City was ordinary gross income as defined in [the predecessor of *§ 61*], and whether, in any event, petitioner sustained a loss through cancellation of the lease which is recognized [under the statute].

Petitioner acquired the property, a lot and ten-story office building, by devise from his father in 1928. At the time he became owner, the premises were leased to a firm which had sublet the main floor to the Irving Trust Co. In 1927, five years before the head lease expired, the Irving Trust Co. and petitioner's father executed a contract in which the latter agreed to lease the main floor and basement to the former for a term of fifteen years at an annual rental of $25,000, the term to commence at the expiration of the head lease.

In 1933, the Irving Trust Co. found it unprofitable to maintain a branch in petitioner's building. After some negotiations, petitioner and the Trust Co. agreed to cancel the lease in consideration of a payment to petitioner of $140,000. Petitioner did not include this amount in gross income in his income tax return for 1933. On the contrary, he reported a loss of $21,494.75 on the theory that the amount he received as consideration for the cancellation was $21,494.75 less than the difference between the present value of the unmatured rental payments and the fair rental value of the main floor and basement for the unexpired term of the lease. He did not deduct this figure, however, because he reported other losses in excess of gross income.

The Commissioner included the entire $140,000 in gross income, disallowed the asserted loss, made certain other adjustments not material here, and assessed a deficiency. . . .

Petitioner apparently contends that the amount received for cancellation of the lease was capital rather than ordinary income and that it was therefore subject to [the rules] which govern capital gains and losses. . . .

The amount received by petitioner for cancellation of the lease must be included in his gross income in its entirety. [The predecessor of *§ 61*] expressly defines gross income to include "gains, profits, and income derived from . . . rent, . . . or gains or profits and income from any source whatever." Plainly this definition reached the rent paid prior to cancellation just as it would have embraced subsequent payments if the lease had never been canceled. It would have included a prepayment of the discounted value of unmatured rental payments whether received at the inception of the lease or at any time thereafter. Similarly, it would have extended to the proceeds of a suit to recover damages had the Irving Trust Co. breached the lease instead of concluding a settlement. That the amount petitioner received resulted from negotiations ending in cancellation of the lease rather than from a suit to enforce it cannot alter the fact that basically the payment was merely a substitute for the rent reserved in the lease. . . .

. . . Simply because the lease was "property" the amount received for its cancellation was not a return of capital. . . . Where, as in this case, the disputed amount was essentially a substitute for rental payments which [the predecessor of *§ 61*] expressly characterizes as gross income, it must be regarded as ordinary income, and it is immaterial that for some purposes the contract creating the right to such payments may be treated as "property" or "capital." . . .

We conclude that petitioner must report as gross income the entire amount received for cancellation of the lease. . . .

COMMENTS AND QUESTIONS

Let us use *Hort* to review the issues discussed in this Chapter.

1. Is the taxpayer in *Hort* selling a carved out income interest? No. He sold the premium value of a lease.

2. Did the taxpayer in *Hort* have an investment in the lease itself? Suppose the taxpayer had purchased the land, buildings, and the favorable lease in 1932, and had then been bought out by the tenant, Irving Trust Co. How would the proceeds received from the tenant be taxed in that case?

3. Suppose an investor lends $10,000 at 15% interest and the market interest rate then drops to 10%. The value of the investor's claim thereby increases to $12,000. The investor who sells the claim has $2,000 capital gain. How does this investor differ from the petitioner in *Hort*?

4. A tenant who is bought out by a landlord when rents go up gets capital gain. *Commissioner v. McCue Bros.*, 210 F.2d 752 (2d Cir. 1954). However,

a landlord who is bought out by the tenant when rents go down has ordinary income — that is the *Hort* case. Why does the tenant get capital gain but Hort, the landlord, receive ordinary income?

5. Does it matter that Hort sold less than all he owned, even though it was not a carved out income interest?

CHAPTER 21

DEFERRED PAYMENTS

§ 21.01 TIMING OF GAIN

In prior chapters we focused on what the taxpayer sold. In this chapter we focus on what the taxpayer receives for the sale. We consider *when* gain is taxed, as well as whether it is capital gain or ordinary income. We start first with timing (*when* is gain taxed) and then discuss whether deferred gain is capital gain.

Assume that a taxpayer owns a capital asset with a $60,000 basis. The asset is now worth $100,000. He sells the asset in year 0 for $30,000 cash, payable in year 0 at the time of sale, and five annual installments of $14,000 cash, payable in years 1 to 5. Adequate interest is charged to compensate for deferral of the receipt of cash beyond year 0, the year of sale. In other words, the interest is sufficient to prevent application of the original issue discount rules. The promise to pay the $14,000 installments is in the form of five nonnegotiable notes. There is some market for these notes but it is not very well developed. A seller trying to sell all five notes would probably get a total of $35,000 cash, not their $70,000 face value. The taxpayer normally reports income on the cash method.

The following chart describes four ways in which the $40,000 gain on the sale ($100,000 minus $60,000) might be reported. The choice of methods carries with it certain implications about whether the income is ordinary or capital gain. First focus on why the timing of taxable income is different in each column of the chart and then worry about whether it is ordinary income or capital gain. The text following the chart explains each column.

Timing of $40,000 Gain

YEAR	(1) Installment Method	(2) Closed Transaction-Equivalent of cash	(3) Open Transaction	(4) Closed Transaction-Regulation
0	$12,000	$5,000	0	$40,000
1	5,600	7,000	0	0
2	5,600	7,000	0	0
3	5,600	7,000	12,000	0
4	5,600	7,000	14,000	0
5	5,600	7,000	14,000	0
TOTAL	40,000	40,000	40,000	40,000

[A]—Installment Method

Column 1 is the installment method, allowed by *§ 453.* When used by the taxpayer, it permits deferral of tax, by allowing the taxpayer to spread out his tax payments over the period in which the sales proceeds are collected. In general, this means that as cash is collected, tax will be paid. Tax on gain is therefore deferred beyond the year of sale.

When the installment method is permitted by the statute, that is the method the taxpayer must use, unless he explicitly elects out of the installment method. *§ 453(a),(b),(c),(d).* If the installment method is used, other methods of reporting gain are irrelevant. Columns 2, 3, and 4 are therefore possible choices only if the installment method is not used.

Mechanics. The mechanism for achieving tax deferral under the installment method is as follows. A percentage of each installment payment is taxable. The percentage is the gross profit on the entire transaction divided by the total contract price. *§ 453(c).* Thus, if a taxpayer with a basis of $60,000 sells property worth $100,000 for $30,000 cash and five $14,000 annual installments, 4/10ths of each installment is taxable, because the total gross profit is $40,000 (100,000 minus 60,000) and the total contract price is $100,000.

As a practical matter, the key provision is *§ 453(f)(3),(4),(5),* which excludes evidences of indebtedness from the definition of "payment," unless the debt (1) is payable on demand or (2) is a government or corporate debt and is readily tradable on an established securities market. This means that a taxpayer can usually receive notes but still defer tax.

What property eligible? The installment method is available for sales of most types of property, but there are some important exceptions. First, dealer dispositions of real and personal property are not usually eligible for the installment method. *§ 453(b)(2),(l)(1).*

Second, sale of publicly traded stock or securities (and other property regularly traded on an established market, as determined by Treasury

Regulations) is not eligible for the installment method. The rule was adopted by the Tax Reform Act of 1986 and is probably a reaction to corporate takeovers in which the sellers of publicly traded stock or securities used the installment method. *§ 453(k)(2).* It also prevents the gain on December 31 sales of publicly traded securities from being deferred to the following payment year.

Third, any gain on the sold asset which is recapture income cannot be postponed by using the installment method. *§ 453(i).* For example, if the taxpayer's original cost for tangible personal property was $75,000, but the basis is now $60,000, after $15,000 depreciation, an installment sale for $100,000 in year 0 (with all cash receipts deferred) would result in $15,000 ordinary income in year 0. Basis would then be $75,000 (60000 + 15000) and the additional $25,000 gain would be taxable under the installment method, unless the taxpayer elected otherwise.

There has been some litigation over whether the sale of a contract right, such as the mortgage servicing contracts in *Bisbee-Baldwin*, is eligible for the installment sales provisions. The contracts are not capital assets, but there is no reason why they should not be "property" within the meaning of *§ 453.* The purposes of the capital gains and installment method provisions are different. The lack of an investment or the absence of a lock-in effect might justify denial of a preferential tax rate, but what has that got to do with timing tax payments to coincide with cash payments received in installments? The word "property" can mean different things in *§§ 1221/1231* and *§ 453. Realty Loan Corp. v. Commissioner,* 54 T.C. 1083 (1970), *aff'd*, 478 F.2d 1049 (9th Cir. 1973), agrees with this analysis. *But see Billy Rose's Diamond Horseshoe, Inc. v. United States,* 322 F. Supp. 76 (S.D.N.Y. 1971), *aff'd*, 448 F.2d 549 (2d Cir. 1971).

Charge interest for tax deferral. The problem of tax deferral has attracted considerable attention and the statute has sometimes responded by charging the taxpayer interest on deferred taxes. Thus, rather than eliminating the opportunity to defer taxes, the government charges the taxpayer a price for lending the taxpayer the use of the deferred tax. This is a complication which cannot realistically be imposed on all taxpayers using the installment method. At present, here is what the statute does. *§ 453A.* It is very complex and an example follows the text's explanation.

First, the statute is only concerned with sales for more than $150,000. Second, even sales for more than $150,000 are disregarded, if they are farm or personal use property. Third, the statute is only concerned with taxable years in which unpaid obligations exceeding $5 million arise, and in which more than $5 million of such unpaid obligations are still due at the end of the year. Fourth, the statute then computes the amount of tax deferral on such unpaid obligations, assuming the top tax rate applies. Fifth, interest is not charged on all of the deferred tax — only on the "applicable percentage" of the deferred tax. That percentage is the amount of unpaid obligations over $5 million, divided by the unpaid obligations. Sixth, interest on this amount is charged at the rate applicable to underpayment of taxes.

For example, assume that a corporate taxpayer sells two properties in year 0, both with a $1 million basis and a value of $3 million. The sales proceeds will be collected with adequate interest in year 2. In year 0, over $5 million in face amount of deferred obligations arises and is unpaid, so interest is charged. The gain on such sales that is deferred is $4 million and the top corporate tax rate is 35%. The deferred tax liability is therefore $1,400,000 (.35 times $4 million). The "applicable percentage" is 1/6th ($6 million minus $5 million divided by $6 million), which produces a deferred tax of $233,333 (1/6th times $1,400,000). Interest must therefore be paid on $233,333 at the underpayment rate used for late tax payments.

Sale to related party. There is also a provision which prevents a seller from deferring tax by an installment sale to a relative (for example, parent to child), followed by a sale of the asset by the related installment buyer. If these two sales occur, the first seller (the parent) must report the amount realized by the second seller (the child), up to the first seller's sales price, at the time when the second sale occurs. This prevents the parent from getting cash into the child's hands without paying tax at the parent's tax rate. *§ 453(e).* This rule usually applies only if the related installment buyer sells within two years of acquiring the property.

Loans secured by installment claims. If an installment claim creditor pledges the claim as security for a loan, and the installment sales price exceeds $150,000, the net proceeds of the loan are taxable. *§ 453A(d).* Sometimes loans are taxable!

[B]—Closed transaction; Equivalent of cash

Column 2 is the "closed transaction" method. The transaction is "closed" because the market value of the installment contract is treated as the "equivalent of cash" received as sales proceeds in the year of sale. In the chart, the value of the installment contract is $35,000. Therefore, the amount realized in the sale year is $65,000 (that is, $30,000 cash plus $35,000 market value of the notes).

When should a contract be treated as having a market value which is the equivalent of cash? The following case provides one answer.

COWDEN v. COMMISSIONER

289 F.2d 20 (5th Cir. 1961)

JONES, CIRCUIT JUDGE:

We here review a decision of the Tax Court by which a determination was made of federal income tax liability of Frank Cowden, Sr., his wife and their children, for the years 1951 and 1952. In April 1951, Frank Cowden, Sr. and his wife made an oil, gas and mineral lease for themselves and their children upon described lands in Texas to Stanolind Oil and Gas Company. By related supplemental agreements, Stanolind agreed to make "bonus" or "advance royalty" payments in an aggregate amount of $511,192.50. On execution of the instruments $10,223.85 was payable, the sum of $250,484.31 was due "no earlier than" January 5 "nor later than" January 10, 1952, and $250,484.34 was stipulated to be paid "no earlier than" January 5 "nor later than" January 10, 1953. One-half of the amounts was to be paid to Frank Cowden, Sr. and his wife, and one-sixth was payable to each of their children. In the deferred payments agreements it was provided that:

> "This contract evidences the obligation of Stanolind Oil and Gas Company to make the deferred payments referred to in subparagraphs (b) and (c) of the preceding paragraph hereof, and it is understood and agreed that the obligation of Stanolind Oil and Gas Company to make such payments is a firm and absolute personal obligation of said Company, which is not in any manner conditioned upon development or production from the demised premises, nor upon the continued ownership of the leasehold interest in such premises by Stanolind Oil and Gas Company, but that such payments shall be made in all events."

. . .

The Tax Court stated, as a general proposition, "that executory contracts to make future payments in money do not have a fair market value." The particular facts by which the Tax Court distinguishes this case from the authorities by which the general proposition is established are, as stated in the opinion of the majority:

> ". . . that the bonus payors were perfectly willing and able at the time of execution of the leases and bonus agreements to pay such bonus in an immediate lump sum payment; to pay the bonus immediately in a lump sum at all times thereafter until the due dates under the agreements; that Cowden, Sr., believed the bonus agreements had a market value at the time of their execution; that a bank in which he was an officer and depositor was willing to and in fact did purchase such rights at a nominal discount; that the bank considered such rights to be bankable and to

represent direct obligations of the payor; that the bank generally dealt in such contracts where it was satisfied with the financial responsibility of the payor and looked solely to it for payment without recourse to the lessor and, in short, that the sole reason why the bonuses were not immediately paid in cash upon execution of the leases involved was the refusal of the lessor to receive such payments."

. . .

A promissory note, negotiable in form, is not necessarily the equivalent of cash. Such an instrument may have been issued by a maker of doubtful solvency or for other reasons such paper might be denied a ready acceptance in the market place. We think the converse of this principle ought to be applicable. We are convinced that if a promise to pay of a solvent obligor is unconditional and assignable, not subject to set-offs, and is of a kind that is frequently transferred to lenders or investors at a discount not substantially greater than the generally prevailing premium for the use of money, such promise is the equivalent of cash and taxable in like manner as cash would have been taxable had it been received by the taxpayer rather than the obligation. . . .

The Tax Court stressed in its findings that the provisions for deferring a part of the bonus were made solely at the request of and for the benefit of the taxpayers, and that the lessee was willing and able to make the bonus payments in cash upon execution of the agreements. It appears to us that the Tax Court, in reaching its decision that the taxpayers had received equivalent of cash bonuses in the year the leases were executed, gave as much and probably more weight to those findings than to the other facts found by it. We are persuaded of this not only by the language of its opinion but because, in its determination of the cash equivalent, it used the amounts which it determined the taxpayers could have received if they had made a different contract, rather than the fair market value cash equivalent of the obligation for which the taxpayers had bargained in the contracts which they had a lawful right to make. We are unable to say whether or not the Tax Court, if it disregarded, as we think it should have done, the facts as it found them as to the willingness of the lessee to pay and the unwillingness of the taxpayers to receive the full bonus on execution of the leases, would have determined that the equivalent bonus obligations were taxable in the year of the agreements as the equivalent of cash. This question is primarily a fact issue. There should be a remand to the Tax Court for a reconsideration of the question submitted in the light of what has been said here.

By closing the transaction in the year of sale, the taxpayer recognizes gain or loss on the sale. He must then recover his basis in the claim to future proceeds by reducing the amount of proceeds taxed in future years. The basis in the claim would be the value at which the claim was included in amount realized ($35,000 in the chart example). The chart assumes that this basis is amortized over the five-year collection period. Should there be any taxable gain before the amount collected on the notes exceeds the $35,000 amount realized in the year of sale? *See Phillips v. Frank*, 295 F.2d 629 (9th Cir. 1961).

[C]—Open Transaction

Column 3 is the "open transaction" method. Under this method, no gain is recognized until sales proceeds exceed basis. In effect, all of the basis is allocated to the early collection of the sales proceeds.

In one case, the Tax Court permitted the open transaction method when the value of an installment contract was discounted far below the face value of the contract (as would be true if a face amount $70,000 debt were valued at $35,000). The Court of Appeals reversed, treating the discounted value of the contract as the equivalent of cash in the year of sale, regardless of the discount. *Warren Jones Co. v. Commissioner,* 60 T.C. 663 (1973), *rev'd and remanded*, 524 F.2d 788 (9th Cir. 1975).

[D]—Regulation — Installment method not used

Column 4 is the government's effort to deal with taxpayers who do not elect the installment method. In effect, it closes the transaction, but in a different way from method 2 above. It conclusively presumes that the value of the obligations is at least equal to the value of the property sold minus any other consideration received. In the chart example that presumed value is $70,000 ($100,000 value of property minus $30,000 cash). The Regulation requires this valuation whether or not the obligations have that value under the traditional "equivalent of cash" doctrine. The government's position appears in the following *Treas. Reg. § 15a.453-1(d)(2)(i),(ii).* The subparagraph (iii) referred to in the Regulation deals with contingent payments, such as sales proceeds which are based on profits. We return to contingent payments in a later section.

> (2) *Treatment of an installment sale when a taxpayer elects not to report on the installment method* — (i) In General. A taxpayer who elects not to report an installment sale on the installment method must recognize gain on the sale in accordance with the taxpayer's method of accounting. The fair market value of an installment obligation shall be determined in accordance with paragraph (d)(2)(ii) and (iii) of this section. In making such determination, any provision of contract or local law restricting the

transferability of the installment obligation shall be disregarded. Receipt of an installment obligation shall be treated as a receipt of property, in an amount equal to the fair market value of the installment obligation, whether or not such obligation is the equivalent of cash. An installment obligation is considered to be property and is subject to valuation, as provided in paragraph (d)(2)(ii) and (iii) of this section, without regard to whether the obligation is embodied in a note, an executory contract, or any other instrument, or is an oral promise enforceable under local law.

(ii) *Fixed amount obligations.* (A) A fixed amount obligation means an installment obligation the amount payable under which is fixed. . . . A taxpayer using the cash receipts and disbursements method of accounting shall treat as an amount realized in the year of sale the fair market value of the installment obligation. . . . In no event will the fair market value of the installment obligation be considered to be less than the fair market value of the property sold (minus any other consideration received by the taxpayer on the sale). A taxpayer using the accrual method of accounting shall treat as an amount realized in the year of sale the total amount payable under the installment obligation. . . . Under no circumstances will an installment sale for a fixed amount obligation be considered an "open" transaction. . . .

The whole point of this Regulation is to preclude use of method 2 (closed transaction at discounted value) and method 3 (open transaction), if the installment method is not used by the taxpayer. The question is whether it is a valid regulation.

§ 21.02 ORDINARY INCOME OR CAPITAL GAIN

Assume that the asset sold in the prior discussion is a capital asset or a *§ 1231* asset, with no recapture income. How much of the gain is capital gain and how much is ordinary income under each of the methods of reporting gain set forth in the chart? The answer is quite mechanical, following from the assumptions underlying the method used to report gain. Recall the four methods:

Method 1 - Installment method
Method 2 - Closed Transaction — Equivalent of Cash
Method 3 - Open Transaction
Method 4 - Closed Transaction — Regulation

Method 1. Under the installment method, the gain is capital gain. Under general statutory principles, sales proceeds are capital gain, unless the gain is recapture income. The logic of the installment method is that taxation of sales proceeds is deferred until cash is received, but they are still sales proceeds. Thus, the gain in years 0 through 5 is capital gain under method 1.

Method 3. The open transaction method also treats the cash received as sales proceeds, although basis is allocated differently. The taxable gain is capital gain, but it is deferred until years 3 through 5 in this example. The taxpayer likes this — deferral plus capital gain.

Methods 2 and 4. Under the closed transaction method, the value of the obligations is treated as sales proceeds in the year of sale. Later collections of these obligations are not technically sales proceeds, but there is a statutory provision converting most collections of debt into sales proceeds (*see § 1271(a);* all corporate debt and individual debt issued after June 8, 1997). Thus, there is capital gain (or perhaps loss) in year 0 (the year of sale) in methods 2 and 4. Any gain on collection in later years (years 1 through 5 in the Chart) is likely to be capital gain.

Argument against method 3 (open transaction). Is there anything anomalous about permitting both deferral and capital gain? If one of the major purposes of the capital gains preference is relief from bunching the future risky flow of income which is realized early (when an asset is sold), does it make sense to provide that relief if the sales proceeds are not bunched up in the year of sale (that is, if they are deferred)? What if the payments stretch out over five or ten years? This question is not academic. It has relevance in deciding whether the open transaction method (method 3), which provides the maximum deferral combined with capital gains, should be permitted. If combining deferral and capital gains is anomalous, perhaps the open transaction method should be prohibited. This supports the government position prohibiting the open transaction method in fixed payment obligation situations.

Argument against method 2 (closed transaction — equivalent of cash). Should the taxpayer be allowed to use the method 2 version of the closed transaction, if the taxpayer elects not to use the installment method? Under method 2, the taxpayer reports the fair market value of the claim as the amount realized in the year of sale. And retirement of the debt is probably treated as an exchange of the debt by *§ 1271(a,b)* and therefore as capital gain (assuming the debt was a capital asset). Like Method 3, this combines deferral and capital gain, which seems anomalous. It also requires valuation of the installment claim in year 0, which arguably imposes an unreasonable burden on the tax administration.

§ 21.03 DISTINGUISHING SALES PROCEEDS FROM INTEREST

If a taxpayer defers receipt of sales proceeds and charges inadequate interest, some portion of the sales proceeds should be recharacterized as interest. This is another version of the original issue discount problem, except that the taxpayer (seller) is transferring property, not lending money to the borrower (buyer). The statute should be concerned with two issues: separating out the interest element from the sales proceeds; and whether the interest ought to be accrued annually or taxed only when the sales proceeds are collected.

For example, if a taxpayer sells an asset in year 0 for $600,000 without interest, due in year 5, the taxpayer has in effect loaned the asset's present value to the buyer. Some portion of the $600,000 ought to be interest, and some sales proceeds.

§ 1274. The analytically pure answer in these cases is to treat the asset's fair market value as sales proceeds, which are loaned back to the buyer, and which then accrues original issue discount annually. *§ 1274.* That is, in fact, the rule in some cases, including sales where the property sold is publicly traded stock or securities, or the consideration for the sale is publicly traded securities. In such cases, valuing the property sold by reference to public trading value is easy. *§ 1273(b)(3).* Thus, a sale of land for publicly traded securities worth $350,000 would be treated as a $350,000 sale, followed by a $350,000 loan to the buyer. The lender would then accrue interest annually in accordance with the usual original issue discount rules, and a total of $250,000 interest would be taxed as ordinary income spread out over the five year period. The $350,000 sales proceeds would be taxed in accordance with the accounting method used to report sales — *e.g.*, it could be deferred under the installment method, as discussed earlier. Another case in which valuation would probably be required is a nonrecourse loan in a sale-leaseback transaction (recall the *Estate of Franklin* situation), to prevent a taxpayer from overstating the purchase price and the amount of the loan. *§ 1274(b)(3).*

Valuation of assets is difficult, however, and the statute often does not require the taxpayer to value the loan at the time of the sale. Instead, the sales proceeds and loan amount is identified by measuring the present value of the future payment ($600,000 in the prior example), using an interest rate measured by reference to the rate on federal bonds of similar maturity to the loan period. For example, if the appropriate interest rate were 9%, the $600,000 "sale" would include a $386,357 sale (the statute compounds interest semi-annually; $600,000/1.045^{10} = 386,357$). The rest of the $600,000 is original issue discount. If the taxpayer elected the installment method, the gain on the sale would be reported in year 5. Meanwhile, in years 1 through 5, interest would accrue annually to the seller at the appropriate interest rate on a $386,357 loan.

§ 483. This brief review of the division of "sales" proceeds into a sale and a loan is not complete. Sometimes the statute does not force a cash basis seller to accrue the interest annually (exceptions appear in *§ 1274(c)(3)),* but still requires interest to be separated from sales proceeds. The mechanism to do this is specified by *§ 483.* It is the older of the two imputed interest rules and a taxpayer exempted from *§ 1274* must examine *§ 483* to see if and how it applies. For example, *§ 483* (rather than *§ 1274),* applies to sales of farms by individuals for no more than $1,000,000, sales of principal residences, and sales of anything for less than $250,000.

§ 483 taxes some portion of the sales proceeds as interest, *when the sales proceeds are collected.* The interest is not accrued annually, like original issue discount. The following example illustrates how the computations are made. Assume that the sale is for two $300,000 installments, payable in years 2 and 5, without interest. If the present value of the two installments is $400,000, then *total* interest is $200,000, which is *one third* of the total $600,000 "sales" proceeds. One third of each $300,000 installment is therefore interest (when collected in year 2 and year 5); the $300,000 payments consist of $100,000 interest and $200,000 sales proceeds.

§ 21.04 CONTINGENT PAYMENTS

The open transaction method (Method 3 in the earlier chart) is usually allowed when payments are "contingent." This result is traced to the decision in *Burnet v. Logan,* 283 U.S. 404 (1931). The taxpayer sold stock in exchange for cash plus a promise of future payments contingent on mining ore. The cash received was insufficient to recover the taxpayer's basis in the stock at the time of the sale. The Court did not force the seller to value the contingent payments, allowing gain to be deferred until the payments exceeded basis.

The same 1981 Regulation dealing with fixed payment obligations, cited earlier, also deals with contingent payments. It permits the open transaction method when contingent payments are to be received "only in those rare and extraordinary cases in which the fair market value of the obligation . . . cannot reasonably be ascertained." *Treas. Reg. § 15a.453-1(d)(2)(iii).* This Regulation's bark is probably more severe than its bite. Transactions like *Burnet v. Logan,* involving contingent payments, continue to be reported on the open transaction method.

Contingent payments and installment method. Does the following argument justify the government being stingy in permitting tax deferral for contingent payments under the open transaction method. Before 1980, a court sympathetic with the taxpayer's desire to defer tax on contingent payments could only permit deferral through the open transaction method. In 1980, however, the statute for the first time explicitly permitted taxpayers to report contingent payment sales on the installment method. *§ 453(j)(2).* Before then, the government did not allow the installment method in contingent payment cases because it was too difficult to compute the gain when the amount realized was contingent. (What was the contract price, from which the gross profit percentage would be computed?) After 1980, that changed. The Regulations state that the maximum contract price will be the amount realized for computing the gross profit percentage; if there is no maximum, but there is a set payment period, basis will be allocated evenly over the payment period; in other cases, cost will generally be allocated over 15 years. *Treas. Reg. § 15a.453-1(c).* Now that the taxpayer has a way to defer tax without using the open transaction method, maybe there is less need to permit the open transaction method.

Contingent payments and capital gain. Do contingent payments eligible for the open transaction method produce capital gain? In *Commissioner v. Carter,* 170 F.2d 911 (3d Cir. 1948), a taxpayer owned stock in a corporation which distributed all of its assets to its stockholders in liquidation. She received easy-to-value property which exceeded her stock basis by $20,000, plus oil brokerage contracts which everyone agreed had "no ascertainable market value when distributed." Each contract provided for commissions on future deliveries of oil. Contingencies associated with earning commissions made the amount and time of payment uncertain. Thereafter, taxpayer collected about $35,000 commissions. The court held that these commissions were capital gains, treating them as deferred proceeds from disposition of the stock. Because liquidations are treated like sales, the deferred proceeds were treated as consideration received for the sale of the stock — that is, capital gain. The court stated that "no reason is apparent for taxing [the commissions] as ordinary income." Isn't there a "good reason" to deny capital gain when gain is deferred?

Contingent payments and imputed interest. If deferred contingent payments are sales proceeds, the problem of distinguishing sales proceeds from interest recurs. Adequate interest could be charged on a contingent payment — for example, the seller could insist that payment of 5% of the gross receipts received as payment for sale of a business include an added interest charge at some specified rate. Frequently, however, no such interest is charged. In that case, some portion of each contingent payment is usually converted to interest when the payment is collected. *§ 483(f)(1).* The payment is discounted back to present value at the time of the sale. The difference between the payment and present value is interest. The longer the deferral, therefore, the higher the portion of the payment which is interest. If there is a lot of interest, the opportunity to combine tax deferral and capital gain on contingent sales is significantly reduced.

§ 21.05 DEFERRAL, CAPITAL GAINS, AND PERSONAL SERVICE INCOME

The problem of combining deferral and capital gains has also arisen in connection with personal service income. Employees are always seeking ways to convert personal service income into capital gains. One popular way was to receive property from the employer, often stock of a corporate employer. There would be significant restrictions on the transferability of the stock or on its retention and, further, the property might be subject to a repurchase option at a value significantly below market value. The courts often held that the restrictions prevented the imposition of tax at the time the stock was received, under a generous (pro-taxpayer) reading of the "equivalent of cash" doctrine. Tax would be postponed until the restrictions lapsed, at which time the taxpayers received ordinary income. Moreover, when the restrictions lapsed, the employees were often allowed to report ordinary income equal to the value of the property when it was originally transferred to them. In the usual case, value had increased and the increase in value over the amount taxed as ordinary income would be capital gains when the property was sold.

[A]—Restricted Property

§ 83 alters prior case law. How is the employee in the following problem taxed under *§ 83?* An employee of a corporation received some of the corporation's stock as compensation without charge. The stock is forfeited back to the corporation if the employee changes employers at any time within five years of receiving the stock. Moreover, the forfeiture rule applies even if the stock has been transferred to another owner by the employee. For ten years, the corporation can repurchase the stock from the owner at the value of the stock on the date it was originally transferred to the employee, if the employee tries to sell the stock to an outsider. The value of the stock when transferred to the employee (year 0) is $10,000. It rises to $15,000 when the forfeiture condition is lifted five years later (year 5). In another seven years (year 12), the stock is sold for $23,000.

How could the employee use *§ 83(b)* in the above example? He could elect to include the $10,000 ordinary income in year 0, taking a $10,000 basis in the property. By accelerating tax (eliminating deferral), there is no tax when the forfeiture provisions expire in year 5 and future recognized gain is capital gain.

What effect does *§ 83(h)* have on tax planning? It prohibits the employer's deduction until the employee has income under *§ 83(a)*. The top corporate and individual tax rates are now 35% and 39.6% respectively. Will deferring the employer's deduction discourage providing employees with compensation in the form of restricted property?

Suppose, in the prior example, the employee paid $10,000 for the restricted property in year 0 (that is, an amount equal to its value), instead of receiving it without charge. Would the employee have to report income in year 5 when the sale restriction lapsed and the property was worth $15,000? *Alves v. Commissioner,* 79 T.C. 864 (1982), *aff'd,* 734 F.2d 478 (9th Cir. 1984).

[B]—Options

Another way employers try to provide both deferral and capital gains to employees is by giving the employee an option to buy stock in the employer corporation (or, perhaps, other property owned by the corporation). *§ 83(e)(3),(4)* preserves the prior case law on this issue, as illustrated by this example. In year 0, a corporation grants an employee an option to buy stock for $100 for five years; in year 0, the stock is worth $100 and the option is worth $5. When the stock goes up in value to $120 in year 5, the employee buys it for $100. The case law held that, if the option had a reasonably ascertainable value, its value was taxable as ordinary income in year 0 (that is, $5 ordinary income), but there was no taxable event on the exercise of the option in year 5. This meant that any personal service income inherent in the $20 gain in year 5 was deferred. Moreover, the gain on the sale of the stock (assume a sale for $120 in year 12) was $15 capital gain, not ordinary income (that is, $120 amount realized, minus $105, which is the basis equal to the purchase price plus the taxed option value).

If the option did *not* have an ascertainable value, no tax would be imposed when the option was received in year 0, but then the exercise of the option in year 5 would result in ordinary income on the spread between the purchase price and the value of the stock at the time of exercise — $20 in the example. Because there was usually a significant gain in value between the time the option was granted and its exercise, the government usually found itself arguing that the option had no ascertainable value in year 0. This position is just the opposite of the government's argument in a *Commissioner v. Carter/Burnet v. Logan* type of case, concerning the potential for using the open transaction doctrine, where the government argues that value can be ascertained.

[C]—Incentive stock options

Finally, there is a statutory provision excluding from ordinary income both the value of stock options received from a corporate employer and the value of the spread between the option price and the value of the stock when the option is exercised, if certain requirements are met by the stock option plan. *§ 421, § 422*; *Treas. Reg. 14a.422A-1 (Q & A 1)*. Most important, the employee cannot own more that 10% of the corporation's voting stock, and the option price must equal the value of the stock when the option is granted. *§ 422(b)(4),(6)*. However, stockholders who own more than 10% of the corporation's voting stock are still eligible for the tax break if the option price is at least 110% of the value of the stock at the time the option is granted and the option is exercisable only within 5 years of its grant. *§ 422(c)(5)*. If the taxpayer qualifies under these sections, no gain is taxed until sale, and the gain is (almost certainly) capital gain. The employer cannot deduct any of the value of an incentive stock option. *§ 421(a)(2)*.

PART VI

TIMING — ACCOUNTING METHODS

We have been discussing timing issues throughout the course. For example: (1) realization is a timing issue, built into the definition of § 61 income; (2) and so is the deferral of realized gain and loss through nonrecognition of income rules, discussed in Chapter 18. This Part discusses accounting methods — specifically, cash and accrual methods — which also specify when income and deductions should be reported.

We have given some attention to accounting methods in earlier chapters. The cash and accrual methods were described in Chapter 3, and the installment method was discussed in Chapter 21. Some of the specifics of the cash methods have also been considered. Is a contract, note or contingent profit claim the "equivalent of cash"? Is a property right taxable compensation if it is subject to a significant restriction? This Part looks more closely at what the cash and accrual accounting methods mean and who can use these methods.

Introductory Remarks

[A] What is at stake for taxpayers — Timing

There are two major reasons why taxpayers care about timing issues. First, tax rates may differ from year to year, either because of progressive tax rates, net operating losses, or changes in statutory rates. Second, taxpayers care about tax deferral, even when tax rates are constant.

You have encountered case law and statutory provisions applying the transactional approach, whereby events in one tax year affect tax events in another year. These included: (1) the "tax benefit" rule (*see* § 5.03, *supra*), eliminating tax on recovery of amounts attributable to useless deductions in a prior year (first in the case law and then in *§ 111*); (2) rules (*see* § 5.04, *supra*) selectively permitting taxpayers to deduct repayments at rates applicable to receipts in an earlier tax year (*§ 1341*); and (3) recapture rules (both *§ 1245* (*see* § 11.04, *supra*) and case law recapture in *Hillsboro* (*see* § 13.02[F], *supra*)). Do not conclude, however, that the transactional approach is a complete substitute for adopting accurate timing rules in the first place. Thus, allowing capital expenditures to be expensed is not "corrected" by later including recovery of the prior deduction in ordinary income.

The only way to "correct" prior mistakes is to charge interest on an early tax break, or, conversely, for the government to pay interest if an item was taxed too early. The statute, however, has only a few interest-charge provisions — for example: (1) when large amounts of installment sales arise and are outstanding at the end of the tax year (*§ 453A*; *see* § 21.01[A], *supra*); and (2) *§ 460(a)(2),(b)(3)* (interest due from taxpayer or government, if estimated contract profits reported as income during the early years of contract performance turn out to be larger or smaller than expected, based on information finally available when contract performance is completed; except that taxpayers can elect not to "look back" and recompute contract profits for earlier years when the estimates of expected income turn out not to match actual profits at the end of the contract period, and the difference between estimated and actual profits is no greater than 10%. *§ 460(b)(6)*).

[B] Summary of accounting methods — cash and accrual; clearly reflect income

There are two major accounting methods — the cash and accrual methods.

Cash. Most taxpayers who perform personal services, such as doctors and lawyers, report income on the cash method — that is, when cash is received or paid. The critical issue is defining "cash." As we have seen in earlier discussions, "cash" includes the "equivalent of cash," and we will say more about this later.

Accrual. The accrual method requires income and deductions to be reported when all events fixing the right to receive cash or pay a liability have occurred, except for the passage of time, and the amount can be determined with reasonable accuracy. *Treas. Reg. § 1.446-1(c)(1)(ii)*. The contents of this requirement will also be discussed later.

The significant feature of the accrual method is that income is reported *before* collection and deductions are taken *before* payment. This might be unfair to either the taxpayer or the government, depending on whether the creditor charges adequate interest to account for deferral of collection of payment. For example, a taxpayer who accrues in year 1 a $100,000 income claim due in year 5 is treated unfairly, if the present value of the claim is less than $100,000, because inadequate interest is charged. Conversely, early deduction of a $100,000 debt, without interest, is unfair to the government because the debt's present value is less than $100,000.

Clearly reflect income. The taxpayer's use of any accounting method is subject to the basic requirement that it "clearly reflect income." *§ 446(b)*. For example, even a cash method taxpayer cannot usually deduct a capital expenditure because that would distort income by allowing a deduction for savings. We also saw earlier that some accounting conventions may be followed if they clearly reflect income, even if they appear to violate some technical rule about deductibility. An example was the decision in *Cincinnati Railroad* (*see* § 13.02[E], *supra*), in which small recurring capital expenditures could be expensed.

[C] Mandatory use of accrual accounting

The accrual method is supposed to reflect income more accurately. It tends to match income with the expenses incurred to earn the income. In addition, it usually reflects the taxpayer's net wealth more accurately, because accrued items are economic gains and losses (at least if interest charges are adequate). Nonetheless, some taxpayers have a hard time keeping records to report accrued items. They prefer to wait for cash receipts and payments before reporting the items for tax purposes.

In recent years, the statute has restricted the taxpayers who are allowed to use the cash method. *§ 448*. For example, the following can *not* use the cash method: (1) tax shelters; and (2) corporations whose annual gross receipts in prior years exceeded $5 million. Personal service corporations can, however, use the cash method regardless of gross receipts; this benefits professional corporations owned by lawyers, doctors, etc. Farming corporations are not subject to *§ 448*, but to separate rules found in *§ 447*.

Farming corporations must use the accrual method, unless (1) their annual gross receipts in prior years did not exceed $1 million, or (2) they are "family owned" and their prior annual gross receipts did not exceed $25 million (the "small family farm"). *§ 447*. The raising or harvesting of trees (except fruit and nut trees) is not subject to this rule. *§ 447(a) (last sentence)*. Why not?

In some cases, the cash method is exceedingly generous. Some taxpayers have been allowed to deduct even capital and inventory costs. Farmers, for example, have been allowed to expense some expenditures which would normally be added to basis, such as the cost of raising cattle. These opportunities to expense costs are withdrawn whenever the accrual method is required. For those taxpayers still allowed to use the cash method (*e.g.*, the "small family farm"), however, *§ 263A* must be consulted. It imposes "uniform capitalization rules," which require most inventory and capital costs to be added to basis. Even these rules have exceptions, however. For example, the "uniform capitalization rules" do not apply to cash method farmers who produce animals, or who produce plants with preproductive periods of 2 years or less. *§ 263A(d)(1)(A)*. And, once again, certain trees are exempted. *§ 263A(c)(5)*.

[D] Which transactions must be reported on the accrual method

Sometimes, specific transactions (rather than a specific type of taxpayer), must be reported on the accrual method. We have already seen two examples — (1) accrual of original issue discount, without regard to whether the creditor is a cash method taxpayer (*§ 1272*; *see* § 19.05[A], *supra*); and (2) the Regulation requiring a taxpayer who does not use the installment method to accrue the gain on sale of property (*Treas. Reg. § 15A.453-1(d)(2)(i),(ii)*; *see* § 21.01[D], *supra*). In addition, taxpayers who sell inventory must use the accrual method. *Treas. Reg. § 1.446-1(c)(2)(i).*

[E] Separating unstated interest from present value

When the receipt of cash is postponed and adequate interest is not charged, the tax law must decide whether to separate the unstated interest from the present value of the claim, and then decide whether to accrue either the interest, the present value, both, or neither.

Sale. We have already considered these possibilities in connection with the sale of property in Chapter 21. Before the adoption of *§ 1274*, taxpayers could defer both the present value of sales proceeds and interest, although *§ 483* required the separation of sales proceeds from interest (so that interest would not be taxed as capital gain). Under current law, when *§ 1274* applies, interest must be separated from present value and accrued in accordance with the original issue discount rules. However, the present value can be deferred if the taxpayer uses the installment method.

Use of property. Similar issues arise whenever the taxpayer postpones receipt of cash for anything of value. For example, *§ 467(d)* deals with postponed payments for use of property (that is, rent). When the total payments exceed $250,000 and at least one payment is paid after the year in which the property is used, the present value of the postponed payment must be accrued in the year of use, whether or not the person providing the property is a cash or accrual method taxpayer. In addition, any interest representing the difference between the actual payment and present value must be accrued annually in accordance with the original issue discount rules. In other words, both unstated interest and present value must be accrued. If this section does not apply, the *entire* payment (without separation of the interest and present value) is reported in accordance with the taxpayer's accounting method — in the year the property is used (for an accrual method taxpayer) or, later, when the payment is collected (for a cash method taxpayer).

For example, if collection of $300,000 of rent payable for use of property in year 0 is deferred until year 2, the owner must accrue the present value of the $300,000 in income in year 0, and then accrue interest periodically thereafter. If the rent had been only $200,000, *§ 467* does not apply; a cash basis taxpayer would then report $200,000 in year 2, and an accrual basis taxpayer would report $200,000 in year 0.

Personal services. When the total consideration exceeds $250,000 for personal services, *§ 467(g)* authorizes the Treasury to separate the present value of future payments from interest and accrue the *interest* annually in accordance with original issue discount rules. However, the present value itself is still either accrued or deferred, depending on whether the taxpayer is an accrual or cash method taxpayer.

CHAPTER 22

CASH METHOD

§ 22.01 CASH OR ITS EQUIVALENT

Because the opportunity to use the cash method has been significantly narrowed by the statute, many of the older cases defining cash and its equivalent have only limited current application. Nonetheless, some taxpayers still care a lot about the cash method, primarily taxpayers who render personal services. This section discusses when cash or its equivalent has been received or paid.

[A]—Embodiments of a promise

A mere promise is not the equivalent of cash. If it were, there would be no difference between the cash and accrual method. Promises are, however, often embodied in something which has a marketable value. What happens when a taxpayer receives a note, or the promise is embodied in a contract or other instrument which could be sold for a price? Here are some decisions addressing these questions. *Western Oaks Building Corp. v. Commissioner,* 49 T.C. 365 (1968) (value of the note or contract must be reported if it is "easily negotiable and freely exchangeable in commerce"); *Rev. Rul. 68–606,* 1968–2 C.B. 42 (contract right "freely transferable and readily salable" is equivalent of cash); *Rev. Rul 76–135,* 1976–1 C.B. 114 (notes with $50 face value have $47 market value; $47 taxed when notes received).

Some cases explicitly state that a note or contract is the equivalent of cash, even if its market value is discounted substantially below face value. *Warren Jones v. United States,* 60 T.C. 663 (1973), *rev'd,* 524 F.2d 788 (9th Cir. 1970) (face = $133,000; market value = $76,980). *But see Cowden v. Commissioner,* 289 F.2d 20 (5th Cir. 1961) (claim need not be negotiable to be cash equivalent, as long as market value not discounted substantially more than is indicated by the prevailing interest rate).

Checks are "cash" in their face amount, regardless of what they would sell for. That makes sense in a society where checks typically pass as cash and are recorded that way in a taxpayer's records. *Kahler v. Commissioner,* 18 T.C. 31 (1952) (even though check was received after the close of banking hours on the last business day of the year, it was considered a taxable receipt in the year it was mailed). If the check is deposited but not paid in a later year, there is a loss deduction in the later year. *But see Premji v. Commissioner*, 72 T.C.M. (CCH) 16 (1996) (receipt of a check when the debtor has insufficient bank funds to pay the check is not taxable in the year of receipt; the check was dated the same day as the debtor filed for bankruptcy; whether there are sufficient funds is a question of fact). Do these cases suggest that a check post-dated to a later year would only be taxable in the later year by a cash basis taxpayer?

[B]—Property other than embodiments of promises

A cash method taxpayer who received property, such as ownership of a home in lieu of cash salary, receives a taxable "equivalent of cash." You have already studied the "equivalent of cash" issue in the context of taxpayers who render personal services, and encountered specific statutory rules which replace prior uncertain case law. *§ 83* determines whether a property interest is subject to sufficient restrictions to prevent cash equivalence and how to value such interests (*see* § 21.05[A], *supra*). In addition, certain property interests might not be taxed, whether or not they are the equivalent of cash — *see, e.g.*, *§ 132* (certain in-kind fringe benefits). And *§ 119* (meals and lodging for the convenience of the employer). These sections resolve many of the cash equivalence issues in the personal service context.

The following *Reed* case discusses the "equivalent of cash" doctrine. The actual facts of the case involve sales proceeds, which would probably be dealt with under either the installment method or the closed transaction-Regulation method (methods 1 and 4, discussed in § 21.01, *supra*). The decision is therefore likely to be relevant only when the "equivalent of cash" doctrine still applies. Would it apply if a taxpayer received the property in *Reed* as a dividend, salary, or rent?

REED v. COMMISSIONER

723 F.2d 138 (1st Cir. 1983)

FLOYD R. GIBSON, SENIOR CIRCUIT JUDGE.

[Editor — Cvengros had an option to buy stock from Reed, the taxpayer, which was exercised on November 23, 1973. The closing date for the sale was December 27, 1973. For tax reasons, Reed wanted to postpone tax until the next year. In early December 1973, Reed and Cvengros modified the sale agreement so that the purchase price of a little more than $800,000 would be placed in escrow, as explained below. The taxpayer reported the gain in 1974 and the court agreed.]

. . .Under the terms of the escrow agreement, the stock sales proceeds were to be paid by Cvengros to the escrowee (the American National Bank and Trust Company) at the December 27, 1973 closing and the escrowee was then to make disbursements of the sales proceeds to a number of selling shareholders, including Reed, on January 3, 1974. Under the agreement, these selling shareholders were not entitled to receive interest, investment income or any other incidental benefits (*e.g.*, bank letter of credit) on the sales proceeds while they were in escrow. The agreement provided for no conditions precedent, other than the passage of time, to the January 3, 1974 payment. . . .

B. Economic Benefit

The Commissioner [] contends that in 1973 Reed received a taxable economic benefit by virtue of Cvengros' deposit of the sales proceeds into the escrow account. The Commissioner argues that upon the December 27, 1973 closing, there were no open transactions remaining and Reed's right to future payment from the escrow account was irrevocable, being conditioned only upon the passage of time; hence, Reed received the "cash equivalent" of the sales proceeds deposited in the escrow account. The Commissioner points out that Reed could have assigned his irrevocable right to receive future payment of the escrow funds.

This argument, which was largely embraced by the Tax Court, is predicated upon a misapplication of various cases of Commissioner says espouse the economic benefit doctrine. These cases held that escrow arrangements were ineffective to defer income tax because of the existence of one of two factors, not present in the instant case: (1) the taxpayer received some present, beneficial interest from the escrow account; (2) the escrow arrangement was the product of the taxpayer's self-imposed limitation on funds the taxpayer had an unqualified, vested right to control.

Specifically, *Kuehner v. Commissioner,* 214 F.2d 437 (1st Cir. 1954), the First Circuit case upon which the Commissioner principally relies, held that a taxpayer recognized income when the purchase price was deposited with the escrowee because the taxpayer's interest in the escrowed funds constituted a property interests equivalent to cash. The taxpayer's interest in the escrow fund was so viewed because the taxpayer was entitled to investment income earned while the funds were in escrow and hence enjoyed a complete and present economic interest in the funds. . . .

By contrast, in this case Reed was not entitled to receive the income earned from the investment of funds held by the escrowee, but merely obtained an unconditional promise that he would ultimately be paid on January 3, 1974 in accordance with the deferred payment provision.

The Commissioner, however, seizes upon broad language in *Kuehner* as support for the proposition that one who has an unconditional right to future payment from an irrevocable escrow account receives taxable income in the year the escrow account was created. There are three reasons why we do not interpret *Kuehner* as supporting this proposition. First, as the *Kuehner* court apparently recognized, the deposited escrow funds could be characterized as "the equivalent of cash" only if the taxpayer received a present beneficial interest in such funds— *e.g.,* investment income. . . .

Second, to apply the Commissioner's interpretation of *Kuehner* to this case would be at odds with the well established principle that a deferred payment arrangement is effective to defer income recognition to a cash basis taxpayer, provided it is part of an arms-length agreement between the purchaser and seller. That the cash basis taxpayer's right to receive future payment of the escrowed proceeds may be characterized as unconditional or irrevocable does not render the contractually binding restriction on the time of payment any less substantial. Third, to apply the Commissioner's interpretation of *Kuehner* here would require an extension of the economic benefit doctrine that would significantly erode the distinction between cash and accrual methods of accounting. The economic benefit doctrine, a nonstatutory doctrine emerging from and primarily related to the area of employee deferred compensation, is based on the idea that an individual should be taxed on any economic benefit conferred upon him, to the extent that the benefit has an ascertainable fair market value. However, in applying the economic benefit doctrine to a cash basis taxpayer's contractual right to receive future payment, as we must do here, courts generally go beyond an inquiry into the fair market value of the contract right to ask the separate question of whether the contract right is the equivalent of cash. Without this separate inquiry, the economic benefit doctrine, as applied to a cash basis taxpayer, could be broadly construed to cover all deferred compensation and deferred payment contracts.

In order to meet the cash equivalency requirement for income recognition, a cash basis taxpayer's contractual right to future payment must be reflected in a negotiable note, bond, or other evidence of indebtedness which, like money, commonly and readily changes hands in commerce. . . .

In this case, it is difficult to conceive Reed's contractual right to future payment, even through unconditional and evidenced by an escrow account, as a right which commonly and readily changes hands in commerce. However, even assuming Reed's right to future payment of the escrowed proceeds was readily transferable in commerce, the escrow account was not intended by the parties as present payment of the purchase price, but rather was intended to serve as an added assurance that payment would be made in the next year. As such, the escrow account cannot be characterized fairly as the equivalent of cash to Reed in 1973. We would have to ignore the distinction between cash and accrual methods of accounting to adopt a rule requiring immediate recognition of income by a cash basis taxpayer who has a contractual right to future payment from an escrow account, but who has received no present beneficial interest from that account.

The Commissioner alternatively suggests that Reed received a present beneficial interest in the escrow funds in the sense that he could have assigned his right to receive payment under the agreement. This argument proves either too much or too little. It proves too much because any promise under a contract for deferred payment could conceivably assign his right to receive future payment, provided the contract does not specifically include a non-assignment clause. Hence, to base the economic benefit rule on whether a taxpayer could have assigned his contractual right to future payment would eviscerate the well recognized rule that a taxpayer can defer income recognition pursuant to a bona fide deferred payment agreement. Furthermore, it proves too little in this case because Reed never attempted to make any assignment of his right to receive the escrow funds and thus did nothing to charge himself with any economic benefit to be derived from the funds. . . .

Isn't the court wrong in *Reed*? Doesn't the lack of investment income argue for discounting the cash equivalent, not deferring recognition?

§ 22.02 CONSTRUCTIVE RECEIPT

Cash or its equivalent is "received", not only in the conventional sense of "receipt," but also if it is "constructively" received. The core example of constructive receipt is interest on a bank account which the taxpayer is free to withdraw in year 1 but leaves with the bank. The interest is taxed in year 1. The general idea behind this rule is plain enough. A taxpayer cannot have the legal right to property, but turn his back on it to defer tax.

The "constructive receipt of cash" doctrine does not, however, wipe out the distinction between accrual and cash method taxpayers, which makes for some very artificial distinctions. There is nothing to stop a taxpayer in year 1 from negotiating for a contract which defers income until year 2, even if she had the economic power to contract for a year 1 payment.

In that case, there is no legal right to the payment in year 1. In the bank interest case, the legal right to the property matured in year 1.

The constructive receipt doctrine also does not require taxation of something which is not the "equivalent of cash." Under "cash equivalence" doctrine, "substantial limitations" on receipt prevent taxation. For example, assume a taxpayer invests in a certificate of deposit with a bank and can withdraw interest prior to the date when the deposit comes due, but only by losing almost half the interest. The penalty is a substantial limitation, postponing tax on the interest until the certificate of deposit comes due. *Treas. Reg. § 1.451–2(a)(2); Rev. Rul. 80–157,* 1980–1 C.B. 186.

REV. RUL. 60–31, 1960–1 C.B. 174

Advice has been requested regarding the taxable year of inclusion in gross income of a taxpayer, using the cash receipts and disbursements method of accounting, of compensation for services received under the circumstances described below. . . .

(3) On October 1, 1957, the taxpayer, an author, and corporation Y, a publisher, executed an agreement under which the taxpayer granted to the publisher the exclusive right to print, publish and sell a book he had written. This agreement provides that the publisher will (1) pay the author specified royalties based on the actual cash received from the sale of the published work, (2) render semiannual statements of the sales, and (3) at the time of rendering each statement make settlement for the amount due. On the same day, another agreement was signed by the same parties, mutually agreeing that, in consideration of, and notwithstanding any contrary provisions contained in the first contract, the publisher shall not pay the taxpayer more than 100x dollars in any one calendar year. Under this supplemental contract, sums in excess of 100x dollars accruing in any one calendar year are to be carried over by the publisher into succeeding accounting periods; and the publisher shall not be required either to pay interest to the taxpayer on any such excess sums or to segregate any such sums in any manner.

(4) In June 1957, the taxpayer, a football player, entered into a two-year standard player's contract with a football club in which he agreed to play

football and engage in activities related to football during the two-year term only for the club. In addition to a specified salary for the two-year term, it was mutually agreed that as an inducement for signing the contract the taxpayer would be paid a bonus of 150x dollars. The taxpayer could have demanded and received payment of this bonus at the time of signing the contract, but at his suggestion there was added to the standard contract form a paragraph providing substantially as follows:

> The player shall receive the sum of 150x dollars upon signing of this contract, contingent upon the payment of this 150x dollars to an escrow agent designated by him. The escrow agreement shall be subject to approval by the legal representatives of the player, the Club, and the escrow agent.

Pursuant to this added provision, an escrow agreement was executed on June 25, 1957, in which the club agreed to pay 150x dollars on that date to the Y bank, as escrow and the escrow agent agreed to pay this amount, plus interest, to the taxpayer in installments over a period of five years. The escrow agreement also provides that the account established by the escrow agent is to bear the taxpayer's name; that payments from such account may be made only in accordance with the terms of the agreement; that the agreement is binding upon the parties thereto and their successors or assigns; and that in the event of the taxpayer's death during the escrow period the balance due will become part of his estate. . . .

[U]nder the doctrine of constructive receipt, a taxpayer may not deliberately turn his back upon income and thereby select the year for which he will report it. Nor may a taxpayer, by a private agreement, postpone receipt of income from one taxable year to another. . . .

However, the statute cannot be administered by speculating whether the payor would have been willing to agree to an earlier payment. *See, for example, J.D. Amend, et ux., v. Commissioner,* 13 T.C. 178, *Acquiescence,* C.B. 1950–1, 1, in which the court, citing a number of authorities for its holding, stated:

> It is clear that the doctrine of constructive receipt is to be sparingly used; that amounts due from a corporation but unpaid, are not to be included in the income of an individual reporting his income on a cash receipts basis unless it appears that the money was available to him, that the corporation was able and ready to pay him, that his right to receive was not restricted, and that his failure to receive resulted from exercise of his own choice.

Consequently, it seems clear that in each case involving a deferral of compensation a determination of whether the doctrine of constructive receipt is applicable must be made upon the basis of the specific factual situation involved.

Applying the foregoing criteria to the situations described above, the following conclusions have been reached . . . :

(3) Here the principal agreement provided that the royalties were payable substantially as earned, and this agreement was supplemented by a further concurrent agreement which made the royalties payable over a period of years. This supplemental agreement, however, was made before the royalties were earned; in fact, in was made on the same day as the principal agreement and the two agreements were a part of the same transaction. . . . Therefore, it is [] held that the author concerned will be required to include the royalties in his gross income only in the taxable years in which they are actually received in cash or other property.

(4) . . . In Revenue Ruling 55–727, the taxpayer, a professional baseball player, entered into a contract in 1953 in which he agreed to render services for a baseball club and to refrain from playing baseball for any other club during the term of the contract. In addition to specified compensation, the contract provided for a bonus to the player or his estate, payable one-half in January 1954 and one-half in January 1955, whether or not he was able to render services. The primary question was whether the bonus was capital gain or ordinary income; and in holding that the bonus payments constituted ordinary income, it was stated that they were taxable for the year in which received by the player. However, under the facts set forth in Revenue ruling 55–727 there was no arrangement, as here, for placing the amount of the bonus in escrow. Consequently, the instant situation is distinguishable from that considered in Revenue Ruling 55–727.

In *E.T.Sproull v. Commissioner,* 16 T.C. 244, *aff'd,* 194 Fed.(2d) 541, the petitioner's employer in 1945 transferred in trust for the petitioner the amount of $10,500. The trustee was directed to pay out of principal to the petitioner the sum of $5,250 in 1945 and the balance, including income, in 1947. In the event of the petitioner's prior death, the amounts were to be paid to his administrator, executor, or heirs. The petitioner contended that the Commissioner erred in including the sum of $10,500 in his taxable income for 1945. In this connection, the court stated:

> . . . It is undoubtedly true that the amount which the Commissioner has included in petitioner's income for 1945 was used in that year for his benefit . . . in setting up the trust of which petitioner, or, in the event of his death his estate, was the sole beneficiary. . . .
>
> The question then becomes. . .was "any economic or financial benefit conferred on the employee as compensation" in the taxable year. If so, it was taxable to him in that year. This question we must answer in the affirmative. The employer's part of the transaction terminated in 1945. It was then that the amount of the compensation was fixed at $10,500 and irrevocably paid out for petitioner's sole benefit. . . .

Applying the principles stated in the *Sproull* decision to the facts here, it is concluded that the 150x dollar bonus is includible in the gross income of the football player concerned in 1957, the year in which the club unconditionally paid such amount to the escrow agent.

TP loses

Renegotiating receipt of earned income. *Rev. Rul. 60–31* is about taxpayers deferring income by contract. Such deferral could be analogized to assigning earned income to a relative. If a taxpayer cannot assign earned income to another person for tax purposes, why can the taxpayer assign it to another tax year? This question occurred to the government in *Commissioner v. Oates,* 18 T.C. 570 (1952), *acquiesced in,* 1960–1 C.B. 5, *aff'd*, 207 F.2d 711 (7th Cir. 1953). Pursuant to contract, a taxpayer was entitled to renewal commissions on insurance contracts, but renegotiated the payment dates to defer the income. The government cited the assignment of income cases (*Earl, Eubank*, and *Horst*) to prohibit deferral, but the court held for the taxpayer.

In 1978 the government proposed a regulation (43 Fed. Reg. 4638,4639 (1978), stating that "the amount of a taxpayer's basic or regular compensation fixed by contract, statute, or otherwise" cannot at the taxpayer's option be deferred beyond the year it would be paid but for the taxpayer's exercise of its option. The government stated that it would reconsider *Rev. Rul. 60–31 (example 3)* and its acquiescence in *Oates* after the Regulation was adopted.

The government was, however, stopped in its tracks. The Revenue Act of 1978 stated that inclusion in income of amounts under private deferred compensation arrangements would be determined "in accordance with the principles set forth in regulations, rulings, and judicial decisions . . . which were in effect on February 1, 1978 [prior to the effective date of the proposed Regulation]."

This problem refuses to go away. When tax rates are lowered, taxpayers may try to renegotiate salary to defer receipt. When this happened prior to the 1986 tax reduction, the government issued the following warning. If you were counselling a client, would you think this warning had any teeth?

> ". . .[T]he period of time for which an agreement defers the receipt of income is an important factor in determining whether a taxpayer's

right to receive income is subject to substantial limitation or restriction." *Announcement 87–3,* IR News Release-86–172.

§ 22.03 DEDUCTIBLE PAYMENTS

The definition of "cash payments" which can support a deduction is not symmetrical with the rules defining "cash receipts" which support inclusion.

For example, making cash available to a payee does not in itself constitute a "payment," just because the payee would constructively receive the money. *Vandel Poel, Francis & Co., Inc. v. Commissioner,* 8 T.C. 407 (1947). And giving a note is not the equivalent of a cash payment. *Helvering v. Price,* 309 U.S. 409 (1940); *Rev. Rul. 76–135,* 1976–1 C.B. 114; *Don E. Williams Co. v. Commissioner,* 429 U.S. 569, 578 (1977) (no deduction for giving a note because "the note may never be paid. . . .") The problem in these cases is that the cash method payor has retained too much dominion and control over the payment to justify a deduction.

Checks, unlike notes, are payments by a cash method taxpayer when the check is delivered. *Rev. Rul. 54–465, 1954–2 C.B. 93.*

Suppose a taxpayer makes a payment with a credit card. Is the amount deductible as a cash payment before the credit card bill is paid? Is it like borrowing cash from a bank and making a deductible payment, or like promising to pay in the future? *Rev. Rul. 78-38, 1978-1 C.B. 67* (government accepts analogy of credit card payment to bank loan, reversing prior Revenue Ruling; payment by credit card is deductible).

§ 22.04 RETIREMENT PLANS

The examples in this Chapter often deal with deferred compensation. A common method of providing deferred compensation is through employer retirement plans. How does the prior discussion apply to these plans?

Many of these plans provide more than a promise to the employee. Money is put into a trust fund or paid to an insurance company, which earns investment income, to be distributed to the employee as an annuity or lump sum at a future date. Under usual principles of cash equivalence the employer's contribution would be taxable to the employee when made to the trust fund or the insurance company, subject to deferral under *§ 83* if there were a substantial risk of forfeiture. Absent that risk, there is cash equivalence embodied in a property right, even though payments will not be received until retirement.

The statute does not tax the employee, however, if the contributions are made to a "qualified" retirement plan. In addition, the plan is not taxed on its annual investment income. This permits the employee to defer tax on plan contributions and income until the employee receives cash. At the same time, employers can deduct contributions to these plans without waiting until the employee is taxed.

Qualified plans. *See generally §§ 401-418E.* In general, a "qualified" retirement plan must not discriminate in favor of highly compensated employees regarding coverage and participation, and must meet certain funding and vesting requirements. In addition, there are maximums on total retirement benefits and special nondiscrimination, funding, and vesting rules for "top heavy" plans, which favor key employees. Payments generally must begin no later than the year after which the taxpayer reaches age 70 1/2; and payments cannot begin (unless the taxpayer pays a penalty) before death, disability, or the year in which the taxpayer reaches age 59 1/2 (although there are a few exceptions permitting earlier distribution — such as for medical, education, and first-time home buying expenses). A self-employed individual can adopt a qualified retirement plan for his employees and include himself, without having to turn himself into an employees by incorporating.

In addition, employees can usually elect to have their employers contribute some of their salary to a qualified plan, without having to report the withheld salary as income, subject to dollar limits and nondiscrimination rules.

There are also rules allowing employees who participate in retirement plans run by state and local government and tax exempt employers to defer tax, even though the employees can elect to take cash from the employer rather than have the employer increase contributions to the deferred compensation plan. *§ 457.* Without this provision, the cash option would result in taxing the employee on the foregone cash.

Tax deferred retirement plans are a sub-specialty which consume the entire professional lives of some practitioners and we do little more here than note their existence. The (important) detail is omitted from this summary.

IRAs (deductible now; taxable later). A taxpayer who is *not* a participant in a qualified retirement plan can defer tax by contributing to an Individual Retirement Account (IRA). *§ 219.* The contribution and the income it earns are both deferred (as in a qualified plan) until payment. The maximum annual deduction is, generally, the lesser of $2,000 or the taxpayer's personal service income. The deduction is "above the line" — that is, it is not an itemized deduction. The taxpayer's spouse can also deduct up to $2,000, based on the taxpayer's personal service income (if *neither* spouse is a participant in a qualified retirement plan).

A taxpayer who *is* a participant in a qualified plan can also invest up to $2,000 in a tax deductible IRA per year, subject to phase-out rules based on AGI. The 1997 Tax Act increases the AGI phaseout range for single individuals to $30,000-$40,000 in 1998, and then gradually increases this range until it is $50,000-$60,000 in 2005. For married couples filing jointly, the 1997 law increases the phase-out range to $50,000-$60,000 in 1998, rising to $80,000-$100,000 by 2007.

Rules similar to those applicable to qualified retirement plans restrict early distributions and specify when distributions must begin.

Suppose spouse 1 is married to spouse 2 who is a participant in a qualified retirement plan. Before the 1997 Tax Act, spouse 1 could also deduct up to $2,000 based on the earned income of spouse 2, but was subject to the low phase-out rules noted above. The 1997 law relaxed the phase-out rules so that spouse 1 can make contributions based on spouse 2's earnings, subject to a $150,000-$160,000 phase-out range for the married unit. This will allow many individuals who work at home, but have wage earning spouses, to deduct a $2,000 contribution to an IRA, even though the wage earning spouse cannot (as a plan participant) make such contributions.

Roth IRAs (nondeductible now; exempt later). The 1997 Tax Act adds another IRA, known as "Roth IRAs." Roth IRAs permit *non*deductible contributions out of earned income, up to $2,000. The contribution accumulates income tax-free, *and* the distribution is tax-free under certain circumstances. *§ 408A.*

The contribution limits for Roth IRAs are phased out — for single taxpayers, between AGI of $95,000 and $110,000; for married couples filing jointly, between AGI of $150,000 and $160,000.

The distributions from a Roth IRA are tax free if the distribution occurs after the end of five tax years beginning with the first tax year for which a contribution is made to the IRA; *and* must be made on or after the individual attains age 59 1/2, with the usual exceptions for death or disability, and certain medical, education, and homebuyer expenses.

Nonqualifying distributions come first out of contributions (as a nontaxable return of capital), so there is no tax on the accumulated income until distributions exceed contributions.

Unlike deductible IRAs, contributions can begin after age 70 1/2. Moreover, distributions can be made after age 70 1/2 (unlike qualified employer plans and ordinary IRAs).

The tax law still has an older pre-1997 provision for a *non*deductible contribution to an IRA, which accumulates income tax free *only until* distribution. *§ 408(o).* It is unclear what purpose these IRAs serve after adoption of the Roth IRA (which exempts the interest both as it accumulates *and* when it is distributed).

§ 22.05 INDIRECTLY TAXING CASH METHOD PAYEES ON ACCRUED INCOME

The most important policy issue in this chapter is whether cash method taxpayers should be allowed to defer tax on accrued income until they receives cash. For example, if a cash method taxpayer has an accrued claim in year 0 to collect $100 in year 2, should the tax on the $100 be deferred? The accrued income is an increase in wealth, at least in an amount equal to its present value. If adequate interest is charged on the $100 to account for deferred receipt, then wealth is increased in year 0 by the full $100.

One way to deal with this problem is to force cash method taxpayers to accrue income. Sometimes the statute does require accrual, as explained earlier. But the statute is not always so harsh on cash method taxpayers, especially regarding deferred compensation. The statutory rules about retirement plans even allow tax deferral when the employee has a property interest which is the equivalent of cash and the employee's retirement fund earns interest.

Disallow Payor's deduction until payee is taxed. There is a way to indirectly tax the cash method taxpayer with accrued income, without forcing the taxpayer on to the accrual method. One way is to overtax the accrual method payor by disallowing a deduction until the payee is taxed. The following example illustrates how.

Assume the following. The Payor is willing to pay the payee $121 in year 2. It is now year 0, two years earlier. Both payor and payee are in the 30% tax bracket. If we do not want the payee to defer tax, then the payee should pay tax in year 0 on the present value of the $121. Assuming a 10% interest rate, that amount is $100 ($121/1.1^2$), and the tax is $30. After-tax, the payee would have $70, if forced to accrue the $100. That $70 would earn interest at a 7% after tax rate, producing $80.143 in two years (70 times 1.07^2). Therefore, the benchmark for deciding if we have indirectly taxed the payee is whether we can simulate that result, leaving the payee with $80.143.

Now look at the payor. How much could the accrual method payor deduct in years 0,1, and 2? In year 0, the accrual method payor should deduct $100, the present value of the future payment; in the next two years the payor should also deduct the 10% interest accruing on the $100 owed to the payee. Indeed, the payor might actually set aside the $100 in year 0 and earn interest sufficient to produce $121 in year 2, two years later, as in the typical retirement plan arrangement. If interest rates are 10%, the year 0 set aside and annual interest in years 1 and 2 are as follows:

	Present Value	*Interest*
Year 0	$100	
Year 1		$10
Year 2		$11

Now — disallow the payor's year 0 accrued deduction. That leaves the payor with $70, which it is willing to commit to the payee. Assume that the payor deposits the $70 in the bank and earns 7% interest (still no accrued deduction for the payor), yielding $80.143 at the end of year 2 (70 times 1.07^2). How much will the payor pay the payee in year 2, at which point the payment will be deductible by the payor? The payor will pay the payee an amount which costs the payor $80.143 after taxes? Because the payment is deductible, the payor will pay much more than $80.143 — in fact, an additional amount which equals the value of a deduction. For those of you who are arithmetically, inclined, that payment will be 80.143 divided by.7 (.7 = 1 minus the 30% tax rate), which equals $114.49. The employee in the 30% bracket will then pay tax equal to 30% of that $114.49 sum and have $80.143 left (70% times 114.49 = 80.143). That is the amount the payee would have had if she had been on the accrual method in the first place, able to invest $70 for two years at a 7% after tax rate of return.

So, disallowing the payor's accrued deduction, until the payee reports the income, leaves the cash method employee in the same position as an accrual method employee. Or does it? Suppose the payor is the employer of the teacher of this course. Will loss of an accrued deduction lead it to reduce the $100 commitment to the payee to $70. No. The equivalence only works if the payor and payee are in the same tax bracket.

Tax the interest on the present value twice. The above example suggests another way to indirectly tax the payee to simulate the accrual method. Let the accrual method payor deduct the $100 in year 0, but tax the payor's 10% interest as it is earned. That leaves the following amount for distribution to the payee — $114.49 (100 times 1.07^2). Do not allow the payor any further deduction at the time of distribution in year 2. The $114.49 is taxed in full to the payee in year 2, again leaving the payee with the "correct" amount — $80.143 (70% times 114.49). This approach taxes the interest twice, once when earned, and again when distributed to the payee.

The intuition behind equating a double tax on interest with putting the payee on the accrual method is the following is the following equivalence. Recall from Chapter 3 that deferral of tax on savings equals taxing the savings but exempting the investment income on after tax savings. A double tax on the interest in effect taxes the investment return on after tax savings, and therefore eliminates the deferral advantage that a cash method taxpayer enjoys by not accruing income. (Thus, in year 1, one 30% tax on $10 interest leaves $7, which is the interest that would have been earned on $70 of after tax savings; the second tax on $7 interest takes away the deferral advantage.)

The statute. The statute in fact postpones deductions by an accrual method payor until the payee is taxed in several circumstances. *See § 83 (h)* (no deduction for payor until payee reports gain on receipt of restricted property; interpreted (generously) by the government to allow the payor a deduction for amounts "includ*ible*" in the service provider's income as long as the payor complies with certain reporting requirements. *Treas. Reg. 1.83-6(a)(1),(2)*); *§ 404(a)(5)* (no deduction for payor until payee reports deferred compensation, unless the payments are to a "qualified retirement" plan); *§ 404(b)(2)(A)* (no deduction for most deferred employee benefits, other than deferred compensation, until the payee reports the item or would report it if it were taxable — for example, an employer's commitment to provide medical or unemployment insurance benefits to an employee in a later year). Now do you see one reason why the top corporate tax rate should not be less than the top individual tax rate?

The meaning of *§ 404(a)(5)* — deferring the payor's deduction until the payee reports deferred compensation — was litigated in the following *Albertson's, Inc.,* case. The payor identified part of a deferred payment as deferred compensation and the remainder as interest to account for the deferral, and argued that the deferral rule did not apply to the interest portion.

ALBERTSON'S, INC., V. COMMISSIONER

42 F.3d 537 (9th Cir. 1994) (on rehearing),
cert. denied, 116 S. Ct. 51 (1995)

[Editor — The facts, in simplified form, are as follows. The employer agreed to pay "basic amounts" of deferred compensation to executives, but retained those cash amounts until a future date when the payment would be made. To compensate the employees for the payment delay, the future payments included an interest factor.]

In 1982, Albertson's requested permission from the IRS to deduct the additional [interest] amounts (but not the basic amounts) during the year in which they accrued instead of waiting until the end of the deferral period. In 1983, the IRS granted Albertson's request. Accordingly, Albertson's claimed deductions of $ 667,142 for the additional amounts that had already accrued, even though it had not yet paid the [employees] any sums under the deferred compensation agreements. In 1987, the IRS changed its policy, however, and sought a deficiency for the additional amounts, contending that all amounts provided for in the deferred compensation agreements were deductible only when received by Albertson's employees. Albertson's filed a petition with the Tax Court, claiming that the additional amounts constituted "interest" and thus could be deducted as they accrued.

In a sharply divided opinion, the Tax Court rejected Albertson's position. *Albertson's, Inc., v. Commissioner*, 95 T.C. 415 (1990). The court found that the additional amounts represented compensation, not interest, and were therefore not deductible until the end of the deferral period under I.R.C. § 404(a)(5) & (d).

[Editor — In a footnote, the court described the Tax Court decision, as follows:

The nine-member majority held that the additional amount was not currently deductible because it was not interest. The four-member concurrence argued that the additional amount was interest, but that section 404's timing restrictions applied to both compensation and interest. The five-member dissent argued that the additional amount was interest and that section 404's timing restrictions applied only to compensation. One judge did not participate, and one judge voted in favor of the majority and the concurrence. Thus, twelve judges agreed that the additional amounts were not deductible interest under section 404.]

We reversed the decision of the Tax Court. We held that the additional amounts constituted interest within the definition of I.R.C. § 163(a) and that interest payments were not governed by the timing restrictions of section 404. The government petitioned for rehearing due to the significant fiscal impact of the panel's opinion which it estimates will cause a $ 7 billion loss in tax revenues.

II. REHEARING

We agreed to rehear this issue after lengthy consideration and reflection. In our original opinion, we stated that the plain language of the statute strongly supported Albertson's interpretation and, accordingly, we adopted it. Nevertheless, we expressed sympathy for the Commissioner's argument that Congress intended the timing restrictions of I.R.C. § 404 to apply to all payments made under a deferred compensation plan and recognized that our plain language interpretation seemed to undercut Congress' purpose.

We have now changed our minds about the result we reached in our original opinion and conclude that our initial decision was incorrect. The question is not an easy one, however. We have struggled with it unsuccessfully at least once, and it may, indeed, ultimately turn out that the United States Supreme Court will tell us that it is this opinion which is in error. This is simply one of those cases — and there are more of them than judges generally like to admit — in which the answer is far from clear and in which there are conflicting rules and principles that we are forced to try to apply simultaneously. Such accommodation sometimes proves to be impossible. In some cases, as here, convincing arguments can be made for both possible results, and the court's decision will depend on which of the two competing legal principles it chooses to give greater weight to in the particular circumstance. Law, even statutory construction, is not a science. It is merely an effort by human beings, albeit judges, to do their best with imperfect tools to arrive at a correct result. . . .

In its petition for rehearing, the government, far more forcefully and clearly than it did originally, has articulated the purpose of the timing restrictions outlined in I.R.C. § 404: to encourage employers to invest in qualified compensation plans by requiring inclusions and deductions of income and expense to be "matched" for nonqualified plans. The matching principle, widely recognized to be the key to I.R.C. § 404, provides significant tax incentives for employers to invest in qualified deferred compensation plans, which are nondiscriminatory and ensure that employees receive the compensation promised to them. As the Commissioner forcefully argues, our original interpretation of I.R.C. § 404 undercut the essential purpose of that provision by violating the matching principle and creating a taxation scheme that favors the type of plan that Congress intended to discourage. For this reason, we granted the Commissioner's petition for rehearing. We now withdraw the portion of our earlier opinion that dealt with deferred compensation agreements, and affirm the Tax Court's decision, although not for the reasons upon which the Tax Court majority relied.

III. ANALYSIS

Albertson's again urges this court (1) to characterize the additional amounts as interest as defined by I.R.C. § 163(a), and (2) to find that such "interest" payments are deductible under I.R.C. § 404. However, we have now concluded that, notwithstanding the statutory language on which Albertson's relies, to hold the additional amounts to be deductible would contravene the clear purpose of the taxation scheme Congress created to govern deferred compensation plans. As the Supreme Court noted in *Bob Jones University v. United States*, 461 U.S. 574 (1983), a term in the Code "must be analyzed and construed within the framework of the Internal Revenue Code and against the background of the congressional purposes."

A. A Comparison of Qualified and Nonqualified Plans

An examination of the differences between qualified and nonqualified plans is essential to an understanding of the purpose of the congressional scheme governing deferred compensation agreements. Congress has imposed few restrictions upon nonqualified deferred compensation plans. An employer may limit participation in a nonqualified plan to highly paid executives, and it need not guarantee equal benefits for all participants. In addition, the employer is not required to set aside any funds or provide any guarantees (beyond the initial contractual promise) that its employees will receive the compensation. Thus, promised benefits for unfunded, nonqualified plans are subject to the claims of the employer's general creditors.

Under a qualified plan, in contrast, an employer may not discriminate in favor of officers, shareholders, or highly compensated employees. I.R.C. § 401(a)(4) & (a)(5). In addition, a qualified plan must satisfy minimum participation and coverage standards concerning eligibility and actual rates of participation. I.R.C §§ 401(a)(2) & (a)(26), 410. The amounts which an employer may contribute to qualified plans and the benefits which qualified plans may provide are also restricted. I.R.C. §§ 401(a)(17), 415.

A qualified plan also provides significant guarantees that employees will receive the compensation promised to them. It generally must be funded through a trust. I.R.C. § 401(a). Neither the corpus nor the income of the trust may be diverted for any purpose; they can only be used for the exclusive benefit of the participants. I.R.C. § 401(a)(2). Under certain qualified plans, the employer's contributions must meet strict funding requirements, and minimum standards govern the vesting of participants' benefits. I.R.C. §§ 401(a)(1) & (a)(7), 411, 412; *see also* 29 U.S.C. § 1082.

It is clear that few employers would adopt a qualified deferred compensation plan, with all of its burdensome requirements, if the taxation scheme favored nonqualified plans or treated nonqualified and qualified plans similarly. Although qualified plans provide significant benefits to employees, they allow employers little flexibility in structuring a plan, require them to provide extensive coverage, prevent them from discriminating in favor of highly compensated employees, and involve a significant initial outlay of funds. Thus, the extensive regulations Congress has imposed upon qualified plans would serve little purpose unless employers had an incentive to adopt such plans. As we discuss in the next part, section 404 provides the incentive necessary to encourage employers to adopt qualified plans by providing significantly more favorable tax treatment of qualified plans than of nonqualified ones.

QP get more favorable tax treatment

The most significant difference between the two types of plans, for purposes of tax deductibility, is that under a qualified plan the employer must turn over annually to a third party the basic amounts that are deferred and may not use those amounts for the employer's own benefit. Thus, the employer, in effect, is required to make the deferred payments at the time the employee is earning the compensation. It is only the employee's right to receive the funds that is delayed. In contrast, an employer with a nonqualified plan is not required to turn any funds over to anyone until the end of the deferred compensation period. Such an employer may use those funds for its own purposes for a period of many years. In a nonqualified plan, it is not only the employee's right to receive the funds that is deferred; the employer's obligation to part with the funds is deferred as well. If one could simply retain the funds and receive tax benefits similar to those one would receive if those amounts were paid out, there would clearly be little incentive to establish a qualified plan.

B. The Purpose of Section 404

Congress enacted section 23(p), the forerunner to section 404, in 1942. Prior to 1942, corporations were allowed to deduct [deferred compensation] expenses as they accrued each year, even though employees did not recognize any income until a subsequent taxable year. In 1942, Congress eliminated this favorable treatment for deductions relating to "nonqualified" deferred compensation agreements[]. In so doing, Congress forced employers who chose to retain their funds for their own use to wait until the end of the deferral period, when these amounts were includible in plan participants' taxable income, before they could take deductions for deferred compensation payments. However, employers who maintained a "qualified" plan that met the rigorous requirements of the Internal Revenue Code (and now ERISA), including turning over the sums involved to a trust fund (or purchasing an annuity), were allowed to continue to take the annual deductions even though their employees would not receive the deferred compensation until a later year.

1. The Matching Principle

Congress provided a single explanation for the timing restrictions of section 404: to ensure matching of income inclusion and deduction between employee and employer under nonqualified plans. As both the House and Senate Reports note, "if an employer on the accrual basis defers paying any compensation to the employee until a later year or years . . . he will not be allowed a deduction until the year in which the compensation is paid."

Commentators have widely agreed that this "matching principle" is the key to section 404. [Discussion omitted]

2. The Significance of the Matching Principle

The significance of section 404's matching principle becomes evident when one compares the treatment of qualified and nonqualified plans under that section. Because section 404 requires employer deductions for contributions to nonqualified plans to be "matched," an employer cannot take tax deductions for payments to its employees until the [employees] include those payments in their taxable income — that is, until the employees actually receive the compensation promised to them.

Qualified plans, in contrast, are not governed by the matching principle and consequently generate concurrent tax benefits to employers. Although employees are not taxed upon the benefits they receive from the plan until they actually receive them, an employer's contributions to a qualified plan are deductible when paid to the trust. I.R.C. §§ 402(a)(1) & 404(a). Thus, the employer may take an immediate, unmatched deduction for any contribution it makes to a qualified plan.

By exempting contributions to qualified plans from the matching principle, Congress compensates employers for meeting the burdensome requirements associated with qualified plans by granting them favorable tax treatment. The current taxation scheme thus creates financial incentives for employers to contribute to qualified plans while providing no comparable benefits for employers who adopt plans that are unfunded or that discriminate in favor of highly compensated employees.

C. The Effects of Albertson's Proposal

Albertson's maintains that section 404 only requires that the basic amounts of compensation be matched; it argues that all additional amounts paid to compensate an employee for the time value of money represent "interest" payments for which an employer may take an immediate deduction. In light of the clear purpose underlying section 404 — to encourage employers to create qualified plans for their employees — we decline to ascribe such an intention to Congress.

. . . Albertson's proposal appears to undermine the effectiveness of the timing restrictions by reducing the significance of the incentive structure created by section 404. In order to adopt Albertson's proposal and allow employers to take current deductions for additional "interest" payments, we would be required to conclude that Congress created a system in which employers could deduct a substantial portion of the nonqualified deferred compensation package long before its employees had received any of those funds. For example, when the additional amounts are calculated for a compensation package deferred over a fifteen-year period using an interest rate similar to that used by Albertson's, an employer can classify more than seventy percent of the deferred compensation package as "interest payments."

D. Albertson's Response

Albertson's has not been able to refute the argument that its interpretation of section 404 undercuts the provision's central purpose. Equally important, it offers us no reason why Congress would have wanted to treat the "interest" part of the deferred compensation package differently from the basic amounts for tax purposes.

Instead, Albertson's rests its argument upon its contention that, because the plain language of § 404 only refers to "compensation" rather than "interest," the employers have a statutory right to deduct the additional amounts as interest under § 163. In this connection, Albertson's points out that section 404 prohibits deduction under sections 162 and 212 but not under section 163, and it is the latter section that governs the deduction of interest. Albertson's argument as to the plain language of the statute is a strong one. We certainly agree that the additional payments resemble "interest" and that, under a literal reading of the statutory language, the deduction of interest is not affected by section 404. However, holding such payments to be deductible "interest" under section 404 would lead to an anomalous result: a taxation scheme designed to make nonqualified plans less attractive would in many cases provide incentives for adopting such plans, and a provision intended to apply the matching principle to nonqualified deferred compensation agreements would exempt substantial portions of [the employee's payments] from its application.

In the end we are forced, therefore, to reject Albertson's approach. We may not adopt a plain language interpretation of a statutory provision that directly undercuts the clear purpose of the statute. . . . In reaching our conclusion, we followed the Supreme Court's approach in *United States v. American Trucking Ass'ns.*, 310 U.S. 534 (1940). There the Court noted that "when [a given] meaning has led to absurd results . . . this Court has looked beyond the words to the purpose of the act. Frequently, however, even when the plain meaning did not produce absurd results but merely an unreasonable one" plainly at variance with the policy of the legislation as a whole,' this Court has followed that purpose, rather than the literal words. . . ."

In rejecting Albertson's appeal, we take heed of the Supreme Court's instructions concerning the proper interpretation of the Internal Revenue Code when the plain language of the provision leads to an unreasonable result and directly contradicts its underlying purpose: the provision "must be analyzed and construed within the framework of the Internal Revenue Code and against the background of the congressional purposes." For the reasons we have expressed, we conclude that, despite the literal wording of the statute, Congress could not have intended to exclude interest payments, a substantial part of the deferred compensation package, from the rule prohibiting deductions until such time as the employee receives the benefits. Indeed, the matching principle would not be much of a principle if so substantial a part of the deferred compensation package were excluded from its operation.

IV. CONCLUSION

In sum, we decline to adopt Albertson's interpretation of I.R.C. § 404. Whether or not the additional amounts constitute interest, allowing Albertson's to deduct them prior to their receipt by their employees would contravene the clear purpose of the taxation scheme governing deferred compensation agreements. Accordingly, we vacate the portion of our original opinion dealing with deferred compensation agreements and affirm the Tax Court's holding that Albertson's may not currently deduct the additional amounts.

The issue in *Albertson's, Inc.,* can be usefully looked at from the point of view of the various ways to indirectly tax a cash method employee on accrued income. Assume a 30% tax rate on both employer and employee. As the example in the text explains, if an employer is willing to set aside $100 compensation for an employee in year 0, and pay interest on the deferred amount (assume 10% is the going rate), the employee will be indirectly taxed on the accrued deferred compensation, *if* the employer cannot deduct the $100 and the interest until the employee is paid. Remember that the employee, without deferral of $100 compensation, would get $70 after-tax, which would accrue after-tax interest at 7% for two years — producing $80.143. If the employer loses a deduction, the employer will only set aside $70 and accrue interest at 7%, producing $80.143 after two years. Because the amount paid to the employee is now deductible, the employer in the 30% bracket will pay the employee $114.49, yielding the employee $80.143 (70% times $114.49) at an after-tax cost of $80.143 to the employer.

If the employer is allowed to accrue a deduction *for the interest* before payment to the employee, the employee will *not* be indirectly taxed on the $100 of year 0 accrued income. For example, the employer can set aside $70 after-tax, which accrues *10%* interest for two years — equal to $84.70, consisting of $70 plus $14.70 interest. When this amount is paid to the employee, the interest cannot be deducted again, but the rest of the payment will be deductible. Instead of $70, the employer in the 30% bracket will pay $100, plus the $14.70 of previously deducted interest, or a total of

$114.70 (which is more than the $114.49 that the employee should get). This leaves the employee, after 30% tax, with $80.29, instead of $80.143. This seems like a small amount only because the interest in this example accrued for only two years. If the interest had been tax-deferred for twenty years, the employee would end up with about 30% more in after-tax income than if the interest had not been tax-deferred.

CHAPTER 23

ACCRUAL METHOD

§ 23.01 INTRODUCTION

Income and deductions accrue when all events have occurred fixing the right or liability, except for the passage of time, and the amount can be determined with reasonable accuracy (the "all events" test). *Treas. Reg. § 1.446–1(c)(1)(ii).* When are all events "fixed"; when is there "reasonable accuracy"? What happens when cash is received or paid before a liability would otherwise have accrued? This Chapter addresses these questions, first with income and then with deduction items.

Relation of tax to financial accounting. Before answering these specific questions, read the following discussion from *Thor Power Tool Co. v. Commissioner,* 439 U.S. 522 (1979), about the differences between accrual under tax and financial accounting.

> The taxpayer's major argument [] is based on the Tax Court's clear finding that the [deduction] conformed to "generally accepted accounting principles." [Taxpayer] points to language in *Treas. Reg. § 1.446–1(a)(2),* to the effect that "[a] method of accounting which reflects the consistent application of generally accepted accounting principles . . . *will ordinarily be regarded* as clearly reflecting income" (emphasis added) . . . . These provisions, [taxpayer] contends, created a presumption that an inventory practice conformable to "generally accepted accounting principles" is valid for income tax purposes. Once a taxpayer has established this conformity, the argument runs, the burden shifts to the Commissioner affirmatively to demonstrate that the taxpayer's method does not reflect income clearly. Unless the Commissioner can show that a generally accepted method "demonstrably distorts income," or that the taxpayer's adoption of such method was "motivated by tax avoidance," the presumption in the taxpayer's favor will carry the day . . . .
>
> . . . We believe [] that no such presumption is present. Its existence is insupportable in light of the statute, the Court's past decisions, and the differing objectives of tax and financial accounting.
>
> First, . . . § 1.446–1(a)(2) of the Regulations states categorically that "no method of accounting is acceptable unless, in the opinion of the

Com'ner decides what is an acceptable method

Commissioner, it clearly reflects income" (emphasis added). Most importantly, the Code and Regulations give the Commissioner broad discretion to set aside the taxpayer's method if, "in [his] opinion," it does not reflect income clearly. This language is completely at odds with the notion of a "presumption" in the taxpayer's favor. The Regulations embody no presumption; they say merely that, in most cases, generally accepted accounting practices will pass muster for tax purposes. And in most cases they will. But if the Commissioner, in the exercise of his discretion, determines that they do not, he may prescribe a different practice without having to rebut any presumption running against the Treasury.

(2) *case law*

Second, the presumption [taxpayer] postulates finds no support in this Court's prior decisions "[W]e are mindful that the characterization of a transaction for financial accounting purposes, on the one hand, and for tax purposes, on the other, need not necessarily be the same." *Frank Lyon Co. v. United States,* 435 U.S. 561, 577 (1978). *See Commissioner of Internal Revenue v. Idaho Power Co.,* 418 U.S. 1, 15 (1974). Indeed, the Court's cases demonstrate that divergence between tax and financial accounting is especially common when a taxpayer seeks a current deduction for estimated future expenses or losses. *E.g., Commissioner of Internal Revenue v. Hansen,* 360 U.S. 446 (1959) (reserve to cover contingent liability in event of nonperformance of guarantee); *Brown v. Helvering,* 291 U.S. 193 (1934) (reserve to cover expected liability for unearned commissions on anticipated insurance policy cancellations)

(3) *financial tax acctg*

Third, the presumption petitioner postulates is insupportable in light of the vastly different objectives that financial and tax accounting have. The primary goal of financial accounting is to provide useful information to management, shareholders, creditors, and others properly interested; the major responsibility of the accountant is to protect these parties from being misled. The primary goal of the income tax system, in contrast, is the equitable collection of revenue; the major responsibility of the Internal Revenue Service is to protect the public fisc. Consistently with its goals and responsibilities, financial accounting has as its foundation the principle of conservatism, with its corollary that "possible errors in measurement [should] be in the direction of understatement rather than overstatement of net income and net assets." In view of the Treasury's markedly different goals and responsibilities understatement of income is not destined to be its guiding light. Given this diversity, even contrariety, of objectives, any presumptive equivalency between tax and financial accounting would be unacceptable.

This difference in objectives is mirrored in numerous differences of treatment. Where the tax law requires that a deduction be deferred until "all the events" have occurred that will make it fixed and certain, *United States v. Anderson,* 269 U.S. 422, 441 (1926), accounting principles typically require that a liability be accrued as soon as it can reasonably be estimated. Conversely, where the tax law requires that income be recognized currently under "claim of right," "ability to pay," and "control" rationales, accounting principles may defer accrual until a later year so that revenues and expenses may be better matched. Financial accounting, in short, is hospitable to estimates, probabilities, and reasonable certainties; the tax law, with its mandate to preserve the revenue, can give no quarter to uncertainty. This is as it should be. Reasonable estimates may be useful, even essential, in giving shareholders and creditors an accurate picture of a firm's overall financial health; but the accountant's conservatism cannot bind the Commissioner in his efforts to collect taxes. "Only a few reserves voluntarily established as a matter of conservative accounting," Mr. Justice Brandeis wrote for the Court, "are authorized by the Revenue Acts." *Brown v. Helvering,* 291 U.S., at 201–202.

Finally, a presumptive equivalency between tax and financial accounting would create insurmountable difficulties of tax administration. Accountants long have recognized that "generally accepted accounting principles" are far from being a canonical set of rules that will ensure identical accounting treatment of identical transactions. "Generally accepted accounting principles," rather, tolerate a range of "reasonable" treatments, leaving the choice among alternatives to management. . . . Variances of this sort may be tolerable in financial reporting, but they are questionable in a tax system designed to ensure as far as possible that similarly situated taxpayers pay the same tax. If management's election among "acceptable" options were dispositive for tax purposes, a firm, indeed, could decide unilaterally — within limits dictated only by its accountants — the tax it wished to pay. Such unilateral decisions would not just make the Code inequitable; they would make it unenforceable.

§ 23.02 INCOME ITEMS

What principles do courts use to decide whether income should be accrued — preventing mismatches between income and deductions; preventing manipulation by a taxpayer of the year of recognition; avoiding administrative problems in deciding whether and how much to accrue; anything else? Do any of these principles conflict?

[A]—No cash received

In the following cases you are almost certain to have trouble coming up with a clear rule about how the "all events" test is applied to accrue income items. Do you find a distinction based on uncertainty regarding the liability vs. uncertainty regarding the amount of the claim? If so, do you think the distinction makes sense?

CONTINENTAL TIE & LUMBER CO. v. UNITED STATES

286 U.S. 290 (1932)

MR. JUSTICE ROBERTS delivered the opinion of the Court.

. . . The railway company [petitioner] is a short-line carrier whose road was in possession and control of the United States and operated by the Director General of Railroads from December 28, 1917, to June 3, 1918, when it was relinquished, and thereafter throughout the remainder of the period of federal control operated by its owner. Approximately $ 25,000 of the additional income determined by the Commissioner consisted of a payment to the railway pursuant to an award of the Interstate Commerce Commission under the terms of section 204 of the Transportation Act 1920. This section provided for such an award and payment to a railroad which during any part of the period of federal control competed for traffic, or connected, with one under federal control, and sustained a deficit in operating income for that portion of the period during which it operated its own railroad. The act directed the Commission to compare the results of such operation with those of the test period, defined as the three years ending June 30, 1917; and, if less favorable during the period of federal control than during the test period, to award an amount calculated as prescribed by the section. The Commission made an award and the Secretary of the Treasury paid the railway.

The petitioner asserted [] that the sum received . . . was not taxable for 1920, as held by the Commissioner, but for 1923, the year in which the amount was determined and paid . . . .

The petitioner kept its accounts upon the accrual basis. The government insists, and the Court of Claims held, that the right to payment having ripened in 1920, the taxpayer should have returned the estimated award under section 204 as income for that year. The petitioner replies that a determination whether it would receive any award under the section and, if so, the amount of it, depended on so many contingencies that no reasonable estimate could have been made in 1920, and that the sum ultimately ascertained should be deemed income for 1923, the year of the award and payment.

The Transportation Act took effect on February 28, 1920. On June 10 the Interstate Commerce Commission issued general instructions governing the compilation and submission of data by carriers entitled to awards under section 204. The petitioner correctly states that at the date of the act's adoption no railroad had a vested right in any amount; until the Commission made an award nothing could be paid, no proceeding was available to compel an allowance, or to determine the elements which should enter into the calculation. In short, says the petitioner, the carrier had no rights, but was dependent solely upon the Commission's exercise of an unrestrained discretion, and until an award was made nothing accrued. But we think that the function of the Commission under the act was ministerial, to ascertain the facts with respect to the carrier's operating income by a comparison of the experience during the test period with that during the term of federal control. The right to the award was fixed by the passage of the Transportation Act. What remained was mere administrative procedure to ascertain the amount to be paid. Petitioner's right to payment ripened when the act became law. What sum of money that right represented is, of course, a different matter.

The petitioner says that at the date of the passage of the act it was impossible to predict that any award would be made to the railway, and, assuming one would eventuate, its amount could not be estimated, for the reason that the principles upon which awards were to be made had to be settled by the Commission and were not finally formulated until 1923. The government insists that, while adjustments or settlement of principles by the Commission might vary the amount to be awarded, the petitioner's case presented problems not differing from those confronting many business concerns which keep accounts on an accrual basis and have to estimate for the tax year the amount to be received on transactions undoubtedly allocable to such year. Admitting there might be differences and discrepancies between the railway's estimate and the amount awarded by the Commission, these, says the government, could, as in similar cases, have been adjusted by an additional assessment or a claim for refund after final determination of the amount due.

The case does not fall within the principle that, where the liability is undetermined in the tax year, the taxpayer is not called upon to accrue any sum (*Lucas v. American Code Co.*, 280 U. S. 445), but presents the problem whether the taxpayer had in its own books and accounts data to which it could apply the calculations required by the statute and ascertain the quantum of the award within reasonable limits.

The carriers kept their accounts according to standards prescribed by the Commission; and these necessarily were the source of information requisite for ascertainment of the results of operation in the two periods to be compared. In the calculation for two such brief periods allowance had to be made for the fact that certain operating charges entered in the books would not accurately reflect true income. Such, for instance, were maintenance charges and those to reserve accounts. The enormous increase in labor and material costs after the expiration of the test period had also to be considered in comparing charges for costs of repairs and renewals in the two periods. Section 204 incorporated by reference the terms of section 209 applicable to the method of treating such items, and the latter in turn referred to the relevant provisions of section 5(a) of the standard operating contract between the Director General and the various railroads. As might have been expected, the general principles thus formulated did not cover in detail questions of fact, the solution of which required is some degree the exercise of opinion and judgment. Thus difference might fairly arise as to when reserve accounts ought to be closed out, as to how much of the sum actually expended for maintenance within a given time was properly allocable to that period, and how much to later years; at what price renewals and replacements should be charged in view of the rapidly mounting cost of material; what factor of difference should be allowed for the efficiency of labor in the pre-war and postwar periods. The petitioner points to the fact that these questions were raised by the railroads under section 209, that the Commission gave extended consideration to them, and that, as respects sundry of them, the applicable principles were not settled until 1921, 1922, and 1923. Petitioner might have added that the Commission, while attempting as far as possible to formulate general principles applicable to large groups of carriers, found it necessary in addition to consider the peculiar conditions and special circumstances affecting individual carriers in order in each case to do justice to the carrier and to the United States. But in spite of these inherent difficulties we think it was possible for a carrier to ascertain with reasonable accuracy the amount of the award to be paid by the Government. Subsequent to its order of June 10, 1920, the Commission made no amendment or alteration of the rules with respect to the information to be furnished under section 204. Obviously the data had to be obtained from the railway's books and accounts and from entries therein all made prior to March 1, 1920. These accounts contained all the information that could ever be available touching relevant expenditures. The petitioner was promptly informed by the terms of section 209, as supplemented by the instructions issued by the Commission, of the method to be followed in allocating charges to operation during periods under inquiry. It does not appear that a proper effort would not have obtained a result approximately in accord with that the Commission ultimately found.

Much is made by the petitioner of the fact that, as a result of representations by the carriers, the Commission from time to time during 1921, 1922, and 1923 promulgated rulings respecting the method of adjusting book charges to actual experience, and it is asserted that petitioner could not in 1920 have known what these rulings were to be. But it is not clear that, if the taxpayer had acted promptly, an award could not have been made during 1920, or at least the principles upon which the Commission would adjust the railway's accounts to reflect true income have been settled during that year sufficiently to enable the railway to ascertain with reasonable accuracy the amount of the probable award. . . .

GLOBE CORPORATION v. COMMISSIONER

20 T.C. 299 (1953)

[Editor — Taxpayer manufactured aerial target assemblies for the government. The price paid for packaging and preservation services was to be negotiated after delivery, with provision for appeal to the head of the government department if negotiations failed. Items were delivered in 1945, and taxpayer submitted a $ 165,893.07 bill for services, which was questioned by the government. A settlement was reached in 1946 for $ 75,525.92, attributable to the 1945 deliveries. The court does not accrue the income in 1945. Is the decision distinguishable from *Continental Tie?*]

BRUCE, JUDGE: . . .

. . . Petitioner kept its books and filed its income tax returns on the calendar year basis and the accrual method of accounting. The sole question presented therefore is whether the income in question accrued within the year 1945 as contended by respondent, or in 1946 as contended by petitioner . . . .

The situation here presented is not to be confused with that in *Dumari Textile Co.,* 47 B.T.A. 639, *aff'd,* 142 F.2d 897, relied on by respondent. In that case the taxpayer, on the accrual basis, was reimbursed in 1938 for a processing tax burden borne by it on account of the floor stock tax. Payment was made to taxpayer pursuant to section 602 of the Revenue Act of 1936. The Board held, following *Continental Tie & Lumber Co. v. United States,* 286 U.S. 290, that the payment received by taxpayer in 1938 accrued in 1936 because the right to the payment ripened when the statute authorizing it was enacted. The Board stated in its opinion:

The statute provided that:

> "There shall be paid to any person who, at the first moment of January 6, 1936, held for sale or other disposition . . . any article

> processed . . . from a commodity subject to processing tax, an amount computed as provided in subsection (b), . . ." Thus, the payment under this section was mandatory if petitioner held any article within the scope of the section. The right to receive the payment was not contingent on any future event. *Everything had happened which could have happened from which to determine the amount of the payment.* There remained only the necessity of filing the claim and proving the facts to the Commissioner of Internal Revenue for petitioner to become entitled to the payment. These requirements, obviously, had no bearing on when the payment accrued since they did not affect the *amount.* [Emphasis supplied.]

The Board went on to say: "This was purely a matter of computation under the express direction of the statute." Both the *Dumari Textile Co.* and *Continental Tie & Lumber Co.* cases are distinguishable from the situation before us in that here more than a mere calculation or computation was required to fix the amount to be accrued. Rather there remained a negotiation between the parties upon terms not as yet agreed upon. There was no formula, method, or particular data which both could accept as the basis of the final agreement. Also the amount finally arrived at as the fair and just compensation to be paid was required to be set forth in an amendment to the contract before payment could be made.

Thus we conclude from the whole record that petitioner was not able to ascertain with reasonable accuracy the amount to accrue until 1946 when the negotiations were completed and the change orders or amendments were executed. That amount was, therefore, not fixed and definite until 1946, at which time it was properly accrued. Such accrual is not precluded by the fact that the items of cost, representing labor, material, and overhead, pertaining to these items were accrued by petitioner in 1945 and reflected in the computation of taxable income for that year. As to such amounts, liability and amount were fixed in that year.

COMMENTS AND QUESTIONS

1. In *Lucas v. North Texas Lumber Co.,* 281 U.S. 11 (1930), the seller and buyer entered into an executory contract to sell timber land on December 30, 1916. The buyer declared itself ready to close the transaction and pay the purchase price "as soon as the papers were prepared." The

seller-taxpayer did not prepare the papers necessary to effect the transfer or make tender of title or possession or demand the purchase price in 1916. Tax was lower in 1916 than 1917 so the taxpayer argued for 1916 accrual. The Court disagreed, stating:

> . . . The title and right of possession remained in [the seller] until the transaction was closed. Consequently unconditional liability of vendee for the purchase price was not created in that year. The entry of the purchase price in respondent's accounts as income in that year was not warranted. Respondent was not entitled to make return or have the tax computed on that basis, as clearly it did not reflect 1916 income.

HOLDING:

Does the decision in *North Texas Lumber* give taxpayers too much control over when to report income? Notice that the taxpayer (unusually) wanted to report income in an earlier year.

2. The cases obviously have difficulty figuring out when uncertainty prevents accrual. In one situation, the statute deals specifically with this issue. *§ 448(d)(5)* prevents accrual of any portion of personal service income which experience indicates will not be collected, *but only if* there is no interest or penalty for untimely payment.

[B]—Cash received

[i] American Automobile Ass'n v. United States

AMERICAN AUTOMOBILE ASS'N v. UNITED STATES

367 U.S. 687 (1961)

MR. JUSTICE CLARK delivered the opinion of the Court.

In this suit for refund of federal income taxes the petitioner, American Automobile Association, seeks determination of its tax liability for the years 1952 and 1953. Returns filed for its taxable calendar years were prepared on the basis of the same accrual method of accounting as was used in keeping its books. The Association reported as gross income only that portion of the total prepaid annual membership dues, actually received or collected in the calendar year, which ratably corresponded with the number of membership months covered by those dues and occurring within the same taxable calendar year. The balance was reserved for ratable monthly accrual over the remaining membership period in the following calendar year as deferred or unearned income reflecting an estimated future service expense to members. The Commissioner contends that petitioner should have reported in its gross income for each year the entire amount of membership dues actually received in the taxable calendar year without regard to expected future service expense in the subsequent year. The sole point at issue, therefore, is in what year the prepaid dues are taxable as income.

IRS:

(Matthew Bender & Co., Inc.) (Pub. 870)

issue: in what yr. are prepaid dues taxable?

In auditing the Association's returns for the years 1952 through 1954, the Commissioner, in the exercise of his discretion under § 41 of the Internal Revenue Code of 1939 [Editor — Now § 446], determined not to accept the taxpayer's accounting system. As a result, adjustments were made for those years principally by adding to gross income for each taxable year the amount of prepaid dues which the Association had received but not recognized as income, and subtracting from gross income amounts recognized in the year although actually received in the prior year.

. . . For many years, the association has employed an accrual method of accounting and the calendar year as its taxable year. It is admitted that for its purposes the method used is in accord with generally accepted commercial accounting principles. The membership dues, as received, were deposited in the Association's bank accounts without restriction as to their use for any of its corporate purposes. However, for the Association's own accounting purposes, the dues were treated in its books as income received ratably over the 12-month membership period. The portions thereof ratably attributable to membership months occurring beyond the year of receipt, *i.e.,* in a second calendar year, were reflected in the Association's books at the close of the first year as unearned or deferred income. Certain operating expenses were chargeable as prepaid membership cost and deducted ratably over the same periods of time as those over which dues were recognized as income.

The Court of Claims bottomed its opinion on *Automobile Club of Michigan v. Commissioner,* 1957, 353 U.S. 180, finding that "the method of treatment of prepaid automobile club membership dues employed (by the Association here was,) . . . for Federal income tax purposes,'purely artificial.' " 181 F. Supp. 255, 258. It accepted that case as "a rejection by the Supreme Court of the accounting method advanced by plaintiff in the case at bar." *Ibid.* The Association does not deny that its accounting system is substantially identical to that used by the petitioner in *Michigan.* It maintains, however, that *Michigan* does not control this case because of a difference in proof, *i.e.,* that in this case the record contains expert accounting testimony indicating that the system used was in accord with generally accepted accounting principles; that its proof of cost of member service was detailed; and that the correlation between that cost and the period of time over which the dues were credited as income was shown and justified by proof of experience. The holding of *Michigan,* however, that the system of accounting was "purely artificial" was based upon the finding that "substantially all services are performed only upon a member's demand and the taxpayer's performance was not related to fixed dates after the tax year." 353 U.S. 180, 189, note 20. That is also true here . . . .

The Association further contends that the findings of the court below support its position. We think not. The Court of Claims' only finding as to the accounting system itself is as follows:

> "22. The method of accounting employed by plaintiff during the years in issue has been used regularly by plaintiff since 1931 and is in accord with generally accepted commercial accounting principles and practices, and was, prior to the adverse determination by the Commissioner of the Internal Revenue, customarily and generally employed in the motor club field."

This is only to say that in performing the function of business accounting the method employed by the Association "is in accord with generally accepted commercial accounting principles and practices." It is not to hold that for income tax purposes it so clearly reflects income as to be binding on the Treasury. Likewise, other findings merely reflecting statistical computations of average monthly cost per member on a group or pool basis are without determinate significance to our decision that the federal revenue cannot, without legislative consent and over objection of the Commissioner, be made to depend upon average experience in rendering performance and turning a profit. Indeed, such tabulations themselves demonstrate the inadequacy from an income tax standpoint of the pro rata method of allocating each year's membership dues in equal monthly installments not in fact related to the expenses incurred. Not only did individually incurred expenses actually vary from month to month, but even the average expense varied — recognition of income nonetheless remaining ratably constant. Although the findings below seem to indicate that it would produce substantially the same result as that of the system of ratable monthly recognition actually employed, we consider similarly unsatisfactory, from an income tax standpoint, allocation of monthly dues to gross monthly income to the extent of actual service expenditures for the same month computed on a group or pool basis. . . .

Whether or not the Court's judgment in *Michigan* controls our disposition of this case, there are other considerations requiring our affirmance. They concern the action of the Congress with respect to its own positive and express statutory authorization of employment of such sound commercial accounting practices in reporting taxable income. In 1954 the Congress found dissatisfaction in the fact that as a result of court decisions and rulings, there have developed many divergencies between the computation of income for tax purposes and income for business purposes as computed under generally accepted accounting principles . . . . As a result, it introduced into the Internal Revenue Code of 1954 § 452 and § 462, which specifically permitted essentially the same practice as was employed by the Association here. Only one year later, however, in June 1955, the Congress repealed these sections retroactively. It appears that in this action Congress first overruled the long administrative practice of the Commissioner and holdings of the courts in disallowing such deferral of income for tax purposes and then within a year reversed its own action. This repeal, we believe, confirms our view that the method used by the Association could be rejected by the Commissioner. While the claim is made that Congress did not "intend to disturb prior law as it affected permissible accrual accounting provisions for tax purposes," H.R. Rep. No. 293, 84th Cong., 1st Sess. 4–5, the could fact is that it repealed the only law incontestably permitting the practice upon which the Association depends. To say that, as to taxpayers using such systems, Congress was merely declaring existing law when it adopted § 452 in 1954, and that it was merely restoring unaffected the same prior law when it repealed the new section in 1955 for good reason, is a contradiction in itself, "varnishing nonsense with the charm of sound." Instead of constituting a merely duplicative creation, the fact is that § 452 for the first time specifically declared petitioner's system of accounting to be acceptable for income tax purposes, and overruled the long-standing position of the Commissioner and courts to the contrary. And the repeal of the section the following year, upon insistence by the Treasury that the proposed endorsement of such tax accounting would have a disastrous impact on the Government's revenue, was just as clearly a mandate from the Congress that petitioner's system was not acceptable for tax purposes. To interpret its careful consideration of the problem otherwise is to accuse the Congress of engaging in sciamachy. We are further confirmed in this view by consideration of the even more recent action of the Congress in 1958, subsequent to the decision in *Michigan, supra.* In that year § 455 was added to the Internal Revenue Code of 1954. It permits publishers to defer receipt as income of prepaid subscriptions of newspapers, magazines and periodicals. An effort was made in the Senate to add a provision in § 455 which would extend its coverage to prepaid automobile club membership dues. However, in conference the House Conferees refused to accept this amendment. Senator Byrd explained the rejection of the amendment to the Senate (104 Cong. Rec., Part 14, p. 17744):

> "It was the position of the House conferees that this matter of prepaid dues and fees received by nonprofit service organizations was a part of the entire subject dealing with the treatment of prepaid income and that such subject should be left for study of this entire problem . . . ."

It appears, therefore, that, pending its own further study, Congress has given publishers but denied automobile clubs the very relief that the Association seeks in this Court.

To recapitulate, it appears that Congress has long been aware of the problem this case presents. In 1954 it enacted § 452 and § 462, but quickly repealed them. Since that time Congress has authorized the desired accounting only in the instance of prepaid subscription income, which, as was pointed out in *Michigan,* is ratably earned by performance on "publication dates after the tax year." 353 U.S. 180, 189, note 20. It has refused to enlarge § 455 to include prepaid membership dues. At the very least, this background indicates congressional recognition of the complications inherent in the problem and its seriousness to the general revenue. We must leave to the Congress the fashioning of a rule which, in any event, must have wide ramifications. The Committees of the Congress have standing committees expertly grounded in tax problems, with jurisdiction covering the whole field of taxation and facilities for studying considerations of policy as between the various taxpayers and the necessities of the general revenues. The validity of the long-established policy of the Court in deferring, where possible, to congressional procedures in the tax field is clearly indicated in this case. Finding only that, in light of existing provisions not specifically authorizing it, the exercise of the Commissioner's discretion in rejecting the Association's accounting system was not unsound, we need not anticipate what will be the product of further "study of this entire problem."

Affirmed.

MR. JUSTICE STEWART, whom MR. JUSTICE DOUGLAS, MR. JUSTICE HARLAN and MR. JUSTICE WHITTAKER join, dissenting.

In *Automobile Club of Michigan* the Court pointed out that the method of accounting employed by the taxpayer was "purely artificial," so far as the record there showed. Here, by contrast, the petitioner proved, and the Court of Claims found, that the method of accounting employed by the petitioner during the years in issue was in accord with generally accepted commercial accounting principles and practice, was customarily employed by similar taxpayers, and, in the opinion of qualified experts in the accounting field, clearly reflected the petitioner's net income. I do not understand that the Court today questions either that proof or those findings.

The Court thus holds that the Commissioner is authorized to disregard and override a method of reporting income under which prepaid dues are deferred in direct relation to the taxpayer's costs under its membership contracts. The effect of the Court's decision is to allow the Commissioner to prevent an accrual basis taxpayer from making returns in accordance with the accepted and clearly valid accounting practice of excluding from gross income amounts received as advances until the right to such amounts is earned by rendition of the services for which the advances were made. To permit the Commissioner to do this, I think, is to ignore the clear statutory command that a taxpayer must be allowed to make his returns in accord with his regularly employed method of accounting, so long as that method clearly reflects his income.

The result, I am afraid, will be to engender far-reaching confusion and injustice in the administration of the Internal Revenue Laws. . . .

As to the enactment and repeal of § 452 and § 462, upon which the Court places so much reliance, there are, at the outset, obvious difficulties in relying on what happened in 1954 and 1955 to ascertain the meaning of § 41 of the 1939 Code. [Editor — now *§ 446*.] But these problems aside, I think that the enactment and subsequent repeal of § 452 and § 462 give no indication of Congressional approval of the position taken by the Commissioner in this case. If anything, the legislative action leads to the contrary impression.

[Editor — The dissent explains that these statutory provisions permitted the taxpayer to change to an accounting method which deferred prepaid income and accrued estimated expenses without getting the Commissioner's permission and that this could create a large revenue loss. The loss would occur because, in the year when these statutory provisions went into effect, prepaid income could be deferred but expenses attributable both to prepaid income taxed in prior years and to estimated future expenses would be deductible. The repeal of these provisions was meant to prevent this loss, but not to prevent deferral of prepaid income under a consistent method of accounting which did not create revenue loss potential. There was even legislative history explicitly stating that "the Treasury Department will not consider the repeal of section 452 as any indication of congressional intent as to the proper treatment for prepaid subscriptions and other items of prepaid income, either under prior law or under other provisions of the 1954 code."]

The net effect of compelling the petitioner to include all dues in gross income in the year received is to force the petitioner to utilize a hybrid accounting method — a cash basis for dues and an accrual basis for all other items. For taxpayers generally the enforcement of such a hybrid accounting method may result in a gross distortion of actual income, particularly in the first and last years of doing business. On the return for the first year in which advances are received, a taxpayer will have to report an unrealistically high net income, since he will have to include unearned receipts, without any offsetting deductions for the future cost of earning those receipts. On subsequent tax returns, each year's unearned prepayments will be partially offset by the deduction of current expenses attributable to prepayments taxed in prior years. Even then, however, if the taxpayer is forbidden to correlate earnings with related expenditures, the result will be a distortion of normal fluctuations in the taxpayer's net income. For example, in a year when there are low current expenditures because of fewer advances received in the preceding year, the result may be an inflated adjusted gross income for the current year. Finally, should the taxpayer decide to go out of business upon fulfillment of the contractual obligations already undertaken, in the final year there will be no advances to report and many costs attributable to advances received in prior years. The result will be a grossly unrealistic reportable net loss.

The Court suggests that the application of sound accrual principles cannot be accepted here because deferment is based on an estimated rate of earnings, and because this estimate, in turn, is based on average, not individual, costs. It is true, of course, that the petitioner cannot know what service an individual member will require or when he will demand it. Accordingly, in determining the portion of its outstanding contractual obligations which have been discharged during a particular period (and hence the portion of receipts earned during that period), the petitioner can only compare the total expenditures for that period against estimated average expenditures for the same number of members over a full contract term. But this use of estimates and averages is in no way inconsistent with long-accepted accounting practices in reflecting and reporting income.

As the Government has pointed out in past litigation, "many business concerns . . . keep accounts on an accural basis and have to estimate for the tax year the amount to be received on transactions undoubtedly allocable to such year." *Continental Tie & Lumber Co. v. United States,* 286 U.S. 290, 295–296. Similarly, the deduction of future expenditures which have already accured often requires estimates like those involved here. Finally, it is to be noted that the regulations under both the 1939 and 1954 Codes permit various methods of reporting income which require the use of estimates. In the absence of any showing that the estimates used here were faulty, I think the law did not permit the Commissioner to forbid the use of standard accrual methods simply upon the ground that estimates were necessary to determine what the rate of deferral should be.

Similarly, it is not relevant that the petitioner "defers receipt . . . of dues to a taxable period in which no, some, or all the services paid for by those dues may or may not be rendered." The fact of the matter is that what the petitioner has an obligation to provide, *i.e.,* the constant readiness of services if needed, will with certainty be provided during the period to which deferment has been made. Averages are frequently utilized in tax reporting. In computing the value of work in process, in distributing overhead to product cost, and in various other areas, the use of averages has long been accepted. The use of an "average cost" is particularly appropriate here where the dues are earned by making services continuously available. The cost of doing so must necessarily be based on composite figures.

For these reasons I think that the petitioner's original returns clearly reflected its income, that the Commissioner was therefore without authority under the law to override the petitioner's accounting method, and that the judgment should be reversed.

QUESTIONS — STATUTORY INTERPRETATIONS

1. How can legislative action taken in 1954 and 1955, after the tax years at issue, influence interpretation of a prior law?

2. Even assuming that later legislation is relevant regarding prior law, does congressional permission in 1954 to defer prepaid income imply that prior law did not allow it? Don't people (and legislatures) sometimes affirm something for the future, without any implication about prior rules?

3. Can we learn anything about taxing prepaid income generally from the fact that, in 1958, Congress permitted publishers to defer prepaid income in *§ 455*?

[ii] Post-AAA Developments

The *AAA* case has not been the last word on deferring prepaid income.

Case law. In *Artnell v. Commissioner,* 400 F.2d 981 (7th Cir. 1968), advance payments for baseball tickets could be deferred because, unlike *AAA,* the performances had to occur on fixed future dates. *See also RCA Corp. v. United States,* 499 F. Supp. 507 (D.N.Y. 1980), *rev'd and remanded,* 664 F.2d 881 (2d Cir. 1981) (lower court had accepted statistical estimates of rate of future performance of service/repair contract as basis for deferring prepaid income).

Statute. In addition to § 455 dealing with publishers, *see § 456* (defer prepaid membership dues, overruling *AAA* on its facts beginning in 1960); *§ 458* (defer prepaid sales proceeds for certain returnable items). Notice that the deferral period permitted by statute is usually short. *§§ 456(e)(2), 458(b)(7).*

Agency rules. In a limited number of situations, the IRS gives up the advantage it won in *AAA,* and permits deferral of prepaid income. *Treas. Reg. § 1.451-5* (deferral of prepaid income on certain inventory sales) is one example. The following Revenue Procedure is another.

REV. PROC. 71-21, 1971-2 C.B. 549

Sec. 2. Background

In general, tax accounting requires that payments received for services to be performed in the future must be included in gross income in the taxable year of receipt. However, this treatment varies from financial accounting conventions consistently used by many accrual method taxpayers in the treatment of payments received in one taxable year for services to be performed by them in the next succeeding taxable year. The purpose of this Revenue Procedure is to reconcile the tax and financial accounting treatment of such payments in a large proportion of these cases without permitting extended deferral in the time of including such payments in gross income for Federal income tax purposes. Such reconciliation will facilitate reporting and verification of such items from the standpoint of both the taxpayers affected and the Internal Revenue Service.

Sec. 3 Permissible Methods

.01 An accrual method taxpayer who receives a payment for services to be performed by him in the future and who includes such payment in gross income in the year of receipt is using a proper method of accounting.

.02 An accrual method taxpayer who, pursuant to an agreement (written or otherwise), receives a payment in one taxable year for services, where all of the services under such agreement are required by the agreement as it exists at the end of the taxable year or receipt to be performed by him before the end of the next succeeding taxable year, may include such payment in gross income as earned through the performance of the services, subject to [certain] limitations . . . . However, if the inclusion in gross income of payments received is properly deferred under the preceding sentence and for any reason a portion of such services is not performed by the end of the next succeeding taxable year, the amount allocable to the services not so performed must be included in gross income in such next succeeding year, regardless of when (if ever) such services are performed.

.03 . . . [A] payment received by an accrual method taxpayer pursuant to an agreement for the performance by him of services must be included in his gross income in the taxable year of receipt if under the terms of the agreement as it exists at the end of such year:

(a) Any portion of the services is to be performed by him after the end of the taxable year immediately succeeding the year of receipt; or

(b) Any portion of the services is to be performed by him at an unspecified future date which may be after the end of the taxable year immediately succeeding the year of receipt . . . .

.06 In any case in which an advance payment is received pursuant to an agreement which requires the taxpayer to perform contingent services, the amount of an advance payment which is earned in a taxable year through the performance of such services may be determined (a) on a statistical basis if adequate data are available to the taxpayer; (b) on a straight-line ratable basis over the time period of the agreement if it is not unreasonable to anticipate at the end of the taxable year of receipt that a substantially ratable portion of the services will be performed in the next succeeding taxable year; or (c) by the use of any other basis that in the opinion of the Commissioner, results in a clear reflection of income.

.11 The amount of any advance payment includible as gross receipts in gross income in the taxable year of receipt by a taxpayer under the foregoing rules shall be no less than the amount of such payment included as gross receipts in gross income for purposes of his books and records and all reports (including consolidated financial statements) to shareholders, partners, other proprietors or beneficiaries and for credit purposes.

limitation

financial stmts

.12 The above rules may be illustrated in part as follows:

(1) On November 1, 1970, A, a calendar year accrual method taxpayer in the business of giving dancing lessons, receives a payment for a one-year contract commencing on that date which provides for 48 individual, one-hour lessons. Eight lessons are provided in 1970. Under the method prescribed in section 3.02, A must include 1/6 of the payment in income for 1970, and 5/6 of such payment in 1971, regardless of whether A is for any reason unable to give all the lessons under the contract by the end of 1971.

(2) Assume the same facts as in Example 1 except that the payment is received for a two-year contract commencing on November 1, 1970, under which 96 lessons are provided. The taxpayer must include the entire payment in his gross income in 1970 since a portion of the services may be performed in 1972 . . . .

In *Barnett Banks of Florida, Inc. v. Commissioner*, 106 T.C. 103 (1996), the taxpayer asked the court to apply *Rev. Proc. 71–21* to a company's receipt of annual credit card fees. The government argued that the fees were for extension of credit in the nature of additional interest or loan commitment fees and that, even if they were for services, the taxpayer should not be allowed to rely on *Rev. Proc. 71–21* to defer the income. The court held that the payments were for services, eligible for deferral under *Rev. Proc. 71–21*. The services included loss-protection for cardholders who lost their wallets or purses; life insurance in conjunction with the use of the card to purchase an airline ticket; and rental car insurance provided when the cardholder charged the rental to the card.

The court also noted that, if the card issuer canceled the card, the taxpayer refunded the annual fee on a pro rata basis for the remaining months in the one-year period. It distinguished *Signet Banking Corp. v. Commissioner*, 106 T.C. 117 (1996), which held for the government, on the ground that the cardholder agreement in that case provided that the membership fee was nonrefundable. It is unclear why refundability is relevant (*Rev. Proc. 71–21* does not talk about refundability), unless it goes to the question of whether the payment is for services or an extension of credit in the first place — that is, a refund suggests that the fee is for services.

The court rejected the government's argument that the Revenue Procedure should not be applied to the service income, because that would be "an abuse of [administrative] discretion." The case is especially interesting as an example of holding the IRS to its published rules, even though they are not Regulations, under an "abuse of discretion" standard.

[iii] Discussion

Loans vs. prepaid income. Why should the government ever be concerned with preventing deferral of prepaid income? After all, not all cash is taxable when received. Loans are not taxed because there is a corresponding repayment obligation. How does prepaid income differ from a loan? Assume a taxpayer receives $ 100 in year 1, and expects to incur related expenses of $ 40 in both years 1 and 2 to earn the money. How would the taxpayer compute deferred income? Would it estimate total expenses and use that to allocate income over future years (*e.g.,* incurring one half the expenses annually causes one half the $ 100 to be reported annually)?

Deposits. Is a deposit more like a loan or prepaid income? In *C.I.R. v. Indianapolis Power & Light Company,* 493 U.S. 203 (1990), an electric utility company received deposits in year 1, if the customer could not meet credit standards. The company paid 6% interest on deposits held for one year or more. If the customer did not pay the bill, the deposit was used to meet the customer's obligation. The Court did not tax the deposit when received, distinguishing a deposit from an advance prepayment, as follows:

> . . . An advance payment, like the deposits at issue here, concededly protects the seller against the risk that it would be unable to collect money owed it after it has furnished goods or services. But an advance payment does much more: it protects against the risk that the purchaser

will back out of the deal before the seller performs. From the moment an advance payment is made, the seller is assured that, so long as it fulfills its contractual obligation, the money is its to keep. Here, in contrast, a customer submitting a deposit made no commitment to purchase a specified quantity of electricity, or indeed to purchase any electricity at all. IPL's right to keep the money depends upon the customer's purchase of electricity, and upon his later decision to have the deposit applied to future bills, not merely upon the utility's adherence to its contractual duties. Under these circumstances, IPL's dominion over the fund is far less complete than is ordinarily the case in an advance-payment situation.

Suppose no interest had been paid by the taxpayer on the deposit? Would *§ 7872* impute any interest on the transaction? Who would be taxed on the interest?

In *Houston Industries Inc. v. U.S.*, 125 F.3d 1442 (Fed. Cir. 1997), the court applied the *Indianapolis Power & Light* case to a situation in which an electric utility charged customers based on estimated use of electricity and later reconciled this prepayment with accurate usage figures. Any overpayments were either credited against future bills or repaid, in each case with interest. The court held that the taxpayer had no guarantee of being able to keep the overpayments and that they were, therefore, not income.

Taxing the payee to get at the payor. There is something troublesome about taxing prepaid income. Maybe the reason for taxing prepaid income has more to do with the pay*or* than the payee. We earlier discussed prepayment for tuition (and other personal consumption items). We noted that there was likely to be a hidden interest-like element accruing to the payor in the prepayment arrangement that would not be taxed. Would taxing the payee on prepaid income indirectly tax the payor on such interest-like income? Let us see.

Assume that the payor prepays $ 100 in year 0 for services to be provided in year 2, two years later. Assuming a 10% interest rate, the interest element in the transaction is $ 10 and $ 11 in the two successive years (years 1 and 2). If the payor is in the 30% tax bracket, the payor should be taxed on that interest so that there is only a 7% return on the $ 100 investment. That should yield services worth only $ 114.49 (100 times 1.07^2).

Will taxing the *Payee* produce that result for the payor indirectly? Put yourself in the payee's position. You have received $ 100 in year 0, prepaid for services due in year 2 (*e.g.*, for a car repair service contract). Assuming the payee is also in the 30% bracket, that leaves the payee $ 70 to fund whatever benefit the payee will provide the payor in year 2. Of course, that

$ 70 will earn 7% after-tax interest, producing $ 80.143 in year 2. What is the value of services the payee will provide to the payor, assuming that it has $ 80.143 of after tax money, committed to the payor? Remember that the payor gets a deduction in year 2 for its costs in providing benefits to the payor.

§ 23.03 DEDUCTIONS

[A]—Cash paid

In *United States v. Consolidated Edison Co.,* 366 U.S. 380 (1961), an accrual basis taxpayer paid New York property taxes but contested the obligation. Payment was necessary to avoid seizure of property. The question was whether the lack of certainty regarding the debt prevented accrual of the payment. The Court held that:

> "[p]ayment" is not a talismanic word. It may have many meanings depending on the sense and context in which it is used . . . .
>
> Of course, an unconditional "payment" made by a taxpayer in apparent "satisfaction" of an asserted matured tax liability is, without more, plain and persuasive evidence, at least against the taxpayer, that "all the events (have) occur(red) which fix the amount of the tax and determine the liability of the taxpayer to pay it," *United States v. Anderson,* [269 U.S. 422], and that the item so paid and satisfied has accrued . . . .
>
> But where . . . the remittance or "payment" did not admit, but specifically denied, liability for, and was not intended to satisfy, the contested [] assessment, but was, in effect, a mere deposit, "in the nature of a cash bond for the payment of (so much, if any, of the contested) taxes (as might) thereafter (be) found to be due" and was made for the sole purpose of staying — there being no other way to stay — an otherwise possible seizure and sale of the property for the contested tax while its validity was being honestly and diligently contested in the only way allowed by the law of the State, it will not do to say that the taxpayer has made an unconditional "payment" in apparent "satisfaction" of the contested part of an asserted matured tax liability, and thereby rendered it immediately accruable . . . .
>
> We therefore conclude that [the contingent liability] accrued not in the year of remittance, but . . . when the New York court entered its final order determining that liability . . . .

After *Consolidated Edison,* the statute was amended to permit deduction of payments, despite a contest over whether the obligation is due, if the payment would have been deductible in the absence of a contest. *§ 461(f).* Is this statutory amendment permitting a deduction a good rule? (1) Loans are not deductible because of the likelihood of repayment. Is repayment of a contested liability less likely than in the case of a loan? (2) Which rule creates the greatest opportunity for taxpayer manipulation — a deduction in the year of payment or the year of dispute settlement?

[B]—No cash paid

[i] Case law

The accrual of deductions, like accrual of income, is also determined by the all events test. Indeed, the all events test was created in a deduction case. In *United States v. Anderson,* 269 U.S. 422 (1926), an accrual basis taxpayer incurred taxes for 1916 but wanted to deduct them in the year of payment, 1917. (Why was the government arguing for earlier deduction in *Anderson*?)

Applying the "all events" test is as difficult on the deduction as on the income side, especially when there are doubts about whether and how much the taxpayer will owe. Many cases were very tolerant of the taxpayer's claim that the liability was fixed and the amount determinable with reasonable accuracy. These cases, allowing a deduction, often dealt with obligations to a group of employees, even though the ultimate payee and amount to be paid were in doubt. *See, e.g., Lukens Steel Co. v. Commissioner,* 442 F.2d 1131 (3d Cir. 1971) (employer's obligation to contribute to Supplemental Unemployment Compensation plan); *Kaiser Steel Corp. v. United States,* 717 F.2d 1304 (9th Cir. 1983) (estimated reserve to pay Workers Compensation claims to employees). *See also Ohio River Collieries Co. v. Commissioner,* 77 T.C. 1369 (1981) (estimated future mining reclamation costs).

Then the Supreme Court decided the *General Dynamics* case, which appeared more hostile to estimating accrued deductions, at least when the liability was not certain.

UNITED STATES v. GENERAL DYNAMICS CORP.

481 U.S. 239 (1987)

MR. JUSTICE MARSHALL delivered the opinion of the Court.

. . . Beginning in October 1972, General Dynamics became a self-insurer with regard to its medical care plans. Instead of continuing to purchase insurance from outside carriers, it undertook to pay medical claims out of its own funds, while continuing to employ private carriers to administer the medical care plans.

To receive reimbursement of expenses for covered medical services, respondent's employees submit claims forms to employee benefits personnel, who verify that the treated persons were eligible under the applicable plan as of the time of treatment. Eligible claims are then forwarded to the plan's administrators. Claims processors review the claims and approve for payment those expenses that are covered under the plan.

Because the processing of claims takes time, and because employees do not always file their claims immediately, there is a delay between the provision of medical services and payment by General Dynamics. To account for this time lag, General Dynamics established reserve accounts to reflect its liability for medical care received, but still not paid for, as of December 31, 1972. It estimated the amount of those reserves with the assistance of its former insurance carriers . . . .

It is fundamental to the "all events" test that, although expenses may be deductible before they have become due and payable, liability must first be firmly established . . . .

We think that this case [] involves a mere estimate of liability based on events that have not occurred before the close of the taxable year, and therefore the proposed deduction does not pass the "all events" test. We disagree with the legal conclusion of the courts below that the last event necessary to fix the taxpayer's liability was the receipt of medical care by covered individuals. A person covered by a plan could only obtain payment for medical services by filling out and submitting a health expense benefits claim form. Employees were informed that submission of satisfactory proof of the charges claimed would be necessary to obtain payment under the plans. General Dynamics was thus liable to pay for covered medical services only if properly documented claims forms were filed. Some covered individuals, through oversight, procrastination, confusion over the coverage provided, or fear of disclosure to the employer of the extent or nature of the services received, might not file claims for reimbursement to which they are plainly entitled. Such filing is not a mere technicality. It is crucial to the establishment of liability on the part of the taxpayer . . . .

This is not to say that the taxpayer was unable to forecast how many claims would be filed for medical care received during this period, and estimate the liability that would arise from those claims. Based on actuarial data, General Dynamics may have been able to make a reasonable estimate of how many claims would be filed for the last quarter of 1972. But that alone does not justify a deduction . . . .

General Dynamics did not show that its liability as to any medical care claims was firmly established as of the close of the 1972 tax year, and is therefore entitled to no deduction. The judgment of the Court of Appeals is

Reversed.

The dissent was unable to distinguish this case from *United States v. Hughes Properties, Inc.*, 476 U.S. 593 (1986), where an accrual method casino operator was allowed to deduct amounts guaranteed for payment on "progressive" slot machines but not yet won by a playing patron. The jackpot on a progressive slot machine increases as more money is gambled and, under Nevada law, a casino operator is prohibited from reducing the jackpot amount. The Court held that all events had occurred to determine the liability despite the fact that the jackpot might not be won for as long as four years. The fact that the casino might go out of business, lose its license, or go bankrupt was irrelevant, because these occurrences are always potential threats to payment of an accrued debt and do not prevent accrual.

The dissent also dismissed the majority's emphasis on the fact that no liability arose until the employee filed a medical claim, viewing the failure to file as a " 'merely formal contingenc[y], or [one] highly improbable under the known facts,' that this Court has viewed as insufficient to preclude accrual and deductibility." Indeed, in *Anderson,* a tax deduction was accrued prior to assessment, and in *Continental Tie,* income was accrued when "what remained was mere administrative procedure to ascertain the amount to be paid." Similarly, in *Hughes,* "the filing and processing of a claim is purely routine and ministerial, and in the nature of a formal contingency . . . ."

[ii] The problem and possible solutions

We could dwell on cases about when liability is fixed and when the amount can be determined with reasonable accuracy, but statutory changes in 1984 have drastically reduced the significance of the dispute. The legislative action was prompted by two concerns. First, there were administrative difficulties in estimating accrued deductions, illustrated by the above cases.

Second, the statute did not generally require accrued amounts to be discounted to present value. *See Burnham Corp. v. Commissioner,* 90 T.C.

953 (1988), *aff'd,* 878 F. 2d 86 (2d Cir. 1989) (government concedes that the "clearly reflect income" requirement in *§ 446(b)* does not require discounting to present value). Occasionally, a case held that a large payment due far in the future could not be accrued prior to payment, undoubtedly influenced by concern over the difference between face and present value. *See Mooney Aircraft, Inc. v. United States,* 420 F.2d 400 (5th Cir. 1969) (no accrual of debt due 15 years later, because it would create a mismatch between income and expenses and might never be paid, despite the fixed liability); *Ford Motor Co. v. Commissioner*, 102 T.C. 87 (1994) (taxpayer cannot, in 1980, deduct $504,000 due 42 years later; the present value of the obligation is only $141,124; the value of the deduction, assuming a 40% tax rate, was $201,600, an amount in excess of the present value). And, a few specific statutory provisions separately identified present value, both to tax income and limit deductions. *See § 467* (deduction of deferred rental obligations over $ 250,000 limited to present value). But these provisions were not adequate to deal with the general problem of accrued deductions which were excessive because the estimates were too high and not discounted to present value.

Before you read about the statutory "solution," consider the different times at which future obligations might be deducted. Assume an obligation to pay $ 121 in year 2, and 10% interest rates. Financially, present value in year 0 is $ 100, with $ 10 and $ 11 interest accruing in years 1 and 2. Here are three deduction possibilities:

	Year 0	Year 1	Year 2
Method 1	−121		
Method 2			−121
Method 3	−100	−10	−11

Method 1 is too generous. It allows a future debt to be deducted in year 0, without discounting.

Method 3 is the theoretically accurate method. It discounts the future debt to present value, deducting present value in year 0, and deducting interest as it accrues annually. The problem is administrative — estimating the correct amount to be discounted.

Method 2 defers the deduction until year 2, the year of payment. This is too severe, but the statute, discussed below, often adopts this approach. This solves the problem of estimating future expenses by waiting until payment. But it defers the deduction for too long, compared to the correct method 3.

[iii] Statutory and regulations solutions — economic performance

The statutory solution specifies that the all events test is not satisfied any *earlier* than "*economic performance.*" *§ 461(h).* When does "economic performance" occur?

Payment to creditor. For many liabilities, economic performance occurs only when payment is made to the person to whom the liability is owed. The statute so states for Workers Compensation and tort liability. *§ 461 (h)(2)(C)* (overriding the *Kaiser Steel* case, *supra,* which permitted accrual of an estimated reserve for Workers Compensation liability). Proposed Regulations expand the payment requirement to include many other liabilities, including those for breach of contract, violation of law, rebates, awards, prizes, taxes, and jackpots (overriding *Hughes Properties* regarding jackpots, discussed in *General Dynamics*). *Treas. Reg. § 1.461–4(g)(2–7).*

"Payment" generally occurs only when (1) the payor has made the kind of cash payment which would support a deduction by a cash basis taxpayer (this excludes giving a note), and (2) the payee has actually received the payment (under cash or cash equivalency doctrine), or constructively received the payment. *Treas. Reg. § 1.461–4(g)(1)(i),(ii)(A-B).*

This "payment" rule is method number 2, above — which, in the example, postponed the deduction until $ 121 was paid in year 2.

Payment to third party. Under the rules outlined so far, economic performance does *not* occur when a taxpayer makes payment to a third party to be held for future payment to the creditor. Such third parties might include a trust, escrow holder, or court-administered fund. This is a puzzling rule. If the debtor has irrevocably committed the present value of the future debt by making payment to a third party, there is no uncertainty regarding either the amount or fact of payment. Consequently, the amount paid (and therefore the deduction) is not likely to exceed present value. Why shouldn't that present value be deductible when paid to a third party?

This question also occurred to Congress and has produced *§ 468B.* Payments to "designated settlement funds," which are certain *court*-established funds to extinguish tort liabilities, are deductible. The fund's investment income is taxed at *§ 1(e)* rates. In addition, the Regulations under *§ 468B* define as economic performance (and therefore allow a deduction for) payments to certain additional "qualified settlement funds" beyond those identified explicitly in the statute. These include funds created by government order, not just court-established funds (*e.g.*, arbitration awards) to extinguish liabilities for breach of contract and violations of law, including environmental laws, not just tort liability. *Treas. Reg. § 1.468B-1(a),(c)(1,2),(e).*

Notice that the deduction for payments to these funds is not as generous as Method 3, discussed earlier, where the taxpayer with a $121 year 2 obligation could accrue the present value of $100 in year 0 and the $10 and $11 interest obligations in years 1 and 2. Unlike Method 3, the "fund taxation" rules tax the investment income earned by the fund. If the taxpayer wants to fund a year 2 payment of $121 with a year 0 deductible payment, it must contribute $105.69 (105.69 times $1.07^2 = 121$). The year 0 payment must be larger than $100 to produce $121 in year 2 because the investment income is taxed each year.

The Treasury at one time proposed regulations to allow a deduction for payments to other types of funds, including payments to an escrowee, trustee, or court to discharge contested liabilities, but these proposals were not adopted.

Structured settlements. The rules about payments to a third party do not eliminate the favorable treatment of "structured settlements" involving physical injury or physical sickness, which allow a debtor to use Method 3. That method permits the deduction of payments to an insurance company to fund future obligations discharging certain personal injury tort liability, *and* permits the income earned on the structured settlement fund to go untaxed. *See § 130; Treas. Reg. § 1.461–6(a).*

Economic performance other than by payment. In some situations, economic performance occurs under the statute at a time *different* from payment. First, when the taxpayer's liability arises out of providing services or property *to the taxpayer,* economic performance occurs when the services or property are provided *to the taxpayer.* For example, the taxpayer's 1990 payment of $10,000 for advertising services, which are not provided until 1992, is not deductible until 1992. *§ 461(h)(2)(A); Treas. Reg. § 1.461-4(d)(2)(i),-4(d)(6) (Example 6).*

Second, when liability of the taxpayer requires the *taxpayer to provide* property or services to someone else, economic performance occurs *as the taxpayer provides* the property or services. For example, assume a taxpayer is obligated in 1991 to pay for future repairs of a leased airplane, and the repairs are done in 1993. Payment to a fund in 1991 to secure future repairs is not deductible until 1993. *§ 461(h)(2)(B); Treas. Reg. § 1.461-4(d)(4),-4(d)(6) (Example 7).*

Exception for recurring items. *§ 461(h)(3)* permits the deduction of debt in the accrual year (without waiting for economic performance), if (1) the debt is a "recurring item" paid soon after the end of the accrual year, and if (2) the item is (a) not "material" or (b) accrual would more properly match expenses and income. The Regulations give this example: the deduction in year 1 of an obligation accrued that year to refund the purchase price to dissatisfied consumers who register their claims before the end of the year, as long as they receive the refund before September 15 of year 2.

Remember— other accounting rules still apply. These rules about economic performance state that a deduction will not occur any earlier than economic performance. They do not supersede other rules postponing deductions, such as the following:

(1) *No deduction before payee reports income.* Sometimes the payor's deduction cannot precede the payee's reporting of income. For example, accrued vacation pay is not deductible until reported by the employee (*§ 404(a)(5)),* even though the employee's services have been provided to the employer. Economic performance with respect to the accrued liability occurs when the services are provided to the employer but the deduction is still postponed. *Treas. Reg. § 1.461–4(d)(6) (Example 1).*

(2) *Costs added to basis.* Sometimes an expenditure must be added to basis. Economic performance regarding accrued debt will not support deduction of a capital expenditure or inventory cost prior to the time when such costs are deductible.

TABLE OF CASES

[References are to pages.]

A

B

C

[References are to pages.]

D

E

F

[References are to pages.]

G

H

I

[References are to pages.]

[References are to pages.]

[References are to pages.]

U

V

W

Z

TABLE OF INTERNAL REVENUE CODE

[References are to pages.]

[References are to pages.]

[References are to pages.]

[References are to pages.]

[References are to pages.]

Internal Revenue Code—Cont.

Internal Revenue Code—Cont.

[References are to pages.]

[References are to pages.]

Internal Revenue Code—Cont.

TABLE OF ADMINISTRATIVE MATERIALS

[References are to pages.]

TREASURY REGULATIONS

Treasury Regulations

Treasury Regulations—Cont.

(Matthew Bender & Co., Inc.) (Pub.870)

[References are to pages.]

REVENUE PROCEDURES

Revenue Procedures

REVENUE RULINGS

Revenue Rulings

Revenue Rulings—Cont.

INDEX

[References are to pages.]

A

[References are to pages.]

[References are to pages.]

C

[References are to pages.]

[References are to pages.]

[References are to pages.]

D

[References are to pages.]

[References are to pages.]

[References are to pages.]

E

F

[References are to pages.]

G

H

I

[References are to pages.]

[References are to pages.]

[References are to pages.]

[References are to pages.]

[References are to pages.]

[References are to pages.]

R

S

[References are to pages.]

[References are to pages.]

[References are to pages.]

U